APPLYING CULTURAL ANTHROPOLOGY

An Introductory Reader

NINTH EDITION

Aaron Podolefsky
Buffalo State (SUNY)

Peter J. Brown
Emory University

Scott M. Lacy
Fairfield University

APPLYING CULTURAL ANTHROPOLOGY: AN INTRODUCTORY READER, NINTH EDITION

Published by McGraw-Hill, a business unit of The McGraw-Hill Companies, Inc., 1221 Avenue of the Americas, New York, NY, 10020. Copyright © 2013 by The McGraw-Hill Companies, Inc. All rights reserved. Printed in the United States of America. Previous editions © 2009, 2007, and 2003. No part of this publication may be reproduced or distributed in any form or by any means, or stored in a database or retrieval system, without the prior written consent of The McGraw-Hill Companies, Inc., including, but not limited to, in any network or other electronic storage or transmission, or broadcast for distance learning.

Some ancillaries, including electronic and print components, may not be available to customers outside the United States.

This book is printed on acid-free paper.

1 2 3 4 5 6 7 8 9 0 QDB/QDB 1 0 9 8 7 6 5 4 3 2

ISBN: 978-0-07-811703-9
MHID: 0-07-811703-8

Senior Vice President, Products & Markets: *Kurt L. Strand*
Vice President & General Manager: *Michael Ryan*
Vice President, Content Production & Technology Services: *Kimberly Meriwether David*
Managing Director: *Gina Boedeker*
Sponsoring Editor: *Patrick Brown*
Director of Developmental Services: *Lisa Pinto*
Development Editor: *Penina Braffman*
Marketing Manager: *Alexandra Schultz*
Director, Content Production: *Terri Schiesl*
Project Manager: *Melissa M. Leick*
Buyer: *Jennifer Pickel*
Designer: *Studio Montage, St. Louis, MO*
Cover Image: *Author's Image/PunchStock*
Typeface: *10/12 Palatino LT Std*
Compositor: *Laserwords Private Limited*
Printer: *Quad/Graphics*

All credits appearing on page or at the end of the book are considered to be an extension of the copyright page.

Library of Congress Cataloging-in-Publication Data

Applying cultural anthropology : an introductory reader / [edited by] Aaron Podolefsky,
    Peter J. Brown, Scott M. Lacy.—9th ed.
        p. cm.
    ISBN 978-0-07-811703-9 (pbk.)
    1. Applied anthropology. 2. Ethnology. I. Podolefsky, Aaron.
    II. Brown, Peter J. III. Lacy, Scott M.
GN397.5.A68 2012
301—dc23
                                                                                        2012021952

The Internet addresses listed in the text were accurate at the time of publication. The inclusion of a website does not indicate an endorsement by the authors or McGraw-Hill, and McGraw-Hill does not guarantee the accuracy of the information presented at these sites.

www.mhhe.com

This book is dedicated to Soloman Sangare, Burama Sangare, and the people of Dissan, Mali, who taught me the power of anthropology as an instrument for social justice and mutual compassion.

—Scott M. Lacy

Contents

Fieldwork

Kinship and Family

Ritual and Religion

Food and Agriculture

Gender and Sexuality

Medical Anthropology

Money and Work

Law and Conflict

Environment, Poverty, and Development

Globalization and Culture Change

Theme Finder for Chapters

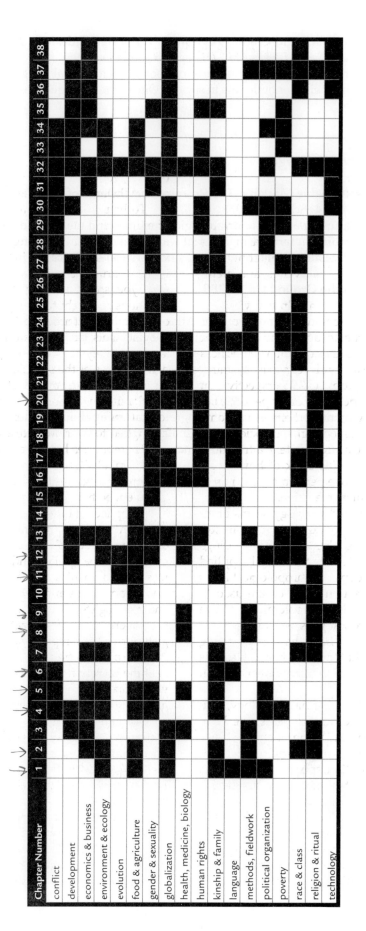

Denotes theme present in chapter

To the Student

An introductory course in any discipline is full of new terminology, concepts, and facts. Sometimes students forget that these new ideas and vocabulary are actually intellectual tools that can be put to work for analyzing and solving problems. In preparing this book, we have selected readings that will show you how anthropological concepts, discoveries, and methods can be applied in today's world.

The study of anthropology can help you view the world in a completely different way than you ever have before. You can come to appreciate the great diversity of human cultures and the interrelatedness of economic, sociopolitical, and religious systems. Anthropology can give you a broad perspective on humanity and help you understand other people's beliefs and customs. In doing so, it can help you become a better citizen in an increasingly global society. But your motivation need not be completely altruistic—there are many examples in this book of how cross-cultural awareness can improve performances in business, negotiations, and clinical medicine.

The fascinating side of anthropology seems obvious to most educated people, but there is also a lesser-known practical side of the discipline. The readings we have selected demonstrate that practical, applied side. Many of the articles depict anthropological ideas and research methods in action—as they are used to understand and solve practical problems. We have included articles on anthropologists working outside the academic setting to show how they are applying anthropology. We believe that the fundamental lessons of anthropology can be applied to many careers and all areas of human endeavor.

To benefit from the study of anthropology, you need to study effectively. Over the years, we have found that students often read assignments without planning, and this actually makes studying less efficient. Before you read a selection, spend a few moments skimming it to get an idea of what it is about, where it is going, and what you should look for. This kind of preliminary reading is a poor idea for mystery novels but is essential for academic assignments. Without this preparation, the article may become a hodgepodge of facts and figures; details may be meaningless because you have missed the big picture. By planning your reading, you can see how the details are relevant to the central themes of an article.

To help you plan your reading, at the beginning of each article we have included questions and a list of glossary terms. Looking at these questions in advance, you may gain an idea of what is to come and why the article is important. This will help make the time you spend reading more fruitful. Most of the questions highlight the central themes of the selection or draw your attention to interesting details. Some of the questions, however, do not have straightforward answers—they are food for thought and topics for debate. Some of the selections refer directly to current discussions of extreme poverty, hunger, obesity, HIV/AIDS, religion, and environmental studies. Our idea is to challenge you to think about how anthropology can be applied to your own life and education.

These articles have been selected with you, the student, in mind. We hope they convey our excitement about the anthropological adventure, and we trust that you will find them both enjoyable and thought provoking.

"Applied anthropology" most often refers to a situation in which a client hires an anthropologist to do research that will help the client resolve a particular problem. Some applied anthropologists run their own research companies that bid and win research contracts from clients and funding agencies; other applied anthropologists work directly for corporations and nongovernmental organizations. Applied anthropologists write their reports specifically for their clients. A good place to find out about applied anthropology is at the Society for Applied Anthropology's Web site, www.sfaa.net. There are many master's degree programs in this field. You may also run across the term "public anthropology" in your studies. This refers to anthropological research and writing that engages important public issues (like many of those addressed in this book) and whose audience is the lay educated public. As "public scholars," anthropologists want to communicate their perspective on contemporary issues and influence public opinion and policy. A good place to find out what is happening in public anthropology is through the Web site of the American Anthropological Association (www.aaanet.org) or the Public Anthropology Web site (www.publicanthropology.org).

If you are interested in reading more about applied anthropology, there are several excellent books available, such as *Applied Anthropology: A Practical Guide,* by Erve Chambers; *Applied Anthropology: An Introduction,* by John van Willigen; *Anthropological Praxis: Translating Knowledge into Action,* by Robert M. Wulff and Shirley J. Fiske; *Applied Anthropology in America,* by Elizabeth M. Eddy and William L. Partridge; and *Making Our Research Useful,* by John van Willigen, Barbara Rylko-Bauer, and Anne McElroy. If you are interested in medical matters, you may want to consult *Understanding and Applying Medical Anthropology,* by Peter J. Brown, or *Anthropology and Public Health,* by Robert Hahn. You may also want to look at the journals *Human Organization* and *Practicing Anthropology,* both of which are published by the Society for Applied Anthropology. The National Association of Practicing Anthropologists (NAPA) also publishes interesting works on specific fields such as medical anthropology.

To the Instructor

Introductory anthropology has become an established part of the college curriculum, and through this course our profession communicates with a large and diverse undergraduate audience. Members of that audience differ in experience, academic concentration, and career aspirations. For those students considering anthropology as a major or minor, we need to provide (among other things) a vision of the future, a view of anthropological work to be done in the public domain as well as within academia. For them, we need to provide some answers to the question, "What can I do with a degree in anthropology?" For students majoring in other areas, such as business, engineering, nursing, or psychology, we need to address the question, "How can anthropological insight or research methods help me understand and solve human problems?" If we can provide such a service, we increase the likelihood that students will find creative solutions to the professional problems that await them, and we brighten the future for our anthropology students by underscoring the usefulness of an anthropological perspective in attempts to solve the practical problems of today's world.

Over the years, we have found that many introductory texts do little more than include a chapter on applied anthropology at the end of the book. This suggests, at least to students, that most of anthropology has no relevance to their lives. Such treatment also implies that the application of anthropological knowledge is a tangent or afterthought—at best an additional subject area, such as kinship or politics.

We disagree. We believe that the applications of anthropology cut across and infuse all the discipline's subfields. This book is a collection of articles that provide examples of both basic and applied research in cultural anthropology.

One of our primary goals is to demonstrate some of the ways our discipline is used outside the academic arena. We want anthropology to be seen as a field that is interesting as well as relevant to the real world. Like the public at large, students seem well aware that the subject matter of anthropology is fascinating, but they seem unaware of both the fundamental questions of humanity addressed by anthropologists and the practical applications of the field. Increased public awareness of the practical contributions of anthropology is a goal that we share with many in the profession. In fact,

this is a major long-term goal of the American Anthropological Association.

Since we first started editing these readers in 1989, the general field of anthropology has changed in precisely this direction of emphasizing public relevance. "Public anthropology" refers to anthropological research and writing that engages important public issues (like many of those addressed in this book) and whose audience is the lay educated public. Our discipline has a long history in this regard, as in the work of Franz Boas on racial discrimination and Margaret Mead's famous articles in *Redbook* magazine. As "public scholars," anthropologists must communicate their perspective on contemporary issues and influence public opinion and policy. In this age of globalization and increased cultural intolerance often linked to religious fundamentalism, the basic messages of public anthropology are more important than ever. Being an effective public anthropologist is just being a great teacher in a larger classroom. A good place to find out what is happening in public anthropology is through the Web site of the American Anthropological Association (www.aaanet.org) or the Public Anthropology Web site (www.publicanthropology.org).

Although people distinguish between basic and applied research, much of anthropology falls into a gray area, having elements of both. Many selections in this book fall into that gray zone—they are brief ethnographic accounts that contain important implications for understanding and resolving problems. We could have included a large number of articles exemplifying strictly applied cultural research—an evaluation report of agency performance, for example. Although this sort of research is fascinating and challenging to do, it is usually not exciting for students to read. We have selected articles that we believe are fascinating for students and convey the dual nature (basic/applied) of social science research. We think that it is not the scholarly writing style that is most important, but rather the content of the research as a way to get students to think and to challenge their own assumptions about the world.

Anthropological research is oriented by certain basic human values. These include being against ethnocentrism, racism, ignorance, and inequality. Anthropology is about understanding and appreciating human similarities and difference. Such an understanding can lead students to new attitudes—like tolerance for cultural difference, commitment to human equality, stewardship of the environment, appreciation of the past, and personal dedication to the continued and honest pursuit of knowledge.

Any student who completes an introductory course in anthropology should learn that anthropological work, in its broadest sense, may include (or at least contribute to) international business, epidemiology, program evaluation, social impact studies, conflict resolution, organizational analysis, market research, and nutrition research—even though their introductory anthropology texts make no mention of those fields. The selections in this book should help students understand why anthropology is important in today's world and also make the course more memorable and meaningful.

FEATURES OF THIS EDITION

- To spark student discussion and thinking about controversial issues and issues of public policy, we have included selections dealing with contemporary topics like fair trade, world hunger, gay marriage, and HIV/AIDS. These selections are clearly anthropological in perspective and approach. When students are able to relate the concepts and examples of anthropology to current debates, they recognize the value of their education.

- We chose readings that complement typical courses in introductory cultural anthropology and that reflect new directions in cultural anthropology. The sequence of articles follows the organization of standard anthropology textbooks, grouped under headings with terms such as fieldwork, gender and sexuality, and ritual and religion, rather than headings based on areas of applied anthropology like economic anthropology or the anthropology of development. At the same time, we include headings such as environment, poverty, and development and law and conflict, reflecting growth and development in the anthropological discipline and purview. Had we meant this book as a reader on applied anthropology, our organization would have been different. Although this book could be used by students in courses on applied anthropology (as earlier editions have been), those students are not our intended audience. For this reason, we have not provided extensive discussion of the history or definition of applied anthropology.

- For students interested in pursuing applied cultural anthropology on their own, there are a number of fine books. These include *Applied Anthropology: A Practical Guide,* by Erve Chambers; *Applied Anthropology: An Introduction,* by John van Willigen; *Anthropological Praxis: Translating Knowledge into Action,* by Robert M. Wulff and Shirley J. Fiske; *Applied Anthropology in America,* by Elizabeth M. Eddy and William L. Partridge; and *Making Our Research Useful,* by John van Willigen, Barbara Rylko-Bauer, and Anne McElroy. Students interested in medical matters may want to consult *Understanding and Applying Medical Anthropology,* by Peter J. Brown, or *Anthropology and Public Health* by Robert Hahn.

- To emphasize how anthropology can be put to work in different settings, we include examples of anthropologists whose careers involve applying anthropology outside the university setting.

- To help students better understand the subject matter, we include a number of pedagogical aids: introductions, a list of glossary terms, and guiding questions for each article; a world map that pinpoints the locations of places and peoples discussed in the articles; and, for easy reference, an extensive glossary and index.

- A **Theme Finder feature,** which follows the table of contents, allows instructors and students to identify critical cross-chapter themes, including race and class, environment, globalization, human rights, poverty, and technology.

NEW TO THIS EDITION

In this edition, we added ten new articles that refer to contemporary social issues such as economic inequality, poverty and hunger, and environment and ecology. The new selections also deal with hot-button issues like the integration of traditional healers in biomedical treatments for diseases like tuberculosis and HIV/AIDS. Throughout this edition, we have also emphasized the human dimensions of globalization.

Throughout the book we have continued our enduring commitment to the discussion of race. We include several articles that help students understand that race is a cultural construction, not a biological fact. In this regard, students need to understand that, as a cultural construction, whiteness brings with it certain privileges that endure—despite progress—since the emergence of the Civil Rights Movement and the election of the first African American president. Racism, sexism, severe economic inequality, and intolerance for cultural difference are enduring problems in our society.

The readings in this book are subdivided into traditional anthropological categories, such as kinship and family, ritual and religion, and globalization and culture change. In each category you will find reading selections that demonstrate not only the relevance of anthropology theory and methods in the understanding of human problems but also the application of anthropology to specific problems or issues.

ACKNOWLEDGMENTS

We are grateful to the many instructors who returned questionnaires evaluating the selections: C. Adams, Indiana University; S. Adrian, University of Arizona; N. Allison, Toccoa Falls College; L. Ammons, Assumption College; P. Barlett, Emory University; K. Barlow, University of Minnesota; E. Bigler, Rhode Island College; B. Bigony, University of Wisconsin at Menomonie; G. Bogdan, Orange Coast College; A. Bolyanatz, Wheaton College; C. Bretell, Southern Methodist University; J. Brown, Oakland University; D. Bruner, University of North Carolina at Greensboro; J. Cahoon, College of St. Scholastica; D. Chasin, Newport Beach, CA; J. Coggeshall, Clemson University; K. Costa, Fall River, MA; Philip E. Coyle, Western Carolina University; J. Culbert, San Diego State University; D. Darlington, Western Wyoming Community College; S. Dauria, Bloomsburg University; J. Dempsey, Phoenix, AZ; D. Duchon, Georgia State University; M. Findlay, California State University at Chico; T. Fitzgerald, University of North Carolina at Greensboro; M. Fong, Chaffey College; P. Fontane, St. Louis College of Pharmacy; F. Freedman, Syracuse University; D. Gamble, Southwest Baptist University; D. Gibson, El Camino College; D. Gordon, Fort Lewis College; T. Greaves, Bucknell University; Amy Harper, Central Oregon Community College; C. Hartse, Olympic College; T. Headland, Summer Institute of Linguistics; E. Hegeman, John Jay College, City University of New York; M. Helms, University of North Carolina at Greensboro; J. Herron, Ottawa, KS; B. Howell, University of Tennessee at Knoxville; C. Hull, Grand Valley State University; S. Jen, California State University at Fresno; B. Joans, Merritt College; C. Johnson, Indiana University Northwest; C. Kahrs, Saddleback Community College; P. Kilbride, Bryn Mawr College; S. Kus, Rhodes College; S. Lamb, Brandeis University; G. Landsman, State University of New York at Albany; J. Levi, Carleton College; P. Little, University of Kentucky; W. Lohrer, California State University at Chico; K. Lorenz, Shippensburg University; Cherylynn MacGreagor, University of Houston-Downtown; K. Maines, Pennsylvania State University; B. Mathieu, West Los Angeles College; M. Mazzarelli, Massachusetts Bay Community College; C. McCall, Hiwassee College; J. McCall, Southern Illinois University at Carbondale; C. Moyers, Cabrillo College; B. Nelson, University of Utah; C. Nowak, Chicago, IL; B. Pate, University of Tennessee; K. Piatt, Babson College; K. Porter, Rochester, NY; M. Pulford, University of Wisconsin at Superior; Francis Ellen Purifoy, University of Louisville; S. Rachelle, Mt. San Jacinto College; R. Rajner, University of Toledo; S. Rasmussen, University of Houston; Paul Roach, Century College—St. Paul; S. Rorbakken, University of Iowa; J. Ryan, Texas Christian University; B. Schmitz, Orange Coast College; D. Seelow, State University of New York at Old Westbury; D. Shepherd, Rubbindale, MN; V. Smith, California State University at Chico; J. Stimpfl, University of Nebraska at Lincoln; H. Swanson, Mohave Community College; M. Taylor, University of Memphis; T. M. Taylor, University of South Colorado; J. Thompson, Tennessee Wesleyan College; J. Tizon, University of Southern Maine; K. Wilcoxson, University of Sioux Falls; P. Wohlt, Ball State University; Z. Zelazo, Montclair State University.

Finally, we thank the following reviewers of this edition for their helpful comments and suggestions: Rosann Bar, Caldwell College; Anna Bellisari, Wright State University; Monica Cable, Franklin & Marshall College; Josephine Caldwell Ryan, University of Texas at Arlington; Flemming Daugaard-Hansen, University of Florida; Sallie Han, SUNY Oneonta; Mary Carol Hopkins, Northern Kentucky University; Andrew Kinkella, Moorpark College; Sarah Lamb, Brandeis University; Sarah Sportman, University of Connecticut; Sharon Stratton, University of Tennessee Chattanooga; and Penny Verin-Shapiro, California State University Fresno.

Aaron Podolefsky

Peter J. Brown

Scott M. Lacy

INTRODUCTION

Understanding Humans and Human Problems

To the uninitiated, the term *anthropology* conjures up images of mummies' tombs, Indiana Jones, and treks through steaming jungles or over high alpine peaks. Anthropologists agree that their chosen field is exciting, that they have been places and seen things that few experience firsthand, and that they have been deeply and emotionally involved in understanding the human condition. At the same time, however, the vision of anthropology presented by Hollywood has probably done more to obscure the true nature of the profession than it has to enlighten the public about what we really do.

Providing an accurate image of anthropology and anthropological work is both simple and complex. Essentially, anthropology is the study of people, or more properly, of humankind. But, you may say, many disciplines study people: psychology, sociology, history, biology, medicine, and so on. True, but anthropology is different in that it seeks to integrate these separate and perhaps narrower views of humanity. To understand ourselves, we need to join these disparate views into a single framework, a process that begins with our biological and evolutionary roots, explores the development of culture through the prehistoric and historical periods, probes the uniquely human ability to develop culture through communication, and examines the diversity of recent and present-day cultures that inhabit the globe.

From this conception of the *holistic* and *comparative* study of humankind emerge what are termed the four fields of anthropology: biological (or physical) anthropology, archaeology, anthropological linguistics, and cultural anthropology. Some universities offer an introductory course that covers all four subfields. Other schools cover the subfields in two or three separate introductory courses. Each approach has its advantage. The former may more fully integrate the biocultural and historical dimensions of humanity; the latter allows students to explore each subfield in greater depth. This book introduces you to cultural anthropology and how they are used in today's world.

Another way to divide the discipline—in fact almost any discipline—is into *basic* and *applied* research. These categories are important in this reader because

we would like students to appreciate both the basic and the applied sides of anthropology. A survey of natural and social scientists and engineers conducted by the U.S. Census Bureau for the National Science Foundation used the following definitions of these fundamental concepts: *Basic research* is study directed toward gaining scientific knowledge primarily for its own sake. *Applied research* is study directed toward gaining scientific knowledge in an effort to meet a recognized need.

Anthropology is a discipline concerned primarily with basic research. It asks "big" questions concerning the origins of humankind, the roots of human nature, the development of civilization, and the functions of our major social institutions (such as marriage and religion). Nevertheless, anthropologists have put the methods and skills developed in basic research to use in solving human problems and fulfilling the needs of society. Anthropologists have, for example, worked with medical examiners in the identification of skeletal remains. They have also helped communities preserve their cultural heritage and businesses and government agencies understand the social impact of programs or development projects.

Although the application of anthropology has a long history, it has until recent years remained in the shadows of pure or basic research. The last twenty-five years have seen a change. Anthropologists have moved beyond their traditional roles in universities and museums and now work in a broad range of settings. They are employed in many government agencies, in the private sector, and in a variety of nonresearch capacities (such as administrator, evaluator, or policy analyst).

In response to the growing opportunities for anthropologists outside academia and to the demands of students, an increasing number of master's degree and doctoral programs provide training specifically in the applications of anthropology. This is not to say that the employment ads list jobs titled "anthropologist." Rather, for those interested in anthropology, there are increasing opportunities to find careers that draw on anthropological training and skills. Profiles of people in nonacademic careers (consumer marketing, high-tech industry, and refugee policy) can be found in this reader. At the same time, studies have shown that there will be increasing job opportunities for anthropologists in universities and colleges during the next decade and beyond.

These new opportunities are particularly evident in this era of multiculturalism and in the increasing public recognition that our society must be a culturally diverse social mosaic. Exploration of this reality has always been the domain of cultural anthropology; a usual pedagogical goal of teachers of cultural anthropology is to increase a student's appreciation and tolerance of cultural differences. Living in a multicultural society presents real challenges of social tensions caused by chronic persistent ethnocentrism, racism, and economic inequality. But living in a multicultural society also brings a cultural richness, a luxuriant wealth, to our lives.

School administrators, engineers, doctors, business leaders, lawyers, medical researchers, and government officials have become aware that the substantive knowledge, the unique perspective, and the research skills of anthropologists are applicable to practical problems—in the United States as well as other countries.

As we explore anthropology, keep in mind the interplay between and interdependence of basic cultural research and the applications of anthropological knowledge and research methods to the solution of human problems.

CULTURAL ANTHROPOLOGY

Cultural anthropology is concerned with the description and analysis of people's lives and traditions. In the past, cultural anthropologists almost always did research in far-off "exotic" societies, but today we have expanded our research interests to include our own societies. Cultural anthropology can add much to both the basic and the applied scientific understanding of human behaviors and beliefs. The study and interpretation of other societies—of their traditions, history, and view of the world—is inherently interesting and important because it documents the diversity of human lifestyles. The anthropological approach to understanding other societies also has practical value for addressing contemporary human problems and needs.

The concept of *culture* is central to anthropology. It refers to the patterns of economy, social organization, and belief that are learned and shared by members of a social group. Culture is traditional knowledge that is passed down from one generation to the next. Although generally stable over time, culture is flexible and fluid, changing through borrowing or invention. The influential American anthropologist Franz Boas championed the concept of culture for understanding

human diversity; culture, Boas argued, is distinct from biological "race" or language. Anthropologists believe that all cultural lifestyles have intrinsic value and validity. Other societies deserve to be studied and understood without being prejudged using our own narrow (and sometimes intolerant) beliefs and values; this universal tendency to prejudge based on the supposed superiority of one's own group, called *ethnocentrism,* is something everyone should avoid.

Culture is the crowning achievement of human evolution. To understand ourselves is to appreciate cultural diversity. Dependence on culture as our primary mechanism of survival sets humans apart from other members of the animal kingdom. This dependence is responsible for the tremendous evolutionary success of our species, which has grown in population (sometimes to the point of overpopulation) and can inhabit nearly every niche on the planet.

The paradox of culture is that, as we humans learn to accept our own cultural beliefs and values, we unconsciously learn to reject those of other peoples. At birth, we are capable of absorbing any culture and language. We are predisposed to cultural learning, but we are not programmed to adopt a particular culture. As we grow, our parents, our schools, and our society teach us what is right and wrong, good and evil, acceptable and unacceptable. At the subconscious level, we learn the symbolic meanings of behavior and through them interpret the meanings of actions. Beliefs, values, and symbols must be understood within the context of a particular culture. This is the principle of *cultural relativity.* At the same time, culture supplies us with the cognitive models—software programs, if you will—that allow us to perceive or "construct" a particular version of reality. Culture permeates our thinking and our expectations; this is the principle of *culture construction.*

In addition to the concept of culture, the anthropological approach to the study of human behavior and belief has two essential characteristics: a holistic approach and a comparative framework. The *holistic approach* means that anthropologists see a particular part of culture—for example, politics, economy, or religion—in relation to the larger social system. Individuals are viewed, not in isolation, but as part of an intricate web of social relationships. Although an anthropological study may have a particular focus, the holistic approach means that the broader cultural context is always considered important because the different parts of a cultural system are interrelated. When, for example, the economy or the technology changes, other aspects of the culture will change as well.

The *comparative framework* means that explanations or generalizations are achieved through cross-cultural research. Questions about humanity cannot be based on information from a single society or a single type of society such as the industrial societies of the United States and Europe. Such a limited framework is simply too narrow for understanding the big picture that basic anthropological research seeks. By studying others within a comparative framework, we can better understand ourselves. If other cultures are a mirror in which we see ourselves, then anthropology is a mirror for humankind.

The broad generalizations about culture and society that we have been talking about are based on detailed knowledge of the world's cultures. To gain this knowledge, anthropologists go to the people. Often accompanied by spouses and children, we pack our bags and travel to far-off lands—to the highlands of New Guinea, the frozen Arctic, the savannas of Africa, or the jungles of South America. Increasingly, anthropologists are bringing their research methods and comparative, holistic perspective, into the cities and suburbs of America, the American schoolroom, and the corporate jungle. This "research adventure" has become the hallmark of cultural anthropology.

The research methods used by the cultural anthropologist are distinctive because they depend, to a large extent, on the firsthand experiences and interpretations of the field researcher. Cultural anthropologists conduct research in natural settings rather than in laboratories or over the telephone. This method for studying another society is often called *participant observation, ethnography,* or *qualitative methods.* The goal of describing, understanding, and explaining another culture is a large task. It is most often accomplished by living in the society for an extended period, by talking with people, and, as much as possible, by experiencing their lives.

One important tool that cultural anthropologists depend on in field research is *language.* They need to learn the local languages not only for their own survival in the field but, more important, because language is a key to understanding someone else's culture. Many anthropologists study descriptive linguistics to make it easier for them to learn an unwritten language in the field. By looking at speech and language in Apache culture (Selection 6) or the complex problems of male-female miscommunication (Selection 15), anthropologists can learn a great deal about the culture they are studying.

The fieldwork experience usually involves a kind of culture shock in which the researcher questions his or her own assumptions about the world. In this way, fieldwork is often a rewarding period of personal growth. In their work, anthropologists expect to find that other people's behavior, even when it seems bizarre when seen from the outside, makes sense when viewed from the people's own point of view. This is why anthropological research often means letting people speak

for themselves. While doing research, the anthropologist often thinks of herself or himself as a child—as being ignorant or uninformed and needing to be taught by the people being studied. This approach often involves in-depth interviewing with a few key informants and then interpreting (and writing about) that other culture for the researcher's own society. The ethnographic method, pioneered and developed in anthropology, is now being used in a range of applied areas, including marketing, management research, and school evaluation. Although ethnography is an important research style, the selections in this book demonstrate that many different methods are used in anthropology today.

The applications of cultural anthropology are diverse. Internationally, anthropologists are involved in programs of technical assistance and economic aid to Third World nations. These programs address needs in such areas as agriculture and rural development; health, nutrition, and family planning; education; housing and community organizing; transportation and communication; and energy. Anthropologists do many of the same things domestically as well. They evaluate public education, study agricultural extension programs, administer projects, analyze policy (such as U.S. refugee resettlement programs), and research crime and crime prevention, for example.

In the private sector, cultural anthropologists can add a fresh perspective to market research. They analyze office and industrial organization and culture. They create language and cultural training workshops for businesspeople and others who are going overseas. These workshops reduce the likelihood of cross-cultural misunderstanding and the problems of culture shock for the employee and, often more important, for his or her family. Cultural anthropologists also conduct market research in the United States to understand cultural dimensions in advertising and client-agency relations (Selection 26).

Applied anthropological work can be divided into four categories. In the first group, applied research and basic research look very much alike, except that the goal of applied research is more directly linked to a particular problem or need. For example, in Selection 31, Aaron Podolefsky studies the causes of the re-emergence of tribal warfare in New Guinea. Such studies provide planners and policymakers with important insights for understanding the problem. This knowledge can help in the design and implementation of programs that help bring an end to warfare in the region.

In the second category, anthropologists may work as researchers for a government agency, corporation, or interest group on a specific task defined by the client.

In the third category, anthropologists work as consultants to business and industry or to government agencies that need in-depth cultural knowledge to solve or prevent a problem. Anthropologists often act as cultural brokers, mediating and translating between groups who are miscommunicating not because of their words but because of cultural meanings.

Finally, a few anthropologists have developed and administered programs. Richard Reed (Selection 33) worked with Paraguay's indigenous Guaraní communities to create forest reserves to protect native people's rights to their traditional lands. Reed's work demonstrates the complexity of applying anthropology to develop and administer projects in which cultural understanding is a fundamental component.

A great deal of anthropological work remains to be done, although this seems to be a well-kept secret. People have a far easier time focusing on the individual as the level of analysis. When divorce, drug abuse, or suicide affects small numbers of people, we may look to the individual and to psychology for answers. When divorce rates climb to 50 percent of all marriages and the suicide rate increases tenfold, however, we must look beyond the individual to forces that affect society at large. Because we are so immersed in our own culture, we have difficulty seeing it as a powerful force that guides—even controls—our behavior. We begin these readings, therefore, with several selections that convey the hidden, but powerful, nature of culture.

The readings in this book are subdivided into traditional anthropological categories, such as ritual and religion; kinship and family; and gender and sexuality. In each category you will find reading selections that demonstrate not only the relevance of anthropology theory and methods in the understanding of human problems but also the application of anthropology to specific problems or issues.

[Handwritten margin notes: "- possibility to be foragers?" and "Is this a pastoralist society?"]

Shakespeare in the Bush

Laura Bohannan

Communication is an essential characteristic of human social life. Through language we socialize our children and pass down cultural values from generation to generation. Communication forms and defines relations among individuals as well as among groups. Because communication is so natural, we seldom ask a critical question: When we speak, does the listener understand?

At a minimum, communication involves a sender, a receiver, and a shared code for exchanging information. When an individual or a group sends a message, the sender anticipates that those who receive the message will interpret and understand the message in the way the sender intended. Miscommunication is, of course, an unfortunately common phenomenon that can lead to fistfights, divorces, and wars.

What most of us do not appreciate is the degree to which culture affects our interpretation of messages. As Laura Bohannan tells the tale of *Hamlet,* we gradually discover how particular behaviors or events can have very different meanings in different places. What is interesting is that the miscommunication of interpretational differences is not a result of poor language or translation abilities. Miscommunication is not a result of speaking too quickly or not loudly enough. It reflects cultural differences.

As you read this selection, ask yourself the following questions:

- What were the author's original beliefs about the universality of the classics—such as *Hamlet?*
- How did the Tiv elders react to the marriage of Hamlet's mother to his uncle? How was this different from Hamlet's own emotional reaction?
- Why do the Tiv believe that a chief should have more than one wife?
- As the author tells the story, consider how the elders interpret various actions to fit Tiv culture and in so doing redefine the central meaning of the play.

The following terms discussed in this selection are included in the Glossary at the back of the book:

age grade	levirate
agnatic	polygyny
chiefdom	socialization
cultural relativism	

Just before I left Oxford for the Tiv in West Africa, conversation turned to the season at Stratford. "You Americans," said a friend, "often have difficulty with Shakespeare. He was, after all, a very English poet, and one can easily misinterpret the universal by misunderstanding the particular."

I protested that human nature is pretty much the same the whole world over; at least the general plot and motivation of the greater tragedies would always be clear—everywhere—although some details of custom might have to be explained and difficulties of translation might produce other slight changes. To end an argument we could not conclude, my friend gave

me a copy of *Hamlet* to study in the African bush: it would, he hoped, lift my mind above its primitive surroundings, and possibly I might, by prolonged meditation, achieve the grace of correct interpretation.

It was my second field trip to that African tribe, and I thought myself ready to live in one of its remote sections—an area difficult to cross even on foot. I eventually settled on the hillock of a very knowledgeable old man, the head of a homestead of some hundred and forty people, all of whom were either his close relatives or their wives and children. Like the other elders of the vicinity, the old man spent most of his time performing ceremonies seldom seen these days in the more accessible parts of the tribe. I was delighted. Soon there would be three months of enforced isolation and leisure, between the harvest that takes place just before the rising of the swamps and the clearing of new

Bohannan, Laura. "Shakespeare in the Bush." *Natural History* (Aug./Sept. 1966). Reprinted by permission of Denis Bohannan.

farms when the water goes down. Then, I thought, they would have even more time to perform ceremonies and explain them to me.

I was quite mistaken. Most of the ceremonies demanded the presence of elders from several homesteads. As the swamps rose, the old men found it too difficult to walk from one homestead to the next, and the ceremonies gradually ceased. As the swamps rose even higher, all activities but one came to an end. The women brewed beer from maize and millet. Men, women, and children sat on their hillocks and drank it.

People began to drink at dawn. By midmorning the whole homestead was singing, dancing, and drumming. When it rained, people had to sit inside their huts: there they drank and sang or they drank and told stories. In any case, by noon or before, I either had to join the party or retire to my own hut and my books. "One does not discuss serious matters when there is beer. Come, drink with us." Since I lacked their capacity for the thick native beer, I spent more and more time with *Hamlet.* Before the end of the second month, grace descended on me. I was quite sure that *Hamlet* had only one possible interpretation, and that one universally obvious.

Early every morning in the hope of having some serious talk before the beer party, I used to call on the old man at his reception hut—a circle of posts supporting a thatched roof above a low mud wall to keep out wind and rain. One day I crawled through the low doorway and found most of the men of the homestead sitting huddled in their ragged clothes on stools, low plank beds, and reclining chairs, warming themselves against the chill of the rain around a smoky fire. In the center were three pots of beer. The party had started.

The old man greeted me cordially. "Sit down and drink." I accepted a large calabash full of beer, poured some into a small drinking gourd, and tossed it down. Then I poured some more into the same gourd for the man second in seniority to my host before I handed my calabash over to a young man for further distribution. Important people shouldn't ladle beer themselves.

"It is better like this," the old man said, looking at me approvingly and plucking at the thatch that had caught in my hair. "You should sit and drink with us more often. Your servants tell me that when you are not with us, you sit inside your hut looking at a paper."

The old man was acquainted with four kinds of "papers:" tax receipts, bride price receipts, court fee receipts, and letters. The messenger who brought him letters from the chief used them mainly as a badge of office, for he always knew what was in them and told the old man. Personal letters for the few who had relatives in the government or mission stations were kept until someone went to a large market where there was a letter writer and reader. Since my arrival, letters were

brought to me to be read. A few men also brought me bride price receipts, privately, with requests to change the figures to a higher sum. I found moral arguments were of no avail, since in-laws are fair game, and the technical hazards of forgery difficult to explain to an illiterate people. I did not wish them to think me silly enough to look at any such papers for days on end, and I hastily explained that my "paper" was one of the "things of long ago" of my country.

"Ah," said the old man. "Tell us."

I protested that I was not a storyteller. Storytelling is a skilled art among them; their standards are high and the audiences critical—and vocal in their criticism. I protested in vain. This morning they wanted to hear a story while they drank. They threatened to tell me no more stories until I told them one of mine. Finally, the old man promised that no one would criticize my style "for we know you are struggling with our language." "But," put in one of the elders, "you must explain what we do not understand, as we do when we tell you our stories." Realizing that here was my chance to prove Hamlet universally intelligible, I agreed.

The old man handed me some more beer to help me on with my storytelling. Men filled their long wooden pipes and knocked coals from the fire to place in the pipe bowls; then, puffing contentedly, they sat back to listen. I began in the proper style, "Not yesterday, not yesterday, but long ago, a thing occurred. One night three men were keeping watch outside the homestead of the great chief, when suddenly they saw the former chief approach them."

"Why was he no longer their chief?"

"He was dead," I explained. "That is why they were troubled and afraid when they saw him."

"Impossible," began one of the elders, handing his pipe on to his neighbor, who interrupted, "Of course it wasn't the dead chief. It was an omen sent by a witch. Go on."

Slightly shaken, I continued. "One of these three was a man who knew things"—the closest translation for scholar, but unfortunately it also meant witch. The second elder looked triumphantly at the first. "So he spoke to the dead chief saying, 'Tell us what we must do so you may rest in your grave,' but the dead chief did not answer. He vanished, and they could see him no more. Then the man who knew things—his name was Horatio—said this event was the affair of the dead chief's son, Hamlet."

There was a general shaking of heads round the circle. "Had the dead chief no living brothers? Or was this son the chief?"

"No," I replied. "That is, he had one living brother who became the chief when the elder brother died."

The old men muttered: such omens were matters for chiefs and elders, not for youngsters; no good could come of going behind a chief's back; clearly Horatio was not a man who knew things.

"Yes, he was," I insisted, shooing a chicken away from my beer. "In our country the son is next to the father. The dead chief's younger brother had become the great chief. He had also married his elder brother's widow only about a month after the funeral."

"He did well," the old man beamed and announced to the others, "I told you that if we knew more about Europeans, we would find they really were very like us. In our country also," he added to me, "the younger brother marries the elder brother's widow and becomes the father of his children. Now, if your uncle, who married your widowed mother, is your father's full brother, then he will be a real father to you. Did Hamlet's father and uncle have one mother?" *cultural cross references*

His question barely penetrated my mind; I was too upset and thrown off balance by having one of the most important elements of *Hamlet* knocked straight out of the picture. Rather uncertainly I said that I thought they had the same mother, but I wasn't sure—the story didn't say. The old man told me severely that these genealogical details made all the difference and that when I got home I must ask the elders about it. He shouted out the door to one of his younger wives to bring his goatskin bag.

Determined to save what I could of the mother motif, I took a deep breath and began again. "The son Hamlet was very sad because his mother had married again so quickly. There was no need for her to do so, and it is our custom for a widow not to go to her next husband until she has mourned for two years."

"Two years is too long," objected the wife, who had appeared with the old man's battered goatskin bag. "Who will hoe your farms for you while you have no husband?"

"Hamlet," I retorted without thinking, "was old enough to hoe his mother's farms himself. There was no need for her to remarry." No one looked convinced. I gave up. "His mother and the great chief told Hamlet not to be sad, for the great chief himself would be a father to Hamlet. Furthermore, Hamlet would be the next chief: therefore he must stay to learn the things of a chief. Hamlet agreed to remain, and all the rest went off to drink beer."

While I paused, perplexed at how to render Hamlet's disgusted soliloquy to an audience convinced that Claudius and Gertrude had behaved in the best possible manner, one of the younger men asked me who had married the other wives of the dead chief.

"He had no other wives," I told him.

"But a chief must have many wives! How else can he brew beer and prepare food for all his guests?"

I said firmly that in our country even chiefs had only one wife, that they had servants to do their work, and that they paid them from tax money.

cultural differences

It was better, they returned, for a chief to have many wives and sons who would help him hoe his farms and feed his people; then everyone loved the chief who gave much and took nothing—taxes were a bad thing.

I agreed with the last comment, but for the rest fell back on their favorite way of fobbing off my questions: "That is the way it is done, so that is how we do it."

I decided to skip the soliloquy. Even if Claudius was here thought quite right to marry his brother's widow, there remained the poison motif, and I knew they would disapprove of fratricide. More hopefully I resumed, "That night Hamlet kept watch with the three who had seen his dead father. The dead chief again appeared, and although the others were afraid, Hamlet followed his dead father off to one side. When they were alone, Hamlet's dead father spoke."

"Omens can't talk!" The old man was emphatic.

"Hamlet's dead father wasn't an omen. Seeing him might have been an omen, but he was not." My audience looked as confused as I sounded. "It was Hamlet's dead father. It was a thing we call a 'ghost.'" I had to use the English word, for unlike many of the neighboring tribes, these people didn't believe in the survival after death of any individuating part of the personality.

"What is a 'ghost'? An omen?"

"No, a 'ghost' is someone who is dead but who walks around and can talk, and people can hear him and see him but not touch him."

They objected. "One can touch zombis."

"No, no! It was not a dead body the witches had animated to sacrifice and eat. No one else made Hamlet's dead father walk. He did it himself."

"Dead men can't walk," protested my audience as one man.

I was quite willing to compromise. "A 'ghost' is the dead man's shadow."

But again they objected. "Dead men cast no shadows."

"They do in my country," I snapped.

The old man quelled the babble of disbelief that arose immediately and told me with that insincere, but courteous, agreement one extends to the fancies of the young, ignorant, and superstitious, "No doubt in your country the dead can also walk without being zombis." From the depths of his bag he produced a withered fragment of kola nut, bit off one end to show it wasn't poisoned, and handed me the rest as a peace offering.

"Anyhow," I resumed, "Hamlet's dead father said that his own brother, the one who became chief, had poisoned him. He wanted Hamlet to avenge him. Hamlet believed this in his heart, for he did not like his father's brother." I took another swallow of beer. "In the country of the great chief, living in the same homestead, for it was a very large one, was an important elder who was

the need to relate when relaying a story w/ differences in culture

often with the chief to advise and help him. His name was Polonius. Hamlet was courting his daughter, but her father and her brother . . . (I cast hastily about for some tribal analogy) warned her not to let Hamlet visit her when she was alone on her farm, for he would be a great chief and so could not marry her."

"Why not?" asked the wife, who had settled down on the edge of the old man's chair. He frowned at her for asking stupid questions and growled, "They lived in the same homestead."

"That was not the reason," I informed them. "Polonius was a stranger who lived in the homestead because he helped the chief, not because he was a relative."

"Then why couldn't Hamlet marry her?"

"He could have," I explained, "but Polonius didn't think he would. After all, Hamlet was a man of great importance who ought to marry a chief's daughter, for in his country a man could have only one wife. Polonius was afraid that if Hamlet made love to his daughter, then no one else would give a high price for her."

"That might be true," remarked one of the shrewder elders, "but a chief's son would give his mistress's father enough presents and patronage to more than make up the difference. Polonius sounds like a fool to me."

"Many people think he was," I agreed. "Meanwhile Polonius sent his son Laertes off to Paris to learn the things of that country, for it was the homestead of a very great chief indeed. Because he was afraid that Laertes might waste a lot of money on beer and women and gambling, or get into trouble by fighting, he sent one of his servants to Paris secretly, to spy out what Laertes was doing. One day Hamlet came upon Polonius's daughter Ophelia. He behaved so oddly he frightened her. Indeed"—I was fumbling for words to express the dubious quality of Hamlet's madness— "the chief and many others had also noticed that when Hamlet talked one could understand the words but not what they meant. Many people thought that he had become mad." My audience suddenly became more attentive. "The great chief wanted to know what was wrong with Hamlet, so he sent for two of Hamlet's age mates (school friends would have taken long explanation) to talk to Hamlet and find out what troubled his heart. Hamlet, seeing that they had been bribed by the chief to betray him, told them nothing. Polonius, however, insisted that Hamlet was mad because he had been forbidden to see Ophelia, whom he loved."

"Why," inquired a bewildered voice, "should anyone bewitch Hamlet on that account?"

"Bewitch him?"

"Yes, only witchcraft can make anyone mad, unless, of course, one sees the beings that lurk in the forest."

I stopped being a storyteller, took out my notebook and demanded to be told more about these two causes

of madness. Even while they spoke and I jotted notes, I tried to calculate the effect of this new factor on the plot. Hamlet had not been exposed to the beings that lurk in the forest. Only his relatives in the male line could bewitch him. Barring relatives not mentioned by Shakespeare, it had to be Claudius who was attempting to harm him. And, of course, it was.

For the moment I staved off questions by saying that the great chief also refused to believe that Hamlet was mad for the love of Ophelia and nothing else. "He was sure that something much more important was troubling Hamlet's heart."

"Now Hamlet's age mates," I continued, "had brought with them a famous storyteller. Hamlet decided to have this man tell the chief and all his homestead a story about a man who had poisoned his brother because he desired his brother's wife and wished to be chief himself. Hamlet was sure the great chief could not hear the story without making a sign if he was indeed guilty, and then he would discover whether his dead father had told him the truth."

The old man interrupted, with deep cunning, "Why should a father lie to his son?" he asked.

I hedged: "Hamlet wasn't sure that it really was his dead father." It was impossible to say anything, in that language, about devil-inspired visions.

"You mean," he said, "it actually was an omen, and he knew witches sometimes send false ones. Hamlet was a fool not to go to one skilled in reading omens and divining the truth in the first place. A man-who-sees-the-truth could have told him how his father died, if he really had been poisoned, and if there was witchcraft in it; then Hamlet could have called the elders to settle the matter."

The shrewd elder ventured to disagree. "Because his father's brother was a great chief, one-who-sees-the-truth might therefore have been afraid to tell it. I think it was for that reason that a friend of Hamlet's father—a witch and an elder—sent an omen so his friend's son would know. Was the omen true?"

"Yes," I said, abandoning ghosts and the devil; a witch-sent omen it would have to be. "It was true, for when the storyteller was telling his tale before all the homestead, the great chief rose in fear. Afraid that Hamlet knew his secret, he planned to have him killed."

The stage set of the next bit presented some difficulties of translation. I began cautiously. "The great chief told Hamlet's mother to find out from her son what he knew. But because a woman's children are always first in her heart, he had the important elder Polonius hide behind a cloth that hung against the wall of Hamlet's mother's sleeping hut. Hamlet started to scold his mother for what she had done."

There was a shocked murmur from everyone. A man should never scold his mother.

"She called out in fear, and Polonius moved behind the cloth. Shouting, 'A rat!' Hamlet took his machete and slashed through the cloth." I paused for dramatic effect. "He had killed Polonius!"

The old men looked at each other in supreme disgust. "That Polonius truly was a fool and a man who knew nothing! What child would not know enough to shout, 'It's me!'" With a pang, I remembered that these people are ardent hunters, always armed with bow, arrow, and machete; at the first rustle in the grass an arrow is aimed and ready, and the hunter shouts "Game!" If no human voice answers immediately, the arrow speeds on its way. Like a good hunter Hamlet had shouted, "A rat!"

I rushed in to save Polonius's reputation. "Polonius did speak. Hamlet heard him. But he thought it was the chief and wished to kill him to avenge his father. He had meant to kill him earlier that evening . . ." I broke down, unable to describe to these pagans, who had no belief in individual afterlife, the difference between dying at one's prayers and dying "unhousell'd, disappointed, unaneled."

This time I had shocked my audience seriously. "For a man to raise his hand against his father's brother and the one who has become his father—that is a terrible thing. The elders ought to let such a man be bewitched."

I nibbled at my kola nut in some perplexity, then pointed out that after all the man had killed Hamlet's father.

"No," pronounced the old man, speaking less to me than to the young men sitting behind the elders. "If your father's brother has killed your father, you must appeal to your father's age mates; *they* may avenge him. No man may use violence against his senior relatives." Another thought struck him. "But if his father's brother had indeed been wicked enough to bewitch Hamlet and make him mad that would be a good story indeed, for it would be his fault that Hamlet, being mad, no longer had any sense and thus was ready to kill his father's brother."

There was a murmur of applause. *Hamlet* was again a good story to them, but it no longer seemed quite the same story to me. As I thought over the coming complications of plot and motive, I lost courage and decided to skim over dangerous ground quickly.

"The great chief," I went on, "was not sorry that Hamlet had killed Polonius. It gave him a reason to send Hamlet away, with his two treacherous age mates, with letters to a chief of a far country, saying that Hamlet should be killed. But Hamlet changed the writing on their papers, so that the chief killed his age mates instead." I encountered a reproachful glare from one of the men whom I had told undetectable forgery was not merely immoral but beyond human skill. I looked the other way.

"Before Hamlet could return, Laertes came back for his father's funeral. The great chief told him Hamlet had killed Polonius. Laertes swore to kill Hamlet because of this, and because his sister Ophelia, hearing her father had been killed by the man she loved, went mad and drowned in the river."

"Have you already forgotten what we told you?" The old man was reproachful. "One cannot take vengeance on a madman; Hamlet killed Polonius in his madness. As for the girl, she not only went mad, she was drowned. Only witches can make people drown. Water itself can't hurt anything. It is merely something one drinks and bathes in."

I began to get cross. "If you don't like the story, I'll stop."

The old man made soothing noises and himself poured me some more beer. "You tell the story well, and we are listening. But it is clear the elders of your country have never told you what the story really means. No, don't interrupt! We believe you when you say your marriage customs are different, or your clothes and weapons. But people are the same everywhere; therefore, there are always witches and it is we, the elders, who know how witches work. We told you it was the great chief who wished to kill Hamlet, and now your own words have proved us right. Who were Ophelia's male relatives?"

"There were only her father and her brother." Hamlet was clearly out of my hands.

"There must have been many more; this also you must ask of your elders when you get back to your country. From what you tell us, since Polonius was dead, it must have been Laertes who killed Ophelia, although I do not see the reason for it."

We had emptied one pot of beer, and the old men argued the point with slightly tipsy interest. Finally one of them demanded of me, "What did the servant of Polonius say on his return?"

With difficulty I recollected Reynaldo and his mission. "I don't think he did return before Polonius was killed."

"Listen," said the elder, "and I will tell you how it was and how your story will go, then you may tell me if I am right. Polonius knew his son would get into trouble, and so he did. He had many fines to pay for fighting, and debts from gambling. But he had only two ways of getting money quickly. One was to marry off his sister at once, but it is difficult to find a man who will marry a woman desired by the son of a chief. For if the chief's heir commits adultery with your wife, what can you do? Only a fool calls a case against a man who will someday be his judge. Therefore Laertes had to take the second way: he killed his sister by witchcraft, drowning her so he could secretly sell her body to the witches."

I raised an objection. "They found her body and buried it. Indeed Laertes jumped into the grave to see his sister once more—so, you see, the body was truly there. Hamlet, who had just come back, jumped in after him."

"What did I tell you?" The elder appealed to the others. "Laertes was up to no good with his sister's body. Hamlet prevented him, because the chief's heir, like a chief, does not wish any other man to grow rich and powerful. Laertes would be angry, because he would have killed his sister without benefit to himself. In our country he would try to kill Hamlet for that reason. Is this not what happened?"

"More or less," I admitted. "When the great chief found Hamlet was still alive, he encouraged Laertes to try to kill Hamlet and arranged a fight with machetes between them. In the fight both the young men were wounded to death. Hamlet's mother drank the poisoned beer that the chief meant for Hamlet in case he won the fight. When he saw his mother die of poison, Hamlet, dying, managed to kill his father's brother with his machete."

"You see, I was right!" exclaimed the elder.

"That was a very good story," added the old man, "and you told it with very few mistakes. There was just one more error, at the very end. The poison Hamlet's mother drank was obviously meant for the survivor of the fight, whichever it was. If Laertes had won, the great chief would have poisoned him, for no one would know that he arranged Hamlet's death. Then, too, he need not fear Laertes' witchcraft; it takes a strong heart to kill one's only sister by witchcraft.

"Sometime," concluded the old man, gathering his ragged toga about him, "you must tell us some more stories of your country. We, who are elders, will instruct you in their true meaning, so that when you return to your own land your elders will see that you have not been sitting in the bush, but among those who know things and who have taught you wisdom."

2

Eating Christmas in the Kalahari

Richard Borshay Lee

✳ pastoralist society (handwritten annotation)

An *economy* is a social system for the production, exchange, and consumption of goods and services. Using this definition, anthropologists believe that all human societies have economies and that economic systems can work without money and markets.

People in food-foraging societies, like the !Kung San described in this selection, have received much attention by anthropologists. To a large degree, this is because they represent (at least by analogy) the original lifestyle of our ancestors. A major discovery of research on food foragers is that their life is not "nasty, brutish, and short." In fact, the food forager's diet might be an ideal one for people living in industrialized societies.

In the hunter-gatherer economy, anthropologists have discovered that the exchange of goods is based on rules of gift giving or reciprocity. In this selection, Richard Lee tells of his surprise at the !Kung San's lack of appreciation of a Christmas gift. As we have already seen, a group's customs and rules about appropriate social behavior can reflect important cultural values. When people act in unexpected ways, anthropologists see this as an opportunity to better understand their culture and world view. That is the case in this selection.

All people give gifts to each other, but there are rules and obligations about those gifts. In our own society, there are rules about the polite way to receive a present. We are supposed to act appreciative (even if we hate the gift) because the gift is less important than the social relationship at stake. The !Kung break those rules, but in the process, Richard Lee discovers that there are important cultural messages behind their "impoliteness."

As you read this selection, ask yourself the following questions:

- Why did Richard Lee feel obligated to give a valuable gift to the !Kung at Christmas? Why did they think he was a miser?

- Why did the !Kung people's insults about the impending gift bother the anthropologist so much? Were the people treating him in a special way?

- What does Lee mean by saying, "There are no totally generous acts?" Do you agree?

- What are some cultural rules about gift giving in our own society?

The following terms discussed in this selection are included in the Glossary at the back of the book:

cultural values   hunter-gatherers
economy   reciprocal gift
egalitarian society

The !Kung Bushmen's knowledge of Christmas is thirdhand. The London Missionary Society brought the holiday to the southern Tswana tribes in the early nineteenth century. Later, native catechists spread the idea far and wide among the Bantu-speaking pastoralists, even in the remotest corners of the Kalahari Desert. The Bushmen's idea of the Christmas story, stripped to its essentials, is "praise the birth of white man's god-chief:" what keeps their interest in the holiday high is the Tswana-Herero custom of slaughtering an ox for his Bushmen neighbors as an annual goodwill gesture. Since the 1930s, part of the Bushmen's annual round of activities has included a December congregation at the cattle posts for trading, marriage brokering, and several days of trance dance feasting at which the local Tswana headman is host.

As a social anthropologist working with !Kung Bushmen, I found that the Christmas ox custom suited my purposes. I had come to the Kalahari to study the hunting and gathering subsistence economy of the !Kung, and to accomplish this it was essential not to

Lee, Richard Borshay. "Eating Christmas in the Kalahari" from *Natural History* (Dec. 1969):14–22, 60–64; copyright © Natural History Magazine, Inc. 1969. Reprinted with permission.

provide them with food, share my own food, or interfere in any way with their food-gathering activities. While liberal handouts of tobacco and medical supplies were appreciated, they were scarcely adequate to erase the glaring disparity in wealth between the anthropologist, who maintained a two-month inventory of canned goods, and the Bushmen, who rarely had a day's supply of food on hand. My approach, while paying off in terms of data, left me open to frequent accusations of stinginess and hardheartedness. By their lights, I was a miser.

The Christmas ox was to be my way of saying thank you for the cooperation of the past year; and since it was to be our last Christmas in the field, I determined to slaughter the largest, meatiest ox that money could buy, insuring that the feast and trance dance would be a success.

Through December I kept my eyes open at the wells as the cattle were brought down for watering. Several animals were offered, but none had quite the grossness that I had in mind. Then, ten days before the holiday, a Herero friend led an ox of astonishing size and mass up to our camp. It was solid black, stood five feet high at the shoulder, had a five-foot span of horns, and must have weighed 1,200 pounds on the hoof. Food consumption calculations are my specialty, and I quickly figured that bones and viscera aside, there was enough meat—at least four pounds—for every man, woman, and child of the 150 Bushmen in the vicinity of /ai/ai who were expected at the feast.

Having found the right animal at last, I paid the Herero £20 ($56) and asked him to keep the beast with his herd until Christmas day. The next morning word spread among the people that the big solid black one was the ox chosen by /ontah (my Bushman name; it means, roughly, "whitey") for the Christmas feast. That afternoon I received the first delegation. Ben!a, an outspoken sixty-year-old mother of five, came to the point slowly.

"Where were you planning to eat Christmas?"

"Right here at /ai/ai," I replied.

"Alone or with others?"

"I expect to invite all the people to eat Christmas with me."

"Eat what?"

"I have purchased Yehave's black ox, and I am going to slaughter and cook it."

"That's what we were told at the well but refused to believe it until we heard it from yourself."

"Well, it's the black one," I replied expansively, although wondering what she was driving at.

"Oh, no!" Ben!a groaned, turning to her group. "They were right." Turning back to me she asked, "Do you expect us to eat that bag of bones?"

"Bag of bones! It's the biggest ox at /ai/ai."

"Big, yes, but old. And thin. Everybody knows there's no meat on that old ox. What did you expect to eat off of it, the horns?"

Everybody chuckled at Ben!a's one-liner as they walked away, but all I could manage was a weak grin.

That evening it was the turn of the young men. They came to sit at our evening fire. /gaugo, about my age, spoke to me man-to-man.

"/ontah, you have always been square with us," he lied. "What has happened to change your heart? That sack of guts and bones of Yehave's will hardly feed one camp, let alone all the Bushmen around /ai/ai." And he proceeded to enumerate the seven camps in the /ai/ai vicinity, family by family. "Perhaps you have forgotten that we are not few, but many. Or are you too blind to tell the difference between a proper cow and an old wreck? That ox is thin to the point of death."

"Look, you guys," I retorted, "that is a beautiful animal, and I'm sure you will eat it with pleasure at Christmas."

"Of course we will eat it: it's food. But it won't fill us up to the point where we will have enough strength to dance. We will eat and go home to bed with stomachs rumbling."

That night as we turned in, I asked my wife, Nancy, "What did you think of the black ox?"

"It looked enormous to me. Why?"

"Well, about eight different people have told me I got gypped; that the ox is nothing but bones."

"What's the angle?" Nancy asked. "Did they have a better one to sell?"

"No, they just said that it was going to be a grim Christmas because there won't be enough meat to go around. Maybe I'll get an independent judge to look at the beast in the morning."

Bright and early, Halingisi, a Tswana cattle owner, appeared at our camp. But before I could ask him to give me his opinion on Yehave's black ox, he gave me the eye signal that indicated a confidential chat. We left the camp and sat down.

"/ontah, I'm surprised at you; you've lived here for three years and still haven't learned anything about cattle."

"But what else can a person do but choose the biggest, strongest animal one can find?" I retorted.

"Look, just because an animal is big doesn't mean that it has plenty of meat on it. The black one was a beauty when it was younger, but now it is thin to the point of death."

"Well I've already bought it. What can I do at this stage?"

"Bought it already? I thought you were just considering it. Well, you'll have to kill it and serve it, I suppose. But don't expect much of a dance to follow."

My spirits dropped rapidly. I could believe that Ben!a and /gaugo just might be putting me on about the black ox, but Halingisi seemed to be an impartial critic. I went around that day feeling as though I had bought a lemon of a used car.

In the afternoon it was Tomazo's turn. Tomazo is a fine hunter, a top trance performer . . . and one of my most reliable informants. He approached the subject of the Christmas cow as part of my continuing Bushman education.

"My friend, the way it is with us Bushmen," he began, "is that we love meat. And even more than that, we love fat. When we hunt we always search for the fat ones, the ones dripping with layers of white fat: fat that turns into a clear, thick oil in the cooking pot, fat that slides down your gullet, fills your stomach and gives you a roaring diarrhea," he rhapsodized.

"So, feeling as we do," he continued, "it gives us pain to be served such a scrawny thing as Yehave's black ox. It is big, yes, and no doubt its giant bones are good for soup, but fat is what we really crave and so we will eat Christmas this year with a heavy heart."

The prospect of a gloomy Christmas now had me worried, so I asked Tomazo what I could do about it.

"Look for a fat one, a young one . . . smaller, but fat. Fat enough to make us //gom (evacuate the bowels), then we will be happy."

My suspicions were aroused when Tomazo said that he happened to know a young, fat, barren cow that the owner was willing to part with. Was Tomazo working on commission, I wondered? But I dispelled this unworthy thought when we approached the Herero owner of the cow in question and found that he had decided not to sell.

The scrawny wreck of a Christmas ox now became the talk of the /ai/ai water hole and was the first news told to the outlying groups as they began to come in from the bush for the feast. What finally convinced me that real trouble might be brewing was the visit from u!au, an old conservative with a reputation for fierceness. His nickname meant spear and referred to an incident thirty years ago in which he had speared a man to death. He had an intense manner; fixing me with his eyes, he said in clipped tones:

"I have only just heard about the black ox today, or else I would have come earlier. /ontah, do you honestly think you can serve meat like that to people and avoid a fight?" He paused, letting the implications sink in. "I don't mean fight you, /ontah; you are a white man. I mean a fight between Bushmen. There are many fierce ones here, and with such a small quantity of meat to distribute, how can you give everybody a fair share? Someone is sure to accuse another of taking too much or hogging all the choice pieces. Then you will see what happens when some go hungry while others eat."

The possibility of at least a serious argument struck me as all too real. I had witnessed the tension that surrounds the distribution of meat from a kudu or gemsbok kill, and had documented many arguments that sprang up from a real or imagined slight in meat distribution. The owners of a kill may spend up to two hours arranging and rearranging the piles of meat under the gaze of a circle of recipients before handing them out. And I knew that the Christmas feast at /ai/ai would be bringing together groups that had feuded in the past.

Convinced now of the gravity of the situation, I went in earnest to search for a second cow; but all my inquiries failed to turn one up.

The Christmas feast was evidently going to be a disaster, and the incessant complaints about the meagerness of the ox had already taken the fun out of it for me. Moreover, I was getting bored with the wise-cracks, and after losing my temper a few times, I resolved to serve the beast anyway. If the meat fell short, the hell with it. In the Bushmen idiom, I announced to all who would listen:

"I am a poor man and blind. If I have chosen one that is too old and too thin, we will eat it anyway and see if there is enough meat there to quiet the rumbling of our stomachs."

On hearing this speech, Ben!a offered me a rare word of comfort. "It's thin," she said philosophically, "but the bones will make a good soup."

At dawn Christmas morning, instinct told me to turn over the butchering and cooking to a friend and take off with Nancy to spend Christmas alone in the bush. But curiosity kept me from retreating. I wanted to see what such a scrawny ox looked like on butchering, and if there was going to be a fight, I wanted to catch every word of it. Anthropologists are incurable that way.

The great beast was driven up to our dancing ground, and a shot in the forehead dropped it in its tracks. Then, freshly cut branches were heaped around the fallen carcass to receive the meat. Ten men volunteered to help with the cutting. I asked /gaugo to make the breast bone cut. This cut, which begins the butchering process for most large game, offers easy access for removal of the viscera. But it allows the hunter to spot-check the amount of fat on an animal. A fat game animal carries a white layer up to an inch thick on the chest, while in a thin one, the knife will quickly cut to the bone. All eyes fixed on his hand as /gaugo, dwarfed by the great carcass, knelt to the breast. The first cut opened a pool of solid white in the black skin. The second and third cut widened and deepened the creamy white. Still no bone. It was pure fat; it must have been two inches thick.

"Hey /gau," I burst out, "that ox is loaded with fat. What's this about the ox being too thin to bother eating? Are you out of your mind?"

"Fat?" /gau shot back. "You call that fat? This wreck is thin, sick, dead!" And he broke out laughing. So did everyone else. They rolled on the ground, paralyzed with laughter. Everybody laughed except me; I was thinking.

I ran back to the tent and burst in just as Nancy was getting up. "Hey, the black ox. It's fat as hell! They were kidding about it being too thin to eat. It was a joke or something. A put-on. Everyone is really delighted with it."

"Some joke," my wife replied. "It was so funny that you were ready to pack up and leave /ai/ai."

If it had indeed been a joke, it had been an extraordinarily convincing one, and tinged, I thought, with more than a touch of malice as many jokes are. Nevertheless, that it was a joke lifted my spirits considerably, and I returned to the butchering site where the shape of the ox was rapidly disappearing under the axes and knives of the butchers. The atmosphere had become festive. Grinning broadly, their arms covered with blood well past the elbow, men packed chunks of meat into the big cast-iron cooking pots, fifty pounds to the load, and muttered and chuckled all the while about the thinness and worthlessness of the animal and /ontah's poor judgment.

We danced and ate that ox two days and two nights; we cooked and distributed fourteen potfuls of meat and no one went home hungry and no fights broke out.

But the "joke" stayed in my mind. I had a growing feeling that something important had happened in my relationship with the Bushmen and that the clue lay in the meaning of the joke. Several days later, when most of the people had dispersed back to the bush camps, I raised the question with Hakekgose, a Tswana man who had grown up among the !Kung, married a !Kung girl, and who probably knows the culture better than any other non-Bushman. *ethnocentrism*

"With us whites," I began, "Christmas is supposed to be the day of friendship and brotherly love. What I can't figure out is why the Bushmen went to such lengths to criticize and belittle the ox I had bought for the feast. The animal was perfectly good and their jokes and wisecracks practically ruined the holiday for me."

"So it really did bother you," said Hakekgose. "Well, that's the way they always talk. When I take my rifle and go hunting with them, if I miss, they laugh at me for the rest of the day. But even if I hit and bring one down, it's no better. To them, the kill is always too small or too old or too thin; and as we sit down on the kill site to cook and eat the liver, they keep grumbling, even with their mouths full of meat. They say things like, 'Oh, this is awful! What a worthless animal! Whatever made me think that this Tswana rascal could hunt!'"

"Is this the way outsiders are treated?" I asked.

"No, it is their custom; they talk that way to each other too. Go and ask them."

/gaugo had been one of the most enthusiastic in making me feel bad about the merit of the Christmas ox. I sought him out first.

"Why did you tell me the black ox was worthless, when you could see that it was loaded with fat and meat?"

"It is our way," he said smiling. "We always like to fool people about that. Say there is a Bushman who has been hunting. He must not come home and announce like a braggart, 'I have killed a big one in the bush!' He must first sit down in silence until I or someone else comes up to his fire and asks, 'What did you see today?' He replies quietly, 'Ah, I'm no good for hunting. I saw nothing at all (pause) just a little tiny one.' Then I smile to myself," /gaugo continued, "because I know he has killed something big.

"In the morning we make up a party of four or five people to cut up and carry the meat back to the camp. When we arrive at the kill we examine it and cry out, 'You mean to say you have dragged us all the way out here in order to make us cart home your pile of bones? Oh, if I had known it was this thin I wouldn't have come.' Another one pipes up, 'People, to think I gave up a nice day in the shade for this. At home we may be hungry but at least we have nice cool water to drink.' If the horns are big, someone says, 'Did you think that somehow you were going to boil down the horns for soup?'

"To all this you must respond in kind. 'I agree,' you say, 'this one is not worth the effort; let's just cook the liver for strength and leave the rest for the hyenas. It is not too late to hunt today and even a duiker or steenbok would be better than this mess.'

"Then you set to work nevertheless; butcher the animal, carry the meat back to the camp and everyone eats," /gaugo concluded.

Things were beginning to make sense. Next, I went to Tomazo. He corroborated /gaugo's story of the obligatory insults over a kill and added a few details of his own.

"But," I asked, "why insult a man after he has gone to all that trouble to track and kill an animal and when he is going to share the meat with you so that your children will have something to eat?"

"Arrogance," was his cryptic answer.

"Arrogance?"

"Yes, when a young man kills much meat he comes to think of himself as a chief or a big man, and he thinks of the rest of us as his servants or inferiors. We can't accept this. We refuse one who boasts, for someday his pride will make him kill somebody. So we always speak of his meat as worthless. This way we cool his heart and make him gentle."

"But why didn't you tell me this before?" I asked Tomazo with some heat.

"Because you never asked me," said Tomazo, echoing the refrain that has come to haunt every field ethnographer.

The pieces now fell into place. I had known for a long time that in situations of social conflict with Bushmen I held all the cards. I was the only source of tobacco in a thousand square miles, and I was not incapable of cutting an individual off for noncooperation. Though my boycott never lasted longer than a few days, it was an indication of my strength. People resented my presence at the water hole, yet simultaneously dreaded my leaving. In short I was a perfect target for the charge of arrogance and for the Bushman tactic of enforcing humility.

I had been taught an object lesson by the Bushmen; it had come from an unexpected corner and had hurt me in a vulnerable area. For the big black ox was to be the one totally generous, unstinting act of my year at /ai/ai and I was quite unprepared for the reaction I received.

As I read it, their message was this: There are no totally generous acts. All "acts" have an element of calculation. One black ox slaughtered at Christmas does not wipe out a year of careful manipulation of gifts given to serve your own ends. After all, to kill an animal and share the meat with people is really no more than the Bushmen do for each other every day and with far less fanfare.

In the end, I had to admire how the Bushmen had played out the farce—collectively straight-faced to the end. Curiously, the episode reminded me of the *Good Soldier Schweik* and his marvelous encounters with authority. Like Schweik, the Bushmen had retained a thoroughgoing skepticism of good intentions. Was it this independence of spirit, I wondered, that had kept them culturally viable in the face of generations of contact with more powerful societies, both black and white? The thought that the Bushmen were alive and well in the Kalahari was strangely comforting. Perhaps, armed with that independence and with their superb knowledge of their environment, they might yet survive the future.

3

Maxwell's Demons
Disenchantment in the Field

Janet McIntosh

Nearly 700 years ago, Berber explorer Ibn Battuta traveled more than 75,000 miles across the world from West Africa to China and Southeast Asia. Centuries before Franz Boas and Bronislaw Malinowski, Battuta recorded ethnographic notes and cultural observations of the people and places he visited. When he arrived at the Swahili Coast of Africa, he could see that the region's major port cities were international trading centers that linked East Africa with Asia, Europe, and the Middle East. When he notes that the city of Mombasa had no "native-grown" grain, he shows that this cosmopolitan urban center fed its population through trade not farming.

As early as 500 C.E. merchants from India, the Middle East, Persia, and elsewhere began to settle on the Swahili Coast, trading and intermarrying with local Bantu populations. Like New York and Tokyo, the Swahili Coast's urban centers attracted entrepreneurs and travelers from afar. Eventually, the culturally diverse populations in cities like Mombasa, Mogadishu, and Kilwa developed Kiswahili, a hybird language that combined a local Bantu language named Sabaki with other languages including Arabic and Persian. Through centuries of trade, Swahili entrepreneurs exported goods from the African interior and imported good from the Indian Ocean trade.

Since the golden age of the Swahili Coast, the region has fallen under the control of a number of foreign rulers, including the Portuguese, Omani, and European colonization. From their intercultural roots and their geopolitical centrality in the Indian Ocean trade, Swahili cultures have endured and adapted to centuries of international exchange and influence. A centuries-old experiment in globalization and cultural hybridity, the Swahili culture fuses African, Arab, Asian, and European traditions and history.

In this chapter, anthropologist Janet McIntosh examines cultural change among the Giriama people of coastal Kenya. McIntosh delves so deeply into the world of the Giriama that she begins to question her disbelief in supernatural phenomena and spirits. Ethnographers distinguish themselves as anthropologists by living and learning from within their study communities. Because we frequently pivot between emic and etic explanations of human behavior, during a field study, and even throughout one's career, it's not surprising that anthropologists will sometimes see the world through the eyes of their research populations.

As you read this selection, ask yourself the following questions:

- Who was Mipoho, and what was her prophecy (prediction) about the future of the Giriama?
- How did the wanganga react when the author refused their offers to predict her future? Why?
- Compare and contrast the authors visits with two diviners: Tresea and Karissa.
- How did Mohammed determine that the author wrote "umbrella" during their divination session? Did Mohammed use supernatural powers or a sleight-of-hand magic trick?
- How do Maxwell's ideas on a Revival Faith of Giriama change over the course of his fieldwork with the author?
- Using a specific example from this chapter, what does the author mean when she says that our pact as anthropologists is to go "there" without ever leaving "here"?

The following terms discussed in this section are included in the Glossary in the back of the book:

authenticity	*emic*
diviner	*etic*
divination	*waganga*

McIntosh, Janet. "Maxwell's Demons: Disenchantment in the Field." *Anthropology and Humanism* 29 (2004):63–77. Copyright © 2004 by the American Anthropological Association. Reproduced with permission of Blackwell Publishing Ltd.

Contemporary ethnographers are surely among the most introspective of social scientists, increasingly conscious of our political and epistemological relationships with those we study. We pore over anthropology's past with chagrin, shuddering to read of its sometime complicity in colonialism. Many aspire to shift the discipline on its moral axis, devoting their work to addressing and redressing the dynamics of power and suffering (see, e.g., Scheper-Hughes 1995). Many, too, have occupied themselves with the limitations of the ethnographer's perspective, writing their position and prejudices into their accounts to mitigate their authority as observers (Clifford and Marcus 1986; Lawless 1992). But despite these valiant efforts, muddy terrain awaits the ethnographer who ventures into the field. The ethical currents in anthropology clarify the importance of conscience but do not establish where the limits of the fieldworker's influence should lie. The reflexive turn gives us license to reflect on our roles as we write but does not specify how we are to navigate the differences between the ethnographer as a human being "on the ground" and the professional identity that ethnographers must at some point inhabit to succeed in the academy. And no amount of reflection can do away with the discomfiting dynamic that can arise between ethnographers and their informants when each comes at the world with a radically different epistemology, and each, through exposure, may come to change the other. Such dilemmas, I find, can be particularly acute when the agnostic, humanist ethnographer places her spyglass up against the religious convictions that make up her field assistant's world.

My account is set in a township called Malindi that extends along the Indian Ocean on the coast of Kenya. The town itself has only a few paved roads; one of these passes the stone-built quarter that houses well-to-do Arabs and Swahili, while others trace the beachfront, passing the large expatriate mansions and luxury hotels so important to an increasingly fragile town economy. Unpaved routes, pitted with rocks that ruin the axles of Malindi's decrepit fleet of Toyota taxis, weave through the residential areas occupied by Giriama and members of other ethnic groups, many of them migrants in search of labor. If you make your way out of the town center to the south-west road, you pass the mud huts of outlying Giriama villages before veering down toward Mombasa.

You can learn a lot about social life in Malindi by planting yourself in the outdoor market and watching peoples' feet. The expensive sneakers usually belong to Western backpackers who bumble through the marketplace, wearing shorts and bulging money belts, looking for a cold soda and a *samosa*, a tasty fried dumpling. Swahili and Arab women are hard to mistake. Beneath their long black robes one catches glimpses of henna or red toenail polish, and many wear open-toe shoes that use straps and sparkling vinyl to declare an expensive femininity. Upwardly mobile men and women who have converted to Christianity may take advantage of the trade in secondhand clothes from the West, donning uncomfortable looking pumps or cheap loafers. And the Giriama men and women who come from rural homesteads carrying baskets of surplus mango, cassava, and bananas wear exhausted-looking flip-flops or no shoes at all.

Beyond the market, houses of Christian and Muslim worship are scattered through town. Passers-by can hear a *muezzin* intoning the call to prayer from a powerful mosque loudspeaker, or the sound of children reciting prayers in *madrasa*, or Quranic school. On Sunday morning, the church just a few doors down might resound with Christian songs accompanied by the tambourine, or the intense tumult of an entire congregation speaking in the voice of the Holy Spirit. Traditional Giriama belief and ritual, meanwhile, is more muted, its shrines tucked away in rural spaces. Yet its presence is broadcast through smaller, subtler cues: the talismans on the arms of Giriama women or the occasional sign advertising traditional healing.

I arrived in Malindi in 1998 to begin dissertation research on the ethnic, religious, and linguistic relationships between Giriama and Swahili. I knew I would need an assistant to help with interviews and translations, and I met him quite by accident while staying at a guest house on the outskirts of town. One day during my Kigiriama lesson, my instructor and I sat in the sun on rickety folding chairs just outside the main door as she tried to help me get my tongue around the language. I was learning the word for "good" when a high male voice through the wall began to correct my pronunciation with a snappy air:

"No, you don't have it yet. Say it like this: 'to-TOH-to.'"

"To-TOH-to," I said to the wall, obediently.

I ducked around the doorframe into the guest house office to find a tall man, probably in his early 20s, sitting at a table and holding a battered-looking book. He was so thin the loose end of his belt passed behind his back and dangled out again in front, but he had buttoned and linked his cuffs with panache unusual for a village youth, and he appeared to have grown out his hair a little and brushed it back with pomade. He introduced himself as Maxwell.

When I told Maxwell that I was interested in ethnic relations and changes in religious practices on the coast, he processed my words quickly. "If you're looking for someone to help you see what has become of our religion," he said, "I'm the one you want."

He jabbed at the table with his index finger. "Our people have been seduced by imported gods. I'm the only one in my family who still believes in the original Giriama way. I want to know everything there is to know about our traditional powers, our true nature, and when I'm done, I'm going to start a movement called 'The Revival Faith of Giriama.'"

These days, of course, the phrase "true nature" is likely to raise the hairs on the neck of most cultural anthropologists, who have been schooled to view the notion of authenticity warily, as a strategic and often highly politicized construction (Dominguez 1986; Fienup-Riordan 1988; Hobsbawm and Ranger 1983). I wasn't interested in cultural purity; in fact, quite the opposite—I was interested in how locals were negotiating cultural contact and change. But Maxwell felt that his heritage was being ground away, and his wish to embark on a search for an uncontaminated religious identity seemed to be one element of the social flux I was trying to understand. He was also smart, and he talked a blue streak. I thought he might keep me company during the long days of fieldwork.

So we entered "the field" together, walking in the same direction, but with wildly mismatched lines of sight. My gaze was fixed on the human plane—the arena of ethnic and religious politics—while Maxwell's would target the supernatural world, to figure out how to harness its powers. "I'm going to see which of the diviners and healers are the most powerful," he anticipated. "I'll learn the best methods for contacting the ancestors. I'll find out who the spirits really are." Once he understood all that, he said, he would recruit the people who had the best powers, to help him bring the Giriama back to their spiritual home. Maxwell made it abundantly clear that he was collecting my wages only to empower himself and, ultimately, his followers. 'I hate white people," he reminded me, and so distanced himself from the image he held most in contempt: the obsequious, disadvantaged African swallowing whole the opinions of a white employer.

According to customary Giriama belief and practice, the world is populated by invisible forces that cross-cut one another, each with a purpose of its own. Spirits and ancestors roam the earth, at turns mischievous, malevolent, and helpful, while an overarching deity named Mulungu controls the rains and the broader sweep of fate. Human beings can intercept these powers and steer them to their own ends, propitiating the ancestors so that they bring good fortune, soliciting the help of spirits in rituals, and harnessing evil creatures for their curses. Those who mediate best between the visible and invisible worlds are the diviners and healers called *"waganga."*

The status of waganga is heavily disparaged by many of the Muslim Swahili and Arabs who have long populated the coastal towns. In the early 19th century, Swahili and Giriama commonly intermarried and the distinction between them was fluid and indeterminate. But in the context of European colonialism and its aftermath, both groups have been politically and economically motivated to reify ever sharper boundaries between themselves and the Giriama (Cooper 1980; Willis 1993). Today, Arabs and Swahili tend to view Giriama ways as heathen and polluting, a narrative internalized by quite a few Giriama (McIntosh 2004). In the 19th century, a Giriama prophetess named Mipoho was said to have prophesied the coming of yet another threat to Giriama ways. Mipoho stood in a circle of beating drums and begin to sink, bolt upright, into the ground, as she intoned her warning. A people as pale as butterflies would come, bringing metal flying craft, vehicles that roll along the ground, and social catastrophe. Giriama youth would scorn and betray their elders, and great draughts of smoke would issue from their mouths. Soon after the earth reclaimed Mipoho, the first Western missionaries arrived, followed during the next decades by colonials and white tourists. Giriama custom was thoroughly marginalized by the colonial and postcolonial economy, while children betrayed the beliefs and practices of their elders with draughts of cigarette smoke issuing from their mouths. Today, some young Giriama pursue status however they can, through the accumulation of the boom boxes and T-shirts that might align them with some version of modernity; through affiliation with Christianity; or, less commonly, through conversion to Islam. There are still many who engage in Giriama rituals, but they are therefore burdened by not one but two disapproving foreign gods.

The force of this disapproval was particularly evident on one field trip Maxwell and I took to a rural secondary school about forty kilometers southwest of Malindi, where we had planned to interview some students. When we arrived we found that that the headmaster had changed the terms of our appointment. We could speak to his students, but only on condition that all 50 of them were present at once. As I looked on helplessly, a crush of teenagers in crisp blue and white uniforms filed into a classroom, jamming the desks together like a blockade. I explained that I was not a missionary but had come to have a "conversation" about religion. The students tossed their pencils into the air and snickered behind their hands, while I succumbed to a sinking feeling that this conversation would never get off the ground.

"How many of you would say you are Christians?" I blushed as I asked; truly, this was fieldwork at its crudest. There was a tentative pause, then a shuffling of uprising hands from most of the students.

"How many would say you are Muslims?" Everyone else, it seemed.

"And how many of you also believe in the traditional Giriama ancestors, the spirits, and the Giriama god, Mulungu?" I heard a chair scrape across the concrete floor, and a blur of murmurs rose like steam and hung in the air for what felt like an eternity. At last the teacher raised his hand from the back of the classroom. "Madam, they are not going to answer a question like that, because they feel shy."

I leapt on his observation. "This is what I'm trying to study! If they feel shy, I want to understand why."

"Because these things are evil. The Christians have told us it is devil worship." The state, too, in fact. The colonial government of Kenya passed Witchcraft ordinances in 1909, 1918, and 1925, and since then the slippery Western category of "witchdoctor" has been used to target benign diviners and healers on an ad hoc basis. During his tenure, President Moi deflected challenges to the Christian state by setting up a special commission to eradicate "devil worship." The Swahili term *sheitani* can be translated as either "spirit" or "devil," and the national press frequently aligns any spirit belief at all with Satanic forces. I decided to take this on.

"Giriama spirits are known to be both good and bad," I ventured, "so why would you call them all devils?"

"Because it's evil to summon them or use them," the teacher replied impatiently. "In fact, it's evil to believe in them."

I nearly opened my mouth to contradict him. I had no objection to cultural change, but I did bristle at the way Giriama were shamed, even by the state itself, into renouncing their practices. Still, who was I to give them a lecture on their cultural pride? I looked at Maxwell. He was leaning against a desk with his hipbone, arms folded, his body in a tall, delicate curve. "Here, Janet, let me help," he said. He strode to the front of the classroom with preternaturally long steps, his trousers flapping like sails behind him. The students straightened and looked sharp for the first time since we had come in. Maxwell scanned the room with his eyes and began to orate as if powered by another source, some lightning bolt that touched his slender frame.

"You say you do not believe in spirits? You say you renounce your ancestors?" His upper body tilted and snapped; his long index finger targeted the boys and girls. Christ, Mohammed, and all the proselytizers who came after them became tyrants who were dismantling Africans' self-regard. The students were cowards and pawns in a great global game of exploitation. "You are following foreign gods, gods who do not love you as you are! Mulungu will love you as a Giriama! He will love you even if you smell like sweat!"

By now Maxwell had shifted out of English and Kiswahili, two languages sanctioned for classroom use, into the stigmatized Giriama mother tongue that is banned in many schools but, according to my Giriama friends, hooks into their deepest identity. His cadences began to lilt steeply. His voice dipped to a near-whisper as he described a man who worked in the tourism industry and began to neglect his ancestors—then it rose again to a shout as he recounted how the embittered, rampaging spirits immolated the man's home and struck his wife with typhoid. "Your ancestors are waiting for you to remember them! The spirits call for their palm wine, and you are out at the church wearing white people's clothes!" The students were saucer eyed with fear.

Eventually Maxwell held out his palms before him. "Now," he said, his eyebrows fierce with anticipation: "Do you believe in these things? These Giriama spirits and ancestors, are they real?"

"Yes," chorused the students.

"Do these things exist?" He was triumphant, but he wanted it said again, to seal the agreement.

"Yes. Yes, they do." The students looked at him gravely.

"I am going to start a movement, something to return us to the God who loves us and the spirits and ancestors who know us and watch us every day. I am going to call it 'The Revival Faith of Giriama.' Some day I want you all to be my followers."

We walked home side by side, Maxwell striding fast and looking distant, lost in the thought of things to come.

After several months of working together, Maxwell and I began to focus on Giriama waganga themselves, interviewing them and sitting in on their rituals, often in a smoky corner of their mud and thatch homes. To spend so much time with this group of professionals was to invite a unique set of dilemmas. Most waganga expected a small gift or fee in exchange for our conversations—a perfectly reasonable demand, I felt. Unfortunately, many also insisted that they tell me my own fortune, a path I resisted because it unnerved me in a way I found hard to articulate. The waganga, however, found my position ungenerous. I was extracting information from them, so why shouldn't they extract it from me? Didn't I trust them? Was I hiding something, perhaps a Christian agenda?

Maxwell noticed these tensions growing during an interview with a particularly reluctant diviner, and on the way home he turned to me. "I know you don't want to have your fortune told," he said, "but I would like to have it done to myself." His relationships with certain family members had been deteriorating, and he was suffering from headaches that only seemed to get worse. He often bought a small handful of aspirins from a roadside kiosk so he could get through the day. He had suspected for some time that he had been bewitched, and now it was time to consult a specialist so he could know for sure.

The research improved after that. The diviners seemed to feel useful as they probed Maxwell's past and future, and Maxwell and I advanced our respective projects as we observed the details of ritual procedure, including the way that powerful ethnic spirits, especially Arabs and Swahili, would possess the waganga's bodies in a cloud of incense to offer diagnoses and suggest ritual remedies. Quite a few suggested Maxwell had been bewitched, but their attributions of guilt varied widely. These discrepancies hardly bothered me; my purpose was not to test the diviners but to understand their cultural roles and the ways in which they used language and responded to social change. I took notes about deftly improvised ritual content while theorizing about the fact that the diviners' spirits often spoke in tongues borrowed from prestigious social groups.

Maxwell was full of questions, eager to talk about what we witnessed. When he asked me why the spirits spoke with such an odd timbre—sometimes nasal, sometimes high pitched, sometimes stuttering—it was hard for me not to tell him about the observations of Judith Irvine (1982), whose cross-cultural survey documents the breadth of linguistic markers that can signal the presence of a spirit. Apparently almost any sound that deviates from normal talk—being slower, faster, oddly pitched, and so on—can mark the source of the sound as extra-ordinary. I told Maxwell about it. "You mean she thinks the spirits themselves aren't talking? That it is just people changing their voices?" Maxwell asked, skeptically. I tried to explain that Irvine's point was not to debunk possession per se, but Maxwell suspected what kind of premise we anthropologists were starting with. He wasn't wrong. When Maxwell asked why so many spirits came from powerful or feared ethnic groups, I told him of the many ethnographies that suggest spirit possession is a human invention that can allow people creatively to process their histories and social roles and, sometimes, to exact redress from those with more power (Boddy 1989; Giles 1995; Lewis 1971; Masquelier 2001; Stoller 1984). Maxwell resisted this: "If the spirits are just inventions people use to help themselves, why do they sometimes punish people by making them sick?"

Between receiving dispatches of anthropological theory from me, Maxwell became obsessed with the diviners' veracity. I noticed that he began to apply a quasi-scientific measuring stick to evaluate them. He wondered why he got a different reading from each diviner, and his interest in finding the "most powerful" ones had expanded into a vociferous condemnation of hucksters. I assumed that he took them as an offense to Giriama tradition and a threat to his revival movement.

Drawn as Maxwell was to extremes, he was most impressed by the diviners who delivered high drama. When he was at the height of his anxiety about his own bewitchment, we made an appointment with Tresea, who had urged us for weeks to come and see what she is capable of. Tresea and her husband eagerly led us into a small hut and offered us two wooden chairs at the edge of the room. Tresea sat close by our feet on a floor mat, her legs extending straight before her. She draped a cloth over her head and tucked a wand of incense beneath it, inhaling the smoke and rocking gently. We waited in silence for what felt like an eternity. Finally, almost imperceptibly, her rocking movements intensified like a pendulum picking up momentum, until her torso began to hurtle back and forth heavily, her head flopping as if her neck might break. It was easy to imagine that she was being pitched around by some tremendous force. After a couple of perilous minutes, Tresea's movements slowed. She seemed to gather herself and tottered to her feet, still breathing heavily. Her eyes looked strange and out of focus. She oriented towards each of us in turn, shaking our hands while offering an Arabic greeting in a protracted, eerie voice: "Asaaaalaaaaam aleikuuum . . . Asaalaaam aleikuuum." Maxwell extended his hand in a sudden, rabbity motion, looking toward the doorway as if to check his escape route. Her husband, sitting next to me, offered the formulaic ritual greeting: "Taireni! Which spirit are you?"

In a stuttering monotone, the spirit announced itself: "Mi-mi-kat-a-mainiiiii . . . Mi-kat-a-mai-niiiiiii."

"The Liver-Cutter." I'd heard of many spirits but never this one, and I felt a small tightening in the pit of my stomach. Only a week earlier, a local doctor had told me I looked a bit jaundiced, so I had had my blood tested. It turned out my liver was off-kilter and they couldn't be sure why. Tresea's husband looked at us.

"What do you want to ask?" he said. Tresea sat and began to tilt violently to and fro again. Maxwell drew his torso back in a steep diagonal line. I glanced at his face; he looked stricken.

"Maxwell, go on! Talk to her!" I was afraid that Tresea, or Tresea's spirit, would take offense, and the momentum of her possession would dissolve.

"I'm afraid," he hissed in my direction. In an uncharacteristically timid voice, Maxwell beseeched the spirit for advice. The spirit launched into a peculiar blend of Swahili and Arabic, while wrenching Tresea's torso in circles.

"I can see you at some point in the past. You're having problems with work. There's a woman . . . she's short and fat. She loves you but you don't love her back, and now she really wants to hurt you." Maxwell would need to arrange an elaborate ritual to reverse the jilted woman's curse. It involved several expensive items, including two chickens and some rare spices. He took notes on a scrap of paper, checking and double checking the prescription until the spirit seemed to lose patience and turned its attention to me.

"You who sit in silence," it said, ominously. "You do not know me, but you will soon enough." Tresea's husband looked at me meaningfully.

"Now," the spirit added, "I ask your permission to leave." We offered our thanks and the spirit fled, leaving Tresea's body in a state of collapse. After a few seconds she heaved, spat some phlegm onto the earth, and crawled onto a bed to stretch out, eyes closed.

Later, as we walked out into the piercing sunlight, Maxwell turned to me. "Did you see how that spirit abused her body? Did you hear how it spoke? Everything it said was exactly right, exactly." Maxwell told me that several months earlier a small, rounded woman had vied for his attentions, but he told her he wasn't interested in her. As she turned to go, she remarked cryptically that he'd be sorry for rejecting her, and it had left him with a bad feeling. So it was she who had cursed him, dragging his fortunes down. He would implement the ritual antidote immediately, and things would start to improve. He seemed relieved.

"If you still have doubts about whether these spirits exist, Janet, you must know by now they are real."

Did I have doubts? I thought about the house where I lived. In the late afternoon, the cool whitewashed walls provided relief from the arduous day—but by night, it became an eerie place, barricaded under the threat of armed robbery, and teeming like a miniature Jurassic Park. Gecko lizards dangled near the lights to catch giant moths; bats hung on the beams over my desk to peer at me; black millipedes as thick as my finger marched across the floor. I once opened the bathroom door to find a stick insect so large it looked like a piece of kindling with wings. In this strange crucible, sleep had taken on an unearthly quality; my antimalarial medication, notorious for neurological side-effects, converted my worst fears into exceptionally vivid nightmares. Every night a new horror visited me under my mosquito net: a river of army ants, a python, a Somali gunman. Most unnerving of all, a little Arab boy, a spirit incarnate, would come to float over my head or sit at the foot of my bed, lingering for a few seconds even after I had opened my eyes.

Some odd things had also begun to happen around the house—minor incidents, but they spooked me. One night, for example, I woke sensing that something strange had happened and turned to look at my alarm clock. It had come to a standstill five minutes earlier. How had I sensed that time had stopped, when my clock was designed to run silently? On another night, I awoke to a great crash—a cast-iron frying pan was on the kitchen floor, and there was no ac-

counting for how it had gotten there from the counter. The missionaries next door were already convinced I was playing with fire in my research—demonic spirits were reaching me, and I needed to embrace Christ to save myself. I began to think that the membrane separating disbelief from belief was thinner than I had realized, and that my subconscious was making brief forays to the other side.

One evening, I secured the house before I went to bed in the usual way, padlocking an iron door on an outside courtyard, then a heavy wooden door at the front of the house, and finally a metal gate that shut me into the second floor. After an hour of fitful insomnia, I got up to get a glass of water from the kitchen. I flipped on the lights and went to open the gate at the top of the stairs, but when I put the key in the lock it seemed to put down roots as if possessed. It simply would not budge. I began to conjure an image of myself trapped there days later—parched, wilting, still scrabbling at the lock—when suddenly the electricity went off with a soft pop, and I was enveloped in darkness. Fear and confusion gathered in my chest and a thought ran through my mind of its own accord: "Who has bewitched me?" Could I have angered the Liver-Cutter by summoning it in bad faith, using it for research without quite believing in it? I felt a wave of queasiness before groping again for the key with jittering hands. All at once the lights sprang on and the lock released the key like a dog opening its mouth, sending me tumbling backward.

Shortly after meeting the Liver-Cutter, Maxwell and I went to visit Karissa, one of the few male diviners in Maxwell's village, renowned for recovering lost and stolen objects. Maxwell was feeling spent—plumbed too often and too intensely by the spirits, perhaps—so we settled on a neutral problem for Karissa to solve: The heavy rains were coming soon and I had lost my umbrella the day before. An old man with a kindly face and grizzled hair, Karissa wore a striped cloth loosely wrapped around his waist beneath his massive caramel-colored chest, scarified with the horizontal welts of a boyhood initiation ceremony. He invited us into a dark hut and seated us on low stools. Maxwell and I told him that we wanted to interview him about his work, but that we could also use his help in finding something, if he wished to take us up on it.

"Don't tell me what it is," he said. "I will do my best to tell you." He began to pile lumps of incense into a hollow coconut shell.

Maxwell whispered in my ear: "The really good ones never promise anything for sure. This man has fierce powers."

The familiar incense fumes made me heady by sheer power of association, and I had to dig my fingernails into my flesh to anchor myself. Karissa produced a solid little pouch made of something resembling shoe-leather, sewn together in thick, powerful stitches. He dangled the talisman over the curling white smoke, incanting rapidly under his breath in the Giriama language. After a short while, he looked intently at the talisman and addressed it directly.

"We want to know what has gone missing. Please tell us what has gone missing." The talisman dangled, motionless.

"Was it a radio?" Still the talisman hung without response.

"Was it clothing? A shirt? Was it a shirt? No? A dress? No?" He paused.

"Was it money?" Karissa held his breath, then made an exasperated noise, as if the talisman might be faulty, or willfully misbehaving. "Money? Money?" He paused, and tried once more. "Money?" He sighed.

"Was it a watch?" No response.

"Was it an umbrella?" The talisman started and began to whirl in rapid clockwise circles over the incense. Karissa smiled with satisfaction. Maxwell and I pushed our chairs backward in awe.

On the way home Maxwell and I conferred. Of course we knew Karissa could control the motions of the talisman, in principal. The question was why the talisman had moved when it did. Ever the fraud detector, Maxwell had long since gotten me to agree we would monitor our reactions during divination rituals, trying not to offer unconscious clues in our gaze, our body language, even our breath if we could help it. But it was far from obvious that Karissa had been attending to us for signals.

Not long after that, Maxwell and I were strolling into town when we passed an apartment building with a hand painted sign on the outside wall: "Professor Omar R. Matata: Expert treatment for ills caused by witchcraft. Unwanted spirits chased away. Drop-in Hours Sunday through Friday, 1:00 to 6:00; Saturday any time." A middle-aged man approached us, wearing a torn shirt and carrying a greasy fish wrapped in a newspaper. "Do you know this professor?" I asked, gesturing toward the sign.

"I'm his assistant," he said with pride. "My name is Mohammed." He was not a Giriama—I inferred he was Digo, a culturally related but thoroughly Muslimized people—but I had noticed that by now Maxwell had ceased to be an ethnic purist in his research. He was so riveted by supernatural mysteries, he didn't much mind where they came from, as long as they worked. I avoided reminding him of the Revival Faith of Giriama, thinking it might be a sore point.

The professor was with a client, so we persuaded Mohammed to speak to us in an empty room on the ground floor of his apartment building. "Tell us about this doctor," Maxwell demanded, without preliminaries. "How strong are his powers?"

"He trained far away, in Tanzania, where he got expert material. He can make money appear out of nowhere. And he can read your mind."

"Can you do any of this?" asked Maxwell. Mohammed thought for a moment, then gestured to my notepad with an authoritative air.

"Give me that," he said. He ripped out a thin strip of paper, about a centimeter wide and three centimeters long. "I'm going to leave the room," he said to me. "I want you to write something on that paper— anything you like. Then fold it into a square"—he demonstrated with his fingertips—"and hold onto it."

Mohammed strolled outside and inspected the hem of his shirt. I looked at the slip of paper and wrote the Swahili word for umbrella: *"mwavuli."* Maxwell chuckled. I folded the paper and called Mohammed inside. Wordlessly, he grabbed my notebook and pen, opened to a clean page, and drew a stick figure with a circle around its midsection like a target. He held this effigy and began to incant under his breath, producing a river of strange sounds that suggested secret codes, obscure information, a window into a world of new knowledge.

Mohammed put the effigy drawing on the table. "Now, I want you to throw your folded paper at this spirit seven times." I tossed the folded square tentatively. It landed on the figure's head. "No—" He picked up the paper and threw it directly at the target area: "Like this." I obeyed, and Mohammed continued: "Now, I want you to eat that paper. Chew it well." I popped the square into my mouth and chewed.

"I'll be back," Mohammed said, and, taking a bottle of water, marched out the door. We could hear him outside, incanting and splashing.

When he reemerged, a few drops of water still clinging to his face, he took my notebook and pen out of my hands. "Look at me," he commanded. His eyes drilled into mine. This was clearly some process of reading, and I felt slightly violated. After about thirty seconds he wrenched away, turned to the notebook, and with a heavy, slow hand inscribed a row of seven digits. Then he faced the drawing of the spirit and began to incant again.

"What are you doing?"

"I'm asking the spirit to help me to translate these numbers." Ponderously, he began to write a letter beneath each number: "m"; "w"; "a"; until he had completed the word *mwavuli.* Maxwell shrieked, and we slapped each other's hands with excitement.

Mohammed refused, when we requested it, to transform paper into money, saying he needed to rest. So we walked home, racking our brains to recall when he might have had an opportunity to read the piece of paper. Mohammed had been outside when

I first wrote the word, and he'd never had a chance to unwrap the square of paper before I ate it. Could some people really skirt the laws of physics to read minds and tell fortunes? The idea was disorienting, almost unthinkable, but I entertained it, turning it over and over with chills running up my neck. I was too preoccupied to write any field notes that night; in fact, I'd been distracted from my ethnographic purpose ever since encountering the Liver-Cutter. Just before going to bed, the thought crossed my mind: If Mohammed has such miraculous powers, why is his shirt so badly torn?

Somewhere in the no-man's-land between wakefulness and sleep my subconscious groped through the murk of the day and grabbed hold of something. I sat up. Mohammed had switched the folded square of paper. He had only touched it once, when showing me how to throw it, but if he had another square hidden between his fingers, he could have made a quick replacement. I dug into my bag and pulled out my notebook, opening it to the page where Mohammed had first torn out a strip of paper and handed it to me. The torn space was now six centimeters long, not three.

William James (2002) has famously described the experience of conversion as one in which the mundane world is ruptured by an ecstatic sense of contact with the divine. What I experienced at this moment was something like a mirror image of Jamesian conversion. My growing wonder was translated suddenly into a dull, mechanical grasp of the facts, coupled with the grungy taste of having been deceived. I had to remind myself that "fakery" is not an important theoretical concept in the anthropological study of religion. Michael Lambek (1993), attending an antisorcery ritual in the Comoros Islands, once spotted a healer concealing a sac of fingernails and dirt that he subsequently "extracted" from a patient's body. On speaking to the diviner at length, Lambek realized that the diviner himself believed in sorcery and felt the planted sac had a persuasive effect important to the effect of the ritual. Even the healers who have become victims of sorcery consider this "extraction" necessary to their cure. In kind, I had seen Giriama diviners go to other diviners and healers for help, demonstrating their overarching commitment to the system, whatever their own repertoire of ritual gambits. And as the great theorists have reminded us, there is much to ritual—its causes, consequences, social roles, and expressive capacities—that transcends the simple Western notions of empirical truth and falsity (Rappaport 1979:173–222; Tambiah 1985:123–166; Turner 1967). I realized with faint sadness that I was back on familiar terrain, possessing an abstract respect for the role of religion in others' lives, and a desiccated relationship to it myself.

In the morning, I set out to tell Maxwell. We were accustomed to sharing everything, and I thought he might be impressed by my resolution to Mohammed's puzzle. Instead, something seemed to drop out from under him. His anger was total, almost violent. He made scything motions of denial with his hands as he reacted, then collapsed into a contemplative stupor and announced he could not work for the rest of that day.

When we resumed our research, Maxwell had changed. It was as if the little window of skepticism that had opened in him some months earlier—back when I started to talk about anthropological theory and he started testing the waganga—had never quite closed, and in the end had been just large enough that a strong wind could blow the whole house down. We went to a famous diviner's place to watch a purification ritual: A child was missing some of his hair and his father feared a witch had snipped it off as he slept. Maxwell eyed the circular patch on the child's scalp, leaned over to me, and said flatly into my ear: "ringworm." He began to revise his past encounters with waganga: those who had divined well must have known his problems already from village gossip. He also suspected he had played his own role, assisting and cueing them as they jointly created an increasingly focused narrative about his troubles—a model of Giriama divinatory collaboration strikingly close to that of David Parkin (1979). During our interviews he became offhand and businesslike, even mouthy, setting traps for diviners so he could spot the contradictions in their answers. He became impossibly demanding in his standards for evidence. "I won't be satisfied that they have any powers until they can do something amazing on the spot. Like change this"—he pointed to a cassette—"into a loaf of bread."

Despite his moments of humor, Maxwell seemed emptied out, and sometimes descended into a bitter anomie.

"I don't believe in spirits anymore. There is no supernatural world. There is just . . . what is."

"What about the Revival Faith of Giriama?" I asked. "What about the pride of your people in their customs?"

He thought for a minute. "Maybe," he proposed, "we could have a Revival Faith of Giriama where people still do the rituals for the spirits and the ancestors, and wear the traditional clothes, but they don't have to believe in any of it. So it wouldn't quite be religion, but it would still preserve our custom."

It occurred to me that in the practice known as cultural tourism, some Giriama families already received a hundred shillings a day for preserving their customs. All they had to do was file into a hotel dining room in traditional dress, dragging their goats on a lead and simulating ancestor propitiation with a bottle of palm wine.

Some time later, I left town on my own for a few weeks to do some research in a nearby area. When I returned I happened to walk past the guest house where Maxwell and I had first met, and a large white canvas sign caught my eye.

"PROFESSOR PROFESSOR," it read, "HIGHLY TRAINED TOP PROFESSIONAL DIVINER AVAILABLE FOR CONSULTATION AND HEALING." The announcement followed with a row of characters that looked like a bad approximation of Chinese. "That's funny," I said to myself. "I thought I knew all the diviners working around here." One of the maids, Taabu, approached me.

"Have you heard about Maxwell?" she asked.

"What about him? Is he all right?"

"He's frightening us," she said.

"What do you mean?"

"He has become a very big diviner. Very feared."

I felt a wild flash of disorientation, and broke into confused laughter. "He's become a diviner? What do you mean? Where does he work?" Taabu gestured toward a back room.

Inside the room Maxwell had lined up the familiar accoutrements of divination and healing, with the perfect air of age and mystery. There was a stained gourd, its cork rimmed with blackened honey. There was a paper with a drawing of a bird in flight, radiating rays of some kind, flanked by two winged snakes, all presumably spirit effigies. There was a gizmo, maybe a wand, with feathers at the tip—this I hadn't even seen in our research. Maxwell was pushing the envelope. I tugged at one of the feathers and dissolved into laughter, crumpling against the wall with angry tears pricking my eyes.

Later, Maxwell demonstrated his ritual routines for me with a trickster's delight. He had gleaned almost everything directly from our research findings, and I was both bemused and horrified. If anyone in the village found out he was playing them, and playing with the powers of the spirits, they could have exiled or even killed him. But his dalliance with divination did not last very long. After a while the thrill, or maybe the anger that had propelled him, wore off. He took down his sign, and I rehired him for a couple more months to help me on a project about language that had nothing to do with spirits.

When I left Kenya, Maxwell used the wages I paid him as collateral for a loan to buy a taxi, which promptly broke an axle. He could not pay his debts, and fled south to Tanzania for a time. Judging from the intermittent e-mail messages he sent me, he left Kenya feeling cynical. He was fed up with his hardships, with religion, and with what he now regarded as the false hope purveyed by diviners and healers. And I would not blame him if he were also fed up with me or, perhaps, with the strange mirror I had held up to his convictions that changed them forever. In his disenchantment, Maxwell had been confronted with what he had once most feared: that a cosmos that once spoke vividly to the Giriama people was fading into the background as the generations turned over and the other forces—the Christians, the Muslims, the modernists, sometimes even the anthropologists—continued their march from over the horizon.

I was struck, though not until later, by the extent to which I had been unsettled by Maxwell's own journey into unbelief and his canny manipulation of the rituals that he now considered empty. Part of my discomfort seemed reasonable enough—even Maxwell saw himself as duping his gullible clients. Another part seemed to emerge from my quintessentially Western fixation on belief. I was vexed by the image of a Giriama going through the motions of divination without believing in it, a deep discomfort probably linked, unconsciously, to the Abrahamic assumption that "religion is (or should be) grounded in a solemn kind of faith." But most upsetting to me, I think, was that through his encounter with me Maxwell had lost his will to resist the forces that threatened to engulf a Giriama way of life still prized by some. We ethnographers are trained not to fetishize "cultural authenticity," but we are also prone to root for the underdog. I had admired Maxwell's pride and scrappiness, and his aspirations to lead a revival movement had made him a central allegorical figure (Clifford and Marcus 1986) in my ethnographic tableau about Giriama dilemmas. In abandoning his convictions, Maxwell lost his place as my figurehead of Giriama resistance—and ironically enough, my analytic approach to religion had contributed to his discouragement.

At the same time, I had complicated my own role as ethnographer by dipping my toe for a moment into an ocean of wonder, then withdrawing just as rapidly. At the beginning of fieldwork, when I resisted having my fortune told, I probably had the same ambivalence that many American agnostics might have about a Ouija board or Tarot card reading. We tell ourselves we don't believe that inert objects can prognosticate; yet disbelief is a fragile conceit, for if the wrong card turns up, then perhaps at some level in which the mind is not so tightly harnessed we might start to entertain the uncomfortable possibility of the impossible. It is that much easier to cross this line when context strips us of the social, material, and semiotic points of reference that remind us of who we are or want to be. It is hard to hold the putative self steady in an environment saturated with alternatives. I had seen spirits under my mosquito net in the realm between sleep and wakefulness, with the bats and the millipedes my silent witnesses, and no one there to talk me down. I felt assailed by mysterious health problems and fickle locks, and transported by the very scent of incense, by now so closely associated with diviners' possession. Everyone around me talked about spirits, even implying that spirits were responsible for the peculiar events in my home, and I was close to these people. I liked and empathized with many of them, and I took seriously their commitments. And so, for a few days there, I had begun to float gingerly above all I had known to be true.

Still, context does not so quickly do away with entrenched habits of self-surveillance. I never entirely lost sight of my future reinsertion into a comfortable life in the United States with my partner, my family, my friends, my students, and my fellow academics. Ultimately, this vision reclaimed me with the inevitability of gravity. The Arab child over my bed became a side-effect of my antimalarial pills and a symptom of my suggestibility. The simultaneous failure of the lock and the lights, and the (ultimately benign) liver abnormality echoed by the name of the Liver-Cutter became coincidences. Karissa, in his remarkable detection of my missing umbrella, had revealed not the psychic ability of his talisman, but a refined sensitivity to his clients' unwitting cues.

I almost had to rewrite these stories for myself—my professional future was at stake. For however diverse anthropologists may be, a series of ideological commitments underlie ethnographic scholarship in the West today, and one of these is the notion that gods, spirits, and ancestors should be analyzed as human phenomena, bound up with local social, economic, semiotic, and political arrangements. Some ethnographers may offer the occasional nod to the mysteries of the unknown, and may even harbor deep cosmological commitments in their hearts, but to seriously entertain supernatural entities as real in one's scholarly work would be considered at best a distraction and at worst a disastrous hobbling of one's analytic abilities. Our pact as anthropologists, then, is to go "there" without ever quite leaving "here"; the emic is all very well and good, provided that the etic is close behind. This epistemological demand means that successful scholarship is most easily carried out by a particular kind of self, a self conditioned by what Katherine Ewing (1994) has identified as the powerful taboo against "going native" among those in our discipline.

No wonder my swift return to agnosticism the night after meeting Mohammed brought with it a shade of relief. I was safe again, back where I belonged, back with the assurance of a future in an elite cultural context where others would make room for me because my ontological commitments would fit neatly in. Maxwell, on the other hand, felt loosed from his mast and cast into a state of enduring liminality, left to rely on his wits, on sheer skin-of-his-teeth bricolage, while dogged by the knowledge that no matter how creative his adaptations, they would never give him the sure footing of the privileges I would go home to.

REFERENCES CITED

Boddy, Janice. 1989. Wombs and Alien Spirits: Women, Men, and the Zar Cult in Northern Sudan. Madison: University of Wisconsin Press.

Clifford, James, and George Marcus. 1986. Writing Culture: The Poetics and Politics of Ethnography. Berkeley: University of California Press.

Cooper, Frederick. 1980. From Slaves to Squatters: Plantation Labor and Agriculture in Zanzibar and Coastal Kenya 1890–1925. New Haven, CT: Yale University Press.

Dominguez, Virginia R. 1986. The Marketing of Heritage. American Ethnologist 13(3):546–555.

Ewing, Katherine. 1994. Dreams from a Saint: Anthropological Atheism and the Temptation to Believe. American Anthropologist 96(3):571–583.

Fienup-Riordan, Ann. 1988. Robert Redford, Apanuugpak, and the Invention of Tradition. American Ethnologist 15(3):442–455.

Giles, Linda L. 1995. Sociocultural Change and Spirit Possession on the Swahili Coast of East Africa. Anthropological Quarterly 68(2):89–106.

Hobsbawm, Eric, and Terence Ranger. 1983. The Invention of Tradition. Cambridge: Cambridge University Press.

Irvine, Judith. 1982. The Creation of Identity in Spirit Mediumship and Possession. In Semantic Anthropology. David Parkin, ed. Pp. 241–260. London: Academic Press.

James, William. 2002[1902]. The Varieties of Religious Experience: A Study in Human Nature. Amherst, NY: Prometheus Books.

Lambek, Michael. 1993. Knowledge and Practice in Mayotte: Local Discourses of Islam, Sorcery, and Spirit Possession. Toronto: University of Toronto Press.

Lawless, Elaine J. 1992. "I Was Afraid Someone Like You . . . an Outsider . . . Would Misunderstand": Negotiating Interpretive Differences between Ethnographers and Subjects. Journal of American Folklore 105(417): 302–314.

Lewis, Ioan M. 1971. Ecstatic Religion: An Anthropological Study of Spirit Possession and Shamanism. Harmondsworth, UK: Penguin Books.

Masquelier, Adeline. 2001. Prayer has Spoiled Everything: Possession, Power, and Identity in an Islamic Town of Niger. Durham, NC: Duke University Press.

McIntosh, Janet. 2004. Reluctant Muslims: Embodied Hegemony and Moral Resistance in a Giriama Spirit

Possession Complex. Journal of the Royal Anthropological Institute 10(1):91–112.

Parkin, David. 1979. Straightening the Paths from Wildness: The Case of Divinatory Speech. Journal of the Anthropological Society of Oxford 10(3):147–160.

Rappaport, Roy. 1979. Ecology, Meaning, and Religion. Richmond, CA: North Atlantic Books.

Scheper-Hughes, Nancy. 1995. The Primacy of the Ethical: Propositions for a Militant Anthropology. Current Anthropology 36(3): 409–440.

Stoller, Paul. 1984. Horrific Comedy: Cultural Resistance and the Hauka Movement in Niger. Ethos 12(2): 165–188.

Tambiah, Stanley J. 1985. Culture, Thought, and Social Action. Cambridge, MA: Harvard University Press.

Turner, Victor. 1967. The Forest of Symbols: Aspects of Ndembu Ritual. Ithaca, NY: Cornell University Press.

Willis, Justin. 1993. Mombasa, the Swahili, and the Making of the Mijikenda. Oxford: Clarendon Press.

4

When Brothers Share a Wife

Melvyn C. Goldstein

....

Marriage is a social institution that formalizes certain aspects of domestic relationships. It is an institution that evokes in us deep-seated emotions about questions of right and wrong, good and evil, and traditional versus modern. Within families, arguments may occur about what is appropriate premarital behavior, what is a proper marriage ceremony, and how long a marriage should last. Although these arguments may be traumatic for parents and their offspring, from a cross-cultural perspective, they generally involve minor deviations from cultural norms. In contrast, anthropology textbooks describe an amazing variety of marriage systems that fulfill both biological and social functions. This selection will show just how different things could be.

Social institutions are geared to operate within and adapt to the larger social and ecological environment. The organization of the family must also be adapted to the ecology. For example, the nuclear family is more adapted to a highly mobile society than is an extended family unit that includes grandparents and others. As society increasingly focuses on technical education, career specialization, and therefore geographic mobility for employment purposes, a system has evolved that emphasizes the nuclear family over the extended family. In a similar way, fraternal polyandry in Tibet, as described in this selection, can meet the social, demographic, and ecological needs of its region.

As you read this selection, ask yourself the following questions:

- What is meant by the term *fraternal polyandry*?
- Is fraternal polyandry the only form of marriage allowed in Tibet?
- How do husbands and wives feel about the sexual aspects of sharing a spouse?
- Why would Tibetans choose fraternal polyandry?
- How is the function of fraternal polyandry like that of nineteenth-century primogeniture in England?

The following terms discussed in this selection are included in the Glossary at the back of the book:

arable land
corvée
fraternal polyandry
monogamy

nuclear family
population pressure
primogeniture

....

Eager to reach home, Dorje drives his yaks hard over the 17,000-foot mountain pass, stopping only once to rest. He and his two older brothers, Pema and Sonam, are jointly marrying a woman from the next village in a few weeks, and he has to help with the preparations.

Dorje, Pema, and Sonam are Tibetans living in Limi, a 200-square-mile area in the northwest corner of Nepal, across the border from Tibet. The form of marriage they are about to enter—fraternal polyandry in anthropological parlance—is one of the world's rarest forms of marriage but is not uncommon in Tibetan society, where it has been practiced from time immemorial. For many Tibetan social strata, it traditionally represented the ideal form of marriage and family.

The mechanics of fraternal polyandry are simple. Two, three, four, or more brothers jointly take a wife, who leaves her home to come and live with them. Traditionally, marriage was arranged by parents, with children, particularly females, having little or no say. This is changing somewhat nowadays, but it is still unusual for children to marry without their parents' consent. Marriage ceremonies vary by income and region and range from all the brothers sitting together as grooms to only the eldest one formally doing so. The age of the brothers plays an important role in determining this: very young brothers almost never participate in actual marriage ceremonies, although they typically join the marriage when they reach their midteens.

Goldstein, Melvyn C. "When Brothers Share a Wife" from *Natural History* (March 1987):39–48; copyright © Natural History Magazine, Inc. 1987. Reprinted with permission.

The eldest brother is normally dominant in terms of authority, that is, in managing the household, but all the brothers share the work and participate as sexual partners. Tibetan males and females do not find the sexual aspect of sharing a spouse the least bit unusual, repulsive, or scandalous, and the norm is for the wife to treat all the brothers the same.

Offspring are treated similarly. There is no attempt to link children biologically to particular brothers, and a brother shows no favoritism toward his child even if he knows he is the real father because, for example, his older brothers were away at the time the wife became pregnant. The children, in turn, consider all of the brothers as their fathers and treat them equally, even if they also know who is their real father. In some regions children use the term "father" for the eldest brother and "father's brother" for the others, while in other areas they call all the brothers by one term, modifying this by the use of "elder" and "younger."

Unlike our own society, where monogamy is the only form of marriage permitted, Tibetan society allows a variety of marriage types, including monogamy, fraternal polyandry, and polygyny. Fraternal polyandry and monogamy are the most common forms of marriage, while polygyny typically occurs in cases where the first wife is barren. The widespread practice of fraternal polyandry, therefore, is not the outcome of a law requiring brothers to marry jointly. There is choice, and in fact, divorce traditionally was relatively simple in Tibetan society. If a brother in a polyandrous marriage became dissatisfied and wanted to separate, he simply left the main house and set up his own household. In such cases, all the children stayed in the main household with the remaining brother(s), even if the departing brother was known to be the real father of one or more of the children.

The Tibetans' own explanation for choosing fraternal polyandry is materialistic. For example, when I asked Dorje why he decided to marry with his two brothers rather than take his own wife, he thought for a moment, then said it prevented the division of his family's farm (and animals) and thus facilitated all of them achieving a higher standard of living. And when I later asked Dorje's bride whether it wasn't difficult for her to cope with three brothers as husbands, she laughed and echoed that rationale of avoiding fragmentation of the family land, adding that she expected to be better off economically, since she would have three husbands working for her and her children.

Exotic as it may seem to Westerners, Tibetan fraternal polyandry is thus in many ways analogous to the way primogeniture functioned in nineteenth-century England. Primogeniture dictated that the eldest son inherited the family estate, while younger sons had to leave home and seek their own employment—for example, in the military or the clergy. Primogeniture maintained family estates intact over generations by permitting only one heir per generation. Fraternal polyandry also accomplishes this but does so by keeping all the brothers together with just one wife so that there is only one set of heirs per generation.

While Tibetans believe that in this way fraternal polyandry reduces the risk of family fission, monogamous marriages among brothers need not necessarily precipitate the division of the family estate: brothers could continue to live together, and the family land could continue to be worked jointly. When I asked Tibetans about this, however, they invariably responded that such joint families are unstable because each wife is primarily oriented to her own children and interested in their success and well-being over that of the children of other wives. For example, if the youngest brother's wife had three sons while the eldest brother's wife had only one daughter, the wife of the youngest brother might begin to demand more resources for her children since, as males, they represent the future of the family. Thus, the children from different wives in the same generation are competing sets of heirs, and this makes such families inherently unstable. Tibetans perceive that conflict will spread from the wives to their husbands and consider this likely to cause family fission. Consequently, it is almost never done.

Although Tibetans see an economic advantage to fraternal polyandry, they do not value the sharing of a wife as an end in itself. On the contrary, they articulate a number of problems inherent in the practice. For example, because authority is customarily exercised by the eldest brother, his younger male siblings have to subordinate themselves with little hope of changing their status within the family. When these younger brothers are aggressive and individualistic, tensions and difficulties often occur despite there being only one set of heirs.

In addition, tension and conflict may arise in polyandrous families because of sexual favoritism. The bride normally sleeps with the eldest brother, and the two have the responsibility to see to it that the other males have opportunities for sexual access. Since the Tibetan subsistence economy requires males to travel a lot, the temporary absence of one or more brothers facilitates this, but there are also other rotation practices. The cultural ideal unambiguously calls for the wife to show equal affection and sexuality to each of the brothers (and vice versa), but deviations from this ideal occur, especially when there is a sizable difference in age between partners in the marriage.

Dorje's family represents just such a potential situation. He is fifteen years old and his two older brothers are twenty-five and twenty-two years old. The new bride is twenty-three years old, eight years

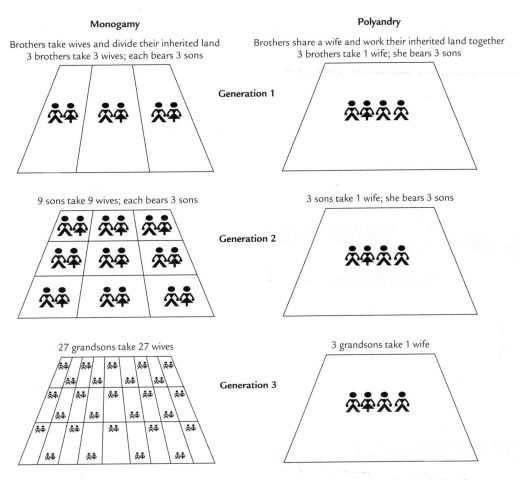

Monogamy

Brothers take wives and divide their inherited land
3 brothers take 3 wives; each bears 3 sons

Polyandry

Brothers share a wife and work their inherited land together
3 brothers take 1 wife; she bears 3 sons

Generation 1

9 sons take 9 wives; each bears 3 sons

3 sons take 1 wife; she bears 3 sons

Generation 2

27 grandsons take 27 wives

3 grandsons take 1 wife

Generation 3

Goldstein, Melvyn C. "When Brothers Share a Wife" from *Natural History* (March 1987):39–48. Illustration reprinted with permission of Joe LeMonnier.

Dorje's senior. Sometimes such a bride finds the youngest husband immature and adolescent and does not treat him with equal affection; alternatively, she may find his youth attractive and lavish special attention on him. Apart from this consideration, when a younger male like Dorje grows up, he may consider his wife "ancient" and prefer the company of a woman his own age or younger. Consequently, although men and women do not find the idea of sharing a bride or a bridegroom repulsive, individual likes and dislikes can cause familial discord.

Two reasons have commonly been offered for the perpetuation of fraternal polyandry in Tibet: that Tibetans practice female infanticide and therefore have to marry polyandrously, owing to a shortage of females; and that Tibet, lying at extremely high altitudes, is so barren and bleak that Tibetans would starve without resort to this mechanism. A Jesuit who lived in Tibet in the eighteenth century articulated this second view: "One reason for this most odious custom is the sterility of the soil, and the small amount of land that can be cultivated owing to the lack of water. The crops may suffice if the brothers all live together, but

if they form separate families they would be reduced to beggary."

Both explanations are wrong, however. Not only has there never been institutionalized female infanticide in Tibet, but Tibetan society gives females considerable rights, including inheriting the family estate in the absence of brothers. In such cases, the woman takes a bridegroom who comes to live in her family and adopts her family's name and identity. Moreover, there is no demographic evidence of a shortage of females. In Limi, for example, there were (in 1974) sixty females and fifty-three males in the fifteen- to thirty-five-year age category, and many adult females were unmarried.

The second reason is also incorrect. The climate in Tibet is extremely harsh, and ecological factors do play a major role perpetuating polyandry, but polyandry is not a means of preventing starvation. It is characteristic, not of the poorest segments of the society, but rather of the peasant landowning families.

In the old society, the landless poor could not realistically aspire to prosperity, but they did not fear starvation. There was a persistent labor shortage throughout

Tibet, and very poor families with little or no land and few animals could subsist through agricultural labor, tenant farming, craft occupations such as carpentry, or by working as servants. Although the per person family income could increase somewhat if brothers married polyandrously and pooled their wages, in the absence of inheritable land, the advantage of fraternal polyandry was not generally sufficient to prevent them from setting up their own households. A more skilled or energetic younger brother could do as well or better alone, since he would completely control his income and would not have to share it with his siblings. Consequently, while there was and is some polyandry among the poor, it is much less frequent and more prone to result in divorce and family fission.

An alternative reason for the persistence of fraternal polyandry is that it reduces population growth (and thereby reduces the pressure on resources) by relegating some females to lifetime spinsterhood. Fraternal polyandrous marriages in Limi (in 1974) averaged 2.35 men per woman, and not surprisingly, 31 percent of the females of child-bearing age (twenty to forty-nine) were unmarried. These spinsters either continued to live at home, set up their own households, or worked as servants for other families. They could also become Buddhist nuns. Being unmarried is not synonymous with exclusion from the reproductive pool. Discreet extramarital relationships are tolerated, and actually half of the adult unmarried women in Limi had one or more children. They raised these children as single mothers, working for wages or weaving cloth and blankets for sale. As a group, however, the unmarried women had far fewer offspring than the married women, averaging only 0.7 children per woman, compared with 3.3 for married women, whether polyandrous, monogamous, or polygynous. While polyandry helps regulate population, this function of polyandry is not consciously perceived by Tibetans and is not the reason they consistently choose it.

If neither a shortage of females nor the fear of starvation perpetuates fraternal polyandry, what motivates brothers, particularly younger brothers, to opt for this system of marriage? From the perspective of the younger brother in a landholding family, the main incentive is the attainment or maintenance of the good life. With polyandry, he can expect a more secure and higher standard of living, with access not only to his family's land and animals, but also to its inherited collection of clothes, jewelry, rugs, saddles, and horses. In addition, he will experience less work pressure and much greater security because all responsibility does not fall on one "father." For Tibetan brothers, the question is whether to trade off the greater personal freedom inherent in monogamy for the real or potential economic security, affluence, and social prestige associated with life in a larger, labor-rich polyandrous family.

A brother thinking of separating from his polyandrous marriage and taking his own wife would face various disadvantages. Although in the majority of Tibetan regions all brothers theoretically have rights to their family's estate, in reality Tibetans are reluctant to divide their land into small fragments. Generally, a younger brother who insists on leaving the family will receive only a small plot of land, if that. Because of its power and wealth, the rest of the family usually can block any attempt of the younger brother to increase his share of land through litigation. Moreover, a younger brother may not even get a house and cannot expect to receive much above the minimum in terms of movable possessions, such as furniture, pots, and pans. Thus, a brother contemplating going it on his own must plan on achieving economic security and the good life not through inheritance but through his own work.

The obvious solution for younger brothers—creating new fields from virgin land—is generally not a feasible option. Most Tibetan populations live at high altitudes (above 12,000 feet), where arable land is extremely scarce. For example, in Dorje's village, agriculture ranges only from about 12,900 feet, the lowest point in the area, to 13,300 feet. Above that altitude, early frost and snow destroy the staple barley crop. Furthermore, because of the low rainfall caused by the Himalayan rain shadow, many areas in Tibet and northern Nepal that are within appropriate altitude range for agriculture have no reliable sources of irrigation. In the end, although there is plenty of unused land in such areas, most of it is either too high or too arid.

Even where unused land capable of being farmed exists, clearing the land and building the substantial terraces necessary for irrigation constitute a great undertaking. Each plot has to be completely dug out to a depth of two to two and a half feet so that the large rocks and boulders can be removed. At best, a man might be able to bring a few new fields under cultivation in the first years after separating from his brothers, but he could not expect to acquire substantial amounts of arable land this way.

In addition, because of the limited farmland, the Tibetan subsistence economy characteristically includes a strong emphasis on animal husbandry. Tibetan farmers regularly maintain cattle, yaks, goats, and sheep, grazing them in the areas too high for agriculture. These herds produce wool, milk, cheese, butter, meat, and skins. To obtain these resources, however, shepherds must accompany the animals on a daily basis. When first setting up a monogamous household, a younger brother like Dorje would find it difficult to both farm and manage animals.

In traditional Tibetan society, there was an even more critical factor that operated to perpetuate fraternal polyandry—a form of hereditary servitude somewhat analogous to serfdom in Europe. Peasants were tied to large estates held by aristocrats, monasteries, and the Lhasa government. They were allowed the use of some farmland to produce their own subsistence but were required to provide taxes in kind and corvée (free labor) to their lords. The corvée was a substantial hardship, since a peasant household was in many cases required to furnish the lord with one laborer daily for most of the year and more on specific occasions such as the harvest. This enforced labor, along with the lack of new land and the ecological pressure to pursue both agriculture and animal husbandry, made polyandrous families particularly beneficial. The polyandrous family allowed an internal division of adult labor, maximizing economic advantage. For example, while the wife worked the family fields, one brother could perform the lord's corvée, another could look after the animals, and a third could engage in trade.

Although social scientists often discount other people's explanations of why they do things, in the case of Tibetan fraternal polyandry, such explanations are very close to the truth. The custom, however, is very sensitive to changes in its political and economic milieu and, not surprisingly, is in decline in most Tibetan areas. Made less important by the elimination of the traditional serf-based economy, it is disparaged by the dominant non-Tibetan leaders of India, China, and Nepal. New opportunities for economic and social mobility in these countries, such as the tourist trade and government employment, are also eroding the rationale for polyandry, and so it may vanish within the next generation.

5

How Many Fathers Are Best for a Child?

Meredith F. Small

Anthropologists study systems of kinship and marriage in many societies for three reasons: first, these issues are very important to the people themselves; second, kinship and marriage are keys for understanding how contemporary cultures work; and finally, because they give us clues as to what patterns of family organization may have existed over the course of human history. As a great deal of anthropological research has revealed, diverse cultures have many different ways of organizing families.

In the United States, we often think of the "traditional" family as a nuclear family: two married parents with their children. Many people ethnocentrically believe that this is the normal or natural family system. Other types of family organization, such as "blended" families, are often described as recent variants. But in fact, the nuclear family model is just one of the many types of kinship organization humans have used at present and in the past—and it is only a relatively recent development in the broader context of human history.

This selection describes a pattern in some South American societies, in which a woman has intercourse with two or more men during her pregnancy and the resulting child is considered as having multiple fathers. This kinship system, like many others across the world, is quite different from the American model of a "traditional" family. However, as this selection argues, this arrangement helps improve children's likelihood of survival in Barí social communities. In the United States, social scientists have shown that having a father present is beneficial for children's development.

As you read this selection, ask yourself the following questions:

- If one father is good, are two or more better? How many fathers are best for a child?
- Why do the Barí believe a child can have more than one father?
- How do Barí women justify taking lovers during pregnancy?
- From an evolutionary perspective, what is the ideal number of fathers for a child to have in Barí society? Why?
- How is the Barí system similar to and different from the system of frequent divorce and court-enforced "child support" payments in modern American society?

The following terms discussed in this selection are included in the Glossary at the back of the book:

multiple paternity
nuclear family
paleoanthropology

Anthropologist Stephen Beckerman was well into his forties before he finally understood how babies are made. He had thought, as most people do, that a sperm from one man and an egg from one woman joined to make a child. But one summer day, as he and his colleague Roberto Lizarralde lounged around in hammocks, chatting with Rachel, an elderly woman of the Barí tribe of Venezuela, she pointed out his error. Babies, she explained, can easily have more than one biological

father. "My first husband was the father of my first child, my second child, and my third child," Rachel said, recalling her life. "But the fourth child, actually, he has two fathers." It was clear that Rachel didn't mean there was a stepfather hanging around or a friendly uncle who took the kid fishing every weekend. She was simply explaining the Barí version of conception to these ignorant anthropologists: A fetus is built up over time with repeated washes of sperm—which means, of course, that more than one man can contribute to the endeavor.

This interview changed not only the way Beckerman and Lizarralde viewed Barí families but also brought into question the very way that anthropologists portray human coupling. If biological fatherhood can be

Small, Meredith F. "How Many Fathers Are Best for a Child?" *Discover* Magazine (March 2003):54–61. Reprinted with permission of the author.

every "father" has a responsibility to the child

shared—an idea accepted by many indigenous groups across South America and in many other cultures across the globe—then the nuclear family with one mom and one dad might not be the established blueprint for a family that we have been led to expect. If so, the familiar story of traditional human mating behavior, in which man the hunter brings home the bacon to his faithful wife, loses credibility. And if the Barí and other groups work perfectly well with more flexible family styles, the variety of family structures that are increasingly common in Western culture these days—everything from single-parent households to blended families—may not be as dangerous to the social fabric as we are led to believe. People in this culture may simply be exercising the same family options that humans have had for millions of years, options that have been operating in other cultures while the West took a stricter view of what constitutes a family.

Stephen Beckerman folds his 6-foot-4-inch frame into a chair and turns to the mountainous topography of papers on his desk at Pennsylvania State University. Once he manages to locate a map under all the piles, he points to a spot on the border between Venezuela and Colombia where he spent 20 years, off and on, with the indigenous Barí Indians. *extracultural turmoil*

The traditional Barí culture, Beckerman explains, has come under attack by outside forces, starting with the conquistadors who arrived in the early sixteenth century. Today Catholic missionaries interact with the Barí, coal and oil companies are trying to seize their land, and drug traffickers and guerrillas are threats. Western influences are apparent: Most families have moved from traditional longhouses to single-family dwellings, and everyone wears modern Western clothes and uses Western goods. However, the Barí continue to practice their traditions of manioc farming, fishing, and hunting, according to Roberto Lizarralde, an anthropologist at the Central University of Venezuela who has been visiting the Barí regularly since 1960. Lizarralde also says that the Barí still have great faith in traditional spirits and ancestral wisdom, including their notion that a child can have multiple biological fathers.

The Barí believe that the first act of sex, which should always be between a husband and wife, plants the seed. Then the fledgling fetus must be nourished by repeated anointings of semen; the woman's body is viewed as a vessel where men do all the work. "One of the reasons women give you for taking lovers is that they don't want to wear out their husbands," Beckerman says. "They claim it's hard work for men to support a pregnancy by having enough sex, and so lovers can help." Just look, the Barí say. Women grow fat during a pregnancy, while men grow thin from all their work.

Anthropologists study a culture's ideas about conception because those ideas have a profound impact on the way people run their lives. In our culture, for example, conceiving children incurs long-term economic responsibility for both the mother and father. We take this obligation so seriously that when a parent fails to provide for a child, it is usually a violation of law. In the Barí system, when a man is named as a secondary biological father he is also placed under an obligation to the mother and the child. In addition, he is expected to give gifts of fish and game. These gifts are a significant burden because the man must also provide for his own wife and primary children.

Beckerman and his colleagues have discovered that naming secondary fathers has evolutionary consequences. A team of ethnographers led by Beckerman, Roberto Lizarralde, and his son Manuel, an anthropologist at Connecticut College who has been visiting the Barí since he was 5 years old, interviewed 114 Barí women past childbearing years and asked them about their full reproductive histories. "These interviews were a lot of fun," Beckerman says, laughing. "Randy old ladies talking about their lovers." In total, the researchers recorded claims of 916 pregnancies, an average of eight pregnancies for each woman. But child mortality was high—about one-third of the children did not survive to age 15. Naming secondary fathers was a critical factor in predicting which babies made it to adulthood. Secondary fathers were involved in 25 percent of pregnancies, and the team determined that two fathers were the ideal number. Children with one father and one secondary father made it to their teens most often; kids with only one father or those with more than two fathers didn't fare as well. The researchers also found that this decrease in mortality occurred not during the child's life but during fetal development: Women were less likely to have a miscarriage or stillbirth if they had a husband and an additional male contributing food. This result was a surprise because researchers had expected that help during childhood would be more important. "The Barí are not hungry; they are not close to the bone. But it must be the extra fat and protein that they get from secondary fathers during gestation that makes the difference," Beckerman explains as he points to photographs of Barí women who look well nourished, even downright plump.

Barí women seem to use this more flexible system of paternity when they need it. Within families, some children have secondary fathers, while their siblings belong to the husband alone. The team discovered that mothers are more likely to take on a secondary father when a previous child has died in infancy. Manuel Lizarralde claims the strategy makes perfect sense, given the Barí belief that the best way to cure a sick child is for the father to blow tobacco smoke over the child's body. "It is easy to imagine a bereaved mother thinking to herself that if she had only provided a secondary father and so more smoke for her dead child, she might have saved him—and vowing to provide that benefit for her next child."

Beckerman says extra fathers may have always been insurance for uncertain times: "Because the Barí were once hunted as if they were game animals—by other Indians, conquistadors, oilmen, farmers, and ranchers—the odds of a woman being widowed when she still had young children were one in three, according to data we gathered about the years 1930 to 1960. The men as well as the women knew this. None of these guys can go down the street to Mutual of Omaha and buy a life insurance policy. By allowing his wife to take a lover, the husband is doing all he can to ensure the survival of his children."

Barí women are also freer to do as they wish because men need their labor—having a wife is an economic necessity because women do the manioc farming, harvesting, and cooking, while men hunt and fish. "The sexual division of labor is such that you can't make it without a member of the opposite sex," says Beckerman. Initially, the researchers worried that jealousy on the part of husbands would make Barí women reticent about discussing multiple sexual partners. "In our first interviews, we would wait until the husband was out of the house," says Beckerman. "But one day we interviewed an old couple who were enjoying thinking about their lives; they were lying in their hammocks, side by side, and it was obvious he wasn't going anywhere. So we went down the list of her children and asked about other fathers. She said no, no, no for each child, and then the husband interrupted when we got to one and said, 'That's not true, don't you remember, there was that guy. . .' And the husband was grinning."

Not all women take lovers. Manuel Lizarralde has discovered through interviews that one-third of 122 women were faithful to their husbands during their pregnancies. "These women say they don't need it, or no one asked, or they have enough support from family and don't require another father for their child," Lizarralde says. "Some even admit that their husbands were not that happy about the idea." Or it may be a sign of changing times. Based on his most recent visits to the Barí, Lizarralde thinks that under the influence of Western values, the number of people who engage in multiple fatherhood may be decreasing. But his father, who has worked with the Barí for more than 40 years, disagrees. He says the practice is as frequent but that the Barí discuss it less openly than before, knowing that Westerners object to their views. After all, it took the anthropologists 20 years to hear about other fathers, and today the Barí are probably being even more discreet because they know Westerners disapprove of their beliefs.

"What this information adds up to," Beckerman says, "is that the Barí may be doing somewhat less fooling around within marriage these days but that most of them still believe that a child can have multiple fathers."

More important, the Barí idea that biological paternity can be shared is not just the quirky custom of one tribe; anthropologists have found that this idea is common across South America. The same belief is shared by indigenous groups in New Guinea and India, suggesting that multiple paternity has been part of human behavior for a long time, undermining all previous descriptions of how human mating behavior evolved.

Since the 1960s, when anthropologists began to construct scenarios of early human mating, they had always assumed that the model family started with a mom and dad bonded for life to raise the kids, a model that fit well with acceptable Western behavior. In 1981 in an article titled "The Origin of Man," C. Owen Lovejoy, an anthropologist at Kent State University, outlined the standard story of human evolution as it was used in the field—and is still presented in textbooks today: Human infants with their big brains and long periods of growth and learning have always been dependent on adults, a dependence that separates the humans from the apes. Mothers alone couldn't possibly find enough food for these dependent young, so women have always needed to find a mate who would stick close to home and bring in supplies for the family. Unfortunately for women, as evolutionary psychologists suggest, men are compelled by their biology to mate with as many partners as possible to pass along their genes. However, each of these men might be manipulated into staying with one woman who offered him sex and a promise of fidelity. The man, under those conditions, would be assured of paternity, and he might just stay around and make sure his kids survived.

This scenario presents humans as naturally monogamous, forming nuclear families as an evolutionary necessity. The only problem is that around the world families don't always operate this way. In fact, as the Barí and other cultures show, there are all sorts of ways to run a successful household.

The Na of Yunnan Province in China, for example, have a female-centric society in which husbands are not part of the picture. Women grow up and continue to live with their mothers, sisters, and brothers; they never marry or move away from the family compound. As a result, sisters and brothers rather than married pairs are the economic unit that farms and fishes together. Male lovers in this system are simply visitors. They have no place or power in the household, and children are brought up by their mothers and by the mothers' brothers. A father is identified only if there is a resemblance between him and the child, and even so, the father has no responsibilities toward the child.

Often women have sex with so many partners that the biological father is unknown. "I have not found any term that would cover the notion of father in the Na language," writes Chinese anthropologist Cai Hua in his book *A Society Without Fathers or Husbands: The Na of China*. In this case, women have complete control over their children, property, and sexuality.

Across lowland South America, family systems vary because cultures put their beliefs into practice in different ways. Among some native people, such as the Canela, Mehinaku, and Araweté, women control their sex lives and their fertility, and most children have several fathers. Barí women are also sexually liberated from an early age. "Once she has completed her puberty ritual, a Barí girl can have sex with anyone she wants as long as she doesn't violate the incest taboo," Beckerman explains. "It's nobody's business, not even Mom's and Dad's business." Women can also turn down prospective husbands.

In other cultures in South America, life is not so free for females, although members of these cultures also believe that babies can have more than one father. The Curripaco of Amazonia, for instance, acknowledge multiple fatherhood as a biological possibility and yet frown on women having affairs. Paul Valentine, a senior lecturer in anthropology at the University of East London who has studied the Curripaco for more than 20 years, says, "Curripaco women are in a difficult situation. The wives come into the village from different areas, and it's a very patrilineal system." If her husband dies, a widow is allowed to turn only to his brothers or to clan members on his side of the family for a new husband.

The relative power of women and men over their sex lives has important consequences. "In certain social and economic systems, women are free to make mate choices," says Valentine. In these cultures women are often the foundation of society, while men have less power in the community. Sisters tend to stay in the same household as their mothers. The women, in other words, have power to make choices. "At the other extreme, somehow, it's the men who try to maximize their evolutionary success at the expense of the women," says Valentine.

Men and women often have a conflict of interest when it comes to mating, marriage, and who should invest most in children, and the winners have sometimes been the men, sometimes the women. As Beckerman wryly puts it, "Anyone who believes that in a human mating relationship the man's reproductive interests always carry the day has obviously never been married."

The Barí and others show that human systems are, in fact, very flexible, ready to accommodate any sort of mating system or type of family. "I think that human beings are capable of making life extremely complicated. That's our way of doing business," says Ian Tattersall, a paleoanthropologist and curator in the division of anthropology at the American Museum of Natural History in New York City. Indeed, such flexibility suggests there's no reason to assume that the nuclear family is the natural, ideal, or even most evolutionarily successful system of human grouping. As Beckerman says, "One of the things this research shows is that human beings are just as clever and creative in assembling their kin relations as they are putting together space shuttles or symphonies."

6

"To Give up on Words"

Silence in Western Apache Culture

Keith H. Basso

Can you imagine working on a four-person cattle crew for several days without being introduced to or speaking with one of the other members, whom you did not know? For the Apache, this is a normal occurrence; they do not feel obligated to introduce strangers to one another. Instead, the Apache believe that when the time is right, the strangers will begin speaking to one another.

Would you find it uncomfortable to go on a date and sit in silence for an hour because you had only recently met your companion? What would you think if after returning home from several months' absence your parents and relatives didn't speak to you for several days? Although these situations seem unusual to us, they are considered appropriate among the Apache. Although it seems natural to us that when people first meet introductions are in order and that when friends and relatives reunite greetings and catching up will immediately follow, this is not the case for all cultures.

Communicating across cultural boundaries can be fraught with uncertainty and misunderstanding. In this classic selection Keith Basso shows how, among the Apache, certain situations call for silence rather than communication and how silence makes sense within its cultural context.

As you read this selection, ask yourself the following questions:

- What are some of the ways silence is used in European American communication, and how are they different from those in Apache culture?
- How are the meaning and function of silence affected by the social and cultural context?
- What is the critical factor in an Apache's decision to speak or keep silent?
- How do Apaches interact upon meeting a stranger, courting, welcoming children home, "getting cussed out," and being with people who are sad?
- Despite the variety of situations in which Apaches are silent, what is the underlying determinant?

The following terms discussed in this selection are included in the Glossary at the back of the book:

hypothesis	*socialization*
informant	*sociolinguistics*
kinship	*status*

It is not the case that a man who is silent says nothing.

—Anonymous

I[1]

Anyone who has read about American Indians has probably encountered statements which impute to them a strong predilection for keeping silent or, as one

Basso, Keith H. "'To Give up on Words': Silence in Western Apache Culture." *Southwestern Journal of Anthropology* 26, no. 3 (Autumn 1970):213–230. Reprinted with permission of the Journal of Anthropological Research and the author.

writer has put it, "a fierce reluctance to speak except when absolutely necessary." In the popular literature, where this characterization is particularly widespread, it is commonly portrayed as the outgrowth of such dubious causes as "instinctive dignity," "an impoverished language," or, perhaps worst of all, the Indians' "lack of personal warmth." Although statements of this sort are plainly erroneous and dangerously misleading, it is noteworthy that professional anthropologists have made few attempts to correct them. Traditionally, ethnographers and linguists have paid little attention to cultural interpretations given to silence or, equally important, to the types of social contexts in which it regularly occurs.

This study investigates certain aspects of silence in the culture of the Western Apache of east-central Arizona. After considering some of the theoretical issues involved, I will briefly describe a number of situations—recurrent in Western Apache society—in which one or more of the participants typically refrain from speech for lengthy periods of time.[2] This is accompanied by a discussion of how such acts of silence are interpreted and why they are encouraged and deemed appropriate. I conclude by advancing an hypothesis that accounts for the reasons that the Western Apache refrain from speaking when they do, and I suggest that, with proper testing, this hypothesis may be shown to have relevance to silence behavior in other cultures.

II

A basic finding of sociolinguistics is that, although both language and language usage are structured, it is the latter which responds most sensitively to extra-linguistic influences (Hymes 1962, 1964; Ervin-Tripp 1964, 1967; Gumperz 1964; Slobin 1967). Accordingly, a number of recent studies have addressed themselves to the problem of how factors in the social environment of speech events delimit the range and condition the selection of message forms (cf. Brown and Gilman 1960; Conklin 1959; Ervin-Tripp 1964, 1967; Frake 1964; Friedrich 1966; Gumperz 1961, 1964; Martin 1964). These studies may be viewed as taking the now familiar position that verbal communication is fundamentally a decision-making process in which, initially, a speaker, having elected to speak, selects from among a repertoire of available codes that which is most appropriately suited to the situation at hand. Once a code has been selected, the speaker picks a suitable channel of transmission and then, finally, makes a choice from a set of referentially equivalent expressions within the code. The intelligibility of the expression he chooses will, of course, be subject to grammatical constraints. But its acceptability will not. Rules for the selection of linguistic alternates operate on features of the social environment and are commensurate with rules governing the conduct of face-to-face interaction. As such, they are properly conceptualized as lying outside the structure of language itself.

It follows from this that for a stranger to communicate appropriately with the members of an unfamiliar society it is not enough that he learn to formulate messages intelligibly. Something else is needed: a knowledge of what kinds of codes, channels, and expressions to use in what kinds of situations and to what kinds of people—as Hymes (1964) has termed it, an "ethnography of communication."

There is considerable evidence to suggest that extra-linguistic factors influence not only the use of speech but its actual occurrence as well. In our own culture, for example, remarks such as "Don't you know when to keep quiet?" "Don't talk until you're introduced," and "Remember now, no talking in church" all point to the fact that an individual's decision to speak may be directly contingent upon the character of his surroundings. Few of us would maintain that "silence is golden" for all people at all times. But we feel that silence is a virtue for some people some of the time, and we encourage children on the road to cultural competence to act accordingly.

Although the form of silence is always the same, the function of a specific act of silence—that is, its interpretation by and effect upon other people—will vary according to the social context in which it occurs. For example, if I choose to keep silent in the chambers of a Justice of the Supreme Court, my action is likely to be interpreted as a sign of politeness or respect. On the other hand, if I refrain from speaking to an established friend or colleague, I am apt to be accused of rudeness or harboring a grudge. In one instance, my behavior is judged by others to be "correct" or "fitting;" in the other, it is criticized as being "out of line."

The point, I think, is fairly obvious. For a stranger entering an alien society, a knowledge of when *not* to speak may be as basic to the production of culturally acceptable behavior as a knowledge of what to say. It stands to reason, then, that an adequate ethnography of communication should not confine itself exclusively to the analysis of choice within verbal repertoires. It should also, as Hymes (1962, 1964) has suggested, specify those conditions under which the members of the society regularly decide to refrain from verbal behavior altogether.

III

The research on which this paper is based was conducted over a period of sixteen months (1964–1969) in the Western Apache settlement of Cibecue, which is located near the center of the Fort Apache Indian Reservation in east-central Arizona. Cibecue's 800 residents participate in an unstable economy that combines subsistence agriculture, cattle-raising, sporadic wage-earning, and Government subsidies in the form of welfare checks and social security benefits. Unemployment is a serious problem, and substandard living conditions are widespread.

Although Reservation life has precipitated far-reaching changes in the composition and geographical distribution of Western Apache social groups, consanguineal kinship—real and imputed—remains the single most powerful force in the establishment and regulation of interpersonal relationships (Kaut 1957; Basso 1970). The focus of domestic activity is the individual "camp," or *gowąą*. This term labels both the occupants and the location of a single dwelling or, as is more apt to be the case, several dwellings built within a few feet of each other. The majority of *gowąą* in Cibecue are occupied by nuclear families. The next largest residential unit is the *gotáá* (camp cluster), which is a group of spatially localized *gowąą*, each having at least one adult member who is related by ties of matrilineal kinship to persons living in all the others. An intricate system of exogamous clans serves to extend kinship relationships beyond the *gowąą* and *gotáá* and facilitates concerted action in projects, most notably the presentation of ceremonials, requiring large amounts of manpower. Despite the presence in Cibecue of a variety of Anglo missionaries and a dwindling number of medicine men, diagnostic and curing rituals, as well as the girls' puberty ceremonial, continue to be performed with regularity (Basso 1966, 1970). Witchcraft persists in undiluted form (Basso 1969).

IV

Of the many broad categories of events, or scenes, that comprise the daily round of Western Apache life, I shall deal here only with those that are coterminous with what Goffman (1961, 1964) has termed "focused gatherings" or "encounters." The concept *situation*, in keeping with established usage, will refer inclusively to the location of such a gathering, its physical setting, its point in time, the standing behavior patterns that accompany it, and the social attributes of the persons involved (Hymes 1962, 1964; Ervin-Tripp 1964, 1967).

In what follows, however, I will be mainly concerned with the roles and statuses of participants. The reason for this is that the critical factor in the Apache's decision to speak or keep silent seems always to be the nature of his relationships to other people. To be sure, other features of the situation are significant, but apparently only to the extent that they influence the perception of status and role.[3] What this implies, of course, is that roles and statuses are not fixed attributes. Although they may be depicted as such in a static model (and often with good reason), they are appraised and acted upon in particular social contexts and, as a result, subject to redefinition and variation.[4] With this in mind, let us now turn our attention to the Western Apache and the types of situations in which, as one of my informants put it, "it is right to give up on words."

V

1. "Meeting strangers" (*nda dòhwáá iłtsééda*). The term, *nda*, labels categories at two levels of contrast. At the most general level, it designates any person—Apache or non-Apache—who, prior to an initial meeting, has never been seen and therefore cannot be identified. In addition, the term is used to refer to Apaches who, though previously seen and known by some external criteria such as clan affiliation or personal name, have never been engaged in face-to-face interaction. The latter category, which is more restricted than the first, typically includes individuals who live on the adjacent San Carlos Reservation, in Fort Apache settlements geographically removed from Cibecue, and those who fall into the category *kii dòhandáágo* (non-kinsmen). In all cases, "strangers" are separated by social distance. And in all cases it is considered appropriate, when encountering them for the first time, to refrain from speaking.

The type of situation described as "meeting strangers" (*nda dòhwáá iłtsééda*) can take place in any number of different physical settings. However, it occurs most frequently in the context of events such as fairs and rodeos, which, owing to the large number of people in attendance, offer unusual opportunities for chance encounters. In large gatherings, the lack of verbal communication between strangers is apt to go unnoticed, but in smaller groups it becomes quite conspicuous. The following incident, involving two strangers who found themselves part of a four-man round-up crew, serves as a good example. My informant, who was also a member of the crew, recalled the following episode:

> One time, I was with A, B, and X down at Gleason Flat, working cattle. That man, X, was from East Fork [a community nearly 40 miles from Cibecue] where B's wife was from. But he didn't know A, never knew him before, I guess. First day, I worked with X. At night, when we camped, we talked with B, but X and A didn't say anything to each other. Same way, second day. Same way, third. Then, at night on fourth day, we were sitting by the fire. Still, X and A didn't talk. Then A said, "Well, I know there is a stranger to me here, but I've been watching him and I know he is all right." After that, X and A talked a lot. . . . Those two men didn't know each other, so they took it easy at first.

As this incident suggests, the Western Apache do not feel compelled to "introduce" persons who are unknown to each other. Eventually, it is assumed, strangers will begin to speak. However, this is a decision that is properly left to the individuals involved, and no attempt is made to hasten it. Outside help in the form of introductions or other verbal routines is viewed as presumptuous and unnecessary. Strangers who are quick to launch into conversation are frequently eyed with undisguised suspicion.

relative to missionaries

A typical reaction to such individuals is that they "want something," that is, their willingness to violate convention is attributed to some urgent need which is likely to result in requests for money, labor, or transportation. Another common reaction to talkative strangers is that they are drunk.

If the stranger is an Anglo, it is usually assumed that he "wants to teach us something" (i.e., give orders or instructions) or that he "wants to make friends in a hurry." The latter response is especially revealing, since Western Apaches are extremely reluctant to be hurried into friendships—with Anglos or each other. Their verbal reticence with strangers is directly related to the conviction that the establishment of social relationships is a serious matter that calls for caution, careful judgment, and plenty of time.

2. "Courting" (*líígoláá*). During the initial stages of courtship, young men and women go without speaking for conspicuous lengths of time. Courting may occur in a wide variety of settings—practically anywhere, in fact—and at virtually any time of the day or night, but it is most readily observable at large public gatherings such as ceremonials, wakes, and rodeos. At these events, "sweethearts" (*zééde*) may stand or sit (sometimes holding hands) for as long as an hour without exchanging a word. I am told by adult informants that the young people's reluctance to speak may become even more pronounced in situations where they find themselves alone.

Apaches who have just begun to court attribute their silence to "intense shyness" (*'isté*) and a feeling of acute "self-consciousness" (*dàyéézí*) which, they claim, stems from their lack of familiarity with one another. More specifically, they complain of "not knowing what to do" in each other's presence and of the fear that whatever they say, no matter how well thought out in advance, will sound "dumb" or "stupid."[5]

One informant, a youth 17 years old, commented as follows:

> It's hard to talk with your sweetheart at first. She doesn't know you and won't know what to say. It's the same way towards her. You don't know how to talk yet . . . so you get very bashful. That makes it sometimes so you don't say anything. So you just go around together and don't talk. At first, it's better that way. Then, after a while, when you know each other, you aren't shy anymore and can talk good.

The Western Apache draw an equation between the ease and frequency with which a young couple talks and how well they know each other. Thus, it is expected that after several months of steady companionship sweethearts will start to have lengthy conversations. Earlier in their relationship, however,

protracted discussions may be openly discouraged. This is especially true for girls, who are informed by their mothers and older sisters that silence in courtship is a sign of modesty and that an eagerness to speak betrays previous experience with men. In extreme cases, they add, it may be interpreted as a willingness to engage in sexual relations. Said one woman, aged 32:

> This way I have talked to my daughter. "Take it easy when boys come around this camp and want you to go somewhere with them. When they talk to you, just listen at first. Maybe you won't know what to say. So don't talk about just anything. If you talk with those boys right away, then they will know you know all about them. They will think you've been with many boys before, and they will start talking about that."

3. "Children, coming home" (*čogoše nakáii*). The Western Apache lexeme *iltá ìnatsáá* (reunion) is used to describe encounters between an individual who has returned home after a long absence and his relatives and friends. The most common type of reunion, *čogoše nakáii* (children, coming home), involves boarding school students and their parents. It occurs in late May or early in June, and its setting is usually a trading post or school, where parents congregate to await the arrival of buses bringing the children home. As the latter disembark and locate their parents in the crowd, one anticipates a flurry of verbal greetings. Typically, however, there are few or none at all. Indeed, it is not unusual for parents and child to go without speaking for as long as 15 minutes.

When the silence is broken, it is almost always the child who breaks it. His parents listen attentively to everything he says but speak hardly at all themselves. This pattern persists even after the family has reached the privacy of its camp, and two or three days may pass before the child's parents seek to engage him in sustained conversation.

According to my informants, the silence of Western Apache parents at (and after) reunions with their children is ultimately predicated on the possibility that the latter have been adversely affected by their experiences away from home. Uppermost is the fear that, as a result of protracted exposure to Anglo attitudes and values, the children have come to view their parents as ignorant, old-fashioned, and no longer deserving of respect. One of my most thoughtful and articulate informants commented on the problem as follows:

> You just can't tell about those children after they've been with White men for a long time. They get their minds turned around sometimes . . . they forget where they come from and get ashamed when they come home because their parents and relatives are poor. They forget how to act with these Apaches and get mad easy.

They walk around all night and get into fights. They don't stay at home.

At school, some of them learn to want to be White men, so they come back and try to act that way. But we are still Apaches! So we don't know them anymore, and it is like we never knew them. It is hard to talk to them when they are like that.

Apache parents openly admit that, initially, children who have been away to school seem distant and unfamiliar. They have grown older, of course, and their physical appearance may have changed. But more fundamental is the concern that they have acquired new ideas and expectations which will alter their behavior in unpredictable ways. No matter how pressing this concern may be, however, it is considered inappropriate to directly interrogate a child after his arrival home. Instead, parents anticipate that within a short time he will begin to divulge information about himself that will enable them to determine in what ways, if any, his views and attitudes have changed. This, the Apache say, is why children do practically all the talking in the hours following a reunion, and their parents remain unusually silent.

Said one man, the father of two children who had recently returned from boarding school in Utah:

Yes, it's right that we didn't talk much to them when they came back, my wife and me. They were away for a long time, and we didn't know how they would like it, being home. So we waited. Right away, they started to tell stories about what they did. Pretty soon we could tell they liked it, being back. That made us feel good. So it was easy to talk to them again. It was like they were before they went away.

4. "Getting cussed out" (*šiłditéé*). This lexeme is used to describe any situation in which one individual, angered and enraged, shouts insults and criticism at another. Although the object of such invective is in most cases the person or persons who provoked it, this is not always the case, because an Apache who is truly beside himself with rage is likely to vent his feelings on anyone whom he sees or who happens to be within range of his voice. Consequently, "getting cussed out" may involve large numbers of people who are totally innocent of the charges being hurled against them. But whether they are innocent or not, their response to the situation is the same. They refrain from speech.

Like the types of situations we have discussed thus far, "getting cussed out" can occur in a wide variety of physical settings: at ceremonial dance grounds and trading posts, inside and outside wickiups and houses, on food-gathering expeditions and shopping trips—in short, wherever and whenever individuals lose control of their tempers and lash out verbally at persons nearby.

Although "getting cussed out" is basically free of setting self-imposed restrictions, the Western Apache fear it most at gatherings where alcohol is being consumed. My informants observed that especially at "drinking parties" (*dá'idlą́ą́*), where there is much rough joking and ostensibly mock criticism, it is easy for well-intentioned remarks to be misconstrued as insults. Provoked in this way, persons who are intoxicated may become hostile and launch into explosive tirades, often with no warning at all.

The silence of Apaches who are "getting cussed out" is consistently explained in reference to the belief that individuals who are "enraged" (*haškéé*) are also irrational or "crazy" (*bìné'idíí*). In this condition, it is said, they "forget who they are" and become oblivious to what they say or do. Concomitantly, they lose all concern for the consequences of their actions on other people. In a word, they are dangerous. Said one informant:

When people get mad they get crazy. Then they start yelling and saying bad things. Some say they are going to kill somebody for what he has done. Some keep it up that way for a long time, maybe walk from camp to camp, real angry, yelling, crazy like that. They keep it up for a long time, some do.

People like that don't know what they are saying, so you can't tell about them. When you see someone like that, just walk away. If he yells at you, let him say whatever he wants to. Let him say anything. Maybe he doesn't mean it. But he doesn't know that. He will be crazy, and he could try to kill you.

Another Apache said:

When someone gets mad at you and starts yelling, then just don't do anything to make him get worse. Don't try to quiet him down because he won't know why you're doing it. If you try to do that, he may just get worse and try to hurt you.

As the last of these statements implies, the Western Apache operate on the assumption that enraged persons—because they are temporarily "crazy"—are difficult to reason with. Indeed, there is a widely held belief that attempts at mollification will serve to intensify anger, thus increasing the chances of physical violence. The appropriate strategy when "getting cussed out" is to do nothing, to avoid any action that will attract attention to oneself. Since speaking accomplishes just the opposite, the use of silence is strongly advised.

5. "Being with people who are sad" (*nde dòbiłgòzóóda bigą́ą́*). Although the Western Apache phrase that labels this situation has no precise equivalent in English, it refers quite specifically to gatherings in which an individual finds himself in the company of someone whose spouse or kinsman has recently died. Distinct from wakes and burials, which follow

delayed reactions, everal
in speech, communication
"TO GIVE UP ON WORDS": SILENCE IN WESTERN APACHE CULTURE 41

immediately after a death, "being with people who are sad" is most likely to occur several weeks later. At this time, close relatives of the deceased emerge from a period of intense mourning (during which they rarely venture beyond the limits of their camps) and start to resume their normal activities within the community. To persons anxious to convey their sympathies, this is interpreted as a sign that visitors will be welcomed and, if possible, provided with food and drink. To those less solicitous, it means that unplanned encounters with the bereaved must be anticipated and prepared for.

"Being with people who are sad" can occur on a foot-path, in a camp, at church, or in a trading post; but whatever the setting—and regardless of whether it is the result of a planned visit or an accidental meeting—the situation is marked by a minimum of speech. Queried about this, my informants volunteered three types of explanations. The first is that persons "who are sad" are so burdened with "intense grief" (dółgozóóda) that speaking requires of them an unusual amount of physical effort. It is courteous and considerate, therefore, not to attempt to engage them in conversation.

A second native explanation is that in situations of this sort verbal communication is basically unnecessary. Everyone is familiar with what has happened, and talking about it, even for the purpose of conveying solace and sympathy, would only reinforce and augment the sadness felt by those who were close to the deceased. Again, for reasons of courtesy, this is something to be avoided.

The third explanation is rooted in the belief that "intense grief," like intense rage, produces changes in the personality of the individual who experiences it. As evidence for this, the Western Apache cite numerous instances in which the emotional strain of dealing with death, coupled with an overwhelming sense of irrevocable personal loss, has caused persons who were formerly mild and even-tempered to become abusive, hostile, and physically violent.

> That old woman, X, who lives across Cibecue Creek, one time her first husband died. After that she cried all the time, for a long time. Then, I guess she got mean because everyone said she drank a lot and got into fights. Even with her close relatives, she did like that for a long time. She was too sad for her husband. That's what made her like that; it made her lose her mind.

> My father was like that when his wife died. He just stayed home all the time and wouldn't go anywhere. He didn't talk to any of his relatives or children. He just said, "I'm hungry. Cook for me." That's all. He stayed that way for a long time. His mind was not with us. He was still with his wife.

> My uncle died in 1911. His wife sure went crazy right after that. Two days after they buried the body, we went

over there and stayed with those people who had been left alone. My aunt got mad at us. She said, "Why do you come back over here? You can't bring my husband back. I can take care of myself and those others in my camp, so why don't you go home." She sure was mad that time, too sad for someone who died. She didn't know what she was saying because in about one week she came to our camp and said, "My relatives, I'm all right now. When you came to help me, I had too much sadness and my mind was no good. I said bad words to you. But now I am all right and I know what I am doing."

As these statements indicate, the Western Apache assume that a person suffering from "intense grief" is likely to be disturbed and unstable. Even though he may appear outwardly composed, they say, there is always the possibility that he is emotionally upset and therefore unusually prone to volatile outbursts. Apaches acknowledge that such an individual might welcome conversation in the context of "being with people who are sad," but, on the other hand, they fear it might prove incendiary. Under these conditions, which resemble those in Situation No. 4, it is considered both expedient and appropriate to keep silent.

6. "Being with someone for whom they sing" (ndebìdádìstááha bigą́ą́). The last type of situation to be described is restricted to a small number of physical locations and is more directly influenced by temporal factors than any of the situations we have discussed so far. "Being with someone for whom they sing" takes place only in the context of "curing ceremonials" (gòjitáł). These events begin early at night and come to a close shortly before dawn the following day. In the late fall and throughout the winter, curing ceremonials are held inside the patient's wickiup or house. In the spring and summer, they are located outside, at some open place near the patient's camp or at specially designated dance grounds where group rituals of all kinds are regularly performed.

Prior to the start of a curing ceremonial, all persons in attendance may feel free to talk with the patient; indeed, because he is so much a focus of concern, it is expected that friends and relatives will seek him out to offer encouragement and support. Conversation breaks off, however, when the patient is informed that the ceremonial is about to begin, and it ceases entirely when the presiding medicine man commences to chant. From this point on, until the completion of the final chant next morning, it is inappropriate for anyone except the medicine man (and, if he has them, his aides) to speak to the patient.[6]

In order to appreciate the explanation Apaches give for this prescription, we must briefly discuss the concept of "supernatural power" (diyí) and describe some of the effects it is believed to have on persons at whom it is directed. Elsewhere (Basso 1969:30) I have defined "power" as follows:

> The term *diyí* refers to one or all of a set of abstract and invisible forces which are said to derive from certain classes of animals, plants, minerals, meteorological phenomena, and mythological figures within the Western Apache universe. Any of the various powers may be acquired by man and, if properly handled, used for a variety of purposes.

A power that has been antagonized by disrespectful behavior towards its source may retaliate by causing the offender to become sick. "Power-caused illnesses" (*kásitį kiyí bił*) are properly treated with curing ceremonials in which one or more medicine men, using chants and various items of ritual paraphernalia, attempt to neutralize the sickness-causing power with powers of their own.

Roughly two-thirds of my informants assert that a medicine man's power actually enters the body of the patient; others maintain that it simply closes in and envelops him. In any case, all agree that the patient is brought into intimate contact with a potent supernatural force which elevates him to a condition labeled *gòdiyò'* (sacred, holy).

The term *gòdiyò'* may also be translated as "potentially harmful" and, in this sense, is regularly used to describe classes of objects (including all sources of power) that are associated with taboos. In keeping with the semantics of *gòdiyò'*, the Western Apache explain that, besides making patients holy, power makes them potentially harmful. And it is this transformation, they explain, that is basically responsible for the cessation of verbal communication during curing ceremonials. Said one informant:

> When they start singing for someone like that, he sort of goes away with what the medicine man is working with (i.e., power). Sometimes people they sing for don't know you, even after it (the curing ceremonial) is over. They get holy, and you shouldn't try to talk to them when they are like that . . . it's best to leave them alone.

Another informant made similar comments:

> When they sing for someone, what happens is like this: that man they sing for doesn't know why he is sick or which way to go. So the medicine man has to show him and work on him. That is when he gets holy, and that makes him go off somewhere in his mind, so you should stay away from him.

Because Apaches undergoing ceremonial treatment are perceived as having been changed by power into something different from their normal selves, they are regarded with caution and apprehension. Their newly acquired status places them in close proximity to the supernatural and, as such, carries with it a very real element of danger and uncertainty. These conditions combine to make "being with someone for whom they sing" a situation in which speech is considered disrespectful and, if not exactly harmful, at least potentially hazardous.

VI

Although the types of situations described above differ from one another in obvious ways, I will argue in what follows that the underlying determinants of silence are in each case basically the same. Specifically, I will attempt to defend the hypothesis that keeping silent in Western Apache culture is associated with social situations in which participants perceive their relationships *vis-à-vis* one another to be ambiguous and/or unpredictable.

Let us begin with the observation that, in all the situations we have described, *silence is defined as appropriate with respect to a specific individual or individuals*. In other words, the use of speech is not directly curtailed by the setting of a situation nor by the physical activities that accompany it but, rather, by the perceived social and psychological attributes of at least one focal participant.

It may also be observed that, in each type of situation, *the status of the focal participant is marked by ambiguity*—either because he is unfamiliar to other participants in the situation or because, owing to some recent event, a status he formerly held has been changed or is in a process of transition.

Thus, in Situation No. 1, persons who earlier considered themselves "strangers" move towards some other relationship, perhaps "friend" (*šìdikéé*), perhaps "enemy" (*šìkédndíí*). In Situation No. 2, young people who have relatively limited exposure to one another attempt to adjust to the new and intimate status of "sweetheart." These two situations are similar in that the focal participants have little or no prior knowledge of each other. Their social identities are not as yet clearly defined, and their expectations, lacking the foundation of previous experience, are poorly developed.

Situation No. 3 is somewhat different. Although the participants—parents and their children—are well known to each other, their relationship has been seriously interrupted by the latter's prolonged absence from home. This, combined with the possibility that recent experiences at school have altered the children's attitudes, introduces a definite element of unfamiliarity and doubt. Situation No. 3 is not characterized by the absence of role expectations but by the participants' perception that those already in existence may be outmoded and in need of revision.

Status ambiguity is present in Situation No. 4 because a focal participant is enraged and, as a result, considered "crazy." Until he returns to a more rational condition, others in the situation have no way of predicting how he will behave. Situation No. 5 is similar in that the personality of a focal participant is seen to have undergone a marked shift which makes his actions more difficult to anticipate. In both situations, the status of focal participants is uncertain because of real or imagined changes in their psychological makeup.

In Situation No. 6, a focal participant is ritually transformed from an essentially neutral state to one which is contextually defined as "potentially harmful." Ambiguity and apprehension accompany this transition, and, as in Situations No. 4 and 5, established patterns of interaction must be waived until the focal participant reverts to a less threatening condition.

This discussion points up a third feature characteristic of all situations: *the ambiguous status of focal participants is accompanied either by the absence or suspension of established role expectations.* In every instance, nonfocal participants (i.e., those who refrain from speech) are either uncertain of how the focal participant will behave towards them or, conversely, how they should behave towards him. Stated in the simplest way possible, their roles become blurred with the result that established expectations—if they exist—lose their relevance as guidelines for social action and must be temporarily discarded or abruptly modified.

We are now in a position to expand upon our initial hypothesis and make it more explicit.

1. In Western Apache culture, the absence of verbal communication is associated with social situations in which the status of local participants is ambiguous.

2. Under these conditions, fixed role expectations lose their applicability and the illusion of predictability in social interaction is lost.

3. To sum up and reiterate: keeping silent among the Western Apache is a response to uncertainty and unpredictability in social relations.

VII

The question remains to what extent the foregoing hypothesis helps to account for silence behavior in other cultures. Unfortunately, it is impossible at the present time to provide anything approaching a conclusive answer. Standard ethnographies contain very little information about the circumstances under which verbal communication is discouraged, and it is only within the past few years that problems of this sort have engaged the attention of sociolinguists. The result is that adequate cross-cultural data are almost completely lacking.

As a first step towards the elimination of this deficiency, an attempt is now being made to investigate the occurrence and interpretation of silence in other Indian societies of the American Southwest. Our findings at this early stage, though neither fully representative nor sufficiently comprehensive, are extremely suggestive. By way of illustration, I quote below from portions of a preliminary report prepared by Priscilla Mowrer (1970), herself a Navajo, who inquired into the situational features of Navajo silence behavior in the vicinity of Tuba City on the Navajo Reservation in east-central Arizona.

I. *Silence and Courting:* Navajo youngsters of opposite sexes just getting to know one another say nothing, except to sit close together and maybe hold hands. . . . In public, they may try not to let on that they are interested in each other, but in private it is another matter. If the girl is at a gathering where the boy is also present, she may go off by herself. Falling in step, the boy will generally follow. They may just walk around or find some place to sit down. But, at first, they will not say anything to each other.

II. *Silence and Long Absent Relatives:* When a male or female relative returns home after being gone for six months or more, he (or she) is first greeted with a handshake. If the returnee is male, the female greeter may embrace him and cry—the male, meanwhile, will remain dry-eyed and silent.

III. *Silence and Anger:* The Navajo tend to remain silent when being shouted at by a drunk or angered individual because that particular individual is considered temporarily insane. To speak to such an individual, the Navajo believe, just tends to make the situation worse. . . . People remain silent because they believe that the individual is not himself, that he may have been witched, and is not responsible for the change in his behavior.

IV. *Silent Mourning:* Navajos speak very little when mourning the death of a relative. . . . The Navajo mourn and cry together in pairs. Men will embrace one another and cry together. Women, however, will hold one another's hands and cry together.

V. *Silence and the Ceremonial Patient:* The Navajo consider it wrong to talk to a person being sung over. The only people who talk to the patient are the medicine man and a female relative (or male relative if the patient is male) who is in charge of food preparation. The only time the patient speaks openly is when the medicine man asks her (or him) to pray along with him.

These observations suggest that striking similarities may exist between the types of social contexts in which Navajos and Western Apaches refrain from speech. If this impression is confirmed by further research, it will lend obvious cross-cultural support to the hypothesis advanced above. But regardless of the final outcome, the situational determinants of silence seem eminently deserving of further study. For as we become better informed about the types of contextual variables that mitigate against the use of verbal codes, we should also learn more about those variables that encourage and promote them.

NOTES

1. At different times during the period extending from 1964–1969 the research on which this paper is based was supported by U. S. P. H. S. Grant MH-12691-01, a grant from the American Philosophical Society, and funds from the Doris Duke Oral History Project at the Arizona State Museum. I am pleased to acknowledge this support. I would also like to express my gratitude to the following scholars for commenting upon an earlier draft: Y. R. Chao, Harold C. Conklin, Roy G. D'Andrade, Charles O. Frake, Paul Friedrich, John Gumperz, Kenneth Hale, Harry Hoijer, Dell Hymes, Stanley Newman, David M. Schneider, Joel Sherzer, and Paul Turner. Although the final version gained much from their criticisms and suggestions, responsibility for its present form and content rests solely with the author. A preliminary version of this paper was presented to the Annual Meeting of the American Anthropological Association in New Orleans, Louisiana, November 1969. A modified version of this paper is scheduled to appear in *Studies in Apachean Culture and Ethnology* (ed. by Keith H. Basso and Morris Opler), Tucson: University of Arizona Press, 1970.

2. The situations described in this paper are not the only ones in which the Western Apache refrain from speech. There is a second set—not considered here because my data are incomplete—in which silence appears to occur as a gesture of respect, usually to persons in positions of authority. A third set, very poorly understood, involves ritual specialists who claim they must keep silent at certain points during the preparation of ceremonial paraphernalia.

3. Recent work in the sociology of interaction, most notably by Goffman (1963) and Garfinkel (1967), has led to the suggestion that social relationships are everywhere the major determinants of verbal behavior. In this case, as Gumperz (1967) makes clear, it becomes methodologically unsound to treat the various components of communicative events as independent variables. Gumperz (1967) has presented a hierarchical model, sensitive to dependency, in which components are seen as stages in the communication process. Each stage serves as the input for the next. The basic stage, i.e., the initial input, is "social identities or statuses." For further details see Slobin 1967:131–134.

4. I would like to stress that the emphasis placed on social relations is fully in keeping with the Western Apache interpretation of their own behavior. When my informants were asked to explain why they or someone else was silent on a particular occasion, they invariably did so in terms of *who* was present at the time.

5. Among the Western Apache, rules of exogamy discourage courtships between members of the same clan (*kii àɫhánigo*) and so-called "related" clans (*kii*), with the result that sweethearts are almost always "non-matrilineal kinsmen" (*dòhwàkìɨda*). Compared to "matrilineal kinsmen" (*kii*), such individuals have fewer opportunities during childhood to establish close personal relationships and thus, when courtship begins, have relatively little knowledge of each other. It is not surprising, therefore, that their behavior is similar to that accorded strangers.

6. I have witnessed over 75 curing ceremonials since 1961 and have seen this rule violated only 6 times. On 4 occasions, drunks were at fault. In the other 2 cases, the patient fell asleep and had to be awakened.

REFERENCES

Basso, Keith H. 1966. *The Gift of Changing Woman*. Bureau of American Ethnology, bulletin 196.

———. 1969. *Western Apache Witchcraft*. Anthropological Papers of the University of Arizona, no. 15.

———. 1970. *The Cibecue Apache*. New York: Holt, Rinehart and Winston, Inc.

Brown, R. W., and Albert Gilman. 1960. The Pronouns of Power and Solidarity. In *Style and Language*, ed. T. Sebeok, 253–276. Cambridge: The Technology Press of Massachusetts Institute of Technology.

Conklin, Harold C. 1959. Linguistic Play in Its Cultural Context. *Language* 35: 631–636.

Ervin-Tripp, Susan. 1964. An Analysis of the Interaction of Language, Topic and Listener. In *The Ethnography of Communication*, ed. J. J. Gumperz and D. Hymes, 86–102. *American Anthropologist*, Special Publication, vol. 66, no. 6, part 2.

———. 1967. *Sociolinguistics*. Language-Behavior Research Laboratory, Working Paper no. 3. Berkeley: University of California.

Frake, Charles O. 1964. How to Ask for a Drink in Subanun. In *The Ethnography of Communication*, ed. J. J. Gumperz and D. Hymes, 127–132. *American Anthropologist*, Special Publication, vol. 66, no. 6, part 2.

Friedrich, P. 1966. Structural Implications of Russian Pronominal Usage. In *Sociolinguistics*, ed. W. Bright, 214–253. The Hague: Mouton.

Garfinkel, H. 1967. *Studies in Ethnomethodology*. Englewood Cliffs, N.J.: Prentice-Hall, Inc.

Goffman, E. 1961. *Encounters: Two Studies in the Sociology of Interaction*. Indianapolis: The Bobbs-Merrill Co., Inc.

———. 1963. *Behavior in Public Places*. Glencoe, Ill.: Free Press.

———. 1964. The Neglected Situation. In *The Ethnography of Communication*, ed. J. J. Gumperz and D. Hymes, 133–136. *American Anthropologist*, Special Publication, vol. 66, no. 6, part 2.

Gumperz, John J. 1961. Speech Variation and the Study of Indian Civilization. *American Anthropologist* 63: 976–988.

———. 1964. Linguistic and Social Interaction in Two Communities. In *The Ethnography of Communication*, ed. J. J. Gumperz and D. Hymes, 137–153. *American Anthropologist,* Special Publication, vol. 66, no. 6, part 2.

———. 1967. The Social Setting of Linguistic Behavior. In *A Field Manual for Cross-Cultural Study of the Acquisition of Communicative Competence (Second Draft)*, ed. D. I. Slobin, 129–134. Berkeley: University of California.

Hymes, Dell. 1962. The Ethnography of Speaking. In *Anthropology and Human Behavior*, ed. T. Gladwin and W. C. Sturtevant, 13–53. Washington, D.C.: The Anthropological Society of Washington.

———. 1964. Introduction: Toward Ethnographies of Communication. In *The Ethnography of Communication*, ed. J. J. Gumperz and D. Hymes, 1–34. *American Anthropologist,* Special Publication, vol. 66, no. 6, part 2.

Kaut, Charles R. 1957. *The Western Apache Clan System: Its Origins and Development.* University of New Mexico Publications in Anthropology, no. 9.

Martin, Samuel. 1964. Speech Levels in Japan and Korea. In *Language in Culture and Society*, ed. D. Hymes, 407–415. New York: Harper & Row.

Mowrer, Priscilla. 1970. Notes on Navajo Silence Behavior. MS, University of Arizona.

Slobin, Dan I. (ed.). 1967. *A Field Manual for Cross-Cultural Study of the Acquisition of Communicative Competence (Second Draft).* Berkeley: University of California.

7

How Families Work

Love, Labor and Mediated Oppositions in American Domestic Ritual

Mark Auslander

All human groups engage in rituals that involve both action and meaning. Rituals are often sacred, but they can also be secular. Anthropologists have long noted that rituals are organized group actions or ceremonies that have a set sequence, ritual objects and historical continuity. Many rituals mark the passage of time in either the social life cycle (i.e., riles of passage) or the annual calendar. Rituals are part of cultural "tradition" through which people create meaning through the use of symbols.

Humans use religion and ritual to help them "make sense" of the mysteries, challenges, and paradoxes of their lives. Anthropological research about cultural rituals requires the interpretation of such symbols and symbolic acts so that we can better understand their deeper meaning and social functions. However, the participants themselves seldom engage in such symbolic interpretation because "this is the way we have always done things." Local people sometimes find the anthropologist's symbolic interpretation problematic.

In this selection, Mark Auslander interprets the domestic rituals of middle-class American society as a way to mediate between two opposing parts of life—work and family. In our socioeconomic system, work involves productivity whereas family involves kinship and emotions like love. These two worlds are in structural opposition because they imply different ideas about the purpose of life. He argues that these two worlds are ritually mediated through economic consumption and reciprocal gift-giving.

In a sense, the American nuclear family is designed to self-destruct and regenerate from generation to generation. Family rituals, even if they are relatively recent historical inventions, evoke feelings of nostalgia and tradition even when one family is ending and another beginning. Auslander begins his analysis in the classic anthropological tradition of cross-cultural comparison. He uses an interpretation of a ritual of the Ngoni people of eastern and central Africa as a lens for understanding American domestic rituals like Halloween, Thanksgiving, Christmas, and especially the "White Wedding." As a member of American society, you might have some problems with the anthropological interpretation of your own domestic rituals, but that may be because it is so difficult to see our own culture from within.

As you read this selection, ask yourself the following questions:

- Why do many Americans spend so much money on weddings? On Christmas?

- What idea does the author convey with the double meaning of the title?

- How and why are the rituals of the American "holiday season" focused on children?

- How does the Ngoni mugeniso ritual ease tensions between the two opposing kinship groups in a patrilineal society? Why are cows important?

- How might people react to possible "mistakes" in a ritual like a wedding?

- What is more important—love or work? If you were an anthropologist from Mars, how would you know?

The following terms discussed in this section are included in the Glossary in the back of the book:

ritual	*kinship systems*
rites of passage	*cultural mediation*

Auslander, Mark. "How Families Work: Love, Labor and Mediated Oppositions in American Domestic Ritual." Reprinted by permission of the author.

Sigmund Freud, dark prophet of the bourgeois psyche, once famously defined sanity as the capacity to "love and work." Yet balancing and integrating these fundamental imperatives, paired enterprises that Freud suggestively termed the "parents of human civilization," has not proved easy for middle-class families from Freud's time onwards. The relentless pursuit of getting and spending in the outer world has long threatened to overwhelm the domestic domain, even if the home fires are in principle exempted from the frigid logic of the marketplace. Home may be where the heart is, but declarations of love are deeply embedded in the symbolic media of material consumption and the workplace—whether one chooses to say it with flowers and diamonds or by developing intricate activity schedules for children. For all of its troubling and troubled aspects, modern work has come in many respects to be thought of as the measure of all things, the pre-eminent source of self-worth and fulfillment. Work promises an escape from the complex, fraught psychic terrain of the family so long ago excavated by Freud and his disciples, while leaving many with the sense that in the pursuit of work they have betrayed key obligations to loved ones.

My title, "how families work," evokes these intertwined paradoxes of middle class domestic life. In most societies for most of human history, the reproduction of the family within larger social frameworks has been a directly economic enterprise, since the family was usually a primary productive unit. The work of kinship in most other societies has been profoundly continuous with other forms of work, the processes through which persons transform natural elements into cultural products and through which they exchange abstract signs of their labor and productive capacity—in the form of shells, cattle, women, money or other valued media. In contrast, since the mid 19th century the western bourgeois family has been formally defined as the social unit most directly opposed to the domain of work and commerce. The family has long been idealized as a haven in a heartless world, a secure enclave that protects its members from the predations of wage labor and financial calculation, a clearly-bounded zone within which unconditional love and sentiment reign supreme. "Family time" has in principle long been contrasted with its antithesis, "work time."

Nonetheless, the middle-class family has since its inception been intimately enmeshed within the cultural logics and practical necessities of capitalist labor regimes. In normative terms, "making a living" has usually implied supporting a family. Middle-class wage levels have, in principle at least, been tied to the cultural ideal of home ownership and reproducing a subsequent generation at least at the same

socioeconomic level as its antecedents. Since the high Victorian era the family and home life have been expected to restore and replenish exhausted wage earners, readying them for productive re-engagement in the business world. Middle-class families have been structured, in conjunction with the middle and upper tiers of the educational system, to reproduce a set of dispositions and orientations in each new generation, so as to meet the emerging labor requirements of the managerial and professional markets. Consumer spending for Christmas and other family holidays has for generations been understood as a bedrock of the national economy. In many respects, then, although the site of the "family" is usually formally contrasted with sites of "work," our families are "at work" continuously, laboring to support externally oriented economic productivity while constituting the home as a uniquely privileged site of "love," in both romantic and non-romantic senses of the term.

For over a century, ritual has proven an especially apt medium for dramatizing, and to some extent redressing, this fundamental tension between love and labor in middle class households. Rituals of the family have also served to mediate, with varying degrees of success, a set of related, pervasive oppositions in modern American kinship and society, including those between the (natal) family of orientation and the (affinal) family of procreation, between immediate and extended families, between autonomy and dependence, between the claims of self and community, between nature and culture, and between life and death, as well as across the complex boundaries of generation, class, race and gender. Ritual practices ranging from Christmas and Halloween to family reunions and funerals simultaneously help constitute and crosscut these fundamental categorical distinctions.

The enormous, fraught burdens placed on middle-class "family time" and on the domestic rituals staged within it may be conceived in terms of the contradictory overall social organization of temporality and labor in modern society. Modern conceptions of personhood are fundamentally tied to economically productive labor: the question "what do you do?" is the single most salient inquiry for middle-class Americans about an interlocutor's status and identity. Yet in the chaos of the marketplace, persons continuously risk being rendered anonymous, their labor time commoditized, their contributions rendered abstract or invisible, their projects absorbed without a trace. As businesses go under, jobs are lost and economies shift, familiar guideposts, through which persons might have kept track of their life progress, may swiftly vanish. The bourgeois family system is expected, in a compensatory fashion, to provide an enduring architecture of temporal continuity, telling its members where they have come from and where they are going. The family is, in effect, charged with maintaining coherent temporal scaffolds for making sense of relations between past, present and future, and most directly, with providing its members with reassuring visions of a viable future.

Yet in contrast to earlier bourgeois dynastic families, of the type memorialized by Thomas Mann in his novel *Buddenbrooks,* modern American middle-class nuclear families are structured to self-destruct each generation. As Bradd Shore argues our children are trained, often in subtle ways, to detach themselves from their natal families and homes, even during moments when the values of family continuity and stability appear to be most manifestly celebrated. In family rituals and everyday domestic scenarios, our children are socialized into achieving multiple futures, which are not always mutually consistent. They are told, in effect, that "the family" is as eternal as the Christmas tree or menorah, yet are conditioned to seek ultimate fulfillment by becoming parents themselves and presiding over an independent household of their own. Simultaneously, they learn that real self-definition depends upon economic productivity in the workplace and that adult citizenship is achieved through autonomous commodity consumption, governed by the prevailing fashions of the market.

Not surprisingly, these ambiguous ritual messages yield decidedly ambiguous consequences for family members. At times, those participating in domestic rituals derive a reassuring sense of coordinated wholeness and fulfillment, experiencing lineal continuity that coherently stretches back through the generations to time immemorial. Yet at other times, participation in these rites can provoke profound crises of faith, foregrounding failed attempts to balance love and work, deep anxiety over the validity and sincerity of family relations, and nagging doubts over market-governed definitions of worldly success.

Since the early 1970s, as the overt economic mobilization of American middle class families has dramatically intensified, the double-edged potentials of family rituals to heal or harm have arguably increased. As both parents are increasingly engaged in (or at least looking for) full time employment, and as time available for sentimental expressions seems to be more and more compressed, time-limited ritual occasions have been correspondingly idealized and elaborated. Ironically, as work increasingly invades the home, family rituals are often researched, planned and pursued with work-like intensity, in the apparent hope of restoring the categorical distinctions between work and family, and between labor and love that have long been eroded in practice. In a society that often expresses skepticism over the value of "mere" ritual, the stakes for family ritual—and for the "family time" that these rituals epitomize—may be higher than ever before.

WHAT IS RITUAL AND HOW DOES IT WORK?

Anthropologists have studied ritual since the discipline's inception, and many would regard the study of "ritual" as one of the few, distinctive features of anthropological inquiry left. Yet there is little consensus as to the definition, organization, consequences or ultimate efficacy of ritual action. Most would agree that ritual is a highly structured and prescribed form of action, in which actors tend to deny the ultimate authorship of their acts, ascribing their motive force to an external authority (be it the gods, the ancestors, law, or tradition) and in which participants understand themselves to be in a context significantly different from ordinary life. The internal structure of ritual is often characterized by intensive repetition, reversibility, severe restrictions on improvisation and accessibility, strict regulation of bodily comportment and emotional expression, marked distinctions in the time and place of performance, secrecy or elaborate control over perception (as in masking or the use of esoteric or archaic language and other restricted codes), the use of highly meaningful words and objects, and the simultaneous deployment of multiple (and usually multi-sensory) channels of communication and expression, often including music and dance. Yet many activities that would be generally recognized as "ritual" do not exhibit many of these characteristics, and some actions sharing many of these qualities would not necessarily be classified as "ritual" in the strictest sense.

Perhaps because of the multiple frames and meanings embedded in ritual practice, scholarly discussion of the topic is invariably marked by dispute, hedging and qualifying. Rituals often uphold the established sociocultural order and status quo, tending to socialize persons into taken-for-granted commonplace assumptions about the world. Yet ritual arenas are especially well suited to the ambiguous dramatization of paradox and may challenge, subvert or resist dominant sensibilities and structures of authority. Ritual is often associated with intensive faith, yet ritual performance, notes Rappaport, is not necessarily coincident with belief in any manifest sense of the term. (Consider Niels Bohr's reputed response to a student shocked that he hung a luck-bringing horseshoe in his laboratory: "Of course I don't believe in the horseshoe, but I understand that my lack of belief has no negative impact upon its efficacy!") Ritual tends to integrate practitioners into wider social collectivities, yet there are extensively documented private (non-shared) rituals and ritual activities may dramatize the radical separation of a person or persons from the larger social field. Ritual generally proceeds by imposing radical separations between persons, objects and categories but tends to establish intimate conjoining or unions between that which had been rendered distinct. Ritual is usually thought of as solemn, yet is sometimes playful, hilarious or uproarious. Although in principle conventional and scripted, ritual acts are at times strikingly original, imaginative, and improvisational. Preparation for successful ritual performance often demands intensive concentration, purposeful discipline and conscious reflection upon the rite, yet performances may enable experiential states of altered consciousness in which normal distinctions between act and actor or subject and object are transcended: "the dance dances the dancer."

SOCIAL REPRODUCTION, SOCIAL TIME AND RITUAL MEDIATION: AN AFRICAN EXAMPLE

The extraordinary mutability and diverse potentials of ritual frameworks perhaps help account for the fact that in human societies the world over, rituals mark and help organize significant moments in the developmental cycles of domestic groups and their changing relationships with higher-level social institutions. Social reproduction, never an easy process, is usually predicated on the social repression and regulation of sexuality and other libidinal drives, the exchange of marriage partners between discrete groups, the transfer of rights, property and obligations between generations, and the controlled, phased waxing and waning of relations between close kin. Amidst the inevitable conflicts that result over resources, power and loyalties, actors are often torn in multiple directions. Young and old can easily be overwhelmed by the divergent pressures of the immediate moment. Ritual provides highly evocative mechanisms for bringing underlying conundrums into the open in a structured fashion and rendering them, for the most part, manageable and negotiable. Ritual dramas, which themselves proceed through highly structured temporal sequences, offer persons and groups meaningful guideposts for understanding larger passages of social time, and for apprehending normally inchoate continuities in collective experience. By the same token, rituals of social reproduction at times offer social actors particularly effective platforms upon which to pursue short-term and long-term political strategies within their families and in the wider community.

An extended example drawn from my fieldwork in south-central Africa may help to clarify how ritual action dramatizes and modulates the contradictory processes entailed in the enterprise of reproducing society. The Ngoni of eastern Zambia hold a special ceremony known as the *mugeniso,* around the time that the first-born son of a marriage union is able to walk. In principle, following the rite, strict prohibitions on the new husband eating in the presence of his wife's parents will be relaxed. In accounting for the ceremony, Ngoni informants explain that the first few years of marriage are nearly always tense. The bride, in a prolonged probationary state, is watched carefully by her husband's kin for signs of laziness, disobedience or disloyalty. She may often return to her mother and father's compound, bearing complaints of ill treatment, and her brothers may be tempted to take revenge on their brother-in-law and his agnates. Cattle or monetary bridewealth transactions, which ought to flow at a regular rate from the husband's people to the bride's people, are often stalled, and mutual recriminations and traditional court proceedings between affines (in-laws) are not unusual. The purpose of the mugeniso, it is usually said, is to "heal" or "cool" the burning animosity between the comparatively new affines and to celebrate their common bond, the first male child of the conjugal union.

In the initial phase of the mugeniso ceremony, the husband and wife's families dramatize these underlying tensions by playing at combat over a head cattle. On the morning of the rite, the husband, wife and child, accompanied by members of the husband's patrilineage (a classification often extended to his entire village), should journey to the bride's natal home bringing a bovine, usually an ox, as a gift to the bride's father. In precolonial days, I was told, the members of the military age regiment, to which the husband had belonged before marriage, would escort the procession. Once they come to the edge of the host village, the approaching party brandishes spears, knobkerries and shields and repeatedly hurls themselves towards the wife's natal relatives, who have danced out to greet them, shouting taunts and insults. The wife's people, in turn, stage mock charges upon the "foreigners, attempting to seize the ox and the boy from them.

This physically enacted opposition is to some extent undercut by the choice of ngoma war songs performed by the two parties as they dance, including the song allegedly sung in the 19th century by the Ngoni's traditional enemy, the Bemba, as the Ngoni legions approached, "Tipasile Mkhondo." There is a good deal of exaggerated leaping, laughter, and playful mock dueling as performers sing the words of the song, "Prepare the spears/the spears/we are all going to die/the Ngoni are coming." In time, the host group "captures" the ox, and moments later the two groups merge into one another, singing songs of war victory as they dance together towards the compound of the wife's father. The young boy will usually be invited to dance with his matrilaterals at the head of the procession and his mother's female relatives will loudly ululate their praises as the child enters the compound.

After the maternal grandparents and their kin have formally welcomed the young family and their relations, the young boy is entitled to enter his maternal grandfather's cattle byre and select a single beast for slaughter. In most cases that I have observed or heard about, the boy seems to understand that regardless of his grandfather's protestations and his subtle (or not so subtle) hints to select a modest beast, the child is really expected to pick the plumpest and most desirable animal. Many times, I've heard Ngoni men rapturously and uproariously recount, "Oh, the old man cried, he just cried, when he saw the beast the boy had chosen. It was his favorite animal, but he had no choice. So he just cried!"

After the beast has been slaughtered and the meal prepared, the husband and his family are invited to enter the house of the wife's parents and to eat with them. The husband is scrupulous to avoid establishing direct eye contact with his father-in-law or mother-in-law, and will be very careful not to sit or crouch near the wall of his in-laws' sleeping quarters. In practice, sons-in-law tend not to eat much at this event, but the groundwork is laid for future commensality and collaboration. Both sides of the family take great delight if the first-born boy eats his food with zest. In several cases, I heard the maternal grandfather tell his grandson, only partly in jest, that he was going to keep him in the compound for good, since his father and his agnates were clearly incapable of paying all the promised bridewealth. The exchanges of food, speeches, teasing and laughter usually have the desired effect. "After the mugeniso," I was often told, "the families will be so much easier with each other."

The mugeniso rite thus effectively dramatizes and to some extent defuses a set of underlying tensions between affines through a series of ambiguous enactments. It begins with a tussle over one of the bridewealth cattle, a persistent source of argumentation between the two families. Appropriately, this struggle quickly merges into a struggle over the young boy, the product of the union that has been legalized through bridewealth cattle; in capturing the ox, his matrilaterals in a sense seem to be capturing their sister's child. At one level, the opposition between the two parties is deflected through the singing of a song about the common enemy of the Ngoni, the Bemba, whom they allegedly vanquished. Yet there is a semi-serious edge to this song, as well, which alludes to the Bemba's status, in Ngoni's eyes, as "food of the spear" (chakudya chamkhondo); it is never clear after all, in relations among affines, just whom is going to "eat" (or

subsume) whom. Similarly, the practice of having the young boy lead the procession once it has been unified can be multiply interpreted. It is sometimes explained as showing the underlying unity among the extended family, which has an equal interest in the new offspring. Yet the husband's people usually tend to state that boy is a warrior "conquering" the village of his mother, while the wife's people assert he is "coming back to his real home."

Overlapping, ambiguous interpretive frames are especially evident in the byre episode, which calls forth a complex mixture of seriousness and hilarity. The scenario of the little boy annihilating his grandfather's favorite beast is a miniature rite of reversal, calling to mind a standard bone of contention between younger and older men. Juniors are forever pleading with their elders to slaughter or sell their cattle, yet men of the senior generation are invariably reluctant to do this, for cattle are the foundation of a patriarch's wealth, prestige and influence. Young men complain endlessly of their older male relatives "love only cattle, not their children." Hence the delight taken in seeing a small boy imperiously and successfully demand a beast from a senior man, especially from a man with whom the boy's own father would be loath to quarrel. At the same time, the incident anticipates the eventual passage of generational succession, when the boy will ultimately inherit the patrimony of the ascendant generation and become the master of its herds.

In principle, this episode teaches the boy the lesson that he may always go to his matrilaterals for aid, for they love him unconditionally, in contrast to his agnates who may resent him as a potential competitor for the common resources of the patrilineage. Yet, there is unquestionably an aggressive edge to the pressure on the boy to pick the finest animal, a choice that invariably pleases his agnates, who are thus reassured that the boy has the makings of a virile, assertive male who will not be overly under the spell of his matrilaterals, whom, they suspect, seek to spoil and "soften" the youth.

Ngoni regard it as particularly hilarious (yet also deeply propitious) if the boy picks one of the cattle that had been given as bridewealth for his mother by his father's people. Significantly, his agnates and matrilaterals tend to differ over just what the joke is. The boy "knows his own beasts," the agnates joke, and is "taking his own back." In contrast, matrilaterals proclaim with a smile, "he feels free since he knows he is in his real home now!" Picking one of the bridewealth cattle raises a delightful paradox: the boy is annihilating one of the media through which the legitimacy of his own birth was established and through which he has legally been made a member of his father's patriline. Interestingly, the demonstrable (and I believe sincere) anguish of the maternal grandfather over the loss of a valued bovine is seen as a good omen by both sides of the family. As one agnate of the boy told me, "When the grandfather cries so hard, that means he and the boy will always be good friends!" A maternal uncle of the boy agreed, laughing, "Oh, he will be a wild one, that one!"

Only once the child has symbolically triumphed over his mother's father may relations of avoidance between affines be relaxed. This victory and subsequent transformation of relations are only possible because of the ambiguous status of the child during the rite; he "belongs" to both his father's people and his mother's people. (If the child unambiguously represented his father's patrilineage at this moment, the assault on the matrilaterals' livestock would presumably seem too aggressive.)

Two further points should be emphasized. First of all, the ritual management of the marriage bond in this instance demands the participation of three generations: the tense relationship between adjacent generations (of the father-in-law and his son-in-law) is successfully manipulated by shifting the focus of attention to relations between alternate generations (of the maternal grandfather and his daughter's son). In effect, solidarity between generations one and three helps to secure the reconciliation of affines, especially between generations one and two.

Secondly, note that these generational reconfigurations are effected through the medium of cattle, the overarching embodiment of social and economic value in Ngoni society. Cattle here operate as the pivotal switch point between the social levels of descent and kinship, between the agnatic principle of patrilineal organization and the interpersonal ties of complementary filiation. In regular bridewealth transactions, cattle mark the boundaries of distinct descent groups, dividing the donating family of the husband from the receiving family of the wife. In the mugeniso rite, performed once the marriage has proven its solidity, these former lines of contrast are blurred; in seizing his maternal grandfather's cow, the little boy (the fruit of the marriage union) operates as a bridge between the two families, establishing a new intimacy that is exemplified by their subsequent act of eating together. Although cattle are the enduring source of aggressive conflict among affines, the seized cow in this instance establishes the enduring "love" between the child and his matrilaterals, who welcome the youth to his "real home." Through the selection and slaughter of the second head of cattle, chosen by the daughter's son of the host, this cross-generational affection is partially transferred to the relationship between the host father-in-law and his guest son-in-law. Up until this moment, in effect, father-in-law and son-in-law have

only been linked through the daughter/wife, a highly fraught link suffused with sexual anxiety. (Indeed, many Ngoni insist that it would be akin to incest for affines to eat together before the mugeniso.) Now, the assured presence of a healthy young grandson/son, a common heir, more securely links the two men. Appropriately, all parties celebrate their transformed relationship by safely consuming together the flesh of a slaughtered beast that embodies the salutary three-way relationship between father-in-law, son-in-law and grandson.

HOW DOES RITUAL MEDIATION WORK IN NORTH AMERICA? THE CASE OF THE WEDDING PARTY

At first consideration, the elaborate ritual logic of the Ngoni mugeniso—defusing affinal tension through a highly valued economic medium that is manipulated to dramatize positive cross-generational solidarity—would seem worlds apart from modern American family rituals. Yet the above analysis casts some light on the internal symbolic mechanisms through which structural oppositions are mediated in middle class North America. Consider, as an illustrative example, the functions of the wedding party in the standard American neotraditional "white wedding" ceremony, which emerged in the late 19th and early 20th centuries.

Over the course of the wedding ceremony, the bride and groom must be visibly separated from their natal families (and especially from their parents) and established as a discrete couple capable of eventually being a family of their own. At the same time, enduring bonds of filial love between parent and child must be emphasized and preserved. This phased attenuation is partly accomplished through the performance of generational solidarity among the couple's peers, in the form of the costumed wedding party, who are visibly contrasted with the couple's parents and families of origin seated in the audience. The process somewhat resembles the much more elaborate functions of age-grades or age-sets in some small-scale, age-ranked societies, in which induction into a male or female cohorts is a necessary precondition to marriage and promotion to full social adulthood and in which agemates actively assist in the marriage process. (Recall that in the mugeniso the Ngoni husband is escorted by his former age regiment.) The American wedding party is typically composed of a group of male peers of the groom and a group of female peers of the bride. At the start of many wedding ceremonies, a series of paired bridesmaids and groomsmen often walk down the aisle, in a ritual foreshadowing of the eventual conjugal pairing of the actual bride and groom. Upon reaching the altar each couple of the wedding party will separate and retire to their respective sides of the altar, forming a line of women on the left and a line of men on the right (in some weddings, this division conforms to the distinction between bride's party and groom's party in the seated audience.)

The wedding party, flanking the altar in a gender divided fashion, thus tangibly paves the way for the bridal couple. This line of peers, which may include the couple's siblings, friends, and a few young cousins (or children of the bride or groom from previous marriages or relationships), stands facing the seated audience, which normally includes the couple's parents and other members of ascendant generations. Standing, among other things, signifies the virility and endurance of the youthful wedding party, who function as representatives of the rising generation on the cusp of social maturity. Appropriately, the wedding party is made up of paired cohorts of male and female peers who may be younger than the couple but who are (in most cases) structurally contrasted with the parents' generation. This twinned peer group in effect frames, and helps to create, the charged ritual space of transformation which will moments later be occupied by the couple. The transition to the adult state of marriage is thus accomplished through the simultaneous performance of generational solidarity and opposition. As they stand before the assembled, the couple is established as structurally like the youthful members of the standing wedding party, and structurally unlike their seated parents and natal families, to whom the bride and groom have turned their backs.

From the late Victorian period onwards the potent generational solidarity of the youthful wedding party, which helps in effect to break bonds between the new spouses and their parents, has been predicated on a manifest gender hierarchy. The groom should from the start of the ceremony stand by his best man and the other male members of the wedding party near the altar at the right front of the church or hall, waiting for his bride. She should enter, escorted by her father or another male who "gives her away" and process down the aisle, in full sight of the assembled, who stand in respect as she does so. She is to be met by the groom, who takes her from her guardian and with her faces the altar and the officiant. This procession enacts the classic principles in European kinship of patriarchy and virilocality; the bride is moved out of her father's family into her husband's domain, and is presented as an elaborate, decorated "gift." The walk down the aisle may also enact the European principle of mild hypergamy; the woman is, in principle, lifted up in status through marriage, as she is absorbed into the relatively superior estate of her husband's family.

The maid of honor and bridesmaids receiving the bride are thus in a significant sense differentiated from the best man and groomsmen standing by the groom, in more ways than gender per se. The line of males of the junior, rising generation, of which the groom is a part, constitutes the key fulcrum of ritual action, the base to which the mobile bride is delivered by a male figure of the senior generation. The line of young women bridesmaids offer protective solidarity to their peer, the bride, but inasmuch as they are "maids" they are destined to follow her lead as eventual brides, escorted in their turn to the altar by their own fathers. This motif is explicitly dramatized when the bride's train is held by girl bridesmaids who follow behind her, a vignette that is invariably viewed as adorable and poignant, for it anticipates the little girls' eventual journey down the aisle as brides themselves. (In contrast, little boys who are junior groomsmen would rarely process down the aisle behind the bride, but are rather expected to stand in the line of males at the front of the church by the altar.) The groom and his best man, in contrast, do not walk down the aisle but appear from another entrance to take up their place at the altar. The groom, in receiving his bride, steps forward from the community of his young male peers, while the bride, in effect, is brought forward to stand near her female peers, although she never precisely stands with them.

In this respect, the work of male generational solidarity is to constitute the fixed social base from which the groom emerges, as an exemplary embodiment of society's ascendant generation. (The groom in most cases is dressed in the same attire as his groomsmen, while her bridesmaids should never emulate the bride's attire.) In contrast to the male wedding party's solid public stability, the primary ritual work of female generational solidarity undertaken by the bridesmaids is to support the bride, through prior backstage work of preparing her for public presentation within a private space that is in principle prohibited to men (be it a changing room, powder room or bedroom). Groomsmen embody the public face of the new generation coming into its own; bridesmaids link the less visible domestic realm to public aesthetic displays, but their status as members of the junior generation would appear to be subsumed under the status of their male counterparts, who have "escorted them" down the aisle.

Significantly, the bride, and emphatically not the groom, is the center of aesthetic and affective attention throughout the rite. Thus, while the groom formally embodies the new generation that will in time succeed the parental generation, his separation from his parents is nowhere dramatically enacted during the rite. In contrast, the separation of the bride from her father or male guardian is one of the most remarked upon and poignant aspects of the ceremony, calling forth an almost obligatory sigh or muffled tear from the audience. This visible separation of bride from father at the rite's opening is complemented by the ever-popular moment at the rite's conclusion when the groom lifts the bride's veil and kisses her. In this regard it is striking that while most officiants have foregone the blatantly patriarchal "I now pronounce you man and wife" for the more egalitarian, "I now pronounce you husband and wife," few officiants can resist uttering the phrase, "You may now kiss the bride," which treats the bride as the marked epitome of desire. The audience's relief at this moment is palpable; after the solemnity of the formal ceremony the kiss is usually greeted with applause, appreciative oohs and aahs, and raucous laughter (especially if the groom and bride a little "too" amorous in their embraces).

The net effect of these overlapping oppositions and conjunctions is to moderate or defuse the potentially troubling force of the basic narrative running through the ceremony. Children are being separated from their parents, one generation is succeeding the other, and erotic pairing is being sanctioned, but these points are, if all goes well, never made too emphatically. There would be something too disturbing, I suspect, if both groom and bride were escorted down the aisle by their parents and then simultaneously abandoned them as they took their final steps to the altar. Similarly, beginning the rite with the bride and groom lined up with the entire wedding party facing the audience might lay excessive, troubling emphasis on the structural opposition between the new and old generations. Similarly, it would too painful and unseemly if the groom, receiving the bride from his soon-to-be father-in-law, were immediately to kiss her at the very moment of transfer in the aisle. In turn, although the lifted veil and final kiss do have erotic connotations, overt sexual displays at this moment would be widely deemed inappropriate.

Appropriately, the rather ambiguous confounding of the identities of the wedding couple and their generational peers is typically disambiguated during the reception. The bride and groom may initially sit with the wedding party, but they are expected to circulate through all the tables of guests, reaffirming bonds with friends, parents, parents' friends, and relatives of all ages. The bride and groom should dance together, but the bride and her father should have a special dance as well. Towards the end of the reception, the bride should toss her corsage or bouquet towards the unmarried women present, and the groom should toss the bride's garter towards the unmarried men. Beyond the manifest purpose of "predicting" the next persons to be married, these acts serve to move the bride and groom out of their liminal state ("betwixt and between"

youth and adulthood) into a fully married condition. By ridding themselves of these ritual paraphernalia, imbued with the interstitial qualities of their intermediate status, the couple distinguishes themselves from their former generational cohort, and thereby enters into the more fully adult citizenship status. Generational solidarity, which was necessary to accomplish this rite of passage during its central phase, is somewhat undone at its conclusion in favor of new, enduring solidarity among all married persons.

The wedding rite, then, is not solely a celebration of the bonds of love between the two members of the couple. It is also, more subtly, a public recruitment of new members into the polity of socially and economically productive actors, and to some extent celebrates the periodic integration of an ascendant generational cohort into the larger realm of the senior generations that run society. Hence, the insistence of parents, often in the face of complaints by the marital couple, that their business associates and friends must be included on the invitation list. The bride's protest, "But this is *my* day," may be met with a parent's explanations that the older person in question "has known you all your life," "is a really close colleague," or "might be of help to you someday, you know." For parents at a more advanced stage in the life cycle, in contrast to those a generation younger, the wedding is not simply a drama of love and of the private self but is also a rite of collective social transition, predicated on a cycle of age-based promotion into the socially-sanctioned domain of work.

As in the mugeniso, at least three generations are implicated in the standard American wedding ceremony: the generations of the conjugal couple, of their parents, and of their hoped-for children. The latter are evoked through flower girls and junior groomsmen, the bouquet that the bride carries (usually in front of her abdomen), the rotund shape of the wedding cake, and the ribald toasts about procreation often delivered at the reception. Although there is of course no precise equivalent of the mugeniso cow in the American wedding, this realignment of inter-generational relations does, rather like Ngoni practice, depend on symbolic media that embody supreme exchange value. First and foremost, an implicit exchange underlies the substantial amount of money spent on the ceremony itself. Well into the nineteenth century, middle class marriage was centered on direct and indirect payments of dowry by the bride's parents to the groom. Dowry functioned, among other things, as a form of pre-mortem inheritance, transferring wealth from the senior generation on the bride's side to the new couple (under the husband's dominion) and ultimately to the couple's offspring, the grandchildren of the bride's parents. This logic endures in the common expectation that the bride's parents will pay for the wedding ceremony, initiating the process that ideally will culminate in "giving us grandchildren." Money transferred from generation one to generation two, in effect, will be reciprocated (or, in a sense, see its potential realized) through the eventual production of members of generation three, who will be linked by intimate emotional bonds to the generous grandparents of generation one.

Although the bride's parents traditionally shoulder the bulk of the wedding costs, every member of the wedding participates in this general process of transforming financial value into affective solidarity. All adult wedding guests, regardless of seniority, are expected to purchase and present wedding gifts, which may take the form of cash or physical objects. Through these gifts the guests project aspects of themselves into the new union (in principle, the gift should not favor bride or groom, but should be something that "they can enjoy together"). Simultaneously, each donor vicariously partakes of the hope, love, erotic energy, and unity of the new couple. Widespread ambivalence over bridal registries, which are so often derided as marketing ploys and self-aggrandizing strategies by the wedding couple, partly derives from the inchoate desire to be tangibly, directly linked to grand narrative of the wedding by choosing a gift that partly expresses the identity of the giver as well as the recipient. Nonetheless, in spite of their misgivings, many guests find themselves using the registry, since selecting a gift independently is time consuming and risky. As everyone knows, not making a monetarily-valuable gift simply is not an acceptable option. Economic value, in both its practical and symbolic dimensions, is essential to the making of the new family.

In this light, we should hardly be surprised by the enduring popularity of weddings, even in our era of frequent divorce and extensive premarital cohabitation and procreation. In real life, on television or at the movies, weddings dramatize the trials and triumphs of the self and the family in search of love, fulfillment and fortune. Weddings remain perhaps the most important ritual arena through which the periodic reproduction of society is enacted, through which our public and private lives are integrated, and through which love and work are brought into meaningful coordination, if only for a few precious moments.

ALL IN GOOD TIME: TEMPORAL PROGRESSION AND RITUAL SEQUENCING

As the above analysis suggests, the enduring power of the wedding ceremony lies partly in its capacity to mark and regulate major temporal progressions in individual life cycles and in the mythic life of society. Each ceremony signals the social maturation of persons and evokes the cyclical realignment of generations, in a way that broadly encompasses divergent definitions of social value, variously grounded in love or work, self or community, autonomy or dependence. Wedding participants and guests often find themselves reflecting upon the broader shape of their lives and the changing configurations of their families over time. A woman in her sixties recently explained to me why she cried while watching her niece exchange vows with her new husband: "Suddenly, I saw my mother's face, the way she looked all those years ago on the day I married my husband. And then I started thinking about my son and whether or not he'll ever get together again with his wife and my little grandson." Smiling apologetically, she dabbed her eyes and said, "Weddings just do bring things up, don't they?"

The peculiar nature of temporal experience within American family rituals is largely a function of unusual features in our family system. As noted above, in contrast to virtually all other human kinship and descent systems, middle-class American families self-destruct in a periodic fashion; from an early age, parents train their children for autonomy, having them sleep alone, go to sleepover parties and summer camp, usually go away to college and eventually form a new family unit through a marriage or long-term romantic bond. Rites such as the wedding celebrate and solemnize this profound separation of child from parent, yet also manifest a compensatory longing for continuity and return to an imagined more secure and "authentic" past. This longing is expressed in the standard injunction that the bride wear "something old, something new," and by the emphasis on self-consciously archaic speech acts, practices, adornment and décor at many weddings. Similarly, in recent years, many couples have sought to unearth and incorporate into their weddings Old World or pre-modern practices associated with their ethnic background. In so doing, they attempt to link themselves to much earlier generations at precisely the moment of marked structural rupture from the generation of their parents.

Family time is organized through two major kinds of ritual activity, rites of passage, which mark singular transitions in a person's life, and calendrical ceremonies, which are regularly repeated, usually on an annual basis. In different ways, each of these ritual events dramatizes and mediates core conundrums in American domestic life while providing a tangible temporal framework though which people attempt to make sense of the complex events of their own lives and of their shifting relations with loved ones. Ritual time thus makes it possible to coordinate individual and social transformations, which in everyday life may be experienced as inconsistent, opposed or wildly divergent.

RITES OF PASSAGE: COORDINATING THE TRANSFORMING SELF AND FAMILY THROUGH TIME

The basic structure of rites of passage lends itself to this double temporal burden, signaling coherent transitions in the individual's life while simultaneously making sense of larger transitions in the family and collectivity.

These multilayered dynamics can be made sense of with reference to Van Gennep's classic model of the "tripartite" structure of these commonly occurring rituals, famously developed by Victor Turner. Such rites commence with the radical separation of the person or persons being transformed, often marked through special adornment, locale, or comportment. The subject then enters into a special interstitial or intermediate state, in Turner's terms, "betwixt and between" conventional social statuses or categories: he or she is neither student nor graduate, child nor adult, unmarried nor married, layman nor priest. During this "liminal period" the person undergoing ritual transformation is often subject to special prohibitions and precautions; he or she may be apprehended as especially pure, sacred, stigmatized or polluted, and may be subjected to heightened risks. This in-between period is often characterized by paradoxical or dramatic reversals of ordinary behavior; one needs, in effect, to step outside of normal society in order to alter one's social position. In the final stage of re-aggregation, during which basic principles of social life are celebrated or reinvigorated, the subject is reintegrated into normal life, usually into a different (often higher ranked) social role than that occupied before the rite.

This tripartite sequence and the extraordinary qualities of the liminal phase make these rites highly appropriate for dramatizing transformations in persons other than the rite's formal subjects. Those organizing, performing or attending the rite often take on certain liminal, interstitial qualities during the ceremony and undergo significant (if subtle or backgrounded) transformations and shifts in status. Rites of passage are thus nearly always collective enterprises that proceed upon multiple tracks, establishing important connections and distinctions among varied persons and groups beyond the proximate, central foci of ritual attention.

For example, birth in modern American society has emerged as a multileveled ritual process through which the newborn child is produced as a social person,

the woman giving birth is produced as a socially legitimate mother, the mother and her husband or partner are together produced as a socially legitimate parental couple, the parents and their child or children are produced as a "family" and a wider network of relations with kin and friends are readjusted and coordinated. The elaborate technological management of modern birth and neonatal care has occasioned subtle linguistic and ritual markers for distinguishing between different kinds of newborns, which, if all goes well, culminates in pronouncing this liminal being "a baby ready to go home." Middle-class expectant mothers are usually expected to conform to a self-improving regimen of regulated health and conditioning during pregnancy, and may feel some pressure to demonstrate their moral fitness as mothers by forgoing pain medications during birth and recapturing a trim figure during the postpartum months. Middle-class fathers are widely expected to participate in birthing classes, watch ultrasound images of the fetus with the mother, and serve as "coaches" during birth. In so doing, fathers vicariously partake in the liminal status of the neonate and birthing mother, and are eventually reintegrated along with them into normal space and time, now as a unified nuclear family. To be sure, like all processes of unification this new social entity rests upon subtle role distinctions; even in couples that strive for gender egalitarianism, the father may, within minutes of successful birth, take on the traditional male role of mediating relations between the domestic unit and larger social domains, phoning friends and relations and handing out cigars to passersby and business associates.

Similarly, the rites of christening or bris (the Jewish circumcision), while manifestly directed towards transforming the moral and spiritual status of the infant, also confirm or help establish important shifts in other persons' conditions, especially in generations one and two. The parents are established in front of the family and the religious community as persons of tradition, substance and faith. Grandparents from both side of the family are, if possible, prominent at a christening, and often exhibit considerably warmer, less formal relations with one another than they did at the wedding itself (shades of the mugeniso?). At the Jewish bris, the paternal grandfather usually holds his grandson as the foreskin is excised, evoking a line of patriarchal authority that in principle stretches back through the generations to the original covenant between the Lord and His chosen people. In this ambiguous, liminal position, holding his male flesh and blood in the face of a knife, the grandfather takes on aspects of the early patriarchs themselves, recalling Abraham's abortive sacrifice of Isaac and Moses' role as the first circumciser. In this sense, the bris is equally a rite of passage for the grandfather and his grandson, who emerge from it confirmed respectively as patriarch and novice within the family and the wider community.

Birthdays may be conceived as special kinds of repeated rites of passage, marking progressive phases in the life of the individual person and in the life of the family units to which he or she is attached. In addition to celebrating the physical and mental maturation of a young child, early birthday parties may mark status shifts for young mothers or engender growing solidarity among the parents (especially mothers) in attendance. The birthday party (for the most part, a 20th century invention) manifestly celebrates the pleasure-seeking self (complete with chocolate cake) and is sometimes dismissed as a narcissistic indulgence. Yet the rite also emphasizes the progressive middle class disciplining of the willful self. Through successive birthday parties, children are expected to learn to play with one another, and are socialized into middle class codes of collaboration, appropriate degrees of formality and informality, and principles of reciprocity. For example, I recall that at my fourth birthday party, my young friends James and Leon in turn, by coincidence, each gave me identical plastic Indian headdresses. Thinking that the second headdress was superfluous, I tried to give it back to Leon, but my mother quickly intervened to tell me to graciously accept both gifts, whispering rhetorically to me, "don't you still want to be Leon's friend?" Such staged events and the moral pedagogy they occasion gradually lay the groundwork for the child's later integration into generational cohorts at school and in the workplace.

Sweet sixteen birthday parties, like high school proms, debutante balls or cotillion, celebrate the coming eligibility of young women for marriage and may be interpreted as "dress rehearsals" for eventual wedding ceremonies. In turn, adult birthday parties, especially for "milestone" years such as forty or seventy, may help solidify relations with peers at work and may spark reflections on the changing shape of the family as well as meditations on mortality.

Educational rites, which subtly mediate between the symbolic practices of the internal family and the wider public sector, may also help reconcile individual life trajectories and the developmental cycles of middle class families. School theatricals, concerts, dances, ballet recitals, and sport events are staged as dramas of symbolic detachment, celebrating a student's increasing autonomy from family-bound roles and integration into horizontal peer groups. At the same time, these events often occasion emotionally-laden family gatherings, in which family members are cast in the roles of "supporters" or "audience members" (or in the cases of proms, as "chaperones") and reflect upon the shifting organization of their family. Parents often report a mixture of pleasure and anxiety in seeing their child skillfully perform dramatic roles, which may remind them that the child is capable of becoming a new and different person than the one that they know. As one father recalled, "Of course, I loved seeing my daughter in school plays, but you know as she got older, I had to steel myself each time. The better she got, I was so proud, but I found myself saying to myself, 'she's just not daddy's little girl anymore!'" Perhaps because of this implicit drama of looming separation the most beloved and effective performances by young people often center on the vanishing horizon of childhood experience and coming-of-age narratives of detachment, such as Peter Pan or the Nutcracker.

Multiple, at times discordant planes of experience are also evident in graduation and commencement exercises, which in addition to marking passages in the life of individual students and of student cohorts, help constitute shifting phases in the life of the graduate's family, at times signaling the coming of the "empty nest" for parents, or representing socioeconomic upward mobility for the entire family. While high school and college graduation ceremonies at one level signal a graduate's fitness for entry into the labor force (and in that sense help mediate detachment from one's natal family and the process of eventually founding one's own family), they also often celebrate the authority of the academy and the contemplative life, and in that sense may signal enduring anxiety over the capacity of the "the real world" or marketplace to provide ultimate meaning in life. Individual and family trajectories are both interlaced and juxtaposed in class reunions and homecoming games, which are often characterized by intermingled nostalgic elegies for lost innocence, celebrations of material success and family vitality, and anxiety over failed opportunities.

As suggested above, these multi-track, contradictory processes culminate in the modern wedding. On the hand, the rite simultaneously celebrates the free, co-equal autonomous selfhoods of the individual persons being married, recognizes the gradual ascension of an entire younger generation, and honors the couple's parents (and often their grandparents). At the same time, it subtly re-instantiates principles of patriarchy, attenuates the couple's relationships with their natal families, asserts that the couple is "one flesh," directs them to procreate, and disciplines the parties into the rigors of married life and bourgeois convention. It is striking that these diverse objectives, implicating so many different persons and overlapping relationships, are all dramatized and mediated through obsessive ritual attention to a single person, the bride herself. Dressed in white, she visually dominates the entire proceeding, and becomes, during the central phase of the rite, a veritable vessel of the eternal and the sacred.

(The wedding rite might in this respect be regarded as a curious resurfacing of the ancient cult of the goddess, or a sanitized Protestant rendition of the medieval cult of the virgin.) The blessings of life itself seem to flow from her as marches down the aisle, greeted by an appropriately reverential sighs.

Various objects associated with the bride carry traces of the numinous qualities that temporarily inhabit her; like ritual paraphernalia in other societies these objects are characterized by what Turner terms the "polyvocality" of ritual symbols, the capacity of a given object or act to evoke different meanings or associations at various levels of experience. Initially, her elaborate white dress connotes virginity, purity, aristocratic bearing, demureness and sacredness. Yet later in the ceremony, when her veil is drawn back for the dramatic kiss, her attire takes on more erotic and procreative associations, anticipating her "deflowering" on the wedding night and her hoped-for fertility. (These associations are dramatically accentuated by the increasingly popular practice, at some receptions, of the groom crawling beneath the bride's billowing skirts, to the raucous cheers of onlookers, to retrieve her garter belt.) Similarly, the bouquet she carries down the aisle initially has extensive associations with her hoped-for fertility (a single flower, after all, would usually seem as inappropriate as a single handful of rice). Yet when the bride tosses the bouquet a different set of meanings comes to the fore: she is not discarding hopes of fertility but is rather, as noted above, shedding her liminal state as wife-to-be. She thus dramatizes her new married state through a playful (but ultimately serious) contrast with her unmarried former peers.

At one level, the white wedding cake, the same color as the bride's dress, evokes the sweetness and pleasure of conjugal unity (on the anticipated marital bed), as emphasized in the (quasi-erotic) moment when the bride and groom feed one another, as well as the resplendent and unique status of the couple, as often signified by small dolls of the couple atop the wedding cake. The cake may also be said to signify the collective investment of the assembled guests in the future procreative generativity of the couple and the hoped-for fecundity of the bride's body. After the couple has exchanged bites, all the guests are expected to eat a piece of the cake, in effect sealing through a shared act of commensality their united witnessing of the marriage and their common hopes for fruits of the union. The cake's associations with fecundity are further emphasized by its large, rotund shape (anticipating the bride's pregnant body) and by the practice of saving a piece to be consumed one year after the wedding, the idealized moment when a newborn baby is expected. In turn, the many handfuls of white rice thrown by the wedding party's members simultane-

ously re-emphasize their collective commitment to recognizing the marriage and evoke the union's hoped-for fecundity; appropriately, this action both marks the formal end of the rite and signals the commencement of a new liminal period, the honeymoon, during which the couple is traditionally supposed to initiate the sexual union that will lead to conception and birth.

In short, the bride's body and its symbolic extensions function as polyvalent symbolic media through which all members of the wedding are brought into close relationship with one another and with the mythic narrative of conception, fertility and the regeneration of life. The wedding is thus a supreme bourgeois ritual, producing a tangible, optimistic vision of a viable future, centered on the symbolic "birth" of a new nuclear family.

At the other end of the spectrum, the American funeral rite also centers on a single body, that of the corpse, in order to orchestrate another set of complex social and temporal relationships. The dead person may be thought of as moving from initial separation (through special treatment, including embalming), into the ambiguous liminal status of funeral corpse, to a final state of integration into the domain of the dead (signified through burial or cremation). This close attention to the dead body not only manages the deceased's social transition out of the living world, but separates the mourners as a collective social unit out of ordinary life, placing them into an ambiguous interstitial space and time. They wear special somber clothes, adopt a solemn demeanor, and may even be expected to view or kiss the corpse, before the coffin lid is closed and the service begins. At the rite's conclusion, they are collectively reintegrated into ordinary life, often through actions, such as food and lively conversation at a reception, that emphasize the renewal of life.

The ultimate consequence of the funeral's double tripartite structure is an achieved marked separation between the categories of life and death. Paradoxically, this ritual distance enables subsequent moments of communion between the living and the dead, as in visits to the cemetery, which are often tied to key moments in the annual calendar, such as Christmas, Memorial Day, or Mother's Day.

THE ANNUAL RITUAL CYCLE: INTEGRATIVE AND DISPERSIVE TENDENCIES IN THE "HOLIDAY SEASON"

Rites of passage thus primarily concentrate upon individual life stage transitions, while simultaneously evoking collective transformations in family and kinship configurations. Conversely, calendrical family rites tend to foreground the collective institutional existence of the family, while secondarily highlighting personal life course journeys through successive family spheres.

To some extent, our major calendrical rites can be conceived as compensatory retreats from the external domains of commerce, getting and spending. Anthropologist Gwen Neville suggests that the modern family reunion (a North American practice developed after the Civil War) is an inverted kind of Protestant pilgrimage. The medieval Catholic pilgrim typically set off from a rural kinship-based setting and moved across a sacral landscape into the wider world toward a distant site, often marked by holy relics, through which he or she might come into intimate contact with the divine. In contrast, as Weber argued, the modern Protestant subject moves through a disenchanted landscape, sensing divine election only through disciplined work and persistent self-actualization in the marketplace. Hence, Neville, maintains, the modern longing, epitomized by the family reunion, to return periodically to the bonds of kinship within a nostalgic agrarian setting, such as the "old home place" or a state park. This insight may be extended to other modern calendrical ceremonies, which are also grounded in an imagined agrarian past, including the harvest festival (Thanksgiving and Halloween), the midwinter rite of sun return (Christmas, Kwanza and Hanukah) and spring fertility festivals (Easter and Passover). In contrast to earlier public festivals, however, the celebration of these rites has been privatized since the mid-nineteenth century, more and more confined to the interiors of nuclear family households. During the past century and a half, these rites have been increasingly homogenized, as regional variations have been leveled (although some distinguishing ethnic markers are often reinserted). These annual holidays thus function as apparent refuges from the wider world of work, enclaved from the rationalized calculations of the economy. Yet, paradoxically, the rites also celebrate the integration of the family into the larger nation and economy.

To appreciate the multiple dimensions of calendrical rites, let us briefly concentrate on the annual "holiday season," stretching from Halloween through Christmas. This two month period—centered on the image of pure child surrounded by a loving family—is characterized by mounting mass commodity consumption, during which all Americans are surrounded by the sights and sounds of marketing, from blinking lights, to storefront displays to Christmas carols. Building on Warner, Bellah approaches Thanksgiving as an integrative rite, binding discrete families into the national "civic religion" of shared sacrifice and imputed grace. The turkey might in this light be conceived of as symbolizing both the solidarity of the family (hence the common prohibition on cutting the turkey before all members and branches of the family have assembled at the table!) and the unity of the nation. In partaking of a piece of the turkey (partly consecrated by a common prayer or murmured words of thanks) family members are thus more intimately bound to one another and to their fellow citizens—symbolically integrated into what Benedict Anderson terms the "imagined community" of the nation. In some families, this integration is hierarchically ordered; all "children," including unmarried persons of any age, are confined to the "children's table."

Although commentators have for generations dutifully denounced the "commercialization" of Christmas as contrary to the day' spiritual and religious principles, it is manifestly a festival of mass commodity consumption, arguably the most important context through which the domestic domain is integrated into the broader public sphere. Preparatory mini-pilgrimages to department store or shopping mall Santas are de rigeur in many families. A Christmas morning featuring only homemade toys would hardly count as Christmas; enormous emphasis is placed on obtaining fashionable and expensive industrially manufactured gifts, especially those celebrated in the mass media. The common myth that Santa Claus, and not the parents, miraculously places the gifts under the Christmas tree could be interpreted as poetically evoking the nearly magical status of the commodity at the symbolic heart of the American family system. The gifts, after all, really do come from somewhere else (if not the North Pole) and through interacting with the outer world of the marketplace the parents have translated mere money into expressions of love, the foundation of the family unit. As Nancy Munn perceptively notes, the polyvalent symbol of the wrapped Christmas present effectively conflates two kinds of parental love. The outer colored wrapping evokes nurturing affection, classically associated with maternal love and aesthetics, while the material value of the store-bought gift within the wrapping evokes the parents' monetary contributions, classically associated with the wage-earning working father. Significantly, on Christmas morning, all these gifts, evoking the multiple relationships (parent-parent, parent-child, sibling-sibling) that constitute the nuclear family unit, are assembled around a singular ritual object, the Christmas tree. There should be only one tree per family, topped by one single star, but the tree itself should have been previously decorated through the collaborative work of the entire family, using objects that often evoke previous Christmas celebrations and key persons and events in family history. The idealized tableau of Christmas morning—children and parents delightedly opening gifts under the tree—is an exemplary model of the

American family system, in which close relatives are bound together as a single unit by exchanging tokens of love derived from the wider market-driven culture.

The Christmas tree, while sometimes spoken of as a sign of family continuity, is also a potent sign of rupture between successive nuclear families. Once a new couple has established their own household, they are likely to have a tree of their own, and are considerably less likely to receive presents under their parents' trees in their natal households. Each newly established Christmas tree embodies the virtual sanctification of the new bourgeois home and nuclear family. Santa Claus, significantly, is believed to deposit his gifts at the symbolic core of domestic space, descending the chimney and entering the "living room" through the fireplace/hearth, an eminently maternal site.

These symbolic complexes may be read as striking evidence of the enduring resonance of premodern and pre-Christian symbolism in modern American culture. Levi-Strauss proposes that Father Christmas carries traces of a pagan quasi-shamanic figure, the King of Saturnalia, who embodies the seasonal cycles of death and the regeneration of life. By giving gifts to children—who for the three months following Halloween incarnate the spirits of the Dead—adults propitiate Death and enhance the vitality of the human world. Hence, parents tenderly struggle to maintain children's faith in Santa Claus for as long as possible. "Is it not that, deep within us," asks Levi-Strauss, "there is a small desire to believe in boundless generosity, kindness without ulterior motives, a brief interlude during which all fear, envy and bitterness are suspended? No doubt we cannot fully share the illusion, but sharing with others at least gives us a chance to warm our hearts by the flame that burns in young souls." In a similar vein, ethnographer Cindy Dell Clark observes that Christmas is not so much for children as it is a "a holiday in which other members of the culture socially situate themselves vis-à-vis children." In the wedding rite, as we have seen, the assembled take pleasure in the eventual prospect of the bride's fertility and the birth of children; in turn, on December 25th all are expected to rejoice in the realization of this promise, reveling in dramas of childish energy and vitality.

Pagan symbolism also runs through the rite that inaugurates the holiday season, Halloween, the night during which the souls of the dead were classically thought to roam the earth. Like Christmas, Halloween also centers on children, but with a different set of emphases. Disguised as ghosts, goblins and other supernatural beings, children would seem to function as temporary vessels of the dead traveling from house to house. The requirement that adults give gifts to these masked beings, on penalty of destructive mischief, could be read as an attempt to propitiate the forces of death, at precisely the moment in the northern hemisphere that the darkest and coldest season of the year descends. In this regard, illuminated jack-o-lanterns made of grimacing, carved pumpkins and placed on threshold sites such as porches might be interpreted as polyvalent (and prophylactic) talismans, simultaneously simulating feared goblins and guarding the home against intrusions by the dark spirits of the night.

Perhaps because of this underlying symbolism of inversion, death and disorder, Halloween celebrates the emergence of children's autonomy and individuation over their normative, vertical integration into the social collectivity. In spite (or perhaps because of) parental and mass media anxiety over child abduction and rumors of poisoned candy, children avidly campaign for trick-or-treating, a practice that dates only to the 1930s. Costumed trick-or-treating could be interpreted as a kind of "deep play" a symbolic rehearsal of adolescence and adulthood, as children try on new roles and identities (in the form of masks and costumes, often associated with miraculous powers) and venture out into the wider world, especially into the normally prohibited domains of other households—precisely the kind of sites they will come to know once they leave the nest of their parents' homes. In contrast to the integrative communion meals of Thanksgiving, Christmas, Passover or Easter, Halloween is centered on a kind of anti-meal, candy, which is not consumed in a collective context. As in classic carnival or saturnalia the world is "turned upside down" during Halloween. Children shout out commands to adults, venture out into the darkness, violate social conventions of decorum, flirt with the grotesque by over-eating and hanging toilet paper, and actively seek out frightening experiences. In temporarily taking control of instruments of secrecy, children may be tentatively exploring more pervasive mysteries and secrets of the adult social world. Each year, the complex dance of collaboration and conflict between parents and children over the precise nature of Halloween activities dramatizes in microcosm parents and children's deeper ambivalence over the maturation process: how much dependence or independence is desirable and tolerable?

Like the other family rituals we have considered, Halloween ambiguously dramatizes both the centrifugal and centripetal tendencies in American kinship. On the one hand, the rite exemplifies the child's growing horizontal integration into a socializing peer group, within which solidarity will be increasingly established (especially in adolescence) through carefully calibrated exercises in common risk-taking. On the other hand, Halloween also occasions intimate collaboration and solidarity between parents and children. The whole family often works together on elaborate scary decorations in the front yard, parents help dress the children in costume, and adults increasingly escort their children through the neighborhood on trick-or-treat ventures.

Taken as a whole, then, the entire holiday season may be regarded as a ritual drama evoking and "solving" the forces of dissolution and dispersal that threaten the American kinship system in a society that has radically separated the family from economic production, and which, in so doing, periodically preempts tri-generational households. The season begins on Halloween night, as children make ambiguous, experimental forays out to other households, testing the limits of parental forbearance and anxiety. Grandparents are often not present at Halloween, but the disturbing specters of more distant antecedents, in the form of the dead unleashed from the graveyard, are sensed and must be placated through ritual play. In turn, on Thanksgiving, at least three living generations should ideally be present to engage in joyous commensality. Significantly, Norman Rockwell's now mythic "Freedom from Want" World War II poster prominently displays loving grandparents at the top of the table, and places happy, expectant grandchildren at the table's base, evoking the affective solidarity between generations one and three. Finally, at Christmas, the ritual focus shifts from alternate generations (who may have traveled to be together) to the adjacent generations inhabiting a single nuclear family household. The white-haired Santa Claus makes a purported appearance as a substitute grandfather, but he is not, appropriately, to be seen by the children. In playing at being the grandfatherly Santa Claus, the parents, in effect, transfer the affective solidarity of alternate generations into the compressed nuclear home, reconciling proximate generations at the end of yet another year of inevitable parent-child negotiation and conflict. (One week later, on New Year's Eve, parents are rewarded with a night that is in principle for adults only, marking the final conclusion of the holiday season.)

CONCLUSION: FROM CONTRADICTION TO PARADOX

Rather like the Ngoni mugeniso ceremony, modern middle-class American family rituals poetically encapsulate and work upon a set of pervasive conundrums at the heart of our kinship and economic system, revolving around problematic generational sequencing and ambiguous signs of abstracted exchange value. When these rituals "succeed," the radical formal divides between love and work, between family of origin and family of procreation, and between dependence and autonomy are, in effect, translated from the level of overt contradiction to a more inchoate level of paradoxical coexistence. In the context of a well-performed wedding, for instance, the costumed bride functions as a composite symbolic paradigm that simultaneously evokes separation and union, filial piety and conjugal eroticism, youth and maturity, poignant loss and the joyous regeneration of life. She is in one respect pure and authentic, an oasis of aesthetic perfection unsullied by the crude logic of the market. She is another respect the embodiment of financial solidity and the fruits of hard work, a tangible celebration of the wealth of her parents or of the marital couple itself. She makes her advent in the rite as a child, being passed away from the hand of her father; she disappears from view at its conclusion as a wife clutching her new husband's hand, showered by rice that evokes the new child she will, in principle, bring forth.

In a comparable fashion, Christmas promises to collapse everyday distinctions between emotion and economy, affection and rationality, juniors and seniors. On the one hand, Christmas is the annual culmination of the cult of domesticity, promising a tableau of unconditional love equally available to rich and poor like. On the other hand, Christmas celebrates the cornucopia of commodity consumption, and is the apotheosis of every dream and fantasy the market has to offer. It celebrates the transcendental self, rewarded through gifts and the pleasures of unbridled acquisition, yet locates that self within a coherent familial framework, under the encompassing sign of the Christmas tree. Each Christmas evokes the benevolent presence of grandfatherly figures, even it subtly moves the actual incumbents of generations one off stage, towards the mythical, invisible domain of Mr. and Mrs. Claus at the North Pole. Successive Christmases provide temporal benchmarks as persons move through the life cycle, from their natal family to new nuclear family units, allowing for periodic reflections on the shape of one's life and for what Shore terms "identity-updating."

Our greatest mythic narrative of Christmas, Charles Dickens' *A Christmas Carol*, directly addresses both the intertwining of the market and the holiday and the complex intersections of personal biography and intergenerational temporal sequencing. Scrooge, the embodiment of soulless capitalist rationality, demands that Bob Cratchet work on Christmas Day, then fires him on this day, of all days. He is punished by successive visitations (significantly, brought to him by the dead themselves) of the spirits of Christmas Past, Present and Yet to Come. In his visions of the past, he re-experiences the pain of love lost and friendship betrayed. In the present, he sees the immediate consequences of his action. In the future, he glimpses the possible legacies of his selfishness, in his own unlamented death and in the preventable death of Cratchet's young son, Tiny Tim. Finally, embracing the spirit of Christmas through joyous commodity consumption and distribution, Scrooge saves Tiny Tim and, in so doing, remakes the future and saves himself. He thereby grasps the basic paradox of Christmas and of the sentimental domestic cult: in giving unstintingly to the junior generation that will in time replace both the middle and senior generations, elders actively secure their own vitality and achieve symbolic immortality. Appropriately, it falls to the youngest child, Tiny Tim, to pronounce the closing words of salvation over the elderly Scrooge and the extended family of Christmas revelers: "God bless us, everyone."

As *A Christmas Carol* reminds us, although family rites produce powerful visions of the past, present and future, they do not, in themselves, determine whether or not the future will be bleak or joyous, alienating or transcendent. As most of us have learned, family rituals can trigger moments of devastating isolation, or afford exquisite glimpses of the sublime. Ritual provides microcosmic, condensed models of the contradictory texture of lived experience, yet these models are not fixed templates, but are only the potential building blocks out of which we may, under certain conditions, come to know ourselves, our antecedents and our descendants more deeply. In creatively manipulating these building blocks, we may improvise more effective and meaningful relations with love ones.

Here, then, lies the greatest paradox of our family rituals: in subordinating ourselves to pre-existent structures that we neither fully understand nor control, we are afforded the possibility of discovering novel aspects of ourselves and our relations with others, living and dead. Such visions may be as fleeting as a bride's tossed bouquet, a Christmas gift's wrapping, the menorah's flickering flame, or a tossed clod of earth. Yet it is out of such glimpses that we may fabricate meaningful trajectories of self and collectivity. In our ritual performances, enigmatic dramas of the insolvable puzzles of our common world, we pursue the enduring double task of reconciling our love with our work, our predecessors with our posterity.

REFERENCES

Herve Varenne. *Americans together, structured diversity in a midwestern town.* (New York Teachers' College Press, 1977); Bradd Shore, *Family time: Studying myth and ritual in working families* (Emory Center for Myth and Ritual in American Life, Working Paper 028-03, 2003).

Thomas Mann, *Buddenbrooks: The decline of a family.* Trans. John E. Wood. (New York: Random House, 1994), In a sense, Mann's novel prophesies the emergence of the modern nuclear family.

Bradd Shore, *Family time: Studying myth and ritual in working families* (Emory Center for Myth and Ritual in American Life, Working Paper 028-03, 2003).

Sociologists working in the tradition of Erving Goffman tend to use the term "ritual" in a rather broader sense, to refer to any patterned, repeated behavior. See Goffman, Erving, *Interaction rituals* (Garden City, NY: Anchor Books, 1967).

N.D. Fustel de Coulanges, *The ancient city.* (Baltimore: Johns Hopkins University Press, 1980 [1864]); Emile Durkheim, *The elementary forms of the religious life* (New York: Basic Book, 1915); Claude Levi-Strauss, *Structural anthropology* Volume I (New York: Basic Books, 1966); Pierre Bourdieu, *Outline of a theory of practice.* Trans. Richard Nice (Cambridge and New York: Cambridge University Press, 1977); Maurice Bloch, *Ritual, history and power: Selected papers in anthropology* (London: Atlantic Highlands, NJ: Athlone Press, 1989).

Victor Turner, *The ritual process: Structure and anti structure* (Chicago: University of Chicago Press, 1969); Carlo Ginzburg, *The night battles: Witchcraft and agrarian cults in the 16th and 17th centuries.* Trans. J. & A. Tedeschi (New York: Penguin Books, 1986); Stuart Hall & T. Jefferson (Eds.), *Resistance through rituals: Youth subcultures in post-war Britain* (London: Routledge, 1993); David Lan, *Guns and rain: Guerrillas and spirit mediums in Zimbabwe* (Berkeley: University of California Press. 1985.) Pater Stallybrass and Albon White, *The politics and poetics of transgression* (London: Methuen, 1986); Jean Comaroff, *Body of power, spirit of resistance: The culture and history of a South African people* (Chicago: University of Chicago Press, 1985).

Roy Rappaport, *Ritual and religion in the making of humanity.* (Cambridge, UK: Cambridge University Press, 1999).

Keith Burridge, *New heaven, new earth: A study of millenarian activities* (New York: Schocken Books, 1969); Dick Hebdige, *Subculture: The meaning of style* (London: Methuen, 1979).

Claude Levi-Strauss, *Structural anthropology.* Volume I. (New York: Basic Books, 1966); Valerio Valeri, *Kingship and sacrifice: Ritual and society in ancient Hawaii* (Chicago: University of Chicago Press, 1985); Nancy Jay, *Throughout your generations forever: Sacrifice, religion and paternity* (Chicago: University of Chicago Press, 1992).

J. Huizinga, *Homo Ludens: A study of the play element of culture* (London: Routledge & K. Paul, 1949); Mikhail Bakhtin. *Rabelais and his world.* Trans. Helene Iswolsky (Cambridge, MA: M.I.T. Press, 1968); Clifford Geertz, *The interpretation of cultures* (New York: Basic Books, 1973); Keith Basso, *Portraits of the "the Whiteman": Linguistic play and cultural symbols among the western Apache* (Cambridge and New York: Cambridge University Press, 1979).

Barbara Babcock (ed.), *The reversible world: Symbolic inversion in art and society.* (Ithaca, NY: Cornell University Press, 1978).

Bradd Shore, *Culture in mind: Cognition, culture and the problem of meaning* (New York: Oxford University Press, 1996), p. 50.

For an overview of American middle class ritual, see Mark Auslander, "Rituals of the Family," *Sloan Work Family Encyclopedia,* 2002; http://wfnetwork.bc.edu/encyclopedia_entry.php?id=253.

Many of my Ngoni friends professed horror and disgust upon learning of the American practice of the rehearsal dinner. "How can affines eat together, before a child has even been born? Don't all your families go crazy in time?" a young man asked me.

Ngoni and Bemba retain a joking relationship with one another, and are expected to cavort uproariously at one another's funerals. In some respects, the relationship between affines at the mugeniso resembles a joking relationship, characterized by raucous clowning and muted aggression.

John Gillis, *A world of their own making: Myth, ritual and the quest for family values* (New York: Basic Books, 1996). For an illuminating discussion of French bourgeois rituals of the 19th century, see A. Martin-Fugier, Bourgeois rituals. In M. Perot (ed.), *A history of private life* (Volume 4), pp. 261–337 (Cambridge, MA: Harvard University Press, 1990).

The generational solidarity of the cohorts is usually emphasized, on an evening preceding the wedding, by single-sex reveling at bachelor and bachelorette parties.

The closest equivalents to age-grades in modern American society are class cohorts at school. Not surprisingly, the maid of honor and best man are often high school or college classmates of the bride and groom.

I realize that all these untoward scenarios must have happened in some weddings, but in an ideal, typical sense these enactments would seem to violate the normative constitutive principles of the system.

Arnold van Gennep. *The rites of passage* (London: Routledge, 2004); Victor Turner, Betwixt and between: The liminal period in rites de passage. In Victor Turner, *The forest of symbols. Aspects of Ndembu ritual* (Ithaca, NY: Cornell University Press, 1967).

The enormous ideological and emotional power of such rites of passage, which can provide such deeply meaningful frameworks through the life cycle, is evidenced by the ever-increasing popularity of innovative life-transition rites, ranging from gay and lesbian commitment ceremonies and weddings to Afrocentric coming of age ceremonies. Indeed, one might argue that given the declining formal economic rationale for the nuclear family, the family is pre-eminently a ritual order in modern American society; a "family" could increasingly be defined as a group of people who practice a set of domestic rituals, integrating them both into intimate units and into larger structures of belonging across divides of space and time.

Yaya Ren, personal communication.

R.E. Davis-Floyd, *Birth as an American rite of passage.* (Berkeley: University of California Press, 1992).

Felicity H. Paxton, *America at the Prom: Ritual and regeneration* (Ph.D. Dissertation, University of Pennsylvania, 2000).

Sherry Ortner, Ethnography among the Newark: The class of '58 of Weequakic high school. *Michigan Quarterly Review* 32 (1993), pp. 411–429.

Victor Turner, *The forest of symbols. Aspects of Ndembu ritual* (Ithaca, NY: Cornell University Press, 1967).

Richard Huntington and Peter Metcalfe, *Celebrations of death: The anthropology of mortuary ritual* (Cambridge: Cambridge University Press, 1979); Lloyd Warner, *The living and the dead: A study of the symbolic life of Americans.* (New Haven: Yale University Press, 1959); John Gillis, *A world of their own making: Myth, ritual and the quest for family values.* (New York: Basic Books, 1996).

Gwen Neville Kennedy, *Kinship and pilgrimage: Rituals of reunion in American Protestant culture.* (New York: Oxford University Press, 1987); see also, Gwen Kennedy Neville, Kinship and pilgrimage: Rituals of reunion in American protestant culture (Working Paper 023-03, Emory Center for Myth and Ritual in American Life, 2003).

This argument is developed in reference to Protestant camp meetings by Bradd Shore, in his Spiritual Work, Memory Work: Revival and Recollection at Salem Camp Meeting (Center for Myth and Ritual in American Life, Working Paper 024-03, 2003). For a discussion of American family reunions, with particular attention to African American reunions, see Mark Auslander, Something we need to get back to: Mythologies of origin and rituals of solidarity in African American working families (Working Paper, Emory Center for Myth and Ritual in American Life, 2003).

Warner, op cit; R. Bellah, *Civil religion in America.* In Bellah, *Beyond belief: Essays on religion in a post-traditional word* (pp. 168-187) (New York: Harper and Row, 1970).

Benedict Anderson, *Imagined communities: Reflections on the origins and spread of nationalism.* (London: Verso, 1983)

The Thanksgiving rite also enables degrees of ethnic and family-specific variation. Cuban Americans, for example, may tend to serve as a special shredded turkey dish. Individual extended or nuclear families often consume a particular dish, or follow a particular practice that they consider unique to their family.

L.E. Schmidt, *Consumer rites: The buying and selling of American holidays* (Princeton, NJ: Princeton University Press, 1995).

W.B. Waits, *The modern Christmas in America* (New York: New York University Press, 1993); J.M. Golby & A.M. Purdue, *The making of modern Christmas* (Athens, GA: University of Georgia Press, 1986).

Indeed, Belk argues that Santa is a secular, capitalist transformation of Christ: while the anti-materialist Jesus "reigns in the realm of the spirit," Santa is "first and foremost a symbol of material abundance and hedonistic pleasure." See Ressell W. Belk. A child's Christmas in America: Santa Claus as deity, consumption as religion. *The Journal of American Culture* 10 (1): 87–100. On Christmas and capitalism see also Lloyd Warner, *The living and the dead: A study of the symbolic life of Americans* (New Haven: Yale University Press, 1959); Daniel Miler (Ed.), *Unwrapping*

Christmas (Oxford: Clarendon Press, 1993); L.E. Schmidt, Consumer rites: *The buying and selling of American holidays* (Princeton, NJ: Princeton University Press, 1995); E.H. Pleck, *Celebrating the family: Ethnicity, consumer culture, and family rituals* (Cambridge, MA: Harvard University Press, 2000); R. Horsley, & J. Tracy (Eds.), *Christmas unwrapped. Consumerism, Christ, and culture* (Harrisburg, PA: Trinity Press International, 2001).

Nancy Munn, *Symbolism in a ritual context: Aspects of symbolic action* (1973), pp. 607–608.

Claude Levi-Strauss, Killing Father Christmas. In Daniel Miller, ed., *Unwrapping Christmas* (Oxford: Clarendon Press, 1995).

Claude Levi-Straus, Killing Father Christmas, p. 50.

Cindy Dell Clark, *Flights of fancy, leaps of faith: Children's myths in contemporary America* (Chicago: University of Chicago Press, 1995), p. 40.

Elizabeth H. Pleck, *Celebrating the family: Ethnicity, consumer culture, and family rituals* (Cambridge, MA: Harvard University Press, 2000).

On saturnalia, see Mikhail Bakhtin, *Rabelais and his world*. Trans. Helene Iswolsky (Cambridge, MA: M.I.T. Press, 1968).

Bradd Shore, Autobiographical memory and identity updating Salem Camp Meeting (Emory Center for Myth and Ritual in American Life, Working Paper 048-06, 2006).

8

Body Ritual Among the ~American~ Nacirema

Horace Miner

....

Generations of anthropologists have traveled the globe, reaching to the far corners of the five continents to discover and describe the many ways of humankind. Anthropologists have gathered a diverse collection of exotic customs, from the mundane to the bizarre. Understanding and appreciating other societies requires us to be culturally relative. But people tend to judge others by their own cultural values in a way that is *ethnocentric*. This is because people take their cultural beliefs and behaviors for granted; they seem so natural that they are seldom questioned. Among the most interesting social customs on record are the rituals of the Nacirema. By viewing Nacirema behaviors as *rituals,* we gain insight into their culture and into the meaning of the concept of *culture*. We also gain insight into the problem of ethnocentrism.

Ritual is a cultural phenomenon. Ritual can be found in all societies. It can be defined as a set of acts that follow a sequence established by tradition.

Throughout the world, ritual reflects the fundamental cultural beliefs and values of a society by giving order to important activities and particular life crises like death and birth. Every day, however, mundane rituals are performed unconsciously. In fact, most Nacirema people do these things without being aware of their underlying symbolic meanings. Pay particular attention to the quotation at the end of the selection.

As you read this selection, ask yourself the following questions:

- How do the Nacirema feel about the human body?
- Do you think that the charms and magical potions used by the Nacirema really work?
- Can you list those aspects of social life in which magic plays an important role?
- What is your opinion of the importance of body ritual, and if you went to live among the Nacirema, would you tell them of your opinion?
- Living among the Nacirema, you might find that their behaviors sometimes appear bizarre. Do you think the Nacirema themselves feel this way?

The following terms discussed in this selection are included in the Glossary at the back of the book:

clan   *ethnocentrism*
culture   *ritual*

....

The anthropologist has become so familiar with the diversity of ways in which different peoples behave in similar situations that he is not apt to be surprised by even the most exotic customs. In fact, if all of the logically possible combinations of behavior have not been found somewhere in the world, he is apt to suspect that they must be present in some yet undescribed tribe. This point has, in fact, been expressed with respect to clan organization by Murdock (1949:71). In this light, the magical beliefs and practices of the Nacirema present such unusual aspects that it seems desirable to

→ USA

describe them as an example of the extremes to which human behavior can go.

Professor Linton first brought the ritual of the Nacirema to the attention of anthropologists twenty years ago (1936:326), but the culture of this people is still very poorly understood. They are a North American group living in the territory between the Canadian Cree, the Yaqui and Tarahumare of Mexico, and the Carib and Arawak of the Antilles. Little is known of their origin, although tradition states that they came from the east. According to Nacirema mythology, their nation was originated by a culture hero, Notgnihsaw, who is otherwise known for two great feats of strength—the throwing of a piece of wampum across the river Pa-To-Mac and the chopping down of a cherry tree in which the Spirit of Truth resided.

Miner, Horace. "Body Ritual among the Nacirema." *American Anthropologist* 58 (1956):503–507. www.anthrosource.net.

consumerism ←

Nacirema culture is characterized by a highly developed market economy which has evolved in a rich natural habitat. While much of the people's time is devoted to economic pursuits, a large part of the fruits of these labors and a considerable portion of the day are spent in ritual activity. The focus of this activity is the human body, the appearance and health of which loom as a dominant concern in the ethos of the people. While such a concern is certainly not unusual, its ceremonial aspects and associated philosophy are unique.

The fundamental belief underlying the whole system appears to be that the human body is ugly and that its natural tendency is to debility and disease. Incarcerated in such a body, man's only hope is to avert these characteristics through the use of the powerful influences of ritual and ceremony. Every household has one or more shrines devoted to this purpose. The more powerful individuals in the society have several shrines in their houses and, in fact, the opulence of a house is often referred to in terms of the number of such ritual centers it possesses. Most houses are of wattle and daub construction, but the shrine rooms of the more wealthy are walled with stone. Poorer families imitate the rich by applying pottery plaques to their shrine walls.

While each family has at least one such shrine, the rituals associated with it are not family ceremonies but are private and secret. The rites are normally only discussed with children, and then only during the period when they are being initiated into these mysteries. I was able, however, to establish sufficient rapport with the natives to examine these shrines and to have the rituals described to me.

fridge

The focal point of the shrine is a box or chest which is built into the wall. In this chest are kept the many charms and magical potions without which no native believes he could live. These preparations are secured from a variety of specialized practitioners. The most powerful of these are the medicine men, whose assistance must be rewarded with substantial gifts. However, the medicine men do not provide the curative potions for their clients, but decide what the ingredients should be and then write them down in an ancient and secret language. This writing is understood only by the medicine men and by the herbalists who, for another gift, provide the required charm.

situations

The author of this article used the term *man* to refer to humanity in general. This term is not used by modern anthropologists because, to many people, it reflects an unconscious sexist bias in language and rhetoric. At the time that this article was written, however, the generalized *man* was a common convention in writing. In the interest of historical accuracy we have not changed the wording in this article, but students should be aware that nonsexist terms (*humans*, *people*, *Homo sapiens*, and so on) are preferred.—The Editors.

The charm is not disposed of after it has served its purpose, but is placed in the charm-box of the household shrine. As these magical materials are specific for certain ills, and the real or imagined maladies of the people are many, the charm-box is usually full to overflowing. The magical packets are so numerous that people forget what their purposes were and fear to use them again. While the natives are very vague on this point, we can only assume that the idea in retaining all the old magical materials is that their presence in the charm-box, before which the body rituals are conducted, will in some way protect the worshipper.

Beneath the charm-box is a small font. Each day every member of the family, in succession, enters the shrine room, bows his head before the charm-box, mingles different sorts of holy water in the font, and proceeds with a brief rite of ablution. The holy waters are secured from the Water Temple of the community, where the priests conduct elaborate ceremonies to make the liquid ritually pure.

In the hierarchy of magical practitioners, and below the medicine men in prestige, are specialists whose designation is best translated "holy-mouth-men." The Nacirema have an almost pathological horror of and fascination with the mouth, the condition of which is believed to have a supernatural influence on all social relationships. Were it not for the rituals of the mouth, they believe that their teeth would fall out, their gums bleed, their jaws shrink, their friends desert them, and their lovers reject them. They also believe that a strong relationship exists between oral and moral characteristics. For example, there is a ritual ablution of the mouth for children which is supposed to improve their moral fiber.

The daily body ritual performed by everyone includes a mouth-rite. Despite the fact that these people are so punctilious about care of the mouth, this rite involves a practice which strikes the uninitiated stranger as revolting. It was reported to me that the ritual consists of inserting a small bundle of hog hairs into the mouth, along with certain magical powders, and then moving the bundle in a highly formalized series of gestures.

In addition to the private mouth-rite, the people seek out a holy-mouth-man once or twice a year. These practitioners have an impressive set of paraphernalia, consisting of a variety of augers, awls, probes, and prods. The use of these objects in the exorcism of the evils of the mouth involves almost unbelievable ritual torture of the client. The holy-mouth-man opens the client's mouth, and using the above mentioned tools, enlarges any holes which decay may have created in the teeth. Magical materials are put into these holes. If there are no naturally occurring holes in the teeth, large sections of one or more teeth are gouged out

emphasis on the mouth

so that the supernatural substance can be applied. In the client's view, the purpose of these ministrations is to arrest decay and to draw friends. The extremely sacred and traditional character of the rite is evident in the fact that the natives return to the holy-mouth-men year after year, despite the fact that their teeth continue to decay.

It is to be hoped that, when a thorough study of the Nacirema is made, there will be careful inquiry into the personality structure of these people. One has to but watch the gleam in the eye of a holy-mouth-man as he jabs an awl into an exposed nerve, to suspect that a certain amount of sadism is involved. If this can be established, a very interesting pattern emerges, for most of the population shows definite masochistic tendencies. It was to these that Professor Linton referred in discussing a distinctive part of the daily body ritual which is performed only by men. This part of the rite involves scraping and lacerating the surface of the face with a sharp instrument. Special women's rites are performed only four times during each lunar month, but what they lack in frequency is made up in barbarity. As part of this ceremony, women bake their heads in small ovens for about an hour. The theoretically interesting point is that what seems to be a preponderantly masochistic people have developed sadistic specialists.

The medicine men have an imposing temple, or *latipso*, in every community of any size. The more elaborate ceremonies required to treat very sick patients can only be performed at this temple. These ceremonies involve not only the thaumaturge but a permanent group of vestal maidens who move sedately about the temple chambers in distinctive costume and headdress.

The *latipso* ceremonies are so harsh that it is phenomenal that a fair proportion of the really sick natives who enter the temple ever recover. Small children whose indoctrination is still incomplete have been known to resist attempts to take them to the temple because "that is where you go to die." Despite this fact, sick adults are not only willing but eager to undergo the protracted ritual purification, if they can afford to do so. No matter how ill the supplicant or how grave the emergency, the guardians of many temples will not admit a client if he cannot give a rich gift to the custodian. Even after one has gained admission and survived the ceremonies, the guardians will not permit the neophyte to leave until he makes still another gift.

The supplicant entering the temple is first stripped of all his or her clothes. In everyday life the Nacirema avoids exposure of his body and its natural functions. Bathing and excretory acts are performed only in the secrecy of the household shrine, where they are ritualized as part of the body-rites. Psychological shock results from the fact that body secrecy is suddenly lost

upon entry into the *latipso*. A man, whose own wife has never seen him in an excretory act, suddenly finds himself naked and assisted by a vestal maiden while he performs his natural functions into a sacred vessel. This sort of ceremonial treatment is necessitated by the fact that the excreta are used by a diviner to ascertain the course and nature of the client's sickness. Female clients, on the other hand, find their naked bodies are subjected to the scrutiny, manipulation, and prodding of the medicine men.

Few supplicants in the temple are well enough to do anything but lie on their hard beds. The daily ceremonies, like the rites of the holy-mouth-men, involve discomfort and torture. With ritual precision, the vestals awaken their miserable charges each dawn and roll them about on their beds of pain while performing ablutions, in the formal movements of which the maidens are highly trained. At other times they insert magic wands in the supplicant's mouth or force him to eat substances which are supposed to be healing. From time to time the medicine men come to their clients and jab magically treated needles into their flesh. The fact that these temple ceremonies may not cure, and may even kill the neophyte, in no way decreases the people's faith in the medicine men.

There remains one other kind of practitioner, known as a "listener." This witch-doctor has the power to exorcise the devils that lodge in the heads of people who have been bewitched. The Nacirema believe that parents bewitch their own children. Mothers are particularly suspected of putting a curse on children while teaching them the secret body rituals. The counter-magic of the witch-doctor is unusual in its lack of ritual. The patient simply tells the "listener" all his troubles and fears, beginning with the earliest difficulties he can remember. The memory displayed by the Nacirema in these exorcism sessions is truly remarkable. It is not uncommon for the patient to bemoan the rejection he felt upon being weaned as a babe, and a few individuals even see their troubles going back to the traumatic effects of their own birth.

In conclusion, mention must be made of certain practices which have their base in native esthetics but which depend upon the pervasive aversion to the natural body and its functions. There are ritual fasts to make fat people thin and ceremonial feasts to make thin people fat. Still other rites are used to make women's breasts larger if they are small, and smaller if they are large. General dissatisfaction with breast shape is symbolized in the fact that the ideal form is virtually outside the range of human variation. A few women afflicted with almost inhuman hypermammary development are so idolized that they make a handsome living by simply going from village to village and permitting the natives to stare at them for a fee.

Reference has already been made to the fact that excretory functions are ritualized, routinized, and relegated to secrecy. Natural reproductive functions are similarly distorted. Intercourse is taboo as a topic and scheduled as an act. Efforts are made to avoid pregnancy by the use of magical materials or by limiting intercourse to certain phases of the moon. Conception is actually very infrequent. When pregnant, women dress so as to hide their condition. Parturition takes place in secret, without friends or relatives to assist, and the majority of women do not nurse their infants.

Our review of the ritual life of the Nacirema has certainly shown them to be a magic-ridden people. It is hard to understand how they have managed to exist so long under the burdens which they have imposed upon themselves. But even such exotic customs as these take on real meaning when they are viewed with the insight provided by Malinowski when he wrote (1948:70):

> Looking from far and above, from our high places of safety in the developed civilization, it is easy to see all the crudity and irrelevance of magic. But without its power and guidance early man could not have mastered his practical difficulties as he has done, nor could man have advanced to the higher stages of civilization.

REFERENCES

Linton, Ralph. 1936. *The Study of Man*. New York: D. Appleton-Century Co.

Malinowski, Bronislaw. 1948. *Magic, Science, and Religion*. Glencoe, IL: The Free Press.

Murdock, George P. 1949. *Social Structure*. New York: The Macmillan Co.

9

Ritual in the Operating Room

Pearl Katz

ethnography of the OR

In the 1970s, anthropologist Bruno Latour discovered a tribe with his sociologist colleague Steve Woolgar. Latour's lost tribe was not hidden deep in the Amazon, nor was it tucked away on some remote Pacific Island. Latour and Woolgar discovered this tribe near the beach in southern California. In San Diego, Latour discovered "laboratory people" working at the Salk Institute for Biological Studies. Laboratory people?

From the earliest days of our discipline, anthropologists have studied humankind by living and participating in distant cultures and communities. Many of us continue to devote our careers to international research, but over the decades anthropologists increasingly applied our research methods and theories in more familiar, yet thoroughly fascinating communities. Latour and Woolgar entered the Salk Institute as if it was a remote village in Bolivia. Through a lens Latour calls "anthropological strangeness," the scientists working in Salk laboratories became an "exotic" tribe with complex rituals and customs that outsiders might find strange. Latour and Woolgar observed laboratory life to produce a compelling translation of how the science tribe works to produce facts and papers.

A number of notable anthropologists have used "anthropological strangeness" to study scientists and other familiar research communities. In *Making PCR,* for example, Paul Rabinow researched genetics pioneers who developed a technology that facilitated the mapping of the human genome. Similarly, Sharon Traweek's *Beamtimes and Lifetimes* presents a cross-cultural comparison of high-energy physicists in Japan and the United States. Through anthropology Traweek, Rabinow, and Latour help us see the laboratory with new eyes—eyes that see how cultural dimensions like gender, dress, class, and cooperation affect the production of scientific knowledge. In this chapter, Pearl Katz deploys a similar strategy to analyze the hospital operating room and sterilization rituals.

As you read this selection, ask yourself the following questions:

- What are three ways anthropologists study ritual?
- If you are standing beside a patient on the operating table, what is the ritual for switching places with the person standing next to you?
- Describe the differences among the three major phases of an operation.
- Give an example of how operating room rituals define categories of appropriate and inappropriate behavior.
- What do rituals in the operating room have in common with rituals in other contexts, sacred or secular?
- Considering the severity of surgery, what is the role of joking in the operating room?

The following terms discussed in this section are included in the Glossary in the back of the book:
autonomy
ritual
sacred
secular

Ritual has been defined as standardized ceremonies in which expressive, symbolic, mystical, sacred, and nonrational behavior predominates over practical, technical, secular, rational, and scientific behavior (Beattie 1966; Durkheim 1961; Gluckman 1962; Goody 1961:169; Leach 1968), although anthropologists have acknowledged that rational, technical acts may occur as part of ritual behavior.

The analysis of ritual has assumed various forms. One is to investigate the meanings, types, and structures of the symbols used in rituals (e.g., Turner 1967; 1969). Another is to examine the thought processes that occur in ritual, or how the actors believe in the

Katz, Pearl. "Ritual in the Operating Room." *Ethnology* 20, no. 4 (Oct. 1981):335–350. Reprinted by permission of Ethnology. Copyright © 1981 by The University of Pittsburgh.

effectiveness of the rituals (Jarvie and Agassi 1970), how the thoughts expressed in ritual reflect their social structure (Levi-Strauss 1966), and how thought processes in ritual compare with those in science (Horton 1970). Another form of analysis of ritual focuses upon the structure and function of ritual in society. Van Gennup's (1960) pioneering work describes the ways in which rituals deal with movements of people through passages in time, place, and statuses, and distinctive phases. Gluckman (1962) shows how ritual may exaggerate the distinctions between different events enacted by the same people, and explained some means by which rituals masked conflicts by emphasizing solidarity. Douglas (1966) describes the ways in which ritual resolve anomaly by avoiding the dangers of pollution.

According to these studies of ritual, behavior in an operating room in a modern hospital would not be defined as ritual because it involves predominately technical, rational, and scientific activity. By relegating behavior in an operating room to a nonritual realm, the meanings of the symbols, movements, and thought processes they reveal are not likely to be subject to the same kinds of analyses as they would if they were termed ritual behavior. Even in Horton's (1970) provocative essay, in which he compares traditional and modern thought, traditional thought is conceived as magical, religious, and expressed in ritual; modern thought as secular, technical, and expressed in scientific activity. Although Horton emphasizes the similarities as well as the differences of these two kinds of thinking, he deliberately defines the two thinking styles as embedded in two separate and different contexts.

Recently, some anthropologists (Firth 1972; Moore and Myerhoff 1977) have acknowledged that secular ceremonies may be examined as rituals because they share the symbolic and communicative functions of rituals. In the same spirit this paper examines both ritual and science in one technical context, the hospital operating room. It describes behavior and thinking in the operating room in order to understand the functions of ritual in a scientific context. Specifically, it examines the functions and efficacy of sterility procedures.

Despite the elaborate rituals, and despite the rigorous application of advanced scientific knowledge in the operating room, infections do occur as a result of surgery. In the vast majority of cases the specific cause of these infections remains unknown (Postlethwait 1972:300). In the United States each year there are approximately two million postoperative infections, causing 79,000 deaths among surgical patients (Boyd 1976:78). This paper argues that the elaborate rituals and technical procedures of the modern hospital operating room, manifestly designed to prevent infection, better serve latent functions. Ritual actually contributes to the efficiency of a technical, goal-oriented, scientific activity, such as surgery, by permitting autonomy of action to the participants and enabling them to function in circumstances of ambiguity.

THE OPERATING ROOM

In most modern hospitals the surgical area is isolated from the rest of the hospital, and the operating room is further isolated from other parts of the surgical area. The surgical area may include dressing rooms, lounges, storage rooms, offices, and laboratories as well as operating rooms. Entrance to the surgical area is restricted to those people who are properly costumed and who are familiar with the rituals within. These include surgeons, anesthesiologists, pathologists, radiologists, operating room and recovery room nurses, student doctors, nurses, and ward orderlies who work in that area.[1] The major exception to these occupational roles is that of the surgical patient who, although costumed, is unfamiliar with the rituals. All of the people in the surgery area wear costumes which identify both their general role in the hospital, as well as denoting the specific areas within the surgical area which they are permitted to enter.

The restrictive entrance procedures and costume requirements contribute to the maintenance of cleanliness and prevention of contamination. Identification and separation of cleanliness and dirt are the most important concepts in the operating room. They govern the organization of the activities in surgery, the spatial organization of rooms and objects, the costumes worn, as well as most of the rituals.

The surgical area of University Hospital[2] has four parts: the periphery, outer, middle, and inner areas (see Figure 1). Physical barriers separate these four areas. They function to prevent contamination from dirtier areas to cleaner ones. From outside to inside, these areas are differentiated according to increasing degrees of cleanliness. The periphery, the least clean area, includes the offices of the anesthesiologists, a small pathology laboratory for quick analyses of specimens, dressing rooms for men and women, and lounges for nurses and doctors. To enter the periphery area a person must wear a white jacket for identification as a member of the medical staff.

The outer area is separated from the periphery by a sliding door. Within the outer area, a nurse at the main desk can prevent the door from opening if an unauthorized person tries to enter. Entrance to the outer area is restricted to patients and to those medical personnel who wear blue or green costumes. The largest and most populated part of the outer area

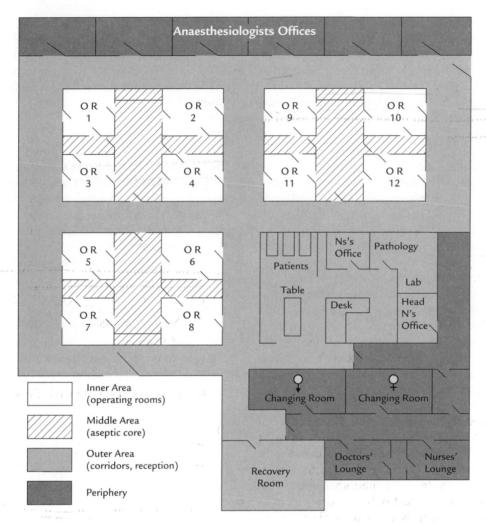

FIGURE 1   Surgical Areas in University Hospital

consists of an open corridor in which the daily operating schedule is posted and a blackboard indicating the current use of operating rooms. Patients awaiting surgery lie in narrow beds lined in a single row along one wall of the open corridor. A nurse, in charge of coordinating the timing and activities in each operating room, sits at an exposed desk in the outer area. She is in continual intercom communication with each operating room. The outer area also contains a large recovery room which houses patients immediately after their surgery is completed.

The middle area consists of three separate areas called "aseptic cores." Each aseptic core contains five doors. One of them links the outer area to the aseptic core. Each of the other four doors leads to an operating room. Each aseptic core contains a long sink, three sterilizing machines (autoclaves), and many carts and shelves containing surgical equipment, sheets, and towels. In order to enter an aseptic core, a person must wear a mask which covers the mouth and nose, coverings for shoes and for hair, and a blue or green outfit.

The innermost area contains the operating rooms and small laundry rooms. In each aseptic core there are four operating rooms and two laundry rooms. Each operating room contains three doors. One door adjoins the outer area and is used exclusively for the patient to enter and leave the operating room. A door with a small glass window connects the aseptic core to the operating room. This is used by the operating room staff. The third door leads to the laundry room which serves as a depository for contaminated clothing and instruments.

PREOPERATIVE RITUALS

One of the more important operating room rituals, scrubbing, takes place in the aseptic core before each operation begins. It is a procedure by which selected personnel wash their hands and lower arms according to rigidly prescribed timing and movements. The purpose of scrubbing is to remove as many bacteria as possible from the fingers, nails, hands, and arms to the elbows. The people who scrub are those who actually carry out, or directly assist in, the surgery; not everyone in the operating room scrubs. The surgeon, assistant surgeon(s), and the scrub nurse, participate in the scrubbing ritual. Medical students and other surgical assistants consider it an honor if they are asked to scrub with a surgeon.

Before a person begins scrubbing he checks the clock in order to time the seven-minute procedure. He turns on the water by pushing a button with his hip, and reaches for a package which contains a nail file, a brush and sponge which is saturated with an antiseptic solution. For two minutes he cleans under each of his nails with the nail file. For two-and-a-half minutes, he scrubs his fingers, hands and arms to his elbows, intermittently wetting the sponge and brush with running water. Using a circular motion he scrubs all of the surfaces of his fingers on one hand, his hand, and, finally, his arm to the elbow. After rinsing that arm thoroughly under running water, he repeats the procedure for two-and-a-half minutes on his second hand. After having scrubbed for seven minutes, he discards the sponge, brush, file, and paper, and turns off the tap water by pressing a button on the sink with his hip.

After scrubbing, the surgeon and his assistant(s) enter the operating room by pushing the door with their hips. They hold their lower arms and hands in an upright position, away from the rest of their bodies. They are forbidden to allow their scrubbed hands and arms to come into contact with any object or person. The scrub nurse hands them a sterile towel to dry their hands. They dry each finger separately, and throw the towel into a container on the floor. The scrub nurse holds the outside, sterile part of a green gown for the surgeon and his assistant(s) to wear. They insert their hands through the sleeves, without allowing their hands to touch the outside of the gown. At this point, their hands, although scrubbed and clean, are not sterile. But the outside of the gown is sterile. After their arms pass through the sleeves, the scrub nurse holds their sterile gloves in place with the open side facing their hands. The surgeon, followed by his assistant, thrusts one hand at a time into each glove. They accomplish this in one quick movement, in which a hand is brought down from its upward position, thrust forward inside the glove and snapped in place over the sleeve. When only one glove is on, the surgeon is not permitted to adjust it with the other hand. However, when the second glove is on, he can adjust his glove and the sleeve of his gown and any other part of the front of the gown.

At this stage, the gown is not completely fastened. In order to fasten his gown, the surgeon unties a tie of his gown at waist level. Although this tie had been sterile, he hands it to the circulating nurse, who has not scrubbed. The circulating nurse brings the tie to the back of his gown. The back is a nonsterile area of the gown. The surgeon helps her reach the back by making a 360° turn, while she holds the tie. The circulating nurse secures this and two more ties to the back of the gown.

PRINCIPLES OF STERILITY AND CONTAMINATION

The rituals of scrubbing, gowning, and gloving suggest some basic principles underlying most of the rituals in the operating room.

1) In the operating room, objects, or parts of objects and people, are classified either as sterile or nonsterile (S = sterile; NS = nonsterile):

    (a) Nonsterile objects are further classified as clean, dirty, or contaminated.

    (b) No part of the circulating nurse or the anaesthesiologist is sterile.

    (c) Parts of the surgeon and the scrub nurse are sterile.

2) To remain sterile, sterile objects may only come into contact with other objects that are sterile (c = contact; > = remains, becomes, or is transformed into; therefore, S c S > S).

3) To remain sterile, sterile objects may not come into contact with anything that is not sterile ($\sim$ = not; therefore, S $\sim$ c NS > S).

4) Nonsterile objects may come into contact with other nonsterile objects, and both remain nonsterile (NS c NS > NS).

5) Sterile objects may be transformed into nonsterile by contact with objects which are nonsterile. This process is called contamination (S c NS > NS).

6) Contaminated objects can only be restored to sterility by either placing them in an autoclave for a specified period of time, or, in the case of a person's clothes, by discarding the contaminated clothes and replacing them with sterile clothes. If gloves become contaminated, rescrubbing for three minutes is required before replacing the gloves and the gown.

Before the operation begins, most sterile objects are either symbolized by the color green or are in contact with an object colored green. Sterile instruments, for example, are placed upon a green towel which lies on a nonsterile tray. Although the green towel has been sterilized, it becomes contaminated at the bottom through contact with the nonsterile tray (S c NS > NS).

The towel remains sterile at the top, however, and the sterile instruments lying on the top remain sterile (S c S > S).

The surgeon, his assistant(s), and the scrub nurse wear sterile gloves and a green or blue gown which is sterile in the front from the waist to the armpits. However, the gown is not sterile in the back nor above the armpits and below the waist in the front. That is why the surgeon unties the tie at the sterile side of his gown with his sterile gloves, and the circulating (nonsterile) nurse holds the tie without touching the surgeon's (sterile) gloves, and brings the tie toward the (nonsterile) back of the surgeon's gown. The sterile tie becomes contaminated when the circulating nurse's hand touches it. It remains contaminated because it is tied in the back of the surgeon's gown.

The potentials for manipulating the overhead light in the center of the operating room illustrate some principles of sterility and contamination. Before the operation begins, the scrub nurse places a sterile handle on the huge, movable, overhead light. This permits the light to be adjusted by the surgeon, his assistant(s), and the scrub nurse through contact with the sterile handle (S c S > S). The circulating nurse and anaesthesiologist, however, are also able to manipulate the light by touching the nonsterile frame of the light (NS c NS > NS).

In order for a person to move to the other side of the person next to him, as the scrubbed members of the operating team stand next to the patient's table, a ritual must be enacted. The person making the move turns 360° in the direction of his move, allowing his back to face the back of his neighbor. This movement prevents his sterile front from coming into contact with his neighbor's nonsterile back (S ∼ c NS > S). Instead, his nonsterile back only comes into contact with his neighbor's nonsterile back (NS c NS > NS).

Before the operation begins each member of the operating team is busily engaged in activities that are essentially similar for each operation. The surgeon and his assistant(s) gown and glove and check last-minute details about the forthcoming operation. The anaesthesiologist checks his tools, his gas supply, and his respirator. He also prepares the instruments for monitoring the patient's vital functions, and prepares the patient for receiving anaesthesia. In the outer area, a nurse checks to insure that the patient is properly identified and his operative site is verified. She independently checks the preoperative instructions written by the surgeon with the administrative order written when the surgery was booked, and asks the surgeon to identify the proposed operation and the precise site of the operation. Finally, she asks the patient to identify his name and the site of the operation.

Within the operating room, the words, "clean," "dirty," "sterile," and "contaminated" assume different meanings according to different stages of the operation. Before the operation begins, the operating room is considered to be clean. Dirty objects have been removed or cleaned. Instruments and clothes which have been contaminated by the previous operation have been removed. Floors, walls, permanent fixtures, and furniture have been cleaned with antiseptic solution. The air in the operating room is continually cleaned during, and between, operations by a filter system.

Fields of sterility and cleanliness within the operating room are mapped out. Everyone in the operating room, with the exception of the patient, is knowledgeable about these fields. Some of the fields, such as that surrounding the patient, are invisible. Other fields are distinguished by the use of sterile paper sheets colored green. The sheets provide only a minimal material barrier against airborne bacteria yet serve as a symbolic shield separating fields of sterility and nonsterility. They are also used to isolate the operative area of the body from the rest of the patient's body. The sheets cover the entire body of the patient leaving a small opening for the operative area, or separate the head end of the patient from the rest of his body. The head end is considered nonsterile and is accessible to the anaesthesiologist and his equipment, which are also nonsterile.

After the patient is rendered unconscious by the anaesthesiologist, the scrub nurse applies an orange-brown antiseptic solution (Providine) onto the patient's skin. She pours the Providine liberally onto the skin, and distributes it with circular movements radiating outward from the center of the operative site. This action is repeated at least once, using a sterile sponge on a long holder which is discarded and replaced with each action. The sterile sponges become contaminated through contact with the patient's nonsterile skin (S c NS > NS). This action, which transforms the sterile sponge into a contaminated sponge, also transforms the dirty body area of the patient into a clean area. When this act is completed, sterile green paper towels are placed on the patient's body, exposing only his aseptic, painted, operative site.

Before the operation begins both nurses lay out and count all the sterile instruments and sponges that are likely to be used. The circulating nurse obtains articles from their nonsterile storage place. When the outside of sealed packages is nonsterile and contains sterile objects inside, the circulating nurse holds the outside of the package. She either thrusts the objects onto a green sterile towel, or asks the scrub nurse to grasp the sterile object by reaching down into the package and lifting the object upwards, with a straight, quick movement. These procedures are followed for each sterile needle, thread, or vial that is wrapped in a nonsterile wrapping in order to prevent contamination of sterile parts by the nonsterile parts of the same package. The two nurses also simultaneously count items that are laid out for use during surgery. The circulating nurse records the amounts of each item that are counted. Each item must be accounted for before the operation is completed, and the last count must concur with the total of the previous counts.

Different operations are classified according to the degree of sterility and contamination likely to be present. At University Hospital there are four categories of operations classified according to decreasing sterility: (1) clean; (2) clean contaminated; (3) contaminated; and (4) dirty. Eye operations, for example, are clean. Most gall bladder operations are clean contaminated. Duodenal operations are contaminated. Colonic operations are dirty. Intestinal operations are considered dirtier than many other operations because the contents of the intestines are highly contaminated with bacteria, requiring additional measurements for vigilance against contamination during the operation. Ritual during most operations is concerned with avoidance of contamination of the patient from the outside. Ritual in operations which are classified as contaminated or dirty are concerned, in addition, with contamination of the patient and the medical staff from inside the patient.

After the completion of dirty operations, the medical staff is required to discard all their outside garments before leaving the operating room. Since the unscrubbed members of the operating team wear only one set of clothing, before the operation they don an additional white, clean, nonsterile gown over their green or blue costome. After the operation is completed they discard the gown.

THE OPERATION

Although extensive variation exists among types of operations, as well as variations among the medical conditions of patients, there is, nevertheless, considerable similarity in the structure of all operations. Operations contain three distinct stages. Specific rituals are performed during these stages. Stage One consists of the incision, or opening. Stage Two consists of the excision and repair. Stage Three consists of the closure.[3]

The operation begins after the anaesthetized patient is draped, all sterilized instruments are counted and placed in orderly rows upon trays, and the nurses and doctors, wearing their appropriate costumes, are standing in their specified places. The anaesthesiologist stands behind the green curtain at the head of the patient, outside of the sterile field. The surgeon stands next to the operative site, on one side of the patient. His assistant usually stands on the opposite side of the patient from that of the surgeon. The scrub nurse stands next to the surgeon, with the pole of an instrument tray between them. The instrument tray is suspended over the patient's body. The circulating nurse stands outside of the sterile field, near the outer part of the operating room.

Silence and tension prevail as the first stage of the operation begins. With a sterile scalpel, the surgeon makes the first incision through the layers of the patient's skin, then discards the scalpel in a sterile basin. He has transformed both the scalpel and the basin from sterile to nonsterile. The transformation takes place because the sterile scalpel touches the patient's nonsterile skin. (The patient's skin, although cleaned with an antiseptic, is not sterile.) The scalpel, which has become nonsterile (S c NS > NS), touches the sterile basin and contaminates the basin (NS c S > NS). The surgeon uses another sterile scalpel to cut through the remaining layers of fat, fascia, muscle, and, in an abdominal operation, the peritoneum. The same scalpel may be used for all the layers underlying the skin because, unlike the contaminated skin, these layers are considered to be sterile.

As the surgeon cuts, he or his assistant cauterizes or ties the severed blood vessels. The patient's blood is considered sterile once the operation has begun. Before the operation, however, the patient's blood is considered to be nonsterile. This was illustrated graphically at University Hospital before a particular emergency operation in which a patient was bleeding externally from an internal hemorrhage. The nurses complained about "the man who is dirtying our clean room!" However, once the operation on this man began, his blood was considered sterile. Sterile instruments which touched his blood during the operation remained sterile (S c S > S) until contaminated by touching something nonsterile.

The rituals enacted during the first stage of the operation involve the transformation of objects defined as sterile and nonsterile, at the same time that the appropriate instruments are made accessible and are being used to make the incisions. The beginning of the first stage, in which the first incision is made, introduces new definitions of sterile and nonsterile. For example, the patient's blood and internal organs, which had been considered nonsterile before the operation, are considered sterile once the operation begins. (The surgeon's blood, however, remains nonsterile.) The patient's skin, although cleansed with antiseptic before the operation, becomes nonsterile once the operation begins and the incision is made (see Figure 2). The rituals also enforce the segregation of sterile and nonsterile objects while the initial incisions are being

Body Category	Outside Operating Room	First Stage (Incision)	Second Stage (Excision)	Third Stage (Closure)
Patient's Washed Skin	C	D	D	C
Patient's Gall Bladder (in gall bladder excision)	D	C	C	D
Patient's Colon (in colon resection)	D	C-OUTSIDE D-INSIDE	C-OUTSIDE D-INSIDE	D
Patient's Feces (in colon resection)	D	D	D	D
Patient's Blood	D	C	C	D
Surgeon's Blood	D	D	D	D

C = Clean
D = Dirty
/// = Discontinuity In Category

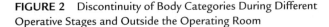

FIGURE 2 Discontinuity of Body Categories During Different Operative Stages and Outside the Operating Room

made. The surgeon typically utters terse commands, usually stating the specific names of the instrument he needs. The scrub nurse immediately places the requested instrument securely in the palm of the surgeon's hand. If the instrument remains clean, the surgeon returns it to the scrub nurse and the scrub nurse places it upon the sterile tray. If it becomes contaminated, as occurs to the skin scalpel after the first incision, the surgeon places it into a container which could only be handled by the circulating nurse.

As the technical tasks become routinized during the first stage of the operation, joking begins. Most of the joking at this stage revolves around the operative procedures which are to be carried out during the next stage: "I can't wait to get my hands on your gallbladder, Mr. Smith." "Okay sports fans, we're going to have some action." The first stage of the operation ends when the first incision has been completed and the organs are exposed. The joking abruptly ends just as the second stage of the operation is about to begin.

The second stage of the operation consists either of repair, implantation or the isolation and excision of the organ, and the anastomosis. (An anastomosis is the connection of two parts of the body which are not normally connected.) This stage contains the greatest amount of tension of the entire operation, and adherence

to ritual is strictly enforced. It begins with the identification and isolation of structures surrounding the organ to be excised. The surgeon identifies vessels, nerves, ducts, and connective tissues, carefully pulling them aside, and preserving, clamping, severing, or tying them. The surgeon utters abrupt, abbreviated commands for instruments to be passed by the scrub nurse, structures to be cut by the assistant(s), basins and materials to be readied by the circulating nurse, and the operating table to be adjusted by the anaesthesiologist. These people respond to the surgeon's commands quickly, quietly, and efficiently. A delayed, or an incorrect, response may be met with noticeable disapproval from the others.

During the second stage of the operation many of the classifications of sterility differ from those of the first stage. In a cholecystectomy (gallbladder removal), for example, the gallbladder is considered to be nonsterile before the operation begins. Yet during the first and second stages the gallbladder is considered to be sterile, before it is severed. Once it is severed, however, although it is considered to be clean, it transforms to nonsterile (see Figure 2). It is placed in a sterile container, but the container becomes contaminated by its contact with the nonsterile gallbladder (S c NS > NS). Because it is nonsterile after it has been removed, it can only be handled by a nonsterile person such as the circulating nurse. But, since the gallbladder is clean and must be examined, it must not be further contaminated from sources outside of the patient. To prevent further contamination, the circulating nurse wears a sterile glove over her nonsterile hand to examine the gallbladder and its contents. The gallbladder is not sterile, but it is not grossly contaminated. It is clean, but nonsterile. It is avoided by the sterile members of the team, yet only touched by the nonsterile members if they wear sterile gloves. The ritual surrounding its removal and examination is complex, and the removed organ is avoided by most members of the operating team because its classification is ambiguous.

Once the gallbladder has been removed, x-rays of its ducts (which remain inside the patient) are taken to determine if gallstones remain. A masked, gowned and lead-shielded radiologist enters the operating room with a large x-ray machine that is draped with green sterile sheets. The surgeon injects a radioopaque dye into the ducts, and everyone, except the radiologist, leaves the room to avoid the invisible x-rays. When the x-rays have been taken, the radiologist and the machine exit, the staff enter, and the operation proceeds.

Although unexpected events may occur at any stage of the operation, they are more likely to occur at the second stage because this stage contains the greatest trauma to the patient's body. If a sudden hemorrhage or a cardiac arrest occurs, the rituals segregating sterile from nonsterile may be held in abeyance, and new rituals designed to control the un-anticipated event take over. If, for example, hemor-rhaging occurs, all efforts are dedicated to locating and stopping the source of hemorrhage and replacing the blood that is lost. Even though immediate replacement of blood is required, rituals are enacted which delay the replacement, yet ensure accurate matching. The anaesthesiologist and the circulating nurse indepen-dently check, recheck, record and announce the blood type, the number and date of the blood bank supply and the operating room request. They glue stickers onto the patient's record and onto the blood bank record. This complex ritual involves repetition, separa-tion and matching records before the blood is trans-fused into the hemorrhaging patient.

If a patient's heart ceases beating, a prescribed rit-ual is enacted by a cardia-carrest team, whose members enter the operating room with a mobile cart, and enact prescribed procedures to recussitate the patient. Con-siderations of preserving the separation of sterility and nonsterility (including most of the rituals previously described) are ignored while this emergency ritual is enacted.

Tension remains high throughout the second stage of the operation. There is virtually no joking or small talk. As the remaining internal structures are repaired and restored in place, some of the tension is lifted, and the routinization of rituals continues. The second stage of the operation ends when all the adjustments to the internal organs are finished and only the suturing of the protective layers for the third stage remains.

The third stage of the operation begins with the final counting of the materials used in surgery. Both nurses engage in this ritual of counting. They simultaneously orally count all the remaining materials, including tools, needles, and sponges. The circulating nurse checks the oral count with her written tally of materials recorded at the beginning of the operation. When the circulating nurse has accounted for each item, she informs the sur-geon that he may begin the closing.

The rituals enacted during this stage of the opera-tion are similar to those enacted during the first stage. The surgeon, or his assistant(s), request specific nee-dles and sutures from the nurses. They sew the patient closed, layer by layer, beginning with the inside layer. Although careful suturing is an essential part of the op-eration, this stage is enacted in a comparatively casual manner. There is considerably less tension than there was during the second stage, and greater toleration for deviations from the rituals. Questions about the procedures are acknowledged and answered. Minor mistakes may be overlooked. If the surgeon touched his nonsterile mask with his sterile glove during this

part of the operation, he would be less likely to reglove and regown than he would if the same incident had occurred during the second stage.

The silence of the second stage is replaced in the third stage by considerable talking, including jokes and small talk. Most of the joking revolves around events which occurred during the second stage and references are made to actual or potential danger dur-ing this stage. "I thought he'd never stop bleeding." "You almost choperated [sic] his spleen by mistake." "Well, I hope he has good term life insurance." Much of the small talk revolves around future activities of the medical staff. The subject of small talk rarely re-lates to the patient. It may involve the next operation, lunch plans, or sports results.

When the closure has been completed, the surgeon signals to the anaesthesiologist to waken the patient. The staff members finish recording information, trans-port the patient to the recovery room, and prepare for the next case. The operation is finished.

DISCONTINUITY AND OPERATING ROOM RITUALS

The observed rituals help to establish the operating room as a separate place, discontinuous from its sur-roundings. They also helped to establish and define categories of appropriate and inappropriate behav-ior. This includes indicating behavior categories and their limits.

The rituals in the operating room and the meaning of many of the words used there are exclusive to that setting. The observed rituals express beliefs and val-ues which are exclusive to the operating room. The use of the words, "clean," "dirty," "contaminated" in the operating room do not correspond to their use else-where. This indicates the existence of discontinuity between the operating room and the outside. Discon-tinuity between the operating room and the outside is also reflected in the restricted entrances, the specific costumes required for entrance, the special language used, the classification and segregation of objects into sterile and nonsterile, and the dispassionate emotional reactions to parts of the human body. A person can be prohibited from entering the operating room if he were not properly dressed, if he transgressed the rules for segregating sterile from nonsterile, and he did not behave in a dispassionate manner upon viewing or touching parts of the body.

The boundaries which separate the operating room from the outside contribute to a particular mental set for the participants, which enable them to participate in a dispassionate manner in activities they would ordinarily view with strong emotion. For example, in the operating room, they look dispassionately upon, and touch internal organs and their secretions, blood, pus, and feces. Outside of the operating room context, these same objects provoke emotions of embarrassment, fear, fascination and disgust in the same persons. Discontinuity was illustrated during a movie shown to the surgeons outside of the surgical area of the hospital. The film illustrated different techniques for draining and lancing pus-filled abcesses. The reactions observed for the surgeons watching this movie were unlike any reactions observed for the same surgeons while they drained abcesses in the operating room. They uttered comments and noises indicating their disgust. They looked away from the screen. Outside of the context of the operating room, with its rituals and its isolation, the same events are experienced differently. In the operating room a purulent lesion is mentally linked to the rituals that are enacted during the act of lancing. The image of the lesion is embedded in the entire operating room context, including the ritual prescriptions for managing that lesion and for organizing the behavior of others in the room. In contrast, outside of the operating room, the image of the lesion is embedded in images of everyday life. In that context, the reaction to the lesion is one of disgust. Outside of the operating room there are no rituals to diffuse their concentration. Moreover, sitting in a darkened room, watching a movie, the viewers are forced to focus on the picture of the lesion. The only opportunity they have to diffuse their focus is to look away, or to make noises indicating their disgust. The operating room, with its focus upon precise rituals, permits diffusion of emotions and encourages discontinuity from everyday life.

The different stages of an operation express discontinuity of mental sets. For example, blood, internal organs, feces, and skin are classified differently during different stages of the operation, and some are different outside of the operating room. Figure 2 illustrates the transformations of the categories, "clean" and "dirty" for parts of the body during different stages of the operation. For each of the parts of the body—the patient's washed skin, gallbladder, colon, feces, blood, and the surgeon's blood—the greatest transformations of dirty and clean categories occurs before the first stage of the operation (the incision), and between the second and third stage (the excision and closure). For example, the patient's blood is considered to be dirty outside of the operating room, yet it is considered to be clean during the first and second stages of the operation. But during the third stage, blood is again classified as dirty. Similarly, the patient's skin, after having been thoroughly cleaned with antiseptic, is considered extremely clean outside of the operating room. However, once the operation begins, the patient's skin is classified as

"dirty." It remains dirty for the first and second stages of the operation. Once closure takes place, during the third stage, the patient's skin is transformed again to "clean."

Rituals exaggerate the discontinuity in the operating room and they proclaim definite categories. An instrument is either sterile or nonsterile; it is never almost sterile or mostly sterile. A person is either scrubbed, gowned, and gloved, and, therefore, sterile, or he is not scrubbed, gowned, or gloved, and, therefore, not sterile. An operation is either in Stage One, Two, or Three, or it has not yet begun, or it has ended. It is never partially begun, nor incompletely ended.

Rituals in the operating room are prescribed for four different kinds of situations: (1) passing through the three stages of surgery, (2) managing unanticipated events, such as cardiac arrest or sudden hemorrhaging, (3) matching information, such as blood types, operative sites or instrument counts, and (4) separating sterile from nonsterile objects. In each of these situations there exists a potential confusion about the appropriate classification of events. There is danger that objects and events can be confused or indistinct or that there is danger of contact of forbidden categories: blood may not be properly matched; the wrong operative site may be selected; an instrument may remain in the patient's body; objects or events may not match or fit; or sterile objects may touch nonsterile ones. For those situations in which behavior categories are not clear, rituals clarify. In a recent textbook for operating room nurses, more than one hundred prescriptions for precise behavior are spelled out in which confusion existed about definitions of categories (Berry and Kohn 1972). At University Hospital, the head operating room nurse claimed that the rituals performed in the operating room "were introduced in response to actual mistakes, problems, conflicts that we had, when how to behave was not clearly spelled out." Rituals in the operating room not only indicate the categories which are potentially confusing, they also indicate the boundaries, or limits, for these categories. Through the use of rituals it is clear to all the participants when Stage One ends and Stage Two begins. It is clear to them which part of the surgeon's body is sterile (between the armpits and waist in front) and which part is not sterile (the remainder). Rituals, then, make salient, and even exaggerate, the boundaries of categories.

Rituals in the operating room have much in common with rituals in other contexts, sacred or secular. Rituals are enacted during periods of transition. In the operating room they are enacted during transitions of events or classifications of objects. Danger is perceived during these periods of transitions. Indeed, Van Gennup (1960) emphasizes the dangers which lie in transitional states because the classification of neither state is clear. When states are not clearly defined, ritual controls the danger. Similarly Douglas (1966) claims that pollution behavior takes place when categories are confused, or when accepted categories are not adhered to, as in anomaly.

Beyond the operating room, rituals also indicate categories and limits or boundaries for these categories. These include rituals which define passages—of time, seasons, stages of life, or passages through different lands—as well as rituals of pollution. Rituals proclaim that something is in one category and not in another. One is an adult, not a child. It is the rainy season, not the dry season. We are in the new land, not the old land. I belong to this kinship group now, not that group. Even the middle, liminal, stage of ritual, which Turner (1969) describes as a kind of limbo, has limits. Although the middle state is neither incorporated into the first stage, nor reintegrated into the last stage, its boundaries are clearly recognized and known to all the participants.

In all societies rituals take place when categories are not clearly defined and when limits of categories are not known. Gluckman (1962) suggests, for example, that primitive societies have more rituals than modern societies because different roles are enacted with the same people in primitive societies. This may be understood as exaggerating the boundaries or limits of each of their roles, precisely because they are unclear. Indeed, ritual is found in modern secular society in those situations in which boundaries are unclear, not only during changes of status, such as marriages and deaths, but also in situations such as entering or leaving a house, installing a political officer, and beginning a team sport.

The operating room observations suggest that through its elaborate, stylized behavioral prescriptions, and obsession with detail, ritual exaggerates the boundaries between categories. Rituals create boundaries because boundaries have been transgressed or are unclear. When boundaries are not precisely defined, confusion may result about which category is operative at a particular time or place. The actors do not know to which situation to respond. Knowing the limits or boundaries gives shape and definition to the categories. Ritual by defining categories and prescribing specific behavior within these categories, creates boundaries. Moreover, when the boundaries are known, autonomy to function can increase (Katz 1968).

AUTONOMY AND RITUAL

At first glance, it seems improbable that ritual, with its emphasis upon specific detailed prescriptions for behavior, may provide autonomy for its participants.

To be sure, it is known that ritual exaggerates and often provides license for behavior which may be prohibited in everyday life (Gluckman 1962). Studies by Katz (1968, 1974, 1976) suggest that autonomy increases when the limits of the system are known and implemented. On this basis one will expect that ritual, by indicating and clarifying boundaries of behavior categories—such as sterile/nonsterile or child/adult—increase the autonomy of the participants. Conversely, when the rituals have not been fully carried out—when a person is not clearly within the prescribed limits—there will be very little autonomy.

For example, when the surgeon enters the operating room after he has scrubbed, but before he has gowned and gloved, he is helpless. He has virtually no autonomy. His scrubbed, clean hands are not clearly classified as sterile, nor as contaminated (although strictly speaking, they are nonsterile). He has to exercise extreme caution lest his hands touch anything. If he touches a sterile object, that object becomes contaminated. If he touches a contaminated object, his hands become further contaminated, and he is required to rescrub. He is so helpless that he can do almost nothing. His hands are raised in a helpless position. He depends upon a nurse to give him a towel and to provide him with a gown and gloves. He is not able to put the gown on himself, nor to tie his gown once it is on. Even when he is gowned, he has no autonomy to touch anything. He cannot pull the sleeve of the gown from his hands. The nurse has to put his gloves on his hands for him. His classification of sterility is confusing because, being half sterile and half nonsterile, he does not clearly fit in either category. His autonomy is severely restricted. The autonomy of others interacting with him is also reduced. Only after he has completely scrubbed, gowned, and gloved, and become unequivocally sterile, does he attain his autonomy. He can move about within the sterile field and touch all sterile objects.

In the operating room, boundaries of categories are likely to become confused if a person is present who does not know the appropriate rituals. When this occurs, autonomy decreases, both for the uninitiated person, and for others who interact with him. On one occasion during surgery in University Hospital, the circulating nurse requested a scrubbed medical student to remove a sterile needle from the nonsterile wrapping which she held in her hand. Although the student knew that the wrapping was nonsterile and the needle was sterile, and he was familiar with many rituals, he did not know the precise ritual required for removing the needle. The ritual required him to grasp the needle between his forefinger and thumb, quickly thrust his fingers upwards, and place the needle upon the sterile tray. The circulating nurse was required to pull downward on the wrapping, discard the wrapping in a contaminated bag, and record the addition of that needle. Neither person had autonomy to deviate from this behavior.

The student succeeded in contaminating his glove and the needle by touching both with the nonsterile wrapping. A great deal of autonomy was lost through his failure to follow the prescribed ritual. The student had to reglove and regown. The circulating nurse had to aid him in regloving and regowning. The needle had to be discarded. Since the needle had contaminated the sterile green towel on the tray, the towel had to be replaced, the sterile contents of the tray removed from the contaminated towel and replaced on the sterile towel. In addition, the circulating nurse had mistakenly recorded the addition of that needle, and, near the end of the operation, it appeared that a needle was missing. All the people present searched for the needle, both inside and outside the patient. This activity delayed the completion of the operation until the circulating nurse realized the source of the mismatching. In this case, the autonomy of most of the staff was restricted because one person did not follow the ritual properly. = extremely important

The surgical patient who is awake can reduce the autonomy of the operating team. The conscious patient has autonomy to express his fears and concerns about the operation. Most members of the medical staff in the operating room regard the waking patient as a hindrance to the smooth performance of preoperative rituals. The waking patient may restrict discussions which are necessary for planning the strategy of the operation. Rendering the patient unconscious deprives the patient of all autonomy, while increasing the autonomy of the staff. The staff gains the autonomy to ignore the patient's psyche, to consider only the parts of his body relevant to the operative procedure, to joke about the patient and his expressions of fear, and to discuss subjects that have nothing to do with the operation. Although the patient loses autonomy, the staff gains autonomy.

It is well known to most laymen that irreverent behavior in the form of jokes and small talk occur in the operating room. Jokes and small talk in the operating room represent autonomous behavior *par excellence*. They are autonomous because they are not a prescribed part of the operative procedure. They often express values which are antithetical to the serious and dangerous nature of the operation itself. Jokes differ from small talk in that jokes explicitly focus on events of surgery (whether real or imagined), whereas small talk revolves around events unrelated to surgery. Both jokes and small talk trivialize the solemnity, significance, discipline and danger that typically accompany surgery. Although the precise content of jokes and small talk in the operating room is unpredictable, their timing is. They are not expressed while transitions take place—when stages are crossed, transformations from sterile to nonsterile occur, or when mismatching or emergencies occur. During transitions danger is often perceived to be present. All attention becomes focused on the rituals which are enacted to restore the boundaries. Jokes and small talk are expressed during those periods in which categories—of stages, sterility, or matching—are clearly defined. They occur when ritual succeeds in restoring and bounding these categories, and activities are routinized. Once the boundaries have been restored by ritual, autonomy flourishes. When the rituals are enacted routinely, the boundaries are defined and autonomy increased.

Jokes and small talk do not occur during periods of transition, when danger is present, although they express concern about these periods. Jokes are not expressed during the times that autonomy is most severely restricted, such as during the transitions. Autonomous behavior of joking and small talk occur after the transitions pass, after the tension subsides, after the rituals have been enacted in their carefully prescribed manner.

Most of the jokes focus on events which occur during transitional or dangerous periods. Jokes about organs to be severed do not occur during the dangerous period while the organ is being severed. Jokes about the incision do not occur while the incision is being made. Jokes about the incision only occur before or after the incision is made. When jokes touched on dangerous or transitional situations, they did so only after rituals had clearly indicated that the situation was over. Only then did the surgical staff make irreverent jokes about the most dangerous and vulnerable aspects of the operation. They made jokes in the crudest terms about internal organs, external appearances, sexual organs, the personality of the patient, or other members of the operating team. But they did not joke about the rituals themselves. The operating room staff treated the rituals with reverence and less questioning than other surgical activities.

Many anthropologists have tried to understand the simultaneous presence of both controlling and autonomous aspects of ritual. Van Gennup (1960), and later, Firth (1972:3) emphasized the controlling and regulating function of ritual. Munn (1969) describes how ritual myths function as social control mechanisms by regulating states and bodily feelings. Turner (1969) describes the presence of elaborate autonomous improvisation within highly structured ritual. Leach (1968:526) suggests that stylization in secular ritual may be either "escetic, representing the intensification of formal restraint, or ecstatic, signifying the elimination of restraint." Gluckman (1970) describes license in ritual as reversals that express behavior outlawed in everyday life. Gluckman (1970:125) also recognizes that license is only permitted in ritual when the limits are known and agreed upon by the participants: "The acceptance of the established order as right and good, and even sacred, seems to allow unbridled license, very rituals of rebellion, for the order itself keeps this rebellion within bounds."

The rituals in the operating room, as well as those described by Gluckman, Leach, and Turner, suggest that the boundaries of behavior are not open to questioning. They are firm. However, within those boundaries there is a great deal of autonomy. In the operating room, the rituals themselves, as signposts indicating boundaries, are not open to question, nor to ridicule. However, within the boundaries considerable autonomy exists. There is autonomy to joke about everything, except the rituals. There is autonomy to question details about the rituals (e.g., how long to scrub), but virtually no autonomy to question the ritual itself (e.g., whether scrubbing was necessary).

CONCLUSION

In modern operating rooms rituals, as stylized, arbitrary, repetitive and exaggerated forms of behavior, occur as integral parts of surgical procedures. Most of the rituals in the operating room symbolize separation of areas containing micro-organisms from areas free of micro-organisms, or separation of realms of cleanliness (sterility, asepsis) from realms of pollution (nonsterility, sepsis, contamination).

Most rituals considered by anthropologists, especially those in sacred settings, express and communicate values, and are linked to institutions of everyday life. Such rituals are amenable to serious questioning of their major premises. It is different, however, with rituals in the hospital operating room. That setting is discontinuous with everyday life, and rituals there have no continuity with values or categories of thought outside of the medical setting. Inspection and introspection of their premises are thereby discouraged or overlooked, but nonetheless neglected. It is through the examination of rituals in extraordinary settings, whether in traditional or modern contexts, that we can become aware of some of the functions of rituals that, heretofore, have largely gone unrecognized in the anthropological literature. The study of the hospital operating room suggests that ritual defines categories and clarifies boundaries between important states by exaggerating the differences between them, doing so precisely where the boundaries normally are not clear and well-defined. It is then that rituals are enacted in order to avoid the confusion that may result when it is uncertain which categories are operative at a particular time.

By imposing exaggerated definitions upon categories, rituals also serve to increase the autonomy of the participants by providing them with an unambiguous understanding of precisely which categories are operative at a certain time. Without the boundaries provided by rituals, participants do not know to which situation to respond. When the boundaries are known, autonomy is increased. Extreme license in ritual is an expression of this. In the operating room irreverent joking, as an example, is only possible after the ritual has succeeded in establishing a boundary between indistinct states. Autonomy is limited, and reverence and awe prevail during transitional states of ritual, when boundaries are not yet firm. When indistinct categories are ritually separated and given sharp definition, ambiguity of behavior is lowered and autonomy enhanced.[4]

NOTES

1. Occasionally others, such as salesmen or filmmakers, are allowed in parts of the surgical area. I was allowed free access to all surgical areas at all times, which included scrubbing and standing next to the surgeons and patient during surgery.

2. University Hospital is a pseudonym for a hospital in North America affiliated with a medical school.

3. The stages are heuristic. I have not encountered surgeons nor surgery texts which describe three distinct stages.

4. For reprints of this article contact Pearl Katz, 2214 Ken Oak Road, Baltimore, MD 21209.

BIBLIOGRAPHY

Beattie, J. 1966. Ritual and Social Change. Man 1:60–74.

———.1970. On Understanding Ritual. Rationality, ed. B. Wilson, pp. 240–268. Oxford. Berry, E. C, and M. L. Kohn. 1972. Introduction to Operating Room Technique. Fourth Edition. New York.

Boyd, W. C. 1976. Surgical Infections. Synopsis of Surgery, eds. R. D. Liechty and R. T. Soper, pp. 78–95. St. Louis.

Douglas, M. 1966. Purity and Danger. London.

Durkheim, E. 1961. The Elementary Forms of Religious Life. New York. (1st English Edition, London 1915).

Firth, R. 1972. Verbal and Bodily Rituals of Greeting and Parting. The Interpretation of Ritual, ed. J. S. La Fontaine, pp. 1–30. London.

Gluckman, M. 1962. Les Rites de Passage. Essays on the Ritual of Social Relations, ed. M. Gluckman, pp. 1–52. Manchester.

Gluckman, M. 1970. Custom and Conflict in Africa. Oxford.

Goody, J. 1961. Religion and Ritual: The Definition Problem. British Journal of Sociology 12:142–164.

Horton, R. 1970. African Traditional Thought and Western Science. Rationality, ed. B. Wilson, pp. 131–I71. Oxford.

Jarvie, I. C., and J. Agassi. 1970. The Problem of Rationality of Magic. Rationality, ed. B. Wilson, pp. 172–193. Oxford.

Katz, F. E. 1968. Autonomy and Organization: The Limits of Social Control. New York.

_____. 1974. Indeterminacy in the Structure of Systems. Behavioral Science 19.

_____. 1976. Structuralism in Sociology: An Approach to Knowledge. Albany.

Leach, E. R. 1968. Ritual. International Encyclopedia of the Social Sciences 13:520–526. New York.

Levi-Strauss, C. 1966. The Savage Mind. London.

Moore, S. F., and B. G. Myerhoff. 1977. Introduction. Secular Rituals, ed. S. F. Moore and B. G. Myerhoff, pp. 3–24. Amsterdam.

Munn, N. 1969. The Effectiveness of Symbols in Murngin Rite and Myth. Forms of Symbolic Action, ed. R. F. Spencer, pp. 178–207. American Ethnologial Society, University of Washington.

Postlethwait, R. W. 1972. Principles of Operative Surgery: Antisepsis, Technique, Sutures, and Drains. Textbook of Surgery: The Biological Basis of Modern Surgical Practice, ed. D. C Sabiston, Jr., pp. 300–318. Philadelphia.

Turner, V. 1967. The Forest of Symbols. Ithaca.

_____. 1969. The Ritual Process: Structure and Anti-Structure. Chicago.

Van Gennup, A. 1960. The Rites of Passage. Chicago.

10

Plastic Red Rituals

There's More to That Cup Than You Think

Krystal D'Costa

How does one describe individual "taste"? For example, why do some people love classical music while others prefer hip hop? Anthropologist Pierre Bourdieu examined the concept of aesthetic taste by analyzing surveys of French citizens from various educational and economic backgrounds. In his book *Distinction*, he found that the aesthetic choices we make are actually learned preferences that separate us from people of different classes. From a young age, according to Bourdieu, you learned to appreciate the cultural values and norms of the social class in which you were raised. When you explore bonding with people outside your soci-economic class, you may experiment with values and aesthetics that are very different from that which you learned at home.

It's one thing to attribute Bourdieu's observations to homophily (people's tendency to bond with similar others, e.g., "birds of a feather…"), but his analysis demonstrates that aesthetic taste plays a central role in separating and reinforcing socieconomic classes. If you were to look in your kitchen, what might the contents of your cupboards and refrigerator reveal about you, your upbringing, or your socieconomic status? Something as simple as the glass you drink from can communicate multiple messages. People who carry refillable water containers instead of small plastic bottles communicate an environmental consciousness and/or a health consciousness. In this chapter, Anthropology-in-Action

Blogger Krystal D'Costa examines culture through the lens of party cups, and she explains that your cup can do a lot more than simply hold your beverage. In fact, selecting the correct cups might just save your next party!

As you read this selection, ask yourself the following questions:

- Why does the author describe the red plastic cup as the great equalizer?
- How does the Sikaiana toddy drinking session promote equality and community?
- How do social rules for drinking differ among the Sikaiana, the Xhosa, and your own family gatherings?
- What does the author mean when she says that social drinking is a ritualized act?
- How would Xhosa or Sikaiana people view the ubiquitous use of disposable party cups in the United States?

The following terms discussed in this section are included in the Glossary in the back of the book:

atoll
beer-drink
toddy
Xhosa

W̲ho here has not enjoyed a cold, refreshing drink from a red plastic cup? Alcoholic and non-alcoholic beverages alike find themselves comfortably enclosed within the confines of the bright red vessel that has

become a ubiquitous American staple. The red plastic cup has appeared at barbecues, picnics, parties, in dugouts and at minor league games, in food cars and at lunch trucks, and even as a last resort at dive bars—and, of course, in college students' dorms and apartments, where it also functions as a key component in drinking games.

How can we understand the widespread adoption of this disposable product? And how does it function to shape the events where it is used?

D'Costa, Krystal. "Plastic Red Rituals: There's More to That Cup Than You Think." Adapted by Krystal D'Costa from her article at http://blogs.scientificamerican.com/anthropology-in-practice/ 2012/01/29/theres-more-to-that-red-plastic-cup-than-you-thought/, January 29, 2012, especially for Applying Cultural Anthropology, 9th ed. Reprinted by permission of the author.

we now culture dictates how a person acts

THE GLASS MATTERS

Among connoisseurs of fine wines and spirits, special attention is given to the drinking vessel, driven by the belief the glass may indeed impact your imbibing experience (D'Costa 2011). For example, there is a reason a red wine glass differs from a white wine glass and that both differ from a champagne flute: the shape of the glass influences the way the beverage behaves once it's poured, and that in turn influences your *experience* of the beverage. The rise of specialty beer glasses capitalizes on this experience. For example, in America the introduction of a handled decagon pint mug in the 1920s kept the drinkers' hands off of the glass itself, which in turn kept the beer cooler longer.

However, glass styles are not impervious to social change. The handled glass was abandoned in the late 1940s in favor of a dimpled glass. Darker beer, which was typically poured in the 10-sided glass, were considered old-fashioned and amber beer, which were rising in popularity, looked better as light hit the dimples in the glass. The dimpled glass would give way to a straighter glass with a slight bulge at the top. The bulge was intended to minimize the chipping that occurred when glassware rubbed together but may have also boosted the aromatic experience of beer. What followed was a proliferation of beer glasses, each claiming to have a specific effect on the beverage contained within. The Tulip style of glasses, for example, is supposed to enhance the aroma of the ale because the slightly narrow neck traps the rich smells emanating from the brew.

Drinking vessels may also denote status. In 16th-century Venice, ownership of fine glassware was a symbol of aristocracy, bearing the requirement that diners possess the sensibilities to properly use the range of elaborate tableware offered to them (McIver 2008). Drinking horns, which were common throughout noble households in medieval Europe, were intricately carved and decorated. In England, they served a double purpose as both drinking vessel and land charter. The vessels could be used to signify the transfer of land, as was the case with the Pusey Horn. The horn was given to the Pusey family by King Cnut as a reward for their role in warning of a Danish attack. The inscription granted the Puseys authority to claim the land. It reads: "I King Knud give thee William Pewse this horn to holde by thy londe" (Jones 1909: 221).

In recent history, the quality of drinking vessels has also signified shifts in economic status. For example, during the American Great Depression, lower quality, machine-produced "Depression glass" created a market for cheap but functional sets that replaced the "elegant" glassware of the luxury market (Nutting 2003). Matching handcrafted pieces could cost a week's pay easily—a factor that drove many fine glassmakers and sellers out of business during this period.

The red plastic cup offers no such enhancement to drinking experience. Nor does it bolster reputation. In fact, to the latter point, it serves as a great equalizer in drinking activities—from the top shelf to the supermarket shelf, the red plastic cup captures and contributes to the spirit of the occasion, often signifying a boisterous and crowd-friendly event. It even detracts from the bitterness of alcohol itself. As any marketing student will tell you, packaging matters! Drinking practices carry their own distinct rules and expectations relating to age, gender, and status. The red plastic cup crosses many of these boundaries to figure prominently in American drinking customs across a range of groups. It helps set expectations and establishes social norms for the gathering.

CONVENIENCE SETS THE TABLE

The most famous of all the red plastic cups is manufactured by Solo, the long time maker of single-use products that are sold almost everywhere today. Founded in 1936, the "paper container" manufacturer first produced a paper cone cup that typically went with water coolers. A wax-lined cup used in the 1950s for fountain sodas and takeaway drinks followed and might be viewed as a precursor to the signature red cup. It created a standard of sturdiness that aided widespread adoption of the product, allowing the red plastic cup—which first appeared in the 1970s—to work its way into popular culture seamlessly. The social movements of this period may have facilitated adoption. For example, during the women's movement as more women entered the workforce disposable tableware could have presented a time saving measure in an increasingly busy household. Solo's simple design for the red cup has been easy for competitors to copy, but in recent years the company has implemented small but noticeable changes (a square bottom, indented grips, and Solo embossed on the side) to add further distinction for customers looking for the Solo brand. The company has expanded its suite of products so that Solo—in cup form or otherwise—permeates all aspects of life, from the office, to coffee from your favorite restaurant chain, to the picnic table.

RITUALIZED CONSUMPTION

Social drinking is a ritualized act. There are certain social codes of consumption that help define the experience by setting expectations and establishing appropriate or acceptable behaviors. Anthropologist

William Donner documented social rules surrounding toddy drinking in Sikaiana, a small Polynesian atoll in the Solomon Islands. Toddy is a generic name for drinks made from fermented palm. In Sikaiana, toddy is made by fermenting the sap of coconut shoots.) Donner found that drinking reorganized the community, allowing boundaries to be renegotiated. Part of this process stems from the ways in which drink is shared. In Sikaiana, toddy distribution follows a rather specific format which helps establish the community as a place of equality:

> "Participants form a circle. The distributor pours a portion and passes it to one person in the group. This person drinks the cup until it is empty, usually in one drink. Then he returns the cup to the distributor and another serving of the exact same size is poured for the next person. This continues until everyone in the group has had a turn and then the distributor starts another round. If a person arrives late, the distributor may offer him a larger portion so that the latecomer can catch up with the people who are already drinking. In larger groups, several cups are passed out simultaneously, but always in a circular fashion so that everyone is given an equal amount to drink" (1994: 250).

Among the Xhosa of southern Africa, beer is also consumed in accordance with a social code. At a beer-drink (a public drinking event), the beer is kept in either cast-iron pots or plastic or wooden containers, and served in tin beakers (billy cans) of various sizes:

> When beer is allocated, the host section's mast of ceremonies points out the size of the beaker because the receivers have certain expectations in this regard based on the current state of their beer-exchange relationship with the givers. So a can of beer given to a neighboring group may be announced with carefully chosen words, such as 'This is your beaker, it is a full iqhwina [seven liters], as it should be when there is a full cask for men" (McAllister 2003: 197).

The drinking vessel is central to the drinking experience. It is an equalizing factor and a measure of consistency for attendees. It also serves as the entry-point for the temporary social community that has gathered. Drinking from the cup confirms attendance at the event and authorizes participation in subsequent event activities—drink and cup possession mediate conversation, singing, dancing, joking and laughing, and even confrontations.

Our red plastic cups work similarly. Cup in hand, we mingle. Liberated by the social permission granted by the red plastic cup, we catch up with old friends and make new ones. It becomes a factor that connects attendees at the event: we *all* have a red plastic cup, so we *all* belong. And we may assert that these cups are ours by writing our name on them, which further makes them a handy tool for socialization.

This sort of possession also minimizes the burden on our hosts to have a bounty of cups available for guests. While we may not share cups as the Xhosa do, there's an understanding that cups are not a limitless resource. The practice also functions to manage alcohol consumption. We get a cup at an event and we're free to fill it with any of the available options. It holds roughly the same amount for everyone—or least it gives the illusion of equality with regard to the ratios in mixed drinks. Among the Sikaiana, the distributor/host determines how much is poured into the cup for each round and how long to wait between rounds:

> Serving large portions and not waiting between rounds will cause the participants to become drunk rapidly. On the other hand, after such a happy state of inebriation has been reached, the distributor may decide to slow the pace of drinking in order to control the level of intoxication and preserve the supply of toddy (Donner 1994: 250).

While we may not necessarily be served in the same way with our red plastic cups (that might be a downer of a party to attend), our named cups provide a way to monitor access to drinks. If you lose your named cup, you might be out of luck. It can also be a signal that the cup-less should perhaps be cut-off, especially when it's clear that the de-cupped has passed beyond happy, joyful drinking to disruptive behavior.

AN OPEN INVITATION

The red plastic cup may have a bit of a party-animal reputation. It's hardly likely you'll be drinking fine wine or quality spirits from a red plastic cup. Or that you'll find a red plastic cup at a banquet or gala. It is a champion of the everyday and the unpretentious. It actively discourages behaviors that might suggest membership in alternative social groups.

The red plastic cup clearly carries with it a sense of appropriate behaviors and expectations: It's not that proper glasses cannot keep the company of the red plastic cup, but that they cannot do so if they bring with them a sense of otherness that distinguishes the user from other members of the group. And given the reputation that drinking vessels have been able to impart, a glass can function to set event attendees apart from each other. A specialty beverage glass would suggest a certain knowledge and understanding that may not be shared among the group, and might detract from participants' ability to freely socialize. A teacup, for example, would suggest that the drinker is experiencing the event differently from others—and create the expectation of more subdued behaviors. The sameness of the cup generates an

blurs cultural lines

openness meant to bypass divisions. The red plastic cup suggests a relaxed, convival atmosphere that invites everyone participate—regardless of the actual contents of the cup.

REFERENCES

Bunimovitz, S., & Greenberg, R. (2004). Revealed in Their Cups: Syrian Drinking Customs in Intermediate Bronze Age. *Canaan Bulletin of the American Schools of Oriental Research* (334): 19–31.

D'Costa, K. "Does Your Beer Glass Matter," *Scientific American—Anthropology in Practice*, August 22, 2011, http://blogs.scientificamerican.com/anthropology-in-practice/2011/08/22/does-your-beer-glass-matter/.

Donner, W. (1994). Alcohol, Community, and Modernity: The Social Organization of Toddy Drinking in a Polynesian Society. *Ethnology*, 33 (3): 245–260.

Jones, E.A. (1909). The Drinking Horns and Silver Plate in the National Museum at Copenhagen. *The Burlington Magazine for Connoisseurs*, 15 (76): 221–232.

Magennis, H. (1985). The Cup as Symbol and Metaphor in Old English Literature. *Speculum*, 60 (3): 517–536.

McAllister, P. (2003). Culture, Practice, and the Semantics of Xhosa Beer-Drinking. *Ethnology*, 42 (3): 187–207.

McIver, K. (2008). Banqueting at the Lord's Table in Sixteenth-Century Venice. *Gastronomica*, 8 (3): 8–11.

Nutting, P. B. (2003). Selling Elegant Glassware During the Great Depression: A. H. Heisey & Company and the New Deal. *The Business History Review*, 77(3): 448–478.

11

The Adaptive Value of Religious Ritual

Richard Sosis

Many anthropologists say that religion and ritual practice are the most fascinating parts of culture. When anthropologists study religion and ritual, however, the questions they ask tend to be very different from those that might concern a theologian, a religious studies scholar, or a potential convert.

Religious beliefs are strongly held because they form the bedrock of the meaning of life; religious rituals reinforce those beliefs. Rather than assessing the truth or falsity of particular religious claims, cultural anthropologists try to understand how religious beliefs and ritual practices shape people's worldviews and their everyday lives. They want to understand those "exotic" beliefs as the believers do. Other anthropologists, especially human behavioral ecologists like the author of this selection, try to explain religion and ritual in a substantially different way. If ritual behaviors are time-consuming, costly, or even painful, then why are they so important roles in most human communities? The author frames this question in evolutionary terms: How might natural selection have favored a human psychology that tends to believe in the supernatural and, by the same token, to engage in costly activities out of commitment to those beliefs?

One possible explanation, the author proposes, has to do with cooperation within a community. If people are linked by a common set of beliefs and a common set of ritual obligations, then they are more likely to cooperate with one another in ways that advance the good of the collective. In this sense, religion and ritual can be described as "adaptive." Religious rituals, the author explains, are thus a form of communication among group members; by participating in rituals, members signal to one another that they identify with the group, that they believe in what it stands for, and that they are prepared to make sacrifices on the group's behalf.

From this perspective, participating in especially challenging forms of ritual behavior—such as praying multiple times each day, carefully controlling one's eating behaviors, dressing in a certain way, or undergoing painful bodily treatments or markings—signals a high level of group commitment. Difficult ritual obligations also deter people with lower levels of commitment ("fakes") from joining the group and "freeloading" on the benefits of group membership. Rituals do not have to have a religious basis in order to have social functions.

While religion and ritual can enhance unity and trust among group members, they can also generate deep-seated animosity toward outsiders. The contemporary world is riddled with religiously motivated conflicts. It becomes much easier to make sense of these conflicts if we keep the double-sided nature of religious affiliation—as a source of unity, on one hand, and as a mechanism of divisiveness, on the other—in mind.

As you read this selection, ask yourself the following questions:

- The author asks, "Why do religious beliefs, practices, and institutions continue to be an essential component of human social life?" How does the author of this selection use his training in behavioral ecology to address this question?
- How have anthropologists' views of the meaning and function of ritual changed since the nineteenth century?
- According to the author, what adaptive problem does ritual behavior solve?
- Within a society, might adherence to religious ritual be more adaptive for some people than others?
- What is the "costly signaling theory of ritual," and what role might it play in the emergence of "demanding religious groups"?

The following terms discussed in this selection are included in the Glossary at the back of the book:

behavioral ecology	*natural selection*
commune	*ritual*
intragroup solidarity	*signaling theory of ritual*
kibbutz	

Sosis, Richard. "The Adaptive Value of Religious Ritual." *American Scientist* (March 2004):166–172. Reprinted with permission of American Scientist.

I was 15 years old the first time I went to Jerusalem's Old City and visited the 2,000-year-old remains of the Second Temple, known as the Western Wall. It may have foreshadowed my future life as an anthropologist, but on my first glimpse of the ancient stones I was more taken by the people standing at the foot of the structure than by the wall itself. Women stood in the open sun, facing the Wall in solemn worship, wearing long-sleeved shirts, head coverings and heavy skirts that scraped the ground. Men in their thick beards, long black coats and fur hats also seemed oblivious to the summer heat as they swayed fervently and sang praises to God. I turned to a friend, "Why would anyone in their right mind dress for a New England winter only to spend the afternoon praying in the desert heat?" At the time I thought there was no rational explanation and decided that my fellow religious brethren might well be mad.

Of course, "strange" behavior is not unique to ultraorthodox Jews. Many religious acts appear peculiar to the outsider. Pious adherents the world over physically differentiate themselves from others: Moonies shave their heads, Jain monks of India wear contraptions on their heads and feet to avoid killing insects, and clergy almost everywhere dress in outfits that distinguish them from the rest of society. Many peoples also engage in some form of surgical alteration. Australian aborigines perform a ritual operation on adolescent boys in which a bone or a stone is inserted into the penis through an incision in the urethra. Jews and Muslims submit their sons to circumcision, and in some Muslim societies daughters are also subject to circumcision or other forms of genital mutilation. Groups as diverse as the Nuer of Sudan and the Latmul of New Guinea force their adolescents to undergo ritual scarification. Initiation ceremonies, otherwise known as rites of passage, are often brutal. Among Native Americans, Apache boys were forced to bathe in icy water, Luiseno initiates were required to lie motionless while being bitten by hordes of ants, and Tukuna girls had their hair plucked out.

How can we begin to understand such behavior? If human beings are rational creatures, then why do we spend so much time, energy and resources on acts that can be so painful or, at the very least, uncomfortable? Archaeologists tell us that our species has engaged in ritual behavior for at least 100,000 years, and every known culture practices some form of religion. It even survives covertly in those cultures where governments have attempted to eliminate spiritual practices. And, despite the unparalleled triumph of scientific rationalism in the twentieth century, religion continued to flourish. In the United States a steady 40 percent of the population attended church regularly throughout the century. A belief in God (about 96 percent), the afterlife (about 72 percent), heaven (about 72 percent) and hell (about 58 percent) remained substantial and remarkably constant. Why do religious beliefs, practices, and institutions continue to be an essential component of human social life?

Such questions have intrigued me for years. Initially my training in anthropology did not provide an answer. Indeed, my studies only increased my bewilderment. I received my training in a subfield known as human behavioral ecology, which studies the adaptive design of behavior with attention to its ecological setting. Behavioral ecologists assume that natural selection has shaped the human nervous system to respond successfully to varying ecological circumstances. All organisms must balance trade-offs: Time spent doing one thing prevents them from pursuing other activities that can enhance their survival or reproductive success. Animals that maximize the rate at which they acquire resources, such as food and mates, can maximize the number of descendants, which is exactly what the game of natural selection is all about.

Behavioral ecologists assume that natural selection has designed our decision-making mechanisms to optimize the rate at which human beings accrue resources under diverse ecological conditions—a basic prediction of *optimal foraging theory*. Optimality models offer predictions of the "perfectly adapted" behavioral response, given a set of environmental constraints. Of course, a perfect fit with the environment is almost never achieved because organisms rarely have perfect information and because environments are always changing. Nevertheless, this assumption has provided a powerful framework to analyze a variety of decisions, and most research (largely conducted among foraging populations) has shown that our species broadly conforms to these expectations.

If our species is designed to optimize the rate at which we extract energy from the environment, why would we engage in religious behavior that seems so counterproductive? Indeed, some religious practices, such as ritual sacrifices, are a conspicuous display of wasted resources. Anthropologists can explain why foragers regularly share their food with others in the group, but why would anyone share their food with a dead ancestor by burning it to ashes on an altar? A common response to this question is that people believe in the efficacy of the rituals and the tenets of the faith that give meaning to the ceremonies. But this response merely begs the question. We must really ask why natural selection has favored a psychology that believes in the supernatural and engages in the costly manifestations of those beliefs.

RITUAL SACRIFICE

Behavioral ecologists have only recently begun to consider the curiosities of religious activities, so at first I had to search other disciplines to understand these practices. The scholarly literature suggested that I wasn't the only one who believed that intense religious behavior was a sign of madness. Some of the greatest minds of the past two centuries, such as Marx and Freud, supported my thesis. And the early anthropological theorists also held that spiritual beliefs were indicative of a primitive and simple mind. In the nineteenth century, Edward B. Tylor, often noted as one of the founding fathers of anthropology, maintained that religion arose out of a misunderstanding among "primitives" that dreams are real. He argued that dreams about deceased ancestors might have led the primitives to believe that spirits can survive death.

Eventually the discipline of anthropology matured, and its practitioners moved beyond the equation that "primitive equals irrational." Instead, they began to seek functional explanations of religion. Most prominent among these early twentieth-century theorists was the Polish-born anthropologist Bronislaw Malinowski. He argued that religion arose out of "the real tragedies of human life, out of the conflict between human plans and realities." Although religion may serve to allay our fears of death, and provide comfort from our incessant search for answers, Malinowski's thesis did not seem to explain the origin of rituals. Standing in the midday desert sun in several layers of black clothing seems more like a recipe for increasing anxiety than treating it. The classical anthropologists didn't have the right answers to my questions. I needed to look elsewhere.

Fortunately, a new generation of anthropologists has begun to provide some explanations. It turns out that the strangeness of religious practices and their inherent costs are actually the critical features that contribute to the success of religion as a universal cultural strategy and why natural selection has favored such behavior in the human lineage. To understand this unexpected benefit we need to recognize the adaptive problem that ritual behavior solves. William Irons, a behavioral ecologist at Northwestern University, has suggested that the universal dilemma is the promotion of cooperation within a community. Irons argues that the primary adaptive benefit of religion is its ability to facilitate cooperation within a group—while hunting, sharing food, defending against attacks and waging war—all critical activities in our evolutionary history. But, as Irons points out, although everyone is better off if everybody cooperates, this ideal is often very difficult to coordinate and achieve. The problem is that an individual is even better off if everyone else does the cooperating, while he or she remains at home enjoying an afternoon siesta. Cooperation requires social mechanisms that prevent individuals from free riding on the efforts of others. Irons argues that religion is such a mechanism.

The key is that religious rituals are a form of communication, which anthropologists have long maintained. They borrowed this insight from ethologists who observed that many species engage in patterned behavior, which they referred to as "ritual." Ethologists recognized that ritualistic behaviors served as a form of communication between members of the same species, and often between members of different species. For example, the males of many avian species engage in courtship rituals—such as bowing, head wagging, wing waving, and hopping (among many other gestures)—to signal their amorous intents before a prospective mate. And, of course, the vibration of a rattlesnake's tail is a powerful threat display to other species that enter its personal space.

Irons's insight is that religious activities signal commitment to other members of the group. By engaging in the ritual, the member effectively says, "I identify with the group and I believe in what the group stands for." Through its ability to signal commitment, religious behavior can overcome the problem of free riders and promote cooperation within the group. It does so because trust lies at the heart of the problem: A member must assure everyone that he or she will participate in acquiring food or in defending the group. Of course, hunters and warriors may make promises—"you have my word I'll show up tomorrow"—but unless the trust is already established such statements are not believable.

It turns out that there is a robust way to secure trust. Israeli biologist Amotz Zahavi observes that it is often in the best interest of an animal to send a dishonest signal—perhaps to fake its size, speed, strength, health, or beauty. The only signal that can be believed is one that is too costly to fake, which he referred to as a "handicap." Zahavi argues that natural selection has favored the evolution of handicaps. For example, when a springbok antelope spots a predator it often *stots*—it jumps up and down. This extraordinary behavior puzzled biologists for years: Why would an antelope waste precious energy that could be used to escape the predator? And why would the animal make itself more visible to something that wants to eat it? The reason is that the springbok is displaying its quality to the predator—its ability to escape, effectively saying, "Don't bother chasing me. Look how strong my legs are; you won't be able to catch me." The only reason a predator believes the springbok is because the signal is too costly to fake. An antelope that is not quick enough to escape cannot imitate the signal because it is not strong enough to repeatedly jump to a certain height. Thus, a display can provide honest information if the signals are so costly

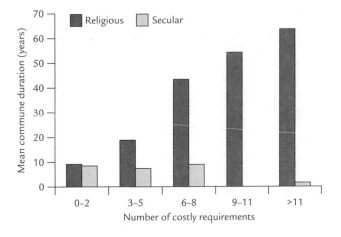

The Adaptive Value of Religious Ritual Behaviors that are constrained. Sosis, Richard. "The Adaptive Value of Religious Ritual." *American Scientist* (March 2004):166–172. Reprinted with permission of American Scientist.

Members' Behavioral Requirements and Commune Longevity

Consumption of:
coffee, alcohol, tobacco, meat, other foods or beverages

Use and ownership of:
photographs, jewelry, certain technology, other material items

Activities:
monogamous marriage, gambling, communication with the outside, living as a nuclear family, maintaining rights to biological children

Behaviors that are required
trial period for membership, surrender of material belongings, learn a body of knowledge, endure public sessions of criticism, certain clothing styles, certain hairstyles, fasting

to perform that lower quality organisms cannot benefit by imitating the signal.

In much the same way, religious behavior is also a costly signal. By donning several layers of clothing and standing out in the midday sun, ultraorthodox Jewish men are signaling to others: "Hey! Look, I'm a *haredi* Jew. If you are also a member of this group you can trust me because why else would I be dressed like this? No one would do this *unless* they believed in the teachings of ultraorthodox Judaism and were fully committed to its ideals and goals." The quality that these men are signaling is their level of commitment to a specific religious group.

Adherence to a set of religious beliefs entails a host of ritual obligations and expected behaviors. Although there may be physical or psychological benefits associated with some ritual practices, the significant time, energy, and financial costs involved serve as effective deterrents for anyone who does not believe in the

teachings of a particular religion. There is no incentive for nonbelievers to join or remain in a religious group, because the costs of maintaining membership—such as praying three times a day, eating only kosher food, donating a certain part of your income to charity and so on—are simply too high.

Those who engage in the suite of ritual requirements imposed by a religious group can be trusted to believe sincerely in the doctrines of their respective religious communities. As a result of increased levels of trust and commitment among group members, religious groups minimize costly monitoring mechanisms that are otherwise necessary to overcome free-rider problems that typically plague communal pursuits. Hence, the adaptive benefit of ritual behavior is its ability to promote and maintain cooperation, a challenge that our ancestors presumably faced throughout our evolutionary history.

BENEFITS OF MEMBERSHIP

One prediction of the "costly signaling theory of ritual" is that groups that impose the greatest demands on their members will elicit the highest levels of devotion and commitment. Only committed members will be willing to dress and behave in ways that differ from the rest of society. Groups that maintain more-committed members can also offer more because it's easier for them to attain their collective goals than groups whose members are less committed. This may explain a paradox in the religious marketplace: Churches that require the most of their adherents are experiencing rapid rates of growth. For example, the Church of Jesus Christ of Latter-day Saints (Mormons), Seventh-day Adventists and Jehovah's Witnesses, who respectively abstain from caffeine, meat, and blood transfusions (among other things), have been growing at exceptional rates. In contrast, liberal Protestant denominations such as the Episcopalians, Methodists, and Presbyterians have been steadily losing members.

Economist Lawrence Iannaccone, of George Mason University, has also noted that the most demanding groups also have the greatest number of committed members. He found that the more distinct a religious group was—how much the group's lifestyle differed from mainstream America—the higher its attendance rates at services. Sociologists Roger Finke and Rodney Stark, of Penn State and the University of Washington, respectively, have argued that when the Second Vatican Council in 1962 repealed many of the Catholic Church's prohibitions and reduced the level of strictness in the church, it initiated a decline in church attendance among American Catholics and reduced the enrollments in seminaries. Indeed, in the late 1950s almost 75 percent of American Catholics were attending Mass weekly, but since the Vatican's actions there has been a steady decline to the current rate of about 45 percent.

The costly signaling theory of ritual also predicts that greater commitment will translate into greater cooperation within groups. My colleague Eric Bressler, a graduate student at McMaster University, and I addressed this question by looking at data from the records of nineteenth-century communes. All communes face an inherent problem of promoting and sustaining cooperation because individuals can free ride on the efforts of others. Because cooperation is key to a commune's survival, we employed commune longevity as a measure of cooperation. Compared to their secular counterparts, the religious communes did indeed demand more of their members, including such behavior as celibacy, the surrender of all material possessions, and vegetarianism. Communes that demanded more of their members survived longer, overcoming the fundamental challenges of cooperation. By placing greater demands on their members, they were presumably able to elicit greater belief in and commitment toward the community's common ideology and goals.

I also wanted to evaluate the costly signaling theory of ritual within modern communal societies. The kibbutzim I had visited in Israel as a teenager provided an ideal opportunity to examine these hypotheses. For most of their 100-year history, these communal societies have lived by the dictum, "From each according to his abilities, to each according to his needs." The majority of the more than 270 kibbutzim are secular (and often ideologically antireligious); fewer than 20 are religiously oriented. Because of a massive economic failure—a collective debt of more than $4 billion—the kibbutzim are now moving in the direction of increased privatization and reduced communality. When news of the extraordinary debt surfaced in the late 1980s, it went largely unnoticed that the religious kibbutzim were financially stable. In the words of the Religious Kibbutz Movement Federation, "the economic position of the religious kibbutzim is sound, and they remain uninvolved in the economic crisis."

The success of the religious kibbutzim is especially remarkable given that many of their rituals inhibit economic productivity. For example, Jewish law does not permit Jews to milk cows on the Sabbath. Although rabbinic rulings now permit milking by kibbutz members to prevent the cows from suffering, in the early years none of this milk was used commercially. There are also significant constraints imposed by Jewish law on agricultural productivity. Fruits are not allowed to be eaten for the first few years of the tree's life, agricultural fields must lie fallow every seven years, and the corners of fields can never be harvested—they must be left for society's poor. Although these constraints appear detrimental to productivity, the costly signaling theory of ritual suggests that they may actually be the key to the economic success of the religious kibbutzim.

I decided to study this issue with economist Bradley Ruffle of Israel's Ben Gurion University. We developed a game to determine whether there were differences in how the members of secular and religious kibbutzim cooperated with each other. The game involves two members from the same kibbutz who remain anonymous to each other. Each member is told there are 100 shekels in an envelope to which both members have access. Each participant decides how many shekels to withdraw and keep. If the sum of both requests exceeds 100 shekels, both members receive no money and the game is over. However, if the requests are less than or equal to 100 shekels, the money remaining in the envelope is increased by 50 percent and divided evenly among the participants. Each member also keeps the original amount he or she requested. The game is an example of a common-pool resource dilemma in which publicly accessible goods are no longer available once they are consumed. Since the goods are available to more than one person, the maintenance of the resources requires individual self-restraint; in other words, cooperation.

After we controlled for a number of variables, including the age and size of the kibbutz and the amount of privatization, we found not only that religious kibbutzniks were more cooperative with each other than secular kibbutzniks, but that male religious kibbutz members were also significantly more cooperative than female members. Among secular kibbutzniks we found no sex differences at all. This result is understandable if we appreciate the types of rituals and demands imposed on religious Jews. Although there are a variety of requirements that are imposed equally on males and females, such as keeping kosher and refraining from work on the Sabbath, male rituals are largely performed in public, whereas female rituals are generally pursued privately. Indeed, none of the three major requirements imposed exclusively on women—attending a ritual bath, separating a portion of dough when baking bread, and lighting Shabbat and holiday candles—are publicly performed. They are not rituals that signal commitment to a wider group; instead they appear to signal commitment to the family. Men, however, engage in highly visible rituals, most notably public prayer, which they are expected to perform three times a day. Among male religious kibbutz members, synagogue attendance is positively correlated with cooperative behavior. There is no similar correlation among females. This is not surprising given that women are not required to attend services, and so their presence

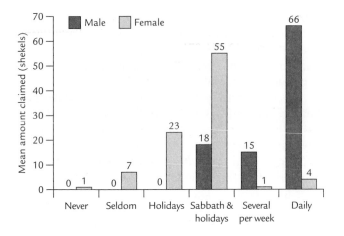

Sosis, Richard. "The Adaptive Value of Religious Ritual." *American Scientist* (March 2004):166–172. Reprinted with permission of American Scientist.

does not signal commitment to the group. Here the costly signaling theory of ritual provides a unique explanation of these findings. We expect that further work will provide even more insight into the ability of ritual to promote trust, commitment and cooperation.

We know that many other species engage in ritual behaviors that appear to enhance trust and cooperation. For example, anthropologists John Watanabe of Dartmouth University and Barbara Smuts at the University of Michigan have shown that greetings between male olive baboons serve to signal trust and commitment between former rivals. So why are human rituals often cloaked in mystery and the supernatural? Cognitive anthropologists Scott Atran of the University of Michigan and Pascal Boyer at Washington University in St. Louis have pointed out that the counterintuitive nature of supernatural concepts is more easily remembered than mundane ideas, which facilitates their cultural transmission. Belief in supernatural agents such as gods, spirits and ghosts also appears to be critical to religion's ability to promote long-term cooperation. In our study of nineteenth-century communes, Eric Bressler and I found that the strong positive relationship between the number of costly requirements imposed on members and commune longevity only held for religious communes, not secular ones. We were surprised by this result because secular groups such as militaries and fraternities appear to successfully employ costly rituals to maintain cooperation. Cultural ecologist Roy Rappaport explained, however, that although religious and secular rituals can both promote cooperation, religious rituals ironically generate greater belief and commitment because they sanctify unfalsifiable statements that are beyond the possibility of examination. Since statements containing supernatural elements, such as "Jesus is the son of God,"

cannot be proved or disproved, believers verify them "emotionally." In contrast to religious propositions, the kibbutz's guiding dictum, taken from Karl Marx, is not beyond question; it can be evaluated by living according to its directives by distributing labor and resources appropriately. Indeed, as the economic situation on the kibbutzim has worsened, this fundamental proposition of kibbutz life has been challenged and is now disregarded by many who are pushing their communities to accept differential pay scales. The ability of religious rituals to evoke emotional experiences that can be associated with enduring supernatural concepts and symbols differentiates them from both animal and secular rituals and lies at the heart of their efficiency in promoting and maintaining long-term group cooperation and commitment.

Evolutionary research on religious behavior is in its infancy, and many questions remain to be addressed. The costly signaling theory of ritual appears to provide some answers, and, of course, it has given me a better understanding of the questions I asked as a teenager. The real value of the costly signaling theory of ritual will be determined by its ability to explain religious phenomena across societies. Most of us, including ultraorthodox Jews, are not living in communes. Nevertheless, contemporary religious congregations that demand much of their members are able to achieve a close-knit social community—an impressive accomplishment in today's individualistic world.

Religion has probably always served to enhance the union of its practitioners; unfortunately, there is also a dark side to this unity. If the intragroup solidarity that religion promotes is one of its significant adaptive benefits, then from its beginning religion has probably always played a role in intergroup conflicts. In other words, one of the benefits for individuals of intragroup solidarity is the ability of unified groups to defend and compete against other groups. This seems to be as true today as it ever was, and is nowhere more apparent than the region I visited as a 15-year-old boy—which is where I am as I write these words. As I conduct my fieldwork in the center of this war zone, I hope that by appreciating the depth of the religious need in the human psyche, and by understanding this powerful adaptation, we can learn how to promote cooperation rather than conflict.

REFERENCES

Atran, S. 2002. *In Gods We Trust*. New York: Oxford University Press.

Iannaccone, L. 1992. Sacrifice and stigma: Reducing free-riding in cults, communes, and other collectives. *Journal of Political Economy* 100: 271–291.

Iannaccone, L. 1994. Why strict churches are strong. *American Journal of Sociology* 99: 1180–1211.

Irons, W. 2001. Religion as a hard-to-fake sign of commitment. In *Evolution and the Capacity for Commitment*, ed. R. Nesse, 292–309. New York: Russell Sage Foundation.

Rappaport, R. 1999. *Ritual and Religion in the Making of Humanity*. Cambridge: Cambridge University Press.

Sosis, R. 2003. Why aren't we all Hutterites? Costly signaling theory and religious behavior. *Human Nature* 14: 91–127.

Sosis, R., and C. Alcorta. 2003. Signaling, solidarity, and the sacred: The evolution of religious behavior. *Evolutionary Anthropology* 12: 264–274.

Sosis, R., and E. Bressler. 2003. Cooperation and commune longevity: A test of the costly signaling theory of religion. *Cross-Cultural Research* 37: 211–239.

Sosis, R., and B. Ruffle. 2003. Religious ritual and cooperation: Testing for a relationship on Israeli religious and secular kibbutzim. *Current Anthropology* 44: 713–722.

Zahavi, A., and A. Zahavi. 1997. *The Handicap Principle*. New York: Oxford University Press.

12

The Worst Mistake in the History of the Human Race

Jared Diamond

What we eat and how we eat are important both nutritionally and culturally. This selection suggests that how we get what we eat—through gathering and hunting versus agriculture, for example—has dramatic consequences. This seems pretty obvious. We all imagine what a struggle it must have been before the development of agriculture. We think of our ancestors spending their days searching for roots and berries to eat, or out at the crack of dawn, hunting wild animals. In fact, this was not quite the case. Nevertheless, isn't it really better simply to go to the refrigerator, open the door, and reach for a container of milk to pour into a bowl of flaked grain for your regular morning meal? What could be simpler and more nutritious?

There are many things that we seldom question; the truth seems so evident and the answers obvious. One such sacred cow is the tremendous prosperity brought about by the agricultural revolution. This selection is a thought-provoking introduction to the connection between culture and agriculture. The transition from food foraging to farming (what archaeologists call the Neolithic revolution) may have been the worst mistake in human history or its most important event. You be the judge. But for better or worse, this cultural evolution has occurred, and the world will never be the same again.

As you read this selection, ask yourself the following questions:

- What is the fundamental difference between the progressivist view and the revisionist interpretation?
- How did the development of agriculture affect people's health?
- What three reasons explain the changes brought about by the development of agriculture?
- How did the development of agriculture affect social equality, including gender equality?

The following terms discussed in this selection are included in the Glossary at the back of the book:

  agricultural development
  civilization
  domestication of plants and animals
  hunter-gatherers
  Neolithic
  paleontology
  paleopathology
  social stratification

To science we owe dramatic changes in our smug self-image. Astronomy taught us that our earth isn't the center of the universe but merely one of billions of heavenly bodies. From biology we learned that we weren't specially created by God but evolved along with millions of other species. Now archaeology is demolishing another sacred belief: that human history over the past million years has been a long tale of progress. In particular, recent discoveries suggest that the adoption of agriculture, supposedly our most decisive step toward a better life, was in many ways a catastrophe from which we have never recovered. With agriculture came the gross social and sexual inequality, the disease and despotism, that curse our existence.

At first, the evidence against this revisionist interpretation will strike twentieth-century Americans as irrefutable. We're better off in almost every respect than the people of the Middle Ages, who in turn had it easier than cavemen, who in turn were better off than apes. Just count our advantages. We enjoy the most abundant and varied foods, the best tools and material

Diamond, Jared. "The Worst Mistake in the History of the Human Race." *Discover Magazine* (May 1987):64–66. Reprinted with permission of the author.

goods, some of the longest and healthiest lives, in history. Most of us are safe from starvation and predators. We get our energy from oil and machines, not from our sweat. What neo-Luddite among us would trade his life for that of a medieval peasant, a caveman, or an ape?

For most of our history we supported ourselves by hunting and gathering: we hunted wild animals and foraged for wild plants. It's a life that philosophers have traditionally regarded as nasty, brutish, and short. Since no food is grown and little is stored, there is (in this view) no respite from the struggle that starts anew each day to find wild foods and avoid starving. Our escape from this misery was facilitated only 10,000 years ago, when in different parts of the world people began to domesticate plants and animals. The agricultural revolution gradually spread until today it's nearly universal, and few tribes of hunter-gatherers survive.

From the progressivist perspective on which I was brought up, to ask "Why did almost all our hunter-gatherer ancestors adopt agriculture?" is silly. Of course they adopted it because agriculture is an efficient way to get more food for less work. Planted crops yield far more tons per acre than roots and berries. Just imagine a band of savages, exhausted from searching for nuts or chasing wild animals, suddenly gazing for the first time at a fruit-laden orchard or a pasture full of sheep. How many milliseconds do you think it would take them to appreciate the advantages of agriculture?

The progressivist party line sometimes even goes so far as to credit agriculture with the remarkable flowering of art that has taken place over the past few thousand years. Since crops can be stored, and since it takes less time to pick food from a garden than to find it in the wild, agriculture gave us free time that hunter-gatherers never had. Thus it was agriculture that enabled us to build the Parthenon and compose the B-minor Mass.

While the case for the progressivist view seems overwhelming, it's hard to prove. How do you show that the lives of people 10,000 years ago got better when they abandoned hunting and gathering for farming? Until recently, archaeologists had to resort to indirect tests, whose results (surprisingly) failed to support the progressivist view. Here's one example of an indirect test: Are twentieth-century hunter-gatherers really worse off than farmers? Scattered throughout the world, several dozen groups of so-called primitive people, like the Kalahari Bushmen, continue to support themselves that way. It turns out that these people have plenty of leisure time, sleep a good deal, and work less hard than their farming neighbors. For instance, the average time devoted each week to obtaining food is only 12 to 19 hours for one group of Bushmen, 14 hours or less for the Hadza nomads of Tanzania. One Bushman, when asked why he hadn't emulated neighboring tribes by adopting agriculture, replied, "Why should we, when there are so many mongongo nuts in the world?"

While farmers concentrate on high-carbohydrate crops like rice and potatoes, the mix of wild plants and animals in the diets of surviving hunter-gatherers provides more protein and a better balance of other nutrients. In one study, the Bushmen's average daily food intake (during a month when food was plentiful) was 2,140 calories and 93 grams of protein, considerably greater than the recommended daily allowance for people of their size. It's almost inconceivable that Bushmen, who eat 75 or so wild plants, could die of starvation the way hundreds of thousands of Irish farmers and their families did during the potato famine of the 1840s.

So the lives of at least the surviving hunter-gatherers aren't nasty and brutish, even though farmers have pushed them into some of the world's worst real estate. But modern hunter-gatherer societies that have rubbed shoulders with farming societies for thousands of years don't tell us about conditions before the agricultural revolution. The progressivist view is really making a claim about the distant past: that the lives of primitive people improved when they switched from gathering to farming. Archaeologists can date that switch by distinguishing remains of wild plants and animals from those of domesticated ones in prehistoric garbage dumps.

How can one deduce the health of the prehistoric garbage makers, and thereby directly test the progressivist view? That question has become answerable only in recent years, in part through the newly emerging techniques of paleopathology, the study of signs of disease in the remains of ancient peoples.

In some lucky situations, the paleopathologist has almost as much material to study as a pathologist today. For example, archaeologists in the Chilean deserts found well preserved mummies whose medical conditions at time of death could be determined by autopsy. And feces of long-dead Indians who lived in dry caves in Nevada remain sufficiently well preserved to be examined for hookworm and other parasites.

Usually the only human remains available for study are skeletons, but they permit a surprising number of deductions. To begin with, a skeleton reveals its owner's sex, weight, and approximate age. In the few cases where there are many skeletons, one can construct mortality tables like the ones life insurance companies use to calculate expected life span and risk of death at any given age. Paleopathologists can also calculate growth rates by measuring bones of people of different ages, examining teeth for enamel defects (signs of childhood malnutrition), and recognizing scars left on bones by anemia, tuberculosis, leprosy, and other diseases.

One straightforward example of what paleopathologists have learned from skeletons concerns historical changes in height. Skeletons from Greece and Turkey show that the average height of hunter-gatherers toward the end of the ice ages was a generous 5'9'' for men, 5'5'' for women. With the adoption of agriculture, height crashed, and by 3000 B.C. had reached a low of only 5'3'' for men, 5' for women. By classical times heights were very slowly on the rise again, but modern Greeks and Turks have still not regained the average height of their distant ancestors.

Another example of paleopathology at work is the study of Indian skeletons from burial mounds in the Illinois and Ohio river valleys. At Dickson Mounds, located near the confluence of the Spoon and Illinois Rivers, archaeologists have excavated some 800 skeletons that paint a picture of the health changes that occurred when a hunter-gatherer culture gave way to intensive maize farming around A.D. 1150. Studies by George Armelagos and his colleagues then at the University of Massachusetts show these early farmers paid a price for their new-found livelihood. Compared to the hunter-gatherers who preceded them, the farmers had a nearly 50 percent increase in enamel defects indicative of malnutrition, a fourfold increase in iron-deficiency anemia (evidenced by a bone condition called porotic hyperostosis), a threefold rise in bone lesions reflecting infectious disease in general, and an increase in degenerative conditions of the spine, probably reflecting a lot of hard physical labor. "Life expectancy at birth in the pre-agricultural community was about twenty-six years," says Armelagos, "but in the post-agricultural community it was nineteen years. So these episodes of nutritional stress and infectious disease were seriously affecting their ability to survive."

The evidence suggests that the Indians at Dickson Mounds, like many other primitive peoples, took up farming not by choice but from necessity in order to feed their constantly growing numbers. "I don't think most hunter-gatherers farmed until they had to, and when they switched to farming they traded quality for quantity," says Mark Cohen of the State University of New York at Plattsburgh, co-editor, with Armelagos, of one of the seminal books in the field, *Paleopathology at the Origins of Agriculture*. "When I first started making that argument ten years ago, not many people agreed with me. Now it's become a respectable, albeit controversial, side of the debate."

There are at least three sets of reasons to explain the findings that agriculture was bad for health. First, hunter-gatherers enjoyed a varied diet, while early farmers obtained most of their food from one or a few starchy crops. The farmers gained cheap calories at the cost of poor nutrition. (Today just three high-carbohydrate plants—wheat, rice, and corn—provide the bulk of the calories consumed by the human species, yet each one is deficient in certain vitamins or amino acids essential to life.) Second, because of dependence on a limited number of crops, farmers ran the risk of starvation if one crop failed. Finally, the mere fact that agriculture encouraged people to clump together in crowded societies, many of which then carried on trade with other crowded societies, led to the spread of parasites and infectious disease. (Some archaeologists think it was crowding, rather than agriculture, that promoted disease, but this is a chicken-and-egg argument, because crowding encourages agriculture and vice versa.) Epidemics couldn't take hold when populations were scattered in small bands that constantly shifted camp. Tuberculosis and diarrheal disease had to await the rise of farming, measles and bubonic plague the appearance of large cities.

Besides malnutrition, starvation, and epidemic diseases, farming helped bring another curse upon humanity: deep class divisions. Hunter-gatherers have little or no stored food, and no concentrated food sources, like an orchard or a herd of cows: they live off the wild plants and animals they obtain each day. Therefore, there can be no kings, no class of social parasites who grow fat on food seized from others. Only in farming populations could a healthy, non-producing elite set itself above the disease-ridden masses. Skeletons from Greek tombs at Mycenae c. 1500 B.C. suggest that royals enjoyed a better diet than commoners, since the royal skeletons were two or three inches taller and had better teeth (on the average, one instead of six cavities or missing teeth). Among Chilean mummies from c. A.D. 1000, the élite were distinguished not only by ornaments and gold hair clips but also by a fourfold lower rate of bone lesions caused by disease.

Similar contrasts in nutrition and health persist on a global scale today. To people in rich countries like the United States, it sounds ridiculous to extol the virtues of hunting and gathering. But Americans are an élite, dependent on oil and minerals that must often be imported from countries with poorer health and nutrition. If one could choose between being a peasant farmer in Ethiopia or a Bushman gatherer in the Kalahari, which do you think would be the better choice?

Farming may have encouraged inequality between the sexes, as well. Freed from the need to transport their babies during a nomadic existence, and under pressure to produce more hands to till the fields, farming women tended to have more frequent pregnancies than their hunter-gatherer counterparts—with consequent drains on their health. Among the Chilean mummies, for example, more women than men had bone lesions from infectious disease.

Women in agricultural societies were sometimes made beasts of burden. In New Guinea farming communities today I often see women staggering under loads of vegetables and firewood while the men walk empty-handed. Once while on a field trip there studying birds, I offered to pay some villagers to carry supplies from an airstrip to my mountain camp. The heaviest item was a 110-pound bag of rice, which I lashed to a pole and assigned to a team of four men to shoulder together. When I eventually caught up with the villagers, the men were carrying light loads, while one small woman weighing less than the bag of rice was bent under it, supporting its weight by a cord across her temples.

As for the claim that agriculture encouraged the flowering of art by providing us with leisure time, modern hunter-gatherers have at least as much free time as do farmers. The whole emphasis on leisure time as a critical factor seems to me misguided. Gorillas have had ample free time to build their own Parthenon, had they wanted to. While post-agricultural technological advances did make new art forms possible and preservation of art easier, great paintings and sculptures were already being produced by hunter-gatherers 15,000 years ago, and were still being produced as recently as the last century by such hunter-gatherers as some Eskimos and the Indians of the Pacific Northwest.

Thus with the advent of agriculture an élite became better off, but most people became worse off. Instead of swallowing the progressivist party line that we chose agriculture because it was good for us, we must ask how we got trapped by it despite its pitfalls.

One answer boils down to the adage "Might makes right." Farming could support many more people than hunting, albeit with a poorer quality of life. (Population densities of hunter-gatherers are rarely over one person per ten square miles, while farmers average 100 times that.) Partly, this is because a field planted entirely in edible crops lets one feed far more mouths than a forest with scattered edible plants. Partly, too, it's because nomadic hunter-gatherers have to keep their children spaced at four-year intervals by infanticide and other means, since a mother must carry her toddler until it's old enough to keep up with the adults.

Because farm women don't have that burden, they can and often do bear a child every two years.

As population densities of hunter-gatherers slowly rose at the end of the ice ages, bands had to choose between feeding more mouths by taking the first steps toward agriculture, or else finding ways to limit growth. Some bands chose the former solution, unable to anticipate the evils of farming, and seduced by the transient abundance they enjoyed until population growth caught up with increased food production. Such bands outbred and then drove off or killed the bands that chose to remain hunter-gatherers, because a hundred malnourished farmers can still outfight one healthy hunter. It's not that hunter-gatherers abandoned their life style, but that those sensible enough not to abandon it were forced out of all areas except the ones farmers didn't want.

At this point it's instructive to recall the common complaint that archaeology is a luxury, concerned with the remote past, and offering no lessons for the present. Archaeologists studying the rise of farming have reconstructed a crucial stage at which we made the worst mistake in human history. Forced to choose between limiting population or trying to increase food production, we chose the latter and ended up with starvation, warfare, and tyranny.

Hunter-gatherers practiced the most successful and longest-lasting life style in human history. In contrast, we're still struggling with the mess into which agriculture has tumbled us, and it's unclear whether we can solve it. Suppose that an archaeologist who had visited us from outer space were trying to explain human history to his fellow spacelings. He might illustrate the results of his digs by a 24-hour clock on which one hour represents 100,000 years of real past time. If the history of the human race began at midnight, then we would now be almost at the end of our first day. We lived as hunter-gatherers for nearly the whole of that day, from midnight through dawn, noon, and sunset. Finally, at 11:54 p.m., we adopted agriculture. As our second midnight approaches, will the plight of famine-stricken peasants gradually spread to engulf us all? Or will we somehow achieve those seductive blessings that we imagine behind agriculture's glittering façade, and that have so far eluded us?

13

The Forgotten Population?

Youth, Food Insecurity, and Rising Global Food Prices

Craig Hadley, Tefera Belachew, David Lindstrom, and Fasil Tessema

Author and food advocate Michael Pollan calls American farmers the most productive people in the history of humankind. Approximately 100 million Americans famers feed more than 300 million Americans. How is it that one farmer (on average) can produce enough to keep 300 bellies fed? This remarkable productivity is a recent development in human history, and it is attributable to our unprecedented consumption of fossil fuels.

In the first half of the twentieth century, the United States needed cheap calories (food) to feed the nation, and government subsidies were awarded to farmers to help bolster production through mechanization and fossil fuels—for operating machines and producing fertilizers and herbicides. As long as petroleum and fossil fuels are cheap, this mechanized farm production produces cheap food, but as fuel prices rise, the cost of food follows. Food prices are at historic highs, and fossil fuel prices are not getting cheaper. This trajectory is headed toward a world with more hunger, unless we rethink how to produce food, in North America and throughout the world.

If mechanized, intensive agriculture based on fossil fuels is growing increasingly inefficient due to rising fuel prices (among other reasons), one emerging alternative is a return (to varying degrees) to human power. Increasing human labor inputs can help mitigate record food and fuel prices, and the U.S. Department of Agriculture is actively recruiting new farmers through programs like Know Your Food, which helps farmers access USDA loans and support. Programs like Know Your Farmer, Know Your Food are developed and launched based on research and data collected specifically for the purpose of understanding how to understand and improve our food system. In this chapter, Hadley and his colleagues conduct innovative anthropological research in Ethiopia to determine how youth suffer and cope with hunger. By applying anthropology to understand complex problems such as the scale and scope of food insecurity among Ethiopian youth, policy makers and nongovernmental organizations can be more effective partners with communities and countries fighting extreme hunger.

As you read this selection, ask yourself the following questions:

- How does food insecurity affect youth?
- How do rising global food costs affect people in Ethiopia?
- How did the authors determine that the prevalence of youth food insecurity is increasing?
- What factors protect Ethiopian youth from food insecurity?
- What is the difference between rural and urban youth perspectives on food?
- What is the Jimma Longitudinal Family Survey of Youth?

The following terms discussed in this section are included in the Glossary in the back of the book:

Ethiopian birr
food insecurity
indicators
social capital
staple foods

Hadley, Craig, Tefera Belachew, David Lindstrom, & Fasil Tessema. "The Forgotten Population? Youth, Food Insecurity, and Rising Prices: Implications for the Global Food Crisis." Reproduced by permission of the American Anthropological Association from *National Association for the Practice of Anthropology Bulletin*, Volume 32, Issue 1, pp. 77–91, November 2009. Not for sale or further reproduction.

The recent and rapid rise in global food prices has led to a increased interest in food insecurity (Benson et al. 2008). Much of the focus has been centered on the vulnerability of mothers and young children, with little attention paid to the possible impacts on the large population of youth in developing countries. Yet, like mothers and children, youth are also likely to experience the poor physical and mental health outcomes, poorer quality diets, worse self-reported health, and lower levels of school attendance that have been attributed to food insecurity. Youth might be at additional risk because food insecurity may also negatively impact on outcomes such as schooling and reproductive health; indeed, evidence is emerging that females in food insecure households are more likely to engage in risky sexual behavior (Weiser et al. 2007). For these reasons, food insecurity is a critical variable to measure and mitigate for youth, who are experiencing a range of social, biological, and mental transitions as they shift into adult roles. Food insecurity is however typically measured at the household level and as a result understanding how food insecurity affects youth is often obscured by the absence of direct measures of food insecurity at the individual level. From a demographic perspective understanding how food insecurity impacts youth is increasingly important as youth represent an increasing proportion of the population in many developing countries, including sub-Saharan Africa (UN Population Fund 2006). Understanding the impact of food insecurity on African youth is also increasingly important from an economic perspective. In the past few years predictions, based on economic trends at the regional and national levels, have suggested broad improvements (mainly in Asia) in food security. In contrast, the predictions for many countries within sub-Saharan Africa were for minimal reductions or even worsening of the food insecurity situation (Benson et al. 2008; Runge et al. 2003). These predictions were based generally on forecasts of economic growth and continuing declines in real food prices. In marked contrast to many other countries, Ethiopia has been experiencing a steady increase in food prices since 2004, culminating in the 2007–08 food crisis spike. Both compared to world markets (Ulimwengu et al. 2009) and to neighboring countries (Honda et al. 2008); the available data lead Ulimwengu and colleagues (2009) to conclude that, "it is obvious that since August 2004 the Ethiopia food price index has been consistently higher than the world index." (See Heady and Fan 2008 for further evidence of the extraordinary food inflation in Ethiopia.) The aim of this chapter is to examine if youth are being impacted by food insecurity, what factors protect them from food insecurity, what factors increase their risk, and the extent to which these factors are consistent over time.

Examining Ethiopia youth during a period of rapid price increases has clear implications for the global food crisis that occurred in 2007–08, and for future food crises. In 2007–08, food prices were increasing at a rapid pace, a trend that stands in stark contrast to the historical decline in food prices, but one that matches what has been occurring in Ethiopia since 2004. Upward pressure on food prices is projected to be felt most acutely by those populations already living at the margins of food security. Ethiopia is one such country with a large proportion of the population living at the margins with approximately 44 percent of its now 80 million people living below the World Bank's poverty line and approximately 40 percent of children under 5 nutritionally stunted. FAO food balance sheets are also suggestive: mean per capita caloric income is estimated at around 2,000 kcal. Although the relative impacts are contested, the global food crisis has its roots in the use of grains for nonfuel purposes, poor harvests, and natural disasters in 2005–06, rising demand for grain-fed meat, and increasing costs of fertilizer. In a prescient analysis, Ford Runge and colleagues (2003) asked what would happen to the prevalence of hunger (a severe state of food insecurity) in sub-Saharan African if the price of staple foods increased such that individuals were able to purchase 10 percent fewer calories, a shift that would be associated with a 20 percent increase in food prices. Under this scenario the total number of food insecure people was projected to increase by 120 million. Few studies have assessed the extent to which rising food prices co-occur with rising levels of food insecurity, and fewer still have examined the impact on adolescents, a large but understudied segment of many developing country populations.

Others studies have suggested that food prices may not have the assumed negative impact on food insecurity. Aksoy and Isik-Dikmelik (2008) argue that low food prices might actually not be pro-poor because a majority of households in developing countries are "marginal" net food buyers. That is, they spend only a fraction of their income on food purchases and therefore would not be adversely affected by rising food prices. Net food buyers also have higher incomes, on average, than net food sellers in the countries that they studied. Higher food prices, they continue, essentially transfer income from the higher income food buyers to poorer net food sellers. The extent to which high food prices cause food insecurity will depend on the proportion of the population that allocates a large fraction of their income on food purchases. In the empirical section of the Aksoy and Isik-Dikmelik paper they note that Ethiopia sits precariously among a subset of countries with a high proportion of vulnerable households or households that spend a significant share of their income on food purchases. For this reason, it is expected that in the Ethiopian case high food prices will have a negative impact on poor households.

The above analyses and arguments are broadly similar to those made in the media and policy-oriented outlets (e.g., Collier 2008:70) as well as discussed by individuals living the study area (see below) suggesting that rural farmers are profiting from the rising food prices. The basic argument is that rural farmers may benefit from selling their crops at higher prices, while urban households will suffer because they are forced to purchase foods at a higher cost. This line of argument is, again, based on the assumption that rural farmers are net food sellers, which may or may not be the case. If true, then the food crisis based on rapid rises in food costs will potentially lead to a reversal in food insecurity trends: urban households may be more likely than rural households to be food insecure. This trend has been noted in the popular media: for instance, one paper quotes a rural cooperative farming president in Ethiopia as saying, "Think of all the poor people in the towns, at least you can feed your family, even if only with some toasted barley. In the cities, there are people that only eat once every two days" (Benequista 2008). The hypothesis that rural farmers are benefiting or at least not feeling the full negative impacts has not yet been tested.

In the face of economic crisis, individuals will enact various coping strategies that may mitigate negative impacts. In the livelihoods literature (Corbett 1988; Devereux 2001) and the anthropological literature (Dirks 1980) scholars have noted that households may rely on their social capital to buffer individual members when the household experiences a shock. By drawing on the resources of other households during difficult times, individuals might not experience food insecurity, or may experience it to a lesser degree. These "horizontal" redistributive networks are hypothesized to be particularly effective when households experience asynchronous shocks. Networks are also likely to be effective when households are linked with other wealthy households that have surplus resources to share out (Hadley et al. 2007). The efficacy

of redistributive networks has been hypothesized to be vulnerable to community-wide shocks; this is referred to as covariate risk. When all members of a community, and hence within a network, experience a shock and no one has surplus resources, then being a member of redistributive networks may not protect households from food insecurity (see, e.g., Adams 1993; Sukkary-Stolba 1989; Devereux 2001). Thus, the global food crisis in addition to increasing the prevalence of food insecurity and shifting sites of vulnerability may also render redistributive networks ineffective. We assess this issue in our analysis below.

Much of the research on food insecurity has focused on mothers and children so little is known about the impact of the crisis on youth. It is possible that households are experiencing heightened levels of food insecurity because of rising food costs but that adolescents may not show evidence of increased food insecurity. This would be the case if adult household members protected or buffered younger household members during periods of food insecurity or during economic crises. Buffering may also be preferentially doled out such that only certain members benefit from this protection (Quisumbing 2003). Such intrahousehold biases in food allocation have been widely noted (although see Haddad et al. 1996). Evidence from Ethiopia and elsewhere suggests that it is often the youngest individuals in a household and girls and women who bear the brunt of food insecurity in households. Consistent with theoretical expectation and the empirical observations, recent popular writings on the global food crisis have also singled out women and children as the most vulnerable to the experience of food insecurity (Benson et al. 2008). Indeed, some evidence from our earlier study in Ethiopia suggests that there is gender bias in the youth experience of food insecurity, but that the bias exists only among the poorest households (Hadley et al. 2008). Theory, the media, and previous results suggest that as the household food security situation deteriorates certain members are buffered potentially at the expense of others.

These various claims about the impact of the global food crisis on food insecurity and the regional and intrahousehold distribution of food insecurity have been difficult to assess, in part because few large-scale surveys include information on food insecurity. Rarer still are surveys that also include an independent assessment of the experiences of food insecurity within households, especially among adolescents. Finally, existing food insecurity assessments are often cross sectional in nature and rely on proxy indicators of food insecurity. Here we use data from a population-representative longitudinal sample of youth in rural, semiurban, and urban settings in Ethiopia to address the following questions:

1. Are adolescents experiencing higher levels of food insecurity because of the rise in food prices?

2. Is the experience of youth food insecurity being felt equally among youth in urban, semiurban, and rural households?

3. Is there any evidence of gender bias in the experience of youth food insecurity?

4. Are redistributive networks equally protective when food prices are rising?

5. Is youth food insecurity associated with poorer health?

METHODS

Study Design and Population

Data for this study come from the ongoing Jimma Longitudinal Family Survey of Youth (JLFSY). The JLFSY began in 2006 and is a longitudinal study of adolescents designed to examine the social and economic determinants of adolescent health and well-being. The study population includes urban, semiurban, and rural settings in and around the town of Jimma, Ethiopia. The town of Jimma, three nearby small towns, and the rural areas around each town were purposively selected to represent a range of ecological and development contexts. Stratified random sampling was used in each of the sites to select households for inclusion in the study. The study had a target sample of 2,100 adolescents and used a two-stage sampling plan. At the first stage, households were randomly sampled from within each study site with the sample size in each site determined by the relative proportion of the study population in the site and the overall target sample size. In the second stage, one adolescent boy and one adolescent girl were randomly selected from each household using a Kish table. This sampling plan produced representative samples of households and adolescent boys and girls ages 13 to 17 in Jimma Town, the three outlying towns, and nine rural peasant associations. The study selected 13 to 17 year olds to capture the major transitions into adulthood experienced by youth (e.g., exit from school, start of work, initiation of sexual activity, entry into marriage, and start of child bearing). Approximately 3,700 households were initially screened, which resulted in a sample of 2,106 boys and girls ages 13 to 17 years. Approximately one and one-half years later the same adolescents were reinterviewed using a similar survey instrument that included the food insecurity items from the baseline survey. In the analysis presented here we use data for 2,084 boys and girls for whom there was no missing information on the variables of interest.

The household questionnaire included a household registry that collected sociodemographic information on all current resident and nonresident household members including information on their weekly income. This information was aggregated to produce a household level measure of income. The second stage adolescent interview was conducted by an interviewer of the same sex as the adolescent respondent and was conducted in private at a later date. The adolescent questionnaire focused on issues related to education, health, and youth experiences of food insecurity. The first round household and adolescent interviews were completed in mid 2005–06 and the second round in 2007. All survey data were doubled entered using SPSS Data Entry templates. All participants provided consent and all study protocols were reviewed by appropriate ethical review boards.

Adolescent Food Insecurity Items

Adolescent insecurity was measured with three items, all of which were adapted from published food insecurity scales used in developing countries (Swindale and Bilinsky 2006). The items were included after much discussion with the interviewing team and pilot testing and reflect what appear to be universal expressions of food insecurity (Swindale and Bilinsky 2006). The items included whether in the three months prior to the interview, the respondent worried about the possibility of a reduction in the food supply, experienced a reduction in the number of meals consumed, or skipped a whole day without eating because of a lack of food or lack of money to buy food. In the analysis presented here, adolescents who responded yes to one or more of the three food insecurity items were considered food insecure.

Socioeconomic Status and Capitals

To predict which youth were most vulnerable to food insecurity, we used in our multivariate analysis the highest education of any member of a household, a measure of household asset ownership, and a measure of the ease with which a household could access a variety of services through informal means. These correspond loosely with human capital, economic capital, and social capital (Yaro 2004). Household asset ownership was measured by a composite index based on ownership of various durable goods and the materials used in the construction of the household's residence. The index was constructed using principal components analysis following a procedure used by the Demographic and Health Surveys. Social capital has been defined by many different scholars, most notably by Bourdieu (1986) and Coleman (1988). Social capital is defined by Bourdieu as "the aggregate of the actual or potential resources which are linked to possession of a durable network of more or less institutionalized relationships of mutual acquaintance and recognition . . . which provides each of its members with the backing of the collectively-owned capital a 'credential' which entitles them to credit" (1986:249). In other words, social capital measures the extent to which an individual can reliably draw on the resources of a network within which he or she is embedded. The social capital construct was measured in the JLFSY survey questionnaire by reading a list of tasks and asking the household head how difficult it would be to get help with each task from someone outside of the household. The questionnaire therefore directly assessed the "credit" an individual had within a large social network by recording expectations of assistance. The tasks included finding someone to watch your children; borrowing a small amount of salt or coffee; getting help with a task like lifting a heavy object or engaging in agricultural work; borrowing 25 kg of flour, maize, teff, or wheat; borrowing money for medicine for a child; and borrowing 10, 50, and 100 Ethiopian birr. Possible responses were very easy, easy, difficult, and very difficult. Reliability analysis on these items revealed a Cronbach's alpha of 0.84, which suggests that the individual items are highly related to one another, and can be summed together to create a single measure of social capital. The measures of capitals were collected at the household level and in the baseline study only.

Statistical Analysis

In general the analytic strategy was to compare the prevalence and distribution of youth food insecurity in the first round and the second round, assess how food insecurity varied between rural, urban, and semiurban sites, and test for gendered differences in the food insecurity experience. Bivariate tests (e.g., the chi-square test) were used to statistically assess whether the observed differences between rounds were significantly different at the 0.05 level of statis-

tical significance. To assess changes in the relationship between independent variables and year of the survey we estimated statistical interactions between year of survey and gender, household income, highest education in the household, household social capital, and whether the household was in a rural setting. All youth contributed data from 2006 and 2007. To account for the nonindependence of the youth's observations we used general estimating equations (GEE) models to calculate corrected standard errors (using SAS ver. 9.1).

RESULTS

Measures of adolescent food insecurity from two survey rounds and household characteristics from the baseline survey were available for 1,874 adolescents, which represent approximately 90 percent of the baseline adolescent sample. Of these, 48 percent ($n = 895$) of these youth were female. At the baseline survey, the mean age of the adolescent sample was 14.8 years. Youth were approximately evenly divided across urban, semiurban, and rural communities. Other characteristics of the study sample have been published elsewhere (Hadley et al. 2008). Household income varied widely across study areas. In the urban setting, mean household income was 171 Birr per week ($SD = 248$ Birr/week; $1 =\sim$9.6 Ethiopian Birr); in the semiurban setting, it was 127 Birr per week ($SD = 196$ Birr/week), and in rural settings it was 39 Birr per week ($SD = 51$ Birr/week). Borrowing the consumption loss estimates from Ulimwengu et al. (2009), a 50 percent increase in food prices would result in a consumption loss of 1,089 Ethiopian Birr for rural households; this represents approximately 54 percent of their household budget. For urban households, a 50 percent price increase would lead to a 949 Ethiopian Birr consumption loss, which represents 10 percent of the household budget. These figures can be interpreted as the Birr needed for a household to maintain stable food consumption levels in the face of rising food prices. Clearly, poor households and rural households would be most affected by food price increases. Although household income and the other capitals were measured only in 2006, shortly before the first round adolescent survey, we expect the relative position of households in the distribution of socioeconomic position to have remained relatively stable over the approximately one and one-half year interval between the first and second round adolescent surveys. The mean highest level of education achieved by anyone in the household was 8.4 years ($SD = 3.6$).

TABLE 1   Proportion of Youth in the JLFSY Reporting Experiencing Each Behavior in the Three Months Prior to the Survey in 2006 and 2007

During the last three months:	2006 (yes,%)	2007 (yes,%)
Were you ever worried that you would run out of food because you did not have food or money to buy food?	17	41
Did you ever reduce the size of your meals because you did not have enough food or money to buy food?	18	40
Did you ever go the whole day without eating because you did not have food or money to buy food?	4.6	6.2

Note: All differences are statistically significant ($p < 0.05$).

Are Youth Food Insecure and Is the Prevalence Increasing?

Yes. As is clear in Table 1 there was a clear increase in the experience of food insecurity among youth. In the 2006 survey round, about 16 percent of youth reported being worried about having enough food. In the 2007 survey round, when the prices of staple crops had increased (Honda et al. 2008), this proportion rose to 42 percent—a more than twofold increase in the prevalence of worrying about having enough food ($p < .01$). Similar increases were evident in the other two indicators of food insecurity: whereas in 2006, 18 percent of youth said that they had to reduce the amount of food they ate because of shortages of food or money, in the 2007 survey round more than 40 percent of youth reported reducing their food consumption ($p < .01$). The proportion of youth who reported missing an entire day of food also increased by more than 25 percent (from 4.9 percent to 6.2 percent; $p < .02$). The prevalence of youth food insecurity (defined as responding yes to at least one of the food insecurity items) was 20 percent in 2006 and 48 percent in 2007; a statistically significant increase ($p < .01$).

Is There Any Evidence of Gender Bias in the Experience of Food Insecurity?

A qualified yes. Boys were more likely to become food insecure. In the 2006 survey round, 15 percent of boys and 25 percent of girls were food insecure ($p < .0001$). Between the 2006 and 2007 study rounds, boys were more likely to become food insecure (29 percent of girls became food insecure vs. 38 percent of boys; $p < .0001$). This increase in boys' food insecurity erased the gender difference in food insecurity identified in the 2006 survey round. In 2007, 50 percent of boys and 46 percent of girls were food insecure, a difference that was statistically significant ($p = .04$).

Is Food Insecurity Being Felt Equally among Youth in Urban, Semiurban, and Rural Households?

No. To assess whether youth in different areas were differentially experiencing the increases in food prices we examined the change in the prevalence of adolescent food insecurity across three different levels of urbanization. This analysis revealed a clear gradient of increased youth food insecurity (see Figure 1; see below for discussion of the wealth differences). In 2006, 23 percent of the urban youth responded yes to at least one of the food insecurity questions, as did 20 percent of semiurban youth and 17 percent of rural youth. In 2007, the food insecurity situation was quite different. There was an 8 percent increase in the prevalence of youth food insecurity among urban youth, but a

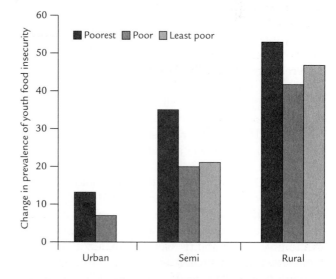

FIGURE 1   Percent increase in the prevalence of youth food insecurity by study locale and relative wealth bracket. Note that there was no change in the prevalence of youth food insecurity among the least poor urban group. In the Y-axis, the change in youth food insecurity occurs between 2006 and 2007.

TABLE 2   Generalized Estimating Equation Estimates of the Probability of Youth Food Insecurity

Variable	Beta	SE	p
Intercept	0.393	0.236	.0957
Social capital (higher = more)	−0.094	0.024	.0001
Year of survey (2007 = 1)	0.329	0.291	.2582
Social capital × Year	0.091	0.030	.0023
Highest education in household	−0.072	0.022	.001
Year × Highest education	−0.042	0.027	.1214
Household wealth index	−0.496	0.091	<.0001
Year × Household wealth index	−0.158	0.115	.17
Gender (Male = 1)	−0.688	0.115	<.0001
Year × Gender	0.766	0.140	<.0001
Semiurban	−0.352	0.151	.0197
Year × Semi urban	0.695	0.178	<.0001
Rural	−1.164	0.213	<.0001
Year × Rural	1.073	0.257	<.0001

27 percent increase in the prevalence of youth food insecurity among semiurban youth, and an astounding 46 percent increase among rural youth. Youth in the poorest households experienced the largest increase in the prevalence of food insecurity. The increases were primarily because of a larger number of youth worrying about food and having to reduce their intake of food. There was no significant change across study locales in the percent of people who reported missing a full day of food because they lacked food or money to buy food.

Do Predictors of Vulnerability Change Over Time?

A qualified yes. Next we fit a logistic model to further explore patterns of vulnerability to youth food insecurity. The logistic regression model predicting food insecurity (yes = 1) included covariates for gender, place of residence, baseline household asset score, baseline highest education in the household, baseline household social capital, and interactions with year of survey (results shown in Table 2). The results replicate what we have shown above and extend our understanding of vulnerability. Gender (male = 1) and the gender × year interaction terms are both significant showing that in 2006, males were less likely to experience food insecurity but that the difference between males and females disappeared by 2007. In 2006, rural and semiurban sites had lower levels of youth food insecurity than did the urban sites, but by 2007, this had reversed so that youth in rural and semiurban areas experienced a significantly greater likelihood of food

insecurity than youth in urban areas. Similarly in 2006, high levels of household social capital were associated with a lower likelihood of youth food insecurity. But in 2007, when more households were experiencing food insecurity or at risk of being food insecure, differences in the occurrence of youth food insecurity across levels of social capital were no longer significant. In all years, however, higher levels of household wealth and high levels of education in the household were protective against youth food insecurity. The wealth effect was most pronounced for the poorest groups.

Do Youth Who Become Food Insecure Also Self-Report Poorer Health?

Yes. Youth health was assessed by self-reports in 2006 and again in 2007. Over 25 percent of youth reported worse health in 2007 than in 2006. Changes in youth health were associated with changes in food insecurity status ($p × 0.002$) in the expected direction. Among those youth who went from being food insecure in 2006 to food secure in 2007, 19.8 percent reported worse health in 2007 than they did in 2006. Among youth who went from being food secure in 2006 to food insecure in 2007, 31 percent reported worse health in 2007. Among youth who were food secure in both study rounds, 23 percent reported poorer health in 2007 than in 2006. Finally, among youth who were food insecure in both rounds, 27 percent reported worse health. The greatest reduction in health status was among those who became insecure and the smallest reduction in health status was among those who became food secure.

DISCUSSION

Our results suggest the environment of dramatically increasing food costs is negatively impacting youth in Ethiopia, a country known for its enduring food security challenges. Our results also show that youth in the poorest households are most affected, and this is especially true in rural areas. The results also show that boys were more likely to become food insecure between survey rounds. We also show that social capital loses its ability to protect youth from food insecurity during the follow-up survey round but traditional indicators of socioeconomic status that do not rely on the surplus of others remain protective. These empirical results suggest that broad generalizations about the current food crisis might obscure important regional and local level variation. They further suggest that predictors of variability in food insecurity reflect a dynamic interaction between local cultural and economic factors and global economic trends.

A limitation of the study is that the food insecurity scale has not been formally validated. However, there are five reasons to believe the scale is valid. Youth's independent assessment of food insecurity is associated with the household head's independent assessment of household food insecurity (Hadley et al. 2008). Youth living in households with lower socioeconomic status are more likely to be food insecure, consistent with theoretical expectations. Response frequencies decline with increasing severity of the item. Youth who respond yes to food insecurity items were less likely to have consumed high quality diets rich in animal source foods (unpublished data). And, the items are similar in nature to those asked elsewhere in the world and are consistent with ethnographic studies of food insecurity in East Africa (Coates et al. 2006). Still, more study is needed of these items and how they operate in large, longitudinal studies.

The evidence we present here clearly demonstrates that rural and semiurban youth are experiencing the brunt of the burden when food prices rise. This is contrary to the claims found among some urban dwellers and those reported in media outlets that suggest a possible reversal in the rural–urban food insecurity pattern. Additional evidence that rural individuals are more affected by food insecurity comes from qualitative data collected in 2008. We undertook a freelisting exercise and asked rural and urban households to list the most powerful barriers to achieving the good life ("turu hiwot" in Amharic; "jireenya gaari" in afaan Oromo). Rural residents were substantially more likely than urban dwellers to report access to food as a barrier to the good life. Finally, rural dwellers expressed concern over the availability and cost of seeds and fertilizer. These results are all consistent with the suggestion of Aksoy and Isik-Dikmelik (2008) that in areas where many households are poor and net-food purchasers, such as Ethiopia, rural dwellers will suffer (see also Ulimwengu et al. 2009 for further support for this idea).

A second key finding is that boys were more likely than girls to become food insecure, although girls were more likely to be food insecure in the baseline round. This gendered shift in food insecurity meant that at the time of the follow-up survey, adolescent boys and girls were equally likely to report experiencing food insecurity. Others have hinted at gendered shifts in vulnerability to food. For instance, famine scholars have long noted that some evidence seems to suggest that during famines, there is a slight female advantage as indicated by lower odds of death relative to men (Macintyre 2002). Macintyre suggests that if the finding is true (and not due to biases in data collection) then it may be due to biological (e.g., greater proportion of body fat) or sociocultural factors. She hypothesizes that women may have greater knowledge of famine foods or, more likely, that a woman's "common role as cook and food preparer may provide some material advantage for them" (Macintyre 2002:250). In the 2006 survey round, girls living in food insecure households were more likely to be food insecure (Hadley et al. 2008). One hypothesis to explain the relatively greater rise in male food insecurity is that girls in poor households experience food insecurity up to a point, and then, rather than experiencing increasing deprivation as the household suffers, other members who had been buffered then become food insecure. We call this the staggered deprivation hypothesis, which to our knowledge has not been formally tested in other settings. It is possible that economically rational households attempt to manage the stress that individual household members experience, rather than allow one member to experience increasing deprivation that would lead to higher costs in terms of lost productivity and health care expenditures. An additional explanation builds on an earlier suggestion we made based on the ethnographic work of Mains (Mains 2007). Mains' work and others suggest that young men had differential access to alternative food and monetary sources. We hypothesized that this allowed young males to achieve a higher level of food security. In the face of the current food crisis, when many people are struggling, access to these alternative food and cash resources may be substantially curtailed. As one informant mentioned, "there are no more invitations in Ethiopia," indicating that people were less often inviting each other to their homes, or to restaurants (personal communication,

Daniel Mains, August 2008). If this were the case, then it would effectively eliminate the pathway through which young males achieved food security in the earlier survey round.

The results of the regression model offer some support here: social capital, while protective of youth food insecurity in 2006 was no longer protective in 2007, and certainly not in mid-2008. Although the household measure of social capital does not directly capture adolescent male's networks, it does suggest that in general the efficacy of social networks has been reduced during the current inflationary period in food prices. Importantly, the other measures of capital and socioeconomic position that are not network based were significant in both years. This suggests that when the entire population suffers a shock, what has been referred to as covariant risk (Devereux 2001), redistributive networks lose their efficacy and social ecologies are reconfigured.

The results for gender and social capital hint at a broader theoretical implication of our study: Patterns of vulnerability are not static. Or, to borrow from Watts and Bohle (1993), in our study the spaces of vulnerability have been reconfigured, and we suspect are continuing to be reconfigured as prices further rise and then fall. Whereas in the baseline round important risk factors appeared to be low material capital, low social capital, and female gender; in the follow-up round gender and social capital were no longer predictive of youth food insecurity. And, rural dwellers who were not at elevated risk in the baseline, were now at heightened risk of food insecurity. Importantly, our study attempts to link these local level factors to larger global processes, and suggests that spaces of vulnerability are patterned by local level gender norms, norms of sharing and reciprocity, and place, and that these in turn are impacted by what is happening at the global level. In this way our study attempts to fill a gap in biocultural anthropology: the link between the global and local (Leatherman 2005).

In terms of direct application, our results suggest that relatively simple to administer instruments may be useful for assessing the impact of economic shocks, including the impact of such events on youth. In this sense, our results are comparable to other work that has used experienced-based measures to assess the impact of economic crises on food insecurity. For instance, Studdert et al. (2001) used a modified version of the Radimer-Cornell scale to show that food insecurity was highly prevalent during the Indonesian economic crisis, which was a time that also saw a rapid and dramatic rise in the price of staple foods. Piaseu and Mitchell (2004) also report high levels of food insecurity among poor urban Thai households during the 1997 economic crisis. Our study differs from these earlier studies in two key ways. First, these studies measured the food insecurity of individuals in the household by asking an adult head of household, whereas the present study explicitly asked youth about food insecurity. It is especially important to assess youth food insecurity through experience-based measures because there are no established anthropometric norms for adolescents in developing counties. Also, collecting dietary data on youths may be difficult through the household head because youth may take meals outside of the house without the household head's knowledge. For younger children dietary recalls using the household head may be appropriate because young children and infants are unlikely to obtain a substantial amount of food on their own. Second, the two other studies that have sought to assess the food insecurity consequences of economic crises have been cross-sectional; the high prevalence of food insecurity identified in these studies is assumed to represent a marked increased over precrises levels. The JLFSY results reported here compare levels of food insecurity among the same individuals at multiple points as food and nonfood prices increase dramatically.

In conclusion, these findings suggest that youth are not adequately buffered from household food insecurity. Lacking data on adult women and young children we cannot say that youth are more or less vulnerable to the food crisis than adults, but our results clearly show that they are vulnerable. Despite this vulnerability, youth seem to be generally forgotten as a vulnerable group. This is unfortunate, as elsewhere we have shown that food insecure youth, especially girls, are more likely to miss school, consume low diversity diets, reported poor health, and lack the energy to carry out everyday activities (Belachew et al. 2008; Hadley et al. 2008). Our results also powerfully demonstrate that patterns of vulnerability are not static and instead reflect a dynamic interplay between the local and the global. That is, predictors of youth food insecurity varied across the study years. This is important because it undermines some of our assumptions about who is vulnerable. Our results, thus, offer a cautionary tale to broad generalities about who is vulnerable to food insecurity during the food crises. Future research would do well to examine pathways through which youth can be targeted. Failure do so many lead to a large population of youth being negatively impacted during a critical period of their lives as they transition into adult roles.

NOTE

Acknowledgments. We gratefully acknowledge the support of the David and Lucille Packard Foundation and the National Science Foundation. We also acknowledge the other Jimma Longitudinal Family Survey of Youth team members Kifle Wolde Michael, Dennis Hogan, Challi Jira, and Abebe Gebre Mariam and all of the participants in the longitudinal study. We also acknowledge the insights of Daniel Mains.

REFERENCES CITED

Adams, Alayne 1993 Food Insecurity in Mali: Exploring the Role of the Moral Economy. IDS Bulletin 24(4):41–51.

Aksoy, M. Ataman, and Aylin Isik-Dikmelik 2008 Are Low Food Prices Pro-Poor? Net Food Buyers and Sellers in Low-Income Countries. Policy Research Working Paper, 4642. Washington, DC: World Bank.

Belachew, Tefera, Craig Hadley, and David Lindstrom 2008 Differentials in Measures of Dietary Quality among Adolescents in Jimma Zone, Southwest Ethiopia. Ethiopian Medical Journal 46(2):123–132.

Benequista, Nicholas 2008 Ethiopia: A Model of African Food Aid is Now in Trouble. Christian Science Monitor, May 6. Electronic document, http://csmonitor.com/2008/0506/p01s06-woaf.html, accessed August 31, 2009.

Benson, Todd, Nicholas Minot, John Pender, Miguel Robles, and Joachim von Braun 2008 Global Food Crisis: Monitoring and Assessing Impact to Inform Policy Responses. Washington, DC: International Food Policy Research Institute (IFPRI).

Bourdieu, Pierre 1986 The Forms of Capital. *In* Handbook of Theory and Research for the Sociology of Education. J. Richardson, ed. Pp. 241–258. New York: Greenwood.

Coates, Jennifer, Edward A. Frongillo, Beatrice L. Rogers, Patrick Webb, Parke E. Wilde, and Robert Houser 2006 Commonalities in the Experience of Household Food Insecurity across Cultures: What are Measures Missing? Journal of Nutrition 136(5):1438S–1448S.

Collier, Paul 2008 The Politics of Hunger. Foreign Affairs 87(6):67–79.

Coleman, James S. 1988 Social Capital in the Creation of Human Capital. American Journal of Sociology 94:S95–S120.

Corbett, Jane 1988 Famine and Household Coping Strategies. World Development 16(9):1099–1112.

Devereux, Stephen 2001 Livelihood Insecurity and Social Protection: A Re-Emerging Issue in Rural Development. Development Policy Review 19(4):507–519.

Dirks, Robert 1980 Social Responses During Food Shortages and Famine. Current Anthropology 21(1):21–44.

Haddad, Lawrence J., Christine Peña, Chizuru Nishida, Agnes R. Quisumbing, and Alison T. Slack 1996 Food Security and Nutrition Implications of Intrahousehold Bias: A Review of Literature. Discussion Paper, 19. Washington, DC: IFPRI.

Hadley, Craig, David Lindstrom, Fasil Tessema, and Tefera Belachew 2008 Gender Bias in the Food Insecurity Experience of Ethiopian Adolescents. Social Science and Medicine 66(2):427–438.

Hadley, Craig, Monique B. Mulder, and Emily Fitzherbert 2007 Seasonal Food Insecurity and Perceived Social Support in Rural Tanzania. Public Health Nutrition 10(6):544–551.

Heady, Derek, and Shenggen Fan 2008 Anatomy of a Crisis: The Causes and Consequences of Surging Food Prices. Washington, DC: IFPRI.

Honda, Jiro, Zaijin Zhan, and Alun Thomas 2008 The Federal Democratic Republic of Ethiopia: Selected Issues, 08–259. Washington, DC: IMF.

Leatherman, Thomas 2005 A Space of Vulnerability in Poverty and Health: Political-Ecology and Biocultural Analysis. Ethos 33(1):46–70.

Macintyre, Kate 2002 Famine and the Female Mortality Advantage. *In* Famine Demography: Perspectives From the Past and Present. T. Dyson and O. O Grada, eds. Pp. 240–260. New York: Oxford University Press.

Mains, Daniel C. 2007 We are Just Sitting and Waiting: Aspirations, Unemployment, and Status among Urban Young Men in Jimma, Ethiopia. Ph.D. dissertation, Department of Anthropology, Emory University.

Piaseu, Noppawan, and Pamela Mitchell 2004 Household Food Insecurity among Urban Poor in Thailand. Journal of Nursing Scholarship 36(2):115–121.

Quisumbing, Agnes R., ed. 2003 Household Decisions, Gender, and Development: A Synthesis of Recent Research. Washington, DC: IFPRI.

Runge, C. Ford, Benjamin Senauer, Philip G. Pardey, and Mark W. Rosegrant 2003 Ending Hunger in Our Lifetime: Food Security and Globalization. Baltimore: John Hopkins University Press.

Studdert, Lisa J., Edward A. Frongillo Jr., and Pascale Valois 2001 Household Food Insecurity was Prevalent in Java during Indonesia's Economic Crisis. Journal of Nutrition 131(10):2685–2691.

Sukkary-Stolba, Soheir 1989 Indigenous Institutions and Adaptation to Famine: The Case of the Western Sudan. *In* African Food Systems in Crisis. Part 1. R. Huss-Ashmore and S. Katz, eds. Pp. 281–294. New York: Gordon and Breach.

Swindale, Anne, and Paula Bilinsky 2006 Development of a Universally Applicable Household Food Insecurity Measurement Tool: Process, Current Status, and Outstanding Issues. Journal of Nutrition 136(5):1449S–1452S.

Ulimwengu, John M., Sindu Workneh, and Zelekawork Paulos 2009 Impact of Soaring Food Price in Ethiopia: Does Location Matter? IFPRI Discussion Paper, 00846. Washington, DC: IFPRI.

UN Population Fund (UNFPA) 2006 State of World Population 2006: United Nations Population Fund. Electronic document, http://www.unfpa.org/upload/lib_pub_file/650_filename_sowp06-en.pdf, accessed August 31, 2009.

Watts, Michael J., and Hans G. Bohle 1993 The Space of Vulnerability: The Causal Structure of Hunger and Famine. Progress in Human Geography 17(1):43–67.

Weiser, Sheri D., Karen Leiter, David R. Bangsberg, Lisa M. Butler, Fiona Percy-de Korte, Zakhe Hlanze, Nthabiseng Phaladze, Vincent Iacopino, and Michele Heisler 2007 Food Insufficiency is Associated with High-Risk Sexual Behavior among Women in Botswana and Swaziland. PLoS Med 4(10):1589–1597.

Yaro, Joseph A. 2004 Theorizing Food Insecurity: Building a Livelihood Vulnerability Framework for Researching Food Insecurity. Norsk Geografisk Tidsskrift-Norwegian Journal of Geography 58(1):23–37.

14

Chinese Table Manners

You Are How *You Eat*

Eugene Cooper

I had been looking forward to this dinner with an important client for over a week. We were going to close the biggest deal of my career. He arrived on time, and I ordered a bit of wine. It was a fancy restaurant and I was trying to behave appropriately; I tucked my napkin neatly on my lap and lifted my wine glass carefully with my little finger extended in the way I had always seen it done. But what began well began to go awry. I looked on in horror as my client ladled a number of different dishes together into a soup bowl, lifted it to his mouth and began to shovel it in. I was so embarrassed by this display of bad manners that I hoped no one I knew would happen by. My face must have betrayed my thoughts, but my client did not let on. He simply asked if I was not enjoying my food because I had left the dishes flat on the table. This took me by surprise, because I realized for the first time that he was looking at me and finding *my* behavior odd. Our smiles became realizations and turned to laughter. Luckily, we had a good sense of humor about our ethnocentrism. Somebody should have warned us; this could have been a real disaster.

Consider yourself warned. Table manners, like a great many everyday events, are heavily laden with cultural meaning. Understanding culturally prescribed behaviors is of practical importance, not merely interesting. More anthropologists need to be involved in cross-cultural training for situations where there is likely to be interaction between people from different cultures or ethnic groups.

As you read this selection, ask yourself the following questions:

- How does one determine which culture's table manners are better? Why do we judge people by their manners?
- What are the important distinctions in Chinese food?
- Which food is the most basic and a necessary part of every Chinese meal? What about your own culture?
- What does it mean in China if you leave your rice bowl on the table while eating from it?
- What is the overriding rule of Chinese table customs?
- How do the Chinese feel about eating alone? Why?

The following terms discussed in this selection are included in the Glossary at the back of the book:

cultural values
ethnology
symbol

"Etiquette of this kind (not putting half eaten meat back in the bowl, [not] wiping one's nose on one's sleeve) is not superficial, a matter for the surface rather than the depths; refined ways of acting are so internalized as to make alternative behavior truly 'disgusting,' 'revolting,' 'nauseous,' turning them into some of the most highly charged and deeply felt of intra-social differences, so that 'rustic' behavior is not merely quaint but barbarous" (Goody 1982:140).

"Probably no common practice is more diversified than the familiar one of eating in company, for what Europeans consider as correct and decent may by other races be looked upon as wrong or indelicate. Similarly, few social observances provide more opportunities for offending the stranger than the etiquette of the table"(Hammerton 1936:23).

Cooper, Eugene. "Chinese Table Manners: You Are *How* You Eat." Reproduced by permission of the Society for Applied Anthropology (SfAA), from *Human Organization* 45, no. 2 (1986):179–184.

Our shrinking world makes encounters with people of other cultures increasingly common in our life experiences. Whether in the conduct of business, in interactions with our "ethnic" neighbors, or as visitors to other countries, we are frequently called on to communicate with others whose assumptions about what constitutes appropriate behavior are widely different from our own.

In such contexts, it is often difficult to know whether habits and customs one takes for granted in one's own home may be creating unfavorable impressions in one's host's home. No less an authority than Confucius, writing more than two thousand years ago, was aware of the potential difficulties involved in intercultural communication, and provided the following advice: "When entering a country inquire of its customs. When crossing a border, inquire of the prohibitions" (Li Chi 1971:17).

Among such customs and prohibitions, those associated with behavior at the table can make an enormous difference in the way one is perceived by a foreign host.

As regards the Chinese in particular, the way one handles oneself at the table gives off signals of the clearest type as to what kind of a person one is, and it is all too easy to offend, as I hope to show. At the same time, however, it is easy enough to equip oneself with a few simple points to bear in mind that will not only pleasantly surprise one's Chinese host, but also convince him or her that one is a sensitive, cultivated, courteous, respectful, and considerate individual.

Surprisingly, for a civilization which has generated so many handbooks of its various cuisines, China has not produced any popular guidebooks for table manners of the Emily Post variety. The field, of course, has for the most part been preempted by the Li Chi—records of etiquette and ceremonial—most of which is said to date from the early Han. Indeed, many of the themes which characterize contemporary Chinese table manners are present in the minute descriptions of behaviors appropriate to people of various stations in all the gradations of Han social structure, such as the prescription to yield or defer. However, one is hard pressed to find a general rough and ready guide to contemporary Chinese table manners of anything more than the most superficial kind, usually present in popular Chinese cookbooks for Western audiences.

The absence of attention to table manners may be the result of the fact that table manners are among those habits most taken for granted—rules no grown-up needs instruction in. A Chinese culinary enthusiast of my acquaintance assures me that table manners are not important in Chinese history, being far outweighed by the scarcity of food generally as the major

issue. Nevertheless, an examination of Chinese table manners provides sufficient contrast with Western table habits in terms of structure and performance, as to make significant features of Chinese etiquette emerge in comparison—features taken for granted by the native.

Those few who have written on the subject (Chang 1977; Hsü and Hsü 1977) generally qualify as bi-cultural individuals with sufficient experience of both Chinese and Western rules to tease out the areas of contrastive significance. My five years of field research (and eating) in Hong Kong, and eight years of marriage to a Chinese woman who taught me Chinese table manners as to a child, also qualify me for the assignment, although my former European colleagues at the University of Hong Kong might question my credentials as an expert on Western etiquette, to be sure.

BASIC STRUCTURES AND PARAPHERNALIA

To begin with, it is useful to consider K. C. Chang's (1977) broad outline of the important distinctions in Chinese food between food (*shih*) and drink (*yin*), and then within the category food, between *fan* (grain/rice) and *ts'ai* (dishes). Chang establishes a hierarchy with grain as the base, vegetables and fruit as next least expendable, and meat as most expendable in the preparation of a meal. Fish would probably fall between vegetables and meat at least as far as contemporary Hong Kong is concerned, particularly if one includes the enormous variety of preserved fish available.

In any event, it is fair to say that a Chinese meal is not a meal without *fan*. The morning food event, at which rice is not normally taken, or if so is taken as gruel, is not thought of as a meal. When Chinese speak of a full day's eating fare, it is two square meals per day rather than three. Thus rice (or grain) defines a meal, and its treatment and consumption are circumscribed in a number of ways.

It will be helpful, however, to lay out the general paraphernalia with which the diner is equipped, and the structure in which it is deployed before returning to the rules governing rice. On this subject, Hsü and Hsü (1977:304) have written:

> The typical Chinese dining table is round or square, the *ts'ai* dishes are laid in the center, and each participant in the meal is equipped with a bowl for *fan*, a pair of chopsticks, a saucer, and a spoon. All at the table take from the *ts'ai* dishes as they proceed with the meal.

> The *ts'ai* dishes are typically shared by all, and must be treated much as common property, whereas

one's bowl is a private place which comes directly in touch with the mouth. The chopsticks are of both the mouth and the table, and mediate between. They are thin, and when employed appropriately only touch the one piece or small quantity a person touches first. Many Westerners find the habit of sharing from a common plate potentially unhygienic, and one might be tempted to dismiss this as a bit of ethnocentricity. However, the point has recently been made by no less an authority than Communist party secretary Hu Yaobang, who called attention to the unsanitary character of traditional Chinese eating habits and urged change.

One employs the chopsticks to take from the common plate and place food in one's bowl, then one raises the bowl to the mouth and pushes food into the mouth with the chopsticks. Hsü and Hsü state, "The diner who lets his *fan* bowl stay on the table and eats by picking up lumps of *fan* from the bowl is expressing disinterest in or dissatisfaction with the food. If he or she is a guest in someone's house, that is seen as an open insult to the host" (1977:304). Since one's bowl is a private place, "good manners do not preclude resting a piece of meat (or other items) in one's bowl between bites" (1977:304). However, one never puts a partially chewed piece of anything back into one of the common plates (I would not have thought this necessary to mention; however, an otherwise culturally sensitive person I know had the audacity to do so recently so it may bear mentioning.) Also, it is extremely poor manners to suck or bite your chopsticks.

In some cases the bowl may be substituted for by a spoon, as, for example, when one goes out to lunch with one's workmates, and each diner is supplied with a flat plate piled high with rice topped with roast pork, chicken, duck and/or *lap cheong* (Chinese sausage), or with a helping of a single *ts'ai* dish (the latter known as *hui fan*).

Eating rice off a flat plate with chopsticks alone is not an easy task. Westerners exasperated with the use of chopsticks often feel their most intense frustration when trying to accomplish this task, and are often reduced to picking up small bits of rice with the ends of their chopsticks and placing them in the mouth. Seeming to pick at one's food in this way is not good manners and marks one as an incompetent foreign devil, confirming in most Chinese minds all of their previous prejudices about *guailos*.

No self-respecting Chinese would attempt to eat rice directly from a flat plate without first piling the rice onto, or scooping the rice into, a spoon. One eats the *ts'ai* or meat with one's chopsticks, but rice is most often carried to the mouth in a spoon. The spoon stands in for the bowl in the mini-context of an individual serving, and one can also think of the bowl itself as serving in the capacity of an enlarged spoon in the context of regular dining as well.

Rice is usually doled out from a common pot by the host or hostess. When someone has filled your rice bowl for you, it is accepted with two hands. To accept rice with one hand suggests disinterest, disrespect, and carelessness. One places the full bowl in front of oneself and waits until everyone has been served. It is very impolite to begin eating before everyone at the table has had his bowl filled with rice. When one has finished the rice in one's bowl, one does not continue to eat of the common *ts'ai* dishes. To eat *ts'ai* without rice in one's bowl is to appear a glutton interested only in *ts'ai*, of which one must consume a great deal to get full without rice. Depending on the degree of intimacy of a relationship, one may, when eating at the home of a friend or acquaintance, rise from the table to refill one's bowl with rice from the rice pot in the kitchen. However, at formal occasions one's host will usually be alert enough to notice when one's rice bowl is empty and move to fill it before one might be forced to request more rice. When one rises to get more rice, the host will usually insist on taking one's bowl and filling it. One may decline such assistance if the host is a close friend by simply saying "I'll serve myself."

At banquets one is expected to fill up on *ts'ai*, and consumption of too much rice may be a sign of disrespect to the quality of the *ts'ai* dishes. No rice should ever be left over in one's bowl at the end of the meal.

> As children we were always taught to leave not a single grain of *fan* in our bowl when we finished. Our elders strongly impressed on us that each single grain of rice or corn was obtained through the drops of sweat of the tillers of the soil (Hsü and Hsü 1977:308).

A corollary of this rule is never to take so much rice, or anything else for that matter, in your bowl as to be unable to finish it. It is also extremely disrespectful of the meal and of one's host to leave bits of rice on the table around one's bowl, and Chinese children are often told that each of these grains will materialize as a pockmark on the face of their future spouse.

As regards the *ts'ai*, it is important to note again that it is arrayed for all to share. Generally speaking, especially on formal occasions, one does not serve oneself without first offering to others, at least those seated immediately to either side. This applies also to the taking of tea, and one generally fills a neighbor's cup before taking tea for oneself. When tea is poured for you, it is customary to tap the table with your fingers to convey your thanks.

The overriding rule of Chinese table customs is deference. Defer to others in everything. Be conscious of the need to share what is placed in common. This means don't eat only from those dishes that you like.

One very common point of instruction from parents to children is that the best mannered person does not allow co-diners to be aware of what his or her favorite dishes are by his or her eating pattern (Hsü and Hsü 1977:304).

When taking from the common dishes one should also only take in such proportions that everyone else will be left with a roughly equivalent amount. It is polite to take the remains of a common *ts'ai* dish after a new dish has been brought out. The desirability of the remains is diminished by the introduction of a new dish, and the remains of the old become fair game. However, it is rather poor manners to incline a common plate toward oneself and scrape the remains into one's bowl. This "looking in the mirror" evokes the idea of narcissistic concern with oneself.

In general, young should defer to old in order of eating, and on formal occasions when guests are present children may even be excluded from the dining table until the adults are finished, or seated at a table separate from the adults. In the household of the boss of the factory where I did my fieldwork, apprentices commonly sat with the boss at the family table, but were relegated to the children's table at the New Year's feast.

A host will usually signal that it is appropriate to begin eating, after each person at the table has taken rice, by picking up his chopsticks and saying "*sik fan.*" When a guest has eaten his fill, he indicates that he is finished by putting down his chopsticks and encouraging others still eating to take their time. They in turn will inquire if the guest is full, and if he is he should say so. Upon finishing one may either remain at the table or leave. A guest of honor is expected to remain until all are finished.

In addition, one should be careful not to take large mouthfuls, to refrain from making noise while chewing, and to try to maintain the same pace of eating as others at the table. In contrast to Western etiquette in which "toothpicks are never used outside the privacy of one's room" (McLean 1941:63), toothpicks are provided at most Chinese tables and it is not impolite to give one's teeth a thorough picking at the table, provided one covers one's mouth with the opposite hand.

Spitting is not good manners at a Chinese table, although this is a rule often honored more in the breach. Spittoons are often provided in Chinese restaurants, both as a repository for waste water and tea used to sterilize one's utensils, and for expectorations of various sorts. Often the contents of the spittoons threaten to get up and walk away, so vile are the contents. The floor is fair game in many restaurants for just about anything remaining in one's mouth not swallowable, such as small bits of bone or gristle. Hong Kong has improved considerably in this regard in recent years, but in working-class restaurants and *daipaidongs*, spitting is still quite common.

INFLECTIONS OF GENERAL PRINCIPLES

Having laid out these basic ground rules, it remains to explore how these rules are inflected in the various contexts in which food events occur in contemporary Hong Kong. These contexts are many and varied, ranging from informal and intimate occasions when the family is together at home for a meal, to the more formal occasions involving elaborate feasts usually held in restaurants. Somewhat intermediate between these are the meals eaten out, but in somewhat less formal contexts—from breakfast taken at *dim saam* houses, lunches taken at foodstalls with workmates, to evening meals prepared in restaurants for individual diners (*hak fan*), and midnight snacks. Expectations as to appropriate comportment at the table will also vary with region of origin, age, and class position.

For example, for Cantonese a full meal usually includes soup, and many Cantonese feel uncomfortable leaving the table without having partaken of soup. The minimal structure of the Cantonese meal includes not just *fan* (grain) and *ts'ai* (dishes), but also soup. This minimal structure is served up in what is known as *hak fan*, a specialty of some restaurants (usually Shanghainese) in which one may choose from a daily set menu of *hak* dishes, served with an extra large bowl of rice and the soup of the day. *Hak fan* is designed for people who must eat alone for some reason, not considered the most desirable circumstances. Two Chinese who knew each other would not sit down at the same table and order two individual dishes of *hak fan*. They would surely grasp the opportunity of sharing the greater variety available to each through social eating.

Jack Goody has likened eating alone to defecating in public (1982:306) because of the absence of the social in meeting essentially biological needs. *Hak fan* assures that even taken alone, the minimum structural entity of a Cantonese meal is available to be consumed. This basic structure is also revealed in a variety of thermos containers used for carrying lunch to work which are equipped with compartments for rice, *ts'ai* and soup. Since the contexts in which food events occur in Hong Kong are so varied, soup is not always the focus of attention. Proceeding through the ordinary day's food events from morning to evening will give us occasion to note context-linked inflections of our general principles.

As mentioned previously, the morning food event does not pass muster as a meal, largely due to the absence of rice. Still, there are a variety of contexts in

which this event may take place. At home, the morning food event usually involves rice from the evening before boiled down to congee with a variety of pickles and condiments tossed in or served on the side. This is usually grabbed quickly in the kitchen on the way out to work, if it is eaten at all, and seldom involves the entire family seated at a single table.

Eaten out, the morning food event may take several forms. Consistent with the quick and superficial character of the event at home is the food event taken at a food stall or *daipaidong,* of which several different types serve suitable breakfast fare—congee (most commonly with preserved egg and pork), *yautiu* (unsweetened fried dough strips), hot *dao-jeung* (soy bean milk), *jucheung fen* (rolled rice noodles), all served with tea, usually in a glass.

Eating at a *daipaidong,* and even in some restaurants, one assumes the probability that the chopsticks, stuffed together in a can and set at the center of the table for individual diners to take, as well as one's cup, bowl, and spoon, will not have been properly washed. A brief ritualized washing usually precedes the meal in which one pours a glass of boiling hot tea into one's glass, stirring the ends of the chopsticks in the water to sterilize them, pouring the still hot water into one's bowl where one's cup and spoon are immersed and sterilized. The wash water is then thrown out, usually on the street in the case of a *daipaidong,* or in a spittoon at a restaurant, and one is prepared to commence eating. Occasionally, one is even provided with a separate bowl for washing one's eating implements, filled by one's waiter with boiling water from a huge kettle.

At a *daipaidong* for breakfast, one usually shares a table with a stranger, or perhaps a neighbor or workmate, depending on whether one eats near home or near work. In any case, one's portion is usually one's own, and the rules of formal dining apply only in the most general terms. Food is usually taken with dispatch, as one is usually rushing to work or to school, and the idea is just to put something in one's stomach to suppress hunger till the first meal of the day—*ng fan* (lunch).

The slightly more formal morning food event is *dim saam,* referred to most often as *yam ch'a* (drink tea). "Drinking tea" again refers to something less than a "meal," although on weekends, taken with one's family at a large table, *dim saam* often involves the consumption of large quantities of buns, dumplings, rice noodles in various shapes, a variety of innards, and the like. One sits down, is approached by one's waiter, or in fancier restaurants by a host or hostess, who will inquire what kind of tea one will be drinking—*sao mei, bo lei, soy sin,* and that old perceived favorite of *guailos*—*heung pien* (jasmine). When the tea arrives the host will fill everyone's cup and the meal may begin.

One acquires food from carts pushed around by young children and/or aged women, and less frequently by older men. One may find oneself sharing a table with strangers, or with regular customers who eat at the same restaurant at the same time every morning. Going to *yam ch'a* on a regular schedule assures one of continuous contact with the usual crowd, and it is common to find oneself seated at the same table with many of the same people each morning. While polite conversation is the general rule, more juicy gossip is not inappropriate as the relationship between morning diners becomes more familiar.

Generally, each diner is aware of what he has consumed, and the position of the plates may be adjusted where they have been ambiguously placed so the waiter can figure the tab. One eats from one's own plates under such circumstances, and pays for one's own plates; however, it is polite to fill the tea cup of one's neighbor from one's own pot if one is acquainted with him or her. There are still some restaurants in Hong Kong which serve tea in a covered bowl, quite literally stuffed with tea, and poured into a cup to be drunk, extremely dark, but the standard tea pot has replaced the bowl as a tea vessel in most restaurants.

A table shared with strangers or neighbors is usually an informal arrangement in which one eats one's own food. However, taking *dim saam* may also be a more formal occasion, especially on weekends, or when one has been *cheng*-ed (asked out). In such circumstances many of the rules of formal dining apply, i.e., the food on the table is common and should only be taken in such proportions that enough is left for others. One may order dishes one likes from the passing wagons, but one should always offer to others before taking from the dish for oneself. The dishes accumulate somewhat at random due to the vagaries of the itinerary of the carts, so there is no formal order to the dishes' arrival, although sweeter dishes are usually taken last.

Dim saam often trails off into lunch on formal or informal occasions, and by noon after the diners have warmed up with a few *dim saam* dishes, it is polite to inquire of one's fellow diners whether a plate of noodles or rice (a real meal) is in order, and if so, to order such dishes from the kitchen from one's waiter. Varieties of *dim saam* are also available from *daipaidong* as well, sometimes served up in individual portions to go.

The midday food event in Hong Kong includes rice or a reasonable substitute (rice noodles, bean noodles, wheat noodles), and is most often taken during a lunch hour break from factory or office labor. A variety of choices confront the Hong Kong worker eating out for lunch. Food stalls serve a variety of dishes, usually in individual portions on flat plates heaped high with rice, and covered with a single *ts'ai* dish.

A glass of tea is usually served, and doubles again as a vessel for sterilizing one's chopsticks and spoon. Blue collar workers I knew in Hong Kong would often consume a full-to-the-brim tea tumbler of high octane spirits with such meals, and trundle back to work with the warm glow and slightly glazed look of a two-martini-lunch executive.

A plate of noodles may also be ordered from stalls specializing in such things. These may be served in individual portions, but given the easy divisibility of noodle dishes it is common for workmates to order a variety of noodle dishes and share them in common. A portion is lifted from the plate to one's bowl; with chopsticks initially, when the noodles are easily grasped in quantity; with help from the spoon as the plate gets progressively emptied. The setting of shared common dishes makes the general rules of the table outlined above once again applicable.

Co-workers will often go out to lunch at large *dim saam* restaurants, catch the tail end of the morning *dim saam* and order a variety of more substantial noodle or rice dishes. Where eating has taken place in common, and occasionally even where individual portions have been served, it is unusual for the check to be divided. Someone usually pays the whole tab. Among workmates, or those who often eat together, there is an implicit assumption that in the long run reciprocity will be achieved. It is not impolite among status equals to grab the check and pay for one's fellow diner, but this is not polite if the status difference is too great. Fights over the check occasionally occur in a way which evokes the potlatches of Northwest Coast Indians in which a status hierarchy is confirmed. Paying the check validates one's status superiority over one's fellow diners. Of course, the wider social setting must also be taken into account. One may be desirous of seeking a favor of an important person, in which case paying the check may serve as a mild form of pressure in which the obligation of reciprocity is finessed, enjoining one's fellow diner to comply with one's request. Food events are first and foremost social events.

The evening meal taken at home usually includes some warmed over *ts'ai* from the previous day's meal plus an increment of newly prepared dishes. It is not good manners to ignore the leftovers, despite the fact that they may not be quite as attractive as when served the day before. The general rules of the table apply, although the intimate setting of the family at home makes their application somewhat less formal. Still and all, parents will most commonly instruct children as to the appropriate forms of behavior at the table in this setting, and the children must show that they understand and are learning. In many working-class homes in Hong Kong it is still common for the men to eat first, with the women joining later and/or hovering over the meal without ever formally sitting down.

At more formal dinners or at banquets or feasts associated with weddings, New Year's, funerals or festivals, the primacy of the *fan* and the secondary character of the *ts'ai* dishes is reversed, with attention devoted to the quality of the *ts'ai* dishes (Hsü and Hsü 1977:307), and rice not served till last. Thus at a banquet one may eat *ts'ai* without rice in one's bowl, and one is expected to fill up on *ts'ai* such that when the rice is finally served, one can only take a token portion, which is to say, this has been a real feast.

> During festivals and especially when acting as hosts all Chinese seem to ignore their sense of frugality and indulge in extravagance. *Ts'ai* dishes are served in abundance. The host or hostess will heap the guests' saucers with piece after piece of meat, fish, chicken and so on, in spite of repeated excuses or even protests on the guests' part. When *fan* is finally served, most around the table are full and can at best nibble a few grains (Hsü and Hsü 1977:307).

By the time the rice has been served at a banquet the diner has already had a share of cold appetizer, several stir fry dishes, or whole chickens, ducks, fish, soup, and a sweet/salty dessert. The emphasis on whole items (with head and tail attached) symbolizes completeness and fullness, and evokes these meanings at the table. One tries to serve fish, *yü*, a homophone for surplus, *yü*, to sympathetically bring about that condition in one's guests.

It is not polite to turn over a fish at the table. Rather, when the side facing up has been finished, the skeleton is lifted off to leave the meat underneath exposed. Apparently, turning over the fish is taboo among boat people, since the fish symbolizes the boat which will capsize sympathetically if a fish is turned over. Waiters in Hong Kong are never sure which of their customers are boat folk and might take offense, so they generally refrain from turning over any fish and apparently the practice has now become general.

A variety of prestige foods, such as shark's fin soup and the various eight precious dishes, are served at banquets more for the social recognition they confer than for the pleasure derived from their consumption (see de Garine 1976:150).

Conceptually, whiskey belongs with grain from which it is distilled and may be taken with food as a rice substitute. On formal occasions in Hong Kong scotch or VSOP Cognac is the rule, served straight in water tumblers, and often diluted with Seven-Up.

Another food event of note in Hong Kong is *siu yeh*—loosely translated as snacks. Usually taken late in the evening, they may include anything from congee, noodles and won ton, to roast pork, duck, or chicken, to *hung dao sa* (sweet red bean soup—hot or iced) and *daofufa* (sweet bean curd usually flavored with almond). *Siu yeh* is usually served in individual portions. If you go out for won ton mein, everyone gets his own bowl. If you order duck's neck soup with rice, you are served an individual helping of soup, and an individual bowl of rice. Depending on the class of restaurant you take your *siu yeh* in, you may or may not find it advisable to wash your utensils with tea.

Itinerant street vendors with wheeled carts dispense a variety of prepared *siu yeh* in some residential neighborhoods, calling housewives and amahs to the street clutching their large porcelain bowls, or doling out cuttlefish parts to schoolchildren on street corners.

In all these contexts the general pattern that emerges is one that centers on deference, in thinking first of the other, in suppressing one's inclination to satiate oneself before the other has had a chance to begin, in humility. One yields to the other before satisfying one's own urges. At the macro level of China's great tradition, one finds such behavior characteristic of the *chün-tzu*, the individual skilled in the *li* (etiquette, rites, and ceremonies). He is one also skilled in the art of *jang*—of yielding, of accomplishing without activity, of boundless generosity, of cleaving to the *li*. There is even something of a Taoist resonance in all this, getting at things indirectly, without obvious instrumental effort.

Generally, it can be stated that the degree to which a Chinese practices the rules of etiquette marks his class position with respect to his fellow Chinese; although the degree to which the behavior of lower-class people at the table is informed by these rules should not be underestimated. Disregard of the rules on the part of a Chinese is regarded with as much distaste by their fellows as the faux pas normally committed by Westerners, except that the latter can be excused by their hopeless, if expected, ignorance.

It does not take much study for a Westerner to perform well enough at the table to impress most Chinese, since their expectations are exceedingly low. Keeping in mind a few simple things without slavishly parading one's knowledge, one can usually avoid provoking disgust and revulsion, and convince one's fellow diners that one is sensitive to others on their own terms, as well as to the world at large. Among the most basic of cultural patterns, learned early in life, the degree to which one observes these patterns has a lot to do with the way one is perceived as a person in Chinese terms.

Simple knowledge of the structural contexts, behavioral expectations, and symbolic associations of food events can provide access across social boundaries that would otherwise be less easily breached, and make it possible to more easily achieve one's goals. Table manners are part of an inventory of symbolic behaviors that may be manipulated, finessed, and encoded to communicate messages about oneself. For the Chinese, as for almost everyone else, you are *how* you eat.

REFERENCES

Chang, K. C. (ed.). 1977. Introduction. In *Food in Chinese Culture*. New Haven: Yale University Press.

de Garine, I. 1976. Food, Tradition and Prestige. In *Food, Man and Society*, eds. D. Walcher, N. Kretchmer, and H. L. Barnett. New York: Plenum Press.

Goody, J. 1982. *Cooking, Cuisine and Class*. Cambridge: Cambridge University Press.

Hammerton, J. A. 1936. *Manners and Customs of Mankind*, Vol. I. New York: W. M. A. Wise.

Hsü, F. L. K., and V. Y. N. Hsü. 1977. Modern China: North. In *Food in Chinese Culture*, ed. K. C. Chang. New Haven: Yale University Press.

Li Chi. 1971. *Chü Li, Part I*. Taipei: World Publishing.

McLean, N. B. 1941. *The Table Graces: Setting, Service and Manners for the American House without Servants*. Peoria, IL: Manual Arts Press.

15

Talk in the Intimate Relationship

His and Hers

Deborah Tannen

Of the 60,000 or so words in the English language, the typical educated adult uses about 2,000. Five hundred of these words alone can convey more than 14,000 meanings. But even with all these alternatives, this is not the central problem of miscommunication in North America. Rather, interethnic and cross-sex conversations may be the root cause of miscommunication because the participants follow different subcultural rules for speaking.

Conversation is a negotiated activity. Within a given culture, conversations rely on unspoken understandings about tone of voice, visual cues, silence, minimal responses (such as "mm hmm"), and a variety of other subtle conventions. A cultural approach to male–female conversations highlights unconscious meaning that can lead members of one group to misinterpret the intent of others. Evidence suggests, for example, that women use the response "mm hmm" to indicate they are listening, whereas men use the same response to indicate they are agreeing. Thus, a man who does not provide such cues may indicate to a female partner that he is not listening, whereas a woman may appear to keep changing her mind when giving the same agreeable cue. In the following selection, linguist Deborah Tannen examines male–female conversation and argues that contrasting communication styles are to blame when long-term relationships fail. Could learning how to read cross-sex, nonverbal cues save one of your relationships?

As you read this selection, consider the following questions:

- What does the author mean when she says that boys and girls grow up in separate worlds, even if they live in the same house?
- According to the author, what are some specific differences in the ways men and women talk to each other?
- What are metamessages, and according to the author, are men or women more attuned to metamessages? Why?
- Can you think of situations from your own life that can be better understood after reading this cultural analysis of cross-sex conversation?

The following terms discussed in this selection are included in the Glossary at the back of the book:

metamessages
complementary schismogenesis
intonation

Male–female conversation is always cross-cultural communication. Culture is simply a network of habits and patterns gleaned from past experience, and women and men have different past experiences. From the time they're born, they're treated differently, talked to differently, and talk differently as a result. Boys and girls grow up in different worlds, even if they grow up in the same house. And as adults they travel in different worlds, reinforcing patterns established in childhood. These cultural differences include differing expectations about the role of talk in relationships and how it fulfils that role. . . .

To see how male–female differences in conversational style can cause misunderstandings that lead to

Tannen, Deborah. Chapter 8: "Talk in the Intimate Relationship: His and Hers" (pp. 133–51) from *That's Not What I Meant!* by Deborah Tannen. Copyright © 1986 by Deborah Tannen. Reprinted by permission of HarperCollins Publishers, and Virago, a division of the Little, Brown Book Group. Excerpts from *Grown Ups* by Jules Feiffer. Copyright © 1982 by Jules Feiffer. Reprinted by permission of Abrams Artists Agency on behalf of Jules Feiffer.

complementary schismogenesis—a mutually aggravating spiral—in close relationships, let's start by seeing what some of those differences are.

HE SAID/SHE SAID: HIS AND HER CONVERSATIONAL STYLES

Everyone knows that as a relationship becomes long-term, its terms change. But women and men often differ in how they expect them to change. Many women feel, "After all this time, you should know what I want without my telling you." Many men feel, "After all this time, we should be able to tell each other what we want."

These incongruent expectations capture one of the key differences between men and women. Communication is always a matter of balancing conflicting needs for involvement and independence, but although everyone has both these needs, women often have a relatively greater need for involvement, and men a relatively greater need for independence. Being understood without saying what you mean gives a payoff in involvement, and that is why women value it so highly.

If you want to be understood without saying what you mean explicitly in words, you must convey meaning somewhere else—in how words are spoken, or by metamessages. Thus it stands to reason that women are often more attuned than men to the metamessages of talk. When women surmise meaning in this way, it seems mysterious to men, who call it "women's intuition" (if they think it's right) or "reading things in" (if they think it's wrong). Indeed, it could be wrong, since metamessages are not on record. And even if it is right, there is still the question of scale: how significant are the metamessages that are there?

Metamessages are a form of indirectness. Women are more likely to be indirect, and to try to reach agreement by negotiation. Another way to understand this preference is that negotiation allows a display of solidarity, which women prefer to the display of power (even though the aim may still be the same—getting what you want). Unfortunately, power and solidarity are bought with the same currency. Ways of talking intended to create solidarity have the simultaneous effect of framing power differences. When they think they're being nice, women often end up appearing deferential and unsure of themselves or of what they want.

When styles differ, misunderstandings are always rife. As their differing styles create misunderstandings, women and men try to clear them up by talking things out. These pitfalls are compounded in talks between men and women because of their different ways of going about talking things out, and their different assumptions about the significance of going about it.

WOMEN LISTEN FOR METAMESSAGES

Sylvia and Harry celebrated their golden wedding anniversary at a country club. Some of the guests were there for the whole weekend, most just for the evening of the celebration: a cocktail party followed by dinner. During dinner, the headwaiter approached Sylvia. "Since we have a rich dessert tonight, and everyone has already eaten at the cocktail party, perhaps you would prefer to cut the anniversary cake at lunch tomorrow?" Sylvia asked the advice of the others at her table. All the men agreed: "Yes, that makes sense. Save the cake for tomorrow." All the women disagreed. "No, the party is tonight. Have the cake tonight." The men were focusing on the message: the cake as food. The women were thinking of the metamessage: serving a special cake frames an occasion as a celebration.

Why are women more attuned to metamessages? Because they are more focused on involvement, that is, on relationships among people, and it is through metamessages that relationships among people are established and maintained. If you want to take the temperature and check the vital signs of a relationship, the barometers to check are its metamessages: what is said and how.

Everyone can see these signals, but whether or not we pay attention to them is another matter—a matter of being sensitized. Once you are sensitized, you can't roll your antennae back in; they're stuck in the extended position.

When interpreting meaning, it is possible to pick up signals that weren't intentionally sent out, like an innocent flock of birds on a radar screen. The birds are there—and the signals women pick up are there —but they may not mean what the interpreter thinks they mean. For example, Mary looks at Larry and asks, "What's wrong?" because his brow is furrowed. Since he was only thinking about lunch, her expression of concern makes him feel under scrutiny.

The difference in focus on messages and metamessages can give men and women different points of view on almost any comment. Harriet complains to Mark, "Why don't you ask me how my day was?" He replies, "If you have something to tell me, tell me. Why do you have to be invited?" The reason is that she wants the metamessage of interest: evidence that he cares how her day was, regardless of whether or not she has something to tell.

A lot of trouble is caused between women and men by, of all things, pronouns. Women often feel hurt when their partners use "I" or "me" in a situation in which they would use "we" or "us". When Mark announces, "I think I'll go for a walk," Harriet feels specifically uninvited, though Mark later claims she would have been welcome to join him. She felt locked out by his use of I?" and his omission of an invitation: "Would you like to come?" Metamessages can be seen in what is not said as well as what is said.

It's difficult to straighten out such misunderstandings because each one feels convinced of the logic of his or her position and the illogic—or irresponsibility—of the other's. Harriet knows that she always asks Mark how his day was, and that she'd never announce, "I'm going for a walk", without inviting him to join her. If he talks differently to her, it must be that he feels differently. But Mark wouldn't feel unloved if Harriet didn't ask about his day, and he would feel free to ask, "Can I come along", if she announced she was taking a walk. So he can't believe she is justified in feeling responses he knows he wouldn't have.

MESSAGES AND METAMESSAGES IN TALK BETWEEN . . . GROWN UPS?

These processes are dramatized with chilling yet absurdly amusing authenticity in Feiffer's *Grown Ups*. To get a closer look at what happens when men and women focus on different levels of talk in talking things out, let's look at what happens in this play.

Jake criticizes Louise for not responding when their daughter, Edie, called her. His comment leads to a fight, even though they're both aware that this one incident is not in itself important.

JAKE: Look, I don't care if it's important or not, when a kid calls its mother the mother should answer.

LOUISE: Now I'm a bad mother.

JAKE: I didn't say that.

LOUISE: It's in your stare.

JAKE: Is that another thing you know? My stare?

Louise ignores Jake's message—the question of whether or not she responded when Edie called—and goes for the metamessage: his implication that she's a bad mother, which Jake insistently disclaims. When Louise explains the signals she's reacting to, Jake not only discounts them but is angered at being held accountable not for what he said but for how he looked—his stare.

As the play goes on, Jake and Louise replay and intensify these patterns:

LOUISE: If I'm such a terrible mother, do you want a divorce?

JAKE: I do not think you're a terrible mother and no, thank you, I do not want a

divorce. Why is it that whenever I bring up any difference between us you ask me if I want a divorce?

The more he denies any meaning beyond the message, the more she blows it up, the more adamantly he denies it, and so on:

JAKE: I have brought up one thing that you do with Edie that I don't think you notice that I have noticed for some time but which I have deliberately not brought up before because I had hoped you would notice it for yourself and stop doing it and also—frankly, baby, I have to say this—I knew if I brought it up we'd get into exactly the kind of circular argument we're in right now. And I wanted to avoid it. But I haven't and we're in it, so now, with your permission, I'd like to talk about it.

LOUISE: You don't see how that puts me down?

JAKE: What?

LOUISE: If you think I'm so stupid why do you go on living with me?

JAKE: *Dammit! Why can't anything ever be simple around here?!*

It can't be simple because Louise and Jake are responding to different levels of communication. [...] Jake tries to clarify his point by overelaborating it, which gives Louise further evidence that he's condescending to her, making it even less likely that she will address his point rather than his condescension.

What pushes Jake and Louise beyond anger to rage is their different perspectives on metamessages. His refusal to admit that his statements have implications and overtones denies her authority over her own feelings. Her attempts to interpret what he didn't say and put the metamessage into the message make him feel she's putting words into his mouth—denying his authority over his own meaning.

The same thing happens when Louise tells Jake that he is being manipulated by Edie:

LOUISE: Why don't you ever make her come to see you?
Why do you always go to her?

JAKE: You want me to play power games with a nine year old? I want her to know I'm interested in her. Someone around here has to show interest in her.

LOUISE: You love her more than I do.

JAKE: I didn't say that.

LOUISE: Yes, you did.

JAKE: You don't know how to listen. You have never learned how to listen. It's as if listening to you is a foreign language.

Again, Louise responds to his implication—this time, that he loves Edie more because he runs when she calls. And yet again, Jake cries literal meaning, denying he meant any more than he said.

Throughout their argument, the point to Louise is her feelings—that Jake makes her feel put down—but to him the point is her actions—that she doesn't always respond when Edie calls:

LOUISE: You talk about what I do to Edie, what do you think you do to me?

JAKE: This is not the time to go into what we do to each other.

Since she will talk only about metamessages, and he will talk only about messages, neither can get satisfaction from their talk, and they end up where they started—only angrier:

JAKE: That's not the point!

LOUISE: It's *my* point.

JAKE: It's hopeless!

LOUISE: Then get a divorce.

Conventional wisdom (and many of our parents and English teachers) tell us that meaning is conveyed by words, so men who tend to be literal about words are supported by conventional wisdom. They may not simply deny but actually miss the cues that are sent by how words are spoken. It they sense something about it, they may nonetheless discount what they sense. After all, it wasn't said. Sometimes that's a dodge—a plausible defence rather than a gut feeling. But sometimes it is a sincere conviction. Women are also likely to doubt the reality of what they sense. If they don't doubt it in their guts, they nonetheless may lack the arguments to support their position and thus are reduced to repeating, "You said it. Yes you did." Knowing that metamessages are a real and fundamental part of communication makes it easier to understand and justify what they feel.

"TALK TO ME"

An article in a popular newspaper reports that one of the five most common complaints of wives about their husbands is "He doesn't listen to me any more." Another is "He doesn't talk to me any more." Political scientist Andrew Hacker noted that lack of communication, while high on women's lists of reasons for divorce, is much less often mentioned by men. Since couples arc parties to the same conversations, why are women more dissatisfied with them than men? Because what they expect is different, as well as what they see as the significance of talk itself.

THE STRONG SILENT TYPE

One of the most common stereotypes of a "real" man is the strong silent type. Jack Kroll, writing about Henry Fonda on the occasion of his death, used the phrases "quiet power", "abashed silences", "combustible catatonia", and "sense of power held in check". He explained that Fonda's goal was not to let anyone see "the wheels go around", not to let the "machinery" show. According to Kroll, the resulting silence was effective on stage but devastating to Fonda's family.

The image of a silent father is common and is often the model for the lover or husband. But what attracts us can become flypaper to which we are unhappily stuck. Many women find the strong silent type to be a lure as a lover but a lug as a husband. Nancy Schoenberger begins a poem with the lines, "It was your silence that hooked me,/so like my father's." Adrienne Rich refers in a poem to the "husband who is frustratingly mute". Despite the initial attraction of such quintessentially male silence, it may begin to feel, to a woman in a long-term relationship, like a brick wall against which she is banging her head.

In addition to these images of male and female behaviour—both the result and the cause of them—are differences in how women and men view the role of talk in relationships as well as how talk accomplishes its purpose. These differences have their roots in the settings in which men and women learn to have conversations: among their peers, growing up.

GROWING UP MALE AND FEMALE

Children whose parents have foreign accents don't speak with accents. They learn to talk like their peers. Little girls and little boys learn how to have conversations as they learn how to pronounce words: from their playmates. Between the ages of five and fifteen, when children are learning to have conversations, they play mostly with friends of their own sex. So it's not surprising that they learn different ways of having and using conversations.

Anthropologists Daniel Maltz and Ruth Borker (…) point out that boys and girls socialize differently. Little girls tend to play in small groups or, even more common, in pairs. Their social life usually centres around a best friend, and friendships are made, maintained, and broken by talk—especially "secrets". If a little girl tells her friend's secret to another little girl, she may find herself with a new best friend. The secrets themselves may or may not be important, but the fact of telling them is all-important. It's hard for newcomers to get into these tight groups, but anyone who is admitted is treated as an equal. Girls like to play cooperatively; if they can't cooperate, the group breaks up.

Little boys tend to play in larger groups, often outdoors, and they spend more time doing things than talking. It's easy for boys to get into the group, but not everyone is accepted as an equal. Once in the group, boys must jockey for their status in it. One of the most important ways they do this is through talk: verbal display such as telling stories and jokes, challenging and sidetracking the verbal displays of other boys, and withstanding other boys' challenges in order to maintain their own story—and status. Their talk is often competitive talk about who is best at what.

FROM CHILDREN TO GROWN UPS

Feiffer's play is ironically named *Grown Ups* because adult men and women struggling to communicate often sound like children. "You said so!" "I did not!" The reason is that when they grow up, women and men keep the divergent attitudes and habits they learned as children—which they don't recognize as attitudes and habits but simply take for granted as ways of talking.

Women want their partners to be a new and improved version of a best friend. This gives them a soft spot for men who tell them secrets. As Jack Nicholson once advised a guy in a movie: "Tell her about your troubled childhood—that always gets 'em." Men expect to *do* things together and don't feel anything is missing if they don't have heart-to-heart talks all the time.

If they do have heart-to-heart talks, the meaning of those talks may be opposite for men and women. To many women, the relationship is working as long as they can talk things out. To many men, the relationship isn't working out if they have to keep working it over. If she keeps trying to get talks going to save the relationship, and he keeps trying to avoid them because he sees them as weakening it, then each one's efforts to preserve the relationship appear to the other as reckless endangerment.

HOW TO TALK THINGS OUT

If talks (of any kind) do get going, men's and women's ideas about how to conduct them may be very different. For example, Diana is feeling comfortable and close to Tom. She settles into a chair after dinner and begins to tell him about a problem at work. She expects him to ask questions to show he's interested; reassure her that he understands and that what she feels is normal; and return the intimacy by telling her a problem of his. Instead, Tom sidetracks her story, cracks jokes about it, questions her interpretation of the problem, and gives her advice about how to solve it and avoid such problems in the future.

All of these responses, natural to men, are unexpected to women, who interpret them in terms of their own habits—negatively. When Tom comments on side issues or cracks jokes, Diana thinks he doesn't care about what she's saying and isn't really listening. If he challenges her reading of what went on, she feels he is criticizing her and telling her she's crazy, when what she wants is to be reassured that she's not. If he tells her how to solve the problem, it makes her feel as if she's the patient to his doctor—a metamessage of condescension, echoing male one-upmanship compared to the female etiquette of equality. Because he doesn't volunteer information about his problems, she feels he's implying he doesn't have any.

Complementary schismogenesis can easily set in. His way of responding to her bid for intimacy makes her feel distant from him. She tries harder to regain intimacy the only way she knows how—by revealing more and more about herself. He tries harder by giving more insistent advice. The more problems she exposes, the more incompetent she feels, until they both see her as emotionally draining and problem-ridden. When his efforts to help aren't appreciated, he wonders why she asks for his advice if she doesn't want to take it.

"YOU'RE NOT LISTENING TO ME"

The other complaint wives make about their husbands is, "He doesn't listen to me any more." The wives may be right that their husbands aren't listening, if they don't value the telling of problems and secrets to establish rapport. But some of the time men feel unjustly accused: "I was listening." And some of the time, they're right. They were.

Whether or not someone is listening only that person can really know. But we judge whether or not we think others are listening by signals we can see—not only their verbal responses but also their eye contact and little listening noises like "mhm," "uh-huh", and "yeah". These listening noises give the go-ahead for talk; if they are misplaced along the track, they can quickly derail a chugging conversation.

Maltz and Barker also report that women and men have different ways of showing that they're listening. In the listening role, women make—and expect—more of these noises. So when men are listening to women, they are likely to make too few such noises for the women to feel the men are really listening. And when women are listening to men, making more such listening noises than men expect may give the impression they're impatient or exaggerating their show of interest.

Even worse, what women and men mean by such noises may be different. Does "uh-huh" or "mhm" mean you agree with what you heard, or just that you heard and you're following? Maltz and Borker contend that women tend to use these noises just to show they're listening and understanding. Men tend to use them to show they agree. So one reason women make more listening noises may be that women are listening more than men are agreeing with what they hear.

In addition to problems caused by differences in how many signals are given, there is bound to be trouble as a result of the difference in how they're used. If a woman cheers a man on in his talk by saying "mhm" and "yeah" and "uh-huh" all over the place, and it later comes out that she disagrees with what he said, he may feel she misled him (thereby reinforcing his stereotype of women as unreliable). Conversely, if a man sits through a woman's talk and follows all she says but doesn't agree, he's not going to shower her with "uh-huh's"—and she's going to think he's not paying attention.

Notice that the difference in how women and men use listening noises is in keeping with their focus in communication. Using the noises to show "I'm listening; go on" serves the relationship level of talk. Using them to show what one thinks of what is being said is a response to the content of talk. So men and women are being stylistically consistent in their interactive inconsistency.

"WHY DON'T YOU TALK ABOUT SOMETHING INTERESTING?"

Sometimes when men and women feel the other isn't paying attention, they're right. And this may be because their assumptions about what's interesting are different. Alison gets bored when Daniel goes on and on about the stock market or the world soccer match. He gets bored when she goes on and on about details of her daily life or the lives of people he doesn't even know.

It seems natural to women to tell and hear about what happened today, who turned up at the bus stop, who called and what she said, not because these details are important in themselves but because the telling of them proves involvement—that you care about each other, that you have a best friend. Knowing you will be able to tell these things later makes you feel less alone as you go along the lone path of a day. And if you don't tell, you are sending a metamessage about the relationship—curtailing it, clipping its wings.

Since it is not natural to men to use talk in this way, they focus on the inherent insignificance of the details. What they find worth telling are facts about such topics as sports, politics, history, or how things work. Women often perceive the telling of facts as lecturing, which not only does not carry (for them) a metamessage of rapport, but carries instead a metamessage of condescension: I'm the teacher, you're the student. I'm knowledgeable, you're ignorant.

A *New Yorker* cartoon shows a scene—probably the source of a thousand cartoons (and a million conversations)—of a breakfast table, with a husband reading a newspaper while the wife is trying to talk to him. The husband says, "You want to talk? Get a newspaper. We'll talk about what's in the newspaper." It's funny because everyone knows that what's in the newspaper is not what the wife wants to talk about.

CONVERSATIONS ABOUT CONVERSATIONS

When women talk about what seems obviously interesting to them, their conversations often include reports of conversations. Tone of voice, timing, intonation, and wording are all re-created in the telling in order to explain—dramatize, really—the experience that is being reported. If men tell about an incident and give a brief summary instead of re-creating what was said and how, the women often feel that the essence of the experience is being omitted. If the woman asks, "What exactly did he say?", and "How did he say it", the man probably can't remember. If she continues to press him, he may feel as if he's being grilled.

All these different habits have repercussions when the man and the woman are talking about their relationship. He feels out of his element, even one down. She claims to recall exactly what he said, and what she said, and in what sequence, and she wants him to account for what he said. He can hardly account for it since he has forgotten exactly what was said—if not the whole conversation. She secretly suspects he's only pretending not to remember, and he secretly suspects that she's making up the details.

One woman reported such a problem as being a matter of her boyfriend's poor memory. It is unlikely, however, that his problem was poor memory in general. The question is what types of material each person remembers or forgets.

Frances was sitting at her kitchen table talking to Edward, when the toaster did something funny. Edward began to explain why it did it. Frances tried to pay attention, but very early in his explanation, she realized she was completely lost. She felt very stupid. And the indications were that he thought so too.

Later that day they were taking a walk. He was telling her about a difficult situation in his office that involved a complex network of interrelationships among a large number of people. Suddenly he stopped and said, "I'm sure you can't keep track of all these people." "Of course I can," she said, and she retraced his story with all the characters in place, all the details right. He was genuinely impressed. She felt very smart.

How could Frances be both smart and stupid? Did she have a good memory or a bad one? Frances's and Edward's abilities to follow, remember, and recount depended on the subject—and paralleled her parents' abilities to follow and remember. Whenever Frances told her parents about people in her life, her mother could follow with no problem, but her father got lost as soon as she introduced a second character. "Now who was that?" he'd ask. "Your boss?" "No, my boss is Susan. This was my friend." Often he'd still be in the previous story. But whenever she told them about her work, it was her mother who would get lost as soon as she mentioned a second step: "That was your tech report?" "No, I handed my tech report in last month. This was a special project."

Frances's mother and father, like many other men and women, had honed their listening and remembering skills in different areas. Their experience talking to other men and other women gave them practice in following different kinds of talk.

Knowing whether and how we are likely to report events later influences whether and how we pay attention when they happen. As women listen to and take part in conversations, knowing they may talk about them later makes them more likely to pay attention to exactly what is said and how. Since most men aren't in the habit of making such reports, they are less likely to pay much attention at the time. On the other hand, many women aren't in the habit of paying attention to scientific explanations and facts because they don't expect to have to perform in public by reciting them—just as those who aren't in the habit of entertaining others by telling jokes "can't" remember jokes they've heard, even though they listened carefully enough to enjoy them.

So women's conversations with their women friends keep them in training for talking about their relationships with men, but many men come to such conversations with no training at all—and an uncomfortable sense that this really isn't their event.

"WHAT DO YOU MEAN, MY DEAR?"

Most of us place enormous emphasis on the importance of a primary relationship. We regard the ability to maintain such relationships as a sign of mental health—our contemporary metaphor for being a good person.

Yet our expectations of such relationships are nearly—maybe in fact—impossible. When primary relationships are between women and men, male–female differences contribute to the impossibility. We expect partners to be both romantic interests and best friends. Though women and men may have fairly similar expectations for romantic interests, obscuring their differences when relationships begin, they have very different ideas about how to be friends, and these are the differences that mount over time.

In conversations between friends who are not lovers, small misunderstandings can be passed over or diffused by breaks in contact. But in the context of a primary relationship, differences can't be ignored, and the pressure cooker of continued contact keeps both people stewing in the juice of accumulated minor misunderstandings. And stylistic differences are sure to cause misunderstandings—not, ironically, in matters such as sharing values and interests or understanding each other's philosophies of life. These large and significant yet palpable issues can be talked about and agreed on. It is far harder to achieve congruence—and much more surprising and troubling that it is hard—in the simple day-to-day matters of the automatic rhythms and nuances of talk. Nothing in our backgrounds or in the media (the present-day counterpart of religion or grandparents' teaching) prepares us for this failure. If two people share so much in terms of point of view and basic values, how can they continually get into fights about insignificant matters?

If you find yourself in such a situation and you don't know about differences in conversational style, you assume something's wrong with your partner or you, or you for having chosen your partner. At best, if you are forward-thinking and generous-minded, you may absolve individuals and blame the relationship. But if you know about differences in conversational style, you can accept that there are differences in habits and assumptions about how to have conversation, show interest, be considerate, and so on. You may not always correctly interpret your partner's intentions, but you will know that if you get a negative impression, it may not be what was intended—and neither are your responses unfounded. If he says he really is interested even though he doesn't seem to be, maybe you should believe what he says and not what you sense.

Sometimes explaining assumptions can help. If a man starts to tell a woman what to do to solve her problem, she may say, "Thanks for the advice but I really don't want to be told what to do. I just want you to listen and say you understand." A man might want to explain, "If I challenge you, it's not to prove you wrong; it's just my way of paying attention to what you're telling me." Both may try either or both to modify their ways of talking and to try to accept what the other does. The important thing is to know that what seem like bad intentions may really be good intentions expressed in a different conversational style. We have to give up our conviction that, as Robin Lakoff put it, "Love means never having to say 'What do you mean?'"

16

Measuring Up to Barbie

Ideals of the Feminine Body in Popular Culture

Jacqueline Urla and Alan C. Swedlund

Cultural ideas about beauty and sexual attractiveness vary across time and between different cultural groups. Feminine ideals of height, weight, appearance, and adornment range from buxom to svelte, from pubescent to maternal, and from scantily clad to ornately garbed. Within this variation, however, some recognizable stereotypes of female beauty have emerged in the postindustrial global culture. Recognizable figures like that of the supermodel, seen from runways in Paris to the cover of magazines in supermarkets, loom large in the definition of women's beauty. Just as recognizable, and particularly American, is the Barbie doll.

Given that Barbie is such an iconic figure, a child's toy, it may be difficult to imagine how she could be a bad girl. Urla and Swedlund discuss Barbie's history and what her plastic frame, boyfriend, and Dream House symbolize. By taking Barbie's measurements and scaling them to life size, they show how unrealistic (even impossible) Barbie really is, especially in comparison with many American women. The authors show that the idea of an "average woman" itself has a history. As a material object of socialization (just like baby dolls that teach mothering) the sexualized Barbie embodies American ideals of femininity, as well as a consumerist model of the "good life" full of fashionable clothing, cars, and swimming pools. Barbie's "hard" body represents self-control and discipline and

sexual attractiveness, but not necessarily reproduction or motherhood.

As you read this selection, ask yourself the following questions:

- What does Barbie symbolize for American girls when they make-believe play about the lives of grown-ups? Why is Barbie fun?

- How is Barbie a consumer? Are desired consumption patterns part of gender socialization?

- How might the "beauty myth" be related to the ideas of the "natural tendencies of the body to decay" that Horace Miner described for the Nacirema people (Selection 8)?

- What does the anthropometry experiment tell us? How is culture involved in the definition of "normal"?

- What is the primary measurable difference between Barbie and a "normal" American woman?

The following terms discussed in this selection are included in the Glossary at the back of the book:

anorexia nervosa   *constructions of femininity*
anthropometry   *late capitalism*

It is no secret that thousands of healthy women in the United States perceive their bodies as defective. The signs are everywhere: from potentially lethal cosmetic surgery and drugs, to the more familiar routines of dieting, curling, crimping, and aerobicizing, women seek to take control over their unruly physical selves.

Urla, Jacqueline, & Alan C. Swedlund. "Measuring Up to Barbie: Ideals of the Feminine Body in Popular Culture." Reprinted by permission of the authors.

Every year at least 150,000 women undergo breast implant surgery (Williams 1992), while Asian women have their noses rebuilt and their eyes widened to make themselves look "less dull" (Kaw 1993). Studies show the obsession with body size and sense of inadequacy starts frighteningly early; as many as 80% of 9 year old suburban girls are concerned about dieting and their weight (Bordo 1991:125). Reports like these, together with the dramatic rise in eating disorders among young women, are just some of the more noticeable fall-out from what Naomi Wolf calls "the beauty myth." Fueled by the hugely profitable cosmetic, weight loss, and fashion industries, the beauty myth's glamorized notions of the ideal body reverberate back upon women as "a dark vein of self hatred, physical obsessions, terror of aging, and dread of lost control" (Wolf 1991:10).

It is this paradox—that female bodies are never feminine enough, that they require deliberate and oftentimes painful refashioning to be what "nature" intended—that motivates our inquiry into the feminine ideal. Neither universal nor changeless, idealized notions of both masculine and feminine bodies have a long history that shifts considerably across time, racial or ethnic group, class, and culture. Body ideals in twenty-first century North America are influenced and shaped by images from classical or "high art," the discourses of science and medicine, as well as a multitude of commercial interests, ranging from mundane life insurance standards, to the more high-profile fashion, fitness, and entertainment industries. Each has played contributing and sometimes conflicting roles in determining what counts as a desirable body for us today. In this essay, we focus our attention on the domain of popular culture and the ideal feminine body as it is conveyed by one of pop culture's longest lasting and most illustrious icons: the Barbie doll.

Making her debut in 1959 as Mattel's new teenage fashion doll, Barbie rose quickly to become the top selling toy in the United States. Several decades and a women's movement later, Barbie dolls remain one of Mattel's biggest selling items netting over one billion dollars in revenues worldwide (Adelson 1992), or roughly one Barbie sold every two seconds (Stevenson 1991).[1] By the nineties, Mattel was estimating that in the United States over 95% of girls between the ages of 3 and 11 own at least one Barbie and that the average number of dolls per owner is seven (Shapiro 1992). Barbie is clearly a force to contend with, eliciting, over the years, a combination of critique, parody, and adoration. A legacy of the post-war era, she remains an incredibly resilient visual and tactile model of femininity for pre-pubescent girls.

It is not our intention to settle the debate over whether Barbie is a good or bad role model for little girls. Though that issue surrounds Barbie like a dark cloud, we are more concerned with how Barbie has been able to survive and remain popular in a period marked by the growth of consumer society, intense debate over gender and racial relations, and changing notions of the body. Our aim, then, is not to offer another rant against Barbie, but to explore how this doll crystallizes some of the predicaments of femininity and feminine bodies in late twentieth-century North America.

A DOLL IS BORN

Parents thank us for the educational values in the world of Barbie . . . They say that they could never get their daughters well groomed before—get them out of slacks or blue jeans and into a dress . . . get them to scrub their necks and wash their hair. Well that's where Barbie comes in. The doll has clean hair and a clean face, and she dresses fashionably, and she wears gloves and shoes that match. (Ruth Handler 1964, quoted in Motz 1983:130)

Legend has it that Barbie was the brainchild of Mattel owner Ruth Handler, who first thought of creating a three dimensional fashion doll after seeing her daughter play with paper dolls. As an origin story, this one is touching and no doubt true. But Barbie was not the first doll of her kind nor was she just a mother's invention. Making sense of Barbie requires that we look to the larger socio-political and cultural milieu that made her genesis both possible and meaningful. Based on a German prototype, the "Lili" doll, Barbie was from "birth" implicated in the ideologies of the cold war and the research and technology exchanges of the military-industrial complex. Her finely crafted durable plastic mold was, in fact, designed by Jack Ryan, well known for his work in designing the Hawk and Sparrow missiles for the Raytheon Company. Conceived at the hands of a military weapons designer-turned-toy inventor, Barbie dolls came onto the market the same year as the infamous Nixon-Khrushchev "kitchen debate" at the American National Exhibition in Moscow. There, in front of the cameras of the world, the leaders of the capitalist and socialist worlds faced off, not over missile counts, but over "the relative merits of American and Soviet washing machines, televisions, and electric ranges" (May 1988:16). As Elaine Tyler May has noted in her study of the Cold War, this much celebrated media event signaled the transformation of American-made commodities and the model suburban home into key symbols and safeguards of democracy and freedom. It was thus with fears of nuclear annihilation and sexually charged fantasies of the perfect bombshelter running rampant in the American imaginary, that Barbie and her torpedo-like breasts emerged into popular culture as an emblem of the aspirations of prosperity, domestic containment, and rigid gender roles that were to characterize the burgeoning post-war consumer economy and its image of the American Dream.

Marketed as the first "teenage" fashion doll, Barbie's rise in popularity also coincided with and no doubt contributed to the post-war creation of a distinctive teenage lifestyle.[2] Teens, their tastes and behaviors, were becoming the object of both sociologists and criminologists, as well as market survey researchers intent on capturing their discretionary dollars. While J. Edgar Hoover was pronouncing "the juvenile jungle" a menace to American society, we have retailers, the music industry, and movie-makers declaring the 13 to 19 year old age bracket "the seven golden years" (Doherty 1988:51–52).

Barbie dolls seemed to cleverly reconcile both of these concerns by personifying the good girl who was sexy, but didn't have sex, and was willing to spend, spend, and spend. Amidst the palpable moral panic over juvenile delinquency and teenagers' new found sexual freedom, Barbie was a reassuring symbol of solidly middle-class values. Popular teen magazines, advertising, television, and movies of the period painted a highly dichotomized world divided into good (i.e. middle class) and bad (i.e. working class) kids: the clean-cut college-bound junior achiever versus the street corner boy; the wholesome American Bandstander versus the uncontrollable bad seed (cf. Doherty 1988; and Frith 1981 for England). It was no mystery where Barbie stood in this thinly disguised class discourse. As Motz writes, Barbie's world bore no trace of the "greasers" and "hoods" that inhabited the many grade B films about teenage vice and ruin. In the life Mattel laid out for her in story books and comics, Barbie, who started out looking like a somewhat vampy, slightly Bardotesque doll, was gradually transformed into a "'soc' or a 'frat'—affluent, well-groomed, socially conservative" (Motz 1983:130). In lieu of back-seat sex and teenage angst, Barbie had pajama parties, barbecues, and her favorite pastime, shopping.

Every former Barbie owner knows that to buy a Barbie was to lust after Barbie accessories: that matching pair of sandals and handbag, canopy bedroom set, or country camper. Both conspicuous consumer and a consumable item herself, Barbie was surely as much the fantasy of U.S. retailers as she was the panacea of middle class parents. For every "need" Barbie had, there was a deliciously miniature product to fulfill it. As Paula Rabinowitz has noted, Barbie dolls, with their focus on frills and fashion, epitomize the way that teenage girls and girl culture in general have figured as accessories in the historiography of postwar culture; that is as both essential to the burgeoning commodity culture as consumers, but seemingly irrelevant to the historical events defining cold war existence (Rabinowitz 1993).

Perhaps what makes Barbie such a perfect icon of late capitalist constructions of femininity is the way in which her persona pairs endless consumption with the achievement of femininity and the appearance of an appropriately gendered body. By buying for Barbie, girls practice how to be discriminating consumers knowledgeable about the cultural capital of different name brands, how to read packaging, and the overall importance of fashion and taste for social status (Motz 1983:131–132). Being a teenage girl in the world of Barbie dolls becomes quite literally a performance of commodity display requiring numerous and complex rehearsals. In making this argument, we want to stress that we are drawing on more than just the doll. "Barbie"

is also the packaging, spin-off products, cartoons, commercials, magazines, and fan club paraphernalia, all of which contribute to creating her persona. Clearly, as we will discuss below, children may engage more or less with those products, subverting or ignoring various aspects of Barbie's "official" presentation. However, to the extent that little girls *do* participate in the prepackaged world of Barbie, they come into contact with a number of beliefs central to femininity under consumer capitalism. Little girls learn, among other things, about the crucial importance of their appearance to their personal happiness and ability to gain favor with their friends. Barbie's social calendar, like her closet, is constantly full, and the stories in her fan magazines show her frequently engaged in preparation for the rituals of heterosexual teenage life: dates, proms, and weddings. A perusal of Barbie magazines, and the product advertisements and pictorials within them, shows an overwhelming preoccupation with grooming for those events. Magazines abound with tips on the proper ways of washing hair, putting on make-up, and assembling stunning wardrobes. Through these play scenarios little girls learn Ruth Handler's lesson about the importance of hygiene, occasion-specific clothing, knowledgeable buying, and artful display as key elements to popularity and a successful career in femininity.

Barbie exemplifies the way in which gender has become a commodity itself, "something we can buy into . . . the same way we buy into a style" (Willis 1991:23). In her insightful analysis of the logic of consumer capitalism, cultural critic Susan Willis pays particular attention to the way in which children's toys like Barbie and the popular muscle-bound "He-Man" for boys link highly conservative and narrowed images of masculinity and femininity with commodity consumption (1991:27). Being or becoming a teenager, having a "grown-up" body, observes Willis, is presented as inextricably bound up with the acquisition of certain commodities, signaled by styles of clothing, cars, music, etc. In play groups and fan clubs (collectors are a whole world unto themselves) children exchange knowledge about the latest accessories and outfits, their relative merit, and how to find them. They become members of a community of Barbie owners whose shared identity is defined by the commodities they have or desire to have. The articulation of social ties through commodities is, as Willis argues, at the heart of how sociality is experienced in consumer capitalism. In this way, we might say that playing with Barbie serves not only as a training ground for the production of the appropriately gendered woman, but also as an introduction to the kinds of knowledge and social relations one can expect to encounter in late capitalist society.

BARBIE IS A SURVIVOR

For anyone tracking Barbie's history, it is abundantly clear that Mattel's marketing strategies have been sensitive to a changing social climate. When the women's movement gained momentum in the seventies, Barbie dolls became a target of criticism (Billyboy 1987; Lord 1994). Mattel responded by giving Barbie new outfits to "reflect the activities and professions that modern women are involved in" (quoted in Harpers, August 2, 1990, p. 20). Just as Barbie graduated from candy striper and ballerina to astronaut and doctor, Mattel also tried to diversify her lily-white image beginning in 1967 with Barbie's first Black friend, "Colored Francie." With the expansion of sales worldwide, Barbie has acquired multiple national guises (Spanish Barbie, Jamaican Barbie, Malaysian Barbie, etc.).[3] In addition, her cohort of "friends" has become increasingly ethnically diversified, as has Barbie advertising, which now regularly features Asian, Hispanic, and Afro-American little girls playing with Barbie. Today, Barbie pals include a smattering of brown and yellow plastic friends, like Teresa, Kira, and Miko who appear on her adventures and, very importantly, can share her clothes.

Perhaps Mattel's most glamorous concession to multiculturalism was Shani who premiered at the 1991 Toy Fair with great fanfare and media attention. Unlike her predecessors who were essentially "brown plastic poured into blond Barbie's mold," Shani, together with her two friends, Asha and Nichelle (each a slightly different shade of brown), and boyfriend Jamal created in 1992, were decidedly Afro-centric, with outfits in "ethnic" fabrics rather than the traditional Barbie pink (Jones 1991). The packaging also announced that these dolls' bodies and facial features were meant to be more realistic of African American women, although as we will see, the differences, while meaningful, don't preclude interchanging clothes with Barbie. Now Mattel announced, "ethnic Barbie lovers will be able to dream in their own image" (*Newsweek* 1990:48). Multiculturalism cracked open the door to Barbiedom and diversity could walk in as long as she was big busted, slim hipped, had long flowing hair, tiny feet, and was very, very thin.[4]

In looking over the course of Barbie's career, it is clear that part of her resilience, continuing appeal, and profitability stems from the fact that her identity is constructed primarily through fantasy and is consequently open to change and reinterpretation. As a fashion model, Barbie continually creates her identity anew with every costume change. In that sense, we might want to call Barbie emblematic of the restless desire for change that permeates post-modern capitalist society (Wilson 1985:63). Not only can her image be renewed with a change of clothes, Barbie is also seemingly able to clone herself effortlessly into new identities—"Malibu Barbie"; "Totally Hair Barbie"; "Teen Talk Barbie"; even Afro-centric Shani—without somehow suggesting a serious personality disorder. Since Barbie is a perpetual teenager, Barbie's owners are at liberty to fantasize any number of life choices for her; she might be a high-powered fashion executive or she just might marry Ken and "settle down" in her luxury condo. Her history is a barometer of changing fashions, changing gender and race relations, and a keen index of corporate America's anxious attempts to find new and more palatable ways of selling the beauty myth and commodity fetishism to new generations of parents and their daughters.

What is striking, then, is that while Barbie's identity may be mutable—one day she might be an astronaut, another a cheerleader—*her hyper-slender, big-chested body has remained fundamentally unchanged over the years*—a remarkable fact in a society that fetishizes the new and improved. Barbie, of course, did acquire flexible arms and legs as we know, her face has changed significantly, and her hair has grown by leaps and bounds (Melosh and Simmons 1986). But her body measurements, pointed toes, and proportions have not altered significantly. It is to that body and to the results of our class experiment in the anthropometry of Barbie that we now turn. But before taking out our calipers on Barbie and her friends to see how their bodies measure up, we want to offer a very brief historical overview of anthropometry to help us understand how the notion of the "average" American female body was debated in post-war United States.

THE MEASURED BODY: NORMS AND IDEALS

The paramount objective of physical anthropology is the gradual completion, in collaboration with the anatomists, the physiologists, and the chemists, of the study of the normal white man under ordinary circumstances.

—Ales Hrdlicka, 1925

Anthropometry, the science of measuring human bodies, belongs to a long line of techniques of the eighteenth and nineteenth centuries—craniometry, phrenology, comparative anatomy—concerned with measuring, comparing, and interpreting variability in the physical dimensions of the human body. Early anthropometry shared with these early sciences the expectation that the body was a window into a host of moral, temperamental, racial, or gender characteristics. It sought to distinguish itself from its predecessors, however, by being more rigorous and standardized in its techniques (Hrdlicka 1939:12). Head shape, especially cranial capacity, was a constant source of special fascination, but by the early part of this century, physical anthropologists, together with anatomists and medical doctors were developing a precise and routine set of measurements for the entire body that they hoped would permit systematic comparison of the human body across race, nationality, and gender.[5]

Anthropometry developed in the United States under the aegis of Ernest Hooton, Ales Hrdlicka, and Franz Boas, located respectively at Harvard, the Smithsonian, and Columbia University. Their main areas of interest were (1) identifying the physical features of racial and or national types, (2) the measurement of adaptation and "degeneracy," and (3) a comparison of the sexes. As is well documented by now, women and non-Europeans did not fare well in these emerging sciences of the body which held white males as the pinnacle of evolution (see the work of Blakey 1987; Gould 1981, Schiebinger 1989; Fee 1979; Russett 1989). Hooton, in his classic book, *Up from the Ape* (1931) regularly likened women and especially non-Europeans of both sexes to non-human primates. Similarly Hrdlicka's 1925 comparative study of male and female skulls went to rather extraordinary lengths to argue that women's brains (presumed at the time to be a sign of intelligence) were actually *smaller* than men's even though his measurements showed females to have a relatively *larger* cranial capacity than that of males.[6]

When it came to defining racial or national types, men, not women, were the most commonly studied.[7] Although Hrdlicka and others considered it necessary to measure both males and females, early physical anthropology textbooks reveal that more often than not it was the biologically male body that was selected to visually represent a particular race or humanity as a whole. Males were, in short, the unspoken prototype, while women's bodies were understood as a sexual subset. Women's bodies were frequently described as deviations from the generic or ideal type: their body fat "excessive;" their pelvis maladaptive to a bipedal (i.e. more evolved) posture; their musculature weak. Scientists seem to agree that what most dictated a woman's physical shape was her reproductive function. All other features were subordinated to and could be explained by this capacity to bear children. Not surprisingly, given this assumption, it was women's, particularly African or non-European women's, reproductive organs, genitalia, and secondary sexual characteristics, that were the most carefully scrutinized and measured (see Fausto-Sterling 1995).

In the United States, we begin to find an attempt to scientifically define a normative "American" female body in the late nineteenth and early twentieth centuries. By the 1860s, Harvard, as well as other universities, had begun to regularly collect anthropometric data on their male student populations, and in the 1890s comparable data began to be collected from the East Coast women's colleges as well. It was thus upper class, largely WASP, young people who were the basis of some of the early attempts to define the measurements of the "normal" American male and female. By basing themselves in elite colleges, "other" Americans—descendants of African slaves, North American Indians, and the many recent European migrants from Ireland, southern Europe, and eastern Europe—were effectively excluded from defining the norm. Rather, their bodies were more often the subject of racist evolutionary-oriented studies concerned with "race crossing," degeneracy, and the effects of the "civilizing" process (see Blakey 1987).

Academia was not the only place where body standards were being developed. By the early part of the twentieth century industry began to make widespread commercial use of practical anthropometry: the demand for standardized measures of the "average" body manifested in everything from designs for labor-efficient workstations and kitchens to standardized sizes in the ready-to-wear clothing industry (cf. Schwartz 1986). Soon insurance companies would enter the scene. Between 1900 and 1920, the first medico-actuarial standards of weight and height began to appear. The most significant of these, the Dublin Standard Table of Heights and Weights, developed in 1908 by Louis Dublin, a student of Franz Boas and statistician for the Metropolitan Life Insurance Company, became the authoritative reference in every doctor's office (cf. Bennett and Gurin 1982:130–138). However, what began as a table of statistical averages soon became a means of setting ideal "norms." Within a few years of its creation, the Dublin table shifted from providing a record of statistically "average" weights to becoming a guide to "desirable" weights which, interestingly enough, began to fall notably below the average weight for most adult women. Historian Joan Brumberg points to the Dublin Table, widely disseminated to doctors and published in popular magazines, together with the invention of the personal or bathroom scale, as the two devices most responsible in America for popularizing the notion that the human figure could be standardized and that abstract and often unrealistic norms could be uniformly applied (1988:232–235).

By the 1940s the search to describe the normal American male and female body in anthropometric terms was being conducted on many fronts fueled by a deepening concern about the physical fitness of the American people. Did Americans constitute a distinctive physical type? Were they physically stronger or weaker than their European ancestors? Could they defend themselves in time of war? And who did this category of "Americans" include? Questions such as these fed into an already long-standing preoccupation with defining a specifically American national character and, in 1945, led to the creation of some of the most celebrated and widely publicized life-size anthropometric statues of the century: Norm and Norma, the average American male and female. These statues, sculpted by Malvina Hoffman, were based on the composite measurements of thousands of white eighteen to twenty-five year old subjects. Both figures were put on display, but it was Norma who received the greatest media attention when the Cleveland Health Museum, which had purchased the pair, decided to sponsor a contest to find the woman in Ohio whose body most closely matched the dimensions of Norma. Under the catchy headline, "Are you Norma, Typical Woman?" the publicity surrounding this contest instructed women how to take their measurements for the contest. Within ten days, 3863 women had sent in their measurements to compete for the $100 prize in U.S. War Bonds that would go to the woman who most resembled the average American girl.

Besides bolstering the circulation of the *Cleveland Plain Dealer,* the idea behind the contest was to promote interest in physical fitness. Norma was described in the press as everything the young American woman should be in a time of war: fit, strong-bodied, and at the peak of her reproductive potential. Newspaper articles emphasized that women had a national responsibility to be fit if America was to continue to excel after the war. Few contestants apparently measured up to the challenge (Shapiro 1945). Only one percent came close to Norma's proportions. Commenting on the search for Norma, Dr. Gebhard, director of the Cleveland Health Museum, was quoted in one of the many newspaper articles as saying that "if a national inventory of the female population of this country were taken there would be as many "4Fs" among the women as were revealed among the men in the draft" (Robertson 1945:4). The contest provided the occasion for many health reformers to voice their concern about the weakening of the "American stock" and to call for eugenic marital selection and breeding.

Norma and Norm were thus always more than statistical composites; they were prescriptive ideals that, like the college studies that preceded them, erased American's racial and ethnic differences. The "average American" of the post-war period was still imagined as a youthful white body. However, there were competing ideals. Health reformers, educators, and doctors who approved and promoted Norma as an ideal for American women were well aware that her sensible, strong, thick-waisted body differed significantly from the tall, slim-hipped bodies of fashion models in vogue at the time.[8] As the post-war period advanced, Norma would be overshadowed by the array of images of fashion models and pin up girls put out by advertisers, the entertainment industry, and a burgeoning consumer culture. These fashion images were becoming increasingly thin in the sixties and seventies while the "average" woman's body was in fact getting heavier.

THE ANTHROPOMETRY OF BARBIE: TURNING THE TABLES

Anthropometry, like the very notion of a "normal" body it has been used to construct, is part of an unsavory history. Nevertheless, in the contemporary cultural context where an impossibly thin image of women's bodies has become the most popular children's toy ever sold, it strikes us it might just be the power tool we need for destabilizing a fantasy spun out of control. It was with this in mind that we asked students in one of our social biology classes to measure Barbie to see how her body compared to the average measurements of young American women of the same period. Besides estimating what Barbie's dimensions would be if she were life-size, we see the experiment as an occasion to turn the anthropometric tables from disciplining the bodies of living women, to measuring the ideals by which we have come to judge ourselves and others. We also see it as an opportunity for students who have grown up under the regimes of normalizing science, students who no doubt have been measured, weighed, and compared to standards since birth, to use those very tools to unsettle a highly popular cultural ideal.

Our initial experiment involved measuring many Barbies and Kens from different decades as well as some of their friends. Here we will only report on the results for Barbie and Ken from the Glitter Beach collection, as well as Jamal and Shani, Barbie's more recent African-American friends. (See Tables 1 and 2.) Mattel had marketed these latter dolls as having a more authentic African-American appearance and a "rounder more athletic" body, and we wanted to test that out.

After practicing with the calipers, discussing potential observational errors, and performing repeated trial runs, we began to record. In scaling Barbie to be life-sized, the students decided to translate her measurements using two standards: (a) If Barbie were a fashion model (5'10") and (b) if she were of average height for women in the United States (5'4"). We also decided to measure Ken in the same way, using an average male stature, which we designated as 5'8", and the more "idealized" stature for men, 6'. We report here only the highlights of the measurements taken on the newer Barbie and newer Ken, Jamal, and Shani, scaled at the fashion-model height. For purposes of comparison, we include data on average body measurements from the standardized published tables of

TABLE 1   Measurements of Glitter Beach Barbie, African-American Shani, and the Average Measurements of the 1988 U.S. Army Women Recruits.[1]

Meas.	Barbie	Shani	U.S. Army "Norma"
Height	5'10"	5'10"	5'4"
Chest Circum.	35"	35"	35.7"
Waist Circum.	20"	20"	31"
Hip Circum.[2]	32.50"	31.25"	38.10"
Hip Breadth	11.6"	11.0"	13.49"
Thigh Circum.	19.25"	20.00"	22.85"

[1]"Norma" is based on 2,208 army recruits, 1,140 of which were white, 922 of which were black.
[2]Hip circumference is referred to as "buttock circumference" in anthropometric parlance.

TABLE 2   Measurements of Glitter Beach Ken, African-American Ken, and the Average Measurements of the 1988 U.S. Army Male Recruits.[1]

Meas.	Ken	Jamal	U.S. Army "Norm"
Height	6'0"	6'0"	5'9"
Chest Circum.	38.4"	38.4"	39.0"
Waist Circum.	28.8"	28.8"	33.1"
Hip Circum.[2]	36.0"	36.0"	38.7"
Hip Breadth	12.2"	12.2"	13.46"
Thigh Circum.	20.4"	20.4"	23.48"

[1]"Norm" is based on 1,774 males, 1,172 of which were white and 458 of which were black.
[2]Hip circumference is referred to as "buttock circumference" in anthropometric parlance.

the 1988 Anthropometric Survey of Army Personnel. We have dubbed these composites for the female and male recruits "Army Norma" and "Army Norm," respectively.

Both Barbie and Shani's measurements at 5'10" reveal the extreme thinness expected of the runway model. Both dolls have considerably smaller measurements than Army Norma *at all points,* even though they are six inches taller than her. When we scaled the dolls to 5'4"—the same as Army Norma—we can see just how skewed the dimensions are: Barbie's chest, waist, and hip measurements come out as 32"–17"–28," clinically anorectic to say the least. We also wanted to see if Mattel had physically changed the Barbie mold in making Shani. Most of the differences we could find appeared to be in the face. Shani's nose is broader and her lips are slightly larger. The only significant difference we found in the bodies was that Shani's back is arched in such a way that it tilts her buttocks up, producing the visual illusion of a higher, rounder, butt . . . Perhaps this is what Mattel was referring to in claiming that Shani has a realistic or ethnically correct body (Jones 1991).

When it came to the male dolls, we did not find the same kind of dramatic difference between them and Army Norm as we did in the female dolls. As the table shows, Ken and Jamal were largely identical to each other, and they were only somewhat slimmer than the average soldier. Visually Ken and Jamal appear very tight and muscular and "bulked out," while the U.S. Army males tend to carry slightly more fat, judging from the photographs and data presented in the 1988 study.

OUR BARBIES, OUR SELVES

I feel like Barbie; everyone calls me Barbie; I love Barbie. The main difference is she's plastic and I'm real. There isn't really any other difference.

—Hayley Spicer, winner of Great Britain's Barbie-Look-Alike competition

Our venture into anthropometry revealed that Barbie has a much more "abnormal" body than does Ken. But her hyper-thin body was by no means exceptional. Studies tracking the body measurements of Playboy magazine centerfolds and Miss America contestants show that between 1959 and 1978 the average weight and hip size for women in both of these groups has decreased steadily while the average weight of women was increasing (Wiseman, Gray, Mosimann, and Ahrens 1992). A follow up study for the years 1979–1988 found this trend continuing into the eighties: approximately 69% of Playboy centerfolds and 60% of Miss America contestants were weighing in at 15% or more below their expected age and height category. In short, the majority of women presented to us in the media as having desirable feminine bodies, were, like Barbie, well on their way to qualifying for anorexia nervosa.

On the surface, at least, it might seem that Barbie's signature thin body would seem at odds with the doll's seemingly endless desire for consumption and self-transformation. Being thin for most women requires repression of desire and self-discipline, neither of which are traits we associate with the consummate shopper. And yet, as Susan Bordo (1990) has argued in regard to anorexia, these two phenomena—hyper-thin bodies and hyper consumption—are very much linked in advanced capitalist economies which depend upon commodity excess. Bodies, says Bordo, are where the regulation of desire is played out most keenly. The imperative to manage the body and to "be all that you can be"—in fact the idea that you can *choose* the body that you want to have—is a pervasive feature of consumer culture. Keeping control of one's body, not getting too fat or flabby, in other words, conforming to gendered norms of fitness and weight, have become signs of an individual's social and moral worth. But as Bordo, Sandra Bartky (1990), and other feminist scholars have been quick to point out, not all bodies are subject to the same degree of scrutiny or the same repercussions if they fail. It is women's bodies and desires in particular where the structural contradictions—the simultaneous incitement to consume and social condemnation for overindulgence—appear to be most acutely manifested in bodily regimes of intense self-monitoring and discipline. Just as it is women's appearance which is subject to greater social scrutiny, so it is that women's desires, hunger, and appetites are seen as most threatening and in need of control in a patriarchal society.

This cultural context is relevant to making sense of Barbie and the meaning her body holds in late consumer capitalism. In dressing and undressing Barbie, combing her hair, bathing her, turning and twisting her limbs in imaginary scenarios, children acquire a very tactile and intimate sense of Barbie's body. Barbie is presented in packaging and advertising as a role model, a best friend, or older sister to little girls. Television jingles use the refrain, "I want to be just like you," while look-alike clothes and look-alike contests make it possible for girls to live out the fantasy of being Barbie. In short, there is every reason to believe that girls (or adult women) link Barbie's body shape with her popularity and glamour.

This is exactly what worries many people. As our measurements show, Barbie's body differs wildly from anything approximating "average" female body weight and proportions. Over the years her wasp-waisted body has evoked a steady stream of critique for having a negative impact on little girls' sense of self-esteem. For example, the release of a Barbie aerobics work-out video for girls in 1992 was met with the following angry letter from an expert in the field of eating disorders:

> I had hoped these plastic dolls with impossible proportions would have faded away in this current health-conscious period; not at all. . . . Move over Jane Fonda. Welcome again, ever smiling breast-thrusting Barbie with your stick legs and sweat-free aerobic routines. I'm concerned about the role model message she is giving our young. Surely it's hard to accept a little cellulite when the culture tells you unrelentingly how to strive for thinness and the perfect body. [Warner 1992)][9]

There is no doubt that Barbie's body contributes to what Kim Chernin (1981) has called "the tyranny of slenderness."[10] But is repression all her hyper-thin body conveys? In her work on how anorectic women see themselves, Susan Bordo writes that, "for anorectics, [the slender ideal] may have a very different meaning; it may symbolize, not so much the containment of female desire, as its liberation from a domestic, reproductive destiny" (Bordo 1990:103).

Similar observations have been made about cosmetic surgery: women often explain their experience as one of empowerment, of taking charge of their bodies and lives (Balsamo 1993; Davis 1991). What does this mean for making sense of Barbie and her long lasting appeal? We would suggest that a sub-text of agency and independence, even transgression, accompanies this pencil-thin icon of femininity. On the one hand, one can argue that Barbie's body displays conformity to dominant cultural imperatives for a disciplined body and contained feminine desires. On the other hand, however, her excessive slenderness can also signify a rebellious manifestation of willpower, a refusal of the maternal ideal, symbolized by pendulous breasts, rounded stomach and hips. Hers is a body of hard edges, distinct borders, and self-control. It is literally impenetrable. While the anorectic woman becomes increasingly androgynous the more she starves herself, Barbie, in the realm of plastic fantasy, is able to remain powerfully sexualized with her large gravity-defying breasts, even while she is distinctly non-reproductive. Like the "hard bodies" in fitness advertising, Barbie's body may signify for women the pleasure of control and mastery both of which are highly valued traits in American society and both of which are predominantly associated with masculinity (Bordo 1990:105). Putting these elements together with her apparent independent wealth can make for a very different reading of Barbie than that of bimbo. To paraphrase one Barbie doll owner: she owns a Ferrari and doesn't have a husband; she must be doing something right.[11]

By invoking these testimonies of anorectic women, we are not trying to suggest that playing with Barbie, or trying to become like Barbie, are paths to empowerment for little girls. Rather we want to signal the complex and contradictory meanings that her body has in contemporary American society. And we also want to underscore that our bodies, whatever the reigning ideal might be, continue to function as a vitally important stage on which gender—as well as race and class—conformity and transgression are played out.[12] It is clear that a next step we would want to take in the cultural interpretation of Barbie is an ethnographic study of Barbie doll owners.[13] It is sensible to assume that the children who play with Barbie are themselves creative users who respond variously to the messages about femininity encoded in her fashions and appearance. In the hands of their adult and child owners, Barbies have become Amazon cave warriors, drag queens, dutiful mommies, and evil axe murderers.[14] As we consider Barbie's many meanings, we should also note that the doll has become a world traveler. A product of the global assembly-line, Barbie dolls owe their existence to the internationalization of the labor market and global flows of capital and commodities that today characterize the toy industry as well as other industries in the post-war era. Designed in Los Angeles, manufactured in Taiwan or Malaysia, distributed worldwide, Barbie[TM] is American-made in name only. Speeding her way into an expanding global market, Barbie brings with her some of the North American cultural subtext we have outlined in this analysis. How this teenage survivor has inserted herself into the cultural landscapes of Mayan villages, Bombay high rises, and Malagasy towns is a rich topic that begs to be explored.

ACKNOWLEDGMENTS

This essay is based on a longer piece of research first published in Urla and Swedlund (1995). Follow-up research we have carried out on the ideal of the thin waist will appear in Orgel, Urla, and Swedlund (in press).

NOTES

1. The statistics and figures provided on sales reflect research carried out in the nineties.

2. While the concept of adolescence as a distinct developmental stage between puberty and adulthood was not new to the fifties, Thomas Doherty (1988) notes that it wasn't until the end of World War II that the term "teenager" became standard usage in the American language.

3. More work needs to be done on how Barbie dolls are adapted to appeal to various national markets. For example, Barbie dolls manufactured in Japan for Japanese consumption are reputed to have noticeably larger, rounder eyes than those marketed in the United States (see Billyboy 1987). For some suggestive thoughts on the cultural implications of the transnational flow of toys like Barbie dolls, TransFormers, and He-Man, see Carol Breckenridge's (1990) brief but intriguing editor's comment to *Public Culture*.

4. On Black Barbies see duCille 1995.

5. Though measurements of skulls, noses, and facial angles for scientific comparison had been going on throughout the nineteenth century, it wasn't until the 1890s that any serious attempts were made to standardize anthropometric measurements of the living body. This culminated in the Monaco agreement of 1906, one of the first international meetings to standardize anthropometric measurement. For a brief review of the attempts to use and systematize photography in anthropometry see Spencer (1992).

6. Hrdlicka argued, rather fantastically, that there was more space between the brain and the cranium in women than in men. Michael Blakey refers to this as Hrdlicka's "air head" hypothesis (1987:16).

7. In her study of eighteenth century physical sciences, Schiebinger (1993) remarks that male bodies (skulls in particular) were routinely assumed to embody the prototype of their race in the various typologies devised by comparative anatomists of the period. "When anthropologists did compare women across cultures, their interest centered on sexual traits—feminine beauty, redness of lips, length and style of hair, size and shape of breasts or clitorises, degree of sexual desire, fertility, and above all the size, shape, and position of the pelvis" (1993:156). In this way, the male body "remained the touchstone of human anatomy," while females were regarded as a sexual subset of the species (1993:159–160).

8. Historians have noted a long-standing conflict between the physical culture movement, eugenicists, and health reformers on the one hand, and the fashion industry on the other that gave rise to competing ideals in American society of the fit and the fashionably fragile woman (e.g. Banner 1983; Cogan 1989).

9. When confronted with these kinds of accusations, Mattel and the fashion industry protest that Barbie dolls, like fashion models, are about fantasy, not reality. "We're not telling you to be that girl" writes Elizabeth Saltzman, fashion editor for *Vogue*. "We're trying to show you fashion" (France 1992:22).

10. In response to this anxiety, Cathy Meredig, an enterprising computer software designer, created the "Happy to be Me" doll. Described as a healthy alternative for little girls, "Happy to be Me" has a shorter neck, shorter legs, wider waist, and larger feet, and a lot fewer clothes,

designed to make her look more like the average woman ("She's No Barbie, Nor Does She Care to Be." *New York Times,* August 15, 1991, C-11).

11. "Dolls in Playland." 1992. Colleen Toomey, producer. BBC.

12. For an illuminating case study of race, class, and gender codings of the female body, see Krause 1998.

13. While not exactly ethnographic, Hohmann (1985) offers a socio-psychological study of how children experiment with social relations during play with Barbies.

14. Barbie has become a somewhat celebrated figure among avant-garde and pop artists, giving rise to a whole genre of Barbie satire known as "Barbie Noire" (Kahn 1991; Ebersole and Peabody 1993). On queer appropriations of Barbie and Ken, see Rand (1995).

REFERENCES

Adelson, Andrea. 1992. And Now, Barbie Looks Like a Billion. *New York Times.* Nov. 26. pg. D3.

Balsamo, Anne. 1993. On the Cutting Edge: Cosmetic Surgery and the Technological Production of the Gendered Body. *Camera Obscura* 28: 207–238.

Banner, Lois W. 1983. *American Beauty.* New York, Knopf.

Bartky, Sandra Lee. 1990. Foucault, Femininity, and the Modernization of Patriarchal Power. In *Femininity and Domination: Studies in the Phenomenology of Oppression,* 63–82. New York: Routledge.

Bennett, William and Joel Gurin. 1982. *The Dieter's Dilemma: Eating Less and Weighing More.* New York: Basic Books.

Billyboy. 1987. *Barbie, Her Life and Times, and the New Theater of Fashion.* New York: Crown Publishers.

Blakey, Michael L. 1987. Skull Doctors: Instrinsic Social and Political Bias in the History of American Physical Anthropology. *Critique of Anthropology* 7(2): 7–35.

Bordo, Susan R. 1990. Reading the Slender Body. In *Body/Politics: Women and the Discourses of Science,* eds. M. Jacobus, E. Fox Keller, and S. Shuttleworth, 83–112. New York: Routledge.

Bordo, Susan R. 1991. 'Material Girl': The Effacements of Postmodern Culture. In *The Female Body: Figures, Styles, Speculations,* ed. L. Goldstein, 106–130. Ann Arbor, MI: The University of Michigan Press.

Breckenridge, Carol A. 1990. Editor's Comment: On Toying with Terror. *Public Culture* 2(2): i–iii.

Brumberg, Joan Jacobs. 1988. *Fasting Girls: The History of Anorexia Nervosa.* New York: New American Library.

Chernin, Kim. 1981. *The Obsession: Reflections on the Tyranny of Slenderness.* New York: Harper.

Cogan, Frances B. 1989. *All-American Girl: The Ideal of Real Woman-hood in Mid-Nineteenth Century America.* Athens and London: University of Georgia Press.

Davis, Kathy. 1991. Remaking the She-Devil: A Critical Look at Feminist Approaches to Beauty. *Hypatia* 6(2): 21–43.

Doherty, Thomas. 1988. *Teenagers and Teenpics. The Juvenilization of American Movies in the 1950's.* Boston: Unwin Hyman.

duCille, Ann. 1995. Toy Theory: Blackface Barbie and the Deep Play of Difference. In *The Skin Trade: Essays on Race, Gender and Merchandising of Difference.* Cambridge: Harvard University Press.

Ebersole, Lucinda and Richard Peabody, eds. 1993. *Mondo Barbie.* New York: St. Martin's Press.

Fausto-Sterling, Anne. 1995. Gender, Race and Nation: The Comparative Anatomy of "Hottentot" Women in Europe, 1815–1817. In *Deviant Bodies: Critical Perspectives on Difference in Science and Popular Culture,* eds. J. Terry and J. Urla. Bloomington: Indiana University Press.

Fee, Elizabeth. 1979. Nineteenth Century Craniology: The Study of the Female Skull. *Bulletin of the History of Medicine* 53: 415–433.

France, Kim. 1992. "Tits 'R' Us." *Village Voice,* March 17, p. 22.

Frith, Simon. 1981. *Sound Effects: Youth, Leisures, and the Politics of Rock'n' Roll.* New York: Pantheon.

Gould, Steven Jay. 1981. *The Mismeasure of Man.* New York: Norton.

Hohmann, Delf Maria. 1985. Jennifer and Her Barbies: A Contextual Analysis of a Child Playing Barbie Dolls. *Canadian Folklore Canadien* 7(1–2): 111–120.

Hooton, E. A. 1931. Up from the Ape. New York: The MacMillan Company.

Hrdlicka, Ales. 1925. Relation of the Size of the Head and Skull to Capacity in the Two Sexes. *American Journal of Physical Anthropology* 8: 249–250.

Hrdlicka, Ales. 1939. *Practical Anthropometry.* Philadelphia: Wistar Institute of Anatomy and Biology.

Jones, Lisa. 1991. Skin Trade: A Doll Is Born. *Village Voice.* March 26, p. 36.

Kahn, Alice. 1991. A Onetime Bimbo Becomes a Muse. *New York Times.* September 29.

Kaw, Eugenia. 1993. Medicalization of Racial Features: Asian American Women and Cosmetic Surgery. *Medical Anthropology Quarterly* 7(1): 74–89.

Krause, Elizabeth. 1998. A Bead of Raw Sweat in a Field of Dainty Perspirers: Nationalism, Whiteness and the Olympic Ordeal of Tonya Harding. *Transforming Anthropology* 7(1).

Lawson, Carol. 1993. Toys Will Be Toys: The Stereotypes Unravel. *New York Times.* February 11. C1, C8.

Lord, M. G. 1994. *Forever Barbie: The Unauthorized Biography of a Real Doll.* New York: William Morrow.

May, Elaine Tyler. 1988. *Homeward Bound: American Families in the Cold War Era.* New York: Basic Books.

Melosh, Barbara and Christina Simmons. 1986. Exhibiting Women's History. In *Presenting the Past: Essays on History and the Public,* eds. Susan Porter Benson, Stephen Brier, and Roy Rosenzweig. Philadelphia: Temple University Press.

Motz, Marilyn Ferris. 1983. 'I Want to Be a Barbie Doll When I Grow Up': The Cultural Significance of the Barbie Doll. In *The Popular Culture Reader,* 3rd ed, eds. Christopher D. Geist and Jack Nachbar, 122–136. Bowling Green: Bowling Green University Popular Press.

Newsweek. 1990. Finally, Barbie Dolls go Ethnic. *Newsweek* (August 13), p. 48.

Orgel, Mary, Jacqueline Urla and Alan Swedlund. In press. Surveying a Cultural Waist-land: Biological Poetics and Politics of the Female Body. In *Anthropology United: Challenging Bio-Social Reductivisms,* eds. Susan McKinnon and Sydel Silverman. University of Chicago Press.

Rabinowitz, Paula. 1993. Accessorizing History: Girls and Popular Culture. Discussant Comments, Panel #150: "Engendering Post-war Popular Culture in Britain and America. "Ninth Berkshire Conference on the History of Women. Vassar College, June 11–13.

Rand, Erica. 1994. "We Girls Can Do Anything, Right Barbie? Lesbian Consumption in Postmodern Circulation." In *Lesbian Postmodern,* ed. Laura Doan, 189–209. New York: Columbia.

Rand, Erica. 1995. *Barbie's Queer Accessories.* Durham and London: Duke University Press.

Robertson, Josephine. 1945. Theatre Cashier, 23, Wins Title of "Norma." *Cleveland Plain Dealer.* September 21, pp. 1, 4.

Russett, Cynthia Eagle. 1989. *Sexual Science: The Victorian Construction of Womanhood.* Cambridge, MA: Harvard University Press.

Schiebinger, Londa. 1989. *The Mind Has No Sex: Women in the Origins of Modern Science.* Cambridge: Harvard University Press.

Schiebinger, Londa. 1993. *Nature's Body: Gender in the Making of Modern Science.* Boston: Beacon Press.

Schwartz, Hillel. 1986. *Never Satisfied: A Cultural History of Diets, Fantasies and Fat.* New York: The Free Press.

Shapiro, Eben. 1992. 'Totally Hot, Totally Cool.' Long-Haired Barbie Is a Hit. *New York Times.* June 22. p. D-9.

Shapiro, Harry L. 1945. *Americans: Yesterday, Today, Tomorrow.* Man and Nature Publications. (Science Guide No. 126). New York: The American Museum of Natural History.

Spencer, Frank. 1992. Some Notes on the Attempt to Apply Photography to Anthropometry during the Second Half of the Nineteenth Century. In *Anthropology and Photography: 1860–1920,* ed. Elizabeth Edwards, 99–107. New Haven, CT: Yale University Press.

Stevenson, Richard. 1991. Mattel Thrives as Barbie Grows. *New York Times.* December 2.

Urla, Jacqueline and Alan Swedlund. 1995. The Anthropometry of Barbie: Unsettling Ideals of the Feminine Body in Popular Culture. In *Deviant Bodies: Critical Perspectives on Difference in Science and Popular Culture,* eds. J. Terry and J. Urla, 277–313. Bloomington: Indiana University Press.

Warner, Patricia Rosalind. 1992. Letter to the Editor. *Boston Globe.* June 28.

Williams, Lena. 1992. Woman's Image in a Mirror: Who Defines What She Sees? *New York Times.* February 6. A1; B7.

Willis, Susan. 1991. *A Primer for Daily Life.* London and New York: Routledge.

Wilson, Elizabeth. 1985. *Adorned in Dreams: Fashion and Modernity.* London: Virago.

Wiseman, C., Gray, J., Mosimann, J., and Ahrens, A. 1992. Cultural Expectations of Thinness in Women: An Update. *International Journal of Eating Disorders* 11(1): 85–89.

Wolf, Naomi. 1991. *The Beauty Myth: How Images of Beauty Are Used Against Women.* New York: William Morrow.

17

Do Muslim Women Really Need Saving?

Anthropological Reflections
on Cultural Relativism and Its Others

Lila Abu-Lughod

Religious differences, including the moral and socio-cultural assumptions subsumed by religion, are extremely important for understanding our globalizing world. After September 11, 2001, the United States went to war in Afghanistan to fight the Taliban, the ruling group in that country, who were believed to be harboring al Qaeda operatives. In addition to the search for Osama bin Laden, a major rationale for going to war was to "liberate" Afghani women from the Taliban. In U.S. political and media discourses, the *burqa*, a black head-to-toe cotton veil mandated by the Taliban for women in public places, became a symbol of women's oppression in Afghanistan.

Prior to invasion by the United States, Afghanistan had a difficult and war-torn history. For years the country was wracked with civil wars, which were made worse by the fact that the United States and the USSR armed rival Afghani factions as pawns in the Cold War. (The Taliban became a powerful group during that period in part because of American financial support for the Islamic radicals.) When the Taliban took control of most of Afghanistan in the late 1990s, many Afghans were cautiously optimistic, hoping that the country might finally experience some peace after years of civil war.

In this selection, anthropologist Lila Abu-Lughod argues that the "liberation of women" rationale for going to war was ethnocentric, and that the focus on the *burqa* ignored issues that may be more important to Afghani women, such as living in an area free from war. Important historical and political connections were ignored by U.S. political leaders, she argues, in favor of the simplistic East-West dichotomy that was used to justify

invasion. American cultural beliefs about the "other" can be exploited in attempts to sway public opinion.

Although it has largely fallen from the headlines, the United States has continued to maintain a significant military presence in Afghanistan. Poor security and lack of basic infrastructure have remained pressing problems in most of the country. A positive future for Afghanis—women and men—is far from assured.

As you read this selection, ask yourself the following questions:

- What was "colonial feminism"? Why was it problematic?

- Why might some women choose to wear a veil?

- In this selection, Abu-Lughod asks, "Can we only free Afghan women to be like us, or might we have to recognize that even after 'liberation' from the Taliban, they might want different things than we would want for them? What do we do about that?" How would you answer this question?

- Why it is problematic to associate feminism with the West?

- How might Americans try to help Afghani women in ways that do not involve "saving" them?

The following terms discussed in this selection are included in the Glossary at the back of the book:

burqa	*Islam*
colonialism	*Muslim*
cultural relativism	*purdah*
ethnocentrism	

What are the ethics of the current "War on Terrorism," a war that justifies itself by purporting to liberate, or save, Afghan women? Does anthropology have anything to offer in our search for a viable position to take regarding this rationale for war?

I want to point out the minefields—a metaphor that is sadly too apt for a country like Afghanistan, with the world's highest number of mines per capita—of this obsession with the plight of Muslim women. I hope to show some way through them using insights from anthropology, the discipline whose charge has been to understand and manage cultural difference.

The question is why knowing about the "culture" of the region, and particularly its religious beliefs and treatment of women, was more urgent than exploring the history of the development of repressive regimes in the region and the U.S. role in this history. Such cultural framing, it seemed to me, prevented the serious exploration of the roots and nature of human suffering in this part of the world. Instead of political and historical explanations, experts were being asked to give religio-cultural ones. Instead of questions that might lead to the exploration of global interconnections, we were offered ones that worked to artificially divide the world into separate spheres—recreating an imaginative geography of West versus East, us versus Muslims, cultures in which First Ladies give speeches versus others where women shuffle around silently in burqas.

Most pressing for me was why the Muslim woman in general, and the Afghan woman in particular, were so crucial to this cultural mode of explanation, which ignored the complex entanglements in which we are all implicated, in sometimes surprising alignments. Why were these female symbols being mobilized in this "War against Terrorism" in a way they were not in other conflicts? Laura Bush's radio address on November 17 reveals the political work such mobilization accomplishes. On the one hand, her address collapsed important distinctions that should have been maintained. There was a constant slippage between the Taliban and the terrorists, so that they became almost one word—a kind of hyphenated monster identity: the Taliban-and-the-terrorists. Then there was the blurring of the very separate causes in Afghanistan of women's continuing malnutrition, poverty, and ill health, and their more recent exclusion under the Taliban from employment, schooling, and the joys of wearing nail polish. On the other hand, her speech reinforced chasmic divides, primarily between the "civilized people throughout the world" whose hearts break for the women and children of Afghanistan and the Taliban-and-the-terrorists, the cultural monsters who want to, as she put it, "impose their world on the rest of us."

Most revealingly, the speech enlisted women to justify American bombing and intervention in Afghanistan and to make a case for the "War on Terrorism" of which it was allegedly a part. As Laura Bush said, "Because of our recent military gains in much of Afghanistan, women are no longer imprisoned in their homes. They can listen to music and teach their daughters without fear of punishment. . . . The fight against terrorism is also a fight for the rights and dignity of women" (U.S. Government 2002).

These words have haunting resonances for anyone who has studied colonial history. Many who have worked on British colonialism in South Asia have noted the use of the woman question in colonial policies where intervention into sati (the practice of widows immolating themselves on their husbands' funeral pyres), child marriage, and other practices was used to justify rule. As Gayatri Chakravorty Spivak (1988) has cynically put it: white men saving brown women from brown men. The historical record is full of similar cases, including in the Middle East. In *Turn of the Century Egypt,* what Leila Ahmed (1992) has called "colonial feminism" was hard at work. This was a selective concern about the plight of Egyptian women that focused on the veil as a sign of oppression but gave no support to women's education and was professed loudly by the same Englishman, Lord Cromer, who opposed women's suffrage back home.

Sociologist Marnia Lazreg (1994) has offered some vivid examples of how French colonialism enlisted women to its cause in Algeria. She describes skits at awards ceremonies at the Muslim Girls' School in Algiers in 1851 and 1852. In the first skit, written by "a French lady from Algiers," two Algerian Arab girls reminisced about their trip to France with words including the following:

> Oh! Protective France: Oh! Hospitable France! . . .
> Noble land, where I felt free
> Under Christian skies to pray to our God: . . . .
> God bless you for the happiness you bring us!
> And you, adoptive mother, who taught us
> That we have a share of this world,
> We will cherish you forever! [Lazreg 1994:68–69]

These girls are made to invoke the gift of a share of this world, a world where freedom reigns under Christian skies. This is not the world the Taliban-and-the-terrorists would "like to impose on the rest of us."

Just as I argued above that we need to be suspicious when neat cultural icons are plastered over messier historical and political narratives, so we need to be wary when Lord Cromer in British-ruled Egypt, French ladies in Algeria, and Laura Bush, all with military troops behind them, claim to be saving or liberating Muslim women.

POLITICS OF THE VEIL

I want now to look more closely at those Afghan women Laura Bush claimed were "rejoicing" at their liberation by the Americans. This necessitates a discussion of the veil, or the burqa, because it is so central to contemporary concerns about Muslim women. This will set the stage for a discussion of how anthropologists, feminist anthropologists in particular, contend with the problem of difference in a global world. In the conclusion, I will return to the rhetoric of saving Muslim women and offer an alternative.

It is common popular knowledge that the ultimate sign of the oppression of Afghan women under the Taliban-and-the-terrorists is that they were forced to wear the burqa. Liberals sometimes confess their surprise that even though Afghanistan has been liberated from the Taliban, women do not seem to be throwing off their burqas. Someone who has worked in Muslim regions must ask why this is so surprising. Did we expect that once "free" from the Taliban they would go "back" to belly shirts and blue jeans, or dust off their Chanel suits? We need to be more sensible about the clothing of "women of cover," and so there is perhaps a need to make some basic points about veiling.

First, it should be recalled that the Taliban did not invent the burqa. It was the local form of covering that Pashtun women in one region wore when they went out. The Pashtun are one of several ethnic groups in Afghanistan and the burqa was one of many forms of covering in the subcontinent and Southwest Asia that has developed as a convention for symbolizing women's modesty or respectability. The burqa, like some other forms of "cover" has, in many settings, marked the symbolic separation of men's and women's spheres, as part of the general association of women with family and home, not with public space where strangers mingled.

Twenty years ago the anthropologist Hanna Papanek (1982), who worked in Pakistan, described the burqa as "portable seclusion." She noted that many saw it as a liberating invention because it enabled women to move out of segregated living spaces while still observing the basic moral requirements of separating and protecting women from unrelated men. Ever since I came across her phrase "portable seclusion," I have thought of these enveloping robes as "mobile homes." Everywhere, such veiling signifies belonging to a particular community and participating in a moral way of life in which families are paramount in the organization of communities and the home is associated with the sanctity of women.

The obvious question that follows is this: If this were the case, why would women suddenly become immodest? Why would they suddenly throw off the markers of their respectability, markers, whether burqas or other forms of cover, which were supposed to assure their protection in the public sphere from the harassment of strange men by symbolically signaling to all that they were still in the inviolable space of their homes, even though moving in the public realm? Especially when these are forms of dress that had become so conventional that most women gave little thought to their meaning.

To draw some analogies, none of them perfect, why are we surprised that Afghan women do not throw off their burqas when we know perfectly well that it would not be appropriate to wear shorts to the opera? At the time these discussions of Afghan women's burqas were raging, a friend of mine was chided by her husband for suggesting she wanted to wear a pantsuit to a fancy wedding: "You know you don't wear pants to a WASP wedding," he reminded her. New Yorkers know that the beautifully coiffed Hasidic women ... are wearing wigs. This is because religious belief and community standards of propriety require the covering of the hair. They also alter boutique fashions to include high necks and long sleeves. As anthropologists know perfectly well, people wear the appropriate form of dress for their social communities and are guided by socially shared standards, religious beliefs, and moral ideals, unless they deliberately transgress to make a point or are unable to afford proper cover. If we think that U.S. women live in a world of choice regarding clothing, all we need to do is remind ourselves of the expression, "the tyranny of fashion."

What had happened in Afghanistan under the Taliban is that one regional style of covering or veiling, associated with a certain respectable but not elite class, was imposed on everyone as "religiously" appropriate, even though previously there had been many different styles, popular or traditional with different groups and classes—different ways to mark women's propriety, or, in more recent times, religious piety. Although I am not an expert on Afghanistan, I imagine that the majority of women left in Afghanistan by the time the Taliban took control were the rural or less educated, from nonelite families, since they were the only ones who could not emigrate to escape the hardship and violence that has marked Afghanistan's recent history. If liberated from the enforced wearing of burqas, most of these women would choose some other form of modest headcovering, like all those living nearby who were not under the Taliban—their rural Hindu counterparts in the North of India (who cover their heads and veil their faces from affines) or their Muslim sisters in Pakistan.

Even *The New York Times* carried an article about Afghan women refugees in Pakistan that attempted to educate readers about this local variety (Fremson 2001). The article describes and pictures everything from the now-iconic burqa with the embroidered eyeholes, which a Pashtun woman explains is the proper dress for her community, to large scarves they call chadors, to the new Islamic modest dress that wearers refer to as *hijab*. Those in the new Islamic dress are characteristically students heading for professional careers, especially in medicine, just like their counterparts from Egypt to Malaysia. One wearing the large scarf was a school principal; the other was a poor street vendor. The telling quote from the young street vendor is, "If I did [wear the burqa] the refugees would tease me because the burqa is for 'good women' who stay inside the home" (Fremson 2001:14). Here you can see the local status associated with the burqa—it is for good respectable women from strong families who are not forced to make a living selling on the street.

The British newspaper *The Guardian* published an interview in January 2002 with Dr. Suheila Siddiqi, a respected surgeon in Afghanistan who holds the rank of lieutenant general in the Afghan medical corps (Goldenberg 2002). A woman in her sixties, she comes from an elite family and, like her sisters, was educated. Unlike most women of her class, she chose not to go into exile. She is presented in the article as "the woman who stood up to the Taliban" because she refused to wear the burqa. She had made it a condition of returning to her post as head of a major hospital when the Taliban came begging in 1996, just eight months after firing her along with other women. Siddiqi is described as thin, glamorous, and confident. But further into the article it is noted that her graying bouffant hair is covered in a gauzy veil. This is a reminder that though she refused the burqa, she had no question about wearing the chador or scarf.

Finally, I need to make a crucial point about veiling. Not only are there many forms of covering, which themselves have different meanings in the communities in which they are used, but also veiling itself must not be confused with, or made to stand for, lack of agency. As I have argued in my ethnography of a Bedouin community in Egypt in the late 1970s and 1980s (1986), pulling the black head cloth over the face in front of older respected men is considered a voluntary act by women who are deeply committed to being moral and have a sense of honor tied to family. One of the ways they show their standing is by covering their faces in certain contexts. They decide for whom they feel it is appropriate to veil.

To take a very different case, the modern Islamic modest dress that many educated women across the Muslim world have taken on since the mid-1970s now both publicly marks piety and can be read as a sign of educated urban sophistication, a sort of modernity (e.g., Abu-Lughod 1995, 1998; Brenner 1996; El Guindi 1999; MacLeod 1991; Ong 1990). As Saba Mahmood (2001) has so brilliantly shown in her ethnography of women in the mosque movement in Egypt, this new form of dress is also perceived by many of the women who adopt it as part of a bodily means to cultivate virtue, the outcome of their professed desire to be close to God.

Two points emerge from this fairly basic discussion of the meanings of veiling in the contemporary Muslim world. First, we need to work against the reductive interpretation of veiling as the quintessential sign of women's unfreedom, even if we object to state imposition of this form, as in Iran or with the Taliban. (It must be recalled that the modernizing states of Turkey and Iran had earlier in the century banned veiling and required men, except religious clerics, to adopt Western dress.) What does freedom mean if we accept the fundamental premise that humans are social beings, always raised in certain social and historical contexts and belonging to particular communities that shape their desires and understandings of the world? Is it not a gross violation of women's own understandings of what they are doing to simply denounce the burqa as a medieval imposition? Second, we must take care not to reduce the diverse situations and attitudes of millions of Muslim women to a single item of clothing. Perhaps it is time to give up the Western obsession with the veil and focus on some serious issues with which feminists and others should indeed be concerned.

Ultimately, the significant political-ethical problem the burqa raises is how to deal with cultural "others." How are we to deal with difference without accepting the passivity implied by the cultural relativism for which anthropologists are justly famous—a relativism that says it's their culture and it's not my business to judge or interfere, only to try to understand. Cultural relativism is certainly an improvement on ethnocentrism and the racism, cultural imperialism, and imperiousness that underlie it; the problem is that it is too late not to interfere. The forms of lives we find around the world are already products of long histories of interactions.

We need to look closely at what we are supporting (and what we are not) and to think carefully about why.... I do not know how many feminists who felt good about saving Afghan women from the Taliban are also asking for a global redistribution of wealth or contemplating sacrificing their own consumption radically so that African or Afghan women could have some chance of having what I do believe should be a universal human right—the right to freedom from the structural violence of global inequality and from the ravages of war, the everyday rights of having enough to eat, having homes for their families in which to live and thrive, having ways to make decent livings so their children can grow, and having the strength and security to work out, within their communities and with whatever alliances they want, how to live a good life, which might very well include changing the ways those communities are organized.

. . . For that, we need to confront two more big issues. First is the acceptance of the possibility of difference. Can we only free Afghan women to be like us or might we have to recognize that even after "liberation" from the Taliban, they might want different things than we would want for them? What do we do about that? Second, we need to be vigilant about the rhetoric of saving people because of what it implies about our attitudes.

Again, when I talk about accepting difference, I am not implying that we should resign ourselves to being cultural relativists who respect whatever goes on elsewhere as "just their culture." I have already discussed the dangers of "cultural" explanations; "their" cultures are just as much part of history and an interconnected world as ours are. What I am advocating is the hard work involved in recognizing and respecting differences—precisely as products of different histories, as expressions of different circumstances, and as manifestations of differently structured desires. We may want justice for women, but can we accept that there might be different ideas about justice and that different women might want, or choose, different futures from what we envision as best (see Ong 1988)? We must consider that they might be called to personhood, so to speak, in a different language.

Reports from the Bonn peace conference held in late November to discuss the rebuilding of Afghanistan revealed significant differences among the few Afghan women feminists and activists present. RAWA's position was to reject any conciliatory approach to Islamic governance. According to one report I read, most women activists, especially those based in Afghanistan who are aware of the realities on the ground, agreed that Islam had to be the starting point for reform. Fatima Gailani, a U.S.-based advisor to one of the delegations, is quoted as saying, "If I go to Afghanistan today and ask women for votes on the promise to bring them secularism, they are going to tell me to go to hell."

One of the things we have to be most careful about in thinking about Third World feminisms, and feminism in different parts of the Muslim world, is how not to fall into polarizations that place feminism on the side of the West. I have written about the dilemmas faced by Arab feminists when Western feminists initiate campaigns that make them vulnerable to local denunciations by conservatives of various sorts, whether Islamist or nationalist, of being traitors (Abu-Lughod 2001). As some like Afsaneh Najmabadi are now arguing, not only is it wrong to see history simplistically in terms of a putative opposition between Islam and the West (as is happening in the United States now and has happened in parallel in the Muslim world), but it is also strategically dangerous to accept this cultural opposition between Islam and the West, between fundamentalism and feminism, because those many people

within Muslim countries who are trying to find alternatives to present injustices, those who might want to refuse the divide and take from different histories and cultures, who do not accept that being feminist means being Western, will be under pressure to choose, just as we are: Are you with us or against us?

My point is to remind us to be aware of differences, respectful of other paths toward social change that might give women better lives. Can there be a liberation that is Islamic? And, beyond this, is liberation even a goal for which all women or people strive? Are emancipation, equality, and rights part of a universal language we must use?

Might other desires be more meaningful for different groups of people? Living in close families? Living in a godly way? Living without war? I have done fieldwork in Egypt over more than 20 years and I cannot think of a single woman I know, from the poorest rural to the most educated cosmopolitan, who has ever expressed envy of U.S. women, women they tend to perceive as bereft of community, vulnerable to sexual violence and social anomie, driven by individual success rather than morality, or strangely disrespectful of God.

BEYOND THE RHETORIC OF SALVATION

Let us return, finally, to my title, "Do Muslim Women Need Saving?" The discussion of culture, veiling, and how one can navigate the shoals of cultural difference should put Laura Bush's self-congratulation about the rejoicing of Afghan women liberated by American troops in a different light. It is deeply problematic to construct the Afghan woman as someone in need of saving. When you save someone, you imply that you are saving her from something. You are also saving her *to* something. What violences are entailed in this transformation, and what presumptions are being made about the superiority of that to which you are saving her? Projects of saving other women depend on and reinforce a sense of superiority by Westerners, a form of arrogance that deserves to be challenged. All one needs to do to appreciate the patronizing quality of the rhetoric of saving women is to imagine using it today in the United States about disadvantaged groups such as African American women or working-class women. We now understand them as suffering from structural violence. We have become politicized about race and class, but not culture.

Could we not leave veils and vocations of saving others behind and instead train our sights on ways to make the world a more just place? The reason respect for difference should not be confused with cultural relativism is that it does not preclude asking how we, living in this privileged and powerful part of the world, might examine our own responsibilities for the situations in which others in distant places have found themselves. We do not stand outside the world, looking out over this sea of poor benighted people, living under the shadow—or veil—of oppressive cultures; we are part of that world. Islamic movements themselves have arisen in a world shaped by the intense engagements of Western powers in Middle Eastern lives.

A more productive approach, it seems to me, is to ask how we might contribute to making the world a more just place. A world not organized around strategic military and economic demands; a place where certain kinds of forces and values that we may still consider important could have an appeal and where there is the peace necessary for discussions, debates, and transformations to occur within communities. We need to ask ourselves what kinds of world conditions we could contribute to making such that popular desires will not be overdetermined by an overwhelming sense of helplessness in the face of forms of global injustice. Where we seek to be active in the affairs of distant places, can we do so in the spirit of support for those within those communities whose goals are to make women's (and men's) lives better (as Walley has argued in relation to practices of genital cutting in Africa [1997])? Can we use a more egalitarian language of alliances, coalitions, and solidarity, instead of salvation?

Even RAWA, the now celebrated Revolutionary Association of the Women of Afghanistan, which was so instrumental in bringing to U.S. women's attention the excesses of the Taliban, has opposed the U.S. bombing from the beginning. They do not see in it Afghan women's salvation but increased hardship and loss. They have long called for disarmament and for peace-keeping forces. Spokespersons point out the dangers of confusing governments with people, the Taliban with innocent Afghans who will be most harmed. They consistently remind audiences to take a close look at the ways policies are being organized around oil interests, the arms industry, and the international drug trade. They are not obsessed with the veil, even though they are the most radical feminists working for a secular democratic Afghanistan. Unfortunately, only their messages about the excesses of the Taliban have been heard, even though their criticisms of those in power in Afghanistan have included previous regimes. A first step in hearing their wider message is to break with the language of alien cultures, whether to understand or eliminate them. Missionary work and colonial feminism belong in the past. Our task is to critically explore what we might do to help create a world in which those poor Afghan women, for whom "the hearts of those in the civilized world break," can have safety and decent lives.

ACKNOWLEDGMENTS

I want to thank Page Jackson, Fran Mascia-Lees, Tim Mitchell, Rosalind Morris, Anupama Rao, and members of the audience at the symposium "Responding to War," sponsored by Columbia University's Institute for Research on Women and Gender (where I presented an earlier version), for helpful comments, references, clippings, and encouragement.

REFERENCES

Abu-Lughod, Lila. 1986. *Veiled Sentiments: Honor and Poetry in a Bedouin Society.* Berkeley: University of California Press.

——. 1995. Movie Stars and Islamic Moralism in Egypt. *Social Text* 42: 53–67.

——. 1998. *Remaking Women: Feminism and Modernity in the Middle East.* Princeton: Princeton University Press.

——. 2001. Orientalism and Middle East Feminist Studies. *Feminist Studies* 27(1): 101–113.

Ahmed, Leila. 1992. *Women and Gender in Islam.* New Haven, CT: Yale University Press.

Alloula, Malek. 1986. *The Colonial Harem.* Minneapolis: University of Minnesota Press.

Brenner, Suzanne. 1996. Reconstructing Self and Society: Javanese Muslim Women and "the Veil." *American Ethnologist* 23(4): 673–697.

El Guindi, Fadwa. 1999. *Veil: Modesty, Privacy and Resistance.* Oxford: Berg.

Fremson, Ruth. 2001. Allure Must Be Covered. Individuality Peeks Through. *New York Times*, November 4: 14.

Global Exchange. 2002. Courage and Tenacity: A Women's Delegation to Afghanistan. Electronic document, http://www.globalexchange.org/tours/auto/2002-03-05_CourageandTenacityeAWomensDele.html. (Accessed February 11).

Goldenberg, Suzanne. 2002. The Woman Who Stood Up to the Taliban. *The Guardian*, January 24. Electronic document, http://222.guardian.co.uk/afghanistan/story/0,1284, 63840.

Hirschkind, Charles, and Saba Mahmood. 2002. Feminism, the Taliban, and the Politics of Counter-Insurgency. *Anthropological Quarterly*, Volume 75(2): 107–122.

Lazreg, Marnia. 1994. *The Eloquence of Silence: Algerian Women in Question.* New York: Routledge.

MacLeod, Arlene. 1991. *Accommodating Protest.* New York: Columbia University Press.

Mahmood, Saba. 2001. Feminist Theory, Embodiment, and the Docile Agent: Some Reflections on the Egyptian Islamic Revival. *Cultural Anthropology* 16(2): 202–235.

Mir-Hosseini, Ziba. 1999. *Islam and Gender: The Religious Debate in Contemporary Iran.* Princeton: Princeton University Press.

Moghissi, Haideh. 1999. *Feminism and Islamic Fundamentalism.* London: Zed Books.

Najmabadi, Afsaneh. 1998. Feminism in an Islamic Republic. In *Islam, Gender and Social Change*, eds. Yvonne Haddad and John Esposito, 59–84. New York: Oxford University Press.

——. 2000. (Un)Veiling Feminism. *Social Text* 64: 29–45.

Ong, Aihwa. 1988. Colonialism and Modernity: Feminist Representations of Women in Non-Western Societies. *Inscriptions* 3–4: 79–93.

——. 1990. State Versus Islam: Malay Families, Women's Bodies, and the Body Politic in Malaysia. *American Ethnologist* 17(2): 258–276.

Papanek, Hanna. 1982. Purdah in Pakistan: Seclusion and Modern Occupations for Women. In *Separate Worlds*, eds. Hanna Papanek and Gail Minault, 190–216. Columbus, MO: South Asia Books.

Safire, William. 2001. On Language. *New York Times Magazine*, October 28: 22.

Spivak, Gayatri Chakravorty. 1988. Can the Subaltern Speak? In *Marxism and the Interpretation of Culture*, eds. Cary Nelson and Lawrence Grossberg, 271–313. Urbana: University of Illinois Press.

Strathern, Marilyn. 1987. An Awkward Relationship: The Case of Feminism and Anthropology. *Signs* 12: 276–292.

U.S. Government. 2002. Electronic document, http://www. whitehouse.gov/news/releases/2001/11/20011117. Accessed January 10.

Van Sommers, Annie and Samuel Zwemer. 1907. *Our Moslem Sisters: A Cry of Need from Lands of Darkness Interpreted by Those Who Heard It.* New York: Fleming H. Revell Co.

Walley, Christine. 1997. Searching for "Voices": Feminism, Anthropology, and the Global Debate over Female Genital Operations. *Cultural Anthropology* 12(3): 405–438.

18

Gay Marriage and Anthropology

Linda S. Stone

On September 21, 1996, the U.S. Congress passed, and President Bill Clinton signed, the Defense of Marriage Act. This federal law states that: (a) the federal government shall not recognize same-sex or polygamous marriages for any purpose and (b) no state is obliged to recognize a same-sex marriage conducted or recognized in another state. Political historians note that the law was passed, largely because congressional opponents of same-sex marriage feared that their states would be forced to recognize same-sex marriages performed in states that legalized such marriages.

Nearly two-decades later, 38 states have passed constitutional provisions defining marriage as between a man and woman. On the other side, 8 states provide marriage licenses to same-sex couples. As national debates over gay marriage continue, discussions of a federal marriage amendment have surfaced that would define marriage as the union of man and woman. However, popular support for such an amendment appears to be waning. A week after President Barack Obama and Vice-President Joe Biden spoke publicly—and for the first time—in favor of marriage equality, 53% of all Americans agreed that gay and lesbian marriage should be legal (ABC News/Washington Post Poll. May 2012).

Debates on gay marriage and civil unions will continue in Washington, D.C., in state legislatures, and in religious communities across the nation, and anthropologists are ready to help inform such debates. In this selection, Linda Stone describes how the idea of marriage is not as universal as many people may assume. In fact, when one looks at cross-cultural analyses of marriage, the only universal to be found is that people from different parts of the world define marriage in unique ways. Cultural diversity and New Reproductive Technologies, such as surrogate motherhood and in-vitro fertilization, reveal that marriage is a social construction, not a human universal based exclusively on biology or anatomy.

As you read this selection, ask yourself the following questions:

- What do anthropological perspectives contribute to contemporary debates on gay marriage?
- How has the development on New Reproductive Technologies conceptually fragmented motherhood?
- How do anthropologists account for the variation of marriage as practiced throughout the world?
- What are some of the differences in the way humans practice marriage throughout the world?
- What are some of the different ways that anthropologists have defined marriage?

The following terms discussed in this selection are included in the Glossary at the back of the book:

affinal	kinship
blended family	marriage

Politicians and the public in the United States today are raising a question once pursued by anthropologists in the 1950s, namely, what should we mean by marriage? The politically charged issue concerns whether or not a constitutional definition of marriage can exclude same-sex couples. With over a century of experience in the study of kinship and marriage worldwide, anthropology can offer perspectives on this debate that may be of interest to our students or the general public.

CAN MARRIAGE BE DEFINED?

Many politicians claim that those advocating gay and lesbian marriage are trying to *re*define marriage. But what anthropologists have learned is that from a global, cross-cultural perspective, "marriage" is in the first place extremely difficult, some would say impossible, to define. One anthropologist, Edmund Leach, tried to define marriage in his 1955 article "Polyandry, Inheritance and the Definition of Marriage" published in *MAN*. Leach quickly gave up this task, concluding that no definition could cover all the varied institutions that anthropologists regularly consider as marriage. Rejecting Leach's conclusion, Kathleen Gough attempted to define marriage cross-culturally in 1959 as an institution conferring full "birth status rights" to children (*The Nayars and the Definition of Marriage. Royal Anthropological Institute of Great Britain and Ireland* 89:23–34). Gough's definition of marriage was convoluted—notable, in her own words, for its "inevitably clumsy phraseology"—since it covered monogamy, polygyny, polyandry, and same-sex marriage. But most important, its core feature—conferring of birth status rights on children—does not old up cross-culturally.

It is true that virtually every society in the world has an institution that is very tempting to label as "marriage," but these institutions simply do not share common characteristics. Marriage in most societies establishes the legitimacy or status rights of children, but this is not the case, for example, among the Navajo where children born to a woman, married or not, become full legitimate members of her matriclan and suffer no disadvantages. "Marriage" around the world most often involves heterosexual unions, but there are important exceptions to this. There are cases of legitimate same-sex marriages as, for example, woman-woman marriage among the Nuer and some other African groups. Here, a barren woman divorces her husband, takes another woman as her wife, and arranges for a surrogate to impregnate this woman. Any children from this arrangement become members of the barren woman's natal patrilineage and refer to the barren woman as their father. Among some Native American groups, males who preferred to live as women (*berdache*) adopted the names and clothing of women and often became wives of other men.

Marriage usually involves sexual relationships between spouses. Yet this was not true of Nuer woman-woman marriages and we find in European history cases of "celibate marriages" among early Christians. Often spouses are co-resident but very often this is not the case. A separate residence of husbands in "men's houses," away from their wives and children, has been common in many places. Among the polyandrous/polygynous Nayar of India, wives and husbands remained in their own natal groups with husbands periodically "visiting" their wives and with children raised by their mothers and mothers' brothers. Indeed the only feature of marriage that is apparently universal is that they will create affinal (in-law) relationships, or alliances, a fact that Lévi-Strauss and others considered to lie behind the origin of human marriage. But even here, affinal relationships are themselves quite varied in their nature and importance across societies. Thus, in terms of child legitimacy, sex of spouses, sexual activity, residence, and so on, what we see around the world in terms of marriage is most notable for its variation.

VARIATION AND CHANGE

Anthropologists have accounted for this variation in a number of ways, looking to economic, ecological, demographic, and historical processes. For example, polyandry, especially in Himalayan regions, is now well understood as, in part, related to the benefits of low population growth in areas of scarce environmental resources (Nancy Levine, *The Dynamics of Polyandry*, 1981). On a broader scale, Jack Goody has contributed to our understanding of marriage variations by drawing comparisons between Eurasian monogamy (with dowry) and sub-Saharan African polygyny (with bridewealth). His work, published in *Production and Reproduction* (1976), has shown important connections that marriage forms have with agricultural practices, the development (or lack of development) of socioeconomic classes, marriage payments, and patterns of property inheritance throughout the history of Africa and Eurasia.

Anthropological studies of kinship and marriage can also provide an understanding that within any society, marriage and the family will change over time. Whereas in the United States legal marriages have been traditionally monogamous unions between a woman and a man, the nature of marriage, the domestic economy, husband-wife relationships, parent-child relationships, family structure, and household structure have seen considerable transformation since the 1700s (Stephanie Coontz, *The Social Origins of Private Life*, 1988). Relevant transformations of marriage and the family have been, in particular, occurring in the United States since the 1960s. Here we have seen rising rates of divorce, resulting in greater numbers of single-parent households. A rise in remarriage following divorce has additionally brought about the growth of so-called blended families, consisting of various combinations of step-parents, step-children, and step-siblings. Many United States children today are raised in two separate households, where one or both may consist of a previous parent and a newer set of step-relations.

The development of New Reproductive Technologies (such as, surrogate motherhood, in-vitro fertilization, frozen embryos) meanwhile, has conceptually fragmented motherhood. We can today distinguish a birth mother from a genetic mother from a legal mother; all three "mothers" may be one, two, or even three separate women. By contrast, fatherhood, once considered "uncertain" compared with motherhood, can now be made certain, one way or another, through DNA testing.

FROM BIOLOGY TO CHOICE

Perhaps the most profound change of all, and one undoubtedly linked with the above transformations of kinship and the family, is a perceptible change in the cultural construction of kinship in the United States. An earlier emphasis on kinship as based on biological connection (what David Schneider termed "shared biogenetic substance" in *American Kinship*, 1980), is giving way to a new conception of kinship as a relation based on personal choice and commitment (Linda Stone, Introduction, Contemporary Directions in Kinship, *Kinship and Family*, 2004). The United States is, in many respects, culturally embracing a wider variety of family forms and an expanded construction of kinship through choice and self-definition as much as through biology.

It is within these new dimensions of family variation and choice as a basis of kinship that, I think, we can best view the movement for legalization of same-sex marriage. From an anthropological perspective that focuses on the whole of humanity, what same-sex couples seeking legal marriage in the United States are trying to do is not to redefine marriage. They are seeking legal recognition in the United States for doing what people around the world have always done, that is, to construct marriage for themselves.

19

"Strange Country This"
An Introduction to North American Gender Diversity

Will Roscoe

Because of the colossal and tragic impact of European conquest in North America, our understanding of the full history of Native America is incomplete. However, the documented history of the tribes we do know about teaches us a significant lesson, namely that these first nations are far more diverse than the singular term Native America suggests. Nevertheless, despite different adaptive strategies, political structures, and cultural lives, alternative gender roles was one of the few widely shared features of Native American societies.

Two-spirit people, or berdaches, are people who fulfill mixed gender roles. Unlike contemporary terms like gay, lesbian, bisexual, and transgender, the term two-spirit represents people whose societies respectfully understand them as both male and female. Two-spirit people have been documented in over 150 North American tribes as people who make critical contributions to their communities. The two-spirit identity was widely understood as the result of divine intervention, and it encompassed much more than sexual preferences. Two-spirit males and females typically specialized in the work of the opposite sex; some berdache women were highly-respected warriors, while some berdache men were known as skilled beadworkers and matchmakers.

In this selection Will Roscoe explains the two-spirit tradition in Native North America including how two-spirit people differed from region to region and

nation to nation. Understanding different ways people understand gender diversity demonstrates the power of culture over biology in terms of how we construct gender and sexuality.

As you read this selection, ask yourself the following questions:

- What role does sexuality play in berdache identities?

- Is it accurate to define the berdache as homosexual?

- What roles did "two-spirit" people play in Native American societies?

- How has the term berdache evolved and why has it become an accepted anthropological term for third/fourth gender Native Americans? Should anthropologists continue to use this term?

- What is the difference between the third and fourth genders?

- What are some of the differences between Native American alternative genders as found in different geographic regions?

The following terms discussed in this selection are included in the Glossary at the back of the book:

asexual	*Defense of Marriage Act*
berdache	*third/fourth gender*

In 1833, Edwin T. Denig came up the Missouri River to the country of the Crow Indians in Montana to spend the next twenty-three years of his life as a trader for the American Fur Company. He found himself in an unknown land, surrounded by unfamiliar cultures. Of

Roscoe, Will. "'Strange Country This': An Introduction to North American Gender Diversity." From *Changing Ones: Third and Fourth Genders in Native North America*. Published 1998, St. Martin's Griffin, pp. 3–22. Copyright © Will Roscoe, 1998. Reproduced with permission of Palgrave Macmillan.

all the differences he encountered none seemed more alien to him than native practices regarding sexuality and gender. Among the Crow Indians, Denig found that some of the most important and respected individuals were men and women who in American and European societies would be condemned, persecuted, jailed, even executed. Their lifestyles would be called immoral and perverse, their sexuality deemed unnatural.

And yet, among the Crows, men who dressed as women and specialized in women's work were accepted and sometimes honored; a woman who led men into battle and had four wives was a respected chief. As Denig wrote, "Most civilized communities recognize but two genders, the masculine and feminine. But strange to say, these people have a neuter," and with a note of exasperation he added, "Strange country this, where males assume the dress and perform the duties of females, while women turn men and mate with their own sex!"

The social universe of native North America was nowhere more at odds with that of Europe and Anglo-America than in its diverse gender roles. Denig's was not a new discovery. Europeans had been encountering "berdaches"—as third and fourth gender people have come to be called in the anthropological literature—since the days of Spanish conquest, and they reacted much as Denig did: with amazement, dismay, disgust, and occasionally, when they weren't dependent on the natives' goodwill, with violence. As Cabeza de Vaca wrote of his sojourn with the Karankawa Indians of Texas in 1540, "In the time that I continued among them, I saw a most brutish and beastly custom, to wit, a man who was married to another, and these be certaine effeminate and impotent men, who goe clothed and attired like women, and performe the office of a woman." Some years earlier, when Vasco Núñez de Balboa encountered forty *pathicos fœmineo amictu* (male homosexuals dressed as women) in Panama, he had them put to the dogs. The scene is illustrated in sadomasochistic detail in Théodor De Bry's famous *Collectiones peregrinationum*. "A fine action of an honourable and Catholic Spaniard," commented one historian a hundred years later.

In 1986, when the U.S. Supreme Court upheld Georgia's sodomy law, the majority opinion cited "millennia of moral teaching" against homosexuality in support of its decision. Ten years later, when legislation called the Defense of Marriage Act was proposed by a twice divorced congressman and signed into law by an admitted adulterer, it was said that no society that allowed people of the same sex to marry has or could survive, that American values were grounded in Judeo-Christian principles that precluded tolerance of same-sex love and gender difference.

In truth, the ground American society occupies once may have been the queerest continent on the planet. The original peoples of North America, whose principles are just as ancient as those of Judeo-Christian culture, saw no threat in homosexuality or gender variance. Indeed, they believed individuals with these traits made unique contributions to their communities. As a Crow tribal elder said in 1982, "We don't waste people the way white society does. Every person has their gift." In this land, the original America, men who wore women's clothes and did women's work became artists, innovators, ambassadors, and religious leaders,

and women sometimes became warriors, hunters, and chiefs. Same-sex marriages flourished and no tribe was the worse for it—until the Europeans arrived. In this "strange country," people who were different in terms of gender identity or sexuality were respected, integrated, and sometimes revered. How could this be? . . .

The evidence of multiple genders in North America offers support for the theory of social constructionism, which maintains that gender roles, sexualities, and identities are not natural, essential, or universal, but constructed by social processes and discourses. At the same time, it challenges certain assumptions of recent work in postmodern cultural studies, feminism, and queer theory. The only societies many of today's influential cultural theorists have considered have been those of the West (and primarily northwest Europe and North America). Few have ever considered cross-cultural evidence; many show a marked disinclination for empirical evidence of any kind. Consequently, certain elements of Western beliefs and epistemology have been essentialized as universal features of human societies. These include assumptions that "sex" and "gender" are relevant categories in all societies and that sexuality and gender are (always) analytically distinguishable; that sexes and genders are binary and dichotomous and that, by extension, only heterosexuality or the attraction between opposites is natural; that ideology and cultural beliefs regarding gender are always essentialist while gender identities and sexualities are always constructed; and that the fluidity of human desire and the ambiguities of human categories make stable identities and cultural continuity impossible. All of these assumptions are called into question by the example of native multiple genders. As we will see, native beliefs about gender and sexuality were avowedly constructionist, acknowledging the malleability of human desire and identity. At the same time, North American multiple genders emerge as roles with great historical depth and continuity, with parallels in societies worldwide.

THE BERDACHE OR ALTERNATIVE GENDER ROLE

The estimated four hundred tribal groups in North America at the time of European contact represented a diverse array of environmental adaptations, subsistence strategies, social organizations, family structures, languages, and religions. They ranged from the egalitarian, loosely organized bands of Inuit hunter-gatherers in the arctic, to the populous farmers and village dwellers of the southeast, who were organized into castes and ruled by chieftains. Many other North American societies combined hunting and gathering with digging stick horticulture. (True agrarian societies, on the other hand, based on intensive food production with draught animals, were not present.)

Rather than technology, native societies emphasized knowledge, especially familiarity with the environment. Consequently, intuitive forms of knowledge were highly developed. Visions, dreams, and trance states were valued as sources of information, direction, ability, and fortune. Ideals of balance, harmony, and integration between humans and nature were widespread. However, those drawn to native religions because of their apparent resonance with Western environmental and New Age tenets would do well to remember the central role of violence in Plains Indian religions and the concern with wealth among Northwest Coast groups.

Most North American societies were only weakly stratified. In the typical tribal social organization leaders were selected (or confirmed) based on competence, and social control was achieved largely through face-to-face interaction. Work roles were organized on the basis of gender. Within these systems, women made important, sometimes the most important, economic contributions to their families' subsistence. Although the life choices and personal autonomy of women made important, sometimes the most important, economic contributions to their families' subsistence. Although the life choices and personal autonomy of women varied significantly from matrilineal groups like the Hopis, Zunis, and Iroquois to the warrior-dominated Plains tribes, opportunities for women to acquire prestige and take leadership roles existed in every group.

Alternative gender roles were among the most widely shared features of North American societies. Male berdaches have been documented in over 155 tribes. In about a third of these groups, a formal status also existed for females who undertook a man's lifestyle, becoming hunters, warriors, and chiefs. They were sometimes referred to with the same term for male berdaches and sometimes with a distinct term—making them, therefore, a fourth gender. (Thus, "third gender" generally refers to male berdaches and sometimes male and female berdaches, while "fourth gender" always refers to female berdaches. Each tribe, of course, had its own terms for these roles, like boté in Crow, nádleehí in Navajo, winkte in Lakota, and alyha: and hwame: in Mohave.) Because so many North American cultures were disrupted (or had disappeared) before they were studied by anthropologists, it is not possible to state the absolute frequency of these roles. Those alternative gender roles that have been documented, however, occur in every region of the continent, in every kind of society, and among speakers of every major language group. The number of tribes

in which the existence of such roles have been denied (by informants or outsider observers) are quite few. Far greater are those instances in which information regarding the presence of gender diversity has simply not been recorded.

"Berdache" has become the accepted anthropological term for these roles despite a rather unlikely etymology. It can be traced back to the Indo-European root *welð, "to strike, wound," from which the Old Iranian *varta-, "seized, prisoner," is derived. In Persia, it referred to a young captive or slave (male or female). The word entered western European languages perhaps from Muslim Spain or as a result of contact with Muslims during the Crusades. By the Renaissance it was current in Italian as bardascia and bardasso, in Spanish as bardaje (or bardaxe), in French as berdache, and in English as "bardash" with the meaning of "catamite"—the younger partner in an age-differentiated homosexual relationship. Over time its meaning began to shift, losing its reference to age and active/passive roles and becoming a general term for male homosexual. In some places, it lost its sexual connotations altogether. By the mid-nineteenth century, its use in Europe lapsed.

In North America, however, "berdache" continued to be used, but for a quite different purpose. Its first written occurrence in reference to third and fourth gender North American natives is in the 1704 memoir of Deliette. Eventually, its use spread to every part of North America the French entered, becoming a pidgin term used by Euro-Americans and natives alike. Its first use in an anthropological publication was by Washington Matthews in 1877. In describing Hidatsa miáti he wrote, "Such are called by the French Canadians "berdaches."' The next anthropological use was in J. Owen Dorsey's 1890 study of Siouan cults. Like Matthews, he described "berdache" as a French Canadian frontier term. Following Alfred Kroeber's use of the word in his 1902 ethnography of the Arapaho, it became part of standard anthropological terminology.

Although there are important variations in berdache roles, which will be discussed below, they share a core set of traits that justifies comparing them:

- Specialized work roles—Male and female berdaches are typically described in terms of their preference and achievements in the work of the "opposite" sex and/or unique activities specific to their identities.

- Gender difference—In addition to work preferences, berdaches are distinguished from men and women in terms of temperament, dress, lifestyle, and social roles.

- Spiritual sanction—Berdache identity is widely believed to be the result of supernatural intervention in the form of visions or dreams, and/or it is sanctioned by tribal mythology.

- Same-sex relations—Berdaches most often form sexual and emotional relationships with non-berdache members of their own sex.

The most visible marker of berdache gender status was some form of cross-dressing, although this occurred much less consistently than is usually assumed. In some tribes, male berdaches dressed distinctly from both men and women. In other cases, berdaches did not cross-dress at all or only partly. Cross-dressing was even more variable in the case of female berdaches. Often, they wore men's clothing only when hunting or in battle. Similarly, despite the common description of berdaches as "doing the work of the opposite sex," they more often engaged in a combination of men's and women's activities, along with pursuits unique to their status.

Berdaches are also frequently attributed with spiritual powers. This was especially common in tribes, such as those of the Plains, with a vision complex, in which visions or dreams were considered life-defining and believed to convey power. Such beliefs not only justified alternative gender identities, they endowed those identities with special prestige. Even in societies lacking the vision complex, such as the Pueblos of the Southwest, alternative gender roles were sanctioned by tribal myths and portrayed in ceremonies.

The process by which third gender identity was adopted and/or acknowledged varied, but one dominant pattern emerges cross-culturally. Recognition of berdache orientation typically occurred when a boy showed interest and aptitude in women's work or a girl persistently engaged in the activities of boys and men. Significantly, these preferences manifested well before puberty, so that sexual behavior was a less important defining trait. In tribes with a vision complex, supernatural intervention was sometimes credited with determining berdache status, but a close reading of ethnographic and historic reports reveals that in many cases childhood cross-gender interests and skills preceded visions, which merely served to confirm alternative gender identity. Another process has been reported for certain arctic and subarctic groups, in which children were sometimes assigned cross- or mixed-sex identities at birth, which might be modified after puberty. Latitude was still allowed, however, for individual preferences. In those instances when men were required to cross-dress because they were considered cowards or because they were captives, a distinction from true berdache status was recognized.

Unfortunately, there are few accounts of berdache sexuality. This has led some to claim that berdaches were asexual or that the sexual aspects of alternative genders were not important. Harriet Whitehead has argued that "sexual object choice is part of the gender configuration, but its salience is low; so low that by itself it does not provoke the reclassification of the individual to a special status," and Clemmer has concluded, "The berdache was not only—and sometimes not at all—a sexual role." Ironically, in those cases for which detailed evidence about individual berdaches exists (such as Osh-Tisch and Hastíín Klah), almost nothing has been recorded about their sexuality and personal relationships. However, when the sexual preferences of berdaches have been reported, a definite pattern emerges. Male and female berdaches were sexually active with members of their own sex and this behavior was part of the cultural expectations for their role.

Indeed, some male berdaches were very active sexually. The Navajo *nádleehí* Kinábahí told Willard Hill that "she" had had sex with over one hundred different men. The Sauk and Fox tribe held an annual dance in which a berdache, or *aya'kwa*, appeared surrounded by all "her" lovers, and Lakota *winkte* bestowed bawdy nicknames as a souvenir of sexual encounters with them. In fact, Lakota warriors sometimes visited *winkte* before going to battle as a means of increasing their own masculinity. In the early eighteenth century, Ojibway men had sex with the berdache Ozaw-wen-dib (Yellowhead), himself an accomplished warrior, "to acquire his fighting ability and courage, by having intimate connection with him." In a similar vein, an Omaha chief once claimed he could change the weather because he had had sex four times with a male berdache.

The active sex life of berdaches led them to be considered fortuitous in all matters relating to sex and romance. Navajo *nádleehí*, Cheyenne *he'eman*, and Omaha *mi^{n}nquga* were matchmakers, while the Mohave believed both male *alyha:* and female *hwame:* were lucky in love. If Mohave berdaches became shamans, they specialized in the treatment of sexual diseases. Pawnee berdaches provided men with love charms for attracting women, while a carved fan from the eastern Sioux depicts male berdaches in a ritual scene associated with the love magic of the elk. (In the Oto origin myth, the figure Elk is described as a berdache.) The autobiography of a Kwakiutl chief provides a rare description of a sexual encounter with a male berdache: "This man, her name was Frances . . . , she caught hold of me, and when I went there she throwed me right into her bed. My, she was strong—awful strong!"

In forming relationships with non-berdache members of their own sex, third and fourth gender natives were "homosexual" in the Western definition of that term. The native view of such relations was more complex, however. Because berdaches were considered members of a distinct gender, native epistemologies classified relationships with them differently than those between individuals who had the same gender identity. Nor were their non-berdache partners labeled in any way; their gender identities and sexualities remained those of men or women. At the same time, knowledge of berdaches' anatomical sex was never denied, and the sexual acts performed with them were recognized (with distinct terms) as different from heterosexual acts. Some male berdaches had relationships with women, although in most cases they were men who were already warriors and husbands who became berdaches on the basis of a vision or dream. Finally, a few berdaches may not have been sexually active at all, although institutionalized celibacy was a foreign concept in native cultures. The only sexual relationships berdaches are not known to have formed are ones involving other berdaches.

The primary characteristic of third gender sexuality in the native view was not its same-sex nature, but the fact that it was nonprocreative. That is, rather than an opposition of heterosexuality to homosexuality, native beliefs opposed reproductive to nonreproductive sex. (This is especially apparent in the case of native terms for berdaches that literally mean "sterile" or "impotent.") Reproductive sex was engaged in to obtain children and fulfill one's kinship role. Nonreproductive sex was engaged in for pleasure and emotional rewards. As such, sexual pleasure was valued in its own right—it forged relationships, it was entertaining, it was necessary for good health. In these belief systems, third and fourth genders represented special instances of nonprocreative sexuality and romantic love. Given the relative absence of restrictions on their sexual availability within a kinship-based social organization, individuals in these roles had more opportunities to engage in sexual activity than did men or women. Although long-term relationships between berdaches and non-berdaches were considered marriages, they do not seem to have been the product of alliance politics between families, to have involved bridewealth or brideservice, or to have been governed by restrictions on the social status of the partners. When such relationships dissolved the disputes involved were usually limited to the couple alone, not their families or clans.

Of all the cultural associations of alternative genders, perhaps the least understood is their relationship to warfare. Many observers have attempted to account for male berdaches by suggesting that the role was a social status imposed on men too weak or cowardly to live up to tribal standards of masculinity. This can

be disproved on several grounds. Landes's Dakota informants, for example, clearly distinguished between men who were uninterested in or afraid of warfare and berdaches "who had a dream." In fact, male berdaches regularly participated in many aspects of warfare. This ranged from accompanying war parties to provide support, entertainment, and luck, to joining in the fighting, handling enemy scalps, and directing victory ceremonies. Indeed, some berdaches, such as the Crow Osh-Tisch, the Ojibway Yellowhead, and the Southern Piegan, Piegan Woman, were renowned for their war exploits, while the Sioux remember a berdache who tricked the Sans Arc band into putting down their weapons just as their enemies attacked. Third and fourth gender figures appear as warriors in myths and tales, as well. In fact, most native belief systems ultimately viewed berdaches and successful warriors in similar terms—both were the beneficiaries of supernatural power.

The associations of alternative genders with death, whether through roles as undertakers and mourners in California, or as participants in victory or "scalp" dances, is striking. They point to a nexus of beliefs difficult to grasp from a Western perspective, in which nonprocreative sexuality and fertility, creativity and inspiration, and warfare and death are linked, and these links are represented by third and fourth gender persons.

That berdaches were accepted and integrated members of their communities is underscored throughout the ethnographic literature and confirmed by contemporary natives. In some tribes, alternative genders enjoyed special respect and privileges. In a few cases, berdaches were feared because of their supernatural power. If they were scorned, hated, or ridiculed, it was usually for individual reasons and not because of their gender difference, at least until the twentieth century. In some cases, joking relationships have been mistakenly interpreted as evidence of nonacceptance. In fact, individuals in tribal societies were often subject to teasing precisely because they had high status. In other cases, accounts attributing natives with hostility toward berdaches can be shown to reflect the judgments of Euro-Americans or of informants influenced by Christianity. As Drucker observed, "Most of the informants were inclined to be reticent about sexual matters, apparently feeling that they would be putting themselves in a bad light by discussing such things. This attitude accounts for most of the denials of the existence of berdaches aboriginally. I was told repeatedly that such individuals ('jotes') were to be found 'only among Mexicans.'" What is needed at this point is an analysis of a tribe either definitely lacking such a role or hostile to gender difference based on pre-contact values.

There are no reliable data at present concerning the numbers of berdaches in native populations, although careful work in census records and oral histories may make it possible to make estimates for some tribes in the late nineteenth century. In small groups, with populations of a few hundred, there might have been only one or two berdaches in a given generation. In larger communities, their numbers were sufficient for them to be recognized as a social group (as among the Timucua, Hidatsa, Crow, and Cheyenne). Among the Hidatsa of the upper Missouri River, there was said to be fifteen to twenty-five *miáti* in a village, and among the Yuki of California as many as thirty in the tribe. In any case, the importance of a social role for a given society is not a function of the number of individuals who occupy it—the number of chiefs and medicine people was in most cases no greater than that of berdaches, but no one would dispute their importance to tribal society and history.

Some of the points made so far apply to alternative genders for females as well. As Medicine notes, "warrior women," like male berdaches, occupied "socially sanctioned role alternatives." These were "normative statuses which permitted individuals to strive for self-actualization, excellence, and social recognition in areas outside their customary sex role assignments. Blackwood has argued that alternative female roles were socially and ontologically on par with male roles in the sense of being distinct, lifelong identities. Still, it is clear that female alternative genders were not mirror opposites of those for males, nor were alternative gender roles the only avenue by which women engaged in male pursuits.

Important differences existed between alternative genders in various tribes, as a regional survey reveals:

Southeast. The reports of René Goulaine de Laudonnière and Jacques Le Moyne, who arrived in Florida in 1564 on an expedition to assert French claims to the region, provide a fairly detailed description of male berdaches among the Timucua Indians. Le Moyne painted two pictures of them and engravings based on these paintings were published by Theodore De Bry. One depicts two pairs carrying corpses on stretchers, while two others carry sick or injured persons on their backs. The engraving is captioned "Hermaphrodites as Laborers," and the accompanying text relates that because they are strong, "hermaphrodites" (a term frequently used by Europeans who often assumed without evidence that berdaches were intersexed) accompany warriors to battle to carry provisions and tend to the injured. A second engraving depicts "curly-haired hermaphrodites" bearing baskets of game, fish, and crocodiles to a storehouse.

Alternative gender males among the Karankawa and Coahuiltec Indians of the Texas Gulf Coast also participated in warfare. According to Cabeza de Vaca, "*Hombres amarionadas impotentes,*" while dressing and living like women, carried heavy burdens and were larger than other males. In the eighteenth century, Dumont de Montigny observed a role for males called the "chief of women" among the Natchez of the lower Mississippi. They did women's work, including crafts and gardening, assisted on war parties, and had sex with men. Unfortunately, these early reports are the most detailed available for Southeast tribes, although alternative gender statuses appear to have been present among the the Creek, Chickasaw, Choctaw, Caddo, and Cherokee.

Northeast and woodlands. Although there are no definite reports of alternative gender roles among the Algonkian-speaking and Iroquoian tribes of the Northeast, among the Algonkian Illinois of the Mississippi Valley the status of *ikoueta*, or male berdaches, seems to have been fairly high, judging from the accounts of French explorers and travelers in the late seventeenth century. Males entered the role based on their preference for women's work. They went to war, sang at religious ceremonies, gave advice at councils, and were considered "manitou," or holy. According to Marquette, "Nothing can be decided without their advice. Nearly all the French observers commented on their sexuality—*ikoueta* practiced "sodomy"—typically in the context of a general denunciation of Illinois morality. Similar roles also have been documented among the Winnebago, Sauk and Fox, Miami, and Potawatomi. Among these groups visions or dreams were believed to play a role in determining berdache identity. The Potawatomi considered such individuals "extraordinary." Indeed, the widespread occurrence of this role among Algonkian-speakers of the Plains (the Cheyenne, Arapaho, Blackfoot, and Gros Ventre) and in the subarctic region makes its apparent absence among eastern Algonkians all the more suspect.

Plains. Whereas the traditional cultures of tribes east of the Mississippi were severely disrupted long before the rise of anthropology, the cultures of the Plains have been more systematically studied, and the literature occasionally provides detailed glimpses of alternative gender roles. Table 1 summarizes this evidence for four tribes: the Crow; their relatives, the Hidatsa; the Lakota; and the Cheyenne.

The North American vision complex reached its apex among Plains tribes. Men sought visions that would enable them to kill game and enemies, women sought visions as sources of designs and inspiration for their arts, and male berdaches among the Mandan, Lakota, Assiniboine, Arapaho, Omaha, Kansa, Osage, and Oto had dreams and visions of female deities or the moon that confirmed their identity and gave them distinct abilities. The Osage term for berdache, *mixu'ga*

TABLE 1   Cultural Associations of Plains Male Berdaches

	Lakota	Crow	Hidatsa	Cheyenne	Other tribes
Dreams/ visions	had dreams of Double Woman	had dreams that transformed	had dreams of Woman Above or "mysterious women"		Assiniboine, Oto, Osage, Arapaho, Kansa, Mandan, Ojibwa
Moon	were influenced by moon				Omaha, Pawnee, Sauk/Fox, Osage, Kansa, Oto
Power	were holy, foretold future, brought luck	some were medicine people	had special power	were doctors	Arapaho, Sauk/Fox
Religion	led some ceremonies	selected sun dance pole	had role in sun dance and other rites; were members of Holy Women Society	led scalp dance	
Sexuality	had sex with men and gave them obscene names	had sex with men	lived with men	were matchmakers	Omaha (matchmakers), Pawnee (love magic)
Crafts	were skilled in quill- and beadwork	excelled in crafts	were industrious in crafts	were talented	Ponca
Warfare	joined war parties	joined war parties		joined war parties	

(and its cognates in Omaha, Kansa, and Oto), literally means "moon-instructed" (from *mi*, "moon" and *xu'ga*, "to instruct"). The most frequently cited skills were those of beading, quillwork, and the manufacture and decoration of myriad products made from animal skins. As Benedict related, "The Dakota had a saying, 'fine possessions like a berdache's,' and it was the epitome of praise for any woman's household possessions." These productive skills were a function of supernatural power—both contact with it and possession of it.

Creativity was only one of the forms this power could take. Lakota *winkte* could also predict the future, and they had auspicious powers in relation to childbirth and childrearing that included bestowing names that were considered lucky. The religious dimension of alternative gender roles was perhaps most fully developed among the Hidatsa and Mandan, horticultural village dwellers, and the Cheyenne, who were former village dwellers. Coleman argues that the reason *he'emane'o* directed the all-important victory dance was because they embodied the central

principles of Cheyenne religion, which were balance and synthesis.

Arctic and subarctic. Saladin d'Anglure has described the extremely flexible gender system of the central arctic Inuit, in which arbitrary gender assignments along with individual preferences result in complex and varied "gender histories" for many individuals. Boys and girls are raised in accordance with the gender of one or more names selected for them before their birth. Consequently, some children are raised with cross- or mixed-gender identities. Upon reaching puberty or adulthood they may choose to alter such identities or retain them. Saladin d'Anglure considers such individuals (who are often shamans, as well) to be members of a distinct third gender. In addition, the Inuit believe some infants, called *sipiniq*, change their anatomical sex at birth. (Similar beliefs have been reported for the Bella Coola and the Tlingit.) The Athapaskan-speaking Dene Tha (Slavey or Beaver Indians of Canada) have a related belief in the possibility of cross-sex reincarnation. Among the Ingalik, an Athapaskan group of the Alaskan interior, both male and female berdaches have been reported, and male berdaches often had shamanic powers.

Russian explorers, traders, and missionaries were well aware of gender diversity among Alaskan natives. The explorer Lisiansky reported that a Russian priest almost married an Aleut chief to a berdache before being informed that the "bride" was male. Among the Chugach and Koniag, Pacific Eskimo (Yup'ik) groups, such individuals were believed to be "two persons in one." Despite Russian attempts to suppress the role, third gender individuals were esteemed and encouraged by their families, who considered them lucky. Many were shamans. Early observers reported that some feminine boys were raised as girls from childhood by families lacking a daughter.

In the vast subarctic region, alternative genders have been reported for the Athapaskan-speaking Kaska and among the widely dispersed Cree and Ojibway. The linguistic relationship between terms for male berdaches in Algonkian-speaking groups (including the Fox and Illinois) is evident.

Northwest Coast and Columbia Plateau. Among the Northwest Coast Haisla, berdaches were reportedly "fairly common." A supernatural berdache was portrayed in masked dances by the neighboring Bella Coola. Among the Eyak, however, berdaches did not have supernatural power and their status was low. Alternative male genders have been widely reported for the Columbia Plateau region but with few details. Among the Flathead of western Montana and the Klamath of southern Oregon, berdaches were often shamans. The career of one Klamath *tw!ĭnnă'ĕk*, known as Muksamse'lapli, or White Cindy, has been briefly described by Spier and by McCleod.

West and Southwest. Male and female alternative genders have been documented throughout the Great Basin, California, Colorado River, and Southwest culture areas. They are consistently described as doing the work of the other sex, less consistently as crossdressing. As elsewhere, they formed relationships with non-berdache members of their own sex. Among some groups (Shoshone, Ute, Kitanemuk, Pima-Papago), families held a kind of initiation rite to confirm male berdache identity. The child was placed in a circle of brush with a bow and a basket (men's and women's objects, respectively). The brush was set on fire, and whichever object the boy picked up as he ran away served to identify his gender preference. The choice of the basket signified male berdache status. Among the Shoshone, who acquired horses and adopted a Plains-oriented lifestyle, male berdaches joined war parties.

In California, third/fourth gender individuals often had ceremonial roles relating to death and burial. Among the Yokuts and Tubatulabal, and possibly the Chumash, male berdaches served as undertakers, handling and burying the deceased and conducting mourning rites. Berdaches also participated in mourning rites among the Monache (Mono), Pomo, Miwok, Achumawi, Atsugewi, and Shasta. Among the Wappo, Mattole, Hupa, Chilula, Tolowa, Maidu, Achumawi, Shasta, and Modoc, male berdaches, and less often female berdaches, were sometimes shamans. One of the last chiefs of the Kawaiisu was a third gender male.

Alternative roles for males (but apparently not females) existed among the Pueblo communities of Isleta, San Felipe, San Juan, Santa Ana, Santo Domingo, Tesuque, Acoma, Laguna, Zuni, and Hopi. Among the western Pueblos, man-woman kachinas, or gods, were portrayed in masked dances and ceremonies. The Zuni *lhamana* We'wha was a religious specialist who regularly participated in ceremonies. Other Pueblo berdaches are described primarily in terms of their specialization in pottery and other pursuits of women.

Alternative gender roles also existed among the Papago and Pima of the Southwest and northern Mexico. Like Plains berdaches, Papago *wiik'ovat* taunted the scalps brought home by warriors, and they were visited for sexual liaisons by men to whom they gave obscene nicknames. A fire test was employed to confirm their identity.

20

It Takes a Village Healer

Can Traditional Medicine Remedy Africa's AIDS Crisis?

Matthew Steinglass

....

In 2012, President Obama surprised the international community when he selected anthropologist, physician, and Dartmouth University President Dr. Jim Yong Kim as his nominee for president of the World Bank. The World Bank is an international institution charged with reducing global poverty. Made up of nearly 200 member countries, the bank manages two institutions: one focuses on poverty reduction in poor to middle-income nations, while the other exclusively works with in the most impoverished countries in the world. So why would President Obama nominate an anthropologist to run these institutions?

Drawing on his training as a physician and anthropologist, Dr. Kim helped develop an innovative treatment program for multi-drug-resistant tuberculosis in Peru, and he helped negotiate lower prices for critical medicines in impoverished countries. These projects evolved into decades of international initiatives and programs that creatively integrated sociocultural and medical research to deliver large-scale, complex treatment for diseases like tuberculosis and HIV/AIDS. Dr. Kim's nomination has roots in his medical anthropology legacy of integrating the fight against disease with the fight against poverty. In recent decades, medical anthropology has grown into one of the fastest-growing branches of the anthropology tree, largely because this multi-disciplinary approach has generated effective, data-driven strategies for addressing global health priorities like HIV/AIDS, tuberculosis, and malaria.

The ever-growing popularity of medical anthropology is outpaced only by the creative applications of this mixed-methods approach. Today, medical anthropologists study nearly every facet of human health, from cultural inequalities in health care to the psychotropic ethnobotany of shamans. In this medical anthropology selection, Matthew Steinglass examines the impact of traditional healers in the fight against HIV/AIDS in Africa.

As you read this selection, ask yourself the following questions:

- Why did the WHO invite traditional healers like Toudji-Dandje to policy meetings?
- What kinds of research do medical anthropologists do?
- What's the difference between an herbalist healer and a diviner-medium?
- How are traditional healers "modernizing" in African cities?
- Compared with Uganda, why has Togo had such a difficult time curbing the HIV/AIDS crisis?

The following terms discussed in this section are included in the Glossary in the back of the book:

diviner	*World Health*
gris-gris	*Organization (WHO)*
manioc	*UNAIDS*

....

On a hot Sunday evening, in a manioc field near the village of Gboto in the small West African nation of Togo, a group of men in city clothes rustle through the brush, periodically stopping to look at bits of uncovered root. At the center of the group stands a stout, gray-haired man in an embroidered African shirt,

Steinglass, Matthew. "It Takes a Village Healer: Anthropologists Believe Traditional Medicine Can Remedy Africa's AIDS Crisis. Are They Right?" *Lingua Franca* 11, no. 3 (April 2001). Reprinted by permission of the author.

giving directions. He doesn't seem to be finding what he's looking for. Then he stops and points to a bush with wide leaves.

"This is called *ahonto*," he says. "It's good for renal problems." But it isn't the plant he needs.

A few dozen yards further on, he pushes into a thicket and motions toward one of his companions, a muscular field hand carrying a machete. The field hand thrusts his machete into the ground, digs until he encounters a root, and then begins to slice away at it. It takes a few minutes of brisk whacking before he comes up with a length of smooth, tan tuber. The man in the embroidered shirt holds it up, examines it, and nods.

"This is *hetsi*," he says with satisfaction.

The man in the embroidered shirt is Dr. Kokou Coco Toudji-Bandje, an African healer who concocts herbal remedies for a variety of ailments. One of these remedies is something he calls Tobacoak's. He believes it is a "natural antiretroviral." More specifically, he says Tobacoak's "destroys HIV in the blood." Over the past ten years, Toudji-Bandje has used Tobacoak's to treat over three thousand AIDS patients. Most of them, he says, have gotten better—and some have been completely cured.

Toudji-Bandje is not the only herbal healer in Africa who claims the ability to cure AIDS, but he is one of the best known. Patients fly from as far away as Congo to see him. He has a large air-conditioned villa-cum-office in Togo's capital city, Lomé. He has a Mercedes and a white Toyota van. According to a few other doctors who have looked into his finances, he has tremendous amounts of money. The one thing Toudji-Bandje does not actually have is an M.D., but he doesn't seem to miss it much.

Most members of the Western intellectual community consider people like Toudji-Bandje part of Africa's AIDS problem, not its solution. The dimensions of that problem are by now depressingly familiar: HIV-positive rates in southern Africa run to 20 percent and higher. More than twenty-five million sub-Saharan Africans are already infected, and hundreds of millions more are at risk. No one knows what will happen to the social fabric in these countries when cumulative death rates climb into double digits. Under the circumstances, you might think that anyone who would distract attention from HIV education and prevention efforts by claiming to have cured the disease with an herbal concoction is not the kind of guy international organizations should be working with.

If so, you would have been surprised to see Toudji-Bandje at last December's crucial meeting of the Africa Development Forum, in Addis Ababa, where a continent-wide AIDS strategy was under development. Toudji-Bandje came with the official Togolese delegation, and the World Health Organization paid his way. He was representing a constituency that the WHO believes should be an integral part of the campaign against AIDS in Africa: traditional healers.

The WHO's support for collaboration between traditional healers and Western-style public-health systems in Africa actually dates back well before the AIDS epidemic. Public-health experts have advocated such collaboration since the 1970s, drawing on arguments that range from the practical (the crippling lack of M.D.s and trained nurses in the developing world) to the ideological (a refusal to privilege Western biomedical science over alternative systems of medical belief). And some of the most enthusiastic advocates of collaboration with traditional healers have been those Western academics whose job it is to study them: medical anthropologists.

Medical anthropology's slice of the academic pie consists in studying different cultures' beliefs and practices relating to health and disease. A typical medical anthropologist might spend his time sitting in the homes of Bono healers in north-central Ghana, looking into how they deal with diarrhea: what diseases they associate with the symptom (*ayamtuo*, *asonkyere*), what they think causes the diseases (unclean substances, contagion), how they treat the diseases (herbal solutions, enemas), and how their disease typologies match up with those of Western medicine (malaria, food poisoning). An anthropologist studying the Manica of Mozambique would find a completely different conception of diarrhea than that of the Bono: The disease might be attributed to a disturbance of a child's "internal snake," to exposure to heat, or to a father touching his still-breastfeeding child after committing adultery and then failing to wash his hands. With its multitude of ethnic groups, who speak more than eight hundred different languages and construct who knows how many startlingly innovative theories of diarrhea, Africa provides medical anthropologists a never-ending supply of thesis fodder.

Back in the 1960s and early 1970s, some medical anthropologists claimed that African traditional healers were a vanishing breed in need of protection from the onslaught of modernity. Today, anyone who talked that way would be laughed out of the lecture hall. Modernity doesn't seem to be doing too well in Africa. Traditional healers, on the other hand, are going strong. There are quite possibly more than two million healers in Africa, and an estimated 80 percent of sub-Saharan Africans consult them. In some countries, these healers outnumber Western-style medical professionals by around forty to one.

If you go into an average village in Togo looking for biomedical health care, you're likely to find an almost empty dispensary, staffed perhaps one or two days a week by a poorly trained community health worker. The same village might have three or four traditional healers within easy walking distance, each ensconced in an attractive compound with flags flying from the roof. And while the community health worker often has a social standing equivalent to that of a cashier at Dairy Queen, traditional healers are generally among the most powerful and respected members of village society.

Medical anthropologists typically divide healers into two main categories: herbalists and diviner-mediums. The healers' work ranges from administering herbal treatments to eradicating spirit possession to dream interpretation. When it comes to answering the obvious questions—Do the diseases diagnosed by traditional healers actually exist? Do the healers' practices help sick patients?—medical anthropologists are supposed to remain strictly nonjudgmental. And yet, they are typically Westerners, who share a basically biomedical understanding of disease etiology. Medical anthropologists handle this clash of worldviews the same way any of us handle conversations with people whose outlooks differ radically from our own: They finesse the issues. They try not to bring them up. They concentrate on areas of agreement.

The problem is that medical anthropologists' particular area of concentration happens to be one in which certain questions can't be finessed. When children are dying of diarrhea-induced dehydration, and you, as a Westerner, think you know how to save them, you can't sit back and watch a traditional healer apply a treatment you believe to be ineffective. You want to do something.

Starting in the late 1970s, some medical anthropologists began doing more than studying traditional healers—they started working with them. Some saw training traditional healers in Western-style biomedicine as a potential solution to Africa's drastic shortfall of trained healthcare personnel. Others thought traditional healers might know things—about medicinal herbs, or about how to deliver care in a spiritually wholesome fashion—that Western doctors didn't. Twenty years later, these same medical anthropologists are spearheading the drive to include traditional healers in AIDS prevention and care. One of the first was Edward C. Green, an independent anthropologist whose 1994 book, *AIDS and STDs in Africa: Bridging the Gap Between Traditional Healing and Modern Medicine,* made the clearest case yet for bringing healers on board in the fight against AIDS.

Green's book drew on his experience in South Africa, where he had established a program that trained traditional healers as educators for AIDS prevention. Such programs, Green was convinced, could be crucial to stopping the spread of HIV. In fact, he wrote in his book, any successful effort to fight AIDS in Africa would have to include "some sort of collaborative action program involving traditional healers."

Traditional healers pervade African societies, Green stressed; instead of ignoring them, doctors and health educators should view them as an untapped resource. His research showed that while Africans rely on doctors and hospitals to treat many illnesses, most believe that traditional healers are better than doctors at curing sexually transmitted diseases. At least part of the reason is that unlike doctors, healers tend to take a "holistic" approach, treating the patient's spiritual and physical well-being together. With a terminal disease like AIDS, the spiritual side becomes very important. In any event, Green reasoned, patients consult traditional healers whether or not the healers have been educated in AIDS prevention. Untrained healers might spread inaccurate information or engage in harmful practices. Moreover, Green asserted, traditional healers are eager to learn about Western medical ideas, and they put what they learn to good use.

Green's controversial ideas largely stemmed from a single core belief: African societies are not a tabula rasa onto which Western biomedicine can simply be imposed. Traditional healers embody the indigenous African medical culture, which cannot be ignored. As Green would later write, "It is Western medicine that is 'alternative' for most Africans."

These ideas were surprisingly new to the debate on AIDS in Africa, but they weren't new to Green. He had been dealing with them for most of his professional career—a career that neatly parallels the history of medical anthropology's efforts to bring traditional healers into the public-health mainstream.

The WHO first declared itself in favor of increased collaboration with traditional healers in 1977. That same year, Green, then an assistant professor of anthropology at West Virginia University, got an offer from Population Action International to go to West Africa to research population growth in the Sahel region. At some point during the trip, he had "a moment of epiphany," he says. "I was in Niger, I think, and somebody said, 'You know, we have a terrible malnutrition problem among pregnant women, and we have one good source of protein: chicken eggs. But there's a taboo against pregnant women eating eggs. Now, if we could just get an anthropologist in here to figure out a way around that taboo.'" Green laughs. "... I thought, gee whiz, you know, I could be applying what I know to life-and-death issues on a grand scale, instead of teaching anthropology to recalcitrant students who are fulfilling a social-science obligation."

Green never did get around to tackling the egg problem, but later in the same trip he had a second epiphany. At a cocktail party in Ghana, he ran into Michael Warren, a medical anthropologist from Iowa State. Warren was setting up one of the first serious programs to train traditional healers in Western health-care techniques. Called Primary Health Training for Indigenous Healers Programme (PRHETIH), Warren's project eventually trained hundreds of traditional healers in a few simple biomedical health-care precepts: diagnosing and treating diarrhea, malnutrition, febrile convulsions, and the like.

By the early 1980s, Green had transformed himself into a medical anthropologist, trading in his recalcitrant college students for eager witch doctors. Having completed a study of traditional healers' responses to Swaziland's first cholera outbreak, he worked with the United States Agency for International Development (USAID) to make recommendations for integrating traditional healers into the Swazi public-health-care system. "We did a survey, and we found that something like 99 percent of the healers wanted to learn Western medical techniques," he says. "So I showed these results to the medical association of Swaziland, thinking all these doctors would be so happy that the traditional healers want to learn! And I finished my presentation, and the questions from the doctors were: Why aren't these guys in jail? They're practicing medicine without a license. Why isn't someone arresting them?"

Nevertheless, Green and a Swazi colleague, Dr. Lydia Makhubu, managed to set up some workshops. "The first healers came in disguise, dressed as civilians," he says. "By the second or third workshop, they were coming in full regalia, dressed in feathers and beads, and waving their . . . paraphernalia. Out of the closet, as it were."

Through the rest of the 1980s and into the 1990s, Green worked all over Africa on projects related to traditional medicine—in Nigeria, Liberia, South Africa, and Mozambique. With another USAID grant, Green set up a program in South Africa in 1992 to train thirty healers as trainers-of-trainers in HIV prevention. These healers would each be expected to train thirty other healers, and so on, hopefully reaching twenty-seven thousand healers by the third generation. The training sessions described the etiology of AIDS in terms culturally meaningful to traditional healers. White blood cells were described as healers' apprentices who guard the master healers, T-cells. During sex, the enemy, HIV, sneaks in and kills the master healers, takes their places, and tricks the apprentices into thinking they are still taking orders from their superiors. The enemy orders the apprentices to let in more and more HIV, until finally the enemy takes over the whole body.

When Green evaluated the traditional healers who had completed the program, he found that their knowledge about AIDS had significantly increased. They were willing to recommend and supply condoms to patients. They were eager to counsel patients against sexual promiscuity, which many healers already con-

sidered dangerous. And they understood that AIDS could be transmitted by sharing the same razor for ritual scarification, but not by sharing a spoon.

By this time, Green was far from the only one running such programs. In 1992, a medical anthropologist named Rachel King, working with Médecins Sans Fronti'res in Uganda, had started a program called Traditional and Modem Health Practitioners Together Against AIDS (THETA). The program initially trained just seventeen healers, but it did so intensively: fifteen months of training, three days a month. Before the program, according to King, healers were "reluctant to discuss AIDS with their clients, because they feared losing them." After the program, healers promoted and distributed condoms to their clients, counseled them on "positive living," and staged AIDS-education performances using music and theater. Evaluators compared the rate of condom use in areas where THETA had been active with the rate in non-THETA areas. It was 50 percent versus 17 percent.

Eight years later, THETA is still going strong, and Uganda is an unparalleled AIDS success story. In 1993, Uganda had an overall HIV-positive rate that reached 14 percent, one of the highest in Africa at the time. As of 2000, Uganda had cut that rate to about 8 percent. It is the only country in the world ever to have fought double-digit HIV-positive rates back down into single digits.

Of course, many things had to go right for that to happen: Uganda's AIDS prevention programs were strong in every sector, involving religious leaders from every major community, including both Christians and Muslims. (In 1989 the mufti of Uganda officially declared a jihad on AIDS.) Community AIDS education projects honeycombed the country, working in every demographic group from market women to bicycle-taxi boys. Uganda had sub-Saharan Africa's first voluntary and anonymous HIV testing program and its first nationwide, multisectoral AIDS prevention coordinating body. Most important, the country's president made a firm political commitment to stopping AIDS. Still, Green feels that THETA served as an invaluable model for other programs in Uganda. "I'm not going to say it's the thing that stopped AIDS in Uganda—there is no one thing, there never is," he says. "But I think it was significant."

Throughout the 1990s, local and foreign governments, as well as NGOs, set up collaborative programs with traditional healers in Botswana, Malawi, Mozambique, Tanzania, and Zambia. Medical anthropology's efforts to integrate traditional healers into the fight against AIDS appeared to be succeeding. But there was one problem: None of these other countries had actually managed to stop the spread of HIV. Green's program in South Africa did not prevent infection rates there from zooming up toward the 20 percent mark, and they're still climbing. In Botswana the rate has been estimated as high as 36 percent.

What happened? In 1999, one of the grand old men of African demographic research, John C. Caldwell, a professor emeritus at the Australian National University at Canberra, presided over a conference on resistance to sexual behavior change in the face of AIDS. In a paper he delivered at the conference, Caldwell put the problem this way:

There is a mystery at the heart of the African epidemic, which urgently needs explanation.... Much lower HIV seroprevalence levels and AIDS deaths have led elsewhere to marked changes in sexual behaviour and to an early decline in HIV incidence.... In northern Thailand the first evidence of the arrival of the AIDS epidemic led to brothels closing as clients' numbers dwindled, even before government interventions were put in place....

There is now some evidence of the beginning of sexual behaviour change in Uganda and of declining HIV incidence and prevalence. Research elsewhere in sub-Saharan Africa shows no such change.... At first it was thought possible to explain this lack of change in terms of inadequate information.... Over time, this explanation has become ever less tenable. The Demographic and Health Survey program had shown that among men, 98 percent knew of AIDS in 1991–92 in Tanzania and 99 percent in 1998 in Kenya. For women, levels of knowledge were 93 percent in Tanzania in 1991–92 and 99 percent in Zambia in 1992 and in Kenya in 1998. The great majority knew of the dangers of sexual transmission.

So why didn't they do anything to protect themselves?

Zeidan Hammad is an internal-medicine specialist at CHU-Tokoin Hospital, the main public hospital in Lomé. The Lebanese-born Hammad was trained in Cuba, and as he walks me through the hospital's rather decrepit white-stucco facilities, he grumbles about the staff's idea of a sterile environment.

"They spread the clean linen out on the ground to dry," he says, waving at multicolored sheets draped across the bushes and dusty grass in the hospital courtyard. "They like that it dries faster that way. You know, in Cuba, there was no money for anything, but they kept things clean!"

The first stop on Hammad's tour is the HIV testing lab, and for this, at least, he has nothing but praise. The lab's two machines, for performing the ELISA and Western Blot tests for HIV, are in perfect, spotless condition, and the staff is efficient and professional. The tests, which cost about three dollars each, are administered in strict privacy, and results are made available to no one but the patient. The lab processes hundreds of results every month.

Next stop on the tour is Ward 4, the long-term-care ward. Only eight of the ward's beds are occupied. That, explains Dr. Hammad, is because the hospital does not treat AIDS patients. "There's nothing we can do for them here," he says. "If they're rich, they go off to Europe. If they're poor, we send them home to die."

It's not entirely true that the hospital can do nothing. Hammad can treat the opportunistic infections that attack AIDS patients in the early stages of HIV infection, and if their immune systems have not deteriorated too badly, he can prolong their lives. And this is where Hammad's frustration with traditional healers manifests itself.

"I have people come to me with problems that suggest they may be HIV positive, and I tell them, go get tested and then come back," he says. "And then they disappear for six months. I go to the test lab and ask, what happened to this person? And they say, yes, we tested him. Then suddenly six months later the person shows up in my office again, practically on the point of death. And he says, 'Oh, I tested HIV positive, so I went to the traditional healer, but it didn't work. So I went to another healer, but it didn't work either.' So now they're back, and now I can't do anything for them. It's too late. Educated people! And they go to these healers! It's crazy!"

If Hammad and Green were to discuss the value of traditional healers in African health care, they would probably have a hard time keeping their voices down. But sixty years ago, doctors and anthropologists were more united in their frustration with traditional African medical culture. In fact, one of the foundational texts of medical anthropology is E.E. Evans-Pritchard's 1937 classic, *Witchcraft, Oracles and Magic Among the Azande*. The book is essentially a limit case of a culture with which Westerners cannot collaborate. When Habermas or Rorty wants an illustration of a worldview that rests on axioms so different from our own that communication between the two cultures is virtually impossible, they turn to Evans-Pritchard's Azande. According to Evans-Pritchard, the reason the Azande worldview is so inimical to the Western one is that it considers diseases, and other misfortunes, to be caused by sorcery. Whether or not Evans-Pritchard thought the Azande believed all diseases to be caused by sorcery has been an ongoing argument in anthropology for sixty years now. Another ongoing argument has been the question of whether Evans-Pritchard's observations about the Azande hold for the rest of Africa as well.

Until fairly recently, most anthropologists felt that they do. G.P. Murdock, whose *Africa: Its Peoples and Their Culture History* is a seminal ethnography of the continent, wrote in 1980 that mystical retribution and sorcery are the main African explanations for disease. George Foster, whose 1976 paper "Disease Etiologies in Non-Western Medical Systems" is another classic of the field, wrote in 1983 that "personalistic" explanations of disease—that is, you get sick because someone, human or demonic, wants you to get sick—predominate in Africa. Most other anthropologists and social scientists, both Western and African, agreed.

Some social-science researchers have blamed the persistence of personalistic theories of disease causation for the failure of Africans to alter their sexual behavior in the face of AIDS. These scholars have hypothesized that Africans' failure to use condoms or limit their number of sexual partners stems partly from the belief that you don't get AIDS unless an enemy wants you to get it. The idea that personalistic ideas about disease are reducing the ability of ordinary Africans to cope with AIDS is even more widespread among doctors like Hammad. Doctors and public health officials, both Western and African, widely blame the failure of HIV prevention in Africa on local belief in witchcraft, sorcery, and *gris-gris* (black magic).

But they are working with a previous generation's understanding of African traditional medicine. In recent years, anthropologists have reassessed the importance of witchcraft to the African view of disease. In the 1970s, Michael Warren, the founder of the PRHETIH project, began arguing that the Bono of Ghana actually saw most diseases as impersonally caused—that is, caused by environmental factors, whether natural or supernatural, rather than by the malign will of another human being or a deity. Over the years more and more anthropologists have made similar findings with other African ethnic groups.

Anthropologists such as Harriet Ngubane, Mary Douglas, Michael Gelfand, and David Hammond-Tooke reported that ideas of contagion and pollution were actually widespread among many African societies. Some Africans believed that diseases were caused by tiny, invisible insects, or that illness was transmitted by contact with impure substances such as feces or menstrual blood. Shona healers in Zimbabwe practiced variolation, the rubbing of fluid from an infected person's pustule into a cut on a non-infected person, to stimulate an immune response. Practices in other ethnic groups might not have been so obviously biomedically effective, but the important thing was that they were based on impersonal theories of disease causation: You contracted a disease because you happened to come into contact with someone or something, not because a person or deity was using magic against you.

Green ascribes the overemphasis on witchcraft by earlier anthropologists in part to "xenophilia"—an attraction to the more exotic and flamboyant elements of African medical culture. (*Witchcraft Among the Azande* is a much sexier title than, say, *Pollution Beliefs Among the Azande.*) He also thinks many researchers were

not thinking clearly about how to classify beliefs. For example, African survey respondents, asked to explain the causes of certain diseases, may reply, "It's the will of God." This has often been classified by researchers as a "supernatural" or personalistic response. But does it have to be? A Western oncologist might utter the same words when asked why a child contracts leukemia.

There are, undeniably, traditional healers who believe AIDS can be caused by witchcraft. In one oft-cited case in Zambia, a community's devastation by AIDS in the early 1990s led it to consult a "witch finder," who allegedly poisoned some fifteen suspected witches. In a Liberian survey, 13 percent of healers, local leaders, and health workers interviewed named witchcraft as a cause of STDs. But that put witchcraft well behind promiscuity, stepping in urine, or sex with an infected person.

The witchcraft question is important because it bears on the possibility of collaboration. If traditional healers believe that diseases are caused by witchcraft, there is not much you can do with them, from a biomedical perspective. They belong, as one doctor who worked in a district hospital in Africa for thirty-three years put it, to "a system that is irreconcilable with our own." But if traditional healers do not ascribe diseases to sorcery—even if they think illnesses are caused by tiny insects, by imbalances in semimystical forces of heat, by interference with the body's "internal snake," whatever—then you can work with that. You can describe the AIDS virus as a variety of the tiny invisible insects many indigenous medical traditions describe. You can build on many medical traditions' belief that promiscuous or adulterous sex results in pollution. You can collaborate.

More or less. Some medical anthropologists feel that even if traditional healers believe in naturalistic theories of disease causation, working with them is an iffy proposition.

In 1991, Peter Ventevogel, a Dutch medical student working on a master's thesis in medical anthropology, went to Ghana to follow up on Warren's famous PRHETIH project. The project had shut down in 1983, and Ventevogel wanted to find out what the healers had retained from their training. His findings, published in 1996 as *Whiteman's Things: Training and Detraining Healers in Ghana,* were interesting: On the one hand, the healers seemed to retain what they had learned in the workshops to a remarkable extent. On the other hand, they didn't actually seem to be putting that knowledge to use. They had learned that diarrhea could result in dehydration, and often remembered the formula for mixing oral rehydration salts, but almost none of them were actually doing it. They continued to treat diarrhea with herbal enemas, which biomedicine considers actively harmful. "PRHETIH was a powerful force attempting to change healers by training them," Ventevogel wrote. "But the healers formed an intractable counterforce, resisting training by 'detraining' themselves."

"The healers don't write their knowledge down and systematically compare it with each other," explains Ventevogel, now a psychiatrist in Amsterdam, in an interview. "The terms and beliefs differ in every village, in fact even in the same village. Their way of thinking is different from ours. I respect traditional healers, but you can't just mix Western scientific medicine and traditional healers up in a soup and expect to get something that makes any sense."

Unlike Ventevogel, Green thinks traditional medical beliefs are largely consistent within ethnic groups and even across them. But there is one of Ventevogel's critiques with which few people on the front lines would disagree. "Training traditional healers," Ventevogel writes, "is no panacea for a failing Western health care system." And in this belief, Ventevogel is joined by one of the more flamboyant medical anthropologists working on AIDS today: Dr. Paul Farmer.

Paul Farmer runs a free clinic in a desperately poor region of rural Haiti. He also teaches at the Harvard Medical School and consults on numerous international infectious-disease projects, largely dealing with AIDS and tuberculosis. He made his mark in the AIDS field with a 1992 book called *AIDS and Accusation*, based on his experiences as an anthropologist in Haiti during the 1980s. One of the book's chief arguments was that the spread of AIDS in Haiti had been misattributed to "cultural factors"—particularly the belief in voodoo—when in fact it stemmed from socioeconomic causes: the country's vicious poverty, its lack of an adequate biomedical health-care system, and its exposure to a sex tourism trade that catered to Americans. Farmer did find that local interpretations of AIDS hinged on allegations of sorcery. But he didn't think that belief in sorcery was what was making the villages vulnerable. He thought they were vulnerable because they were poor.

Farmer doesn't think the spread of AIDS in Africa can be blamed on African traditional medical culture. The very notion, in Farmer's view, is merely a smokescreen behind which the rich West can evade responsibility for Africa's AIDS catastrophe. At the same time, he thinks that the newer emphasis on working with traditional healers has also served as an excuse for the West's failure to provide the world's poor with decent scientific medical care. We could stop AIDS in Africa, Farmer is saying—but we don't, because we don't want to spend the money.

This argument has become all the sharper recently, as generic antiretroviral drugs from Brazilian and Indian companies have pushed the cost of treatment ever lower. The recent offer by the Indian pharmaceutical company Cipla to supply Médecins Sans Fronti'res with an antiretroviral cocktail treatment for $350 per patient per year puts certified antiretrovirals into the same price class as the herbal remedy of Toudji-Bandje, whose six-month course of treatment costs $430. If Farmer is right—if the barriers to stopping AIDS in Africa are about money, not culture—then the cheaper the drugs get, the greater the pressure on the West will be to intervene.

Green spots a problem with Farmer's thesis. "The richest countries in Africa have the highest HIV rates," he says emphatically. "And the richest people in each country have the highest HIV rates." This may be an exaggeration, but there does seem to be some positive correlation between HIV rates and a nation's income. Botswana and South Africa are among the countries with the highest HIV-positive rates in southern Africa. The highest rate in West Africa is in Ivory Coast. These are the richest countries in their respective zones.

Early in the epidemic, some studies showed HIV rates rising with markers such as education level and travel. AIDS often seemed to hit the richer, more urban classes first. It struck the men who had the money to employ prostitutes. And, of course, their wives. As the epidemic wore on, these correlations became far less pronounced. After all, some of the poorest nations in sub-Saharan Africa—Zambia and Malawi, for example—also have extraordinarily high rates of infection. Still, most anthropologists agree that many rich, educated Africans continue to use traditional healers, though sometimes in conjunction with bio-medical doctors and often in secret.

Whatever his differences with other anthropologists, Farmer agrees that collaborating with healers can be worthwhile. "I bet I work with them as much as anybody," he remarks. But he doesn't see healers as the repositories of a culture's accumulated medical wisdom. "When they're sick, they don't often go to each other," he says. "They come to see me."

In fact, Farmer doesn't just think traditional healers are ineffective. He thinks they're not really traditional: "It may have been different in Central America, Africa, and Asia in the past, but now you see that most 'traditional' healers use antibiotics, and a weird amalgam of modernity and the products of a globalizing economy."

Many anthropologists have noticed that "traditional" healers in Africa are undergoing a strange process of mutation as the continent modernizes. Lots of them still wear traditional robes, carry staffs with ivory heads, and preside over smoke-filled huts surrounded by mud fetishes. But more and more of them are putting on lab coats, hanging certificates on the wall, selling their products in labeled bottles, or even administering injections. Green has documented the common practice of adding mashed-up ampicillin pills to "traditional" herbal medicines.

A perfect example of this sort of "weird amalgam" is Toudji-Bandje, the inventor of Tobacoak's. Toudji-Bandje, the secretary general of Togo's National Association of Traditional Healers, learned his herbal lore from his aged traditional-healer uncle. He also calls himself "Doctor." He has applied for a patent for Tobacoak's. He sends samples of his patients' blood to a laboratory in France to be tested for viral load. He has a catchy brand name for his product. And he calls it an "antiretroviral." Since when is "antiretroviral" a traditional African medical concept?

Toudji-Bandje's patients don't appear to care whether his theory of disease etiology is autochthonous, import, or creole. If anything, the mixture of North and South enables him to claim authority from both sources. What really matters to his patients is simply that someone is telling them he can cure their illness. And they believe the treatment works. "It completely eliminates my fever," says one patient, who declines to give his name. "When I take the medicine, I can eat. Whether it will cure me completely, I don't know. I haven't been taking it long enough. "

"I tested positive in 1992," says a Mr. Kpodar, who claims to have been Toudji-Bandje's second AIDS patient. "I told my wife, and she tested positive too. I begged her to take Toudji-Bandje's medicine, but her family wouldn't let her. She died in 1993. The product saved my life." Toudji-Bandje claims that his remedy is effective in 86 percent of patients. But no third party has examined Toudji-Bandje's data, let alone conducted an independent study of his patients.

In Togo, AIDS is not yet completely out of control. But it's about to be. Togo's current rate of infection runs to 5.98 percent of adults aged fifteen to forty-nine, and a UNAIDS official confirms that HIV rates are rising. There have been active AIDS education and prevention programs in Togo since the late 1980s. But they don't seem to have had much effect.

"I've been trying to get traditional healers involved," says Bridget McHenry, a Peace Corps volunteer working in a village called Yometchin, in Togo's southern Maritime Region. "Some refuse. Some are psyched to do it. But most healers don't believe AIDS can't be cured. And they diagnose a lot of AIDS cases as the result of gris-gris."

Peace Corps volunteers in Togo are fairly pessimistic about the possibility of changing local sexual behavior, and they ascribe much of the blame to belief in gris-gris. But few of them know anything about gris-gris. They give the impression of being lost in a culture they don't understand—precisely the situation Green thinks should be avoided. And if you ask them whether they think it would have been useful to have some training in traditional medical ideas before going into villages as AIDS educators, most say no.

"It's different in every village," says Kim Williams, a volunteer in a Plateau Region village called Akpakpakpe. "You have to really listen closely to understand it at all, and they think you're an idiot. "

"And they know you're not one of them," adds McHenry. "They know you don't believe it. You'll always be yovo"—a foreigner.

Williams nods in agreement.

Each Peace Corps volunteer is paired with a homologue, or counterpart, from a local Togolese NGO or governmental agency. At a recent meeting, the homologues made it clear they're not interested in collaborating with traditional healers either.

"The healers say they can cure AIDS," says one homologue. "But of course they can't. They deceive people."

"They deny the disease exists," says another. "They say it's an old African sickness traditionally known as dikanaku. It's 'get-thin-and-die' in Ewe."

Although the WHO and UNAIDS are both developing programs directed toward traditional healers in Togo, the country's medical establishment regards traditional practitioners with ambivalence. On the one hand, there are doctors, like Hammad, who blame traditional healers for preventing Togolese from coming to terms with AIDS. But Messanvi Gbeassor, a biologist at Lomé's Université du Bénin, has good relations with healers. "We even work with their national association," he says. Gbeassor also carried out some tests on Toudji-Bandje's product, with tantalizingly positive results.

As for the Togolese government, its PNLS—Programme National de Lutte contre le SIDA—claims to have an active program for collaboration with traditional healers. If you try to find out more about this program, you will be directed to the PNLS headquarters, a spacious villa in a sleepy residential section of town. The building appears to be devoid of activity, other than the whir of air conditioners and a couple of boys out front listening to the radio. On the first floor, in a bare, grimy office, a small old man will deflect your questions repeatedly, and then, rummaging through the room's single cabinet, will at last come up with a copy of a statement of program goals from 1992, which announces the intention to hold training sessions with traditional healers.

If there is one single reason for Togo's lamentable performance in stopping HIV, it is illustrated in the condition of the PNLS. Unlike Uganda, Togo's government has not made an overwhelming political commitment to the struggle against AIDS. The president, General Gnassingbe Eyadema, has paid lip service to the cause, but he has not committed sufficient resources to it or made it a top priority. "What's lacking here," says

Moustapha Sidatt, the WHO's resident representative in Togo, "is political will." Sidatt has an ambitious plan to establish a nationwide association of traditional practitioners, which would inspect their practices to determine that they are not harmful, and would issue membership cards backed by the government and the WHO.

Sidatt would also like to start testing the products of traditional healers who claim to treat AIDS or its associated opportunistic infections. "We're trying to approach them, to gain their confidence," he says. "We have some laboratories here at the university, and virology laboratories abroad, which can test their products. There are many things we would like to do. But that requires a political decision from the government."

If you drive east on the highway from Lomé, toward Aneho and Ouidah, you will see little flags fluttering along the roadside in various colors. The flags are advertisements for traditional healers, and the different colors—white, green, black—symbolize the different practices available: herbal solutions, traditional vaccination (herbs inserted directly into cuts in the skin), sorcery, exorcism. Just a few miles outside of Lomé you'll come upon the freshly painted clinic of Madame Leocadie Ashorgbor.

Ashorgbor provides herbal remedies. She learned them from her husband, from whom she is now estranged. She does not know where her husband trained, but some of the remedies are probably time-tested elements of Togolese culture. Still, her husband's recipes aren't all Ashorgbor relies on. "You have to have the gift," she says. "The gift comes from God." Ashorgbor doesn't heal through prayer, but the formulas for some of her herbal remedies come to her in revelations.

What would a medical anthropologist like Green make of Ashorgbor? Well, he would probably find her very interesting, but also a bit confusing. Can Western medicine collaborate with people like her to fight AIDS? If not, why not? "I don't claim working with traditional healers is easy," says Green. "I just think, looking at the public-health benefits, it's a good thing to do."

Ashorgbor agrees. "I think it's a good idea," she says of the WHO's initiative to organize Togo's traditional practitioners. "Depending on how it's done. You know, we traditional therapists are hard people to work with. We get all those herbs up in our heads, and we get a little bit crazy."

21

The Viral Superhighway

George Armelagos

Anthropologists look at human health through the wide-angled lens of our species's long evolutionary history, our biology in a world of microorganisms, and the remarkable medical achievements of our culture. Anthropologists try to see the "big picture."

As recently as the 1970s, epidemiologists—scientists who study the spread of disease—were publicly saying that the age of infectious disease was a thing of the past. At that time, it appeared that the world's major killers, including polio, smallpox, and tuberculosis, were under control—or at least that biomedical science had developed the methods to get them under control. But that has not been the case. Recent decades have seen the emergence of a growing list of new infectious diseases (like HIV/AIDS and SARS) as well as the resurgence of old diseases (like tuberculosis and malaria).

This selection, written by a leading biological anthropologist, shows how pathogenic microorganisms evolve along with humans (and other species) in conjunction with major shifts in patterns of human residence, technological development, and travel. The author identifies three major shifts in the overall pattern of human disease, or "epidemiological transitions," and links them with three major episodes in human prehistory and history.

The first shift involved the domestication of plants and animals that made humans change from nomadic hunting and gathering to sedentary agricultural patterns of residence. The second epidemiological transition was associated with the improvements in nutrition, hygiene, and medicine that accompanied the Industrial Revolution in the nineteenth century and has been characterized by the decline of infectious disease and an increase in chronic disease in the developed world. This second transition has primarily happened in rich countries. The third epidemiological transition, taking place as we speak, is the result of contemporary patterns of globalization, ranging from global warming and other forms of environmental degradation to new patterns of global travel and commerce.

Another major contributor to this third shift is the emergence of drug-resistant strains of common diseases. As the selection illustrates, the pathogens that cause infectious disease, like all other living organisms, are constantly evolving and adapting to new environments. This new development—drug-resistant strains of common microbes—is one of the most frightening possibilities humans now face. However, contemporary human societies can take concrete steps to counter the threats posed by the "viral superhighway." Taking those steps, however, will require concerted effort by political leaders, public health experts, and by all of us.

As you read this selection, ask yourself the following questions:

- How is population health influenced by culture?

- What is an "epidemiological transition"?

- The author describes not one but three epidemiological transitions over the course of human history. When did each of these transitions occur in Europe and the United States, and how can each be explained?

- How is globalization involved in the increasingly rapid spread of infectious disease?

- What steps can we take to protect ourselves, and future generations, against the dangers posed by the widening "viral superhighway"?

The following terms discussed in this selection are included in the Glossary at the back of the book:

diseases of civilization   *pathogen*
epidemiological transition

So the Lord sent a pestilence upon Israel from the morning until the appointed time; and there died of the people from Dan to Beer-sheba seventy thousand men.

—2 Sam. 24:15

Swarms of crop-destroying locusts, rivers fouled with blood, lion-headed horses breathing fire and sulfur: the Bible presents a lurid assortment of plagues, described as acts of retribution by a vengeful God. Indeed, real-life epidemics—such as the influenza outbreak of 1918, which killed 21 million people in a matter of months—can be so sudden and deadly that it is easy, even for nonbelievers, to view them as angry messages from the beyond.

How reassuring it was, then, when the march of technology began to give people some control over the scourges of the past. In the 1950s the Salk vaccine, and later, the Sabin vaccine, dramatically reduced the incidence of polio. And by 1980 a determined effort by health workers worldwide eradicated smallpox, a disease that had afflicted humankind since earliest times with blindness, disfigurement, and death, killing nearly 300 million people in the twentieth century alone.

But those optimistic years in the second half of our century now seem, with hindsight, to have been an era of inflated expectations, even arrogance. In 1967 the surgeon general of the United States, William H. Stewart, announced that victory over infectious diseases was imminent—a victory that would close the book on modern plagues. Sadly, we now know differently. Not only have deadly and previously unimagined new illnesses such as AIDS and Legionnaires' disease emerged in recent years, but historical diseases that just a few decades ago seemed to have been tamed are returning in virulent, drug-resistant varieties. Tuberculosis, the ancient lung disease that haunted nineteenth-century Europe, afflicting, among others, Chopin, Dostoyevski, and Keats, is aggressively mutating into strains that defy the standard medicines; as a result, modern TB victims must undergo a daily drug regimen so elaborate that health-department workers often have to personally monitor patients to make sure they comply [see "A Plague Returns," by Mark Earnest and John A. Sbarbaro, September/October 1993]. Meanwhile, bacteria and viruses in foods from chicken to strawberries to alfalfa sprouts are sickening as many as 80 million Americans each year.

And those are only symptoms of a much more general threat. Deaths from infectious diseases in the United States rose 58 percent between 1980 and 1992. Twenty-nine new diseases have been reported in the past twenty-five years, a few of them so bloodcurdling and bizarre that descriptions of them bring to mind tacky horror movies. Ebola virus, for instance, can in just a few days reduce a healthy person to a bag of teeming flesh spilling blood and organ parts from every orifice. Creutzfeldt-Jakob disease, which killed the choreographer George Balanchine in 1983, eats away at its victims' brains until they resemble wet sponges. Never slow to fan mass hysteria, Hollywood has capitalized on the phenomenon with films such as *Outbreak*, in which a monkey carrying a deadly new virus from central Africa infects unwitting Californians and starts an epidemic that threatens to annihilate the human race.

The reality about infectious disease is less sensational but alarming nonetheless. Gruesome new pathogens such as Ebola are unlikely to cause a widespread epidemic because they sicken and kill so quickly that victims can be easily identified and isolated; on the other hand, the seemingly innocuous practice of overprescribing antibiotics for bad colds could ultimately lead to untold deaths, as familiar germs evolve to become untreatable. We are living in the twilight of the antibiotic era: within our lifetimes, scraped knees and cut fingers may return to the realm of fatal conditions.

Through international travel, global commerce, and the accelerating destruction of ecosystems worldwide, people are inadvertently exposing themselves to a Pandora's box of emerging microbial threats. And recent rumblings about biological terrorism have highlighted the appalling potential of disease organisms for being manipulated to vile ends. But although it may appear that the apocalypse has arrived, the truth is that people today are not facing a unique predicament. Emerging diseases have long loomed like a shadow over the human race.

People and pathogens have a long history together. Infections have been detected in the bones of human ancestors more than a million years old, and evidence from the mummy of the Egyptian pharaoh Ramses V suggests that he may have died from smallpox more than 3,000 years ago. Widespread outbreaks of disease are also well documented. Between 1347 and 1351 roughly a third of the population of medieval Europe was wiped out by bubonic plague, which is carried by fleas that live on rodents. In 1793, 10 percent of the population of Philadelphia succumbed to yellow fever, which is spread by mosquitoes. And in 1875 the son of a Fiji chief came down with measles after a ceremonial trip to Australia. Within four months more than 20,000 Fijians were dead from the imported disease, which spreads through the air when its victims cough or sneeze.

According to conventional wisdom in biology, people and invading microorganisms evolve together: people gradually become more resistant, and the microorganisms become less virulent. The result is either mutualism, in which the relation benefits both species, or commensalism, in which one species benefits without harming the other. Chicken pox and measles, once fatal afflictions, now exist in more benign forms. Logic would suggest, after all, that the best interests of an organism are not served if it kills its host; doing so would be like picking a fight with the person who signs your paycheck.

But recently it has become clear to epidemiologists that the reverse of that cooperative paradigm of illness can also be true: microorganisms and their hosts sometimes exhaust their energies devising increasingly powerful weaponry and defenses. For example, several variants of human immuno-deficiency virus (HIV) may compete for dominance within a person's body, placing the immune system under ever-greater siege. As long as a virus has an effective mechanism for jumping from one person to another, it can afford to kill its victims [see "The Deadliest Virus," by Cynthia Mills, January/February 1997].

If the competition were merely a question of size, humans would surely win: the average person is 10^{17} times the size of the average bacterium. But human beings, after all, constitute only one species, which must compete with 5,000 kinds of viruses and more than 300,000 species of bacteria. Moreover, in the twenty years it takes humans to produce a new generation, bacteria can reproduce a half-million times. That disparity enables pathogens to evolve ever more virulent adaptations that quickly outstrip human responses to them. The scenario is governed by what the English zoologist Richard Dawkins of the University of Oxford and a colleague have called the "Red Queen Principle." In Lewis Carroll's *Through the Looking Glass* the Red Queen tells Alice she will need to run faster and faster just to stay in the same place. Staving off illness can be equally elusive.

The Centers for Disease Control and Prevention (CDC) in Atlanta, Georgia, has compiled a list of the most recent emerging pathogens. They include:

- *Campylobacter*, a bacterium widely found in chickens because of the commercial practice of raising them in cramped, unhealthy conditions. It causes between two million and eight million cases of food poisoning a year in the United States and between 200 and 800 deaths.

- *Escherichia coli* 0157:H7, a dangerously mutated version of an often harmless bacterium. Hamburger meat from Jack in the Box fast-food restaurants that was contaminated with this bug led to the deaths of at least four people in 1993.

- Hantaviruses, a genus of fast-acting, lethal viruses, often carried by rodents, that kill by causing the capillaries to leak blood. A new hantavirus known as *sin nombre* (Spanish for "nameless") surfaced in 1993 in the southwestern United States, causing the sudden and mysterious deaths of thirty-two people.

- HIV, the deadly virus that causes AIDS (acquired immunodeficiency syndrome). Although it was first observed in people as recently as 1981, it has spread like wildfire and is now a global scourge, affecting more than 30 million people worldwide.

- The strange new infectious agent that causes bovine spongiform encephalopathy, or mad cow disease, which recently threw the British meat industry and consumers into a panic. This bizarre agent, known as a prion, or "proteinaceous infectious particle," is also responsible for Creutzfeldt-Jakob disease, the brain-eater I mentioned earlier. A Nobel Prize was awarded to the biochemist Stanley B. Prusiner of the University of California, San Francisco, for his discovery of the prion.

- *Legionella pneumophila*, the bacterium that causes Legionnaires' disease. The microorganism thrives in wet environments; when it lodges in air-conditioning systems or the mist machines in supermarket produce sections, it can be expelled into the air, reaching people's lungs. In 1976 thirty-four participants at an American Legion convention in Philadelphia died—the incident that led to the discovery and naming of the disease.

- *Borrelia burgdorferi*, the bacterium that causes Lyme disease. It is carried by ticks that live on deer and white-footed mice. Left untreated, it can cause crippling, chronic problems in the nerves, joints and internal organs.

How ironic, given such a rogues' gallery of nasty characters, that just a quarter-century ago the Egyptian demographer Abdel R. Omran could observe that in many modern industrial nations the major killers were no longer infectious diseases. Death, he noted, now came not from outside but rather from within the body, the result of gradual deterioration. Omran traced the change to the middle of the nineteenth century, when the industrial revolution took hold in the United States and parts of Europe. Thanks to better nutrition, improved public-health measures, and medical advances such as mass immunization and the introduction of antibiotics, microorganisms were brought under control. As people began living longer, their aging bodies succumbed to "diseases of civilization:" cancer, clogged arteries, diabetes, obesity, and osteoporosis. Omran was the first to formally recognize that shift in the disease environment. He called it an "epidemiological transition."

Like other anthropologists of my generation, I learned of Omran's theory early in my career, and it soon became a basic tenet—a comforting one, too, implying as it did an end to the supremacy of microorganisms. Then, three years ago, I began working with the anthropologist Kathleen C. Barnes of Johns Hopkins University in Baltimore, Maryland, to formulate an expansion of Omran's ideas. It occurred to us that his epidemiological transition had not been a unique event. Throughout history human populations have undergone shifts in their relations with disease—shifts, we noted, that are always linked to major changes in the way people interact with the environment. Barnes and I, along with James Lin, a master's student at Johns Hopkins University School of Hygiene and Public Health, have since developed a new theory: that there have been not one but three major epidemiological transitions; that each one has been sparked by human activities; and that we are living through the third one right now.

The first epidemiological transition took place some 10,000 years ago, when people abandoned their nomadic existence and began farming. That profoundly new way of life disrupted ecosystems and created denser living conditions that led, as I will soon detail, to new diseases. The second epidemiological transition was the salutary one Omran singled out in 1971, when the war against infectious diseases seemed to have been won. And in the past two decades the emergence of illnesses such as hepatitis C, cat scratch disease (caused by the bacterium *Bartonella henselae*), Ebola, and others on CDC's list has created a third epidemiological transition, a disheartening set of changes that in many ways have reversed the effects of the second transition and coincide with the shift to globalism. Burgeoning population growth and urbanization, widespread environmental degradation, including global warming and tropical deforestation, and radically improved methods of transportation have given rise to new ways of contracting and spreading disease.

We are, quite literally, making ourselves sick.

When early human ancestors moved from African forests onto the savanna millions of years ago, a few diseases came along for the ride. Those "heirloom" species—thus designated by the Australian parasitologist J.F.A. Sprent because they had afflicted earlier primates—included head and body lice; parasitic worms such as pinworms, tapeworms, and liver flukes; and possibly herpes virus and malaria.

For 99.8 percent of the five million years of human existence, hunting and gathering was the primary mode of subsistence. Our ancestors lived in small groups and relied on wild animals and plants for their survival. In their foraging rounds, early humans would occasionally have contracted new kinds of illnesses through insect bites or by butchering and eating disease-ridden animals. Such events would not have led to widespread epidemics, however, because groups of people were so sparse and widely dispersed.

About 10,000 years ago, at the end of the last ice age, many groups began to abandon their nomadic lifestyles for a more efficient and secure way of life. The agricultural revolution first appeared in the Middle East; later, farming centers developed independently in China and Central America. Permanent villages grew up, and people turned their attention to crafts such as toolmaking and pottery. Thus when people took to cultivating wheat and barley, they planted the seeds of civilization as well.

With the new ways, however, came certain costs. As wild habitats were transformed into urban settings, the farmers who brought in the harvest with their flint-bladed sickles were assailed by grim new ailments. Among the most common was scrub typhus, which is carried by mites that live in tall grasses, and causes a potentially lethal fever. Clearing vegetation to create arable fields brought farmers frequently into mite-infested terrain.

Irrigation brought further hazards. Standing thigh-deep in watery canals, farm workers were prey to the worms that cause schistosomiasis. After living within aquatic snails during their larval stage, those worms emerge in a free-swimming form that can penetrate human skin, lodge in the intestine or urinary tract, and cause bloody urine and other serious maladies. Schistosomiasis was well known in ancient Egypt, where outlying fields were irrigated with water from the Nile River; descriptions of its symptoms and remedies are preserved in contemporary medical papyruses.

The domestication of sheep, goats, and other animals cleared another pathway for microorganisms. With pigs in their yards and chickens roaming the streets, people in agricultural societies were constantly vulnerable to pathogens that could cross interspecies barriers. Many such organisms had long since reached commensalism with their animal hosts, but they were highly dangerous to humans. Milk from infected cattle could transmit tuberculosis, a slow killer that eats away at the lungs and causes its victims to cough blood and pus. Wool and skins were loaded with anthrax, which can be fatal when inhaled and, in modern times, has been developed by several nations as a potential agent of biological warfare. Blood from infected cattle, injected into people by biting insects such as the tsetse fly, spread sleeping sickness, an often-fatal disease marked by tremors and protracted lethargy.

A second major effect of agriculture was to spur population growth and, perhaps more important, density. Cities with populations as high as 50,000 had developed in the Near East by 3000 B.C. Scavenger species such as rats, mice, and sparrows, which congregate wherever large groups of people live, exposed city dwellers to bubonic plague, typhus, and rabies. And now that people were crowded together, a new pathogen could quickly start an epidemic. Larger populations also enabled diseases such as measles, mumps, chicken pox, and smallpox to persist in an endemic form—always present, afflicting part of the population while sparing those with acquired immunity.

Thus the birth of agriculture launched humanity on a trajectory that has again and again brought people into contact with new pathogens. Tilling soil and raising livestock led to more energy-intensive ways of extracting resources from the earth—to lumbering, coal mining, oil drilling. New resources led to increasingly complex social organization, and to new and more frequent contacts between various societies. Loggers today who venture into the rain forest disturb previously untouched creatures and give them, for the first time, the chance to attack humans. But there is nothing new about this drama; only the players have changed. Some 2,000 years ago the introduction of iron tools to sub-Saharan Africa led to a slash-and-burn style of agriculture that brought people into contact with *Anopheles gambiae*, a mosquito that transmits malaria.

Improved transportation methods also help diseases extend their reach: microorganisms cannot travel far on their own, but they are expert hitchhikers. When the Spanish invaded Mexico in the early 1500s, for instance, they brought with them diseases that quickly raged through Tenochtitlán, the stately, temple-filled capital of the Aztec Empire. Smallpox, measles, and influenza wiped out millions of Central America's original inhabitants, becoming the invisible weapon in the European conquest.

In the past three decades people and their inventions have drilled, polluted, engineered, paved, planted, and deforested at soaring rates, changing the biosphere faster than ever before. The combined effects can, without hyperbole, be called a global revolution. After all, many of them have worldwide repercussions: the widespread chemical contamination of waterways, the thinning of the ozone layer, the loss of species diversity. And such global human actions have put people at risk for infectious diseases in newly complex and devastating ways. Global warming, for instance, could expose millions of people for the first time to malaria, sleeping sickness, and other insect-borne illnesses; in the United States, a slight overall temperature increase would allow the mosquitoes that carry dengue fever to survive as far north as New York City.

Major changes to the landscape that have become possible in the past quarter-century have also triggered new diseases. After the construction of the Aswan Dam in 1970, for instance, Rift Valley fever infected 200,000 people in Egypt, killing 600. The disease had been known to affect livestock, but it was not a major problem in people until the vast quantities of dammed water became a breeding ground for mosquitoes. The insects bit both cattle and humans, helping the virus jump the interspecies barrier.

In the eastern United States, suburbanization, another relatively recent phenomenon, is a dominant factor in the emergence of Lyme disease—10,000 cases of which are reported annually. Thanks to modern earth-moving equipment, a soaring economy, and population pressures, many Americans have built homes in formerly remote, wooded areas. Nourished by lawns and gardens and unchecked by wolves, which were exterminated by settlers long ago, the deer population has exploded, exposing people to the ticks that carry Lyme disease.

Meanwhile, widespread pollution has made the oceans a breeding ground for microorganisms. Epidemiologists have suggested that toxic algal blooms—fed by the sewage, fertilizers, and other contaminants that wash into the oceans—harbor countless viruses and bacteria. Thrown together into what amounts to a dirty genetic soup, those pathogens can undergo gene-swapping and mutations, engendering newly antibiotic-resistant strains. Nautical traffic can carry ocean pathogens far and wide: a devastating outbreak of cholera hit Latin America in 1991 after a ship from Asia unloaded its contaminated ballast water into the harbor of Callao, Peru. Cholera causes diarrhea so severe its victims can die in a few days from dehydration; in that outbreak more than 300,000 people became ill, and more than 3,000 died.

The modern world is becoming—to paraphrase the words of the microbiologist Stephen S. Morse of Columbia University—a viral superhighway. Everyone is at risk.

Our newly global society is characterized by huge increases in population, international travel, and international trade—factors that enable diseases to spread much more readily than ever before from person to person and from continent to continent. By 2020 the world population will have surpassed seven billion, and half those people will be living in urban centers. Beleaguered third-world nations are already hard-pressed to provide sewers, plumbing, and other infrastructure; in the future, clean water and adequate sanitation could become increasingly rare. Meanwhile, political upheavals regularly cause millions of people to flee their homelands and gather in refugee camps, which become petri dishes for germs.

More than 500 million people cross international borders each year on commercial flights. Not only does that traffic volume dramatically increase the chance a sick person will infect the inhabitants of a distant area when she reaches her destination; it also exposes the sick person's fellow passengers to the disease, because of poor air circulation on planes. Many of those passengers can, in turn, pass the disease on to others when they disembark.

The global economy that has arisen in the past two decades has established a myriad of connections between far-flung places. Not too long ago bananas and oranges were rare treats in northern climes. Now you can walk into your neighborhood market and find food that has been flown and trucked in from all over the world: oranges from Israel, apples from New Zealand, avocados from California. Consumers in affluent nations expect to be able to buy whatever they want whenever they want it. What people do not generally realize, however, is that this global network of food production and delivery provides countless pathways for pathogens. Raspberries from Guatemala, carrots from Peru, and coconut milk from Thailand have been responsible for recent outbreaks of food poisoning in the United States. And the problem cuts both ways: contaminated radish seeds and frozen beef from the United States have ended up in Japan and South Korea.

Finally, the widespread and often indiscriminate use of antibiotics has played a key role in spurring disease. Forty million pounds of antibiotics are manufactured annually in the United States, an eightyfold increase since 1954. Dangerous microorganisms have evolved accordingly, often developing antibiotic-resistant strains. Physicians are now faced with penicillin-resistant gonorrhea, multiple-drug-resistant tuberculosis, and *E. coli* variants such as 0157:H7. And frighteningly, some enterococcus bacteria have become resistant to *all* known antibiotics. Enterococcus infections are rare, but staphylococcus infections are not, and many strains of staph bacteria now respond to just one antibiotic, vancomycin. How long will it be before run-of-the-mill staph infections—in a boil, for instance, or in a surgical incision—become untreatable?

Although civilization can expose people to new pathogens, cultural progress also has an obvious countervailing effect: it can provide tools—medicines, sensible city planning, educational campaigns about sexually transmitted diseases—to fight the encroachments of disease. Moreover, since biology seems to side with microorganisms anyway, people have little choice but to depend on protective cultural practices to keep pace: vaccinations, for instance, to confer immunity, combined with practices such as hand-washing by physicians between patient visits, to limit contact between people and pathogens.

All too often, though, obvious protective measures such as using only clean hypodermic needles or treating urban drinking water with chlorine are neglected, whether out of ignorance or a wrongheaded emphasis on the short-term financial costs. The worldwide disparity in wealth is also to blame: not surprisingly, the advances made during the second epidemiological transition were limited largely to the affluent of the industrial world.

Such lapses are now beginning to teach the bitter lesson that the delicate balance between humans and invasive microorganisms can tip the other way again. Overconfidence—the legacy of the second epidemiological transition—has made us especially vulnerable to emerging and reemerging diseases. Evolutionary principles can provide this useful corrective: in spite of all our medical and technological hubris, there is no quick fix. If human beings are to overcome the current crisis, it will be through sensible changes in behavior, such as increased condom use and improved sanitation, combined with a commitment to stop disturbing the ecological balance of the planet.

The Bible, in short, was not far from wrong: We do bring plagues upon ourselves—not by sinning, but by refusing to heed our own alarms, our own best judgment. The price of peace—or at least peaceful coexistence—with the microorganisms on this planet is eternal vigilance.

22

Culture and the Evolution of Obesity

Peter J. Brown

As a people, Americans rank as one of the fattest societies in history. This epidemiological fact remains despite the tremendous amount of money, effort, and worry that Americans put into diet, exercise, and the quest for the perfect body. For some people, particularly teens and young adults, the quest to be thin can become such an obsession that they develop life-threatening eating disorders, like anorexia nervosa. But in other cultures, young women may go to great lengths to try to gain weight to look attractive. There are no universal standards of physical beauty; in fact, there is considerable cross-cultural variation. Culture defines normality.

How do conditions like obesity come to be expressed? Biologists usually say that it is a combination of genes and environment. There is good evidence that genes predispose people toward conditions, but there is seldom evidence that the chain of causation is entirely genetic. A complete explanation must be both biological and cultural. In other words, if a condition like obesity is caused by an interaction of genetic and cultural/behavioral predispositions, then both the genes and culture must be the product of evolutionary processes.

In this selection, Peter Brown provides a cross-cultural and evolutionary analysis of how both biological and cultural factors in obesity evolved. This analysis explains the sociological distribution of obesity today. It also emphasizes that peripheral body fat (characteristic of women) is a small health hazard compared to abdominal fat (characteristic of men).

Dietary patterns are obviously shaped by culture. But human tendencies to value meat, fatty foods, and sweets must be understood in the context of our evolutionary past.

As you read this selection, ask yourself the following questions:

- Have you ever noticed that there are gender differences in the locality of fat storage in the body? Why would this be the case?

- Why are fat people ridiculed and discriminated against in the United States? Are these social reactions worse for men or for women?

- What does the author mean when he says that in a rich society, slenderness can be an individual symbol of conspicuous consumption?

- Given the difference in health risk between peripheral body fat and central body fat, why might weight not be the best way to measure one's risk?

- Why do humans like foods that are "bad" for them?

The following terms discussed in this selection are included in the Glossary at the back of the book:

adipose tissue	gender dimorphism
cultural ideals	ideal body images
culture	obesity
epidemiology	sexual dimorphism
food scarcity	

Brown, Peter J. "Culture and the Evolution of Obesity." *Human Nature* 2 (1991):31–57. Copyright © 1991 by Walter de Gruyter, Inc., New York. With kind permission from Springer Science+Business Media.

T he etiology or cause of obesity can be understood in the context of human cultural and genetic evolution. The cause of human obesity and overweight involves the interaction of genetic traits with culturally patterned behaviors and beliefs. Both these genes and culture traits, remarkably common in human societies, are evolutionary products of similar processes of selection related to past food scarcities. This idea is not new: The notion of "thrifty phenotypes rendered detrimental by progress" was introduced more than a quarter-century ago. In recent years, the evidence for the existence of genes that enable individuals to use food energy efficiently and store energy reserves in the form of fat has been increasingly impressive; those individuals with "fat phenotypes" are likely to develop adult obesity (Stunkard et al. 1986, 1990).

It is important to recognize that these "thrifty" genes are, at least in the human context, necessary but not sufficient factors in the causation of obesity. In actuality, the new discoveries in the genetics of obesity highlight our ignorance about the role of nongenetic or cultural factors, which are usually subsumed in the term *environment* in the medical literature. The purpose of this paper is to examine why and how cultures have evolved behaviors and beliefs that appear to predispose individuals to develop obesity. I believe that an anthropological model of culture has significant advantages over the commonly used undifferentiated concept of "environment" for generating hypotheses about behavioral causes of obesity. This cultural approach is particularly useful for improving our understanding of the social epidemiological distribution of obesity.

It is valuable to raise an obvious question at the outset: Why do people find it very difficult to reduce their intake of dietary fat and sugar even when the medical benefits of this behavioral change are well known to them? The answer is not obvious, since neither the physiological nor the cultural attraction of these foods is well understood. The proximate mechanisms for this attraction are linked to brain physiology and biochemistry (Wurtman and Wurtman 1987). The ultimate answers are linked to our evolutionary heritage. Human predispositions to obesity are found in both genetic and cultural traits that may have been adaptive in the context of past food scarcities but are maladaptive today in the context of affluence and constant food surpluses.

THE PROBLEMS OF OBESITY AND OVERWEIGHT

Throughout most of human history, obesity was neither a common health problem nor even a realistic possibility for most people. Today, particularly in affluent societies like the United States, obesity is very common, affecting about 12 percent of adult men and women; overweight is even more common, affecting an additional 20 to 50 percent of adult Americans depending on the definitions used (Bray 1987). Not only are overweight and obesity relatively common conditions in our society, they are also extremely complex and intractable. Obesity is a serious public health problem because of its causal connection to major causes of morbidity and mortality from chronic diseases, including cardiovascular disease, type 2 diabetes mellitus (NIDDM), and hypertension. On the individual level, obesity and overweight bring with them an enormous amount of personal psychological pain. The fact that the obese are subjected to significant social and economic discrimination is well documented.

Fat is extraordinarily difficult to shed because the body guards its fat stores. The evidence concerning the effectiveness over a 5-year period of diet therapies indicates that nearly all of the weight that is lost through diets is eventually regained. The remarkable failure of diet therapies has made some researchers rethink their commonsensical theory of obesity as being caused by overeating; the clinical evidence of the past 40 years simply does not support this simplistic notion.

Even in the absence of scientific data about the effectiveness of diet therapy, the diet and weight-loss industry in the United States is remarkably successful in its ability to capture the hope and money of people who perceive themselves to be overweight. This industry thrives because of a complex of cultural beliefs about the ideal body and sexual attractiveness rather than medical advice and the prevention of chronic diseases per se. The American cultural concern about weight loss and the positive valuation of slenderness for women of the middle and upper classes are difficult to overemphasize. Chernin (1981) has referred to this cultural theme as an "obsession" and the "tyranny of slenderness." In this light, it is impossible to claim that obesity is purely a medical issue.

OBESITY AND HUNGER

It is important to remember that for most citizens of the world today, as it has been in the past, the possibility of obesity is remote whereas the possibility of hunger is close to home. There is a palpable irony in the fact of an epidemic of obesity in a world characterized by hunger. For example, in the United States an estimated 20 million people are hungry because they are on a "serious diet"; generally these people are of the middle and upper classes, and most are women. At the same time in the same rich nation, another estimated 20 million Americans are hungry and poorly nourished largely because they lack sufficient money; generally these people are elderly, homeless, or rural inhabitants. This sad symmetry in the estimates of voluntary and involuntary hunger in the United States is a valuable starting point for a discussion of the etiology of obesity. From an evolutionary standpoint, past food shortages have acted as powerful agents of natural selection, shaping both human genetics and behavior.

A theory of the etiology of obesity must not only account for the influences of genes and learned behaviors but also explain its social distribution. Before the problem of causation is addressed, it is worthwhile to examine the nature of human obesity.

CHANGING DEFINITIONS OF OBESITY

The most basic scientific issues regarding obesity are, in fact, controversial. The definitions of obesity and overweight have been the subject of substantial medical debate, in part because they must be based on inferred definitions of normality or "ideal" body proportions. Although obesity refers to excessive adiposity (fat deposits), the most common measurement is not of fat tissue at all but an indirect inference based on measures of stature and total body weight (Bray 1987).

The social history of height and weight standards in the United States is interesting. Until recently, the task of defining both obesity and ideal weights has been the domain of the life-insurance industry. The most well-known table of desirable weights was developed by the Metropolitan Life Insurance Company using correlation statistics between height/weight and mortality among insurance applicants. Ideal weights were based on data from 25-year-old insurance applicants, despite the nonrepresentative nature of the "sample" pool and the fact that in most human populations, individuals increase in weight until around age 50. Obesity was defined as 120 percent of the Ideal Body Weight (IBW), and overweight was defined as 110 percent IBW. Individual life-insurance applicants outside the recommended weight range were required to pay a surcharge on insurance premiums. In 1959, the concept of "frame size" was introduced, although the resulting categories were never given operational definitions using anthropometric measures.

Definitions of obesity have changed throughout history. From 1943 to 1980, definitions of "ideal weights" for women of a particular height were consistently lowered, while those for men remained approximately the same. In 1983, a major debate on the definition of obesity began when Metropolitan Life revised its tables upward, based on new actuarial studies of mortality. Many organizations and experts in the diet industry, including experts in medical fields, rejected these new standards.

In the current medical literature, weight and height tables have been replaced by the Body Mass Index (BMI), defined as body weight (in kilograms) divided by the square of body height (in meters). BMI (W/H^2) is strongly correlated with total body fat, and a value greater than 30 is generally considered obese. Current recommendations include slight increases in BMI with age (Bray 1987). Nevertheless, there continues to be little agreement on precise definitions of either overweight or obesity.

An important added dimension to the questions of definition of obesity involves the distribution of fat around the body trunk or on the limbs. Central or trunk body fat distribution is closely correlated with serious chronic diseases, such as cardiovascular disease, whereas peripheral body fat in the hips and limbs does not carry similar medical risks. Because of this clinically important distinction, measures of fat distribution like waist to hips ratio (WHR), wherein lower WHR values indicate lower risk of chronic disease consequences, will be a valuable addition to future definitions of obesity.

FOUR FACTS ABOUT THE SOCIAL DISTRIBUTION OF OBESITY

Humans are among the fattest of all mammals, and the primary function of our fat is to serve as an energy reserve. The nonrandom social distribution of adiposity within and between human populations may provide a key to understanding obesity. Four facts about this social distribution are particularly cogent for an evolutionary reconstruction: (1) the gender difference in the total percent and site distribution of body fat, as well as the prevalence of obesity; (2) the concentration of obesity in certain ethnic groups; (3) the increase in obesity associated with economic modernization; and (4) the powerful and complex relationship between social class and obesity. Any useful theory concerning the etiology of obesity must account for these social epidemiological patterns.

Sexual Dimorphism

Humans show only mild sexual dimorphism in variables like stature. Males are only 5 to 9 percent taller than females. The sample of adults from Tecumseh, Michigan, seen in Figure 1, are typical. Men are larger than women in height and total body mass, but women have more subcutaneous fat as measured by skinfold thicknesses in 16 of 17 sites (the exception is the suprailiac region—so-called "love handles"). The greatest degree of sexual dimorphism is found in the site of distribution of fat tissue; women have much more peripheral fat in the legs and hips (Kissebah et al. 1989). This difference is epidemiologically important because the greater proportion of peripheral fat in females may be associated with reduced morbidity compared to males with identical BMI values.

Sex differences are also seen in the prevalence of obesity. Despite methodological differences in the categorization of obesity, data from the 14 population surveys shown in Figure 2 indicate that in all of the studies, females have a higher prevalence of obesity than males. A greater risk of obesity for females appears to be a basic fact of human biology.

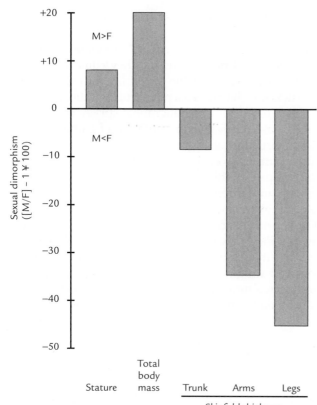

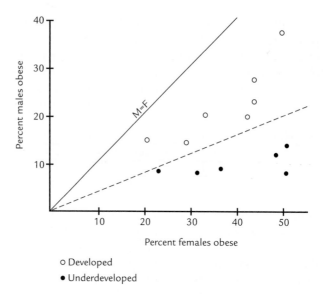

FIGURE 2 Gender differences in prevalences of obesity in 14 populations by general industrial development. Operational definitions of obesity differ between studies. See Brown and Konner (1987) for references. The unbroken line demarcates equal male-female obesity prevalences. The broken line indicates an apparent distinction in gender proportions of obesity in developed and underdeveloped countries. From Brown, P.J., & M. Konner. "An Anthropological Perspective on Obesity." *Annals of the New York Academy of Sciences* 499 (1987):29–46. Copyright © 1987 by The New York Academy of Sciences. Reprinted by permission of John Wiley & Sons, Inc.

FIGURE 1 Sexual dimorphism in stature, body mass, and fat measures among white Americans aged 20 to 70 in Techumseh, Michigan. Sexual dimorphism is calculated by comparing male and female means; positive figures refer to greater male measures. Skinfold thicknesses are means of four sites on the trunk or five sites on the arms and legs; the mean dimorphism for all 17 fat measures is –19 percent. From Brown, P.J., & M. Konner. "An Anthropological Perspective on Obesity." *Annals of the New York Academy of Sciences* 499 (1987):29–46. Copyright © 1987 by The New York Academy of Sciences. Reprinted by permission of John Wiley & Sons, Inc.

Economic Modernization

The social distribution of obesity varies among societies, depending on their degree of economic modernization. Studies of traditional hunting and gathering populations report *no obesity.* In contrast, numerous studies of traditional societies undergoing the process of economic modernization demonstrate rapid increases in the prevalence of obesity. Trowell and Burkitt's (1981) 15 case studies of epidemiological change in modernizing societies conclude that obesity is the first of the "diseases of civilization" to appear. The rapidity with which obesity becomes a common health problem in the context of modernization underscores the critical role of cultural behaviors in the causation of obesity, since there has been insufficient time for changes in gene frequencies.

Figure 2 also suggests that variations in the male-female ratio of obesity prevalence are related to economic modernization. In less industrially developed societies female obesity is much more common than male obesity, but in more affluent societies the ratio is nearly equivalent. Recent World Health Organization data on global obesity also support this observation (Gurney and Gorstein 1988).

Cultural changes with modernization include the seemingly invariable pattern of diet in industrial countries—decreased fiber intake and increased consumption of fat and sugar. Modernization is also associated with decreased energy expenditures related to work, recreation, or daily activities. From the perspective of the populations undergoing economic modernization, increasing average weight might be seen as a good thing rather than a health problem.

Ethnicity

The idea that particular populations have high rates of a genotype that predisposes individuals to obesity and related diseases is not new but is now supported by a convincing body of adoption and twin data (Stunkard et al. 1986, 1990) and by studies of particular obesity-prone populations like the Pima Indians (Ravussin et al. 1988). In the United States, ethnic groups with elevated rates of obesity include African Americans (particularly in the rural South), Mexican Americans, Puerto Ricans, Gypsies, and Pacific Islanders (Centers for Disease Control 1989).

The fact that certain ethnic groups have high rates of obesity is not easy to interpret because of the entanglement of the effects of genetic heredity, social class, and cultural beliefs. The association of obesity with ethnicity is not evidence for the exclusive role of genetic transmission, since social factors like endogamy (marriage within the group) or group isolation are critical for defining the population structure—that is, the social system through which genes are passed from generation to generation.

Social Class

Social class (socioeconomic status) can be a powerful predictor of the prevalence of obesity in both modernizing and affluent societies, although the direction of the association varies with the type of society. In developing countries, there is a strong and consistent *positive association* between social class and obesity for men, women, and children; correspondingly, there is an inverse correlation between social class and protein-calorie malnutrition. In heterogeneous and affluent societies, like the United States, there is a strong *inverse correlation* of social class and obesity for females. The association between obesity and social class among women in affluent societies is not constant through the life cycle. Economically advantaged girls are initially fatter than their low-income counterparts, but the pattern is reversed beginning at puberty. For females, social class remains the strongest social epidemiological predictor of obesity.

OBESITY AND HUMAN EVOLUTION

Human biology and behavior can be understood in the context of two distinct processes of evolution. Biological evolution involves changes through time in the frequency of particular genes, primarily because of the action of natural selection on individuals. Cultural evolution involves historical changes in the configurations of cultural systems, that is, the learned patterns of behavior and belief characteristics of social groups. Cultural evolution includes the striking and rapid transformation of human lifestyles from small food-foraging societies to large and economically complex states in a span of less than 5,000 years.

The Context of Food Scarcities

Food shortages have been very common in human prehistory and history; in fact, they could be considered a virtually inevitable fact of life for most people. As such, they have been a powerful evolutionary force.

A cross-cultural ethnographic survey of 118 nonindustrial societies (with hunting and gathering, pastoral, horticultural, and agricultural economies) found some form of food shortages for *all* of the societies in the sample (Whiting 1958). Shortages occur annually or even more frequently in roughly half of the societies, and every 2 to 3 years in an additional 24 percent. The shortages are "severe" (i.e., including starvation deaths) in 29 percent of the societies sampled. Seasonal availability of food results in a seasonal cycle of weight loss and weight gain in both hunting and gathering and agricultural societies, although the fluctuation is substantially greater among agriculturalists.

Scarcity and Cultural Evolution

A hunting and gathering economy was characteristic of all human societies for more than 95 percent of our history, yet it is represented by only a handful of societies today. In general, food foragers enjoy high-quality diets, maintain high levels of physical fitness, suffer the risk of periodic food shortages, and are generally healthier than many contemporary populations that rely on agriculture. Without romanticizing these societies, the evidence is persuasive enough to suggest a "paleolithic prescription" of diet and exercise for the prevention of chronic diseases (Eaton et al. 1988). This recommendation refers to the quality of preindustrial diets and not to their dependability or quantity.

Approximately 12,000 years ago, some human groups shifted from a food-foraging economy to one of food production. This economic transformation allowed the evolution of urban civilizations. Many archaeologists believe that people were "forced" to adopt the new agricultural economy because of ecological pressures from population growth and food scarcities or because of military coercion. The archaeological record clearly shows that agriculture was associated with nutritional stress, poor health, and diminished stature (Cohen and Armelagos 1984). The beginning of agriculture is also linked to the emergence of social stratification, a system of inequality that improved the Darwinian fitness of the ruling class relative to that of the lower classes. Social inequality, particularly differential access to strategic resources, plays a critical role in the distribution of obesity in most societies.

Certain ecological zones appear to be prone to severe food shortages. For example, archaeological analysis of tree rings from the southwestern United States shows that the prehistoric past was characterized by frequent and severe droughts. The impressive agricultural societies of the prehistoric Southwest had expanded during an extended period of uncharacteristically good weather and could not be maintained when the lower and more characteristic rainfall patterns resumed. Ecological conditions leading to severe scarcity may have acted as strong forces of selection for "thrifty" genotypes.

Scarcity and Genetic Evolution

Since food shortages were ubiquitous for humans under natural conditions, selection favored individuals who could effectively store calories in times of surplus. For most societies, these fat stores would be called on at least every 2 or 3 years. Malnutrition increases infectious disease mortality, as well as decreasing birth weights and rates of child growth. The evolutionary scenario is this: Females with greater energy reserves in fat would have a selective advantage over their lean counterparts in terms of withstanding the stress of food shortages, not only for themselves but also for their fetuses or nursing children. Humans have evolved the ability to "save up" food energy for inevitable food shortages through the synthesis and storage of fat.

Selection has favored the production of peripheral body fat in females, whose reproductive fitness is influenced by the nutritional demands of pregnancy and lactation. This peripheral fat is usually mobilized after being primed with estrogen during the late stages of pregnancy and during lactation. In addition, a minimal level of fatness increases female reproductive success because of its association with regular cycling and early menarche (Frisch 1987).

In this evolutionary context the usual range of human metabolic variation must have produced many individuals with a predisposition to become obese; yet they would, in all likelihood, never have had the opportunity to do so. Furthermore, in this context there could be little or no natural selection against this tendency. Selection could not provide for the eventuality of continuous surplus simply because it had never existed before.

CULTURE AND ADAPTATIONS TO FOOD SCARCITY

Food scarcities have shaped not only our genes but also, and perhaps more important, human cultures. Because the concept of culture is rarely considered in medical research on obesity, and because I am suggesting that this concept has advantages over the more common and undifferentiated term *environment*, it is

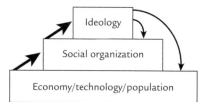

FIGURE 3 A materialist model of culture. From Brown, Peter J. "Culture and the Evolution of Obesity." *Human Nature* 2 (1991):31–57. Copyright © 1991 by Walter de Gruyter, Inc., New York. With kind permission from Springer Science+Business Media.

necessary to review some basic aspects of this anthropological term. *Culture* refers to the learned patterns of behavior and belief characteristic of a social group. As such, culture encompasses *Homo sapiens'* primary mechanism of evolutionary adaptation, which has distinct advantages of greater speed and flexibility than genetic evolution.

Cultural behaviors and beliefs are usually learned in childhood and they are often deeply held and seldom questioned by adults, who pass this "obvious" knowledge and habits to their offspring. In this regard, cultural beliefs and values are largely unconscious factors in the motivation of individual behaviors. Cultural beliefs define "what is normal" and therefore constrain the choices of behaviors available to an individual.

One useful way of thinking about culture in relation to obesity is a cultural materialist model as seen in Figure 3. This model divides culture into three layers. The material foundation of a cultural system is the economic mode of production, which includes the technology and the population size that the productive economy allows and requires. Population size is maintained by the social system, sometimes called the mode of reproduction. Contingent on the first layer is the system of social organization, which includes kinship patterns, marriage and family practices, politics, and status differentiation. Contingent on the social structure is the ideology or belief system, including ideas, beliefs, and values, both secular and sacred. Most anthropologists believe that the ideology is an extremely important part of culture, in part because it rationalizes and reinforces the economy and social structure. Ideology enables people to make sense of their world and to share their common world view through symbols. As such, ideology includes sacred concepts from religion as well as secular concepts (with symbolic components) like health or sexual attractiveness.

A culture is an integrated system: A change in one part causes changes in the other layers. The materialist model indicates that the direction of causal change is from the bottom layer upward (the solid arrows in Figure 3). An economic change, like the invention of agriculture or the Industrial Revolution, has drastic implications for population size, social organization, and associated beliefs. On the other hand, most people within a society tend to explain things from the top down. Of course, people can hold contradictory beliefs and values that are not necessarily linked to their actual behavior.

CULTURAL PREDISPOSITIONS TO OBESITY

Obesity is related to culture in all three levels of the materialist model.

Productive Economy and Food Scarcity

Humans have evolved a wide variety of cultural mechanisms to avoid or minimize the effects of food scarcities. The most important adaptation to scarcity is the evolution of systems of food production and storage. As noted previously, the primary weakness of preindustrial systems of food production is a vulnerability to food shortages. The universality of food shortages discussed above is largely because of the technological limitations in food production and storage.

On the other hand, the energy-intensive (and energy-inefficient) system of agriculture in industrialized societies produces large surpluses of food. These agricultural surpluses are seldom used to eliminate hunger; rather they are used to transform and process foods in particular ways—often to add calories, fat, or salt. For example, we feed "extra" grain to beef cattle to increase the proportion of fat in their meat; consumers say that this overfeeding makes the meat "juicy." Similarly, potatoes are transformed into french fries and potato chips. From a nutritional standpoint the original vegetable is actually reduced to a vehicle for fat and salt. Endemic hunger exists even in the most affluent societies, where it is caused not by poor production but by inequitable distribution.

Technological changes associated with cultural evolution almost exclusively reduce the energy requirements of human labor. In general, cultural evolution has meant the harnessing of greater amounts of energy through technology (one aspect of the mode of production). To prevent obesity, people in developed societies must burn energy through daily workouts rather than daily work.

Reproduction and Energy Expenditure

The concept of the *mode of reproduction* is also related to predispositions to obesity. Pregnancy and lactation represent serious and continuing energy demands on women in societies that have not undergone the demographic transition. Industrial and nonindustrial societies differ in terms of the historical changes from high to low fertility and the reduction of mortality attributable to infectious disease. Higher numbers of pregnancies and longer periods of breast-feeding place high energy demands on women, especially if they cannot supplement their diet during these critical periods. As a result, women suffer greater risk of protein-energy malnutrition. Conversely, with fewer pregnancies and the reduction of breast-feeding, women in industrial societies have less opportunity to mobilize peripheral fat stores and suffer greater risk of obesity. In contemporary societies like the United States, mothers in lower social classes tend to have more children and to feed their infants with bottled formula rather than breast milk. Use of infant formulas allows women to retain their fat stores. These different social patterns in reproduction may play a role in the inverse association of obesity and social class for females.

Social Structure and Obesity

Characteristics of social organization may function as predispositions to obesity. In highly stratified and culturally heterogeneous societies, the distribution of obesity is associated with ethnicity and social class. Marriage patterns typically illustrate ethnic or social class endogamy, that is, marriage within the group. In the United States, members of ethnic minorities choose marriage partners from the same group at extremely high rates. This social practice may concentrate the genetic predispositions to conditions like obesity in particular subpopulations. Similarly, data suggest a pattern of "assortative mating" by social class as well as body type (particularly stature), which may be related to the genetic etiology of obesity. Genetic admixture with Native American groups of the Southwest has been suggested as a cause of elevated rates of type 2 diabetes mellitus and obesity among Mexican Americans (Gardner et al. 1984).

The pervasive and complex relationship between obesity and social class, or socioeconomic status (SES), is important. SES is related to particular behavior patterns that cause obesity. This statement underemphasizes the fact that these learned behaviors are *characteristic* of particular social groups or classes. In other words, the cultural patterns of social class groups are primary, not the individual behaviors themselves.

From a cross-cultural perspective, the general association between obesity and social position is positive: The groups with greater access to economic resources have higher rates of obesity. This pattern is logical and expected because socially dominant groups with better access to strategic resources should have better nutrition, better health, and consequently greater reproductive success.

As discussed earlier, the remarkable and important exception is women in industrial societies, who exhibit a strong *inverse* correlation between obesity and social class. The challenge for researchers is to explain why and how upper-class women in industrial societies remain thin. For many women the ideal of thinness requires considerable effort, restrained eating, and often resources invested in exercise. The social origins of the ideal of thinness in American women are associated with historical changes in women's economic roles, marriage patterns, and family size.

Low-income people in industrial societies might be considered well off by worldwide standards, and this access to resources is reflected in obesity prevalences. Yet in the context of perceived relative deprivation and economic stability, many people in societies like the United States live in stressful conditions—just one paycheck away from hunger. In terms of life priorities, economic security may be a higher and more immediate objective than more elusive goals like an "ideal body" or even long-term health. Amid the daily stresses of poverty, food may be the most common avenue of pleasure and psychological relief. Ethnographic studies of low-income urban black communities in the United States show a social emphasis on food sharing as a tool for marking family ties and demonstrating community cohesiveness.

Cultural Beliefs as Predispositions to Obesity

The third and possibly most important level of the model of culture shown in Figure 3 encompasses cultural symbols, beliefs, and values. Aspects of ideology relevant to the etiology of obesity include the symbolic meaning of fatness, ideal body types, and perceived risks of food shortages.

Fatness is symbolically linked to psychological dimensions, such as self-worth and sexuality, in many societies of the world, but the nature of that symbolic association is not constant. In mainstream U.S. culture, obesity is socially stigmatized, but for most cultures of the world, fatness is viewed as a welcome sign of health and prosperity. Given the rarity of obesity in preindustrial societies, it is not surprising that they lack ethnomedical terms for obesity. Much more attention is placed on "thinness" as a symptom of starvation, like among the !Kung San (Lee 1979), or in contemporary Africa as a sign of AIDS (sometimes called "the slim disease"). In the context of the AIDS epidemic, plumpness is indeed a marker of health.

Perhaps it is large body size, rather than obesity per se, that is admired as a symbol of health, prestige, prosperity, or maternity in agricultural societies. The Tiv of Nigeria, for example, distinguish between a very positive category, "too big" *(kehe)*, and an unpleasant condition "to grow fat" *(ahon)* (Bohannan and Bohannan 1969). The first is a compliment because it is a sign of prosperity; the second is a rare and undesirable condition.

For women, fatness may also be a symbol of maternity and nurturance. In traditional societies in which women attain status only through motherhood, this symbolic association increases the cultural acceptability of fatness. A fat woman, symbolically, is well taken care of, and in turn she takes good care of her children. Fellahin Arabs in Egypt describe the proper woman as fat because she has more room to bear the child, lactates abundantly, and gives warmth to her children. The cultural ideal of thinness in industrial societies, in contrast, is found where motherhood is not the sole or even primary means of status attainment for woman. The idea that fat babies and children are healthy children is very widespread. Food can be treated as a symbol of love and nurturance; in some cultures it may be impolite for a guest to refuse food that has been offered, but it is taboo to refuse food from one's mother.

In the industrialized United States, ethnic variation in culturally accepted definitions of obesity is significant. Some Mexican Americans have coined a new term, *gordura mala* (bad fatness), because the original term *gordura* continues to have positive cultural connotations (Ritenbaugh 1982). For this group cultural identity has a stronger and independent effect on risk of obesity than socioeconomic status. An ethnographic study of the cultural meanings of weight in a Puerto Rican community in Philadelphia (Massara 1989) documents the positive associations and lack of social stigma of obesity. Additional quantitative evidence suggests significant differences in ideal body preferences between this ethnic community and mainstream American culture. Positive evaluations of fatness may also occur among lower-class African Americans and Mexican Americans. These ethnic groups are heterogeneous, however, and upwardly mobile ethnics tend to resemble mainstream American culture in their attitudes about obesity and ideal body shape.

In a low-income housing project in Atlanta, Georgia, a sociological interviewer was asked by a group of obese black women, "Don't you know how hard it is to keep this weight *on*?" Their views of the advantages of a large body included being given respect and reduced chances of being bothered by young "toughs" in the neighborhood. For these women, fatness was part of their positive self-identity, and if a friend lost weight she was thought to look sickly. Among lower-income groups, the perceived risk of a food shortage—not for the society as a whole but for the immediate family—may be very important, especially if lack of food was personally experienced in the past. The perception of the risk of future "bad times" and insufficient food is the reality upon which people act.

FATNESS AND CROSS-CULTURAL STANDARDS OF BEAUTY IN WOMEN

Culturally defined standards of beauty vary between societies. In a classic example, Malcom (1925) describes the custom of "fattening huts" for elite Efik pubescent girls in traditional Nigeria. A girl spent up to 2 years in seclusion and at the end of this rite of passage possessed symbols of womanhood and marriageability—a three-tiered hairstyle, clitoridectomy, and fatness. Fatness was a primary criterion of beauty as it was defined by the elites, who alone had the economic resources to participate in this custom. Similarly, fatter brides demand significantly higher bridewealth payments among the Kipsigis of Kenya (Borgerhoff Mulder 1988).

Among the Havasupai of the American Southwest, if a girl is thin at puberty, a fat woman "stands" (places her foot) on the girl's back so she will become attractively plump. In this society, fat legs and, to a lesser extent, arms are considered essential to beauty. The Tarahumara of northern Mexico consider fat legs a fundamental aspect of the ideal feminine body; an attractive woman is called a "beautiful thigh." Among the Amhara of Ethiopia in northern East Africa, thin hips are called "dog hips" in a typical insult (Messing 1957).

It is difficult to know how widespread among the world's cultures is the association of plumpness and beauty. A preliminary indication can be found through a cross-cultural survey based on data from the Human Relations Area Files (a cross-indexed compilation of ethnographic information on more than 300 of the most thoroughly studied societies). The results of this survey are summarized in Table 1. Although conclusions made from these data are weak because of the small number and possibly nonrepresentative nature of the cases, as well as the fact that most ethnographies are difficult to code on this variable, some preliminary generalizations are possible. Cultural standards of beauty do not refer to physical extremes. No society on record has an ideal of extreme obesity. On the other hand, the desirability of "plumpness" or being "filled out" is found in 81 percent of the societies for which this variable can be coded. This standard, which probably includes the clinical categories of overweight and mild obesity, apparently refers to the desirability of fat deposits, particularly on the hips and legs.

Although cross-cultural variation is evident in standards of beauty, this variation falls within a certain range. American ideals of thinness occur in a setting

TABLE 1   Cross-Cultural Standards of Female Beauty

	Number of Societies	Percent of Societies
Overall body		
Extreme obesity	0	0
Plump/moderately fat	31	81
Thin/abhorrence of fat	7	19
Breasts		
Large or long	9	50
Small/abhorrence of large	9	50
Hips and Legs		
Large or fat	9	90
Slender	1	10
Stature		
Tall	3	30
Moderate	6	60
Small	1	10

Source: From Brown, P.J., & M. Konner. "An Anthropological Perspective on Obesity." *Annals of the New York Academy of Sciences* 499 (1987):29–46. Copyright © 1987 by The New York Academy of Sciences. Reprinted by permission of John Wiley & Sons, Inc.

in which it is easy to become fat, and preference for plumpness occurs in settings in which it is easy to remain lean. In context, both standards require the investment of individual effort and economic resources; furthermore, each in its context involves a display of wealth. Cultural beliefs about attractive body shape in mainstream American culture place pressure on females to lose weight and are involved in the etiology of anorexia and bulimia.

IDEAL BODY-TYPE, SIZE, AND SYMBOLIC POWER IN MEN

The ethnographic record concerning body preferences for males is extremely weak, yet preliminary research suggests a universal preference for a muscular physique and for tall or moderately tall stature. In general, members of all human societies appear to admire large body size as an attribute of attractiveness in men, because it symbolizes health, economic success, political power, and social status. "Big men," political leaders in tribal New Guinea, are described by their constituents in terms of their size and physical well-being: He is a man "whose skin swells with 'grease' [fat] underneath" (Strahern 1971). The spiritual power (*mana*) and noble breeding of a Polynesian chief is expected to be seen in his large size. In American society vestiges of a similar idea remain; for example, a "fat cat" is a wealthy and powerful man who can "throw his weight around." The political metaphor of weight and power in American society has been explored by social historians. Most male college students in the United States, in contrast with women, want to gain weight because it is equivalent to gaining muscle mass and physical power in a process called "bulking up."

CONCLUSIONS

Two sets of conclusions can be drawn from this discussion of culture and its relationship to obesity—one practical and one theoretical. First, recognition of cultural variation in beliefs and behaviors related to obesity needs to be incorporated into health programs aimed at reducing the prevalence of obesity. The second conclusion regards the need for more research on the role of culture, as it interacts with genes, on the etiology of obesity.

The Importance of Culture in Health Interventions

Existing cultural beliefs must be taken into account in the design and implementation of health promotion projects. In an obesity prevention campaign in a Zulu community outside of Durban, one health education poster depicted an obese woman and an overloaded truck with a flat tire, with a caption "Both carry too much weight." Another poster showed a slender woman easily sweeping under a table next to an obese woman who was using the table for support; it had the caption "Who do you prefer to look like?" The intended message of these posters was misinterpreted by the community because of a cultural connection between obesity and social status. The woman in the first poster was perceived to be rich and happy, since she was not only fat but had a truck overflowing with her possessions. The second poster was perceived as a scene of an affluent mistress directing her underfed servant.

Health interventions must be culturally acceptable, and we cannot assume that people place the highest priority on their health. The idea of reducing *risk factors* for chronic diseases that may develop later may not be an effective strategy for populations who do not feel empowered or who live in a fundamentally risky world.

Implications for the Etiology of Obesity

The frequency of past food shortages, the social distribution of obesity, and the cultural meanings of fatness, when taken together, suggest a biocultural hypothesis of the evolution of obesity. Both genetic and cultural predispositions to obesity may be products of the same evolutionary pressures, involving two related processes: first, genetic traits that cause fatness were selected because they improved chances of survival in the face of food scarcities, particularly for pregnant and nursing women; second, in the context of unequal access to food, fatness may have been socially selected because it is a cultural symbol of social prestige and an index of general health. Under Western conditions of abundance, our biological tendency to regulate body weight at levels above our ideal cannot be easily controlled even with a reversal of the widespread cultural ideal of plumpness.

This evolutionary model is obviously congruent with the current etiological theory about obesity, which combines genetic predispositions with "environmental" causes. Recent research both in epidemiology and human laboratory research demonstrates without a doubt the central role of genetic heredity in the etiology of obesity. Similar genetic evidence exists for variables like the distribution of fat on the body and basal metabolic rates. To an anthropologist, these important studies are welcome and expected.

The recent advances in understanding the genetic bases of obesity remind us, however, of our ignorance about the precise role of the "environment." One problem is that "environment" has been poorly defined and treated as if it were idiosyncratic for every individual or family. Another problem is that "environment" is essentially treated as a residual category—one that cannot be explained by genetic heredity. This paper has attempted to show how the anthropological concept of culture may be useful in conceptualization of the different components of the "environment" and the generation of hypotheses for future research in behavioral medicine.

The most convincing demonstrations of a strong genetic component for obesity have been in populations with relatively high levels of cultural homogeneity. In social contexts like Denmark, Iowa, or among Pima Indians, the influence of culture—including learned behaviors and beliefs—is minimized by the sample selected for study in order to emphasize the importance of genotypical variation. Essentially, cultural variation has been treated as if it were "noise." An essential goal in future research must be the identification of specific cultural factors—whether economic, social, or ideological—that predispose people to obesity.

From the standpoint of the prevention of obesity, it is critical to stress that genetic predisposition is not destiny. Genetic predispositions to obesity have apparently been maintained in populations throughout most of our species' history, yet it has rarely been expressed phenotypically. Culture is adaptive because it can be changed. Habitual patterns of behavior—of an individual or an entire society—can be changed to reduce morbidity and mortality linked to obesity and overweight. These changes must include social and political efforts to reduce the risk of hunger and food scarcity, even in affluent societies.

REFERENCES

Bohannan, P., and L. Bohannan. 1969. *A Source Notebook on Tiv Religion.* New Haven, CT: Human Relations Area Files.

Borgerhoff Mulder, M. 1988. Kipsigis Bridewealth Payments. In *Human Reproductive Behavior,* eds. L. Betzig, M. Borgerhoff Mulder, and P. Turke, 65–82. Cambridge: Cambridge University Press.

Bray, G. A. 1987. Overweight Is Risking Fate: Definition, Classification, Prevalence and Risks. In *Human Obesity,* eds. R. J. Wurtman and J. J. Wurtman. *Annals of the New York Academy of Sciences* 499: 14–28.

Brown, P. J., and M. Konner. 1987. An Anthropological Perspective on Obesity. In *Human Obesity,* eds. R. J. Wurtman and J. J. Wurtman. *Annals of the New York Academy of Sciences* 499: 29–46.

Centers for Disease Control. 1989. Prevalence of Overweight—Behavioral Risk Factor Surveillance System, 1987. *Morbidity and Mortality Weekly Report* 38: 421–423.

Chernin, K. 1981. *The Obsession: Reflections on the Tyranny of Slenderness.* New York: Harper & Row.

Cohen, M. N., and G. J. Armelagos, eds. 1984. *Paleopathology at the Origins of Agriculture.* New York: Academic Press.

Eaton, S. B., M. Shostak, and M. Konner. 1988. *The Paleolithic Prescription.* New York: Harper & Row.

Frisch, R. E. 1987. Body Fat, Menarche, Fitness and Fertility. *Human Reproduction* 2: 521–533.

Gardner, L. I., M. P. Stern, S. M. Haffner, S. P. Gaskill, H. Hazuda, and J. H. Relethford. 1984. Prevalence of Diabetes in Mexican Americans. *Diabetes* 33: 86–92.

Gurney, M., and J. Gorstein. 1988. The Global Prevalence of Obesity—An Initial Overview of Available Data. *World Health Statistics Quarterly* 41: 251–254.

Kissebah, A. H., D. S. Freedman, and A. N. Peiris. 1989. Health Risks of Obesity. *Medical Clinics of North America* 73: 111–138.

Lee, R. B. 1979. *The !Kung San: Men, Women, and Work in a Foraging Society.* Cambridge, MA: Harvard University Press.

Malcom, L. W. G. 1925. Note on the Seclusion of Girls Among the Efik at Old Calabar. *Man* 25: 113–114.

Massara, E. B. 1989. *Que Gordita! A Study of Weight Among Women in a Puerto Rican Community.* New York: AMS Press.

Messing, S. D. 1957. *The Highland Plateau Amhara of Ethiopia.* Ph.D. dissertation, Department of Anthropology, University of Pennsylvania, Philadelphia.

Ravussin, E., S. Lillioja, and W. C. Knowler, et al. 1988. Reduced Rate of Energy Expenditure as a Risk Factor for Body-Weight Gain. *New England Journal of Medicine* 318: 467–472.

Ritenbaugh, C. 1982. Obesity as a Culture-Bound Syndrome. *Culture, Medicine and Psychiatry* 6: 347–361.

Strahern, A. 1971. *The Rope of Moka.* New York: Cambridge University Press.

Stunkard, A. J., T. I. A. Sorenson, C. Hanis, T. W. Teasdale, R. Chakaborty, W. J. Schull, and F. Schulsinger. 1986. An Adoption Study of Obesity. *New England Journal of Medicine* 314: 193–198.

Stunkard, A. J., J. R. Harris, N. L. Pedersen, and G. McClearn. 1990. The Body-Mass Index of Twins Who Have Been Reared Apart. *New England Journal of Medicine* 322: 1483–1487.

Trowell, H. C., and D. P. Burkitt. 1981. *Western Diseases: Their Emergence and Prevention.* Cambridge, MA: Harvard University Press.

Whiting, M. G. 1958. *A Cross-Cultural Nutrition Survey.* Doctoral dissertation, Harvard School of Public Health, Cambridge.

Wurtman, R. J., and J. J. Wurtman, eds. 1987. *Human Obesity.* Annals of the New York Academy of Sciences 499.

23

Pocahontas Goes to the Clinic

Popular Culture as Lingua Franca in a Cultural Borderland

Cheryl Mattingly

Technical competence may be a critical component of medical practice, but it alone cannot heal. In U.S. hospitals and clinics, medical technology and practice depend on the ability of patients and physicians to trust, communicate, and understand each other. In urban hospitals, patients, doctors, and other medical personnel may share similar goals, but they may not share the same languages and ethnicities. Linguistic and ethnic diversity have transformed the medical clinic into a cultural borderland, which now more than ever demands anthropological perspectives.

Sickle-cell patients in the United States often experience the negative effects of medical treatment undermined by a lack of sociocultural understanding. Sickle-cell anemia is a serious condition in which red blood cells can become stiff, sticky, and sickle-shaped; clumps of sickle cells can block blood flow and lead to chronic pain, infection, and organ failure. This medical condition affects African Americas, Hispanic Americans, as well as populations from Africa, South America, Central America, India, Saudi Arabia, and Caribbean and Mediterranean countries. Because sickle-cell anemia impacts African Americans and Hispanic Americans, the legacies of racial and ethnic divisions in the United States often creep into the treatment of sickle-cell patients. For example, the chronic pain associated with sickle-cell anemia leads some clinicians to inappropriately label African American teenage boys with sickle-cell as "med-seeking" patients.

Establishing effective communication and understanding between patients and caregivers is complicated by ethnic divisions, differences in language, and racial/ethnic stereotyping. Nonetheless, creative clinicians find ways to bridge the cultural borderlands of the medical clinic. In this selection, Cheryl Mattingly examines how global icons like Disney characters and Spider Man help patients and doctors create trust and communicative contexts for healing.

As you read this selection, ask yourself the following questions:

- How is the medical clinic a "border zone?" What is a border zone?

- What is a healing drama and how do they apply to medical practice?

- How do cultural misunderstandings influence medical care?

- How does culture in the hybrid environment of a borderland differ from culture in a more homogeneous context?

- How is the practice of culture a practice of othering?

- In what ways can race and class impact the quality and efficacy of medical treatment?

The following terms discussed in this selection are included in the Glossary at the back of the book:

indigenized   *othering*
lingua franca   *sickle-cell anemia*

The first time I met Pocahontas in a hospital was in the mid-1990s. Of course, as a U.S. citizen, I had known her since childhood. But I had forgotten all about her until she appeared, quite unexpectedly, in hospitals in Chicago and Los Angeles where I was carrying out research. She looked very different than I remembered.

Older, and less, well, historical. She had been dusted off, Disneyfied, transformed into a gorgeous teen-age beauty with a head of the most magnificent black hair and a body as enviably proportioned as Barbie. She could sing too. And it was Disney who sent her to the clinic. For not only was she a larger-than-life fig-ure in a popular animated movie, she was packaged into craft sets, costumes, dolls, and an array of other cultural artifacts that began to find their way into all sorts of children's places—including children's hos-pitals. She traveled internationally as well. I saw her once, resplendently arrayed, hair flowing, on a large poster board in a duty free shop at the Copenhagen airport. Internet chat rooms carried on worldwide con-versations about her adventures. Pocahontas had gone global.

This apparently frivolous example of the circula-tion of global goods has special and, indeed, profound significance in the context of health care, as I have gradually come to realize. Drawing from ethnographic research carried out over the past nine years among African American families who have children with severe illnesses and disabilities, I examine how chil-dren's popular culture, exported by such mass media empires as Disney, operates in the fraught borderland that constitutes the urban clinic. Children's films and television programs provide characters and plights that are creatively localized in health care encounters. A child's beloved character can offer a kind of narrative shadow, a cultural resource that children, families, and health care professionals readily turn to in the ongoing task of creating socially shared meaning, especially the sort of meaning that has to do with trying to positively shape a child's future.

Stories, it has long been noted, tend to provoke the imagination. They spur us to consider life in the sub-junctive mode (Bruner 1986, 2002), in terms of a "what if" universe of possibilities. Thus, it is not surprising that anthropologists have looked at the way stories created by global media inspire new imaginative con-structions of lives and worlds. The study of media has been intimately connected to the reinvention of culture as a contested space, a point of particular relevance to this article. Media is often treated as a force for con-structing a distinctive identity—for creating boundar-ies and marking distinctions—but here I explore it as a vehicle for creating commonalities. Its role as media-tor between the worlds of family and clinic takes on special importance in clinical encounters marked by differences in race and social class. Children's popu-lar culture offers resources for building bridges among groups who perceive themselves as Other but who are compelled to collaborate because of the need to tend to a sick or disabled child. A Disneyfied Pocahontas is only one of the mass-marketed figures that plays

an important role in the clinic, especially in creating "common ground" between the world of the hospital and home, and among the various key actors who care for severely ill or disabled children. Global icons like these can function as a lingua franca, offering a lan-guage of publicly available symbols on which families, health professionals, and children can draw to signal a common heritage or to create shared imaginative space across racial, class, and sufferer–healer divides. Why is a trade language so necessary in the U.S. urban hospital?

WHEN CULTURE IS A BORDERLAND: THE URBAN CLINIC

Urban hospitals constitute an example of what is argu-ably the most visible site in anthropology these days— the border zone, which James Clifford describes as a place of "hybrid cosmopolitan experiences" (1997:25). Border zones have emerged as part of the refigura-tion of culture, a shift from the discipline's traditional task of elucidating "the crystalline patterns of a whole culture" to a focus on "the blurred zones in between" (Rosaldo 1989:209). Anthropologists have been mov-ing from the heartlands to the borders for quite some time. This has meant a shift away from studying iso-lated communities in favor of geographic areas—such as urban centers or national border zones, which are characterized by ethnic pluralism and a fast changing cultural scene. It has also meant paying special atten-tion to sites of heightened commerce among actors who are culturally diverse. A focus on border zones is part of a fertile rethinking of traditional concepts of culture by anthropologists and culture theorists.

In a borderland, culture emerges more vividly as a space of encounter than of enclosure. For many, culture has come to designate a noisy, pluralistic, contested, ever-changing public sphere, rather than a substance, com-mon property, or a shared commitment to a way of life. This perspective emphasizes connections—including media-created connections—that are often political and often unexpected among these diverse communi-ties and commodities.[1] Viewed in this way, culture is not to be found in a group's shared set of beliefs and values so much as in its practices of drawing contrasts and boundaries with other groups as well as challeng-ing those contrasts. This sort of cultural world is char-acterized by politically charged, difference-making exchanges among actors.

The clinical world has often been recognized as contested terrain. The urban hospital is a place in which misreadings and conflicts routinely arise. The United States is growing rapidly more ethnically diverse, and this means that health care increasingly involves providing treatment for diverse populations. Urban health care in the United States is characterized by a dizzying array of languages, nationalities, racial identifications, social classes, and religions.[2] It has been well documented that ethnic diversity is accompanied by unequal access to health care. Racism also plays a key role in adverse health outcomes. African Americans continue to be one of the least well-served minority groups, a recognition that has provoked examination of the connections between race and health.[3]

A great deal of the work in medical anthropology has explored transactions within biomedical encounters marked by cultural confusions and misunderstandings—border talk, in fact. But the figure of clinic as border zone takes on a decidedly less familiar cast when situated within the recent debates about culture, place, and space that have arisen among scholars far removed from anything clinical—those who have been delivering, or responding to, challenges concerning the location of culture in the face of a globalizing and decolonizing world. This work offers an intriguing vantage point for examining the border activities of health care practices. In this discursive context, the familiar figure of the misunderstood patient emerges as startlingly emblematic, an exemplary citizen of that new nation, the land of the culturally in-between. If the practice of culture is, in part, the practice of Othering, of identifying cultural (and racial) difference in a thousand subtle and unconscious ways, this is of special importance in clinical encounters. Failures of communication are magnified to intense proportions in situations characterized by both perceptions of difference and high stakes. Cultural identities constructed by race, class, gender, and other potentially stigmatizing markers take on profound meaning here. What might, in another context, be a small slight or a confusing conversation, can, under these heightened circumstances, take on enormous importance. To feel neglected by one's doctor when one's child is seriously ill is not the same as being ignored by the grocery clerk.

The primary research that informs this article is a longitudinal ethnography that began in Los Angeles in January 1997 and is still ongoing. It has been carried out by an interdisciplinary team of anthropologists and occupational therapists. We initially recruited 30 African American families from the Los Angeles area whose children (ages from birth to eight) were being treated in several clinical sites. Most, although not all families, were low income. Eighteen of those initially recruited have continued to participate. Others joined subsequently as some families left the study for various reasons (e.g., moving out of state). All families now participating have been part of the project for at least three years.

This continuity of families has allowed us to come to know the ebbs and flows of chronic illness and to witness what that means in the never-ending process of negotiating health care with shifting casts of health professionals and changing bureaucratic processes. The research has involved accompanying families to clinical visits, observing and sometimes videotaping those encounters, and separately interviewing participants about what they perceived happened in the encounters. We have also observed and videotaped children and families at home and in the community, especially at key family events. This kind of longitudinal design has revealed a great deal about clinical encounters as events in family lives and about multiple perspectives between families and clinicians as these develop and change over time.

In this article, I provide examples and quotations from clinicians and family members that exemplify some themes that have arisen repeatedly in our data and are important to the arguments I make here. The data I cite come not only from my own interviews and observations but also from research conducted by other members of the research team.[4]

Not surprisingly, a key issue for families concerns whether or not they can trust their clinicians. The most minute nuances and gestures of health professionals (esp. doctors) are routinely scrutinized, becoming a subject of storytelling and puzzling. What are they trying to tell me? parents wonder. What are they hiding? Do they treat me this way because I'm black? A man without a job? A single mother? Do they think I'm a "ghetto mom"? Do they think I'm abusing my child? Are they experimenting on my child? Are they ignoring me because I'm on Medicaid? Do they think I'm not strong enough, bright enough, educated enough, to hear the truth? These are the sorts of questions asked by families in our research, and they are asked again and again. If cultures are spaces in which cultural differences are constructed and Othering is an everyday occurrence, this is profoundly consequential when a child's health or life is on the line.

THE HAZARDS OF BORDER CROSSING

If health encounters operate in a "border zone," all the key actors—especially minority patients and families—are attempting to cross borders. When children have chronic medical conditions, successful treatment demands cooperation and alliance building among children, family members, and professionals.[5] This can be a daunting task for all involved, especially when clients have had a difficult time receiving decent health care, as is the case with many of the families in this study. When stigmatizing class and racial categorizations arise, or are suspected of arising, tensions intensify. Mistrust on all sides tends to run high. Othering tactics practiced by clinicians are often subtle and largely unconscious, becoming most visible when patients, including parenting kin, are perceived as noncompliant. Explicit racial designations are rarely used, but there is a common taxonomy of "difficult clients" that is often attached to low-income minorities, a language so polite that its stigmatizing influences are largely undetected by clinicians. In our research with children, negative labels are often affixed to the parents rather than the children themselves. In addition to obvious negative markers—such as the "abusive, noncompliant, or neglectful parent"—there is a language of compassion that can also serve to create difference: the "overwhelmed parent," the "too many things going on at home parent," the "doesn't really understand the clinical picture" parent, or the "still in denial" parent.

One of the most insidious features of these categories is that when people have been placed in one of them, their capabilities and strengths are hidden from view. This problem is exacerbated by the fact that health care encounters are based on expert models of service delivery: Clients have problems, professionals have problem-solving expertise. This too, can make it difficult for professionals to see the need to identify their clients' strong points or to learn from them. In addition to the problematic categories that abound in informal health care discourse, professionals also learn narrative strategies that can effectively disguise the abilities of clients. They operate with a common set of narrative scripts or work to construct stories that "make sense" of problematic or difficult clients in a way that leaves little room for the client to emerge as an agent, to influence the framing of the problem or the path of treatment (Mattingly 1998b). Although these problematic features of health care are by no means peculiar to minority populations, they are certainly intensified for minorities in which racial designations are likely to influence the clinical encounter.

One place this has emerged with startling clarity in our study is with children suffering from sickle-cell disease. The sickle-cell clinic has been the place where race is most openly discussed by clinical staff as well as parents. One mother in our study remarked that children with this disease are "not being treated with dignity and respect" in many hospitals, a lack of respect that includes parents as well. Because of some humiliating experiences at the hospital in which her child had been a patient for years, she transferred her daughter to another hospital, even though they lacked the same level of expertise in treating sickle-cell disease. She put it this way: "I'm not a radical. I'm not a feminist. . . . I just think you should be treated a certain way, and I should be treated like the person next to me who maybe is a different skin color."

Several clinicians in our study concurred. One physician who has treated sickle-cell patients for 25 years (and who happens to be white) angrily noted the dismissive way clinical staff tend to view sickle cell, a dismissiveness that also extended to the clinicians who treat such children:

> I'll tell you I don't even listen to them, the attendings. They say, "Ah well, we have a chemotherapy patient coming in so we need to send your sickle patient off the floor because this patient's more important." You know? And I won't tell you what I'd like to say to them. . . . There's very much the attitude that well, this is something that anybody can take care of and it's just like pneumonia. And they don't really believe that there's anything in particular, that special expertise, that's going to help you take care of these kids. And you find out real quick that that's not true.

A vivid illustration of problematic, race-based categorizing is the "med-seeking" label regularly attached to those with sickle-cell disease who go into a pain crisis. Adolescent African American boys, in particular, are often refused crucial pain medication or are seen as crazy, violent, or drug seeking when in a pain crisis. The physician quoted above told the following story in an interview:

> Try being a 17-year-old black male with severe pain going into an emergency room and asking for narcotics and see how far you get. . . . Some of the best advice that I ever heard was from an adult with sickle cell, this is from family day that we had a few years ago. And this adult said, "What you need to do is when you're totally fine, you're not in the middle of a crisis, go to the emergency room and ask to meet the head of the emergency room and sit down for five minutes with him and say, "Hi, my name is blank, remember me? I was an extremist the other night and I'm just on my way to my law firm today, but you know, but on the way to the business I own or the job I have doing X, Y, Z, I wanted to stop in and let you know that I don't always go around in my undershirt and underwear screaming, asking for narcotics."

An African American social worker we also interviewed in this same clinic echoed this: "As soon as the house staff hears there's a sickle-cell patient, something goes up that says, 'I've got a kid here that's drug-seeking, you know, manipulating,' without actually doing any assessment of the child."

The difficulty of not being heard or of being subjected to racially based Othering, although especially articulated with sickle-cell disease, pervades clinical encounters. How do families, children, and clinicians attempt to cross a clinical border zone heightened by racial wariness and mistrust? They cultivate border-crossing skills: They learn to "read the minds" of professional Others, and in light of those readings, to devise strategies to present themselves as worthy of care. Border crossing can be very tricky business because African American clients routinely must be noncompliant to get the care they or their children need. Learning to read the culture of a clinic and of an individual health professional means learning how to execute the right kind of noncompliance that will lead to getting care rather than being turned away or, worse, reported to the social worker as a "problem parent." One mother explained how she has learned to "shuffle through and play this politicking thing"—that is, to appear compliant even in situations in which she knows more about her child's disease than the professional and may privately disregard what the clinician tells her to do. In situations in which she felt she must fight directly, even when she was proved medically correct, she was then faced with yet more "shuffling" and "playing" the "politicking thing" to reestablish good relationships with estranged clinicians. In other words, she had to apologize and act grateful even when she was right to challenge professionals:

> A lot of times you, as parents, you kind of specialize in a disease. You know a lot more than the doctor knows and it's scary when you have doctors that say, "Oh, I'm Dr. So and So" and . . . then they say something off the wall and you know that they are completely wrong. And how do you deal with a doctor and his ego? And so that's part of the game that I've mentioned before. You have to know how to shuffle through and play this politicking thing when you shouldn't have to do that.

CHILDREN'S POPULAR CULTURE AS LINGUA FRANCA

It is within this charged and wary context that the power of children's popular culture needs to be understood. If failed encounters produce and reinforce narratives of the stigmatized Other, successful ones counter these powerful narratives by producing ones in which clinicians and patients come to share, if sometimes fleetingly, a narrative of mutuality and belonging.[6] So, for instance, when an oncologist stops an examination to ask a parent about his or her Thanksgiving and to recount a story about problematic in-laws at the dinner, the oncologist speaks, in an important way, to a shared world of values and practices. The ability of professionals to recognize, acknowledge, and build on commonalities that cross lines of race, class, and culture is as important as recognizing the existence of race-based stereotyping or cultural difference.

Common worlds are routinely created in clinic interactions, drawing on cultural resources that are familiar to all the parties. For clinicians who have sustained relationships with clients, the ability of the actors to call on the small things—a joke remembered, a movie just seen, a disastrous Thanksgiving dinner—can be extremely powerful in forging bonds across formidable social divides. The importance of doing this has been noted repeatedly in the African American community with whom we have been involved. When things go very well in a clinical interaction, as they sometimes do, an important ingredient is that patients, clinicians, and even family caregivers are able to "read" one another well enough to create a shared narrative. That is, they are able to participate as actors in an unfolding story they help construct, one for which they have real commitment and one that embodies or suggests healing possibilities. This is what I have elsewhere called a "healing drama" (Mattingly 1998a, 2000; Mattingly and Lawlor 2001). Healing dramas need not depend on the possibility of curing; in fact, they can embrace death. But they do depend on moments in which shared experiences are created between professionals and clients. Such moments can draw members together even when they come from diverse social positions.

As it turns out, popular culture as offered up by mass media plays a critical role in facilitating the construction of these shared narratives. Global popular culture is often drawn on by families and health professionals to develop a shared story of hope. By *shared*, of course, I do not mean that health professionals and clients come to see or experience things in the same way, but that, at minimum, there is sufficient consensus to agree about treatment options and other practical matters and there is a sense that everyone is working in the best interest of the child. At times, though, there is a kind of collective imagining that goes far beyond this minimal level. Stories from children's popular culture are woven into clinic life and into interactions with home health professionals. They become part of stories acted out or referred to, especially during rehabilitation therapies that try to incorporate treatment into some form of child play. Rehabilitation therapists and aides mention that to treat children, they find that they need to watch the same movies that children are seeing simply to be able to understand them in therapy. Children repeat phrases or initiate actions in therapy that imitate their favorite film stories.

It is no surprise that characters from Disney films turn up with such regularity in pediatric hospitals and find their way into all kinds of clinical sessions. Disney has been the primary exporter of children's popular culture for decades, a matter that has long provoked critiques from, for example, critical social theorists of the well-known Frankfurt School.[7] The power of mass media to shape cultural identities has also been a topic of central concern within contemporary culture theory. Stuart Hall, for example, has argued that mass media is a primary vehicle for ideological production, a means through which groups construct images of their lives (Hall 1997). Mass media might be colonizing but ethnographic studies of the actual practices of cultural production and reception help to complicate the picture of media as ideology machine. Such studies reveal the way that the global is made "local" in specific contexts and show that the meaning of a media text is not given by the text itself but by the processes through which it is taken up and consumed by particular interpretive communities (Abu-Lughod 1991; Metcalf 2001; Rapp and Ginsburg 2001). Reception theories in media studies have been at pains to argue that meaning is a complex and local practice of negotiation between the world of the text and the world of the audience. It is a historically particular and local invention (see Spitulnik 1993 for a review of this literature). In other words, the audience does not merely consume, it "poaches," as Michel de Certeau (1984) puts it, helping to construct meaning through its practices of consumption.

CONSUMING POPULAR CULTURE: CHILDREN AND FAMILIES

Children's popular culture (esp. Disney) is everywhere in the lives of this African American community. Disney and other popular culture products have a fundamental role in the ongoing (playful) practice of these children as they imagine themselves in various scenes, playing various parts. In these playful constructions of possible selves, characters gleaned from Disney (as well as other media) stories provide easily adapted cultural material. Children often try out characters borrowed from scenes in movies or television shows, inviting adults to play their appropriate part in the scenarios they set in motion. The cultural space of Disneyland itself profoundly feeds the imagination of children, shaping a sense of life possibilities even if they are only possibilities that can be played with. For example, one critically ill four-year-old declared, in a fit of wishful thinking, "My daddy's gonna take me to Disneyland with—with Michael Jackson."[8]

When young children identify with certain characters in movies and television programs, it is not simply that they like those characters. Rather, they become those characters, at least for moments at a time, and they do so with particular delight when they can find others who will cooperate. Identifications with a particular character are social achievements, for it takes not only the child but the support of those around her for this identity to become "real." It requires cooperative efforts if these characters are to be incorporated in the scenes of everyday life. Identity play may be initiated or actively discouraged by parents or other adults. When a three-year-old boy declared that he was one of the "Power Puff Girls," his mother laughingly told us how she dissuaded him from this identification; he received no social support for seeing himself as a girl. This identity work is far from passive; it is actively carried out through a variety of efforts, often orchestrated by parents, in which the ongoing connection of their child with a popular character is ensured. Parents tell other important adults—including clinicians—about their child's favorite movie characters, thus widening the net of those who participate in the co-construction of a child as fantasy figure. They take their children to Disneyland or even far away Orlando's Walt Disney World to meet "their" special character. They dress children up as these characters for special occasions like birthdays and Halloween. They buy the dolls, coloring books, underwear, lunch boxes, tee shirts, stickers, pillow cases, curtains, and other merchandise that import the character into everyday life. They organize elaborate children's birthday parties to which dozens of people (including many adults) are invited and at which they recreate scenes from the movie in which their child's favorite character stars.

It is striking how consistently a child (or parent) chooses a character similar to the child in gender, racial or ethnic identity, or even disability. Even more intriguing, the kinds of adventures these characters face have their parallels in key events in a child's life. The happy endings that characterize children's movies and television programs offer hopeful visions of a child's future in "real life." Fascinatingly, this match may result from a striking mismatch, where a superhero possesses exactly the qualities that a child conspicuously lacks but longs for. Movie plots and life plots have a curious symmetry, although most often a symmetry by which a character's extraordinary or magical abilities provide a wishful identification for a child.

CONSUMING CHILDREN'S POPULAR CULTURE: THE CLINICAL COMMUNITY

Pediatric clinicians routinely draw on popular culture to connect with children. This is most apparent and most elaborate in rehabilitation therapies in which clinicians struggle to get children to cooperate with what can be painful or difficult exercises. Especially in acute hospital settings, there is a certain desperation in calling on this trade language. Often there is little time to get to know children who must be asked to participate in activities that are likely to frighten or pain them. Over the years, we have interviewed a number of physical and occupational therapists about their use of Disney and other mass media narratives in clinical work. I include some of the comments they have made in our interviews about how and why children's popular culture figures so pervasively in health care encounters. One occupational therapist mentioned that she always looks at children's shoes to see what character or movie they like. Another therapist said,

> It's not like you have a couple of sessions to develop rapport. You're seeing them just that one time and the parents say, "There's this issue and you absolutely have to get this assessment done right now." And the doctor wants to know what you think right then. And you have to develop a rapport very quickly. And that's when you just grab whatever you can that you can just kind of key into them with.

Certain favorite characters are woven into therapy sessions. Many come from Disney films because, as an occupational therapist noted dryly, "They have a pretty big corner on the market." When there is time to listen, a physical therapist pointed out, it is possible to "let them [the children] lead you," which is the very best way to work. A physical and occupational therapist at a pediatric burn unit reflected on the importance of these characters for the children they treated. The therapist noted, mimicking the children, "Different kids, especially at different ages, tend to attach to different things. Like the girls, like we had so many little girl patients that were really into, like, Snow White."

This attachment is used by clinicians as a "motivator" during therapy sessions. A physical therapist offered this example:

> I think we use it as a motivator if they indicate to us that that's something they really like to do. Like my one little girl, Anita, who loves, loves Snow White. I mean it was something. So we would call her Snow White and we would say . . . let's have you walk like a Princess Snow White and we'll go over and see if we can drop little things for the little seven dwarfs.

Children's popular culture can provide a "key" into the world of a child's imagination, a world in which the clinician can become an ally rather than an enemy, and one in which a child can do things impossible in ordinary life. To illustrate, I offer the following example. One occupational therapist told a story about how she came to incorporate "Spiderman" into her sessions with a child suffering severe sensory

motor problems. This eight-year-old boy was so afraid of heights he slept with his mattress on the floor and refused to play on swings, slides, or monkey bars on the playground. As a result, he spent many lonely hours at school recess and home while his friends and schoolmates played together. During their first clinic session, she found him extremely shy, remembering that "when Manny first entered the clinic, he had his face buried into his mother's side and he would not turn around or make eye contact with me." After several false starts that yielded only silence, the therapist noticed he was wearing a "Spiderman" shirt and shoes. She decided "it was worth a try" to see if Spiderman could draw him out. When she produced a Spiderman coloring book, "a smile began to creep over his face." Coloring the Spiderman book together began their many Spiderman adventures. As Manny colored, he told her of Spiderman's great feats and enemies, and out of this, as she put it, "a pact had been formed for future therapy sessions" for in all subsequent sessions "Spiderman played a prominent role." Manny donned a special Spiderman vest for therapy time. There was one session the therapist described in some detail because she saw it as a turning point in her work with the boy. For this session, she used a rope hammock swing (a typical piece of therapy equipment for children with sensory motor difficulties), which she announced was a spider's web. (The Spiderman's web, in fact.) After much coaxing, Manny eventually climbed into the web with her, although he was so frightened that his teeth chattered. To distract him, she sang the Spiderman Song, which she also recited for me. This song includes such telling lines as

> Can he swing from a thread?
> Take a look overhead.
> Hey there, there goes the Spiderman!

Manny gradually calmed as he heard the song, which allowed the therapist to begin a game of throwing beanbags at various Spiderman "enemies" (beanie babies she had set up in different spots around the therapy room). She took on the voices of these hapless enemies as Manny bashed them with beanbags. He became so enthusiastic that, in an unprecedented moment, he insisted they swing higher and higher so that even while he was in a "tornado" he could "fight against evil." This therapist was convinced that Manny's capacity to become Spiderman in these therapy episodes was critical to her success with him, as evidenced by his willingness to take on such terrifying challenges as swinging high above ground.

Notably popular icons are extremely versatile cultural resources. The same character can take on different meanings for different children. Whereas for Manny, it is Spiderman's brave capacities to, for example, "swing from a thread" that are salient, for another child facing a different sort of disabling condition, other features become central. For example, Spiderman also became a favorite cultural icon for a boy in our study forced to wear medical masks to treat a severe burn injury to his face. In this case, Spiderman's identity as a "masked hero" is emphasized; in Manny's case, it is his skill at gravity defying leaps through space.

CONCLUSION

Popular culture provides a common language for adults and children, a set of public symbols that they can draw on to try to connect with one another. Even comparative strangers, like health professionals, can readily draw on them to connect to a child they do not know and who is, likely as not, afraid of them.

Globally circulated and mass-produced texts are made meaningful in local ways and offer powerful cultural resources that serve local ends. Popular culture offers characters and plots that are remade, "indigenized" as Arjun Appadurai (1991, 1996) says, to fit specific needs and circumstances. As the Spiderman examples illustrate, the meaning of a popular media text does not reside in the text-in-itself and can never be reduced to mere "consumption"; it always involves situated constructions that do practical work for particular actors.

Popular-culture stories and heroes provide potent vehicles for overcoming the dreary, frightening, or embattled relations between clinicians and patients and do so in a way that supports hope. When clinicians draw on these loved characters in their interactions with children, they may be connecting with children and parenting kin in a far more powerful way than they sometimes realize. When clinicians speak to families only in the medicalized language of statistical probabilities, especially if prognoses are poor, mistrust is easily heightened. It is not that clients want to be lied to or have medical information withheld. But they are also concerned that clinicians support a subjunctive reading of their child's chances and that they make every effort, even for, as parents sometimes say, "a little black kid" (Mattingly 2004). How can families come to trust that professionals have not "given up" on their children, despite the fact that they have severe disabilities and are African American? In the racial climate of the United States, this is not a question that can be asked and answered directly. Clues must be indirect. It is here that, in its own oblique and playful way, the lingua franca of children's popular culture—when exemplified by, for example, a joking exchange between a nurse and mother about how quickly Spiderman recovered from surgery (the very

same surgery a child has just undergone)—suggests possibilities that go far beyond the ostensible topic. In a wary place like the urban clinic, when people are struggling to connect across all kinds of barriers, a Pocahontas or a Spiderman, one might say, travels well.

ACKNOWLEDGMENTS

I would like to thank members (past and present) of the research team: Erica Angert, Nancy Bagatell, Jeanine Blanchard, Jeannie Gaines, Lanita Jacobs-Huey, Teresa Kuan, Stephanie Mielke, Ann Neville-Jan, Melissa Park, Carolyn Rouse, Katy Sanders, and Kim Wilkinson. Particular, heartfelt thanks goes to my long-time research partner, Mary Lawlor. Thanks also to the Narrative Study Group for comments on drafts of this article: Linda Garro, Elinor Ochs, Janet Hoskins, Marjorie Goodwin, Gelya Frank, Nancy Lutkehaus and again, Mary Lawlor. I gratefully acknowledge support by Maternal and Child Health Bureau (MCJ #060745) and National Center for Medical Rehabilitation Reasearch, National Institute of Child Health and Human Development, National Institutes of Health (1RO1HD38878, 2RO1HD38878).

NOTES

1. A number of scholars have explored how mass media produces connections and even diasporic communities in ways that further complicate any simple use of the term *culture* (Abu-Lughod 1991; Appadurai 1991; Diouf 2000; Erlmann 1996; Mbembe 1992; Metcalf 2001; Pollock et al. 2000; Price 1999; Schein 2002).

2. See Good et al. 2002, Cooper-Patrick et al. 1999, and Doescher et al. 2000.

3. In a careful review of research findings on health disparities, an Institute of Medicine Committee reported that

   minorities are less likely than whites to receive needed services, including clinically necessary procedures. These disparities exist in a number of disease areas, including cancer, cardiovascular disease, HIV/AIDS, diabetes, and mental illness, and are found across a range of procedures, including routine treatments for common health problems. [Institute of Medicine 2002:2; see also Good et al. 2002]

   Although health disparities for all minorities as compared to whites have been consistently documented, African Americans are routinely subjected to the greatest racial stereotyping and to the least access to health services (Bailey 1991; James 1994; Whitehead 1997). Some research indicates this is regardless of social class, education, economic status, or type of health care coverage (Dressler 1993; Good et al. 2002). Other research challenges this in claiming that social class plays a larger role than race, per se, in quality of health care (e.g., Lareau 2002). In any case, it is clear that when race and class are confounded, as they are for most of the families we have been following, receiving good health care services is an on-going challenge. For further discussion of the connection between race and health, see also Barbee 1993; Jackson 1993; Porter 1994; and Wailoo 2001.

4. For the sake of simplicity and to help protect confidentiality of informants, throughout the article, when quoting participants, I refer to the research team collectively, as in "we interviewed" or "we observed," rather than identifying particular researchers.

5. General concern to improve the capacity of clinicians to communicate with minority clients has spurned a vast, cross-disciplinary literature on "cultural competence" (Brach and Fraser 2000; Guarnaccia and Rodriguez 1996; Lopez 1997; Pierce and Pierce 1996) and on "culturally compatible interventions" (Takeuchi et al. 1995).

6. This point was brought home with force in the way the African American families in our study talked about the meaning of September 11th. They underscored not only the concern to be designated as different from Euro-Americans but also the need to be recognized as sharing a common national culture and heritage (Mattingly et al. 2002).

7. See Henry Giroux's (1999) critique of the Disney empire for a fascinating, and more recent, exposition along these lines.

8. As Giroux states, Disney is hardly a monolithic empire. Rather, he explains,

> The Disney culture offers potentially subversive moments and pleasures in a range of contradictory and complex experiences. In fact, any approach to studying Disney must address the issue of why so many kids and adults love Disney and experience its theme parks, plays, and travel opportunities as a counterlogic that allows them to venture beyond the present while laying claim to unrealized dreams and hopes. [1999:5]

REFERENCES

Abu-Lughod, Lila. 1991. Writing against Culture. In *Recapturing Anthropology: Working in the Present*, ed. Richard Fox, 137–162. Santa Fe: School of American Research Press.

Appadurai, Arjun. 1991. Global Ethnoscapes: Notes and Queries for a Transnational Anthropology. In *Recapturing Anthropology: Working in the Present*, ed. Richard Fox, 191–210. Santa Fe: School of American Research Press.

———. 1996. *Modernity at Large: Cultural Dimensions of Globalization*. Minneapolis: University of Minnesota Press.

Bailey, Eric. 1991. Hypertension: An Analysis of Detroit African-American Health Care Treatment Patterns. *Human Organization* 50(3): 287–296.

Barbee, Evelyn. 1993. Racism in U.S. Nursing. *Medical Anthropology Quarterly* 7(4): 346–362.

Brach, C., and I. Fraser. 2000. Can Cultural Competency Reduce Racial and Ethnic Health Disparities? A Review and Conceptual Model. *Medical Care Research and Review* 57(Suppl. 1): 181–217.

Bruner, Jerome. 1986. *Actual Minds, Possible Worlds*. Cambridge, MA: Harvard University Press.

———. 2002. *Making Stories: Law, Literature, Life*. New York: Farrar, Straus, and Giroux.

Clifford, James. 1997. *Routes: Travel and Translation in the Twentieth Century*. Cambridge, MA: Harvard University Press.

Cooper-Patrick, L., J. Gallo, J. Gonzales, H. Vu, N. Powe, C. Nelson, and D. Ford. 1999. Race, Gender, and Partnership in the Patient-Physician Relationship. *Journal of the American Medical Association* 282(6): 583–589.

de Certeau, Michel. 1984. *The Practice of Everyday Life*. S. Rendall, trans. Berkeley: University of California Press.

Diouf, Mamadou. 2000. The Senegalese Murid Trade Diaspora and the Making of a Vernacular Cosmopolitanism. S. Rendall, trans. *Public Culture* 12: 679–702.

Doescher, M., B. Saver, P. Franks, and K. Fiscella. 2000. Racial and Ethnic Disparities in Perceptions of Physician Style and Trust. *Archives of Family Medicine* 9(10): 1156–1163.

Dressler, William. 1993. Health in the African American Community: Accounting for Health Disparities. *Medical Anthropology Quarterly* 7(4): 325–345.

Erlmann, Veit. 1996. The Aesthetics of the Global Imagination: Reflections on World Music in the 1990s. *Public Culture* 8: 467–487.

Giroux, Henry. 1999. *The Mouse That Roared: Disney and the End of Innocence*. Lanham, MD: Rowman and Littlefield.

Good, Mary-Jo DelVecchio, C. James, Byron Good, and A. Becker. 2002. The Culture of Medicine and Racial, Ethnic, and Class Disparities in Healthcare. Pp. 594–625. Report by the Institute of Medicine on Unequal Treatment. Washington, DC: National Academy Press.

Guarnaccia, P., and O. Rodriguez. 1996. Concepts of Culture and Their Role in the Development of Culturally Competent Mental Health Services. *Hispanic Journal of Behavioral Sciences* 18: 419–443.

Hall, Stuart. 1997. *Representation: Cultural Representations and Signifying Practices*. London: Sage.

Institute of Medicine. 2002. *Unequal Treatment: What Healthcare Providers Need to Know about Racial and Ethnic Disparities in Healthcare*. Washington, DC: National Academy Press.

Jackson, Eileen. 1993. Whiting-Out Difference: Why U.S. Nursing Research Fails Black Families. *Medical Anthropology Quarterly* 7(4): 363–385.

James, Sherman. 1994. John Henryism and the Health of African-Americans. *Culture, Medicine and Psychiatry* 18: 163–182.

Lareau, Annette. 2002. Invisible Inequality: Social Class and Childrearing in Black Families and White Families. *American Sociological Review* 67: 747–776.

Lopez, Steven. 1997. Cultural Competence in Psychotherapy: A Guide for Clinicians and Their Supervisors. In *Handbook of Psychotherapy Supervision*, ed. C. E. Watkins Jr., 570–588. New York: John Wiley and Sons.

Mattingly, Cheryl. 1998a. *Healing Dramas and Clinical Plots: The Narrative Structure of Experience.* Cambridge: Cambridge University Press.

_____. 1998b. In Search of the Good: Narrative Reasoning in Clinical Practice. *Medical Anthropology Quarterly* 12(3): 273–297.

_____. 2000. Emergent Narratives. In *Narrative and the Cultural Construction of Illness and Healing*, eds. Cheryl Mattingly and Linda Garro, 181–211. Berkeley: University of California Press.

_____. 2004. Performance Narratives in Clinical Practice. In *Narrative Research in Health and Illness*, eds. B. Hurwitz, T. Greenhalgh, and V. Skultans, 73–94. London: Blackwell Publishing.

Mattingly, Cheryl, and Mary Lawlor. 2001. The Fragility of Healing. *Ethos* 29(1): 30–57.

Mattingly, Cheryl, Mary Lawlor, and Lanita Jacobs-Huey. 2002. Narrating September 11: Race, Gender, and the Play of Cultural Identities. *American Anthropologist* 104(3): 743–753.

Mbembe, Achille. 1992. The Banality of Power and the Aesthetics of Vulgarity in the Postcolony. *Public Culture* 4: 1–30.

Metcalf, Peter. 2001. Global "Disjunctive" and the "Sites" of Anthropology. *Cultural Anthropology* 16(2): 165–182.

Pierce, Robert, and Lois Pierce. 1996. Moving toward Cultural Competence in the Child Welfare System. *Children Youth Services Review* 18(8): 713–731.

Pollock, Sheldon, Homi Bhabha, Carol Breckenridge, and Dipesh Chakrabarty. 2000. Cosmopolitanisms. *Public Culture* 12: 577–589.

Porter, Cornelia. 1994. Stirring the Pot of Differences: Racism and Health. *Medical Anthropology Quarterly* 8(1): 102–106.

Price, Monroe. 1999. Satellite Broadcasting as Trade Routes in the Sky. *Public Culture* 11: 69–85.

Rapp, Rayna, and Faye Ginsburg. 2001. Enabling Disability: Rewriting Kinship, Reimagining Citizenship. *Public Culture* 13(3): 533–556.

Rosaldo, Renato. 1989. *Culture and Truth: The Remaking of Social Analysis*. Boston, MA: Beacon.

Schein, Louisa. 2002. Mapping Hmong Media in Diasporic Space. In *Media Worlds: Anthropology on New Terrain*, eds. Faye Ginsburg, Lila Abu-Lughod, and Brian Larkin, 229–244. Berkeley: University of California Press.

Spitulnik, Debra. 1993. Anthropology and the Mass Media. *Annual Review of Anthropology* 22: 293–315.

Takeuchi, D., S. Sue, and M. Yeh. 1995. Return Rates and Outcomes from Ethnicity-Specific Mental Health Programs in Los Angeles. *American Journal of Public Health* 85: 638–643.

Wailoo, Keith. 2001. *Dying in the City of the Blues: Sickle Cell Anemia and the Politics of Race and Health*. Chapel Hill: North Carolina University Press.

Whitehead, Tony. 1997. Urban Low-Income African American Men, HIV/AIDS, and Gender Identity. *Medical Anthropology Quarterly* 11(4): 411–417.

24

Anthropologist Takes Inner-City Children on Shopping Sprees

Elizabeth Chin

As exciting as long-term fieldwork in far away places may sound, it is exceptionally difficult work. Before reaching into our toolkit of qualitative and quantitative methods, anthropologists arrive in a new research community with immediate priorities like establishing living arrangements, improving your local language skills, and acquiring permission to conduct research activities. These are difficult skills to teach, so since the earliest days of ethnographic field research, anthropologists have shared a poorly kept secret to help earn the confidence and trust of a new study community: children hold the keys to the village.

Like Boas and the lessons he reported learning from Inuit youth, Evans-Pritchard (during a trouble-laden East African field study), found hope and a helping hand with local youth who had the time and curiosity to tolerate a troubled anthropologist. In fact, after his helpers desert him, it is a young person who eventually helps Evans-Pritchard get to the site that becomes the subject of his famous ethnography, *The Nuer.* In the book, he recalls with happiness one site where he passed several days fishing and learning language with Nuer youth.

When reading classic ethnographies like *The Nuer*, the authors may not explicitly describe their interaction with local youth as a formal research method. Nonetheless, anthropologists often refer to the significant contributions of young people during field research. Whether it's Boas, Evans-Pritchard, or any number of more contemporary anthropologists, children often play a critical role in our research and field experiences. If you enter a community that is entirely different from the ones in which you are familiar, you become a child the moment you step into the village. You'll need help learning to talk and show respect. You'll need help getting food and shelter if this is a rural village without rentals or shops. You may even need a lesson on how to bathe and use local latrines (techniques, norms). As a curious outsider in a new community, the anthropologist relies on children as peers who are willing and able to spend countless hours practicing language, learning village roads or forest, or maybe identifying major families that make up the community. In this selection, anthropologist Elizabeth Chin develops a unique way to conduct anthropological research with children; she takes them on $20 shopping sprees. How would you spend your $20, and what would your purchases say about you?

As you read this selection, ask yourself the following questions:

- Why did the author take children on shopping trips?

- Using specific examples from the text, explain why the author describes the shopping trips as a "passage into the entire lives of children."

- How did their families influence the children's consumer decisions?

- Were the children impulsive and careless with their $20, or were they careful consumers? How did they learn or develop this behavior?

- What kinds of items did children buy for themselves, and what items did they purchase to give as gifts?

The following terms discussed in this section are included in the Glossary in the back of the book:
consumption
discourse
ethnographic
participant observation

When I asked Davy if he would like to go on a shopping trip with me, he tilted his head to the side, smiling, and looked at me without speaking for several moments. He seemed to want to speak, but couldn't. We sat, me hunkered up in a fifth-grade-sized chair, my knees knocking up against the underside of a fifth-grade-sized table in the reading corner of Davy's classroom. "Yeah," he said, his almost-changing voice creaky and thin, his tone rising to make his answer sound more like a question. He looked away and then peeked back at me, as if he had a suspicion that I would disappear while his head was turned. "Yeah."

By far, most of my research was conducted in a participant-observer mode in homes, at school, and in the neighborhood. This work was central to documenting and understanding the consumer lives of African American children in New Haven, because it immersed me in children's daily lives. However, I also needed to get a close, concentrated look at these children's spending and shopping, precisely in order to understand how the rest of what I was seeing and doing was enmeshed with aspects of consumption. I knew that hanging around with kids might never get me to the corner store with them, much less into the mall, food court, or some secret consumer site. Here, I decided to construct my own opportunities and take children on shopping trips. My aim was to guarantee that I would be able to watch each child shopping, to see which stores they wanted to go to, to see what they bought, and to watch the process of evaluating merchandise, dealing with other shoppers, and negotiating the particular forms of public space presented by malls and stores. These events were conceived of and designed as a foil to the happenstance of more regular participant observation, controlled and controllable (though not experimental), and, frankly, as a relief from the anxiety of waiting for something obviously significant to happen in the course of the everyday.

The methodology of the shopping trips was simple: I provided the children with twenty dollars each and said they could spend it where they liked, on whatever they liked. I conducted twenty-three shopping trips in all, one of which was incomplete. (Most of the following discussion focuses on twenty completed shopping trips, excluding two excursions with teenage girls.) Taking place toward the end of two years of field research, the trips were not particularly natural in that they did not replicate or even attempt to replicate the kind of experience that kids might have with adults within their own social spheres. As a result, I cannot make the argument that these trips are an indication of how such children really do spend their money when they have it, but the strength of the patterns that do emerge provides a firm basis for understanding some of the social and cultural dynamics at work in these children's lives.[1] The basic facts of the shopping trips did not mesh with children's everyday experiences in any case, since most caretakers did not give their children money and then take kids on a shopping trip where the child was free to dictate just about everything: when and where to shop, when and where to eat, when to leave. As Kiana explained to me in her poetic and whimsical way when I asked her to explain to me how her experience with me was different from her usual shopping excursions:

When you're with a grown-up, boy, it's different. "No, stay here. No, no you wait until I get out of the store." I don't like that. I like it when I go with people who just let me be freely in the store to buy whatever I want to buy.

How was it today?

Terrific. Yeah.

How do you feel?

I feel good. Because usually when I come from shopping I'm tired, but I'm not today because it's different . . . but you see, you let me be freely—so that's how it's different.

In letting Kiana "be freely" I did not represent or exercise the kind of adult authority familiar to these children: I was not a mother, aunt, teacher, or older sibling. My dogged refusal to curb their often rambunctious behavior, despite severe temptation on my part, made me even less credible as a grown-up, if the disapproving looks of shop clerks and other adults were any indicator. Although my initial intention was to trail behind kids, seeing what they did, this plan was thwarted by children's consistent efforts to draw me into social interaction with them. I could not remain apart from the shopping but was almost continually required by children to be an active and opinionated participant. This was, for them, an integral part of the shopping dynamic: social relationships. This discussion I had with Cherie as she wondered whether to buy a cap gun was typical in many ways (though Cherie's wit was particularly quick):

Oooh, $2.99. Should I get it?

You like it?

I'm asking you.

Do you like that?

Kind of.

What would you do with it?

Murder my brother [a mischievous grin].

The children who went shopping represent a varied group of friends, siblings, cousins, and classmates because I found myself being asked to take sisters, cousins, and friends along as well. I viewed these requests as important information in and of itself and in response chose not to insist that children shop individually with me. When they asked me, I allowed them to go in pairs or even small groups. Kids were also remarkably adept at ensuring that I could not refuse these requests, which were usually made by girls. More than once, when I arrived at a girl's house to take her out shopping she would run up to me saying, "My friend [sister, cousin] is staying with me, can she come, too?"

In most cases children were caught up in thinking about family members and caretakers even while shopping alone with me, and these absent people exerted a force on children's shopping trips that was in many respects far more powerful than my own influence.[2] Several kids spoke of having been told by mothers and grandmothers to be sure to buy one thing or another. To my surprise, they never attempted to enlist me in surreptitiously derailing those instructions. Likewise, other children, after having made one practical purchase or another, would remark with great satisfaction and anticipation, "My mommy is going to be so happy that I bought this!" From the outset, then, the effort to understand these children's consumption was not possible if I insisted on considering their choices as being generated out of self-interest and personal desire—the starting point for so much theory on consumption in general and shopping in particular. The process of consumption was for these children based quite overtly on a complex and sometimes convoluted web of social relationships—especially to kin, but also including each other, friends, myself, and those they came into contact with while they shopped, as well as occasional imaginary figures.

Through their shopping excursions, kids were engaging with their families, neighborhoods, city, and culture rather than exiting from those social entanglements. Children used shopping as a way to create relationships and, rather than being self-contained packages of information, the shopping trips were a passage into the entire lives of these children.[3] These shopping trips represent a convergence point of social, cultural, economic, and political processes through which children continually navigate. Understanding them ethnographically requires connecting the purchases to children's larger worlds. Although Davy bought only two items when he went shopping with me, those purchases are revealing when understood in the larger ethnographic context, and in the circumstances of his everyday life.

SHOPPING EXCURSIONS

Davy

There is stark and apparent simplicity to Davy's purchases when presented in tabular form (see table 1). The items, their prices, and the place where they were bought are not all that surprising: this was a ten-year-old boy on a shopping spree. But what Davy bought cannot speak on its own about his personal concerns and motivations, or the circumstances and forces shaping them. Why walkie-talkies? Why Toys-R-Us? Understanding the things Davy bought takes us into his life at school, at home, and in New Haven.

Davy had arrived in Lucy Aslan's classroom in the middle of the school year. The oldest of four children, Davy came from a home fraught with difficulties. Sometimes he would come to school and sleep all morning, and when asked what was wrong would answer that his mother, who was in her early twenties, had not come home all night and he'd had to take care of his younger siblings, the youngest still in diapers. Money was tight for his family, and though a simple uniform of white shirt and blue pants was required at the school, Davy did not have the proper outfit. A couple of months after Davy joined the class, the classroom aide took him downtown and bought him a basic set of school clothes and a sweater. He came to class the next day wearing his new uniform and beaming broadly. Davy's pleasure in being able to dress both according to the school code and like his classmates was openly visible and reflected his new ability to fit in with everyone else.

Davy was painfully eager to communicate with teachers and other children but seemed not quite to know how, and his end of any conversation was usually monosyllabic. My pictures from the field seemed always to catch him on the edge of things, hands in pockets, tall for his age, leaning in longingly toward a group of kids who were doing something that he was not quite part of. Davy was not at the edges of things because the rest of the class was leaving him out; the other kids really seemed to like him, and several students made special efforts to help him with his math or his reading, both subjects he liked but was struggling with. It just seemed that Davy did not know how to make contact with people or that he was afraid.

TABLE 1 Davy's Purchases

Item	Prices	Store
1 set walkie-talkies	$12.99	Toys-R-Us
batteries	$ 4.29	Toys-R-Us

On his shopping trip, Davy spent his twenty dollars at Toys-R-Us, a store that he had never visited before. He did not even know the store's name and at the beginning of our trip had asked if we could go shopping "where Ronnie and Kareem went." These two boys were classmates of Davy's and had been talking with him about their trip, which we had done the day before. Once we were in Toys-R-Us, Davy's trip did not take long. He seemed to take little notice of the abundant merchandise and, though he was unfamiliar with the store's layout, he found and quickly settled on his choice: a walkie-talkie set. Together with the batteries the walkie-talkies required, the total cost came to just over twenty dollars (I routinely paid small sums over the twenty dollars if they resulted from sales tax, which many children could not calculate or did not anticipate). The problem was, as we moved along another aisle Davy also found Wolverine, an X-Men action figure, which he had told me before we began shopping he had planned to buy. These action figures were tremendously popular among the boys in the classroom, and most of them had two or three of the most coveted ones. The boys would often congregate together in front of Ronnie's house to play X-Men after school. Though the boys freely lent figures back and forth during these play sessions, Davy did not have a figure of his own. Having Wolverine would have let him enter into these play sessions at a new level, just as being able to come to school in the same uniform his classmates wore allowed him to meld more fully with the group, if even only visually. Although Davy knew the walkie-talkies and batteries would cost all the money he had, he spent several minutes standing in the store aisle, holding Wolverine, the batteries, and the walkie-talkies all together, unable to decide which thing to leave behind. It seemed as if he was hoping if he wished hard enough the prices would magically change. Finally, he reluctantly put Wolverine back on the shelf.

As I stood there watching Davy struggle with this decision, I experienced some of the most painful moments of my research. The Wolverine figure, after all, cost under five dollars. It was hardly expensive, but it was more than Davy could buy. More than being a single moment where he faced frustration and disappointment and had to curb his desire, this boy's dilemma in the Toys-R-Us aisle was also the story of his life. Davy's wants were modest. He did not pine for the $200 Sega Genesis video game system, but a five-dollar action figure; he did not want flashy and expensive brand-name clothes, but rather a simple school uniform consisting of a white shirt and blue pants. Clothing, sleep, food, and time with his mother all seemed to be hard to come by in Davy's world. Just as the five-dollar Wolverine figure was more than he

could afford, it was more than he could expect that his entirely reasonable and limited wants would be fulfilled, since even his basic needs seemed to be inconsistently provided for.

Davy's very first visit to the largest, most prevalent, and most economically successful toy retailer in the world needs to be understood in the context of the circumstances that shaped his life. Although scholars and middle-class observers tend to interpret a lack of contact with consumer culture as a sort of uncontaminated state, a freedom, or a benefit, Davy's limited consumer experience was not a sign of his being sheltered from the venal world of consumerism and hence kept pure in relation to it. That Davy had never before visited what is arguably one of the central sites of childhood experience in the United States is at once a *sign* of exclusion and a *form* of exclusion from one of the wealthiest societies now on the globe. An experience like Davy's is made possible when children and whole communities are multiply isolated, just as its residents are multiply oppressed: socially, economically, educationally, productively, and also in terms of consumption. Toys-R-Us, like any major site of consumption, is thus not a great equalizer, as has been argued, for instance, in the case of the department store (Williams 1982). Davy entered that store bringing his history with him, and his entrance into the mecca of children's consumption did nothing at all to change the objective circumstances of his life experientially or objectively, if even for a few moments. The equality of consumers' money as it enters the shop's till does not extend to the consumers themselves: their particular life experiences and expectations shape their relationships with the store itself, its merchandise, and its personnel.

In the interaction with toys on the shelves, Davy's experience was forged *within* his own life situation, complete with the economic, social, and material difficulties with which he was so consistently confronted. These elements came together in Davy's life in particular ways in relation to Toys-R-Us. Located several freeway miles away from Newhallville and nearly inaccessible by public transportation, this store lay far beyond his reach, given that his family had no car. More to the point, his mother could not afford to buy many toys for her children in any case. Davy's actions and decisions while in Toys-R-Us struck me as being most forcefully aimed at social goals rather than being more blatantly consumerist. It was through watching and thinking about incidents like that with Davy that I became convinced that consumption is at its base a social process, and one that children use in powerful ways to make connections between themselves and the people around them. Davy's decision to buy the walkie-talkies is an especially poignant example of the effort to create social connectedness through the process of consumption, and most Newhallville kids expressed similar desires and intentions as they considered merchandise, compared prices, compiled their purchases, and spent their money. This tendency or potential has been remarked upon by others (Williams 1988; Willis 1991) with a special focus on the utopian elements of children's consumption practices. Without attempting to deny or even downplay the prosocial and utopian elements of these kids' consumption—elements that are too often overlooked—my aim is to explore also the contradictions and the limitations of children's efforts to forge social relationships through consumption. It is not consumption itself that poses the primary obstacle for Newhallville children in these endeavors. Rather, it is social inequality itself, in its many forms and guises, that continually shapes these children's consumption, purchases, motivations, wishes, and fantasies.

Davy, who struggled every day to communicate and to connect verbally with the people around him, had chosen, it seems, the perfect vehicle for allowing him to accomplish what seemed so difficult for him. The walkie-talkies were a toy that required another person in order to be enjoyed, and a toy that required him to speak in order to play with them. The walkie-talkies seemed to suit his particular dilemma perfectly: they were a vehicle that allowed him to talk to people but at the same time did not require him to be too close in order to make contact. Davy told me when I asked that he planned to use the walkie-talkies with his little brother, and this detail is also important. Davy had chosen a toy that by its very nature needed to be shared, not just because he wanted to connect and communicate with others; although he was the only child in his family to be taken on a shopping trip, he wanted to come home with something his other siblings could enjoy with him. Davy's choice of toy and playmates can be seen to fit in with his already established caretaking role in relationship to his younger siblings. His projected choice of playmates was not inevitable, and he did not really have to choose his little brother—he could have planned to use the walkie-talkies with his friends Ronnie and Kareem, for instance.

Even the Wolverine figure that he yearned for gives more insight on the nature of Davy's social longings than it helps to understand his material desires, if these things must be considered separately at all. Having his own Wolverine figure would have provided him a way to enter into social relationships with other boys in the neighborhood, as he would have been able to come to the play sessions with a toy of his own and thus level the playing field a bit. The struggle Davy experienced while standing in the Toys-R-Us aisle with only twenty dollars to spend was not focused on a selfish desire to have more stuff. These objects were avenues through which he could attempt to forge more

complex, more meaningful, and stronger social relationships with his siblings and with his friends. His struggle was less about whether to buy walkie-talkies or Wolverine than it was deciding which relationships he wanted to foster and strengthen: those with friends, or those with family.

There exists a gap between efforts like Davy's to create and foster relationships with friends and family through consumption, and the ability to successfully accomplish these efforts. For poor and working-class kids, the constraints on access to the material realms of the consumer world are many. Though Davy's choice of merchandise on his shopping trip reveals a multilayered complexity regarding his careful attention to siblings, sharing, caretaking, and building friendships, one wonders what Davy did when the expensive batteries inevitably lost their power. How would he replace the five-dollar batteries? Where could he buy them? Unlike the Wolverine figure he put aside, the walkie-talkies required ongoing purchases in order to keep them going. The continuing effectiveness of his choice—walkie-talkies as a medium of social connection—was also predicated on his continuing ability to consume. Children and adults of all classes are increasingly faced with the dilemma that social participation requires greater and greater levels of consumption, whether of food, services, merchandise, or images. For children who are not only poor or working class, but also racial minorities, this dilemma has especially devastating consequences. Pervasive media images and popular beliefs portraying the consumer engagement of these kids as fundamentally violent and out of control, fueled by greed and drugs, are among the most destructive of these consequences not only because they have a well-demonstrated power to skew perceptions as well as public policy, but also because, like all forms of racist discourse, they are a dehumanizing force.

Shaquita

When I went to pick her up for her shopping trip, Shaquita emerged from her house lurching like a ten-year-old Quasimodo: her small cousin had grabbed hold of her leg and attached herself to it with a toddler's grim determination. Shaquita had to trick the little girl into going back into the house, then lunged out the door, quickly shutting it behind her as the child's wails rose in pitch and volume behind it. We could hear the little girl's shrieks as we crossed the street, and even as we drove away.

The dedication that Shaquita's cousin showed her was not unusual. In her classroom Shaquita was known for her sensitivity and generosity to others and could

TABLE 2   Shaquita's Purchases

Item	Price	Store
1 pair gold-colored slip-ons	$9.99	Payless Shoes
1 pair denim mules	$6.99	Payless Shoes
1 package foam rollers	$2.09	Rite-Aid Drugs
1 bag bubblegum	$ .99	Rite-Aid Drugs

always be counted on as the one who would comfort or stand by another kid in a crisis. Shaquita's father had been living in California "since I was a little baby," and though he called and sent her cards sometimes, she did not see him. She lived with her older sister and younger brother in her maternal grandparents' home and had been there for about five years, since the time her mother had entered the Army. Out of the Army now, Shaquita's mother lived across town in a city housing project, and the children visited her regularly. "My mother wanted us back," she said, "but my grandmother asked if we could stay there and help her." Her grandmother, a domestic worker, had just received her General Equivalency Diploma that year and the family was still celebrating her achievement. Deeply connected to an extensive kinship network, Shaquita was particularly close to her godmother, who took her on trips "down South," and who often bought her new clothes when she needed them. Shaquita's godmother was a member of the church the family attended, and the church played a big part in the family's life.

The first purchase Shaquita made was two pairs of shoes at Payless (see table 2). She had originally gone into the shoe store to find herself sneakers for camp but couldn't find any sneakers she liked. She did find a pair of $6.99 denim mules that she liked very much, though, and bought those for herself. As a birthday gift, Shaquita bought her mother a pair of golden slip-ons for $9.99. With the remainder of her twenty dollars she bought a 99-cent bag of bubblegum that she planned to share with her older sister and some hair-rollers made of pink foam for her grandmother for $2.09. Shaquita spent more than half her money on gifts, all for female kin who play central roles in her life.

In her explanation about why she and her siblings continued to live with their grandparents even after their mother had returned from the Army, Shaquita emphasized she was wanted, that their mother had asked to have her children back, but their grandmother wanted to keep them. Shaquita never said much about what she herself preferred to do, but she seemed happy and secure in her grandparents' home, even as she longed for and missed being with her mother. Looking at these gifts in more detail sheds light on the nature of the different relationships that Shaquita had or hoped to have with her mother and grandmother.

Shaquita told me before we began our trip that her mother wanted some gold sandals and that she wanted to buy her these for a birthday gift. There is a fantasy aspect to these shoes, with their golden color, and their special-event feel. These qualities dovetail with aspects of Shaquita's actual relationship with her mother, where visits were special events. At $9.99, the shoes cost Shaquita about half of her money, and to some degree this is an indication of the degree to which Shaquita wanted to impress her mother, draw her in, and get close to her. Perhaps, like Dorothy's ruby slippers, the golden shoes are a way for Shaquita to get back to an idealized home.

In comparison to the shoes, the pink foam rollers Shaquita bought her grandmother have a down-to-earth usefulness. Shaquita had good reason to think her grandmother would really be glad she had chosen to buy her rollers, since she and her sister were always "borrowing" them. This choice emerged as well from the detailed knowledge we gain of those we live with—knowledge that is gained from pulling one person's hair off a hair curler in order to use it oneself, using the same toothpaste and soap, from changing each others' sheets. This gift, so eminently practical, is particularly appropriate for a female primary caretaker, who is so often expected to forego luxuries herself in order to provide for those around her. The rollers were in this way a powerful symbolic contrast to the golden shoes, and their practicality attested to the everyday intimacy Shaquita shared with her grandmother as opposed to the more richly imagined relationship she contemplated with her mother. The contrast also "speaks" of the differences between Shaquita's relationship with her mother as an important emotional figure and with her grandmother as primary caretaker.

If the golden shoes helped to create the kind of relationship Shaquita imagined she could have with her mother, the rollers allowed Shaquita to demonstrate that she understood her grandmother's generosity and care by reciprocating it. Shaquita could have decided to solve the roller shortage problem by buying some for herself; then she would not have had to use her grandmother's anymore. But in doing this she would have been broadcasting an entirely different message than she did by coming home with a gift. If she had said she was buying the new rollers for herself, Shaquita would have asserted not only her right to use her grandmother's things, but also that she felt it was not her responsibility to replace the things she used. Rather than taking this approach, Shaquita chose to make a gesture that could show her understanding of her obligations as a household member, a gesture that showed she was aware of the kinds of things her grandmother needed. With her sister, however, there could he more give and take, and Shaquita bought a

99-cent bag of bubblegum that they could share. In an omission worth noting, Shaquita bought no gifts for the male members of the household, her brother and grandfather. In fact, no child bought a gift for a male friend or relative.

Cherie

Thinking about mothers' wants and needs was an important element in kids' lives, and several children aside from Shaquita bought gifts for their mothers. Cherie spent nearly all of her money ($14.99 to be exact) on a pair of sneakers for her mother (table 3). The rest of her money was spent on candy, but she gave most of it away to family members, spending less than five dollars on herself. In Cherie's purchases, once again the deep sense of mutual obligation, and even debt, between family members played a central role. For Cherie, as well as for other kids, these obligations and debts were often at once sustaining and joyful as well as painful, onerous, and highly charged. I sometimes suspected that the lesson imparted to children and imparted by them was a coercive generosity: share or else. These harsher aspects of mutual dependence and obligation were an important part of being connected to family and caring for them, and existed simultaneously with the pleasure and satisfaction children received in participating in their families and households.

Cherie, her newborn brother, and mother Deanna shared an attic apartment in a two-family house owned by Deanna's mother. Though Deanna's sister Lynn, a paramedic, did not live at home, she visited her mother often. Deanna received the bulk of her income from state and federal programs and there was some tension between Deanna and her sister, stemming, I thought, from Lynn's steady and comfortable income coupled with her status as a jobholder, versus Deanna's reliance on public assistance. Lynn had no children herself and often gave Cherie expensive gifts: a television set, Sega Genesis game system, and a CD player. These gifts fanned the competitive flames between the sisters. These conflicts occasionally erupted into physical confrontations. Deanna had a scar on her thigh where her sister had once bitten her during a vio-

lent tussle. "Look! She ruined my pretty legs!" Deanna wailed to me in mock anguish as she showed me the marks. Deanna's relationship with her mother also seemed tense, partly out of jealousy over the close relationship between her mother and Deanna's sister, but tension also seemed to emerge around issues of mutual aid and paying of bills. Deanna's rent was largely paid for with a Section 8 voucher, but Deanna felt that her mother expected her to pay too much of the electricity and gas bill. Deanna also did not have a car and felt that her mother was not generous about taking her to the store for grocery shopping, demanding either money or food stamps as payment for the favor.

Cherie's role in this complex web of material and emotional jockeying seemed to be that of an eager, placating human pinball, quick of wit and quick on her feet, working hard to make everyone around her happy and trying to keep out of the way of flashing tempers. She was not, however, just an insecure little victim, and shared a warm and jokey intimacy with her mother, who did not baby Cherie much, speaking and kidding with her like a pal. Deanna was also watchful and protective of her daughter, and my first encounter with Deanna was really an encounter with her disembodied voice—Cherie was outside trying out a new skateboard and Deanna was watching and directing her every move from an upstairs window. But Deanna was moody and prone to drinking, and Cherie seemed ever watchful of her changing disposition.

Cherie's shopping trip reflects these concerns about mediating actual and potential conflicts between these three imposing women in her life and, most of all, anticipating her mother's wants and needs. Even in the planning stages of her shopping trip, Cherie thought she would buy her mother a pair of sneakers "because I took my mother's sneakers because I needed them for junior police." The junior police was part of a community outreach program designed to improve the touchy relations between police and residents of certain New Haven neighborhoods, among them Newhallville. Kids participating in the program went to special events, had educational and training sessions, and wore uniforms. Black shoes were required with Cherie's uniform, and Deanna had given her own black sneakers to her daughter so that she was fully equipped. Cherie knew that replacing those sneakers with the money from this shopping trip would make her mother very happy, and that it would impress her quite a bit:

You're going to try them on to see if they fit your mom?

Yes. She can fit them. She's going to say, "$14.95, child? What were you thinking?"

Why? Is that a lot?

TABLE 3   Cherie's Purchases

Item	Price	Store
1 pair black leather sneakers	$14.99	Payless Shoes
2 containers "juice bar" gum	$ .69 ea	Kay-Bee Toys
2 bags chocolate coins	$ .69 ea	Kay-Bee Toys
1 dish strawberry frozen yogurt	$ 1.35	Food court

It's a lot for me these days, she says. But she'll say, "Thank you for getting them."

I bet she will.

I'll get them for my dear old mother. Because six might be too small, she could grow into these.

You think she will?

Okay. I'm buying my mother a pair of shoes, size six and a half. That's all I'm saying.

Cherie's decision to buy her mother new shoes may have been calculated, in part, to fend off any bad feelings Deanna may have been having about having given her own shoes to her daughter and then having to go without herself. Her "dear old mother" was not her only concern, however, and once Cherie had decided to buy one person in her household a gift, she began to wonder what she should get for her grandmother, aunt, and little brother. She bought some small bags of candy for her aunt and grandmother and did not get anything for her brother. (Cherie's joking comments about buying a cap gun to "murder my brother" hinted at a bit of tension and even jealousy she was feeling at his arrival, which may explain her omission.) After we finished shopping, Cherie spent her last couple of dollars on a strawberry frozen yogurt for herself at the mall's food court. Cherie's shopping trip took less than an hour, and its culminating moment was not the purchases themselves but the distribution of the gifts.

When we returned to Cherie's house, it was already dark outside, and we found her mother, grandmother, aunt, and new baby brother in her grandmother's living room. Cherie's grandmother was holding the new baby, who slept in her lap. Cherie's aunt Lynn was off from work that night and sat sprawled in a living room chair, wearing a baseball cap, acid-washed jeans, and a frown. Deanna had just gotten a perm from her mother, who did under-the-table beauty parlor work out of her home. With a towel over her shoulders and conditioner in her hair, Deanna sat on the couch, watching TV with the others.

Cherie could hardly contain her excitement as we came into the house and, beaming intensely, put the package from Payless down on the couch, saying, "Look what I got!" "What's that?" Deanna said in a high, girl-baby voice. Cherie told her mother that it was a present for her, that she bought it for her on her shopping trip. Deanna answered with a simple, "Thank you," and opened up the box, moving to sit on the floor as she began to try on one of the shoes. Her foot did not seem to go in very well. "They don't fit," she said, scrunching her eyebrows down. Cherie stood almost frozen, not believing that this could be true. Deanna pulled her foot out of the shoe and saw that her thick

athletic sock was hanging over her toes, bunching up inside the shoe. She readjusted her sock, and tried the shoe again. It was a perfect fit. Deanna was all smiles, and Cherie, with evident relief, began passing out bags of chocolate coins to her grandmother and aunt, the enjoyment of this radiating out of her in all directions.

Interpreting the meaning and importance of children's purchases for themselves, which constituted the great majority of purchases overall, is perhaps even more complicated than unraveling the complexities of gifts. For one, children on the whole did not seem driven by their impulses. Kids often managed to buy an astonishing amount for twenty dollars, and overall they were careful, thoughtful, and critical in their buying. Second, when they bought things for themselves, it was not in most cases appropriate to assume that these purchases were self-centered or selfish. Children's purchases for themselves revealed a profound practicality, and the purchase of "needed" items emerged as a central element of kids' shopping. With her twenty dollars Sheila bought a pair of shoes, one package each of socks and underwear, and a bottle of nail polish. Her mother had told her beforehand to be sure and buy socks and underwear with part of her twenty dollars. Marvella, a fourteen-year-old, bought Clearasil, deodorant, and school notebooks with part of her money. Cherelle came prepared with a list that included items such as "gel for the back of my hair" (which she did not buy) and a hair bow to match her school uniform (which she did buy).

Tanika

Tanika had been wearing her brother's sneakers to gym class since she had outgrown her own a few months before. Buying herself sneakers when she needed them was not only practical, but something she found immensely satisfying. "My mother is going to be so happy that she doesn't have to buy me sneakers now," she crowed on the way home in the car (table 4).

Unlike many children in her class, Tanika was not regularly expected to spend part of her own money on things she needed, like socks and underwear. Although Tanika's family was not as economically on the edge as Davy's family, Tanika was keenly aware of the stresses upon her parents generated by running a family and working. Both her parents worked, and they owned their two-family home. This was the first time she had bought sneakers for herself, and easing the burden on her mother's demanding array of responsibilities seemed to be a big part of this decision—in addition, of course, to getting herself some shoes that fit properly and that had not previously belonged to her older brother.

TABLE 4   Tanika's Purchases

Item	Price	Store
1 pair sneakers	$11.00	Payless Shoes
1 pair glasses	$ 3.99	Claire's Accessories
1 t-shirt	$ 5.99	Foxmoor Clothes
1 vest	$ 7.99	Foxmoor Clothes

TABLE 5   Ricky's Purchases

Item	Price	Store
1 tube repair kit	$2.49	Toys-R-Us
8 color changing markers	$1.99	Toys-R-Us
8 colored pencils	$1.99	Toys-R-Us
styrofoam glider plane	$3.99	Toys-R-Us
4 bags of marbles	$1.79 ea	Toys-R-Us
1 marble	$ .99	Toys-R-Us
bubblegum	$ .99	Toys-R-Us

So, now is this something you'd normally do—spend money on buying yourself—have you ever bought yourself sneakers before?

No. I just did it for the first time because I knew I needed sneakers and I wanted them real bad. Because I'm tired of wearing my brother's sneakers and they're ugly.

Is there a reason you haven't gotten new sneakers?

Because she [Tanika's mother] ain't got the time because she works. And she gets off at 4:30 and she goes in at 8:00 and she's tired. Then she takes her nap and then she gets up and cooks—then eats and goes back to sleep. So—that's why she don't have time. . . . On Saturday she'll do it because she don't have to work.

Tanika occasionally earned pocket money by going to work with her mother and helping her out as she cleaned offices in a downtown building. Buying the sneakers was, in part, another way of giving her mother some additional help. Tanika's excitement over the shoes really blossomed when she imagined her mother's reaction to the realization that she would not have to take her free time on a Saturday to go downtown shopping. Using purchases to make caretakers happy, and imagining their pleased reactions, was something that many children found deeply satisfying rather than a chore. In this way they often connected themselves to family and kin even through purchases that were for themselves, rather than being gifts.

Ricky

At Toys-R-Us, Ricky carefully amassed an impressive array of items: a container of bubblegum, four bags of marbles, a set of eight markers, a set of eight colored pencils, a three-foot styrofoam glider plane, and a repair kit for bicycle inner tubes (see table 5). Unlike many children, Ricky did not buy anything that he really planned to share or use with others. A tremendously intelligent and energetic kid with a wicked sense of humor and an insanely goofy laugh, Ricky had been held back in school and was a few years older than his classmates. His major interest was art,

and he continually drew astonishingly accomplished renditions of the Tasmanian Devil and other popular cartoon figures. His family life was crowded and in some ways precarious: earlier in the year he had stolen the proceeds of a classroom art show ($18) to help buy food for his family, and he was repaying his teacher with a small sum once a week. He lived in a three bedroom apartment with his mother, her boyfriend, and three younger siblings. His mother was expecting another child, and their finances were barely adequate to keep the family housed, fed, and clothed.

Ricky's first and highest priority purchase was an inner tube repair kit. For boys in the neighborhood, bikes were a primary avenue to freedom, and they ranged far and wide through the neighborhood and beyond. His tire had a flat, and he wanted to be mobile again. At $2.49 the tube repair kit left Ricky with plenty of money. He checked the price of an inner tube just to compare. "That tube would have cost me $6.99," he said. "It cost a whole lot more and I would only have one of them!" Instead, he pointed out, he paid less and could repair his inner tube several times with the one kit.

Like several other children, Ricky was very clearly focused on getting as much for his money as he possibly could. He loved a Lamborghini model car but realized he would have to buy cement and paint for it. He went so far as to pick all of these things out and carry them around cradled in his arms as we continued up and down the aisles, but he suddenly decided it was too expensive and put everything back. Farther down the aisle, he saw a big styrofoam glider plane. At $3.99 it was about half the price of the model car and certainly gave the impression of getting more for the money, being about three feet long. He decided he wanted to buy art supplies with the remainder of his money. He took a great deal of time evaluating different packages of pens and pencils, their properties, their prices, how many were in a box. He chose things that could be used in more than one way: markers that changed color if treated a certain way, and colored pencils that could be used to do watercolors, too. The marbles were to be added to his marble collection.

Unlike the purchases of many girls, nothing that Ricky bought directly linked him back to his family. This was quite common among boys (except Davy). His purchases remain, like those of most children, practical and well thought out. He wanted to buy the tube repair kit first because he was afraid he would forget if he put it off until later in the trip. One of the most impressive things was Ricky's ability to spread the twenty dollars out so that it satisfied many areas of his interests and activities: the tube repair kit for mobility and peer interaction, the plane for playing, the art supplies for drawing and making things, the marbles to add to an already existing collection.

Teyvon

Teyvon came shopping with me on a Sunday afternoon the day before he was to begin a summer school enrichment program. He spent his entire twenty dollars on an outfit to wear for the first day along with a summer's supply of notebooks, paper, pens, and pencils (table 6). Our first stop was Sam's Dollar Store on the downtown mall's first floor. Teyvon, a skinny kid who always seemed to be pushing his large round-rimmed glasses back up to the bridge of his nose, wasted little time and we spent all of five minutes inside Sam's. Spotting a salesperson right away, he went right up to the man saying, "Excuse me, where are the notebooks?" The man pointed them out and Teyvon chose one. "Excuse me," he shouted out in his raspy, piping voice, "where is the notebook paper?" For a total of $5.37, he bought a notebook, one package of pencils, two packages of pens, and two 200-sheet packages of filler paper.

These purchases of Teyvon's had been carefully planned, and earlier in the week he had scouted potential purchases for his shopping trip, picking out an outfit at a clothing store on lower Chapel Street. We went shopping on a Sunday, however, and when we arrived at the store cootaining his outfit, it was closed. Teyvon did not want to wait and come back another day and instead quickly regrouped, looking for shorts and a t-shirt in the mall stores that were open. In Champs, a sporting goods store, Teyvon once again made a nearly flawless beeline for the salesman, detoured only by a few moments where he gingerly caressed a gold-colored Michael Jordan basketball. "I'm looking for a t-shirt and I have fourteen dollars and seventy cents," he announced to the salesman, who took us over to a rack full of t-shirts. Spotting one he liked, Teyvon felt around for the price tag: $39.95. He dropped the tag and moved on. "There are some shirts that are on

Item	Price	Store
1 10-pack of pencils	$1.00	Sam's Dollar Store
2 10-packs of pens	$1.00 ea.	Sam's Dollar Store
2 packs of notebook paper	$1.00 ea.	Sam's Dollar Store
1 notebook binder	$1.00	Sam's Dollar Store
1 pair shorts	$5.99	SuperBargains
1 Hornets t-shirt	$9.98	Champs Sporting Goods

TABLE 6   Teyvon's Purchases

sale over here," the salesman said. This rack was full of t-shirts decorated with team logos. Teyvon wanted a Celtics t-shirt, but none were on sale. He settled for a black shirt with a white, blue and purple design of the Charlotte Hornets for $9.99. As we were waiting at the counter to pay, Teyvon spotted some baseball caps emblazoned with the Bulls logo. The hats were $21.99. "The price must have gone up when they won," he remarked wryly.

At this point, Teyvon had very little money left, and he still needed a pair of shorts to complete his first-day outfit. He was looking for big, baggy shorts that went down over his knobby knees, preferably in purple or blue to match the shirt. We looked all over the mall, but there were no stores there carrying kids' clothes except for a place called SuperBargains. The shorts there did not come in the right colors, but they did come in the right size and the right price. Teyvon decided on a $5.99 pair of black mesh shorts that had a yellow underlining. When he took the shorts up to the counter, the saleswoman began to ring them up at $4.99, but Teyvon stopped her and told her this was the wrong price. She checked the price, and indeed, Teyvon had been right. With the purchase, it turned out, he had his choice of "silly sippers," drink holders in funny shapes like a bunch of grapes or a banana, with a curly straw attached. He chose a dolphin-shaped silly sipper, saying, "I'll give this to my little cousin."

In Teyvon's case, his focus was on buying things he needed; being able to stretch a limited sum of money to cover both a summer's worth of school supplies and a new outfit was something that continued as he got older. In 1993 he had a job working as a counselor at another summer program. When I spoke with his mother, Vanessa, she told me with evident pride that he had spent his first paycheck (about sixty dollars) buying himself a pair of sneakers, groceries for the family, food for the family cat, and had even started a savings account and was squirreling away funds for a car. "And he didn't buy the regular cat food," Vanessa pointed out emphatically, "he bought the seven-dollar cat food!" At the time, Teyvon was thirteen years old.

Shopping Trips in Children's Cultural Worlds

Just looking at shoe purchases is revealing. Seven girls and one boy bought shoes with a portion of their money, and I became such a familiar sight at the downtown Payless store (a discount shoe chain) that when the store employees saw me approach behind a ten-year-old, they would greet me by asking how my research was coming. The shoe purchases embodied both these priorities of efficiency and buying for need: kids spent anywhere from $3.99 to $14.99 on shoes and often managed to buy several additional items with the money that was left over. Namisha bought her shoes, a pair of blue flats with embroidery on top, to wear to church. Alan bought a pair of sturdy shoes for five dollars and boasted about it for the rest of the day.

In contrast to the brand-name crazed consumers who live in the popular imagination, these children, while interested and knowledgeable about status items, showed not the slightest inability to distinguish between an abstract wish for expensive, status goods and the practical realities of purchasing ability. Though kids demonstrated often and in a variety of ways their detailed knowledge of and interest in brands for clothing, sneakers, food, cars, and so on, they showed little or no interest in purchasing branded merchandise during shopping trips. This gap between abstract wishes and concrete actions is too little noted in the literature on the consumption of kids like these. When the gap is noted, it is primariJy approached in terms of kids' frustration with not being able to buy what they yearn for. While children do harbor these frustrations, the shopping trips also showed that a concern for status items, brands, and fashion does not exist at a constant level and exerts a fluctuating force in children's consciousness.

Sheila and Tarelle, for example, gave me a long and detailed education on the ins and outs of athletic shoes—which brands, models, and colors are "slammin'" and which aren't. Even once inside Payless, Sheila pointed out to me the various "wannabe" models of sneakers lined up on the shelves:

> Sheila tells me that at Payless they have "wannabe" Reeboks, Nikes. She goes to a bunch of sneakers and holds them up one by one, telling me what kinds of wannabes they are. "These are wannabe Huaraches," she says, holding up a pair of sneakers with a cutout top. "They're by Nike."

Sheila and Tarelle even pointed out the sneakers that Tanika had bought earlier for herself, saying that they looked stupid and that they would never wear them. These attitudes did not stop the girls, however, from each buying a pair of shoes in the store: Sheila bought a pair of multicolored Docksider-type shoes,

and Tarelle bought a pair of blue suede clogs. Kids had a keen eye for brands that was undeniable, but it was rivaled by their equally adept eye for bargains.

While on one hand kids would tell me with utter certainty that "everyone" was wearing Air Jordans, and that they really wanted a pair, they would duck into Payless a few minutes later and come out with a ten-dollar pair of shoes or sneakers. I became, upon reflection, very curious about who this supposed "everyone" was since, as I pointed out to Stephen, only two kids at his school actually wore Air Jordans, and he was one of them: this hardly constituted anything approaching "everyone." This was an imaginary "everyone" nonetheless experienced at some level by kids as being real, though not necessarily immediate. This "everyone" is similar to the real but nonexistent amoral and pathological consumer that these kids are so often portrayed as being. In both instances these images possess a powerful influence, one at odds with an on-the-ground situation.

The shopping trips were also striking for what children did not do, even when they were with me, a singularly lenient adult. Family, household, and community dynamics in Newhallville did not foster the kind of wild-child consumer who pitches fits in supermarket aisles and runs amok in Toys-R-Us. A lack of self-control, especially in stores, was not tolerated by the Newhallville caretakers I knew, and when kids pressed their luck by whining, wheedling, or crying they were most often dealt with harshly. As a result kids learned early to keep control. Certain tensions and realities are made visible and present for Newhallville children that for their middle-class counterparts are more often hidden and secret. The cost of being fed, clothed, and cared for is one of these things. Kids in Newhallville are frequently expected to spend part of their allowance, birthday, or Christmas money on buying things for themselves that they need, and their purchases during shopping trips reflect these patterns and expectations. While most kids certainly seemed to be attending to their desires in their shopping, what is most striking is the degree to which practicality on the one hand, and generosity on the other, influenced their shopping trips.

In the presence of caretakers children rarely, if ever, asked for things, whined, or wheedled, and only once during shopping trips did a child attempt such tactics with me. Teyvon, who in the classroom demonstrated world-class cadging abilities, tried his skills out on me during his shopping trip, hounding me to buy him an ice-cream cone. I bought him one, and he later told me he'd just been testing me to see if I'd give in. "You weak!" he crowed, laughingly. More often, rather than Teyvon's calculated exploration of my weak spots, children instead seemed to take care not to impose upon what many saw as my largesse—not only because I was giving them twenty dollars to spend but because I was taking them on an outing and spending time with them when it seemed to them I did not have to. At the outset of each trip I would buy kids a snack and we would sit and chat for a bit. Some children, however, insisted on using a portion of their shopping money, paying for these snacks themselves. As Tarelle said, "I don't want to be spending up all of your money, Miss Chin." Children were extremely careful not to incur debt with me by overtaxing what they saw as my generosity (I usually reminded them they should be thanking the government, not me, for the twenty dollars) and this kind of mental recordkeeping in relation to social and monetary debts was the norm: once Nyzerraye came to visit me at my apartment and got soaked in a sudden downpour. I lent Nyzerraye a pair of socks so that she could have dry feet during her afternoon with me. I told her she could keep them and forgot about it after she went home. A week later, her grandmother sent Nyzerraye back to return the socks, which had been washed, neatly folded, and enclosed in a Ziploc sandwich bag.

Gift-giving was a powerful way for children to strengthen, transform, or maintain relationships with those around them. While Cherie and Shaquita were the only kids to spend more than half of their money on gifts, eight of the twelve girls who came on shopping trips with me bought a gift for someone. In contrast only one boy bought a gift, a small porcelain picture frame decorated with flowers, which he gave to me.[4] This boy was Shaquita's brother and, looking back, I am not surprised that it was this boy who showed this kind of concern—it fits right in with the kinds of priorities and concerns that Shaquita showed in her own shopping trip. The basically gendered aspect of children's gift buying fits in well with expectations at home regarding relationships between friends and family, where the active maintenance of relationships was often managed by girls and women, and the accounting of material and emotional debts brokered by them as well. This is what Michaela di Leonardo has called "the work of kinship" (1987). Though di Leanardo identifies this work as being primarily the province of women, children's purchases here suggest that girls are drawn into this work early: girls bought gifts for their mothers, younger siblings, grandmothers, and, in one case, an infant niece. The purchases showed an intimate understanding of the needs and wants of the people around them and I was especially struck that children seemed to know quite well their mother's shoe and clothing sizes. This sort of intimate knowledge suggests that children do not regard their caretakers just as the givers of care and resources and as therefore somehow able to provide

for all of their own needs as well. Rather, these girls demonstrated the degree to which they understand the very human and real limitations of their caretakers' abilities and recognized their own responsibility for acknowledging or lightening the load. Being able to arrive home after a special outing like the shopping trips with a gift for someone else, especially for a primary caretaker, was a way of demonstrating that kids understood that their membership in the network of kin needed to be active in order to be activated. These gifts were an effort to reciprocate with care and caring and at the same time allowed kids to show that they were competent in meting out material resources in ways that served not only material ends, but social ones as well.

Another aspect in the buying of gifts and its importance for these children was that most of the time kids were not in the position to give gifts of a material kind; the pleasure aroused in children through choosing, buying, and giving gifts should not be taken lightly or discounted. Although I have emphasized above the practical and tactical nature of gift-giving, there was also a distinct and profound gratification that children experienced in being able to give something to someone else. For them, the power to be generous was often a tremendous motivator, not engaged with cynically or out of obligation, but one generating a pleasure and satisfaction unlike that of buying something for themselves. This is not to deny in any way that children found buying things for themselves pleasing and satisfying. Kids loved buying things for themselves, and they did it more often than they bought things for others.

"It would seem that shopping has become about the only area of social action which is defined as clearly not politicized," observes Daniel Miller in an essay entitled "Could Shopping Ever Really Matter?" (1997, 31). What Miller pinpoints in his essay is the long-standing and still influential position of Left-leaning scholars (Right-leaning ones as well) which defines the "mere" act of shopping as vulgar, disconnected from social relations (but somehow not disconnected from political economies), self-referential, surfacey, and inherently apolitical or even antipolitical, a position that he aptly characterizes as "a strange mixture of Marxism with elite criticism of low culture" (44). Just how a socially and culturally organized activity like shopping might be divorced from the social relations of production while remaining firmly rooted in the political economy that has generated it is a question most observers have successfully evaded for decades. More recently, however, the more obvious answer has suggested itself, which is (of course) that shopping cannot be excised from social and cultural relationships, and therefore neither can it be separated from the realm of the political. Miller points out complexities similar to those I have outlined in this chapter in a discussion of the issues surrounding shopping for mundane, everyday items like household disinfectant:

> The atmosphere reflects a gamut of social relations. In one case a daughter-in-law may exact revenge on a dominating mother-in-law by her superior knowledge of changes in the market and constantly implying that her rival's products and choices are out of date or inappropriate. In another context two housewives freely exchange experiences of consumption in order that both should be protected against critical comments from what is regarded as the ignorant bur malevolent world of men. The conversion of shopping knowledge into social relations was most evident in intra-female discussion but may become highly emotive when it is others (especially children) of the household complaining that their expectations have been thwarted. (Miller 1998, 41–42)

Miller's assumption that children are passive and/or receptive in this process is as suspect as the claim that shopping is all about self-gratification and purchase of surface identities. Seen through the context of Newhallville children's life circumstances, the picture that emerges from close observation of what these kids bought when they went on shopping trips with me is one that contrasts greatly with the common assumption and assertion that children are primarily responsive, for instance, voicing their "thwarted desires" but not working to actively satisfy those desires, or the desires (or needs) of others. Even more specifically, poor minority children are often seen as acting on desire but little else, and with often antisocial results.

The major defining factor of these kids' engagement with the consumer sphere is social inequality, and it is understanding the ways in which social inequality shapes their lives, including their shopping lives, which renders visible the political aspects of such "vulgar" activity. Thus the politics of shopping for these children operates at the intimate levels of relationships with mothers, siblings, peers, and caretakers, and at the same time is bound up with "larger" political processes: racism, poverty, residential and economic segregation, and gender bias.

NOTES

1. It has been argued that so-called windfall monies like those 1 provided children for the shopping trips are spent differently than everyday money (Bodkin 1959). However, Bodkin's argument is focused on the spending of adults, not children, who do not generally receive regular wages but often receive various forms of non-wage income in the form of gifts, allowance, or windfall. Zelizer (1989) argues that each of these kinds of "special monies" carries with it particular symbolic and social meanings and implications. The patterns evident in my analysis of these children's shopping trips are not in conflict with the $20 being windfall income or a form of "special money."

2. Some people have suggested to me that perhaps children bought gifts and "spent their money wisely," as they often said in Newhallville, to impress me. Perhaps. Yet if this was the case, an explanation is still needed as to why children thought that gift-giving and careful shopping would be "good" for them, and it is an explanation that leads right back into children's social and kinship networks. In other words, the notion of "observer influence" neither accounts for nor explains the patterns that emerge in looking at children's purchases on these trips.

3. In *A Theory of Shopping*, Daniel Miller (1998) similarly notes that residents of one North London street used shopping as a way to show their love for kin, "express care and concern" (35), attempt to transform or educate household members, among other things. Fischer and Arnold (1990) also document the ways in which women engage in Christmas gift shopping as "more than a labor of love."

4. While Teyvon did not buy the silly sipper he received with his purchase of shorts, he did say he planned to give it away to his cousin, and it can be considered another gift.

25

Just Another Job?

The Commodification of Domestic Labor

Bridget Anderson

Commodification - the transformation of a good or service that can be bought and sold w/ money

For most women, working is a necessity, not an option. There are reasons to celebrate the fact that women have become active participants in the workforce alongside their male counterparts. But this socioeconomic transformation has also created a "double shift" for many women, who work a full day and then return home to the additional unpaid jobs with home, household, and family each night.

Many families try to alleviate this "double shift" by "outsourcing" domestic work to a paid worker. This outsourcing is what the author of this selection means by the "commodification of domestic labor." In other words, domestic labor can be bought and sold like other services or goods. Although domestic labor is an increasingly important commodity in societies throughout western Europe, the United States, and other world regions, it is generally poorly paid. Employers look for potential employees who are willing to work for the lowest wages and, quite frequently, the individuals they hire are migrants from poor, faraway countries.

While the wages middle-income Western families pay their domestic workers may be low by local standards, they are often very high in comparison to wages available in poor countries. As a result, millions of people from countries as diverse as the Philippines, Sri Lanka, Ghana, Nigeria, Columbia, and El Salvador have left their homes and families in order to take their chance of working abroad as a domestic worker. Even educated people with professional experience—among them journalists, teachers, bankers, nurses, and others—are prepared to take on the risks of transnational migration since the benefits are perceived as being so high.

This selection illustrates the difficulties of being a transnational migrant in domestic work. It can be very challenging to work within the intimate space of another person's, or another family's, home—especially within a foreign culture. At the same time is it difficult to live far away from family and friends, including, quite often, one's own children. Relationships between employers and employees are frequently marked by asymmetries of race, nationality, language, class, and citizenship, since many transnational domestic workers have migrated on an undocumented or "illegal" basis. As this selection illustrates, these asymmetries leave transnational domestic workers vulnerable to various forms of discrimination, exploitation, and abuse. Globalization is not just about manufacturing being done in China or call centers in India; globalization hits close to home.

As you read this selection, ask yourself the following questions:

- What is the "commodification of domestic labor"? What factors have contributed to the rise in demand for domestic workers in western Europe?

- Why are so many domestic workers in western Europe transnational migrants from Southeast Asia, West Africa, or eastern Europe?

- From the perspective of the domestic workers the author interviewed, what are the advantages of live-in as opposed to live-out domestic work? What are the disadvantages?

- How do racial stereotypes and other forms of prejudice contribute to the mistreatment of some domestic workers?

- Some employers describe their domestic employees as "one of the family." How might this way of characterizing their employment relationship actually contribute to the exploitation and abuse of the migrant women they employ?

The following terms discussed in this selection are included in the Glossary at the back of the book:

commodification
domestic labor
maternalism

Anderson, Bridget. "Just Another Job? The Commodification of Domestic Labor." Reprinted with permission of the author.

Paid domestic work looks in many ways like just another undesirable job. The hours are long, the pay is low, and the tasks are often regarded as demeaning. The same could be said of hamburger flipping or garbage collection. But there is much to distinguish the culture of domestic labor from other kinds of low-wage work. Significantly, domestic work is deeply embedded in status relationships, some of them overt, but others less so. And these relationships are all the more complex because they fall along multiple axes. They are relationships among women, but often women of different races or nationalities—certainly of different classes. They take place in a space that can be intimate, loving, and private but that can also be a form of social plumage, demonstrating to visitors the home owner's comfort and leisure. And the worker, often a migrant without legal protection or proper papers, may depend on the employer for more than her paycheck, just as the employer depends on the worker for more than her elbow grease.

The demand for domestic workers has been steadily rising in Europe, and although one can point to many economic and demographic forces that may have contributed to this trend—the retrenchment of the welfare state, the rise in the ratio of older to younger people, the feminization of the workforce, the rise in divorce, and the decline of the extended family—they leave a good deal unexplained. For instance, many domestic workers are employed by women who do not work outside their homes. Moreover, many paid domestic workers are cleaners rather than carers. While a working couple might need someone to look after their children or elderly relatives, no one *has* to employ a cleaner in the same way. Ironed clothes, dust-gathering ornaments, polished floors, and clean windows are not necessities; but such markers affirm a household's status by displaying its access to financial and human resources.

The migrant domestic workers I interviewed, many of them through a British support organization called Kalayaan, seemed to spend much of their time servicing lifestyles that their employers would have found difficult and even undesirable to sustain had they undertaken their upkeep themselves. Said Aida, a Filipina live-in in Paris:

> Every day I clean for my madam one pair of riding shoes, two pairs of walking shoes, house shoes. That is every day, just for one person. . . . Plus the children: that's one pair of rubbers and one pair of everyday school shoes. . . . Fourteen pairs of shoes every day. My time is already finished. . . . You will be wondering why she has so many bathrobes, one silk and two cotton. I say, Why does madam have so many bathrobes? Every day you have to hang them up. Every day you have to press the back because it is crumpled.

Siryani, a Sri Lankan live-in in Athens, recounted, "They have a very big house, and white carpet everywhere. They have three dogs. I hate those dogs with long, long hair. Even one hair will show on the white carpet."

When a cleaner is not enabling her employers to enjoy an extravagant lifestyle or an impractically appointed home (would Siryani's employers have had both white carpet and dogs if they'd had to clean their own home?), she allows her middle-class, female employer to devote "quality" time to her children and husband. In effect, employing a cleaner enables middle-class women to take on the feminine role of moral and spiritual support to the family, while freeing her of the feminine role of servicer, doer of dirty work. The employment of a paid domestic worker thereby facilitates status reproduction, not only by maintaining status objects but also by allowing the worker to serve as a foil to the lady of the house. Simply by hiring a domestic worker, the employer lowers the status of the work that employee does. After all, the employer has better or more lucrative things to do with her time.

Many middle-class, heterosexual couples in the United Kingdom employ a cleaner once they have children, thereby averting gender and generational conflict over domestic work.[1] But there is no total amount of domestic work that can be divided fairly between equal partners or delegated to someone who is paid to do it. When one does not have to do the work oneself, standards change. Eliska, a Czech au pair in the United Kingdom recounted, "Her teenage daughter changes her clothes five, six times a day and leaves them on the floor. I have to pick them up, wash them, iron them, put them away. I cannot tell her, Tasha, you cannot change your clothes so many times. And my employer does not notice."

Economic explanations, then, fail to fully account for the popularity of domestic workers in middle- to upper-class European households, because they fail to consider the status implications of hiring such workers. Similarly, the prevalence of migrant labor in this sector cannot be attributed only to avoidance of tax and national insurance, for there is a supply of cheap, non-migrant female laborers willing to work off the books. Despite the relatively high wages of Polish workers in Berlin, they still account for a significant proportion of domestic workers. Filipina workers are the most popular in Athens, and they are also the most expensive.

Significantly, migrant workers are more willing than local ones to live with their employers. Live-in workers may be considerably less expensive than live-out workers, in some cases because their board and lodging are set against their wages, but especially because employers get more labor and greater flexibility

disguised slavery and extreme racism

exploitation of illegal immigrants

for their money. Whatever hours a live-in nanny and housekeeper is supposed to work, there is virtually no time when she can comfortably refuse to "help" her employer with a household task. Domestic workers and au pairs commonly complain of having to be available at both ends of the day, early in the morning for children and late at night for entertaining guests. It is a question not simply of long hours but of permanent availability. Said Teresa, a Filipina domestic in Athens:

> You're working the minute you open your eyes until the minute you close your eyes. You keep your strength and your body going so that you will finish your work. . . . You keep waiting on your employers until they go to sleep because, although you finish your work, for example you finish ironing everything, putting the children or the elder person to bed, even if you put them to bed at ten o'clock, there are still other members of the family. So you keep on observing, "Oh, can I sleep or maybe they will call me to give them food or to give them a yogurt.". . . And even if you are sleeping you sometimes feel that you are still on duty.

A 1998 survey of thirty-nine Kalayaan members found that although the workers were well organized and belonged to a trade union, only 18 percent worked eight hours or less a day. Nearly 30 percent averaged more than twelve hours a day.

Although the long hours, low pay, and lack of privacy render live-in domestic work extremely unpopular among the population in general, migrants, particularly new arrivals, can find it advantageous: problems of accommodations and employment are solved in one, and the worker can both minimize expenses and acclimatize herself to a new language and culture. Moreover, housing is more than a place to live: it is shelter from the police, and many new arrivals are undocumented and terrified of deportation. Employers appreciate live-in migrants because, unlike local domestic workers, migrants cannot leave their employers to go tend to their own sick children or other family obligations. Undocumented workers in particular have extremely limited access to their own families or, really, to any life outside the employing home.

Such women, however, isolated in private households, without papers or legal protection, are strikingly vulnerable to abuse. Their work can be singularly degrading: cleaning cats' anuses, flushing employers' toilets, scrubbing the floor with a toothbrush three times a day, or standing by the door in the same position for hours at a time. One worker told a researcher of a particularly degrading experience: "We were three Filipinas, she brought us into the room where her guests were, she made us kneel down and slapped each one of us across the face."[2]

Sadly, these are not isolated instances. Kalayaan keeps annual figures detailing the kinds of difficulties faced by the workers they register. In 1996–1997, 84 percent reported psychological abuse, 34 percent physical abuse, and 10 percent sexual abuse. Additionally, 54 percent were locked in, 55 percent did not have their own beds, and 38 percent were not fed regularly.

Racial stereotypes play a role both in the abuse of domestic workers and in the selection of migrant workers over local citizens in the first place. Certainly, such stereotypes help manufacture a sense of difference between the female employer and her domestic worker: "other" women are presumed suited to such service work, and these others are so alien that some employers actually fear that the migrants' bodies will contaminate their homes. Workers are typically required to wash their clothes separately from those of the family, and they are given their own cutlery and plates. Said Rose, a Ghanaian domestic worker in Athens, of her employer's family, "The daughter wouldn't even accept water from my hand, simply because I am black." Irene, a Filipina I interviewed in Athens, recounted the following story: "I heard children playing house. One child said, 'I am a Daddy.' The other child said, 'I am a Mummy,' and then, 'She is a Filipina.' So what does the child mean? Even the child knows or is already learning that if you are a Filipina, you are a servant inside the house."

Agencies and employers tend to express preferences for specific nationalities of domestic workers, and these preferences often reflect racial hierarchies that rank women by precise shades of skin color. One volunteer from Caritas, the international Catholic social service and relief agency, in Athens told me, "The Ethiopians are very sweet. They are not like the African Africans, who are ugly." Said a worker at an agency in Barcelona, "Moroccans are difficult to place. . . . Their religion is very different, they observe Ramadan. . . . They are very different, though like Peruvians they are brought up to be servile. . . . Filipinas are easiest to place." And according to a community volunteer in Paris, "You know the black people are used to being under the sun, and the people in France think they are very lazy, they are not going very quick, and you know, another breed, but they are very good with children, very maternal."

Some hierarchies are based on particular national or personal prejudices. Greek employers and agencies tend to frown upon Albanians and Ukrainians. In Paris, many employers evince a preference for Haitians, who are generally darker-skinned than the expressly shunned Moroccans and Algerians. Stereotypes differ across European states, but also across households: one household might display an "eccentric" liking

what constitutes bad?

for Congolese, for example, on the basis of household myths of an almost folkloric character. A "bad" experience with a domestic worker might lead a family to generalize about her entire nationality. Consider the comments of this Athens employer:

> I have a problem with women from Ethiopia: they are lazy, and they have no sense of duty, though they are good-hearted. . . . I have a lot of experience. I have had ten girls from Ethiopia. They like to be well-dressed—hair, nails; for that they are good. . . . Then the Albanians—that was terrible. They are liars, always telling lies. And telephone maniacs because they have never had telephones. And they had no knowledge of electrical appliances. For seven months I had that girl. . . . Then I had one from Bulgaria. The Bulgarians are more civilized, more sincere, more concerned about work. But they are very unhappy.

Of course, not all employers are racist or abusive. Some women hire migrants in the hope of helping them. Certainly, migrant workers need the money. Why not match the needs of hard-pressed working mothers, on the one hand, with those of desperate migrants on the other?

Many of the domestic workers I met said that traveling abroad had enabled them to make important contributions to their families back home. But most of the more than four thousand workers at Kalayaan had never intended to come to Britain. Some had migrated first to the Middle East, from where they accompanied their employers to London on business trips or holidays; others had taken jobs in their countries of origin and traveled with their employers to the United Kingdom. While domestic workers who had papers felt that their work brought benefits to their families, others, especially those still undocumented, found the price too high. Said Nora, a Filipina working in London, "My life is worse than before. I'm on this dark road with no way out, that's how I feel. . . . All I want to do is go back home, even though we're very poor. But then, what kind of life will my daughter have?"

Hidden costs become apparent to many workers when they return home. They often feel ill at ease in their home countries, where things have changed in their absence, and where they may feel that they no longer belong. When their families meet them at the airport, these women commonly do not recognize their own kin. They talk of the embarrassment of having sex with husbands who have become virtual strangers, and of reuniting with children who doubt their mothers' love. Often a woman's relatives will have died or moved away. It is thus scarcely surprising that such women are very ambivalent when asked whether they would recommend migration to their daughters. Most migrants would prefer that their daughters did not have to make the choice between hunger and moving abroad.

So is employing a migrant domestic worker an act of sisterhood toward a woman in need or of complicity with abusive power structures? Employers often make contact with Kalayaan after they have seen a television program or read an article exposing the situation of migrant domestic workers in London. They want to help, they explain, and to offer board and lodging in return for "help around the house." A place in a British home is proffered as a kind of charity, and the woman's labor power is a little extra on the side. But even under the best of circumstances, the employer has power over the worker, and this power is greatly increased when the worker is an undocumented migrant. How the employer chooses to exercise that power is up to her.

As Judith Rollins has noted, a kind of "maternalism" sometimes marks these relationships, wherein friendliness between the women works to confirm the employer's sense of her own kindness and of the worker's childlike inferiority. Through kindness, pity, and charity, the employer asserts her power. Nina, an employer in Athens, had hired dozens of migrant domestic workers to care for her very disabled mother over the years, because, she said, "This is the Greek way to help foreigners." She claimed to offer exceptional working conditions (though the wages she told me were extremely low) and a loving household. But her employees, she lamented, have turned out to be gold diggers:

> There is no feeling for what I offer. I'll give you an example of the last woman from Bulgaria. . . . I had a bright idea: "She needs to see her friends." Because I was tired of all the turnover, I gave her Sunday off. . . . Now, every morning, including Sundays, the girl wakes, helps grandmother to the toilet and changes her Pamper. . . . Then she goes, but she must be back before seven P.M. . . . Then after all I do for her, the girl says every Sunday she would like to be back at midnight, and not to do any work—that is, not to change the Pamper in the morning.

This worker was being denied twelve consecutive hours off in a week—an arrangement that would still have placed her hours well above the European legal maximum.

Some employers express their maternalism through gifts, giving their domestic workers mostly unwanted, cast-off household goods. Said Maggie, a Zairean working in Athens, "You need the money to feed your children, and in place of pay they give you old clothes. 'I give you this, I give you this.' They give you things, but me, I need the money. Why? I am a human being."

All of these exercises of power, whether through direct abuse, through the insistence that a worker perform degrading tasks, or through acts of maternalism, expose the relationship between worker and employer as something other than a straightforward contractual one. But that is not the only relationship in the domestic workplace that is fraught with ambiguity and complexity. When we hire someone to care for children or the elderly, we cannot pay simply for the physical labor of care, leaving the emotional labor to those who are genetically linked to those cared for. Magnolia, a Dominican nanny in Barcelona, noted, "Sometimes when they say to me that I should give her lots of love, I feel like saying, well, for my family I give love free, and I'm not discriminating, but if it's a job you'll have to pay me."

Indeed, many parents hire nannies rather than sending their children to day care precisely because they want their children to develop personal, emotional relationships with the people who care for them. But can the emotional labor of care really be bought? The worker may carry out the physical work of care, entering into a sort of intimacy with the children, but her caring engenders no mutual obligations, no entry into a community, and no real human relationship—just money. A worker may care for a child over many years, spending many more hours with that child than the child's natural mother does, but should the employer decide to terminate the relationship, the worker will have no further right to see the child. As far as the employer is concerned, money expresses the full extent of her obligation to the worker. To the worker, this view is deeply problematic; indeed, it denies the worker's humanity and the very depth of her feelings. Juliette, a nanny from Côte d'Ivoire working in Parma, recalled, "I cared for a baby for his first year. . . . The child loves you as a mother, but the mother was jealous and I was sent away. I was so depressed then, seriously depressed. All I wanted was to go back and see him. . . . I will never care for a baby again. It hurts too much."

The idea that the worker can be considered "part of the family" allows some employers to negotiate these difficulties. Interestingly, this language even appears in U.K. immigration legislation with reference to au pairs. But the analogy does not withstand scrutiny. A relative who contracts a long-term illness is not expelled from the family; domestic workers usually are, even if they are given a nice severance package. And although being a part of the family does not entitle the worker to unconditional love or support, it does entitle the employer to encroach on the worker's off-duty hours for "favors." In fact, many employers will invoke either a contractual or a family relationship under different circumstances, depending on what is most convenient. Writes Miranda Miles:

> The disadvantages of being "one of the family" far
> outweighed the advantages. Wages tended to be lower

and erratically paid on the premise that the maid would "understand" their financial situation. Incorporating a domestic worker into the family circle is usually, although not always, a sure way of depressing wages and possibly hiding even the most discreet forms of exploitation involved in the employer-employee relationship.[4]

These are vexed questions, for while informality clearly leaves workers open to exploitation—excessive hours, for instance, or low pay—workers also value having personal relationships with their employers, particularly because domestic work can be highly isolating. In some cases, a woman will decide to work for low wages precisely because she feels that a particular family is "nice" or an employer "treats me as part of the family." Professionalizing employment relations and rendering them more anonymous may therefore introduce new difficulties. Labor is a social, not simply an economic, process.

This is not to say that labor contracts for domestic work are not important. We should welcome the emergence of domestic labor into the realm of recognized and productive work. Professionalization is a means of giving respect to domestic workers as workers, as well as of managing the personal relationships that develop from care work.

Certainly, it is possible to argue for the social significance of care work. Changing an elderly person's incontinence pads is surely as important and as deserving of social respect and status as the work of a stockbroker. But the work of cleaners and housekeepers sometimes occupies a more problematic space. Cleaning can be part and parcel of caring, and tidying up for a disabled person, for instance, can be construed as socially valuable. But many cleaners, like those described at the start of this essay, do work that simply expresses the employer's status, leisure, and power. Can such race-, class-, and gender-based divisions be resolved through contracts? Undocumented migrants, for example, cannot draw boundaries or refuse work they find demeaning. They simply do not have the power. The most effective way to protect them is to make sure that they have basic employment rights, as well as access to the means to implement those rights. For migrants, these rights begin with work permits.

Because both the workers and the employers in this sector tend to be women, it is tempting to draw on notions of sisterhood in order to reform the relationships between employers and employees. But the power relations among these women are very complex, to the point where even acts of kindness work to reproduce an employer's status and self-image, and they do not always, in the end, benefit the worker. This does not mean that employers should not respect their domestic workers but, rather, that they should also be aware that the very act of employing a domestic worker weaves them into a status relationship. Real sisterhood, then, should take concerned women beyond their own homes: it means campaigning and organizing around issues of migration and domestic labor, having as an important first demand that domestic work be treated, in the best sense, like just another job.

NOTES

1. Nicky Gregson and Michelle Lowe, *Servicing the Middle Classes: Class, Gender and Waged Domestic Labour in Contemporary Britain.* London: Routledge, 1994.

2. Margaret Healy, "Exploring the Slavery of Domestic Work in Private Households," unpublished M.A. thesis, University of Westminster, 1994.

3. Judith Rollins, *Between Women: Domestic Workers and Their Employers.* Philadelphia: Temple University Press, 1985.

4. Miranda Miles, Working in the City: The Case of Migrant Women in Swaziland's Domestic Service Sector. In *Gender, Migration and Domestic Service*, ed. Janet Momsen. London: Routledge, 1999.

26

Conflict and Confluence
in Advertising Meetings

Robert J. Morais

....

Not every anthropology student aspires to become a professor, nor do the majority of budding anthropologists dream of a career living and studying with people in remote corners of the world. Over the past twenty-five years, more than half of all new Anthropology PhDs have found employment in nonacademic settings such as nonprofit organizations, government agencies, consulting firms, and multinational corporations such as Intel, Microsoft, Motorola, and Kodak.

Corporate anthropology applies methods and theories from cultural anthropology to reveal and decode consumer cultures. The pioneering anthropologist Bronislaw Malinowski encouraged future generations of social scientists to immerse themselves in their study populations to learn how to see cultures from within. He advocated meticulous note-taking and participant observation as means to discover the difference between what people say versus what they actually do. Similarly, conventional market research may document what consumers say, but anthropological methods can see beyond that which consumers might tell marketers. As anthropologists have discovered, people often tell researchers what they think the researchers want to hear.

Reaching and understanding consumer cultures have become increasingly difficult for businesses as globalization creates access to new markets, and as technology fragments the mass media into countless specialized television networks, websites, and satellite radio stations. The complexity of modern business drives many executives and entrepreneurs to seek anthropological consultants to study consumer

behavior, organizational theory, cross-cultural communication, and management strategies. In this selection, Robert Morais applies anthropological methods to analyze meetings between advertising agencies and their clients. Anthropology can help businesses reach consumers and develop successful new products, but it can also help business executives and account managers understand and improve their relationships with employees, clients, and each other.

As you read this selection, ask yourself the following questions:

- How do advertising meetings fit Van Genep's definition of a rite of passage?

- How does advertising reflect and shape culture?

- How do "creatives" differ from clients and account managers?

- In what ways do seating arrangements in advertising meetings reflect social hierarchies? What other ways are hierarchies performed in advertising meetings?

- Why do clients and account managers sometimes decide not to speak their true feelings? How do account managers read between the lines when clients say one thing but mean another?

The following terms discussed in this selection are included in the Glossary at the back of the book:

cultural validators   liminal period
rite of passage   secret society

....

INTRODUCTION

Advertising professionals have written widely on the creative development process (e.g., Della Femina 1970; Steel 1998); scholars have considered how advertising

reflects and shapes culture (cf. Henry 1963; Lasch 1979; Schudson 1984; Sherry 1987); and, over the past two decades, there has been a burgeoning interest in the value of anthropology to marketing and advertising (Louis 1985; Miller 1990; Denny 1999; Sanders 2002;

Morais, Robert J. "Conflict and Confluence in Advertising Meetings." Reproduced with permission of the Society for Applied Anthropology (SfAA) from *Human Organization* 66, no. 2 (2007):151–159.

Wellner 2002; Wasserman 2003; Monari 2005; Murphy 2005; Ante 2006; Inglessis 2006). Ethnographic accounts of advertising agencies are less common. Notable examinations include Malefyt and Moeran's (2003) collection of essays, Moeran's (1996) study of a Japanese advertising agency, Miller's (1997) description of an agency in Trinidad, and Mazzarella's (2003) account of the relationship between the advertising industry and consumerism in India.

This paper focuses on a critical juncture in the creation of advertising: the meeting between the manufacturer (client) and the agency where advertising ideas are presented, discussed, and selected. I shall argue that these meetings contain the defining attitudes, behaviors, and symbols of the client–agency relationship and will offer an analysis that may help advance the understanding of meetings in other cultural contexts.

ADVERTISING IN PERSPECTIVE

Advertising is one component of a marketing mix that includes a wide range of programs designed to increase brand sales. Underhill (2000:32) argues that "while branding and traditional advertising build brand awareness and purchase predisposition, these factors do not always translate into sales." Yet U.S. manufacturers remain committed to advertising, spending $130 billion on it in 2005 alone (TNS Media Intelligence 2006). Given this level of investment, and the fact that consumers tend not even to recall most advertising one day after they are exposed to it (cf. Schudson 1984:3–4; Steel 1998:xi), companies devote considerable time and money to fielding the best advertising they can develop or risk a disappointing return on their investment. For this reason, most U.S. manufacturers that spend heavily on advertising employ agencies that specialize in the creation of ads rather than generate the ads themselves.

Advertising is a highly competitive industry in the United States; agency firings and account reassignments are common. As Malefyt (2003:139, 142–143) points out, a consequence of this volatility is that "the process of ad production . . . is one directed . . . not so much at the brand, consumer or even rival agencies, but towards the client." This behavior reflects Michell and Sander's (1995) finding that advertising development processes and interpersonal relationships have more influence on agency loyalty than the perceived quality of the creative work. Other studies have examined the roles of agency personnel who create advertising (Hirschman 1989; Young 2000) and interaction across disciplines within agencies and with clients (Kover 1995; Kover and Goldberg 1995). Moeran (1996:79–87)

concentrates on events surrounding a presentation in which an agency is competing to win an account (Johnson 2006). Miller's (1997:182–194) ethnography on the development of an advertising campaign in Trinidad could apply to virtually any advertising agency in the United States. This paper focuses sharply on creative meetings and considers the contrasting objectives, strategies, and tactics of the agency and client personnel who attend these meetings.

METHODOLOGY

In 1981, I left academic anthropology and became an advertising executive. For most of my advertising career I served in account management, later moving to strategic planning and research. In mid-2006, I joined a marketing research and consulting firm. After a quarter of a century of work in the field, this is my first report, supporting Reinharz's (1988:168) contention that "there are few published accounts of (going native) since those who have gone native cease to publish." This paper is based upon participation in thousands of creative meetings between 1981 and 2006 while employed at large and mid-sized American advertising agencies and aligns closely to what Sherry (2003:xii) terms "observant participation" and to Kemper's assertion that "advertising executives are ethnographers in the strict sense of the word" (Kemper 2003:35). Formal and informal discussions with numerous account management and creative colleagues and with marketing management clients expanded my perspective and validated my analysis. The formal interviews were conducted over several months; I have had informal conversations about advertising management throughout my advertising career. Most of the meetings my advertising and client colleagues and I observed involved work for food brands, over-the-counter and prescription pharmaceuticals, personal care items, and household cleaning products manufactured by companies ranging in size from multinational corporations to venture capital funded start-ups. The product categories are a limiting factor of this research because these manufacturers are generally creatively conservative. However, these marketers represent a substantial share of the businesses that advertising agencies serve. The names of the companies, informants, and brands have been withheld to preserve confidentiality.

THE MEETING DEFINED

The meeting as a focus of anthropological inquiry does not have a rich tradition; the most extensive attention paid to meetings by an anthropologist is

Schwartzman's (1989) study on meetings in a mental health organization. Her definition of a meeting is a useful starting point. For Schwartzman (1989:7) a meeting is:

> A communicative event involving three or more people who agree to assemble for a purpose ostensibly related to the functioning of an organization or group, for example, to exchange ideas or opinions, to solve a problem, to make a decision, or negotiate an agreement, to develop policy and procedures, to formalize recommendations . . . a meeting is characterized by talk that is episodic in nature.

Because advertising creative meetings occur in a designated place, the agency's or client's conference room, for a discrete period of time, normally 60 to 90 minutes, they can be viewed analytically as frames (Goffman 1974; Moeran 2005:43–57). Moeran's (2005: 63–79) discussion of frames in a business context is useful for seeing creative meetings not only as a frame within agency life, but also as the key frame for interpreting and understanding agency/client relationships.

THE MEETING PARTICIPANTS

In creative meetings, agency attendees include account managers and the "creatives," or executives directly responsible for creating the advertising. Larger agencies might also include account planners (Malefyt 2003). Client participants are the marketing management employees of the manufacturing company that has hired the agency.

Advertising agency account managers represent the agency to the client, communicate client needs to the agency, and help ensure that agency departments get the work done on strategy, on time, and on budget. They are relationship managers, problem solvers, and communicators. They are more similar to the client than any other agency staffer. As one client said, they "dress and speak like us; they are more like us (than creative people)." Creatives are organized into copy writer–art director teams that develop the advertising ideas. A creative director, with experience in writing or art direction, supervises creative teams. In creative meetings, the creative director is the selling partner of the account team but argues from a creative rather than a business perspective, which is the function of account managers. Creatives are conceptual, imaginative people who invent, design, and produce "the work." They differ temperamentally and stylistically from their MBA-trained clients. Client marketing managers conceive and execute the marketing plan for a brand. Their responsibilities include managing product development, quality control, product distribution to retailers, sales tracking, consumer promotions such as coupons, and developing advertising. In advertising

creative meetings, clients are the gatekeepers for creative work and they must be convinced that the work merits exposure to consumers.

Advertising creative meetings involve the interaction of client and agency teams as two entities, as well as the interaction of members within teams. Hirschman (1989) speaks to both dimensions when, citing Turow (1984:21), she characterizes clients as patrons of the agency (Hirschman 1989:42–43) and then describes the roles of several participants in the creative development process. Miller, remarking on the tension between account managers and creatives in Trinidad, notes that creatives are "artists" and account managers are responsible for clients' "commercial concern" (Miller 1997:188). Even within creative teams, Young (2000) found that copy writers and art directors have different feelings about creative development. Across agency and client lines, within agencies, and, to a lesser extent, within client teams, contrasting responsibilities and attitudes have a major impact on the conduct and outcome of creative meetings.

GOALS: MUTUAL AND OTHERWISE

Agency and client personnel enter creative meetings to reach agreement on the work and advance the most promising creative ideas to the next step in the development process. Clients hope to manage a smooth process within specified time and production cost parameters. They also strive to showcase their professional skills to management. Clients are acutely aware that their comments during creative meetings are heard not only by the agency but also by their superiors, and clients believe that "looking smart" to both the agency and their superiors is critical. As one client said, "If you say what your boss agrees with and he says he agrees, the agency (as well as your boss) thinks you are smart." Agency personnel share the desire to move the process forward seamlessly. They know that the better the clients appear to their own management, the more loyal these clients will be to the agency. Agency staff enter the meeting with a strong desire to sell specific creative work that makes the agency team, and specific individuals within the agency team, look insightful and inventive.

The agency also has an agency-building agenda; imaginative creative work can help win new business. Additionally, creative work is often "pushed" by individuals who want to build their personal "reel" for future jobs. Most importantly, agencies must leave the meeting having preserved, and ideally enchanced, their relationship with the client. A smooth development process, high creative test scores, and positive business results are important. Exhibiting leadership and creativity, managing the meeting, accepting the

TABLE 1   Hierarchy of Agency and Client Goals

Agency	Client
Preserve the relationship	Look smart and capable
Enhance perception of the agency and one's self	Exhibit leadership and control over the meeting
Sell creative work that the agency will be proud to showcase	Manage the overall development process on a timely basis
Sell creative work in the fewest number of presentation rounds	Help develop creative work with which the entire marketing team is comfortable
Get high copy test scores	Get high copy test scores
Grow brand sales	Grow brand sales

final decision with grace, attaining camaraderie, and just "getting it" (i.e., understanding client personality and culture, listening carefully to client comments, and knowing client preferences) all contribute to the larger objective of a stronger agency–client bond and retention of the account. The hierarchy of goals in creative meetings depicted in Table 1 is based on observations and discussions with agency account managers and creatives and client marketing managers.

BEFORE THE MEETING

The creative development process may be initiated because brand sales are softening, the current advertising is reaching consumer exposure "wear out," a launch of a new product is planned, the agency has won a new account, or a client simply wants new creative work. The client or agency crafts a Creative Brief, the blueprint for creative development. Account managers work out a timetable for development, presentation, testing, and production of the creative work. They review the brief with the creative team, and, before the meeting, provide creatives with intelligence regarding the client's intellectual and temperamental terrain.

Creatives are given two to three weeks to develop ideas. Guided by the Brief, they develop concepts that will challenge their clients' comfort levels and ideas they are fairly sure the client will find acceptable. Conservative ideas carry special risks. As one creative director said, "I always give them something I know will sell, but I have to be careful because everything you put on the table is for sale." Account managers, eager to please the client, request safe work and negotiate with creative directors about which work to present to a client. If a creative director insists on presenting a storyboard that the account manager believes is marginally related to the strategy, or "edgy," the account manager asks the creative team to present an execution that is "closer in" strategically or more conservative.

Often the creative team and account manager strike a deal to offer both approaches. The body of work is reviewed first by the creative director, then with the account management team, and finally with agency management. Several rounds of internal agency meetings occur before creative work is presented to the client.

For this paper, I use a meeting that will culminate in a television commercial as the case in point. There is no standard number of television storyboards that are presented in a creative meeting, but a battery of five to eight ideas is typical. Agencies group storyboards into categories based on executional styles (e.g., realistic "slice of life" situations that are problem or solution oriented, celebrity presenters, demonstrations with competitive comparisons, an image driven idea, or a humorous situation). Sorting is also done according to variations on the strategy that emphasize particular understandings about the target consumer. For example, several advertisements for an over-the-counter wart remover might all be written to a "removes warts in one step" consumer promise while varying thematically. One underscores the time mothers save avoiding a visit to the doctor, another focuses on consumer trust of the brand, and still another connects with the embarrassment that people feel when they have warts. Sorting offers an opportunity for the agency to explain its thinking and demonstrate that no stone has been left unturned in the pursuit of creative ideas. Clients find categorization helpful for organizing and evaluating ideas.

When the work is reviewed in the agency's offices, or even while en route to the client's office, the agency team decides which storyboards to recommend. Many marketers field one or more rounds of advertising testing and usually only three to four storyboards will advance to testing; the remainder of the creative work presented is killed in the meeting. Some clients ask that the agency propose a single storyboard for production, which makes the agency recommendation process more difficult. During the internal agency meeting, an account manager may argue for a storyboard that compares a brand directly with a competitor because he or she believes that a senior client desires this approach. An art director–copy writer team may press for an idea that they want to produce for their own portfolios. The creative director may think his or her idea is the most persuasive or so imaginative that it will help the agency win new business. The decision regarding the agency recommendation is usually made jointly by the creative director and the most senior account manager. There will be a top choice, followed by two to three other options.

Meetings with existing clients rarely involve formal rehearsals. The sequence of the storyboard presentation is discussed before the meeting and account managers prepare their "set ups." Senior account managers may telephone their client counterparts to sell them on the quality of the work beforehand. When clients contemplate an upcoming creative meeting, they hope, as one client said, "that the agency has found the Holy Grail, that these guys will tell you how to sell a brand in a way that you have never seen." Agency professionals enter creative meetings with some trepidation. They understand the strategy, the consumer, and the client, but client response to creative work is unpredictable. Agency anxiety derives not only from the looming assessment of their work but also to the clients' impending judgment of the people who created it.

THE MEETING

The men and women who enter the conference room for a creative meeting exchange cordial remarks about family members or weekend activities to ease tension. Senior clients sit near the center of the table, directly across from the agency presenters, and client subordinates take seats on the same side of the table as their bosses. Agency presenters occupy the center positions, directly across from the clients. More senior advertising agency staff often sit to the extreme right or left of center. The meeting, often referred to as a "copy meeting," begins formally when an account manager delivers the "set up," including the meeting objective, which is to review the advertising. The account manager then outlines the anticipated plan for the new creative work. This could include replacing weak advertising, refreshing a successful campaign, or exploring advertising that may succeed current advertising after testing among consumers. The outcome of the meeting is expressed: "When we are in agreement about the strongest approaches, we will conduct focus groups, then field quantitative testing, then place the advertising in a test market, and, if the market test is successful, we will air the new creative nationally." After completing the meeting objectives, an account manager or account planner reads the Creative Brief. The Brief commonly includes:

1. the objective of the advertising;
2. a description of the target market segment to whom the advertising must appeal;
3. insights or observations about the target consumer based on research;
4. the positioning or basic selling proposition for the brand that sets it apart from competition;
5. the core promise that the advertising must make to the consumer to compel purchase;
6. support for the promise that provides to the consumer a reason to believe the promise made;
7. a statement on the tonality of the advertising; and
8. mandatories, or items that must be included in the advertising.

The set up for the meeting conveys that the agency understands the business context, reminds attendees of the strategic blueprint on which the creative work is based, and sets up client expectations by framing the creative work. After the set up is completed, the creative director explains how the creative team undertook the assignment and "explored a wide range of approaches." Creative teams responsible for each idea then expose their ideas to the client. Presenters begin with an explanation of the thinking that took the team from the Creative Brief to the creative execution. For example, a commercial for a nutritional brand might be inspired by an insight that people over 50 want to stay healthy to continue to do the things they have always enjoyed. Creatives often use client buzz words. As one associate creative director said, "When you use their language . . . phrases like 'good recall device'. . . it puts them at ease." The art director describes each storyboard frame, then the copy writer reads the copy. Storyboards are presented one by one in this manner until all of them are exposed. As the storyboards are presented, clients jot down notes based on a mental checklist that makes evaluation of creative work more systematic. Client criteria typically include:

1. Their gut reaction—do they like the idea?
2. Is it consistent with objectives?
3. Is it on strategy?
4. Does it connect with the target consumer?
5. Is it clear?
6. Is it distinctive to the brand?
7. Will it cut through the clutter of other advertisements?

8. Is it competitive?

9. Does it reflect the character of the brand?

10. Is it extendable to a long-term campaign?

11. Are the claims and graphics supportable scientifically and/or legally?

After all of the creative work has been presented, the creative director or a senior account manager summarizes the ideas, groups them into categories, and discusses the storyboards the agency feels have the greatest merit. Agencies never disparage any of the work they present—"We love all of our children equally"—but most clients use the agency recommendation as guidance for their own evaluation, although some clients ignore it. In either case, an agency recommendation provides perspective on the relative strength of the ideas and gives clients time to reflect on the work they have been shown. The agency team has lived with the creative work from inception through several rounds of discussion. As one account manager said, "The agency is intimate with the work. The client is not."

After the agency recommendation has been made, clients offer their reactions to the work. Junior client personnel usually speak first followed by coworkers in ascending rank. Junior staff voice thoughts that correspond to their mental checklist. Senior clients provide more expansive remarks on the fit of the advertising with overall brand business objectives, but even company presidents might comment on a turn of phrase or a product demonstration. During this appraisal, at least one client will express appreciation for the range of thinking and the effort that the agency has expended. This statement is intended to set a positive tone for the ensuing critical comments. Agency professionals know it is mere civility. Some clients prefer to reflect on the creative work, listen to a colleague's comments, and speak only if they have something significant to add, but junior and midlevel clients feel pressure to make cogent remarks. As one client noted, "If you have nothing to contribute, you don't belong in the meeting." A client's career development goals are well served by displaying a grasp of creative concepts and an ability to identify the ideas that have the most potential to grow a brand.

When viewing an array of creative ideas, clients will rarely say, "None of this works; go back to the drawing board." Instead, they declare, "This is an interesting range of ideas," which is code for, "I don't like anything you have shown me." Even when clients reject a storyboard, they may select a phrase or graphic that they encourage the agency to include in the next round of creative development. When clients are responding unfavorably, the hearts of creatives sink, but agency professionals know they must respond to the critique. Not every client comment is addressed. Agencies pay most attention to, as one client phrased it, "the biggest paycheck." Another client said, "Pencils are raised when the senior VP talks." Comments by junior clients are heard, but acted upon only if the most senior client present concurs. When all of the clients have responded, the agency expresses its appreciation for their remarks without appearing sycophantic, answers questions that the client has raised, and challenges criticisms tactfully. The agency recommendation is defended with a balance of conviction and conciliation; the agency must convey that it has a well-reasoned point of view while making it clear that it is receptive to the clients' viewpoint. Agencies differ in how resolute they will be in their defense of creative work. An agency that recommends storyboards A, B, and C over D, E, and F may be told by the senior client that only E is acceptable and another round of creative development is required. Some agencies acquiesce immediately or, in agency parlance, "roll over." Other agencies "push back" until they have convinced the client to accept their argument or they have exhausted all hope that the client can be dissuaded from its own position.

Experienced account managers know the difference between what clients say and what they mean. When a client asks, "Why did you choose that particular graphic?" it is code for "I dislike the graphic." The question format avoids direct conflict. The agency must decide to "fight" for the idea or explain why it chose it and offer to consider alternatives. Account managers, generally more conciliatory than creatives, feel that, as one account manager said, "Creatives would be better off listening and ferreting out the real issues," rather than leaping to the defense of their work.

Senior agency executives feel pressure to sell their work to clients. They may believe in the quality of the creative, but they also want to avoid endless rounds of redevelopment. Account managers take the lead in selling an idea; in addition to their persuasive skills and knowledge of the client's temperament and culture, their personal relationship with a client can help win the agency's case (cf. Moeran 1996:39–68). As they listen to client comments, agency executives consider the source and formulate their response. Does this client want to look smart in front of the boss? Is that client afraid of championing an idea that is outside the threshold of corporate risk? Does he not understand the idea? Does he simply not like it? If a client states that an image campaign is too ethereal and contends that a "slice-of-life" approach would be stronger, and the account manager or creative director knows that this comment is driven by a desire to increase sales quickly with "comfortable" (low risk) creative work, the manager might say, "An image campaign is what our brand needs. If we go this way, we'll be more competitive than ever." Experienced account managers know to stop selling when clients express in tone or intensity that they are closed to further discussion. Moreover, the agency must know how to withdraw gracefully. The client must not be made to feel like a bully; if clients sense that the agency team is beaten down they may request another team within the agency or, worse, consider a new agency. As one creative director phrased it, "A good general knows when to retreat and still retain dignity. You need to be looking to the next meeting, how you will come out in a good position to do better next time." One senior account manager estimated that "You can push clients 10 to 20 percent from where they are, but you will never move them more than 50 percent." When agencies push too hard, frustrated clients may dismiss them because they feel the agency does not understand what they want.

After clients make critical comments, they provide direction to the agency for the next round of creative development. A client will ask that copy be clarified or a product demonstration be simplified. Clear direction is critical. When a client says "I just don't think that tag line works," the agency is not certain what will please the client. When a client says, "I'd like to see a tag line that expresses our brand's superiority over the competition," the agency can craft copy that will be more acceptable in the next round of creative work.

When all of the comments and responses have been voiced, an agency account manager summarizes the agreements reached and the actions that will be taken following the meeting ("Next Steps") along with the timetable for accomplishing them. The happiest outcome for agency and client is to advance the process to focus group assessment or production. A requirement by the client for new creative work or substantial revisions stalls progress. When the former result is achieved, participants congratulate one another and say, "good meeting." Meetings that close without progress are disappointing, but euphemistic phrases such as "Productive meeting" or "We're moving ahead" help mitigate disappointment. Even a "good meeting" may not be good for everyone. Creatives might feel the most conservative work was sold or individual participants may fear they have performed poorly. A meeting succeeds on all fronts when the agency and client concur that the best work was chosen, clients feel they have been listened to, and the agency feels that it, too, has been heard. Everyone smiles and departs knowing that they did their job well. A good meeting means that the agency–client relationship has been preserved and very likely strengthened. When a meeting fails to achieve its stated objectives, agency account managers know that they must telephone their client and reassure them that the next round of work will be better.

AFTER THE MEETING

Minutes after a creative meeting adjourns and the client and agency teams separate, postmortems begin. Clients usually move on quickly to their next task, although there may be a brief conversation about their delight or disappointment in the agency's work. The agency team engages in a more extensive assessment of the meeting, often replaying specific client comments and agency responses. Many account managers feel that an unsatisfactory creative meeting undermines their credibility with the client who may wonder if, as one account manager said, "I have communicated to the creative team what is in the client's head." Creatives must overcome personal demoralization when clients have requested significant changes in their work. As a creative director said, "The advertising will get worse with changes and changes and rewrites and rewrites." One copy writer noted that sometimes "you come back after a meeting and blow off steam. You can't just sit down and start over again until you have done that." After sufficient discussion, account managers review the actions required for the next step in the creative process with the agency team.

UNDERSTANDING CREATIVE MEETINGS: STRUCTURE, SENTIMENT, AND MEETING MANAGEMENT

Despite options like on-line viewing and conference calls, face-to-face advertising creative meetings occur because they allow direct interaction that connects people emotionally as well as intellectually. For agency professionals, creative meetings are ideal venues to sell creative work and enhance client relationships, enabling agencies to better gauge reactions, negotiate with clients, and showcase themselves personally. For clients, the conference room setting is a superior opportunity for personal performance and professional camaraderie. In face-to-face creative meetings, clients can also demonstrate vividly the power and control they have over their agencies.

STATUS AND ROLE

When senior agency executives select flanker positions to the far left or right of the center of the conference table they do so to stress their separateness from other agency staff and to occupy a perch from which to offer commentary during the creative meeting. Their distance from the fray carries other symbolism; it is a vantage point from which they can make the "big picture" statements that demonstrate a mastery of the full business context of the creative work. Seating is also important for agency managers to assess and respond to client reactions, which is why they place themselves within the direct sight line of senior clients.

The sequence and content of client commentary reflect the status and role of the speaker (see Schwartzman 1989:291–293 on social position and speaking sequences in meetings). The lower the status, the earlier one speaks and the more circumspect the comments. Higher-status clients offer their thoughts after lower level managers, giving them the dual advantage of having heard what their colleagues said and additional time to reflect on the creative work.

RULES OF ENGAGEMENT

The agency team is a kind of secret society (Goffman 1959:104) with unwritten rules of engagement in the presence of those outside the society (Meerwarth, Briody, and Devadatta 2005). Internally, as Hirschman (1989:51) observes, "conflict, mutual distrust and power struggles are inherent in the advertising process, but the agency must show a 'united front' to the client" (Kover and Goldberg 1995:55). One of the more egregious sins occurs when an agency representative deviates from the previously agreed upon agency position during a creative meeting. When this agreement is violated, the consequences can be severe. Reprimands of subordinates who diverge from the agency's recommendation are common; cautionary tales tell of employees who transgressed being fired on the return airplane flight after a client meeting. Clients are under less pressure to express a uniform point of view, but most client cultures encourage consensus, and clients know that moving creative work forward requires agreement on the direction they provide to the agency.

READING THE ROOM

Just before a creative meeting, a well-known advertising executive was asked by one of his agency associates what he recommended. His reply: "Read the room." His meaning: assess client reactions as ideas are presented and adjust the agency recommendation to match the ideas that the client will accept. During creative meetings, agency executives do not watch their colleagues present; they watch their clients. They scan faces for confusion, comprehension, and delight. They study eyes and body language. They pay attention to how many notes clients are taking and they watch for client reactions to specific graphics and copy. When the agency summarizes the body of work, when clients comment, when the agency responds and the client counters, agency executives read the room.

Reading the room helps the agency control creative meetings. When a client is perceived as unreceptive to an agency recommendation, an agency executive formulates a defense that shows cognizance of the client's discomfort: "The idea in this board is totally new in this category. It will startle the consumer and it will cut through the clutter of competitive advertising. This approach may make us a bit uncomfortable but it is precisely the kind of advertising the brand needs right now." If the executive senses that the favored board is being judged extremely poorly and even a strong argument will not persuade the client, the executive will cast a glance at colleagues and soften the agency recommendation: "The idea in this board is totally new in this category. It will startle the consumer and it will cut through the clutter of competitive advertising. But, because it is so cutting edge, we should test it among consumers to see if we have gone too far."

One agency creative director described how he visualizes a conference room swaying as arguments veer side to side. He prepares his arguments and chooses a position based on where the room "lands." He may agree or disagree with the prevailing client point of view, but he will choose his statements carefully to ensure that the meeting does not become contentious. The process of reading the room is like comprehending the difference between a wink and a blink (Geertz 1973:6–7). It requires contextual understanding: knowing the psychology of the participants, the strength of the creative work, the corporate cultures, and the relationships of the meeting attendees. The power and accuracy of an individual manager's intuition, of knowing by seeing and listening, is critical.

DEFENDING THE WORK

Clients may criticize creative work because they believe it is off strategy, it fails their checklist of acceptable advertising, or it is inconsistent with "what we know works." A major issue for creative personnel is how to best protect the integrity of their idea when clients feel, as an associate creative director said, that "challenging their beliefs is like challenging their religion." Kover and Goldberg (1995:56–59) describe several strategies that copy writers use to argue for their work, all of which are also applied by art directors and account managers. These tactics include: 1) selling with passion; 2) a frontal attack, which is effective when clients seek highly creative work; 3) creating work that is likely to sell, a risky proposition, as noted earlier; 4) offering the appearance of acceptance, then doing what they wish, which may be effective with small revisions but is not viable when the issue is whether an idea should even be produced; and 5) the "aleatory game," which entails hoping for the best outcome. Experienced agency account managers lower rising temperatures in creative meetings by intervening with phases such as, "That's a good thought. We'll consider that." Agency colleagues and clients depend upon account managers to control meetings; account managers know that an adroit defense of creative work and the ability to defuse difficult situations is a measure of their value.

Although clients often claim they want breakthrough advertising, most clients are nervous that "edgy" creative work will violate the character of their brand, unless the brand character is, by definition, "edgy." Moreover, many creatives feel that clients often "don't get it" when particularly inventive executions are presented, a reaction that Schudson (1984:81) terms "aesthetic insensitivity." Clients' lack of understanding of a creative idea is demonstrated by the common client practice of expressing a wish that selected copy or graphics used in one storyboard also be used in other storyboards. Similarly, when a client feels that an execution has too much humor, the client may ask the agency to "dial it back." As one creative said, "When they change the board, they pull out the one thread that holds it together." Clients' desire for a recitation of a brand's features, attributes, and benefits can snuff out a creative idea. As a creative director said, "The idea gets whittled away by the client's checklist." Clients believe that they own the creative work. When they want changes, the agency should, after discussion, agree to make them. Creatives feel that they, as the inventors of the idea, own it (Hirschman 1989; Kover and Goldberg 1995; Young 2000), which adds tension to creative meetings. As Kover (1995:604) writes, "Copy writers have a 'reputation' in the folklore of the advertising business. They are charged with defending their work and its integrity against any charge, no matter how small." Kover's explanation for this behavior is that "Copy writers do not merely present advertising, they present *themselves*" (Kover 1995:604, emphasis in original). He notes that copy writers speak about their work as if it is "a piece carved from their private being" (ibid.) and Kover and Goldberg (1995:53) remark on the "resentment" that creatives feel when clients alter their work.

How aggressively creatives and account managers defend creative work is contingent upon agency and client cultures. Many clients see challenges to their criticisms as evidence of agency conviction, and they respond positively, as long as the defense is respectful and cordial. Seeing an agency "roll over" when a storyboard is criticized suggests that the agency has little heart for the work, and the client may wonder why the agency presented it. When the agency fights too long and hard, clients become annoyed. Clients also know when agency executives claim, "I agree with everything you have said," they are about to disagree and prolong a discussion. In such situations, clients anticipate that after the meeting they will have a conversation with a senior account manager who will "fix it." If the account manager cannot deliver what the client wants, then that manager risks replacement by one who will. When the choice is between fighting the good fight for the creative work and protecting the agency–client relationship, the latter is the necessary course. Agency executives understand that advertising may be at the intersection of commerce and art, but commerce is the main drag, and clients control the road.

AGREEMENTS

Agreements are the actions that will be taken to revise, test, or produce creative work after a meeting. The word agreement has an egalitarian and conciliatory connotation; it also implies that the client and agency concur on what needs to be done. However, *to agree* does not always mean to be *in agreement*. The recitation of agreements in creative meetings is, in fact, a recitation of client directives. The word agreement fuels the illusion that the client and agency are peers and it smoothes over disagreements that may have occurred during the meetings, but there is no mistake that the clients are in charge.

IMPRESSION MANAGEMENT AND IMPRESSING MANAGEMENT

Presentations by agencies in creative meetings are performances according to Goffman's definition: "all the activity of a given participant on a given occasion which serves to influence in any way the other participants" (Goffman 1959:15) and are "social dramas" (Turner 1974, 1986). As a creative director said, "The spotlight is on you. You have the chance to convince someone that something you have created is worth the world seeing." A central tenet of Goffman's analysis, impression management, is evident throughout creative meetings. Agencies attempt to impress clients with an understanding of the client's business, their devotion to the brand, and their passion for the creative work. An expression of passion can persuade clients that creative work is worthy of acceptance. As a creative director phrased it, "Passion can be contagious." Meeting participants also aim to impress management. Junior clients want to demonstrate to bosses that they are managing the creative development process effectively and, since they know their judgments are being judged, that they bring their share of insights to the meeting. When creative work is received poorly and no progress is made, a midlevel client can "die inside because it makes my life worse. The process is stalled and I'll get slammed." Junior agency personnel want to impress senior staff as well, and all of the agency presenters must impress their clients.

RITES OF PASSAGE

Creative meetings are a rite of passage as classically defined by Van Gennep (1960; Mocran 1996:94). Creative work is separated from its development while in storyboard form; selected ideas are transformed during the meeting by suggested revisions and then returned to the development process for consumer assessment or airing. Creative meetings are the liminal period (Van Gennep 1960:21), "betwixt and between" (Turner 1964; Malefyt 2003:145; Sherry 2005:72–74), during which the transformation occurs. The successful transition of a storyboard from preclient exposure to initiation as a "client approved board" is hailed with as much jubilation as other rites of passage throughout the world. Meeting participants are transformed as well. It is not only the storyboard that is evaluated in creative meetings, it is also the people who created or contributed to the work. Extending the argument from Geertz (1973) that cocks symbolize men and Kover (1995) that storyboards represent copy writers, all of the agency and client personnel who display their imagination, intellect, experience, and professionalism in a creative meeting are as exposed and judged as the advertising ideas. In this sense, approval or disapproval of a body of work and the achievement of goals in creative meetings is not just business. It is personal.

CONCLUSION

Creative meetings are, as Schwartzman notes of all meetings, "sense makers" that help participants "define, represent, and also reproduce social entities and relationships" (Schwartzman 1989:39) and they function as "social and cultural validators" that enhance a sense of community and identity within an organization (Schwartzman 1989:41). Moeran observed this phenomenon in a Japanese advertising agency when he noted that meetings are "frames in which participants made sense of their organization and their actions taken therein" (Moeran 2005:14). Sense-making modes in creative meetings include the comprehension of verbal codes that mollify tense situations, the reading of verbal and nonverbal behavior, the understanding of the subtle machinations surrounding the client–agency balance of power, and the craft of negotiation. Miller (1990), writing about an agency in Trinidad, agrees with Moeran, writing about an agency in Japan, that presentations "define and maintain the advertising community as a whole" (Moeran 1993:88). Schwartzman contends that meetings are organization life "writ small" (Schwartzman 1989:39). Similarly, creative meetings contain the essence of client–agency relationships: conflicting objectives, displays of status, opportunities to show supreme insight, to control without appearing controlling, to demonstrate passion without being combative, to persuade without browbeating, and to accept without embracing. Agencies work hard to preserve creative integrity, but preservation of the client–agency relationship is paramount, for without the relationship, there is no creative presentation.

Despite the conflicts in creative meetings, the confluence of professional and personal objectives makes these meetings a powerful mechanism of action in the advertising industry. They function because they provide a venue for commercial ideas to be challenged and often made stronger, and for participants to achieve goals that secure their positions and advance their careers. In creative development, the agency's desire for art shaped by the demands of commerce meets the clients' need for commerce clothed in seductive art. During creative meetings, the often dazzling fusion of business goals and creativity, and of divergent organizational, attitudinal, and temperamental styles, converge. Some advertising agency executives say, "It's all about the work." Others view their business cynically, as the management of client–agency relationships. Both are correct. The work of the agency is the creative product and the creative meeting itself.

REFERENCES

Ante, Spencer E. 2006. The Science of Desire. *BusinessWeek.* June 6: 99–106.

Della Femina, Jerry. 1970. *From Those Wonderful Folks Who Gave You Pearl Harbor: Front-line Dispatches from the Advertising War*, ed. Charles Sopkin. New York: Simon and Schuster.

Denny, Rita. 1999. Consuming Values: The Culture of Clients, Researchers and Consumers. In *The Race for Innovation*, 375–384. Amsterdam: ESOMAR.

Geertz, Clifford. 1973. *The Interpretation of Cultures*. New York: Basic Books.

Goffman, Erving. 1959. *The Presentation of Self in Everyday Life*. New York: Doubleday.

_____. 1974. *Frame Analysis*. Cambridge, Mass.: Harvard University Press.

Henry, Jules. 1963. *Culture Against Man*. New York: Random House.

Hirschman, Elizabeth C. 1989. Role-Based Models of Advertising Creative and Production. *Journal of Advertising* 18(4): 42–53.

Inglessis, Maria Garcia. 2006. For Marketers or Scholars? *Quirk's Marketing Research Review*, December: 58–62.

Johnson, Steve. 2006. The Rational and Emotional "Tells" to Get the Most from Agency Presentations. *Product Management Today*. January: 26–27.

Kemper, Steven. 2003. How Advertising Makes its Object. In *Advertising Cultures*, eds. Timothy Dewaal Malefyt and Brian Moeran, 35–54. Oxford and New York: Berg.

Kover, Arthur J. 1995. Copywriters' Implicit Theories of Communications: An Exploration. *Journal of Consumer Research* 21: 596–611.

Kover, Arthur J. and Stephen M. Goldberg. 1995. The Games Copywriters Play: Conflict, Quasi-Control, a New Proposal. *Journal of Advertising Research*, July/August: 52–62.

Lasch, Christopher. 1979. *The Culture of Narcissism*. New York: W. W. Norton & Company.

Louis J. C. 1985. It's Anthropological: Research Takes a "Cultural" Bent. *Advertising Age*, January 14: 3:31.

Malefyt, Timothy Dewaal. 2003. Models, Metaphors and Client Relations: The Negotiated Meanings of Advertising. In *Advertising Cultures*, eds. Timothy Dewaal Malefyt and Brian Moeran, 139–163. New York: Berg.

Malefyt, Timothy Dewaal, and Brian Moeran, eds. 2003. *Advertising Cultures*. New York: Berg.

Mazzarella, William T. S. 2003. *Shoveling Smoke: Advertising and Globalization in Contemporary India*. Durham, N.C.: Duke University Press.

Meerwarth, Tracy L., Elizabeth K. Briody, and Devadatta M. Kulkarni. 2005. Discovering the Rules: Folk Knowledge for Improving GM Partnerships. *Human Organization*, 64: 286–302.

Michell, Paul C. N., and Nicholas H. Sanders. 1995. Loyalty in Agency-Client Relations: The Impact of the Organizational Context. *Journal of Advertising Research*, March/April: 9–14.

Miller, Annetta. 1990. You Are What You Buy. *Newsweek*, June 4: 59.

Miller, Daniel. 1997. *Capitalism: An Ethnographic Approach*. New York: Berg.

_____. 2003. Advertising, Production and Consumption as Cultural Economy. In *Advertising Cultures*, eds. Timothy Dewaal Malefyt and Brian Moeran, 75–89. Oxford and New York: Berg.

Moeran, Brian. 1993. A Tournament of Value: Strategies of Presentation in Japanese Advertising. *Ethnos* 54: 73–93.

_____. 1996. *A Japanese Advertising Agency*. Honolulu: University of Hawaii Press.

_____. 2005. *The Business of Ethnography: Strategic Exchanges, People and Organizations*. New York: Berg.

Monari, Gina-Louise. 2005. Anthropology: Not Just for Academia. *MedAdNews*, August: 1, 28.

Murphy, Richard McGill. 2005. Getting to Know You. *Fortune Small Business*, June, 41–46.

Reinharz, Shulamit. 1988. *On Becoming a Social Scientist*. Piscataway, N.J: Transaction Books.

Sanders, Elizabeth. 2002. How "Applied Ethnography" Can Improve Your NPD Research Process. *PDMA Visions* 26(2): 8–11.

Schudson, Michael. 1984. *Advertising, The Uneasy Persuasion*. New York: Basic Books.

Schwartzman, Helen. 1989. *The Meeting*. New York: Plenum Press.

Sherry, John. 1987. Advertising as a Cultural System. In *Marketing and Semiotics: New Directions in the Study of Signs for Salc*, ed. Jean Umiker-Sebeok, 441–461. Berlin: Mouton de Gruyter.

_____. 2003. Foreword: A Word from Our Sponsor—Anthropology. In *Advertising Cultures*, eds. Timothy Dewaal Malefyt and Brian Moeran, xi–xiii. New York: Berg.

_____. 2005. We Might Never Be Post-Sacred: A Tribute to Russell Belk on the Occasion of His Acceptance of the Converse Award. In *16th Paul D. Converse Symposium*, eds. Abbie Griffin and Cele C. Otnes, 67–77. Chicago: American Marketing Association.

Steel, Jon. 1998. *Truth, Lies, and Advertising*. New York: John Wiley & Sons.

TNS Media Intelligence, February 2006. (Industry Report).

Turner, Victor W. 1964. Betwixt and Between: The Liminal Period in Rites de Passage. The Proceedings of the American Ethnological Society, Symposium on New Approaches to the Study of Religion. Pp. 4–20. Washington, D.C.: U.S. Government Printing Office.

_____. 1974. *Dramas, Fields and Metaphors*. Ithaca, N.Y.: Cornell University Press.

_____. 1986. *The Anthropology of Performance*. New York: PAJ Publications.

Turow, Joseph. 1984. *Media Industries: The Production of News and Entertainment*. New York: Longman.

Underhill, Paco. 2000. *Why We Buy*. New York: Touchstone.

Van Gennep, Arnold. 1960. *The Rites of Passage*. Chicago: University of Chicago Press.

Wasserman, Todd. 2003. Watch and Learn. *Adweek*, November 3: 21–22.

Wellner, Alison Stein. 2002. Watch Me Now. *American Demographics*, October: S1–S5.

Young, Charles E. 2000. Creative Differences Between Copy Writers and Art Directors. *Journal of Advertising Research*, May/June: 19–26.

27

Law, Custom, and Crimes against Women

The Problem of Dowry Death in India

John van Willigen and V. C. Channa

Anthropologists find many societies with unusual customs, beliefs, and behaviors. Usually they discover, after careful study and reflection, that these customs perform some useful function within the society, as in the case of polyandry discussed in Selection 4. But is this always the case? Must we assume that simply because a custom exists it is healthy for the members of society? We think not, and the Christians who were fed to lions and the Aztec slaves who were sacrificed to a bloodthirsty god would most likely agree.

Times change; hunters and gatherers plant crops, tribal people rush headlong into peasantry, and small-scale farmers become urban wage earners. Traditions that helped maintain a healthy society in one context may become dysfunctional in another. For better or worse, traditions and beliefs run deep and are almost impossible to unlearn. It is the nature of culture to resist change.

As you will read, the practice of dousing a bride with kerosene and setting her on fire is a horrific example of a traditional dowry system that has gone completely awry. That said, what can be done? Laws, even those that carry serious penalties, are light ammunition against the armor of strongly held cultural beliefs. Governments will solve such problems only through public policy based on in-depth cultural understanding.

As you read this selection, ask yourself the following questions:

- What do you think the authors mean when they suggest that dowry death presents a problem for ethnologists because of ethnological theory's functional cast?

- Why does the institution of dowry make college education problematic for some young women?

- What are the present-day approaches to solving the dowry death problem?

- How can women's access to production roles and property, delocalization of social control, and economic transformation affect the problem of dowry death?

- Dowry-related violence in India is related to a particular socio-cultural perspective on the economic value of women. What might be said about the relationship between the economic position and the social status of women in America?

The following terms discussed in this selection are included in the Glossary at the back of the book:

caste	ethnology
cultural materialism	peasants
demography	sex roles
dowry	

A 25-year-old woman was allegedly burnt to death by her husband and mother-in-law at their East Delhi home yesterday. The housewife, Mrs. Sunita, stated before her death at the Jaya Prakash Narayana Hospital that members of her husband's family had been harassing her for bringing inadequate dowry.

The woman told the Shahdara subdivisional magistrate that during a quarrel over dowry at their Pratap Park house yesterday, her husband gripped her from behind while the mother-in-law poured kerosene over her clothes.

Her clothes were then set ablaze. The police have registered a case against the victim's husband, Suraj Prakash, and his mother.

—Times of India, February 19, 1988

van Willigen, John & Channa, V. C. "Law, Custom, and Crimes against Women: The Problem of Dowry Death in India." Reproduced by permission of the Society for Applied Anthropology (SfAA) from *Human Organization* 50, no. 4 (1991):369–377.

This routinely reported news story describes what in India is termed a "bride-burning" or "dowry death." Such incidents are frequently reported in the newspapers of Delhi and other Indian cities. In addition, there are cases in which the evidence may be ambiguous, so that deaths of women by fire may be recorded as kitchen accidents, suicides, or murders. Dowry violence takes a characteristic form. Following marriage and the requisite giving of dowry, the family of the groom makes additional demands for the payment of more cash or the provision of more goods. These demands are expressed in unremitting harassment of the bride, who is living in the household of her husband's parents, culminating in the murder of the woman by members of her husband's family or by her suicide. The woman is typically burned to death with kerosene, a fuel used in pressurized cook stoves, hence the use of the term "bride-burning" in public discourse.

Dowry death statistics appear frequently in the press and parliamentary debates. Parliamentary sources report the following figures for married women 16 to 30 years of age in Delhi: 452 deaths by burning for 1985; 478 for 1986 and 300 for the first six months of 1987 (Bhatia 1988). There were 1,319 cases reported nationally in 1986 (*Times of India*, January 10, 1988). Police records do not match hospital records for third degree burn cases among younger married women; far more violence occurs than the crime reports indicate (Kumari 1988).

There is other violence against women related both directly and indirectly to the institution of dowry. For example, there are unmarried women who commit suicide so as to relieve their families of the burden of providing a dowry. A recent case that received national attention in the Indian press involved the triple suicide of three sisters in the industrial city of Kanpur. A photograph was widely published showing the three young women hanging from ceiling fans by their scarves. Their father, who earned about 4,000 Rs. [rupees] per month, was not able to negotiate marriage for his oldest daughter. The grooms were requesting approximately 100,000 Rs. Also linked to the dowry problem is selective female abortion made possible by amniocentesis. This issue was brought to national attention with a startling statistic reported out of a seminar held in Delhi in 1985. Of 3,000 abortions carried out after sex determination through amniocentesis, only one involved a male fetus. As a result of these developments, the government of the state of Maharashtra banned sex determination tests except those carried out in government hospitals.

The phenomenon of dowry death presents a difficult problem for the ethnologist. Ethnological theory, with its residual functionalist cast, still does not deal effectively with the social costs of institutions of what might be arguably referred to as custom gone bad, resulting in a culturally constituted violence syndrome.

This essay examines dowry and its violent aspects, and some of the public solutions developed to deal with it in India. Our work consists of a meta-analysis of some available literature. We critique the legal mechanisms established to regulate the cultural institution of dowry and the resultant social evils engendered by the institution, and argue that policies directed against these social evils need to be constructed in terms of an underlying cause rather than of the problem itself. We consider cause, an aspect of the problem infrequently discussed in public debate. As Saini asserts, "legal academicians have shown absolutely no interest in the causal roots of dowry as practiced in contemporary India" (1983:143).

THE INSTITUTION

Since ancient times, the marriage of Hindus has required the transfer of property from the family of the bride to the family of the groom. Dowry or *daan dehej* is thought by some to be sanctioned by such religious texts as the *Manusmriti*. Seen in this way, dowry is a religious obligation of the father of a woman and a matter of *dharma* (religious duty) whereby authority over a woman is transferred from her father to her husband. This transfer takes different forms in different communities in modern India (Tambiah 1973). In public discussion, the term "dowry" covers a wide range of traditional payments and expenses, some presented to the groom's family and others to be retained by the bride. Customs have changed through time. The financial burdens of gifts and the dowry payments per se are exacerbated by the many expenses associated with the marriage celebration itself, but dowry payment is especially problematic because of its open-ended nature. As Tambiah notes, "marriage payments in India usually comprise an elaborate series of payments back and forth between the marrying families" and "this series extends over a long period of time and persists after marriage" (1973:92). Contemporary cases, such as the death of Mrs. Sunita, often revolve around such continued demands.

A daughter's marriage takes a long time to prepare and involves the development of an adaptive strategy on the part of her family. An important part of the strategy is the preparation for making dowry payments; family consumption may be curtailed so as to allow accumulation of money for dowry. Seeing to marriage arrangements may be an important aspect of retirement planning. The dowries that the family receives on behalf of their sons may be "rolled over" to deal with the daughter's requirements. Families attempt to cultivate in both their sons and daughters attributes that will make them more attractive in marriage negotiations. Many things besides dowry are considered in negotiations: "non-economic" factors have demonstrable effect on the expectations for dowry and the family's strategy concerning the dowry process.

Education is a variable to be considered in the negotiation process. Education of young women is somewhat problematic because suitable husbands for such women must also be college educated. The parents of such young men demand more dowry for their sons. A consideration in sending a young woman to college will therefore be her parents' capacity to dower her adequately so as to obtain an appropriate groom. In any case, education is secondary to a man's earning power and the reputation of a woman's family. Education is, however, important in the early stages of negotiation because of the need to coordinate the level of the education of the men and women. Education qualifications are also less ambiguously defined than other dimensions of family reputation. Physical attractiveness is a consideration, but it is thought somewhat unseemly to emphasize this aspect of the decision.

Advertisements in newspapers are used for establishing marriage proposals (Aluwalia 1969, Niehoff 1959, Weibe and Ramu 1971), but contacts are more typically established through kin and other networks. Some marriages may be best termed "self-arranged," and are usually called "love marriages." In these cases, young men and women may develop a relationship independent of their families and then ask that negotiations be carried out on their behalf by family representatives.

Analysis of matrimonial advertisements shows some of the attributes considered to be important. Listed in such advertisements are education, age, income and occupation, physical attributes, *gotra* (a kind of unilineal descent group) membership, family background, place of residence, personality features, consideration of dowry, time and type of marriage, and language.

Consideration of dowry and other expenditures are brought out early in the negotiations and can serve as a stumbling block. Dowry negotiations can go on for some time. The last stage is the actual "seeing of the groom" and the "seeing of the bride," both rather fleeting encounters whose position at the end of the process indicates their relative lack of importance.

Marriage is a process by which two families mutually evaluate each other. The outcome of the negotiations is an expression of the relative worth of the two persons, a man and a woman, and, by extension, the worth of their respective families. This estimation of worth is expressed in marriage expenditures, of which dowry is but a part. There are three possible types of expenditures: cash gifts, gifts of household goods, and expenditures on the wedding celebration itself. The cash gift component of the dowry goes to the groom's father and comes to be part of his common household fund. The household goods are for use by the groom's household, although they may be used to establish a separate household for the newlyweds. When separate accommodations are not set up, the groom's family may insist that the goods do not duplicate things they already have.

Dates for marriages are set through consideration of horoscopes; horoscopy is done by professional astrologers *(pandits)*. This practice leads to a concentration of marriage dates and consequent high demand for marriage goods and services at certain times of the year. During marriage seasons, the cost of jewelry, furniture, clothes, musicians' services, and other marriage related expenditures goes up, presumably because of the concentration of the demand caused by the astrologers.

The expenditures required of the woman's family for the wedding in general and the dowry in particular are frequently massive. Paul reports, for a middle-class Delhi neighborhood, that most dowries were over 50,000 Rs. (1986). Srinivas comments that dowries over 200,000 Rs. are not uncommon (1984).[1]

ETHNOLOGICAL THEORIES ABOUT DOWRY

Dowry had traditionally been discussed by ethnologists in the context of the functionalist paradigm, and much theorizing about dowry appears to be concerned with explaining the "contribution" that the institution makes to social adaptation. The early theoretician Westermarck interpreted dowry as a social marker of the legitimacy of spouse and offspring, and as a mechanism for defining women's social roles and property rights in the new household (Westermarck 1921:428). Murdock suggests that dowry may confirm the contract of marriage (1949). Dowry is interpreted by Friedl as a means to adjust a woman to her affinal home as it rearranges social relationships including the social separation of the man from his parents (1967). Dowry payments are public expressions of the new relationship between the two families, and of the social status of the bride and groom.

Dowry is seen in the social science literature as a kind of antemortem or anticipated inheritance by which a widow is assured of support, and provision for her offspring (Friedl 1967; Goody 1973, 1976). It transfers money to where the women will be and where they will reproduce; as a result, resources are also placed where the children will benefit, given the practice of patrilineal inheritance of immovable, economically valuable property like farm land.

In India, dowry is also seen as an expression of the symbolic order of society. According to Dumont, dowry expresses the hierarchal relations of marriage in India and lower status of the bride (Dumont 1957). The amount of dowry given is an expression of prestige. The capacity to buy prestige through dowry increases the potential for social mobility (Goody 1973). Dowry is a kind of delayed consumption used to demonstrate or improve social rank (Epstein 1960).

There is a significant discontinuity between discussions of dowry in the ethnological theory and in public discourse. Certainly the dowry problem does appear in the writing of contemporary ethnologists, but it is simply lamented and left largely uninterpreted and unexplained.

THE EXTANT SOLUTIONS TO THE PROBLEM

The Dowry Prohibition Act of 1961, as amended in 1984 and 1986, is the primary legal means for regulating the dowry process and controlling its excesses. The laws against dowry are tough. Dowry demand offenses are "cognizable" (require no warrant) and nonbailable, and the burden of proof is on the accused. There are, in fact, convictions under the law.

The act defines dowry as "any property of valuable security given or agreed to be given either directly or indirectly—(a) by one party to a marriage to the other party to a marriage; or (b) by parents of either party to a marriage or by any other person, to either party to the marriage or to any other person" (Government of India 1986:1). The act makes it illegal to give or take dowry, "If any person after the commencement of this act, gives or takes or abets the giving or taking of dowry, he shall be punishable with imprisonment for a term which shall not be less than five years; and with fine which shall not be less than fifteen thousand rupees or the amount of the value of such dowry which ever is more" (Government of India 1986:1). While this section unambiguously prohibits dowry, the third section allows wedding presents to be freely given. Thus the law does not apply to "presents which are given at the time of marriage to the bride (without demand having been made in that behalf)" (Government of India 1986:1). Identical provisions apply to the groom. Furthermore, all such presents must be listed on a document before the consummation of the marriage. The list is to contain a brief description and estimation of the value of the gifts, name of presenting person, and the relationship that person has with the bride and groom. This regulation also provides "that where such presents are made by or on the behalf of the bride or any other person related to the bride, such presents are of a customary nature and the value thereof is not excessive having regard to the financial status of the person by whom, or on whose behalf, such presents

are given" (Government of India 1986:2). Amendments made in 1984 make it illegal for a person to demand dowry with the same penalty as under the earlier "giving and taking" provision. It was also declared illegal to advertise for dowry, such an offense being defined as not bailable, with the burden of proof on the accused person.

This legislation was coupled with some changes in the Indian Penal Code that legally established the concept of "dowry death." That is, "where the death of a woman is caused by any burns or bodily injury or occurs otherwise than under normal circumstances within seven years of her marriage and it is shown that soon before her death she was subjected to cruelty or harassment by her husband or any relative of her husband for, or in connection with, any demand for dowry, such death shall be called 'dowry death,' and such husband or relative shall be deemed to have caused her death" (Government of India 1987:4). The Indian Evidence Act of 1871 was changed so as to allow for the presumption of guilt under the circumstances outlined above. Changes in the code allowed for special investigation and reporting procedures of deaths by apparent suicide of women within seven years of marriage if requested by a relative. There were also newly defined special provisions for autopsies.

To this point, however, these legal mechanisms have proved ineffective. According to Sivaramayya, the "act has signally failed in its operation" (1984:66). Menon refers to the "near total failure" of the law (1988:12). A similar viewpoint is expressed by Srinivas, who wrote, "The Dowry Prohibition Act of 1961 has been unanimously declared to be an utterly ineffective law" (1984:29).

In addition to the legal attack on dowry abuses, numerous public groups engage in public education campaigns. In urban settings, the most noteworthy of these groups are specialized research units such as the Special Cell for Women of the Tata Institute of Social Sciences (Bombay), and the Center for Social Research (New Delhi). Also involved in the effort are private voluntary organizations such as the Crimes Against Women Cell, Karmika, and Sukh Shanti.

These groups issue public education advertising on various feminist issues. The anti-dowry advertisement of the Federation of Indian Chambers of Commerce and Industry Ladies Organization exemplifies the thrust of these campaigns. In the following advertisement, which was frequently run in the winter of 1988 in newspapers such as the *Times of India,* a photograph of a doll dressed in traditional Indian bridal attire was shown in flames.

> Every time a young bride dies because of dowry demands, we are all responsible for her death. Because we allow it to happen. Each year in Delhi hospitals

alone, over 300 brides die of third degree burns. And many more deaths go unreported. Most of the guilty get away. And we just shrug helplessly and say, "what can we do?" We can do a lot.

Help create social condemnation of dowry. Refuse to take or give dowry. Protest when you meet people who condone the practice. Reach out and help the girl being harassed for it. Act now.

Let's fight it together.

As parents, bring up educated, self-reliant daughters. Make sure they marry only after 18. Oppose dowry; refuse to even discuss it. If your daughter is harassed after marriage stand by her.

As young men and women, refuse marriage proposals where dowry is being considered. As friends and neighbors, ostracize families who give or take dowry. Reach out to help victims of dowry harassment.

As legislators and jurists, frame stronger laws. Ensure speedy hearings, impose severe punishments. As associations, give help and advice. Take up the challenge of changing laws and attitudes of society. Let us all resolve to fight the evil. If we fight together we can win.

SAY NO TO DOWRY.

Also engaged in anti-dowry work are peasant political action groups such as Bharatiya Kisan Union (BKU). BKU consists of farmers from western Uttar Pradesh whose political program is focused more generally on agricultural issues. The group sponsored a massive 25-day demonstration at Meerut, Uttar Pradesh, in 1988. The leadership used the demonstration to announce a social reform program, most of it dealing with marriage issues. According to news service reports, "The code of social reforms includes fixing the maximum number of persons in a marriage party at 11, no feasts relating to marriage, and no dowry except 10 grams of gold and 30 grams of silver" (*Times of India*, February 11, 1988). Buses plying rural roads in western Uttar Pradesh are reported to have been painted with the slogan "The bride is the dowry." Private campaigns against dowry occur in the countryside as well as among the urban elites, although it is likely that the underlying motivations are quite different.

POLICY ANALYSIS

Our argument is based on the assumption that social problems are best dealt with by policies directed at the correction of causative factors, rather than at the amelioration of symptoms. While current legal remedies directly confront dowry violence, the linkage between cause and the problematic behavior is not made. Here we develop an argument consisting of three components: women's access to production

roles and property; delocalization of social control; and economic transformation of society. The pattern of distribution of aspects of the institution of dowry and its attendant problems is important to this analysis. Although dowry practices and the related crimes against women are distributed throughout Indian society, the distribution is patterned in terms of geography, caste rank, socioeconomic rank, urban/rural residence, and employment status of the women. In some places and among some people there is demonstrably more violence, more intensity of dowry practices, and more commitment to dowry itself. Much of the distributional data are problematic in one way or another. The most frequent problem is that the studies are not based on national samples. Furthermore, the interpretation of results is often colored by reformist agendas. There is a tendency to deemphasize differences in frequency from one segment of the population to another so as to build support of dowry death as a general social reform issue. Nevertheless, while the data available for these distributions are of inconsistent quality, they are interpretable in terms of our problem.

Women's Access to Production Roles and Property

Dowry violence is most frequent in north India. Some say that it is an especially severe problem in the Hindi Belt (i.e., Uttar Pradesh, Haryana, Punjab, Delhi, Bihar) (Government of India 1974:75). It is a lesser, albeit increasing problem in the south. There is also a north/south difference in the marriage institution itself. To simplify somewhat, in the north hypergamy is sought after in marriage alliances, in which case brides seek grooms from higher rank descent groups within their caste group (Srinivas 1984). In the south, marriages are more typically isogamous.

The literature comparing north and south India indicates important contrasts at both the ecological and the institutional levels. Based on conceptions developed by Boserup (1970) in a cross-cultural comparative framework on the relationship between the farming system and occupational role of women, Miller (1981) composed a model for explaining the significant north-south differences in the juvenile sex ratio [the ratio of males to females ten years of age and below]. The farming systems of the north are based on "dry-field plow cultivation," whereas in the south the farming systems are dominated by "swidden and wet-rice cultivation" (Miller 1981:28). These two systems make different labor demands. In the wet rice or swidden systems of the south, women are very important sources of labor. In the north, women's involvement in agricultural production is limited.

According to Miller, women in the north are excluded from property holding and receive instead a "dowry of movables." In the south, where women are included in the production activities, they may receive "rights to land" (Miller 1981:28). In the north, women are high-cost items of social overhead, while in the south, women contribute labor and are more highly valued. In the north there is a "high cost of raising several daughters" while in the south there is "little liability in raising several daughters." There is thus "discrimination against daughters" and an "intense preference for sons" in the north, and "appreciation for daughters" and "moderate preference for sons" in the south. Miller thus explains the unbalanced-toward-males juvenile sex ratios of the north and the balanced sex ratios of the south (Miller 1981:27–28). The lower economic value of women in the north is expressed in differential treatment of children by sex. Females get less food, less care, and less attention, and therefore they have a higher death rate. In general the Boserup and Miller economic argument is consistent with Engels's thesis about the relationship between the subordination of women and property (Engels 1884, Hirschon 1984:1).

Miller extended her analysis of juvenile sex ratios to include marriage costs (including dowry), female labor participation, and property owning, and found that property owning was associated with high marriage costs and low female labor force participation, both of which were associated with high juvenile sex ratios. That is, the death rate of females is higher when marriage costs are high and women are kept from remunerative employment. Both of these patterns are associated with the "propertied" segment of the population (Miller 1981:156–159). Her data are derived from the secondary analysis of ethnographic accounts. The literature concerning the distribution of dowry practices and dowry death is consistent with these results.

Miller's analysis shows a general pattern of treatment of females in India. Their access to support in various forms is related to their contribution to production (Miller 1981). This analysis does not explain the problem of dowry violence, but it does demonstrate a fundamental pattern within which dowry violence can be interpreted.

The distribution of dowry varies by caste. In her study of dowry violence victims in Delhi, Kumari found that members of the lower ranking castes report less "dowry harassment" than do those in higher ranking castes (Kumari 1988:31). These results are consistent with Miller's argument since the pattern of exclusion of women from economic production roles varies by caste. Women of lower castes are less subject to restrictions concerning employment outside the realm

of reproduction within the household. These women are often poor and uneducated, and are subject to other types of restrictions.

In the framework of caste, dowry practices of higher caste groups are emulated by lower caste groups. This process is known as "Sanskritization" and it may relate to the widely held view that dowry harassment is increasing in lower ranking castes. Sanskritization is the process by which lower ranked caste groups attempt to raise their rank through the emulation of higher rank castes. The emulation involves discarding certain behaviors (such as eating meat or paying bride price) and adopting alternatives (Srinivas 1969). Attitudinal research shows that people of the lower socio-economic strata have a greater commitment to dowry than do those of higher strata (Hooja 1969, Khanna and Verghese 1978, Paul 1986). Although the lower and middle classes are committed to dowry, the associated violence, including higher death rates, is more typically a middle class problem (Kumari 1988).

Employment status of women has an effect on dowry. In her survey of dowry problems in a south Delhi neighborhood, Paul (1986) found that the amount of dowry was less for employed middle class women than it was for the unemployed. This pattern is also suggested by Verghese (1980) and van der Veen (1972:40), but disputed by others (Murickan 1975). This link is also manifested among tribal people undergoing urbanization. Tribal people, ranked more toward the low end of the social hierarchy, typically make use of bride price (i.e., a payment to the bride's family) rather than dowry (Karve 1953). As these groups become more integrated into national life, they will shift to dowry practices to emulate high castes while their women participate less in gainful employment (Luthra 1983). Croll finds a similar relationship in her analysis of post-revolutionary China. She says, "it is the increased value attributed to women's labor which is largely responsible for the decline in the dowry" (1984:58).

Both Kumari (1988) and Srinivas (1984) developed arguments based on non-economic factors. Kumari in effect indicated that if dowry could be explained in economic terms, marriage would be simply a calculation of the value of a woman: if the value were high, bride price would be paid, and if the value were low, dowry transactions would occur. This formulation was presented as a refutation of Madan's dowry-as-compensation argument (Kumari 1988). We agree that reducing this practice to purely economic terms is an absurdity. The argument is not purely economic, but it is certainly consistent with a cultural materialist perspective (Harris 1979) in which symbolic values are shaped by an underlying material relationship that is the basis for the construction of cultural reality.

Delocalization of Social Control

Dowry violence is more frequent in cities (Saini 1983). Delhi has the reputation of having a high frequency of problems of dowry (Srinivas 1984:7). The urban-rural distribution pattern may be a manifestation of the effects of the delocalization of dowry. Dowry, when operative in the relationships among local caste groups in related villages, was to an extent self-regulating through caste *panchayats* (councils) and by the joint families themselves. These groups easily reach into peoples' lives. By contrast, the national level laws have inadequate reach and cannot achieve regulation. While in some areas caste groups continue to function to limit abuses, these groups are less effective in urban settings. Population movements and competition with state level social control mechanisms limit the effectiveness of self-regulation. A government commission study of women's status argues "that because of changed circumstances in which a son generally has a separate establishment and has a job somewhere away from home, the parents cannot expect much help from him, and so they consider his marriage as the major occasion on which their investment in his education can be recovered" (Government of India 1974:74). These views are consistent with the research results reported by Paul, who demonstrates that dowry amounts are higher among people who have migrated to Delhi and those who live in nuclear families, because the families in general and the women in particular are less subject to social constraints (Paul 1986). New brides do not seem to have adequate support networks in urban settings.

Economic Transformation of Society

The custom of dowry has been thrown into disarray by inflationary pressures. The consumer price index for urban non-manual workers has increased from its reference year of 1960 value of 100 to 532 for 1984–85 (Government of India 1987). The media of dowry exchange have changed dramatically because of the increasing availability of consumer goods. It has become increasingly difficult to prepare for giving dowry for a daughter or a sister. Sharma argues that, in part, dowry problems are caused by rapid change in the nature of consumer goods which made it no longer possible to accumulate gift goods over a long period as the latest styles in material goods could not be presented (1984:70–71).

The current regime of individual dowry seeking and giving is constituted as a kind of rational behavior. That is, it is achieved through choice, is consistent with certain values, and serves to increase someone's utility. There are a number of things sought

by the groom's family in these transactions. Wealth and family prestige are especially important. The family prestige "bought" with marriage expenditures, which is relevant to both the bride and groom's side in the transaction, is no doubt very much worth maximizing in the Indian context. From the perspective of the bride's family, dowry payments involve trading present consumption for future earning power for their daughter through acquiring a groom with better qualities and connections. In a two-tier, gender segregated, high unemployment, inflationary economy such as that of India, one can grasp the advantage of investing in husbands with high future earning potential. It is also possible to argue that in societies with symbolic mechanisms of stratification, it is expected that persons will attempt to make public displays of consumption in order to improve their overall performance and so to take advantage of the ambiguities of the status hierarchy system. The demand for both symbolic goods and future earnings is highly elastic. Family connections, education, and wealth seem especially important in India, and they all serve as hedges against inflation and poverty. With women having limited access to jobs and earning lower pay, it is rational to invest in a share of the groom's prospects. If you ask people why they give dowry when their daughters are being married they say, "because we love them." On the other hand, grooms' families will find the decision to forgo dowry very difficult.

SUMMARY

The distributional data indicate that the relationship between the way females are treated in marriage and their participation in economic production is consistent with Miller's development of the Boserup hypothesis. It is assumed that the pattern of maltreatment of females has been subject to various controls operating at the levels of family, caste, and community. Urbanization reduces the effectiveness of these mechanisms, thus increasing the intensity of the problem. This trend is exacerbated by the economic transformations within contemporary Indian society. It is our viewpoint that policies developed to reduce dowry-related violence will fail if they do not increase the economic value of women.

The criminalization of dowry may have been a politically useful symbol, but it has not curtailed the practice. As dowry is attacked, the state has not adequately dealt with the ante-mortem inheritance aspect of the custom. If dowry continues to provide a share of the family wealth to daughters before the death of the parents, then legally curtailing the practice is likely to damage the economic interests of women in the name of protecting them. One might argue that the primary legal remedy for the dowry problem actually makes it worse because it limits the transfer of assets to women. Perhaps this is why research on attitudes toward dowry indicates a continued positive commitment to the institution (Mathew 1987). India is a society in which most people (most particularly the elite) have given and received dowry; most people are even today giving and taking dowries. Declaring dowry a crime creates a condition in which the mass of society are technically criminals. The moral-legal basis of society suffers, and communal, parochial, and other fissiparous forces are encouraged.

To be effective, anti-dowry legislation must make sure that the social utility provided by dowry practices be displaced to practices that are less problematic, and that the apparent causes of the practice be attacked. To do so would mean that attempts to eradicate the social evils produced by the dowry institution need to be based on an examination of women's property rights so as to increase their economic access. Traditional Hindu customs associated with inheritance give sons the right from birth to claim the so-called ancestral properties. This principle is part of the Mitakshara tradition of Hindu law, which prevails throughout India except in Bengal, Kerala, Assam, and northern parts of Orissa. These properties are obtained from father, paternal grandfather, or paternal great-grandfather. According to Sivaramayya (1984:71), "The Hindu Succession Act (the law which controls inheritance) did not abrogate this right by birth which exists in favor of a son, paternal grandson and paternal great grandson. The availability of the right in favor of these male descendants only is a discrimination against daughters." The right is derived from ancient texts. According to Tambiah (1973:95), the Dharmasastras provide that it is "essentially males who inherit the patrimony while women are entitled to maintenance, marriage expenses and gifts." While the Hindu Succession Act abrogates much traditional law, it specifically accepts the principle of male birthright to the property of the joint family. That is, "When a male Hindu dies after the commencement of the Act, having at the time of death an interest in a Mitakshara coparcenary property, his interest in the property shall devolve by survivorship upon the surviving members of the coparcenary and not in accordance with this Act" (Government of India 1985:3). The Hindu Succession Act in its most recent form provides for the intestate or testamentary inheritance of a female of a share of the family property. Yet the prior right of males at birth is not abrogated. Hindu males own a share of the family rights at birth; females can inherit it. Testamentary succession overrides the principle of intestate succession, and therefore the interests of females can be usurped simply by writing a will. The other procedures for a female to renounce an interest in family property are very simple. Moreover, according to Sivaramayya (1984:58), "no specific formality is required for the relinquishment of the interest beyond the expression of a clear intention to that effect." Instruments of relinquishment can be and are forged.

The ante-mortem inheritance function of dowry has been eroded or perhaps supplanted by transfer of goods to the groom's family for their consumption and the expression of the so-called prestige of the family. Indeed social science commentary on dowry in India suggests that this aspect of dowry is relatively unimportant in any case because only a small portion of the total marriage expenditure is under the bride's control. There is evidence that even the clothing and ornaments and other personal property of the bride are being usurped (Verghese 1980). Implementation of a gender-neutral inheritance law as advocated by the Government of India Committee on the Status of Women may serve to increase the economic value of women in general, while it serves as an alternative to the ante-mortem inheritance aspect of dowry. Since dowry constitutes a kind of ante-mortem inheritance, it is logical to change the inheritance laws in conjunction with the restrictions on dowry behavior. Sisters as well as brothers need to have a share in the family wealth from birth, and that right should be associated with legal procedures that increase the difficulty of alienation of property rights. There is no question that such a procedure would serve to erode the stability of the patrilineal family by diluting its economic base.

The Government of India has passed legislation such as the Hindu Succession Act (1956) and the Hindu Adoption and Maintenance Act (1956), both of which inter-alia provide for a woman's right of inheritance from her father. For example, under the Adoption and Maintenance Act, a woman has a claim of rights of maintenance from her husband's father in case she is widowed. Moreover, she has the right to claim inheritance from her deceased husband's estate. In spite of these changes, inheritance provisions are quite different for males and females. The Chief Justice of the Supreme Court of India, Honorable Mr. Justice Y. V. Chandrachud, wrote that in spite of changes, "some inequalities like the right of birth in favor of a son, paternal grandson, and paternal great grandson still persist" (1984:vii). Provision of females with equal rights to inherit ancestral property from birth, or from a bequest, or at the death may reduce dowry problems. Furthermore, property that is allowed to remain in the name of the deceased for any length of time, as is frequently the case in India, should revert to the state. As it stands, property may remain in the name of a deceased ancestor, while his descendants divide it informally among themselves.

The establishment of a gender-neutral inheritance law represents a significant shift in public policy. We argue that there is a link between pro-male property laws and violence toward women. While we assert this position, we also need to recognize that the property laws give coherence and stability to an essential Indian institution, the joint family. The Mitakshara principle of male inheritance rights is both a reflection and a cause of family solidarity. Modifying this principle in an attempt to reduce violence toward women could have a deleterious effect on family coherence. In addition, the fundamental nature of these institutions makes it inconceivable that there would be substantial resistance to these changes. Yet if one considers this issue in historic terms, it is apparent that during the twentieth century, legal change is in the direction of gender neutrality, a process that started with the Hindu Law of Inheritance (Amendment) Act (1929) and the Hindu Succession Act (1956), and continues through judicial decisions to the present (Diwan 1988:384). As Diwan notes in reference to the changes brought by the Hindu Succession Act of 1956, "the Mitakshara bias towards preference of males over females and of agnates over cognates has been considerably whittled down" (1988:358). Such change is not easy. The changes brought with the Hindu Succession Act in 1956 were achieved only after overcoming "stiff resistance from the traditionalists" (Government of India 1974:135). The same report states, "The hold of tradition, however, was so strong that even while introducing sweeping changes, the legislators compromised and retained in some respects the inferior position of women" (Government of India 1974:135). It must be remembered that the texts that are the foundations of contemporary law include legislation (such as the Hindu Succession Act itself), case law, and religious texts, so that the constitutional question is also a question for religious interpretation, despite the constitutional commitment to secularism.

We are advocating further steps toward gender neutrality of the inheritance laws so that women and men will receive an equal share under intestate succession, and have an equal chance to be testamentary heirs. The law should thus be gender-neutral while still permitting a range of decisions allowing property to stay in a male line if the holder of the property so chooses. The required social adjustment could be largely achieved through the decisions of a family, backed by the power of the state. Families could express their preferences, but the state would not serve to protect the economic interests of males. The process could involve the concept of birthright as well as succession at death. We do not choose to engage those arguments, but do point out that the rapid aging of the Indian population may suggest that a full abrogation of the Mitakshara principle of birthright would be the best social policy because doing so would give older people somewhat greater control over their property in an economy virtually devoid of public investment in social services for older people (Bose and Gangrade 1988, Sharma and Dak 1987).

There are precedents for such policy at the state level. In Andhra Pradesh, the Hindu Succession Act was amended to provide for a female's birthright interest in the Mitakshara property. In Kerala, the Mitakshara property concept was legally abrogated altogether. Other gender asymmetries in the laws of India need to be attacked. The overall goal of policy should be to increase the economic value of women.

Ethnological theory directs our attention to social recognition of marriage and property transfer as functionally important features of the institution. The state can provide a means of socially recognizing marriage through registration and licensure. The law expresses no explicit preference for traditional marriage ritual, and it is possible to have a civil marriage under the provisions of the Special Marriage Act (1954) through registration with a magistrate. Nevertheless, this system co-exists parallel with the traditional system of marriage, which is beyond the reach of state control. Other marriages may be registered under this act if the persons involved so choose, and if a ceremony has been carried out. These special marriages are an alternative to an unregistered marriage.

We conclude that a useful mechanism for state control of dowry problems is the establishment of universal marriage registration, which does not exist at the present time. Marriage registration is also called for by the first Round Table on Social Audit of Implementation of Dowry Legislation (Bhatia 1988), which may serve to provide some monitoring of dowry abuses and perhaps to manifest the state's interest in an effective marriage institution. It would be naive to assume that such a policy would be widely honored, but as it is, low-income persons do not get married because they do not have the resources for marriage under the traditional non-state controlled regime. There are numerous reform groups that organize mass marriage ceremonies of village people so as to help them escape the burden of marriage expenditures. The point is that compliance is a large problem even under current circumstances.

In conclusion, we feel that the causes of the dowry problems are a product of the low economic value of women, loss of effective social control of abuse through delocalization, and pressures caused by economic transformation. The traditional family, caste group, and community controls which have been reduced in effectiveness should be replaced by state functions. The foundation of state control is universal marriage registration and licensure. The impact of the economic value of women on the problem is indicated by the transition from bride price to dowry among tribal people. It is also associated with a reduction in the extent of gainful employment and lower dowry amounts demonstrated for employed women. A broad program to increase the economic value of women would be the most useful means of dealing with the problem of dowry. Further restrictions on dowry without providing for a radically different property right for females is probably not in the interests of Indian women, since dowry represents ante-mortem inheritance. This underlying paradox may explain the commitment to dowry revealed in attitudinal research with Indian women, even though it is also an important feminist issue. The alternatives include the abolishment of the legal basis for the joint family as a corporate unit as has been done in Kerala, or the legal redefinition of the joint family as economically duolineal, as has occurred in Andhra Pradesh.

NOTE

1. For purposes of comparison, a mid-career Indian academic might be paid 60,000 Rs. per year.

REFERENCES

Aluwalia, H. 1969. Matrimonial Advertisements in Panjab. *Indian Journal of Social Work* 30: 55–65.

Bhatia, S. C. 1988. Social Audit of Dowry Legislation. Delhi: Legal Literacy Project.

Bose, A. B., and K. D. Gangrade. 1988. *The Aging in India, Problems and Potentialities.* New Delhi: Abhinav.

Boserup, Ester. 1970. *Women's Role in Economic Development.* New York: St. Martin's Press.

Chandrachud, Y. V. 1984. Foreword. In *Inequalities and the Law,* ed. B. Sivaramayya, iv–vi. Lucknow: Eastern Book Company.

Croll, Elisabeth. 1984. The Exchange of Women and Property: Marriage in Post-revolutionary China. In *Women and Property—Women as Property,* ed. Renee Hirschon, 44–61. London/New York: Croom Helm/St. Martin's Press.

Diwan, Paras. 1988. *Modern Hindu Law, Codified and Uncodified.* Allahabad: Allahabad Law Agency.

Dumont, Louis. 1957. *Hierarchy and Marriage Alliance in South Indian Kinship.* London: Royal Anthropological Institute.

Engels, Fredrich. 1884. *The Origin of Family, Private Property and the State.* New York: International.

Epstein, T. Scarlett. 1960. Peasant Marriage in South India. *Man in India* 40: 192–232.

Friedl, Ernestine. 1967. *Vasilika, A Village in Modern Greece.* New York: Holt, Rinehart and Winston.

Goody, Jack. 1973. Bridewealth and Dowry in Africa and Eurasia. In *Bridewealth and Dowry,* eds. Jack Goody and S. J. Tambiah, 1–58. Cambridge: Cambridge University Press.

———. 1976. *Production and Reproduction, A Comparative Study of the Domestic Domain.* Cambridge: Cambridge University Press.

Government of India. 1974. *Towards Equality: Report of the Committee on the Status of Women.* New Delhi: Government of India, Ministry of Education and Social Welfare.

———. 1985. The Hindu Succession Act. New Delhi: Government of India.

———. 1986. The Dowry Prohibition Act, 1961 (Act No. 28 of 1961) and Connected Legislation (as on 15th January, 1986). New Delhi: Government of India.

———. 1987. *India 1986, A Reference Manual.* Delhi: Ministry of Information and Broadcasting.

Harris, Marvin. 1979. *Cultural Materialism: The Struggle for a Science of Culture.* New York: Random House.

Hirschon, Renee. 1984. Introduction: Property, Power and Gender Relations. In *Women and Property—Women as Property,* ed. Renee Hirschon, 1–22. London/New York: Croom Helm/St. Martin's Press.

Hooja, S. L. 1969. *Dowry System in India.* New Delhi: Asia Press.

Karve, Irawati. 1953. *Kinship Organization in India.* Bombay: Asia Publishing.

Khanna, G. and M. Verghese. 1978. *Indian Women Today.* New Delhi: Vikas Publishing House.

Kumari, Ranjana. 1988. Practice and Problems of Dowry: A Study of Dowry Victims in Delhi. In *Social Audit of Dowry Legislation,* ed. S. C. Bhatia, 27–37. Delhi: Legal Literacy Project.

Luthra, A. 1983. Dowry Among the Urban Poor, Perception and Practice. *Social Action* 33: 207.

Mathew, Anna. 1987. Attitudes Toward Dowry. *Indian Journal of Social Work* 48: 95–102.

Menon, N. R. Madhava. 1988. The Dowry Prohibition Act: Does the Law Provide the Solution or Itself Constitute the Problem? In *Social Audit of Dowry Legislation,* ed. S. C. Bhatia, 11–26. Delhi: Legal Literacy Project.

Miller, Barbara D. 1981. *The Endangered Sex, Neglect of Female Children in Rural North India.* Ithaca, NY: Cornell University Press.

Murdock, George P. 1949. *Social Structure.* New York: Macmillan.

Murickan, J. 1975. Women in Kerala: Changing Socioeconomic Status and Self Image. In *Women in Contemporary India,* ed. A. de Souza, 73–95. Delhi: Manohar.

Niehoff, Arthur H. 1959. A Study of Matrimonial Advertisements in North India. *Eastern Anthropologist* 12: 37–50.

Paul, Madan C. 1986. *Dowry and the Position of Women in India. A Study of Delhi Metropolis.* New Delhi: Inter India Publishers.

Saini, Debi. 1983. Dowry Prohibition Law, Social Change and Challenges in India. *Indian Journal of Social Work* 44(2): 143–147.

Sharma, M. L. and T. Dak. 1987. *Aging in India, Challenge for the Society.* Delhi: Ajanta Publications.

Sharma, Ursula. 1984. Dowry in North India: Its Consequences for Women. In *Women and Property—Women as Property,* ed. Renee Hirschon, 62–74. London/New York: Croom Helm/St. Martin's Press.

Sivaramayya, B. 1984. *Inequalities and the Law.* Lucknow: Eastern Book Company.

Srinivas, M. N. 1969. *Social Change in Modern India.* Berkeley, CA: University of California Press.

———. 1984. *Some Reflections on Dowry.* Delhi: Oxford University Press.

Tambiah, S. J. 1973. Dowry and Bridewealth and the Property Rights of Women in South Asia. In *Bridewealth and Dowry,* eds. Jack Goody and S. J. Tambiah, 59–169. Cambridge: Cambridge University Press.

van der Veen, Klaus W. 1972. *I Give Thee My Daughter—A Study of Marriage and Hierarchy Among the Anavil Brahmins of South Gujarat.* Assen: Van Gorcum.

Verghese, Jamila. 1980. *Her Gold and Her Body.* New Delhi: Vikas Publishing House.

Weibe, P. O. and G. N. Ramu. 1971. A Content Analysis of Matrimonial Advertisements. *Man in India* 51: 119–120.

Westermarck, Edward. 1921. *The History of Human Marriage.* London: MacMillan and Co.

28

The Kpelle Moot

James L. Gibbs Jr.

Some scholars argue that law, like marriage, is a major institution found in all societies, although in widely divergent forms. Others argue that law exists only where some individual or group possesses the authority to impose punishments. Debates about what is and what isn't law aside, conflict exists in all societies. Further, all societies have culturally defined mechanisms by which people attempt to settle their differences.

Conflict-management procedures must be geared to meet the needs of particular social systems. In the urban centers of Western society, people live in faceless anonymity. Relations between people can be characterized as single interest. For example, generally a person's landlord is neither kin nor neighbor. The landlord-tenant relationship is not complicated by any other social bonds. A person who has a car accident is unlikely to have run into a friend or a relative. Our legal system, with its narrow focus on the grievance itself, fits our social system of one-dimensional relationships.

In small-scale social systems, people are often involved with one another on multiple levels. A landlord may also be a neighbor and a relative. In such settings, people are born, grow up, grow old, and die in the same community. Because their social relationships are long-term and highly valued, people in such communities need to resolve disputes in a way that maintains good relations.

Today in the United States, government agencies and grassroots organizations are establishing programs—Neighborhood Justice Centers or Dispute Resolution Centers—based on models of consensus and conciliation. According to the *Citizen's Dispute Resolution Handbook*, the potential of local-level conflict resolution was originally recognized in the work of an anthropologist who had described these processes in Africa.

As you read this selection, ask yourself the following questions:

- How are formal courtroom hearings different from moots?
- In what kinds of cases is the formal court effective and in what kinds is it ineffective?
- How is a mediator different from a judge?
- What is the function of the blessing at the beginning of the moot?
- In contrast to the official court, how does the procedure used during the moot facilitate harmony and reconciliation?
- Why does the author consider the moot therapeutic?

The following terms discussed in this selection are included in the Glossary at the back of the book:

clan	multiplex relationships
culture area	palaver
extended family	patrilineal
mediator	single-interest relationship
moot	social control

Africa as a major culture area has been characterized by many writers as being marked by a high development of law and legal procedures.[1] In the past few years research on African law has produced a series of highly competent monographs such as those on law among the Tiv, the Barotse, and the Nuer.[2] These and related shorter studies have focused primarily on formal processes for the settlement of disputes, such as those which take place in a courtroom, or those which are, in some other way, set apart from simpler measures of social control. However, many African societies have informal, quasi-legal, dispute-settlement procedures, supplemental to formal ones, which have not been as well studied, or—in most cases—adequately analysed.

In this paper I present a description and analysis of one such institution for the informal settlement of disputes, as it is found among the Kpelle of Liberia; it is the moot, the *bɛrɛi mu meni saa* or "house palaver."

Gibbs, Jr., James. L. "The Kpelle Moot." *Africa* 33, no. 1 (1963). Reprinted with permission of the author.

Hearings in the Kpelle moot contrast with those in a court in that they differ in tone and effectiveness. The genius of the moot lies in the fact that it is based on a covert application of the principles of psychoanalytic theory which underlie psychotherapy.

The Kpelle are a Mande-speaking, patrilineal group of some 175,000 rice cultivators who live in Central Liberia and the adjoining regions of Guinea. This paper is based on data gathered in a field study which I carried out in 1957 and 1958 among the Liberian Kpelle of Panta Chiefdom in north-east Central Province.

Strong corporate patrilineages are absent among the Kpelle. The most important kinship group is the virilocal polygynous family which sometimes becomes an extended family, almost always of the patrilineal variety. Several of these families form the core of a residential group, known as a village quarter, more technically, a clan-barrio.[3] This is headed by a quarter elder who is related to most of the household heads by real or putative patrilineal ties.

Kpelle political organization is centralized although there is no single king or paramount chief, but a series of chiefs of the same level of authority, each of whom is superordinate over district chiefs and town chiefs. Some political functions are also vested in the tribal fraternity, the Poro, which still functions vigorously. The form of political organization found in the area can thus best be termed the polycephalous associational state.

The structure of the Kpelle court system parallels that of the political organization. In Liberia the highest court of a tribal authority and the highest tribal court chartered by the Government is that of a paramount chief. A district chief's court is also an official court. Disputes may be settled in these official courts or in unofficial courts, such as those of town chiefs or quarter elders. In addition to this, grievances are settled informally in moots, and sometimes by associational groupings such as church councils or cooperative work groups.

In my field research I studied both the formal and informal methods of dispute settlement. The method used was to collect case material in as complete a form as possible. Accordingly, immediately after a hearing, my interpreter and I would prepare verbatim transcripts of each case that we heard. These transcripts were supplemented with accounts—obtained from respondents—of past cases or cases which I did not hear litigated. Transcripts from each type of hearing were analysed phrase by phrase in terms of a frame of reference derived from jurisprudence and ethno-law. The results of the analysis indicate two things: first, that courtroom hearings and moots are quite different in their procedures and tone, and secondly, why they show this contrast.

Kpelle courtroom hearings are basically coercive and arbitrary in tone. In another paper[4] I have shown that this is partly the result of the intrusion of the authoritarian values of the Poro into the courtroom. As a result, the court is limited in the manner in which it can handle some types of disputes. The court is particularly effective in settling cases such as assault, possession of illegal charms, or theft where the litigants are not linked in a relationship which must continue after the trial. However, most of the cases brought before a Kpelle court are cases involving disputed rights over women, including matrimonial matters which are usually cast in the form of suits for divorce. The court is particularly inept at settling these numerous matrimonial disputes because its harsh tone tends to drive spouses farther apart rather than to reconcile them. The moot, in contrast, is more effective in handling such cases. The following analysis indicates the reasons for this.[5]

The Kpelle *bɛrɛi mu meni saa*, or "house palaver," is an informal airing of a dispute which takes place before an assembled group which includes kinsmen of the litigants and neighbors from the quarter where the case is being heard. It is a completely ad hoc group, varying greatly in composition from case to case. The matter to be settled is usually a domestic problem: alleged mistreatment or neglect by a spouse, an attempt to collect money paid to a kinsman for a job which was not completed, or a quarrel among brothers over the inheritance of their father's wives.

In the procedural description which follows I shall use illustrative data from the Case of the Ousted Wife:

> Wama Nya, the complainant, had one wife, Yua. His older brother died and he inherited the widow, Yokpo, who moved into his house. The two women were classificatory sisters. After Yokpo moved in, there was strife in the household. The husband accused her of staying out late at night, of harvesting rice without his knowledge, and of denying him food. He also accused Yokpo of having lovers and admitted having had a physical struggle with her, after which he took a basin of water and "washed his hands of her."
>
> Yokpo countered by denying the allegations about having lovers, saying that she was accused falsely, although she had in the past confessed the name of one lover. She further complained that Wama Nya had assaulted her and, in the act, had committed the indignity of removing her headtie, and had expelled her from the house after the ritual hand-washing. Finally, she alleged that she had been thus cast out of the house at the instigation of the other wife who, she asserted, had great influence over their husband.
>
> Kɔlɔ Waa, the Town Chief and quarter elder, and the brother of Yokpo, was the mediator of the moot, which decided that the husband was mainly at fault, although Yua and Yokpo's children were also in the wrong. Those at fault had to apologize to Yokpo and bring gifts of apology as well as local rum[6] for the disputants and participants in the moot.

The moot is most often held on a Sunday—a day of rest for Christians and non-Christians alike—at the home of the complainant, the person who calls the moot. The mediator will have been selected by the complainant. He is a kinsman who also holds an office such as town chief or quarter elder, and therefore has some skill in dispute settlement. It is said that he is chosen to preside by virtue of his kin tie, rather than because of his office.

The proceedings begin with the pronouncing of blessings by one of the oldest men of the group. In the Case of the Ousted Wife, Gbenai Zua, the elder who pronounced the blessings, took a rice-stirrer in his hand and, striding back and forth, said:

> This man has called us to fix the matter between him and his wife. May γala (the supreme, creator deity) change his heart and let his household be in good condition. May γala bless the family and make them fruitful. May He bless them so they can have food this year. May He bless the children and the rest of the family so they may always be healthy. May He bless them to have good luck. When Wama Nya takes a gun and goes in the bush, may he kill big animals. May γala bless us to enjoy the meat. May He bless us to enjoy life and always have luck. May γala bless all those who come to discuss this matter.

The man who pronounces the blessings always carries a stick or a whisk (*kpung*) which he waves for effect as he paces up and down chanting his injunctions. Participation of spectators is demanded, for the blessings are chanted by the elder (*kpung namu* or "*kpung* owner") as a series of imperatives, some of which he repeats. Each phrase is responded to by the spectators who answer in unison with a formal response, either *e ka ti* (so be it), or a low, drawn-out *eeee*. The *kpung namu* delivers his blessings faster and faster, building up a rhythmic interaction pattern with the other participants. The effect is to unite those attending in common action before the hearing begins. The blessing focuses attention on the concern with maintaining harmony and the well-being of the group as a whole.

Everyone attending the moot wears their next-to-best clothes or, if it is not Sunday, everyday clothes. Elders, litigants, and spectators sit in mixed fashion, pressed closely upon each other, often overflowing onto a veranda. This is in contrast to the vertical spatial separation between litigants and adjudicators in the courtroom. The mediator, even though he is a chief, does not wear his robes. He and the oldest men will be given chairs as they would on any other occasion.

The complainant speaks first and may be interrupted by the mediator or anyone else present. After he has been thoroughly quizzed, the accused will answer and will also be questioned by those present. The two parties will question each other directly and question others in the room also. Both the testimony and the questioning are lively and uninhibited. Where there are witnesses to some of the actions described by the parties, they may also speak and be questioned. Although the proceedings are spirited, they remain orderly. The mediator may fine anyone who speaks out of turn by requiring them to bring some rum for the group to drink.

The mediator and others present will point out the various faults committed by both the parties. After everyone has been heard, the mediator expresses the consensus of the group. For example, in the Case of the Ousted Wife, he said to Yua: "The words you used towards your sister were not good, so come and beg her pardon."

The person held to be mainly at fault will then formally apologize to the other person. This apology takes the form of the giving of token gifts to the wronged person by the guilty party. These may be an item of clothing, a few coins, clean hulled rice, or a combination of all three. It is also customary for the winning party in accepting the gifts of apology to give, in return, a smaller token such as a twenty-five cent piece[7] to show his "white heart" or good will. The losing party is also lightly "fined;" he must present rum or beer to the mediator and the others who heard the case. This is consumed by all in attendance. The old man then pronounces blessings again and offers thanks for the restoration of harmony within the group, and asks that all continue to act with good grace and unity.

An initial analysis of the procedural steps of the moot isolates the descriptive attributes of the moot and shows that they contrast with those of the courtroom hearing. While the airing of grievances is incomplete in courtroom hearings, it is more complete in the moot. This fuller airing of the issues results, in many marital cases, in a more harmonious solution. Several specific features of the house palaver facilitate this wider airing of grievances. First, the hearing takes place soon after a breach has occurred, before the grievances have hardened. There is no delay until the complainant has time to go to the paramount chief's or district chief's headquarters to institute suit. Secondly, the hearing takes place in the familiar surroundings of a home. The robes, writs, messengers, and other symbols of power which subtly intimidate and inhibit the parties in the courtroom, by reminding them of the physical force which underlies the procedures, are absent. Thirdly, in the courtroom the conduct of the hearing is firmly in the hands of the judge but in the moot the investigatory initiative rests much more with the parties themselves. Jurisprudence suggests that, in such a case, more of the grievances lodged between the parties are likely to be aired and adjusted. Finally, the range of relevance applied to matters which are brought out is extremely broad. Hardly anything mentioned is held to be irrelevant. This too leads to a more thorough ventilation of the issues.

There is a second surface difference between court and moot. In a courtroom hearing, the solution is, by and large, one which is imposed by the adjudicator. In the moot the solution is more consensual. It is, therefore, more likely to be accepted by both parties and hence more durable. Several features of the moot contribute to the consensual solution: first, there is no unilateral ascription of blame, but an attribution of fault to both parties. Secondly, the mediator, unlike the chief in the courtroom, is not backed by political authority and the physical force which underlies it. He cannot jail parties, nor can he levy a heavy fine. Thirdly, the sanctions which are imposed are not so burdensome as to cause hardship to the losing party or to give him or her grounds for a new grudge against the other party. The gifts for the winning party and the potables for the spectators are not as expensive as the fines and the court costs in a paramount chief's court. Lastly, the ritualized apology of the moot symbolizes very concretely the consensual nature of the solution.[8] The public offering and acceptance of the tokens of apology indicate that each party has no further grievances and that the settlement is satisfactory and mutually acceptable. The parties and spectators drink together to symbolize the restored solidarity of the group and the rehabilitation of the offending party.

This type of analysis describes the courtroom hearing and the moot, using a frame of reference derived from jurisprudence and ethno-law which is explicitly comparative and evaluative. Only by using this type of comparative approach can the researcher select features of the hearings which are not only unique to each of them, but theoretically significant in that their contribution to the social-control functions of the proceedings can be hypothesized. At the same time, it enables the researcher to pin-point in procedures the cause for what he feels intuitively: that the two hearings contrast in tone, even though they are similar in some ways.

However, one can approach the transcripts of the trouble cases with a second analytical framework and emerge with a deeper understanding of the implications of the contrasting descriptive attributes of the court and the house palaver. Remember that the coercive tone of the courtroom hearing limits the court's effectiveness in dealing with matrimonial disputes, especially in effecting reconciliations. The moot, on the other hand, is particularly effective in bringing about reconciliations between spouses. This is because the moot is not only conciliatory, but *therapeutic*. Moot procedures are therapeutic in that, like psychotherapy, they re-educate the parties through a type of social learning brought about in a specially structured interpersonal setting.

Talcott Parsons[9] has written that therapy involves four elements: support, permissiveness, denial of reciprocity, and manipulation of rewards. Writers such as Frank,[10] Klapman,[11] and Opler[12] have pointed out that the same elements characterize not only individual psychotherapy, but group psychotherapy as well. All four elements are writ large in the Kpelle moot.

The patient in therapy will not continue treatment very long if he does not feel support from the therapist or from the group. In the moot the parties are encouraged in the expression of their complaints and feelings because they sense group support. The very presence of one's kinsmen and neighbors demonstrates their concern. It indicates to the parties that they have a real problem and that the others are willing to help them to help themselves in solving it. In a parallel vein, Frank, speaking of group psychotherapy, notes that: "Even anger may be supportive if it implies to a patient that others take him seriously enough to get angry at him, especially if the object of the anger feels it to be directed toward his neurotic behavior rather than himself as a person."[13] In the moot the feeling of support also grows out of the pronouncement of the blessings which stress the unity of the group and its harmonious goal, and it is also undoubtedly increased by the absence of the publicity and expressive symbols of political power which are found in the courtroom.

Permissiveness is the second element in therapy. It indicates to the patient that everyday restrictions on making anti-social statements or acting out anti-social impulses are lessened. Thus, in the Case of the Ousted Wife, Yua felt free enough to turn to her ousted co-wife (who had been married leviratically) and say:

> You don't respect me. You don't rely on me any more. When your husband was living, and I was with my husband, we slept on the farm. Did I ever refuse to send you what you asked me for when you sent a message? Didn't I always send you some of the meat my husband killed? Did I refuse to send you anything you wanted? When your husband died and we became co-wives, did I disrespect you? Why do you always make me ashamed? The things you have done to me make me sad.

Permissiveness in the therapeutic setting (and in the moot) results in catharsis, in a high degree of stimulation of feelings in the participants and an equally high tendency to verbalize these feelings.[14] Frank notes that: "Neurotic responses must be expressed in the therapeutic situation if they are to be changed by it."[15] In the same way, if the solution to a dispute reached in a house palaver is to be stable, it is important that there should be nothing left to embitter and undermine the decision. In a familiar setting, with familiar people, the parties to the moot feel at ease and free to say *all* that is on their minds. Yokpo, judged to be the wronged party in the Case of the Ousted Wife, in accepting an apology, gave expression to this when she said:

> I agree to everything that my people said, and I accept the things they have given me—I don't have *anything else* about them on my mind. *(My italics.)*

As we shall note below, this thorough airing of complaints also facilitates the gaining of insight into and the unlearning of idiosyncratic behaviour which is socially disruptive. Permissiveness is rooted in the lack of publicity and the lack of symbols of power. But it stems, too, from the immediacy of the hearing, the locus of investigatory initiative with the parties, and the wide range of relevance.

Permissiveness in therapy is impossible without the denial of reciprocity. This refers to the fact that the therapist will not respond in kind when the patient acts in a hostile manner or with inappropriate affection. It is a type of privileged indulgence which comes with being a patient. In the moot, the parties are treated in the same way and are allowed to hurl recriminations that, in the courtroom, might bring a few hours in jail as punishment for the equivalent of contempt of court. Even though inappropriate views are not responded to in kind, neither are they simply ignored. There is denial of *congruent* response, not denial of *any* response whatsoever. In the *bɛrɛi mu meni saa,* as in group psychotherapy, "private ideation and conceptualization are brought out into the open and all their facets or many of their facets exposed. The individual gets a 'reading' from different bearings on the compass, so to speak,[16] and perceptual patterns . . . are joggled out of their fixed positions. . . ."[17]

Thus, Yua's outburst against Yokpo quoted above was not responded to with matching hostility, but its inappropriateness was clearly pointed out to her by the group. Some of them called her aside in a huddle and said to her:

> You are not right. If you don't like the woman, or she doesn't like you, don't be the first to say anything. Let her start and then say what you have to say. By speaking, if she heeds some of your words, the wives will scatter, and the blame will be on you. Then your husband will cry for your name that you have scattered his property.

In effect, Yua was being told that, in view of the previous testimony, her jealousy of her co-wife was not justified. In reality testing, she discovered that her view of the situation was not shared by the others and, hence, was inappropriate. Noting how the others responded, she could see why her treatment of her co-wife had caused so much dissension. Her interpretation of her new co-wife's actions and resulting premises were not shared by the co-wife, nor by the others hearing a description of what had happened. Like psychotherapy, the moot is gently corrective of behavior rooted in such misunderstandings.

Similarly, Wama Nya, the husband, learned that others did not view as reasonable his accusing his wife of having a lover and urging her to go off and drink with the suspected paramour when he passed their house and wished them all a good evening. Reality testing for him taught him that the group did not view this type of mildly paranoid sarcasm as conducive to stable marital relationships.

The reaction of the moot to Yua's outburst indicates that permissiveness in this case was certainly not complete, but only relative, being much greater than in the courtroom. But without this moderated immunity the airing of grievances would be limited, and the chance for social relearning lessened. Permissiveness in the moot is incomplete because, even there, prudence is not thrown to the winds. Note that Yua was not told not to express her feelings at all, but to express them only after the co-wife had spoken so that, if the moot failed, she would not be in an untenable position. In court there would be objection to her blunt speaking out. In the moot the objection was, in effect, to her speaking *out of turn.* In other cases the moot sometimes fails, foundering on this very point, because the parties are *too* prudent, all waiting for the others to make the first move in admitting fault.

The manipulation of rewards is the last dimension of therapy treated by Parsons. In this final phase of therapy[18] the patient is coaxed to conformity by the granting of rewards. In the moot one of the most important rewards is the group approval which goes to the wronged person who accepts an apology and to the person who is magnanimous enough to make one.

In the Case of the Ousted Wife, Kɔlɔ Waa, the mediator, and the others attending decided that the husband and the co-wife, Yua, had wronged Yokpo. Kɔlɔ Waa said to the husband:

> From now on, we don't want to hear of your fighting. You should live in peace with these women. If your wife accepts the things which the people have brought you should pay four chickens and ten bottles of rum as your contribution.

The husband's brother and sister also brought gifts of apology, although the moot did not explicitly hold them at fault.

By giving these prestations, the wrong-doer is restored to good grace and is once again acting like an "upright Kpelle" (although, if he wishes, he may refuse to accept the decision of the moot). He is eased into this position by being grouped with others to whom blame is also allocated, for, typically, he is not singled out and isolated in being labelled deviant. Thus, in the Case of the Ousted Wife, the children of Yokpo were held to be at fault in "being mean" to their step-father, so that blame was not only shared by one "side," but ascribed to the other also.

Moreover, the prestations which the losing party is asked to hand over are not expensive. They are significant enough to touch the pocketbook a little; for the Kpelle say that if an apology does not cost something other than words, the wrong-doer is more likely to repeat the offending action. At the same time, as we noted above, the tokens are not so costly as to give the loser additional reason for anger directed at the other party which can undermine the decision.

All in all, the rewards for conformity to group expectations and for following out a new behaviour pattern are kept within the deviant's sight. These rewards are positive, in contrast to the negative sanctions of the courtroom. Besides the institutionalized apology, praise, and acts of concern and affection replace fines and jail sentences. The mediator, speaking to Yokpo as the wronged party, said:

> You have found the best of the dispute. Your husband has wronged you. All the people have wronged you. You are the only one who can take care of them because you are the oldest. Accept the things they have given to you.

The moot in its procedural features and procedural sequences is, then, strongly analogous to psychotherapy. It is analogous to therapy in the structuring of the role of the mediator also. Parsons has indicated that, to do his job well, the therapist must be a member of two social systems: one containing himself and his patient; and the other, society at large.[19] He must not be seduced into thinking that he belongs only to the therapeutic dyad, but must gradually pull the deviant back into a relationship with the wider group. It is significant, then, that the mediator of a moot is a kinsman who is also a chief of some sort. He thus represents both the group involved in the dispute and the wider community. His task is to utilize his position as kinsman as a lever to manipulate the parties into living up to the normative requirements of the wider society, which, as chief, he upholds. His major orientation must be to the wider collectivity, not to the particular goals of his kinsmen.

When successful, the moot stops the process of alienation which drives two spouses so far apart that they are immune to ordinary social-control measures such as a smile, a frown, or a pointed aside.[20] A moot is not always successful, however. Both parties must have a genuine willingness to cooperate and a real concern about their discord. Each party must be willing to list his grievances, to admit his guilt, and make an open apology. The moot, like psychotherapy, is impotent without well-motivated clients.

The therapeutic elements found in the Kpelle moot are undoubtedly found in informal procedures for settling disputes in other African societies also; some of these are reported in literature and others are not. One such procedure which seems strikingly parallel to the Kpelle *bɛrɛi mu meni saa* has been described by J. H. M. Beattie.[21] This is the court of neighbors or *rukurato rw'enzarwa* found in the Banyoro kingdom of Uganda. The group also meets as an ad hoc assembly of neighbors to hear disputes involving kinsmen or neighbors.[22]

The intention of the Nyoro moot is to "reintegrate the delinquent into the community and, if possible, to achieve reconciliation without causing bitterness and resentment; in the words of an informant, the institution exists 'to finish off people's quarrels and to abolish bad feeling.'"[23] This therapeutic goal is manifested in the manner in which the dispute is resolved. After a decision is reached the penalty imposed is always the same. The party held to be in the wrong is asked to bring beer (four pots, modified downwards according to the circumstances) and meat, which is shared with the other party and all those attending the *rukurato*. The losing party is also expected to "humble himself, not only to the man he has injured but to the whole assembly."[24]

Beattie correctly points out that, because the council of neighbors has no power to enforce its decision, the shared feast is *not* to be viewed primarily as a penalty, for the wrong-doer acts as a host and also shares in the food and drink. "And it is a praiseworthy thing; from a dishonourable status he is promoted to an honourable one . . ."[25] and reintegrated into the community.[26]

Although Beattie does not use a psychoanalytic frame of reference in approaching his material, it is clear that the communal feast involves the manipulation of rewards as the last step in a social-control measure which breaks the progressive alienation of the deviance cycle. The description of procedures in the *rukurato* indicates that it is highly informal in nature, convening in a room in a house with everyone "sitting around." However, Beattie does not provide enough detail to enable one to determine whether or not the beginning and intermediate steps in the Nyoro moot show the permissiveness, support, and denial of reciprocity which characterize the Kpelle moot. Given the structure and outcome of most Nyoro councils, one would surmise that a close examination of their proceedings[27] would reveal the implicit operation of therapeutic principles.

The fact that the Kpelle court is basically coercive and the moot therapeutic does not imply that one is dysfunctional while the other is eufunctional. Like Beattie, I conclude that the court and informal dispute-settlement procedures have separate but complementary functions. In marital disputes the moot is oriented to a couple as a dyadic social system and serves to reconcile them wherever possible. This is eufunctional from the point of view of the couple, to whom divorce would be dysfunctional. Kpelle courts customarily treat matrimonial matters by granting a divorce. While this may be dysfunctional from the point of view of the couple, because it ends their marriage, it may be eufunctional from the point of view of society. Some marriages, if forced to continue, would result in adultery or physical violence at best, and improper socialization of children at worst. It is clear that the Kpelle moot is to the Kpelle court as the domestic and family relations courts (or commercial and labour arbitration boards) are to ordinary courts in our own society. The essential point is that both formal and informal dispute-settlement procedures serve significant functions in Kpelle society and neither can be fully understood if studied alone.[28]

NOTES

1. The fieldwork on which this paper is based was carried out in Liberia in 1957 and 1958 and was supported by a grant from the Ford Foundation, which is, of course, not responsible for any of the views presented here. The data were analyzed while the writer was the holder of a pre-doctoral National Science Foundation Fellowship. The writer wishes to acknowledge, with gratitude, the support of both foundations. This paper was read at the Annual Meeting of the American Anthropological Association in Philadelphia, Pennsylvania, in November 1961.

    The dissertation, in which this material first appeared, was directed by Philip H. Gulliver, to whom I am indebted for much stimulating and provocative discussion of many of the ideas here. Helpful comments and suggestions have also been made by Robert T. Holt and Robert S. Merrill.

    Portions of the material included here were presented in a seminar on African Law conducted in the Department of Anthropology at the University of Minnesota by E. Adamson Hoebel and the writer. Members of the seminar were generous in their criticisms and comments.

2. Paul J. Bohannan, *Justice and Judgment among the Tiv*, Oxford University Press, London, 1957; Max Gluckman, *The Judicial Process among the Barotse of Northern Rhodesia*, Manchester University Press, 1954; P. P. Howell, *A Handbook of Nuer Law*, Oxford University Press, London, 1954.

3. Cf. George P. Murdock, *Social Structure*, Macmillan, New York, 1949, p. 74.

4. James L. Gibbs, Jr., "Poro Values and Courtroom Procedures in a Kpelle Chiefdom," *Southwestern Journal of Anthropology* (in press) [1963, 18:341–350]. A detailed analysis of Kpelle courtroom procedures and of procedures in the moot together with transcripts appears in: James L. Gibbs, Jr., *Some Judicial Implications of Marital Instability among the Kpelle* (unpublished Ph.D. Dissertation, Harvard University, Cambridge, Mass., 1960).

5. What follows is based on a detailed case study of moots in Panta Chiefdom and their contrast with courtroom hearings before the paramount chief of that chiefdom. Moots, being private, are less susceptible to the surveillance of the anthropologist than courtroom hearings; thus I have fewer transcripts of moots than of court cases. The analysis presented here is valid for Panta Chiefdom and also valid, I feel, for most of the Liberian Kpelle area, particularly the north-east where people are, by and large, traditional.

6. This simple distilled rum, bottled in Monrovia and retailing for twenty-five cents a bottle in 1958, is known in the Liberian Hinterland as "cane juice" and should not be confused with imported varieties.

7. American currency is the official currency of Liberia and is used throughout the country.

8. Cf. J. F. Holleman, "An Anthropological Approach to Bantu Law (with special reference to Shona law)" in the *Journal of the Rhodes-Livingstone Institute*, vol. x, 1950, pp. 27–41. Holleman feels that the use of tokens for effecting apologies—or marriages—shows the proclivity for reducing events of importance to something tangible.

9. Talcott Parsons, *The Social System*, The Free Press, Glencoe, Ill., 1951, pp. 314–319.

10. Jerome D. Frank, "Group Methods in Psychotherapy," in *Mental Health and Mental Disorder: A Sociological Approach*, edited by Arnold Rose, W. W. Norton Co., New York, pp. 524–535.

11. J. W. Klapman, *Group Psychotherapy: Theory and Practice*, Grune & Stratton, New York, 1959.

12. Marvin K. Opler, "Values in Group Psychotherapy," *International Journal of Social Psychiatry*, vol. iv, 1959, pp. 296–298.

13. Frank, op. cit., p. 531.

14. Ibid.

15. Ibid.

16. Klapman, op. cit., p. 39.

17. Ibid., p. 15.

18. For expository purposes the four elements of therapy are described as if they always occur serially. They may, and do, occur simultaneously also. Thus, all four of the factors may be implicit in a single short behavioural sequence. Parsons (op. cit.) holds that these four elements are common not only to psychotherapy but to all measures of social control.

19. Parsons, op. cit., p. 314. Cf. loc. cit., chap. 10.

20. Cf. Parsons, op. cit., chap. 7. Parsons notes that in any social-control action the aim is to avoid the process of alienation, that "vicious-cycle" phenomenon whereby each step taken to curb the non-conforming activity of the deviant has the effect of driving him further into his pattern of deviance. Rather, the need is to "reach" the deviant and bring him back to the point where he is susceptible to the usual everyday informal sanctions.

21. J. H. M. Beattie, "Informal Judicial Activity in Bunyoro," *Journal of African Administration*, vol. ix, 1957, pp. 188–195.

22. Disputes include matters such as a son seducing his father's wives, a grown son disobeying his father, or a husband or wife failing in his or her duties to a spouse. Disputes between unrelated persons involve matters like quarrelling, abuse, assault, false accusations, petty theft, adultery, and failure to settle debts. (Ibid., p. 190.)

23. Ibid., p. 194.

24. Beattie, op. cit., p. 194.

25. Ibid., p. 193.

26. Ibid., p. 195. Moreover, Beattie also recognizes the functional significance of the Nyoro moots, for he notes that: "It would be a serious error to represent them simply as clumsy, 'amateur' expedients for punishing wrongdoers or settling civil disputes at an informal, sub-official level." (Ibid.)

27. The type of examination of case materials that is required demands that fieldworkers should not simply record cases that meet the "trouble case" criterion (cf. K. N. Llewellyn and E. A. Hoebel, *The Cheyenne Way*, Norman, Okla., University of Oklahoma Press, 1941; and E. A. Hoebel, *The Law of Primitive Man*, Cambridge, Mass., Harvard University Press, 1954), but that cases should be recorded in some transcript-like form.

28. The present study has attempted to add to our understanding of informal dispute-settlement procedures in one African society by using an eclectic but organized collection of concepts from jurisprudence, ethno-law, and psychology. It is based on the detailed and systematic analysis of a few selected cases, rather than a mass of quantitative data. In further research a greater variety of cases handled by Kpelle moots should be subjected to the same analysis to test its merit more fully.

29

Sacred Barriers to Conflict Resolution

Scott Atran, Robert Axelrod, Richard Davis

In 1993, one-hundred years after the U.S. military overthrew the highly organized and self-sufficient Kingdom of Hawaii, Congress passed a resolution to formally apologize for suppressing the "inherent sovereignty" of the Native Hawaiian people including the deprivation of their rights to self-determination. Five years earlier Congress formally apologized to Japanese Americans for forcibly removing them to internment camps during World War II. More recently, in 2008 congressional representatives discussed a new apology to Native Americans for years of mistreatment including the massacre of more than 300 Lakota men, women, and children at Wounded Knee Creek by the Seventh Calvary.

National apologies are not meant to destabilize and shame American citizens for the historic misdeeds of our government. They are symbolic concessions intended to promote healing and reconciliation following collective injustices which undermine the peace and multicultural harmony of our nation and world. As international conflicts, religious fundamentalism, and economic disparity continue to divide our planet, symbolic concessions and national apologies are essential building blocks to peace. In this selection Atran, Axelrod, and Davis discuss the role of national apologies as precursors to reconciliation in the enduring conflict between Palestine and Israel. As social scientists with methodological approaches for cross-cultural understanding, anthropologists can promote peace through policy-oriented research that demonstrates the symbiotic relationship between material and symbolic concessions.

As you read this selection, ask yourself the following questions:

- How do sacred values differ from material/instrumental values?
- What is the difference between material and symbolic concessions?
- Why do material incentives sometimes fail to promote peaceful resolutions to political and cultural conflicts?
- What are some symbolic concessions made by the U.S. government to facilitate political compromise?
- How might anthropological research contribute to negotiating a peaceful resolution to the Israeli-Palestinian conflict?

The following terms discussed in this selection are included in the Glossary at the back of the book:

 devoted actor   *sacred values*
 rational actor model   *symbolic concession*

Efforts to resolve political conflicts or to counter political violence often assume that adversaries make rational choices. Ever since the end of the Second World War, "rational actor" models have dominated strategic thinking at all levels of government policy and military planning. In the confrontations between nation states, and especially during the Cold War, these models were arguably useful in anticipating an array of challenges and in stabilizing world peace enough to prevent nuclear war. Now, however, we are witnessing "devoted actors" such as suicide terrorists, who are willing to make extreme sacrifices that are independent of, or all out of proportion to, likely prospects of success. Nowhere is this issue more pressing than in the Israeli-Palestinian dispute. The reality of extreme behaviors and intractability of political conflicts there and discord elsewhere—in the Balkans, Kashmir, Sri Lanka, and beyond—warrant research into the nature and depth of commitment to sacred values.

Atran, Scott, Robert Axelrod, & Richard Davis. "Sacred Barriers to Conflict Resolution." *Science* 317, no. 5841 (24 Aug. 2007): 1039–1040. Reprinted with permission from AAAS.

SACRED VALUES

Sacred values differ from material or instrumental ones by incorporating moral beliefs that drive action in ways dissociated from prospects for success. Across the world, people believe that devotion to core values (such as the welfare of their family and country or their commitment to religion, honor, and justice) is, or ought to be, absolute and inviolable. Such values outweigh other values, particularly economic ones.

To say that sacred values are protected from trade-offs with economic values does not mean that they are immune from all material considerations. Devotion to some core values, such as children's well-being or the good of the community, or even to a sense of fairness, may represent universal responses to long-term evolutionary strategies that go beyond short-term individual calculations of self-interest, yet advance individual interests in the aggregate and long run. Other such values are clearly specific to particular societies and historical contingencies, such as the sacred status of cows in Hindu culture or the sacred status of Jerusalem in Judaism, Christianity, and Islam. Sometimes, as with cows or forests, the sacred may represent accumulated material wisdom of generations in resisting individual urges to gain an immediate advantage of meat or firewood for the long-term benefits of renewable sources of energy and sustenance. Political leaders often appeal to sacred values as a way of reducing "transaction costs" in mobilizing their constituents to action and as a least-cost method of enforcing their policy goals.

Matters of principle or "sacred honor," when enforced to a degree far out of proportion to any individual or immediate material payoff, are often seen as defining "who we are." After the end of the Vietnam War, successive U.S. administrations resisted Hanoi's efforts at reconciliation until Hanoi accounted for the fate of U.S. soldiers missing in action. Granted, the issue was initially entwined with rational considerations of balance of power at the policymaking level: The United States did not want to get too close to Hanoi and so annoy Beijing (a more powerful strategically against the Soviet Union). But popular support for the administration's position, especially among veterans, was a heartfelt concern for "our boys," regardless of numbers or economic consequences.

The "who we are" aspect is often hard for members of different cultures to understand; however, understanding and acknowledging others' values may help to avoid or to resolve the hardest of conflicts. For example, at the peaceful implementation of the occupation of Japan in 1945, the American government realized that preserving, and even signaling respect for, the emperor might lessen the likelihood that Japanese would fight to the death to save him.

SYMBOLIC CONCESSIONS

Our research team has measured emotional outrage and propensity for violence in response to peace deals involving compromises over issues integral to the Israeli-Palestinian conflict with Israeli settlers, Palestinian refugees, and Hamas versus non-Hamas students. Our proposed compromises were exchanging land for peace, sovereignty over Jerusalem, the right of Palestinian refugees to return to their former lands and homes inside Israel, and recognition of the validity of the adversary's own sacred values. We found that the use of material incentives to promote the peaceful resolution of political and cultural conflicts may backfire when adversaries treat contested issues as sacred values. Symbolic concessions of no apparent material benefit may be key in helping to solve seemingly intractable conflicts.

These results correspond to the historical sense of experts. One senior member of the National Security Council responded recently, "This seems right. On the settlers [who were to be removed from Gaza], Sharon realized too late that he shouldn't have berated them about wasting Israel's money and endangering soldiers' lives. Sharon told me that he realized now that he should have made a symbolic concession and called them Zionist heroes making yet another sacrifice."

As further illustration that sacred values can be at the heart of deep-seated political disputes, Isaac Ben Israel, a former Israeli Air Force general who currently heads his country's space agency, told us: "Israel recognizes that the [Hamas-led] Palestinian government is still completely focused on what it considers to be its essential principles. . . . For Hamas, a refusal to utter the simple words 'We recognize Israel's right to exist' is clearly an essential part of their core values. Why else would they suffer the international boycott . . . and let their own government workers go without pay, their people go hungry, and their leaders risk assassination?" Ghazi Hamad, a Hamas leader and then-spokesman for the Palestinian government, told us: "In principle, we have no problem with a Palestinian state encompassing all of our lands within the 1967 borders. But let Israel apologize for our tragedy in 1948, and then we can talk about negotiating over our right of return to historic Palestine." In rational-choice models of decisionmaking, something as intangible as an apology could not stand in the way of peace.

Apologies may not be so much deal-makers in themselves as facilitators for political compromise that may also involve material transactions. At its founding in 1948, Israel was in dire economic straits. But Israel and the World Jewish Congress refused to demand compensation directly from Germany for the property of murdered European Jews. Israel insisted that before any money could be considered, Germany must publicly declare contrition for the murder and suffering of Jews at German hands.

An Iranian scholar and former top diplomat remarked recently that "symbolic statements are important if sincere, [and] without reservation. In 2000, [then-Secretary of State Madeleine] Albright seemed to apologize to Iran for past offenses but then said [in a memorandum] 'despite the trend towards democracy, control over the military, judiciary, courts and police remain in unelected hands.' Our leadership interpreted this as a call for a coup."

RECENT DISCUSSIONS

We went to the Middle East in February 2007 to directly probe issues of material trade-offs and symbolic concessions with leaders of the major parties to the Israel-Palestine dispute. We asked 14 interviewees in Syria, Palestine, and Israel to verify statements for citation. No off-the-record statements contradicted these.

Responses were consistent with our previous findings, with one important difference. Previously, people with sacred values had responded "No" to the proposed trade-off; "No" accompanied by emotional outrage and increased support for violence to the trade-off coupled with a substantial and credible material incentive; and "Yes, perhaps" to trade-offs that also involve symbolic concessions (of no material benefit) from the other side. Leaders responded in the same way, except that the symbolic concession was not enough in itself, but only a necessary condition to opening serious negotiations involving material issues as well. For example, Musa Abu Marzouk (former chairman, and current deputy chairman, of Hamas) said "No" to a trade-off for peace without granting a right of return; a more emphatic "No, we do not sell ourselves for any amount," when given a trade-off with a substantial material incentive (credible offering of substantial U.S. aid for the rebuilding of Palestinian infrastructure); but "Yes, an apology is important, but only as a beginning. It's not enough, because our houses and land were taken away from us and something has to be done about that."

Similarly, Binyamin Netanyahu (former Israeli prime minister and current opposition leader in parliament) responded to our question, "Would you seriously consider accepting a two-state solution following the 1967 borders if all major Palestinian factions, including Hamas, were to recognize the right of the Jewish people to an independent state in the region?" with the answer: "Yes, but the Palestinians would have to show that they sincerely mean it, change their textbooks and anti-Semitic characterizations and then allow some border adjustments so that Ben Gurion [Airport] would be out of range of shoulder-fired missiles."

For Israel's former chief hostage negotiator, Ariel Merari, "Trusting the adversary's intentions is critical to negotiations, which have no chance unless both sides believe the other's willingness to recognize its existential concerns." Indeed, recognition of some "existential values" may change other values into material concerns, e.g., "since the PLO's [Palestine Liberation Organization's] recognition of Israel, most Israelis no longer see rule over the West Bank as existential."

We urgently need more scientific research to inform better policy choices. Our findings about sacred values suggest that there may be fewer differences than are publicly acknowledged in the material trade-offs that "moderate" and "radical" leaders in Palestine, Israel, and elsewhere may be willing to make. Overcoming moral barriers to symbolic concessions and their emotional underpinnings may pose more of a challenge but also offer greater opportunities for breakthroughs to peace than hitherto realized.

30

Army Enlists Anthropology in War Zones

David Rohde

In 2007 the U.S. military launched a $41 million project called the Human Terrain System. In hopes of helping U.S. soldiers better understand the cultural landscape in Iraq and Afghanistan, this project places anthropologists in combat zones to advise and help develop counterinsurgency operations.

Each Human Terrain System team consists of a team leader, an area specialist, a social scientist, and a research manager. The only civilian member of the team is the social scientist, typically an anthropologist with specialized knowledge on the region and its people. The team conducts original ground-level research and consults existing documents before presenting their conclusions and counsel to military commanders.

The use of anthropology in war zones is not a novel idea; it has created controversy in previous conflicts including World War II and the Vietnam War. In 1964, for example, a U.S. military project named CAMELOT was ostensibly organized to apply social science research to better understand the conditions which lead to military conflict; critics, however, believed that the military would use the project to destroy populist movements in Latin America, Asia, and elsewhere.

Today, anthropologists from the American Anthropological Association debate the ethics of civilian anthropology in Afghanistan and Iraq. Opponents of the Human Terrain System project argue that collaboration with combat operations violates the association's Code of Ethics which mandates that anthropologists do no harm to the subjects of their research. Advocates, on the other hand, counter that if anthropology can reduce combat casualties and assist civilian victims caught up in the destruction of war, anthropologists should apply their methods and training to reduce human suffering if they can. In this selection, David Rohde portrays both sides of this heated debate.

As you read this selection, ask yourself the following questions:

- What is mercenary anthropology?
- Why do many anthropologists object to using anthropologists in military operations?
- Why do military officials collaborate with anthropologists in combat operations and war zones?
- Is it ethical for professional anthropologists to work in combat operations?

The following terms discussed in this selection are included in the Glossary at the back of the book:

Human Terrain Team	*mercenary*
jirga	*Operation Khyber*

SHABAK VALLEY, AFGHANISTAN

In this isolated Taliban stronghold in eastern Afghanistan, American paratroopers are fielding what they consider a crucial new weapon in counterinsurgency operations: a soft-spoken civilian anthropologist named Tracy.

Tracy, who asked that her surname not be used for security reasons, is a member of the first Human Terrain Team, an experimental Pentagon program that assigns anthropologists and other social scientists to American combat units in Afghanistan and Iraq. Her team's ability to understand subtle points of tribal relations—in one case spotting a land dispute that allowed the Taliban to bully parts of a major tribe—has won the praise of officers who say they are seeing concrete results.

Col. Martin Schweitzer, commander of the 82nd Airborne Division unit working with the anthropologists here, said that the unit's combat operations had been reduced by 60 percent since the scientists arrived in February, and that the soldiers were now able to focus more on improving security, health care, and education for the population.

"We're looking at this from a human perspective, from a social scientist's perspective," he said. "We're not focused on the enemy. We're focused on bringing governance down to the people."

In September, Defense Secretary Robert M. Gates authorized a $40 million expansion of the program, which will assign teams of anthropologists and social scientists to each of the 26 American combat brigades in Iraq and Afghanistan. Since early September, five new teams have been deployed in the Baghdad area, bringing the total to six.

Yet criticism is emerging in academia. Citing the past misuse of social sciences in counterinsurgency campaigns, including in Vietnam and Latin America, some denounce the program as "mercenary anthropology" that exploits social science for political gain. Opponents fear that, whatever their intention, the scholars who work with the military could inadvertently cause all anthropologists to be viewed as intelligence gatherers for the American military.

Hugh Gusterson, an anthropology professor at George Mason University, and 10 other anthropologists are circulating an online pledge calling for anthropologists to boycott the teams, particularly in Iraq.

"While often presented by its proponents as work that builds a more secure world," the pledge says, "at base, it contributes instead to a brutal war of occupation which has entailed massive casualties."

In Afghanistan, the anthropologists arrived along with 6,000 troops, which doubled the American military's strength in the area it patrols, the country's east.

A smaller version of the Bush administration's troop increase in Iraq, the buildup in Afghanistan has allowed American units to carry out the counterinsurgency strategy here, where American forces generally face less resistance and are better able to take risks.

A NEW MANTRA

Since Gen. David H. Petraeus, now the overall American commander in Iraq, oversaw the drafting of the Army's new counterinsurgency manual last year, the strategy has become the new mantra of the military. A recent American military operation here offered a window into how efforts to apply the new approach are playing out on the ground in counterintuitive ways.

In interviews, American officers lavishly praised the anthropology program, saying that the scientists' advice has proved to be "brilliant," helping them see the situation from an Afghan perspective and allowing them to cut back on combat operations.

The aim, they say, is to improve the performance of local government officials, persuade tribesmen to join the police, ease poverty, and protect villagers from the Taliban and criminals.

Afghans and Western civilian officials, too, praised the anthropologists and the new American military approach but were cautious about predicting long-term success. Many of the economic and political problems fueling instability can be solved only by large numbers of Afghan and American civilian experts.

"My feeling is that the military are going through an enormous change right now where they recognize they won't succeed militarily," said Tom Gregg, the chief United Nations official in southeastern Afghanistan. "But they don't yet have the skill sets to implement" a coherent nonmilitary strategy, he added.

Deploying small groups of soldiers into remote areas, Colonel Schweitzer's paratroopers organized jirgas, or local councils, to resolve tribal disputes that have simmered for decades. Officers shrugged off questions about whether the military was comfortable with what David Kilcullen, an Australian anthropologist and an architect of the new strategy, calls "armed social work."

"Who else is going to do it?" asked Lt. Col. David Woods, commander of the Fourth Squadron, 73rd Cavalry. "You have to evolve. Otherwise you're useless."

The anthropology team here also played a major role in what the military called Operation Khyber. That was a 15-day drive late this summer in which 500 Afghan and 500 American soldiers tried to clear an estimated 200 to 250 Taliban insurgents out of much of Paktia Province, secure southeastern Afghanistan's most important road, and halt a string of suicide attacks on American troops and local governors.

In one of the first districts the team entered, Tracy identified an unusually high concentration of widows in one village, Colonel Woods said. Their lack of income created financial pressure on their sons to provide for their families, she determined, a burden that could drive the young men to join well-paid insurgents. Citing Tracy's advice, American officers developed a job training program for the widows.

In another district, the anthropologist interpreted the beheading of a local tribal elder as more than a random act of intimidation: the Taliban's goal, she said, was to divide and weaken the Zadran, one of southeastern Afghanistan's most powerful tribes. If Afghan and American officials could unite the Zadran, she said, the tribe could block the Taliban from operating in the area.

"Call it what you want, it works," said Colonel Woods, a native of Denbo, Pa. "It works in helping you define the problems, not just the symptoms."

EMBEDDING SCHOLARS

The process that led to the creation of the teams began in late 2003, when American officers in Iraq complained that they had little to no information about the local population. Pentagon officials contacted Montgomery McFate, a Yale-educated cultural anthropologist working for the Navy who advocated using social science to improve military operations and strategy.

Ms. McFate helped develop a database in 2005 that provided officers with detailed information on the local population. The next year, Steve Fondacaro, a retired Special Operations colonel, joined the program and advocated embedding social scientists with American combat units.

Ms. McFate, the program's senior social science adviser and an author of the new counterinsurgency manual, dismissed criticism of scholars working with the military. "I'm frequently accused of militarizing anthropology," she said. "But we're really anthropologizing the military."

Roberto J. González, an anthropology professor at San Jose State University, called participants in the program naïve and unethical. He said that the military and the Central Intelligence Agency had consistently misused anthropology in counterinsurgency and propaganda campaigns and that military contractors were now hiring anthropologists for their local expertise as well.

"Those serving the short-term interests of military and intelligence agencies and contractors," he wrote in the June issue of *Anthropology Today*, an academic journal, "will end up harming the entire discipline in the long run."

Arguing that her critics misunderstand the program and the military, Ms. McFate said other anthropologists were joining the teams. She said their goal was to help the military decrease conflict instead of provoking it, and she vehemently denied that the anthropologists collected intelligence for the military.

In eastern Afghanistan, Tracy wanted to reduce the use of heavy-handed military operations focused solely on killing insurgents, which she said alienated the population and created more insurgents. "I can go back and enhance the military's understanding," she said, "so that we don't make the same mistakes we did in Iraq."

Along with offering advice to commanders, she said, the five-member team creates a database of local leaders and tribes, as well as social problems, economic issues, and political disputes.

CLINICS AND MEDIATION

During the recent operation, as soldiers watched for suicide bombers, Tracy and Army medics held a free medical clinic. They said they hoped that providing medical care would show villagers that the Afghan government was improving their lives.

Civil affairs soldiers then tried to mediate between factions of the Zadran tribe about where to build a school. The Americans said they hoped that the school, which would serve children from both groups, might end a 70-year dispute between the groups over control of a mountain covered with lucrative timber.

Though they praised the new program, Afghan and Western officials said it remained to be seen whether the weak Afghan government could maintain the gains. "That's going to be the challenge, to fill the vacuum," said Mr. Gregg, the United Nations official. "There's a question mark over whether the government has the ability to take advantage of the gains."

Others also question whether the overstretched American military and its NATO allies can keep up the pace of operations.

American officers expressed optimism. Many of those who had served in both Afghanistan and Iraq said they had more hope for Afghanistan. One officer said that the Iraqis had the tools to stabilize their country, like a potentially strong economy, but that they lacked the will. He said Afghans had the will, but lacked the tools.

After six years of American promises, Afghans, too, appear to be waiting to see whether the Americans or the Taliban will win a protracted test of wills here. They said this summer was just one chapter in a potentially lengthy struggle.

At a "super jirga" set up by Afghan and American commanders here, a member of the Afghan Parliament, Nader Khan Katawazai, laid out the challenge ahead to dozens of tribal elders.

"Operation Khyber was just for a few days," he said. "The Taliban will emerge again."

31

Contemporary Warfare
in the New Guinea Highlands

Aaron Podolefsky

Within political units—whether tribes or nations—there are well-established mechanisms for handling conflict nonviolently. Anthropologists have described a wide range of conflict resolution mechanisms within societies. Between politically autonomous groups, however, few mechanisms exist. Consequently, uncontained conflict may expand into armed aggression—warfare. In both primitive and modern forms, warfare always causes death, destruction, and human suffering. It is certainly one of the major problems confronting humankind.

New Guinea highlanders can tell you why they go to war—to avenge ghosts or to exact revenge for the killing of one of their own. As we have seen in previous selections, people do not seem to comprehend the complex interrelationship among the various parts of their own social system. Throughout the world, anthropologists find that people do not fathom the causes of their own social behavior. If they did, finding solutions would certainly be a far simpler matter.

The leaders of Papua New Guinea see intertribal fighting as a major social problem with severe economic consequences. Although fighting itself may be age-old, the reemergence of warfare in this area in the 1970s appears to have a new set of causes. In this selection, Aaron Podolefsky shows how the introduction of Western goods may have inadvertently resulted in changes in economic arrangements, marriage patterns, and, ultimately, warfare.

As you read this selection, ask yourself the following questions:

- What is the theoretical orientation (research strategy) of this paper?
- When did tribal fighting re-emerge as a national problem in New Guinea?
- How did intertribal marriage constrain the expansion of minor conflict into warfare?
- How has the rate of intertribal marriage changed? Why did it change?
- How are the introduction of Western goods, trade, marriage, and warfare interrelated?

The following terms discussed in this selection are included in the Glossary at the back of the book:

affinal kin	*hypothesis*
aggression	*lineage*
agnates	*multiplex relationships*
blood relatives	*pacification*
cross-cutting ties	*tribe*
cultural materialism	

After decades of pacification and relative peace, intergroup warfare re-emerged in the Papua New Guinea highlands during the late 1960s and early 1970s, only a few years before national independence in 1975. Death and destruction, martial law, and delay in highlands development schemes have been the outcome.

Most explanations of the resurgence either posit new causes (such as psychological insecurity surrounding political independence from Australian rule or disappointment at the slow speed of development) or attribute the increased fighting to relaxation of government controls which suppressed fighting since the pacification process began. None of the explanations thus far advanced has looked at changes in the structure or infrastructure of highlands societies themselves which could account for behavioral changes in the management of conflict.

This paper employs a cultural materialist strategy in which the efficacy of explanatory models is ranked: infrastructure, structure, and superstructure.[1] From a macrosociological perspective, infrastructural changes unintentionally induced during the colonial era resulted

Podolefsky, Aaron. "Contemporary Warfare in the New Guinea Highlands." *Ethnology: An International Journal of Cultural and Social Anthropology* 23 (1984):73–87. Reprinted by permission of Ethnology.

in changes in the structural relations between groups. These changes reduced existing (albeit weak) indigenous mechanisms constraining conflict. Traditionally, groups maintained differential access to resources such as stone used for axes and salt. Axe heads and salt were produced in local areas and traded for valuables available elsewhere. I argue that the introduction and distribution of items such as salt and steel axes reduced the necessity for trade, thereby altering the need for intertribal marriage as well as reducing extratribal contacts of a type which facilitated marriage between persons of different tribes. The reduction of intertribal marriage, over time, resulted in a decay of the web of affinal and nonagnatic kin ties which had provided linkages between otherwise autonomous tribal political units. Thus, the resurgence of tribal fighting is, in part, a result of the reduction of constraints which might otherwise have facilitated the containment of conflict rather than its expansion into warfare. This view sees warfare as one possible end result of a process of conflict management.

An advantage of this strategy is that it suggests a testable hypothesis which runs counter to conventional wisdom and informed opinion that the rate of intertribal marriage would increase after pacification. Some researchers believed that once tribal fighting ended men would be able to wander farther afield and develop relationships with single teenage girls over a wide area. Pacification, then, might reasonably be expected to result in an increase in intertribal marriage. An increase or lack of change in the rate of intergroup marriage since contact would invalidate the explanation. The hypothesis will be tested on data collected in the Gumine District, Simbu (formerly Chimbu) Province, Papua-New Guinea.

BACKGROUND

Warfare in traditional highlands societies has been regarded as chronic, incessant, or endemic, and is said to have been accepted as a part of social living in most areas. Indeed, the pattern of warfare was one of the most continuous and violent on record.

However, hostilities were neither random nor did highlanders live in a perpetual state of conflict with all surrounding groups. Some neighboring groups maintained relations of permanent hostility and had little to do with one another. In contrast, most neighboring tribes intermarried and attended one another's ceremonies.

Pacification was an early goal of the colonial administration. By the end of the 1930s fighting was rare in the vicinity of Simbu province government stations. By 1940 Australian authority was accepted and attacks on strangers and tribal fighting had nearly ended, although the entire highlands was not pacified until the 1960s. This period also witnessed the introduction of Western goods such as salt and the steel axe.

Change came quickly to New Guinea. Sterling writes in 1943: "Headhunters and cannibals a generation ago, most of the natives of British New Guinea have now become so accustomed to the ways of the whites that they have been trained as workers and even to assist in administering the white man's law."

From the end of World War II through the 1970s, educational and business opportunities expanded, local government and village courts were introduced, and national self-government was attained in 1975. Highlanders came to expect that development would lead to material gains.[2]

Tribal warfare began to reemerge as a significant national problem in about 1970, five years before independence. By 1973 the government had become concerned that the situation might deteriorate to a point that they could no longer effectively administer parts of the highlands. In 1972, according to a government report, 28 incidents involving 50 or more persons were reported in the Western Highlands District. A decade later, Bill Wormsley (1982) reports 60 fights per year in the Enga Province (the figures are of course not directly comparable). Although the level of fighting declined in Enga during 1980 due to the declaration of a state of emergency, it increased again in 1981 and 1982. Martial law has also been declared in the Simbu Province. Deaths lead to payback killing and to demands for compensation payments. Inflated demands for "excess" compensation further compound the problem.

Of the five major theories of warfare outlined by Koch in 1974 (biological evolution, psychological theories, cultural evolution, ecological adaptation, and social-structure analysis), scholars have used only psychological theories and social-structural analysis to explain the recent emergence of tribal warfare.

Some researchers favor explanations which combine the traditional cultural heritage of violence with issues in development. Others seem to argue that the problem lies in the Enga's perception that the government, especially the courts, has become weaker and that this had led to the breakdown in law and order. Rob Gordon notes, however, that the police force in Enga has increased from 72 in 1970 to 300 in 1981, and that the average sentence for riotous behavior has grown from 3 months in 1970 to 9.6 months in 1978–9 with no apparent deterrent effect. Kiaps (field officers), Gordon suggests, have in fact lost power for several reasons. Most interesting from the perspective of the present analysis involves the kiaps' loss of control over access to goods. He (1983:209) states that "The importance that the Enga attach to trade-goods should not be underestimated." An old Engan is quoted as saying "The first Kiaps gave beads, salt, steel axes—everyone wanted it so they all followed the Kiap and stopped fighting. We stopped fighting because we did not want to lose the source of these things." I would add that once they "followed the kiaps" for these goods, previous important trade relations no longer needed to be kept up. In a 1980 study, Gordon also acknowledges problems created by intergroup suspicion, generational conflict exacerbated by education, and decline in men's houses and clan meetings. Similarly, Paula Brown (1982a) believes that pacification was a temporary effect in which fighting was suppressed. The Simbu do not see the government as holding power.

Explanations also combine development problems with psychologically oriented theories. Contemporary violence is sometimes thought to be a protest rising out of psychological strain created by the drastic social change of an imposed economic and political system. In a 1973 paper Bill Standish describes the period leading up to independence as one of stress, tension, and insecurity. He argues that the fighting is an expression of primordial attachments in the face of political insecurity surrounding national independence from Australian colonial rule. Paula Brown (1982a, 1982b) suggests that during the colonial period expectations for the future included security, wealth, and the improvement of life. "Disappointment that these goals have not been realized is expressed in disorder." She suggests that what is needed is a political movement rather than the imposition of Western institutions and suppression of fighting.

The present paper cannot and does not formally refute any of these explanations. Indeed, some make a great deal of sense and fill in part of a very complex picture. However, it is difficult to evaluate the validity of these explanations since very little data are presented. For example, Standish (1973) presents no evidence to assess whether, in fact, the level of stress has changed over time (precontact, postcontact, or independence era), or whether stress is associated with fighting or even with differential levels of awareness about independence, the latter likely expressing itself geographically around centers of population and development.

ETHNOGRAPHIC BACKGROUND— THE MUL COMMUNITY

Mul lies approximately 3 miles east of the Gumine District Headquarters and 32 miles south of Kundiawa, the capital of the Simbu province. The Gumine patrol post was established in 1954. During the early 1960s a dirt road was constructed linking Gumine to the capital and within a few years the road was extended through Mul. Lying at an elevation of about 5,500 feet,

Mul is the central portion of a larger tribal territory which extends steeply from the southern edge of the Marigl Gorge to elevations of 8 to 9,000 feet.

The area is densely populated. Land is either cultivated or fallow in grass or scrub regrowth. Individually owned trees are scattered and there are a yearly increasing number of coffee trees. With 295 persons per square mile on cultivatable land, this density is high compared with other highland groups (see Brown and Podolefsky 1976).

The people of Mul are Simbus. Social relations and cultural patterns follow in most important respects those extensively documented by Paula Brown in numerous publications. I will describe here only those dimensions of organization most directly relevant to the resurgence of tribal fighting.

Mul residents trace kinship through males, and their social groupings are patrilineal. Hierarchical segments link themselves as father/son, while parallel segments are seen as brothers. Individuals, however, are less concerned with this overall construct and tend to interact in terms of group composition and alignments. The likelihood of an individual conflict escalating into warfare is directly related to the structural distance between conflicting parties.

The largest political group to unite in warfare is the tribe, a group of several thousand individuals. Tribes are segmented into clans whose members see themselves as a unified group. Generally, individually owned plots of land tend to cluster and people can point out rough boundaries between adjacent clans. Plots of land belonging to members of a particular subclan tend to cluster within the clan area. The subclan section (or one-blood group) is the first to mobilize for warfare. The potential for expansion of such conflicts depends to a large degree on whether the relative position of the groups in the segmentary system lends itself to opposing alignments at the higher levels of segmentation and upon the past relations between the groups.

Unlike subclan sections in most highlands societies there is no restriction upon fighting between sections of the subclan. Within the subclan section, however, there are moral restrictions on internal fighting. If comembers become extremely angry they may attack with fists, clubs, or staffs, but not with axes, arrows, or spears. These restrictions are related to the notion that members of the subclan have "one-blood," and that this common blood should not be shed.

Segmentary principles operate in situations of cooperation as well as conflict. Members of a subclan section may enclose garden plots within a single fence and cooperate in the construction of men's houses. Brown (1970:99–103) similarly notes that in the central Simbu transactions between clans and tribes are competitive while those within the clan are reciprocal. Generally speaking, in terms of proximity of land holdings and residence, cooperation in gardening and house construction and the willingness to unite in common defense and ceremonial exchange, the solidarity of a social group is inversely related to the position in the segmentary hierarchy.

Cross-cutting these segmentary principles are a variety of interpersonal ties (e.g., affinal and other non-agnatic relations, exchange ties, and personal friendships) which affect behavior in conflict situations. It is these ephemeral or transitory linkages which provide the avenues through which structurally autonomous tribal groups interact.

MARRIAGE AND WARFARE

Marriage and warfare are linked in the minds of New Guinea highlanders. Early writers report indigenous notions that highlanders marry their enemies. The Siane say, "They are our affinal relatives; with them we fight" (Salisbury 1962:25). Enga informants report, "We marry those whom we fight" (Meggitt 1958:278). In an extensive study of Enga warfare, Meggitt (1977:42) supports these assertions by reporting quite strong correlations between rates of intergroup marriage and killing.

While there is little doubt that there is a strong association between marriage and warfare, it is not clear at all that they are causally related in any direct fashion, i.e., warfare causing marriage or marriage causing warfare. It is highly unlikely that warfare causes marriage. Researchers have noted the difficulty in arranging marriages between hostile groups. It is similarly unlikely that marriage causes warfare (although exceptions can certainly be pointed out). While disputes may arise between bride and groom or their families, the relations are generally highly valued and long term. The association between marriage and warfare can be reduced to two separate relationships. First, highlanders most frequently marry their neighbors. Second, highlanders most frequently go to war with their neighbors. This is because in the highlands, where travel is restricted and relations are multiplex, neighbors are the parties most likely to be involved in a dispute. Thus propinquity is causally related to both marriage and warfare; the positive correlation between marriage and warfare is spurious. Indeed, the essence of the argument made here is that if other variables could be "controlled" the association between warfare and marriage would in fact be negative.

The notion that there is no direct (as opposed to inverse) causal relationship between warfare and marriage is critical. Warfare results from precipitating disputes in the absence of sufficiently powerful third party mechanisms and other constraints which control the dispute. One dimension of constraint stems from marriage links.

In her paper "Enemies and Affines," Paula Brown (1964) carefully describes the relevant social relations among the central Simbu. During wedding ceremonies speeches proclaim that the groups of the bride and groom (consisting of subclansmen, some clansmen, kin, and affines) should remain on friendly terms and exchange visits and food. The marriage creates individual ties and obligations outside the clan which, while not institutionalized, are not wholly voluntary. At various stages in the life cycle payments are obligatory. Given the widely documented emphasis on transaction in highlands social relations, it is important to note that whenever a formal food presentation occurs between clans, the donors and recipients are related to one another through marriage. Extratribal relatives play an important role in conflict situations.

> The prevailing hostility between neighboring tribes gives extratribal relatives a special complex role. Men try not to injure their close kin and affines in any conflict between their agnatic group and the group of their relatives, but they may not attempt to prevent or stop hostilities. In any dealings between neighboring tribes, men with connections in both take a leading part; their political sphere of action encompasses both. When intermediaries and peacemakers are required these men are active (Brown 1964:348).

Thus, in Central Simbu, affines played some role in attempting to prevent warfare and were important in restoring peace. No amount of oral history data will tell us how many wars did not occur due to efforts made through these channels. Nor can such data tell us how many wars were shorter or less intense than they would have been had there been fewer cross-cutting ties. The importance of cross-cutting ties is recognized among the densely populated Enga.

> Even while or after two men or groups fight over an issue, others may intervene to urge negotiation and compromise. . . . Whether, however, noncombatants initiate some kind of conciliation or simply stand by and watch the fighting spread depends on a complex set of conditions . . . relevant factors . . . include, for instance, the importance traditionally ascribed to the object in contention (is it a pig or a sweet potato garden?), the number of antagonists, the kinship, affinal, or exchange connections among some or all of them, and between them and interested noncombatants (Meggitt 1977:12).

Moreover, the frequency of intergroup marriage is related to the expansion or containment of a dispute. That is, the more intermarriage the greater the chance that disputes will be handled without violence or that the violence can be contained.

Especially within the tribe, the supporters of each party include men with affines on the other side, most of whom are on good terms with their in-laws and have no wish to offend them. In such cases some men stay out of the fight while others, while participating, avoid meeting their affines in combat. This may serve to confine interclan conflict. Between tribes, similar serious disputes can more easily lead to fighting because fewer men have close ties which restrain them from supporting their fellow tribesmen (Brown 1964:352).

In sum, while there is an apparent correlation between marriage and warfare, marriage, in fact, establishes a social relationship which acts primarily as a constraint upon the expansion of a dispute. Second, as Meggitt suggests, it is not merely the marriage ties between the two groups, but also between them and their allies, i.e., the web of affinal relations. Third, the frequency of marriage, or density of the web, is related to efficacy of conflict management processes.

CHANGING PATTERN OF INTERTRIBAL MARRIAGE

A null hypothesis that the proportion of intertribal marriages has gone up or remained the same can be rejected ($p < 0.001$) on the basis of the data shown in Table 1. Thus, we tend to believe, based upon these data, that there has in fact been an overall decline in intertribal marriage.

The data reveal a statistically significant change in the marriage pattern in the anticipated direction. Figure 1 describes the proportion of marriage ties within and between tribes, before and after Western influence. Comparing the intertribal (between) and intratribal (within) marriage rates in the precontact sample (labeled before), we see that intertribal marriage was nearly three times as frequent as intratribal marriage. Of the 114 marriage ties recorded in the precontact sample, 85 (75 percent) were between members of different tribes while only 29 (25 percent) were

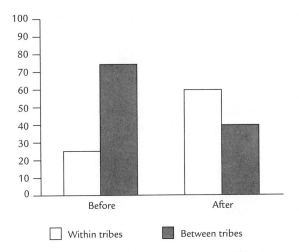

FIGURE 1 Percentage of Marriage Ties. Podolefsky, Aaron. "Contemporary Warfare in the New Guinea Highlands." *Ethnology: An International Journal of Cultural and Social Anthropology* 23 (1984):73–87. Reprinted by permission of Ethnology.

within the tribe. This allowed for a dense network of affinal ties between autonomous political groups. In the recent postcontact period (labeled after), in contrast, the number of intertribal marriages drops below the number of intratribal marriages. Of the 74 marriage ties in the postcontact sample, only 30 (40 percent) were between persons of different tribes while 44 (60 percent) were within the tribe. The intertribal marriage rate in the recent period is nearly half that of the precontact period.

The argument presented in this paper is that the dramatic reduction of intertribal marriage rates had significant implications for the structure of relations between politically autonomous tribal groups.

A Secondary Analysis

Sometimes it is possible to replicate one's findings by performing a secondary analysis on data collected by other researchers.

In 1964, Paula Brown published data on the marriage of some men in the Naregu tribe who live in the central Simbu near the capital of Kundiawa. Data for two clans are divided into previous generations (prior to 1930) and present generation. Brown's categories for marriage ties may be collapsed to match those used above.

What should we expect, a priori? Since Brown did not arrange the data to address this particular question, we expect some differences. Her temporal dichotomy is previous and present generation rather than before and after contact. Europeans did not reach this area until the mid-1930s and Brown's data are

TABLE 1 Marriage Ties by Time Period

	Before Contact		**After Contact**	
	N	%	N	%
Between tribes	85	75%	30	40%
Within tribes	29	25%	44	60%
Total	114	100%	74	100%

chi squared = 21.86 1 df
p < 0.001 (one tail)
phi = .341

Podolefsky, Aaron. "Contemporary Warfare in the New Guinea Highlands." *Ethnology: An International Journal of Cultural and Social Anthropology* 23 (1984):73–87. Reprinted by permission of Ethnology.

TABLE 2   Marriages of Some Men in the Naregu Tribe

	Pre-1930 (Before)		Post-1930 (After)	
	N	%	N	%
Between tribes	154	60%	130	47%
Within tribes	102	40%	144	53%
Total	256	100%	274	100%

chi squared = 8.597 1 df
p < 0.005 (one tail)
phi = .1272
Podolefsky, Aaron. "Contemporary Warfare in the New Guinea Highlands." *Ethnology: An International Journal of Cultural and Social Anthropology* 23 (1984):73–87. Reprinted by permission of Ethnology.

dichotomized at 1930. This means that precontact marriages are included in the present generation sample. Neither do Brown's data allow for a decade of transition. Based upon these differences in the data sets, we would expect the difference between the previous and present samples to be less extreme than the difference between the before and after sample in the Mul data (i.e., we expect a lower measure of association).

The data in Table 2 reveal a statistically significant change in the marriage pattern, although the association is lower (as we expected it would be) than in Mul. The between-tribe marriage rate (in the sample) dropped from 60 to 47 percent. This change was sufficient to draw Brown's attention. While the analysis fits our predictions, we cannot be certain that the change in marriage pattern observed by Paula Brown in central Simbu represents the same process occurring in Mul nearly twenty years later. Nevertheless, the analysis is intriguing. I think Brown was observing the initial stages of a process of change initiated by a reduction in the necessity for trade.[3]

TRADE AND MARRIAGE

Given the conventional wisdom that pacification would lead to greater intertribal contact and, therefore, an increase in the rate of intertribal marriage, it remains to be explained why the proportion of intertribal marriages decreased. In other words, what forces or situations affected the marriage pattern?

Interviews with young men of marriageable age and some of the oldest men in the community elicited two different perspectives. (Unfortunately, it was not possible for me, being a male, to maintain serious conversation with women on this topic.) Young men typically explained that they do not find wives from other areas because they are "tired"; they just do not have any desire to travel the long distances to visit women of other areas when there are women close at hand.

This emic explanation is not particularly satisfactory from an anthropological perspective.

While the older men could not explain why the distribution of marriages in their younger days differed from that of more recent years, they were able to describe the ways young men and women met prospective spouses from other tribes prior to the coming of Europeans scarcely twenty years earlier. The old men reported that when they were young trade was very important. Salt, stone axes, bird of paradise feathers, shells of different kinds, pandanus oil, carpul fur, and the like were traded between tribes during trading expeditions. Figure 2 maps the trade network as described by the older residents of Mul.

When they were young, the old men reported, they would dress in their finest decorations and travel to the places described in Figure 2. The women at these places, they said, would see them arrayed in all their finery and want to marry them. Of course, the situation may not have been quite this straightforward.

These reports drew my attention to the link between intertribal marriage and trade for scarce necessary and luxury resources. What would be the effect of the introduction of European goods upon trade? And could this affect marriage patterns?

According to the old men, pigs from Mul were traded south to the lower elevation, less densely populated areas in return for bird of paradise feathers and carpul fur (see Figure 2). Some of the fur and feathers were traded for cowrie shells with people from Sina. Cowries, in turn, were traded to the Gomgales for kina shells. Carpul fur and pandanus oil were traded to the east for salt. Finally, some of the fur and feathers obtained from the south and the salt obtained from the east were traded to the northeast for stone axes and small shells, which had in turn been brought in from even further off.

Enter the ubiquitous steel axe; exit the stone axe. No one in Mul today would use a stone axe. Indeed, it was difficult to find someone who recalled how to attach stone to handle. The effect was that the primary reason for trade between the peoples of Mul and Era (i.e., the need for stone axes) was eliminated and the Muls' need for fur, feathers, and salt was reduced (what may have begun to increase was a need for cash). Similarly, salt increasingly became more readily available. Nowadays it can be purchased at the store on the government station or in small trade stores which stock, for example, three bags of salt, two packs of cigarettes, a bit of rice, and two or three tins of mackerel. The availability of salt locally eliminates the need to trade for it and further reduces the need for fur. Thus, two of the five trade routes shown on Figure 2 become totally unnecessary and the usefulness of trade items from a third is reduced.

The elimination of the need to trade for necessary scarce resources allowed some trade relations to atrophy.

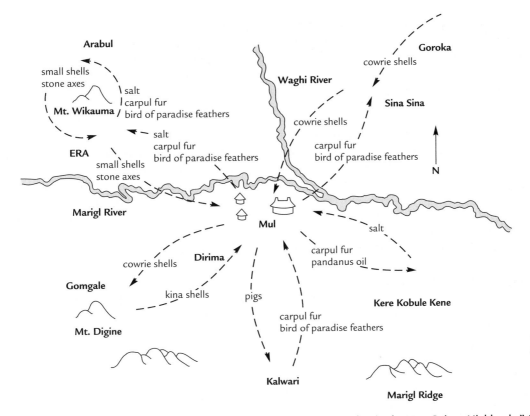

FIGURE 2   Traditional Exchange Network. Podolefsky, Aaron. "Contemporary Warfare in the New Guinea Highlands." *Ethnology: An International Journal of Cultural and Social Anthropology* 23 (1984):73–87. Reprinted by permission of Ethnology.

I use the term *atrophy* since the process was probably one of gradual disuse of trade networks rather than a catastrophic change. The remaining trade relations were reliant upon the need for luxury items such as shells and feathers. Scholars who have done long-term research in New Guinea have described the highlanders' declining interest in these decorative items.

With the introduction of Western goods and the reduction of trade, both the need and the opportunity for intermarriage declined. Intertribal marriage was functional in that it facilitated intergroup economic transactions. While there are a range of rights and obligations as well as affective ties which make marriage into neighboring groups preferable, more distant marriages have recognized importance. This same point was made by Roy Rappaport in his study of the Tsembaga Maring:

> While unions between men and women of a single local group are generally preferred, the Tsembaga recognize certain advantages in marriage to members of other local groups . . . unions with groups north of the Sambai River and south of the Bismarks strengthen trading relationships. Bird-of-paradise plumes and shell ornaments are still obtained from these groups and until the 1950s stone axes from the Jimi Valley were traded for salt manufactured in the Simbai Valley (1969:121).

An early paper on the Siani linked trade and marriage directly by focusing on the exchange of non-utilitarian valuables which occurred at marriage and at the rites of passage for children of the marriage (Salisbury 1956). Valuables were traded in from the coast about 70 miles to the northeast. Trading took the form of ceremonial gift exchange between affines. At the same time, Salisbury reports a statistically significant trend for Siane men to obtain wives from the south and west while their sisters marry into groups from the north and east (the direction from which valuables come).

Even more interesting for the present purpose is Salisbury's report on the effect of the introduction of European wealth goods. The European settlements nearest the Siane were in Goroka and Asaroka, 30 miles to the east and north. Groups nearest these (who were already closer than the Siane to coastal wealth) quickly became wealthy in shells, cloth, and other European goods. Salisbury reports that, as a result of this increased wealth, the movement of women in that direction became more pronounced. He also notes that "Neither the wealth difference nor the movement of women is recognized in Siane idealogy."

Thus, Salisbury clearly links marriage patterns to the need to obtain wealth not locally available, although no mention is made of utilitarian goods. While the initial response to "wealthy neighbors" is to increase "wife giving," it is easy to see that once wealth is more evenly (and locally) distributed this reason for marrying out will no longer be of major consequence.

Particularly in the many areas of the highlands where marriages were arranged by families with minimal, if any, consultation with the bride or groom, consideration of trade relations was likely to play a role in the selection of a spouse. Families had an interest in the establishment or maintenance of trade relations.

At the same time that the function of intertribal marriage for maintaining the economic system in terms of access to necessary resources was eliminated, the decline in trade itself reduced the opportunity to make marriage arrangements between non-adjacent groups. Generally speaking, opportunity for marriage is not random but may be structured by factors such as class, caste, religious affiliation, sorority membership, or political borders. Changes in this structure of opportunity may lead to observable changes in marriage patterns. In other words, a change in the visiting (or trading) pattern between autonomous political groups could affect the structure of opportunity. The importance of opportunity remains whether the individuals are free to choose their own mates or whether such choices are made for them.

In central Simbu elders choose a person's spouse for them and, although they can refuse, the bride and groom usually accept even though they may never have met. Brown (1969) reports that some groups do not intermarry because of the lack of opportunity to make arrangements.

Administrative policy and mission influence may have speeded the process. In some areas, such as South Fore or Manga, Australian patrol officers insisted (or at least strongly urged) that brides consent and that women have a right to choose a spouse. Nowadays in central Simbu more marriages are being initiated by the couples themselves. Choice in a mate is likely to further increase the importance of the structure of opportunity.

In sum, the argument here is that the replacement, by Western goods, of resources secured through trade reduced the economic need (function) for intergroup marriage and the opportunity to arrange such marriages. The effects of these changes were not felt immediately because of the extant relations between groups. Over time fewer and fewer intertribal marriages were arranged to replace those of the passing generation. The net effect was a gradual decay of the web of affinal and non-agnatic ties which cut across tribal boundaries.

CONCLUSION

Gordon (1980) has insightfully pointed out that there is very little sense in talking about or planning development if people live in fear of renewed tribal fighting. Moreover, he notes that this is a testing time for anthropologists "who find that their explanatory models are somewhat inadequate." Indeed, few of the explanations begin from a particular theoretical position nor even a unified conceptual model; there is little discussion of the mechanisms by which suggested "causes" result in the behavior being explained; and, little evidence is presented to test the explanations.

In this paper, I have employed a particular theoretic strategy, namely, cultural materialism, in which the efficacy of explanatory models are ranked: infrastructure, structure, and superstructure.

Prior to contact with the outside world, stone axe heads and salt were produced in local areas where these resources were available. Redistribution was accomplished through trade. One of the functions of intertribal marriage was the facilitation of trade between autonomous political groups. With the early introduction of Western goods, particularly steel axes and salt, local production was discontinued and marriage was no longer necessary to maintain these trade relations. As trade was discontinued, so declined the opportunity to make marriage arrangements between non-adjacent groups. Of course, existing marriage ties facilitated continued contact between groups, but probably less frequently, and there was no pragmatic reason for young people to marry others from distant areas. Particularly in the case of women, where such a marriage necessitated a move far from her natal family, there were distinct disadvantages. Thus, as older people died and fewer marriages were arranged between groups, the web of affinal and non-agnatic kin ties decayed. Intertribal marriages provided a linkage through which groups could communicate, and a mechanism and reason for containing conflict. With the decline in intergroup marriage over time, the likelihood of a dispute expanding into full-scale warfare increased.

This explanation began with infrastructural conditions (production) and showed how they were causally related to structural changes (trade relations) which in turn caused further structural changes (the web of kin ties), finally leading to changes in conflict behaviors. I have tried to explain each of the stages in this temporal process, i.e., the relationship between trade and marriage and the relationship between marriage and warfare.

Scientific hypotheses and models can be tested by examining predictions which can be deduced from them. The model which I have outlined predicts the unlikely occurrence that, with pacification and the ability to wander further afield without the threat of life and limb, intertribal marriage actually declined rather than rose as was thought would be the case. The hypothesis was tested on genealogical data collected in this research site as well as on data published earlier from a different area of the Simbu province. This is but a single case study and there is no statistical reason to extend the findings to other areas of the highlands. However, the inability to falsify the hypothesis in this case lends support to the general efficacy of the explanation.

NOTES

1. Financial support from the National Science Foundation (Grant No. BNS76-218 37) is gratefully acknowledged.

2. For a more extensive discussion of this period with special reference to the resurgence of fighting, see Brown 1982a and 1982b.

3. Paula Brown reports (pers. comm.) that recently many Simbu women are marrying outside the Simbu to men they had met in the district or on visits. She notes that there are, now, advantages for older men having a daughter married to a prestigious outsider. Naregu men who migrate probably also marry outsiders.

    Such marriages further the process described here since, although they are extra-tribal, they do not link neighboring potential enemy groups.

REFERENCES

Brown, P. 1964. Enemies and Affines. *Ethnology* 3:335–356.

——. 1969. Marriage in Chimbu. In *Pigs, Pearlshells and Women*, eds. R. M. Glasse and M. Meggitt, 77–95. Englewood Cliffs, NJ: Prentice-Hall.

——. 1970. Chimbu Transactions. *Man* 5: 99–117.

——. 1982a. Conflict in the New Guinea Highlands. *Journal of Conflict Resolution* 26: 525–546.

——. 1982b. Chimbu Disorder: Tribal Fighting in Newly Independent Papua New Guinea. *Pacific Viewpoint* 22: 1–21.

Brown, P. and A. M. Podolefsky. 1976. Population Density, Agricultural Intensity, Land Tenure, and Group Size in the New Guinea Highlands. *Ethnology* 15: 211–238.

Gordon, R. 1980. Rituals of Governance and the Breakdown of Law and Order in Papua New Guinea. Paper presented at the annual meeting of the American Anthropological Association. Washington, D.C.

——. 1983. The Decline of the Kiapdom and the Resurgence of "Tribal Fighting" in Enga. *Oceania* 53: 205–223.

Howlett, D., et al. 1976. *Chimbu: Issues in Development.* Development Studies Centre Monograph No. 4. Canberra.

Koch, K. 1974. *The Anthropology of Warfare.* Addison-Wesley Module in Anthropology No. 52.

Meggitt, M. 1958. The Enga of the New Guinea Highlands. *Oceania* 28: 253–330.

——. 1977. *Blood Is Their Argument: Warfare Among the Mae Enga Tribesmen of the New Guinea Highlands.* Palo Alto, CA: Mayfield.

Rappaport, R. 1969. Marriage Among the Maring. In *Pigs, Pearlshells and Women*, eds. R. M. Glasse and M. Meggitt, 117–137. Englewood Cliffs, NJ: Prentice-Hall.

Salisbury, R. F. 1956. Asymmetrical Marriage Systems. *American Anthropologist* 58: 639–655.

——. 1962. *From Stone to Steel.* London: Cambridge University Press.

Standish, B. 1973. The Highlands. *New Guinea* 8: 4–30.

Wormsley, W. 1982. Tribal Fighting, Law and Order, and Socioeconomic Development in Enga, Papua-New Guinea. Paper presented at the meeting of the American Anthropological Association. Washington, D.C.

32

Are the Desert People Winning?

Robert Sapolsky

If you could create your own version of an ideal society, what would it look like? Is it a beach culture, or maybe a mountain society? How do people produce food, shelter, and families? This thought exercise requires some creative and holistic anthropological thinking. Approximately 500 years ago, Thomas More wrote his response to this question in a book titled *Utopia*. In 134 pages, More created a fictional island with rich details about its political organization, religious life, and cultural norms. You might like More's Utopia, but buyer beware. In his Utopia there is no private property and every citizen performs a critical trade like carpentry and blacksmithing. Utopia citizens all wear similar and simple clothes, priests can marry, euthanasia is legal, and every family gets two slaves restrained with heavy gold chains. One way people become a Utopia slave is to commit adultery. And don't even think of premarital sex because the punishment is a life-sentence of enforced celibacy.

If you're not liking More's Utopia, you might consider the science fiction of Ursula K. Le Guin. Daughter of the famous twentieth-century anthropologist Alfred Kroeber, Le Guin wrote utopian novels that became a laboratory for imagined worlds with norms that seem unimaginable here on earth. In *The Left Hand of Darkness,* Le Guin creates a wintery and androgynous planet named Gethen. The people of Gethen are neither male nor female, but they do get sexual urges for a few days each month. Depending on the relationship and moment, one partner temporarily takes on a male form, while the other becomes a female; in Gethen biology a person could father children and next give birth to others. In Gethen, Le Guin created a world she could imagine, but had not yet seen—a world in which an androgynous biology eliminates sexual tension, male dominance, and war. Her novels are experiments in the anthropology of utopia.

Unless you've already purchased a ticket to Gethen, you can put some of your anthro-knowledge to work and imagine your own version of an ideal world. To get you started, here is a selection by Robert Sapolsky that examines some curious links between cultural practices and climate. Sapolsky argues that adopting a "desert dweller culture" versus a "forest dweller culture" will predict your society's religion, gender norms, and even your propensity to violence.

As you read this selection, ask yourself the following questions:

- Give two specific examples from the text of how climate/environment is linked with cultural norms.
- What information is contained in Textor's *A Cross Cultural Summary*?
- How does Marvin Ember explain the ecological roots of violence?
- Are desert dwellers or forest dwellers more likely to by polytheistic? Why?
- Are desert dwellers or forest dwellers more likely to harbor beliefs about the inferiority of women? Why?
- Is the forest culture or desert culture more widespread throughout the world? Why is that culture "winning"?
- Would you rather be born into a forest culture or desert culture? Why?

The following terms discussed in this section are included in the Glossary in the back of the book:

ecology
polytheism
utopia

All across the world, the sort of culture you live in has something to do with the ecosystem around it. Traditional tundra societies are more likely to share cultural patterns with each other than with tropical rain forest societies, regardless of whether some descended from a common ancestral culture. High-altitude plateau cultures differ in systematic ways from fishing cultures in island archipelagoes. Some of these correlations are fairly predictable: Tuareg desert nomads are not likely to have 27 different words for types of snow or fishhooks. But as Textor found, some of the correlations are far from predictable and have helped contribute to the sociopolitical mess we now inhabit.

Attempts to link culture with climate and ecology have an old history (Herodotus did it long before Montesquieu), but with the rise of anthropology as a discipline, the effort became scientific. Early efforts were often howlers of dead-white-male racism; every study seemed to generate irrefutable scientific proof that northern European ecosystems produced superior cultures, more advanced morals, technologies, and intellects, and better schnitzel. Much of contemporary social anthropology represents a traumatized retreat from the sins of those intellectual fathers. One solution was to resolutely avoid cultural comparisons, thereby ushering in an era wherein an anthropologist could spend an entire career documenting the puberty rite of one clan of farmers in northeastern Cameroon.

But some anthropologists remained generalists, studying cross-cultural patterns while cautiously treading around ideological bias, and many continued to explore how ecology affects culture. One such pioneer was John Whiting of Harvard, who in 1964 produced a paper entitled "Effects of Climate on Certain Cultural Practices." Comparing data from non-Westernized societies from around the planet, he noted that husbands and wives from cultures in the colder parts of this planet are more likely to sleep together at night than are spouses in the tropics. He also found that cultures in habitats that produce protein-poor diets have the longest restrictions on postpartum sex. Whiting hypothesized that to counterbalance the lack of protein, infants required a longer period of nursing, which placed a premium on well-spaced births.

Other anthropologists explored the ecological roots of violence. In 1982 Melvin Ember of Yale found that certain ecosystems are so stable and benign that families remain intact throughout the year, farming their plot of land or hunting and gathering in the surrounding rich forest. In less forgiving settings, family units often split up for long periods, dividing their herds into smaller groups during dry seasons, for instance, with family members scattered with subflocks on distant pockets of grazing land. In such situations,

warrior classes—as one sees among the pastoralist cowherding Masai of East Africa—are more common. There are advantages to having a communal standing army in case enemies appear when many of the men are away finding grass for the cattle.

In the 1960s, Textor pursued a radically different approach to cross-cultural research. He collated information on some 400 different cultures from around the world and classified them according to nearly 500 traits. What sort of legal system did each culture have? How did its people make a living? Did they believe in an afterlife? Did they weave or know about metallurgy? When at play, did they prefer games of chance or of strategy? Then he fed all these variables about all these cultures into some gigantic paleo-computer, cross-correlated everything, and laid out the significant findings. The result, his monumental *A Cross-Cultural Summary*, offers table after table indicating, among other things, which cultural differences are statistically likely to be linked to ecological differences. While not the sort of book you toss in your knapsack for beach reading, there is something irresistible about thousands of pages of correlations. Where else could you discover that societies that don't work with leather very well are disproportionately likely to have games of skill? How do you explain that one?

From these various anthropological approaches, a basic dichotomy has emerged between two types of societies from very different ecosystems: societies born in rain forests and those that thrive in deserts. Think of Mbuti pygmies versus Middle Eastern bedouin, or Amazonian Indians versus nomads of the Gobi. There turn out to be consistent and permeating differences between the two. Obvious exceptions exist, some quite dramatic. Nonetheless, the correlates are unnerving.

Begin with religious beliefs. A striking proportion of rain forest dwellers are polytheistic, worshipping an array of spirits and gods. Polytheism is prevalent among tribes in the Amazon basin (the Sherenti, Mundurucu, and Tapirape) and in the rain forests of Africa (the Ndorobo), New Guinea (the Keraki and Ulawans), and Southeast Asia (the Iban of Borneo and the Mnong Gar and Lolo of Vietnam). But desert dwellers—the bedouin of Arabia, the Berbers of the western Sahara, the !Kung of the Kalahari Desert, the Nuer and Turkana of the Kenyan/Sudanese desert—are usually monotheistic. Of course, despite allegiances to a single deity, other supernatural beings may be involved, like angels and djinns and Satan. But the hierarchy is notable, with minor deities subservient to the Omnipotent One.

This division makes ecological sense. Deserts teach large, singular lessons, like how tough, spare, and withholding the environment is; the world is reduced to simple, desiccated, furnace-blasted basics. Then picture rain forest people amid an abundance of edible plants and medicinal herbs, able to identify more species of ants on a single tree than one would find in all the British Isles. Letting a thousand deities bloom in this sort of setting must seem natural. Moreover, those rain forest dwellers that are monotheistic are much less likely to believe that their god sticks his or her nose into other people's business by controlling the weather, prompting illness, or the like. In contrast, the desert seems to breed fatalism, a belief in an interventionist god with its own capricious plans.

Another major difference was brought to light by Melvin Ember. Desert societies, with their far-flung members tending goats and camels, are classic spawning grounds for warrior classes and the accessories of militarism: military trophies as stepping stones to societal status, death in battle as a guarantee of a glorious afterlife, slavery. And these cultures are more likely to be stratified, with centralized authority. A cosmology in which an omnipotent god dominates a host of minor deities finds a natural parallel in a rigid earthly hierarchy.

Textor's work highlights other differences between desert and rain forest societies. Purchasing or indenturing wives is far less prevalent among rain forest peoples. And in rain forest cultures, related women tend to form the core of a community for a lifetime, rather than being shipped off to serve the expediency of marriage making. In desert cultures, women typically have the difficult tasks of building shelters and wandering in search of water and firewood, while the men contemplate the majesty of their herds and envision their next raid. Among rain forest cultures, it's the men who are more likely to do the heavy lifting. Rain forest cultures also are less likely to harbor beliefs about the inferiority of women; you won't be likely to find rain forest men giving thanks in prayer that they were not created female, as is the case in at least one notable desert-derived religion. Finally, desert cultures tend to teach their children to be modest about nudity at an earlier age than in rain forest cultures and have more severe strictures against premarital sex.

Which kind of culture would you prefer to get traded to? When it comes to the theistic part, it's six of one, half a dozen of the other to me. As for the other correlates, desert cultures, with their militarism, stratification, mistreatment of women, uptightness about child rearing and sexuality, seem unappealing. And yet ours happens to be a planet dominated by the cultural descendants of the desert dwellers. At various points, the desert dwellers have poured out of the Middle East, defining large parts of Eurasia. Such cultures, in turn, have passed the last 500 years subjugating the native populations of the Americas, Africa,

and Australia. As a result, ours is a Judeo-Christian/ Muslim world, not a Mbuti-Carib/Trobriand one.

So now we have Christians and Jews and Muslims in the wheat fields of Kansas, and in the cantons of the Alps, and in the rain forests of Malaysia. The desert mind-set, and the cultural baggage it carries, has proven extraordinarily resilient in its export and diffusion throughout the planet. Granted, few of those folks still live like nomadic pastoralists, guiding their flocks of sheep with staffs. But centuries, even millennia after the emergence of these cultures, they bear the marks of their desert pasts. Our vanquished enemies in Afghanistan, the Taliban, and our well-entrenched Saudi friends created societies of breathtaking repressiveness. In Jerusalem in recent years, Jewish Orthodox zealots have battled police, trying to close down roads on Saturday, trying to impose their restrictive version of belief. And for an American educator with, say, a quaint fondness for evolution, the power of the Christian right in many parts of this country to dictate what facts and truths may be uttered in a classroom is appalling. Only one way to think, to do, to be. Crusades and jihads, fatwas and inquisitions, hellfire and damnation.

Unfortunately, the rain forest mind-set appears not only less likely to spread than its desert counterpart but also less hardy when uprooted, more of a hothouse attribute. Logging, farming, and livestock grazing are rapidly defoliating Earth. Our age witnesses not only an unprecedented extinction of species but of cultures and languages as well. William Sutherland, a population biologist at the University of East Anglia, has shown that the places on Earth with the most biodiversity are the most linguistically diverse as well and that languages are even more at risk for extinction than are birds or mammals. And so the rain forest cultures, with their fragile pluralism born of a lush world of plenty, deliquesce into the raw sewage of the slums of Rio and Lagos and Jakarta.

What are we to make of the correlations between environment and cultural practices? Think of humans as the primates that we are, and it makes perfect sense. Go discover two new species of monkeys never before seen. Know nothing about them other than that one lives in the trees of an Amazonian forest and that the other walks the arid scrubland of Namibia, and a card-carrying primatologist can predict with great accuracy the differing sex lives of the two species, which is the more aggressive, which is the more territorial, and so on. In this respect, we are subject to the influences of ecology, like any other species.

Still, two big differences make us distinctive. First, human cultures allow far more—and far more dramatic—exceptions to rules than one finds in other primates. After all, our mean old Judeo-Christian/ Muslim world has also produced peaceful Quakers and Sufis. In contrast, no olive baboon, living a savanna life that favors omnivory, has ever opted for vegetarianism as a moral statement.

The second distinctive trait of human culture is its existential bent. We're not just talking about how ecology influences the kind of arrowhead you make or whether, during some ceremonial ritual, you shake the rattle before or after you do the dance with the hyena skull. What's at stake are profound, and defining, human preoccupations: Is there a god or gods, and does your existence matter to Them? What happens when you die, and how do your actions in life affect your afterlife? Is the body basically dirty and shameful? Is the world basically a benevolent place?

In the end, if we want to understand how people find answers to these intensely personal, individuating questions, we must admit some biology in the back door. We already recognize the many ways in which genetics, neurochemistry, and the endocrinology of depression affect whether a person constitutionally views life as a vessel half empty or half full. We are even beginning to glimpse a biology of religious belief itself. There are neurological injuries that cause religious obsessions, neuropsychiatric disorders associated with "metamagical" thinking; there are brain regions that regulate how tightly an organism demands a link between cause and effect, potentially creating room for insight into that odd phenomenon we call faith.

To answer the question, How did I become who I am? we must incorporate myriad subtle and interacting factors, from the selective pressures that shaped our primate gene pool eons ago to the burst of neurotransmitters in the previous microsecond. Maybe it's time to add another biological variable to the list: When our forebears pondered life's big questions, did they do so while contemplating an enveloping shroud of trees or an endless horizon?

33

Two Rights Make a Wrong

Indigenous Peoples Versus Environmental Protection Agencies

Richard Reed

In today's world, environmentalism has become an almost mainstream cultural ideal, as cereal boxes and pop stars beseech us to "save the rainforest." The question of indigenous rights to traditional lands, however, has not received the same degree of popular attention. Indigenous peoples do not have the same political allies as the forests in which they live. In this selection we see that some environmentalists and anthropologists propose combining these two agendas, arguing that the goals of conservation and defending traditional indigenous land use have much in common. For example, both efforts should be aimed at preventing land from being exploited according to models of nonsustainable agrobusiness.

Neither environmental conservation nor indigenous land rights are simple issues, and the alliance between these two sides is far from harmonious. In this selection, anthropologist Richard Reed describes the history of the creation of a national park (or reserve) in Paraguay where, initially, indigenous people were expected both to have access to land for traditional purposes and to be involved in managing and maintaining the park.

Anthropologists began by calling for the creation of the reserve and the inclusion of indigenous people in its management plan. Anthropologists found a powerful ally to make the reserve a reality: The Nature Conservancy, a U.S.-based nonprofit conservation group. Anthropologists were also called on to facilitate communication among indigenous people, biologists, and personnel in a variety of government and nongovernment organizations. Yet while anthropologists are in a privileged position to understand the viewpoint of these different cultures, they are working in a context of unequal power. By the time the national park was created, only those indigenous people who maintained a traditional economic lifestyle, as defined by The Nature Conservancy, were permitted to have access, while the rest of the "acculturated" indigenous people were excluded.

Indigenous people are not fossils or museum exhibits. They have never been in a "natural" state; they have always had an impact on the local ecology. Indigenous people themselves should ideally decide how to practice their culture and respond to changing political, economic, and ecological traditions. Because native groups remain as disempowered today as they were five hundred years ago when the first Europeans arrived, they profoundly distrust all who want to come and help them, including well-intentioned anthropologists. As Reed says, to the indigenous people of this region, The Nature Conservancy is just another in a long history of outsider plantation owners (*latifundistas*). Until indigenous peoples can become actors with a voice in the environmental movement, this promising alliance will continue to be problematic.

As you read this selection, ask yourself the following questions:

- What are the different goals that the two sides in this alliance have? Are these goals incompatible?

- How did the fact that there were at least two indigenous groups involved in this case make the situation more complicated?

- How did anthropologists play a role as "culture brokers" in this scenario? Did their efforts fail? Why?

- Why was The Nature Conservancy so interested in Mbaracayu Park, whereas the World Bank was not?

- What cultural ideals of the "native" are involved in this case?

The following terms discussed in this selection are included in the Glossary at the back of the book:

foraging	*peasants*
horticulture	*shifting agriculture*
indigenistas	*swidden cultivation*
indigenous	yerba mate
latifundistas	yerbateros

Reed, Richard. "Two Rights Make a Wrong: Indigenous Peoples Versus Environmental Protection Agencies." Reprinted with permission of the author.

In lowland Latin America, the struggle to save the forests has forged new alliances between indigenous peoples and environmental foundations. Such alliances link the future of the world's indigenous people with the future of the forests, to the benefit of both. The political and economic capital that environmental agencies bring to the conservation struggle can aid indigenous groups. At the same time, environmental groups gain two things: the indigenous knowledge to understand the complex biological communities in these areas as well as a potent symbol of the importance of the mission (Graham and Conklin 1995).

Problems have begun to surface, however, in the relationship between indigenous peoples and the environmental movement. Agencies find that indigenous populations are often internally divided and that their conflicting demands are difficult to reconcile in the larger fight for environmental protection. Indigenous peoples, in turn, are often dissatisfied with the restrictions imposed by environmental protection organizations.

This article examines a case in which The Nature Conservancy (TNC) and several indigenous groups tried to collaborate in the creation and management of a reserve in northeastern Paraguay. In 1989, TNC purchased 53,000 hectares of the last sustainable stands of subtropical deciduous forest that once covered the Paraguay and Brazil's Paraná Plateau—one of the last open forests for the Aché and the Guaraní peoples. In their fight against colonists and cattle ranchers, the Aché, the Guaraní, and TNC were forced to contend with one another. They also had to contend with misunderstandings based on conceptions of nature and indigenous peoples that emerged as environmentalists and anthropologists negotiated access to and management of the region.

MBARACAYU

Until 1970, far eastern Paraguay was undisturbed by intensive development. The region was protected by plantation owners (*latifundistas*) and multinational corporations that were primarily interested in the limited collection of native *yerba mate* (*Ilex paraguayensis*) and harvesting of hardwood trees. Two indigenous groups occupied the forests, the food-foraging Aché and the horticultural Guaraní. These two groups generally lived in a state of mutual fear and permanent conflict; both have had intermittent contact with *yerba mate* collectors and loggers who penetrated the zone. Throughout history, *latifundistas* restricted colonization of the forest by nonindigenous peoples, but the Guaraní and Aché were tolerated. As a result, the indigenous

groups had free access to sufficient resources to control their own lives.

Over the last twenty years, the forests of eastern Paraguay have been expropriated to satisfy land demands by agro-industrialists and the growing peasant population. Between 1963 and 1976, the Paraguay land reform agency (IBR) distributed about four million hectares to 90,000 families. By 1984, 5.1 million hectares, roughly half of the arable land in eastern Paraguay, had been given to peasant colonists. Foreign investment accompanied colonization. Brazilian, American, and Japanese companies purchased vast areas of forest for clear-cutting and agriculture (Parquet 1985:37). Soybean production and ranching replaced traditional industries in eastern Paraguay. As a result, the forests were reduced by half by 1989, and the rate of continued deforestation in Paraguay was higher than in any other Latin American country (Hanratty and Meditz 1990).

As rural transformation converts Paraguay's subtropical forests into an international breadbasket, the Aché and Guaraní are losing land. As early as the 1970s, voices were raised in defense of Paraguay's indigenous peoples (AIP/Misión 1977). The Aché became an international concern when they were forced to take refuge with missionaries and exploitative patrons (Arens 1976). Anthropologists and *indigenistas* lobbied the national government for land. Although most Aché and Guaraní received guarantees to some land, these *"colonias nacionales"* were insufficient for hunting and shifting agriculture.

In the early 1980s, anthropologists identified a major tract of remaining forested land called "Mbaracayu," which could allow many of the indigenous people to continue traditional hunting and gathering. Since the World Bank then controlled this land (a lumber company had defaulted on a loan), there was hope that this virgin forest could be secured for the indigenous groups.

Traditionally the Guaraní of the region hunted in the forests and collected a variety of goods, including commodities such as *yerba mate* and skins. In 1971, when the land was sold for lumbering, the families living in Mbaracayu were forced from their homes onto adjacent lands. Today, five hundred Guaraní families are located near the land, supplementing their gardens by hunting and gathering on the few large tracts of forest that remain undeveloped.

Mbaracayu also harbored one of the last groups of hunting and gathering Aché. Since being forced out of the forest in 1976, they had been given fields and houses at a religious mission outside the reserve. Nevertheless, the Aché continued their patterns of intermittent nomadic foraging within the dense forests of Mbaracayu.[1]

TIMELINE OF MBARACAYU RESERVE

- 1531–1960: Indigenous people in Paraguay struggle successfully to maintain traditional lifestyles in the forests of eastern Paraguay.
- 1968: Mbaracayu forest is purchased by timber company.
- 1971: Guaraní communities are forced out of Mbaracayu forest by timber company.
- 1974: Timber company goes bankrupt; World Bank acquires Mbaracayu by default.
- 1976: World Bank and Paraguayan government attempt to force Aché out of Mbaracayu forest.
- 1983: Anthropologists approach World Bank to grant Mbaracayu to indigenous groups.
- 1983: World Bank ignores anthropologists (and their own guidelines on indigenous peoples).

- 1989: TNC purchases 53,000 hectares of the last sustainable stands of subtropical deciduous forest in Paraguay.
- 1989: Anthropologists meet with indigenous groups to discuss the creation of the reserve and its management plan.
- 1989: NGO Fundación Moises Bertoni (FMB) is created to manage the reserve.
- 1991: All Guaraní indigenous people are denied access to the reserve.
- 1991: Aché indigenous people are granted limited access to the reserve, provided they maintain their "traditional," "natural" lifestyles as defined by FMB and TNC.

In 1983, anthropologists approached the World Bank to donate the land for use by Paraguayan indigenous people. When calls to Washington came to naught, the bank was instead asked to provide a small portion of the land to the Aché and Guaraní in compliance with the World Bank's own policy of protecting indigenous peoples in the project areas. Bank personnel ignored the requests, suggesting that the whole idea of indigenous use of the land was preposterous.

Seeking allies, some anthropologists approached TNC. The idea quickly became a plan, was then converted into a project, was embedded in a program, and within days had been granted a budget. There was a reason TNC moved quickly. In the 1980s it was searching for the means to internationalize its work, and Mbaracayu offered a unique opportunity. The region harbored plant and animal life that was disappearing from much of southern Brazil, northern Argentina, and eastern Paraguay. Paraguayan land was cheap and the Paraguayan government was an image-conscious dictatorship. It was a case where a little pull and a little money could accomplish a great deal in a short time.

Whereas anthropologists' inquiries to the World Bank were rebuffed, TNC's interest in acquiring Mbaracayu was warmly received. TNC had important Washington connections, had amassed a considerable war chest for the negotiation of land purchase, and could call on a host of international contacts for such complex transactions as debt-for-nature swaps.

As discussions moved forward quickly, TNC proposed that the land be protected by a joint Paraguayan-international effort. In conformity with World Bank guidelines toward indigenous people, the bank requested that TNC develop a management plan for indigenous peoples' use of the region. To design this component of the management plan, anthropologists (the author included) visited each indigenous community, counted the population, and held a meeting to discuss the plan. In Paraguay, a host country agency called Fundación Moises Bertoni (FMB) was developed to orchestrate the land acquisition and manage the park.

This management plan provided the first arena for the negotiation of the conflicting rights of indigenous people and TNC. The Guaraní and Aché saw the creation of the reserve and TNC's interest in their involvement as a means of acquiring what they considered their primordial right, the forests of Mbaracayu. Although the government's interest in helping indigenous groups was limited, the indigenous groups saw new potential in the international ties and power of TNC. For its part, TNC reinforced the impression that Mbaracayu was a site where indigenous groups could maintain their society and culture. Rhetoric surrounding the project emphasized the agencies' sensitivity to indigenous peoples' needs and rights. Introducing Mbaracayu in its own literature, TNC (1996:17) reported that it purchased the area in 1991 "to help the Aché preserve their traditions and to protect one of the last untouched forest wilderness areas in Paraguay."

In designing the reserve management plan, anthropologists proposed that indigenous people could be important to the future of the region. Guaraní and Aché have the greatest knowledge of the local environment, its resources, and their use. More than a simple biological variable in the forest ecosystem, the plan pointed out that traditional economic activities in the area had directly affected the existing forest. Guaraní and Aché hunting, gathering, fishing, and swidden cultivation had patterned the region's flora and fauna. Anthropologists noted that for five centuries Guaraní had collected *yerba* commercially, while protecting and promoting a series of natural yerba stands (*yerbales*). These activities provided Guaraní with a steady income without destroying the forest. Thus, indigenous commercial extraction had "managed" the so-called "natural" environment (Reed 1997).

Given these models of indigenous resource use, the anthropological team suggested that the indigenous residents be integrated into the maintenance and management of the reserve. Aché would continue to hunt and gather; Guaraní would be allowed to continue traditional, commercial *yerba* gathering. In addition, it was proposed that the Aché be employed as "guarde bosques," manipulating the colonists' fear of "savage Indians" to assure that they remained beyond the park's boundaries. In sum, anthropologists suggested that indigenous groups be given access to the resources that they traditionally used, resources that were vital to their continued social and economic independence (Renshaw and Reed 1989:53).

When the proposed indigenous component of the management plan was presented to the Paraguayan reserve management agency, however, discussions were fraught with conflict and misunderstanding. The team of biologists, TNC, and FMB were skeptical of the plan to give indigenous people rights to use park resources. They were concerned that hunting would undermine endangered animal populations, gardens would damage the forest, and commercial gathering would lead to wholesale destruction of forest resources.

The arguments against the plan rested on two points. First, they suggested that Mbaracayu had been unaffected by past human activity. Second, giving Aché and Guaraní rights to continue hunting, field cutting, or commercial collection would degrade the forest environment.

The management plan that was finally written by the FMB attempted to step gingerly between the conflicting demands. It allowed some Aché limited access to the reserve, provided they had no impact on its floral or faunal populations. The majority of the Aché were to be relocated to land that TNC would purchase elsewhere and title directly to the community. The management plan excluded Guaraní from any access to the land. Instead of being treated as an indigenous people with a right to the reserve, they were integrated into an alternative plan to assist local peasants with agricultural extension work projects.

With the establishment of the reserve, most Aché and Guaraní felt they had lost their primordial right to the forest. They greeted the loss with the same fatalism they had exhibited previously when other large areas were removed from their control. The TNC found that their model was easily imposed on the rural region, creating the reality that fit their ideas. By restricting Guaraní

from this last large parcel of forest, they forced them farther into Paraguayan peasant society. Most Aché, in turn, were forced into a plot where a degree of farming was necessary to augment the meager hunting.

DISCUSSION

It would be easy to blame the unhappy result on the parties involved: the environmentalists' insensitivity, the indigenous communities' naivete; the anthropologists' idealism. The reality is more complex. The negotiations surrounding Mbaracayu suffered from a series of erroneous assumptions and conflicting perceptions. Each party created images of the others based on their differing world views. TNC's ideas of forest peoples, the anthropologists' scientific models, and the indigenous groups' attitudes toward the larger power structure all made it impossible for a meaningful dialogue to take place. Consequently, the plan that was implemented reinforced the inequities of power and resources that characterize other relations between small-scale societies and the larger system.

As instructive as it would be to analyze fully all images used in the discussion, the following discussion focuses on the concept of "natural" that dominates much of our thinking about the environment. Despite the word's ubiquity, the concept of nature remains extremely ambiguous. On one hand, it refers to the inherent qualities of things, as in "the nature of." On the other hand, it refers to the original state, as in "the natural world." In the environmental movement, it has taken on both of these meanings. It signifies the world in its original state, following its own (natural) laws and organized according to the (natural) order of things.

In practice, our ideas of nature are most often defined in relation to their opposites; such as grace, in religion; culture, in anthropology; and history, in philosophy. In the environmental debate, our concept of nature is opposed to civilization. In this romantic vision, for which Rousseau can take much of the credit, human civilization destroys the original ideal order of the world. Where French philosophers found the evils of civilization in the growth of the state, today's evil empire is envisioned in the development of expanding technology, markets, and populations. As humans develop the power and need to dominate nature, they destroy its order, its ecological rationality, and its scientific predictability.

Ecologically Noble Savage

The distinction between nature and civilization helps us understand the position of indigenous peoples in the environmental movement. Rousseau suggested that people's natural humanity was destroyed by civilization. As in the seventeenth century, indigenous peoples today are thought to have the capacity to be *either* natural *or* civilized. Presumably, humans in their original state did not destroy nature but lived in conjunction with it—in ideological and biological harmony with the environment in which they lived. Redford (1990) terms this natural conception of humans the "ecologically noble savage."

Anthropologists' own models of indigenous life also promoted the concept of the ecologically noble savage. Since the nineteenth century, anthropologists have portrayed original human societies as in a state of nature. In the ecological anthropology of the 1960s, this perception developed into models of the idealized ecological relationships of indigenous peoples in biotic communities. Indigenous people are presented as elements in stable ecosystems, their adaptive activity perfectly integrated into the larger environment.

As indigenous people enter into agreements with environmental groups in lowland South America, they are preceived within this dichotomy between "natural" and "civilized." In the planning of Mbaracayu, the Aché—who left the mission, shed superfluous clothing, and lived in the forest—were easily defined as forest savages. In the minds of functionaries in Asunción and Washington, they were perceived to be natural elements of the forest ecosystem. Aché culture was described in biological terms in the forest ecosystem. Aché hunters and gatherers were considered as living in harmony with nature, harvesting enough to survive but not seeking to expand or overexploit the flora or fauna.

This conceptualization found expression in the imagery that TNC used in discussing the Aché and advertising their work to the public. Pictures of Aché in TNC articles emphasized the small, light, forest people as a "Stone Age culture." As one publication put it, "For hundreds of years, the Aché roamed over the dense forest in eastern Paraguay, hunting and gathering with no permanent homes and few possessions" (The Nature Conservancy 1996). A writer for *The Nature Conservancy Magazine* almost fully conflates the categories of Aché and animal:

> "Felipe Jakugi scampers 60 feet up a Lapacho tree that sways like a giant waving hand. Jakugi, an Aché Indian, is at home in the treetops of Mbaracayu forest of northeastern Paraguay. For centuries, the Aché have hunted monkeys and escaped enemies in the forest canopy." (Thigpen 1996)

The anthropologists involved with the project (myself included) made full use of the concept of the noble savage. The indigenous component of the management plan depended more on ethnography and theoretical work in tropical ecology (Posey and Baleé 1989,

Treachy 1982) than on the ideas and opinions of the local indigenous communities. It stressed the rationality of traditional indigenous use of natural resources. By arguing that these people would continue to treat the forest as a sacred entity, anthropologists forced the diverse hopes, needs, desires, and plans of all the various individuals of several ethnic groups into one neat political package and then tried to sell it to the environmental agencies.

Ecological Half-Breeds

Few, if any, groups in lowland South America conform to the rigid vision of isolated naturalness. As indigenous people become integrated into the environmental movement, the reality of their attitudes and activities often conflicts with the model of forest people as noble. The vast majority of indigenous peoples enter the market economy for cash crops or wage labor; buy clothes and tools from the world markets; and market natural resources. Once sullied by these activities, they are seen to be forever and utterly changed. Once touched by the market, native peoples are thought to lay down the mantle of noble savage and align with the environmentally destructive society.

Indigenous peoples who fail the litmus test of environmental sensitivity are cast as ignoble savages—ecological half-breeds. Indigenous people in contact with the larger society and international economy are assumed to have acquired only the worst of modern society, having adopted the drives and desires of the poor and destitute. Without considering the long-term implications of these ideas, or their coherence in the face of the actual beliefs of indigenous peoples, researchers assume that these peoples lay down indigenous attitudes en masse as if they were broken tools and pick up new ideas as if they were sharper machetes. These new attitudes are considered destructive and unsustainable in the forest, because forest peoples are believed to be especially vulnerable to irrational desires for commodities. Rousseau, like Marx, pointed to private property as the first step toward both civilization and destruction. Today, we harbor the illusion that exposure to commodities seduces forest peoples into making the most unnecessary demands. With the same smug superiority that is used to describe the sale of Manhattan for a few baubles, we expect indigenous peoples to fall into the commodity trap—machetes and running shorts, followed by unquenchable desires for alcohol, tape players, sunglasses, and a host of other luxuries.

In the case of Mbaracayu, native groups that didn't fit the caricature of the noble savage found no place in TNC's forest. Aché who chose to practice a more complex economy, perhaps integrating swidden cultivation or selling labor for wages, were thought to no longer maintain a "traditional" Aché lifestyle (Thigpen 1996). In fact, as Aché expressed growing discordance over the various options presented by TNC, the population became increasingly divided between those Aché whom TNC considered "real" and those whom they considered somehow less authentic. Those who chose to farm or clear forest were restricted from their native forests and offered a parcel in another region. Only those who subscribed to TNC's model of the Aché were permitted to continue to use Mbaracayu.

TNC considered all Guaraní totally degraded by the larger society. The Guaraní are shifting cultivators; as such, they stepped out of a state of nature and became involved in the market economy, practicing a mix of agriculture, wage labor, and petty commodity production. TNC saw such Guaraní activities as a direct threat to the "virgin" forest that supposedly existed. In many ways, the Guaraní were considered peasants—greedy individuals who acted with unenlightened self-interest, predators who would disrupt the equilibrium of nature and destroy the ecosystem.

THE POLITICAL CONTEXT OF THE DEBATE

The environmental dialogue is locked into a simple dichotomy between the natural and the civilized, despite the many recent advances in theory concerning the complexity of human relations with the environment. Biologists and ecologists are aware that the very concept of "virgin" forest as untouched by human hands ignores millennia of human involvement. Indigenous production has not only been sustained in the forest but is an integral factor in maintaining the "natural" biological diversity (Denevan and Padoch 1987, Hecht and Cockburn 1989). In Mbaracayu, gardening, hunting, and even forestry are important influences on the natural forest ecosystem (Baleé 1992:43). Far from destroying nature, humans have created the natural world.

Anthropologists and ecologists appreciate the resilience of the forest and the tenacity of indigenous cultures, but the new understandings are not readily integrated into the discussion of environmental conservation. Why are misperceptions fostered, and why do simple dichotomies still dominate the dialogue about environmental conservation? An awareness of the political context of dialogue makes it clear that misperceptions are created and reinforced in the contemporary conflict over resources.

Graham and Conklin (1995) point out that the dialogue between indigenous peoples and expanding societies takes place in a frontier area. This "middle ground" is not fully controlled by either the small-scale society or the larger system. Since the time of the Jesuits, the Paraguayan government in Asunción has held tenuous control over its rural area. As recently as the 1880s, Paraguay lost over a third of its territory to Brazil. *Latifundios* were organized to take responsibility for protecting Paraguayan sovereignty. Today, the disassembly of these plantations creates a power vacuum. Brazilian ranchers, Japanese lumber firms, and Paraguayan soybean farmers struggle for remnants of control, and no clear state official has the power to enforce the law.

The dialogue between environmental groups and indigenous peoples is a part of this larger conflict over the resources. As environmental groups move to protect the few remaining stands of forests, they find that they are in conflict not only with developers but also with the claims of primordial rights by indigenous residents. Indigenous groups, on the other hand, find that a new type of plantation owner (*latifundista*) has arrived on the scene. The need to defend their ancestral land demands that they negotiate with this new "developer"—the environmental protection group.

The terms that are chosen in the dialogue over forest rights fall prey to the power relations of the larger system. Worldwide networks of information, international political connections, and a war chest of capital empower environmental groups in the international scramble for land. TNC, World Wildlife Fund, and the Fund for Animals have the economic and political weapons to confront some of the most powerful corporations and many national governments. They hold a vast amount of institutional power in their relations with indigenous groups—relations that reinforce and are reinforced by the terms of the dialogue. By defining indigenous people with respect to a yardstick of savagery, environmental groups can effectively exclude all those who do not conform to their ideal.

Graham and Conklin also point out that it is politically dangerous for environmental groups to ignore indigenous groups. Indians' presence can develop into a political problem if the conflict over resources moves into the national or international consciousness. Environmental groups are better served by defusing confrontation. On the other hand, the involvement of indigenous peoples, even a contentious and divided group such as the Aché, can be a public relations asset. This was clear in the case of Mbaracayu, where TNC was careful to publicize its defense of the Aché along with its program for protecting the environment (The Nature Conservancy 1996).

Indigenous groups have not had the opportunity to establish their own definitions of themselves or their world in the environmental debate. Despite the attempts of anthropologists and Paraguayans to inform the local residents of TNC and its aims, most indigenous people garnered little understanding of the actors involved or the complex negotiations that were taking place over their land. They had little idea of what to expect, alternating between complete belief that they would get to use the land exclusively and a lack of confidence that anything would happen.

This is not to say they were confused. In the case of Mbaracayu, although indigenous groups had only a hazy idea of TNC, its purpose, or its programs, they had a very clear idea of the structure of power in the struggle for the land of Mbaracayu. Their high hopes and cynicism were born of the long history of relationships with *latifundistas*. From the indigenous standpoint, the environmental agency was virtually indistinguishable from previous ranchers and multinational corporations.

As alliances are formed between indigenous groups and environmental agencies, we are called upon to facilitate the dialogue concerning reserves and indigenous peoples. Anthropologists are brought into the debate because of their distinct knowledge and perspective. They not only offer accurate information about the people and places involved but are also in the privileged position of seeing the conflict from two perspectives. These abilities, however, force anthropologists into the conflicting roles of scientist and political actor. Although knowledge gives anthropologists a responsibility to take action, it offers little power in dictating the terms of the debate or deciding the outcome.

Thus it was TNC, not the Aché, Guaraní, or anthropologists, who defined the terms of the debate over indigenous rights to Mbaracayu in the national and international sphere. By defining some indigenous people as threats to the natural environment, TNC could rally support for the reserve and the relocation of those indigenous residents. Those who chose to stay needed to abide by the strictures laid down by the agency. On the other hand, neither the Aché nor the Guaraní had the opportunity either to portray themselves in all the complexities of their indigenous identity or to declaim TNC as a *latifundista* that was taking indigenous land for its own purposes.

In conclusion, environmental groups are integrating indigenous peoples into the day-to-day management of conservation areas. Despite their common ground, agencies and indigenous groups cannot escape confrontation. Even when their short-term objectives are similar, their respective long-term goals are often very different. Whereas agencies seek to protect the forests in perpetuity and seek indigenous peoples' assistance in the endeavor, indigenous groups are fundamentally concerned with their own survival and see the forests as their primary resource in that struggle.

As large areas of the forest are converted to pasture and field, the two groups remain in contention for the remaining undisturbed areas.

NOTE

1. This group has been extensively studied by anthropologists and provided data to further a variety of cultural ecological models (e.g., Hill and Hurtado 1995).

REFERENCES

AIP/Misión (Asociación Indígena del Paraguay and Misión de Amistad). 1977. *Población y tierras indígenas en la región oriental de la República del Paraguay.* Manuscript.

Arens, Richard. 1976. *Genocide in Paraguay.* Philadelphia: Temple University Press.

Baleé, William. 1992. People of the fallow. In *Conservation of Neotropical Forests: Working from Traditional Resource Use,* ed. K. Redford and C. Padoch, 35–58. New York: Columbia.

Clay, Jason. 1988. *Indigenous Peoples and Tropical Forests: Models for Land Use and Management from Latin America.* Cambridge, MA: Cultural Survival.

Denevan, William, and Christine Padoch. 1987. Swidden-fallow agroforestry in the Peruvian Amazon. *Advances in Economic Botany* Number 5. New York: New York Botanical Gardens.

Graham, Laura, and Beth Conklin. 1995. The shifting middle ground: Amazonian Indians and eco-politics. *American Anthropologist* 97(4): 695–710.

Hanratty, Dennis, and Sandra Meditz, eds. 1990. *Paraguay: A Country Study.* Washington, DC: U.S. Government Printing Office.

Hecht, Susanna, and Andrew Cockburn. 1989. *The Fate of the Forest.* New York: Verso.

Hill, Kim, and A. Magdalena Hurtado. 1995. *Aché Life History: The Ecology and Demography of a Foraging People.* New York: Aldine de Gruyter.

Laino, Domingo. 1997. *Paraguay: Fronteras y penetracion brasileña.* Asunción: Ediciones Cerro Cora.

The Nature Conservancy. 1996. Profiles: Maracayu. *The Nature Conservancy.* Nov./Dec.

Padoch, Christine et al. 1985. Amazonian agroforestry: A market oriented system in Peru. *Agroforestry Systems* 3(1): 47–58.

Parquet, Reinerio. 1985. *Las Empresas Transnacionales en la economia del Paraguay.* Unpublished manuscript prepared for Unidad Conjunta CEPAL/CET: Buenos Aires.

Posey, Darrell, and William Baleé. 1989. Resource management in Amazonia. *Advances in Economic Botany* Number 7. New York: New York Botanical Gardens.

Redford, Kent. 1990. The ecologically noble savage. *Orion Nature Quarterly* 9(3): 25–29.

Reed, Richard. 1997. *Forest Dwellers, Forest Protectors: Indigenous Models for International Development.* Boston: Allyn and Bacon.

Renshaw, John, and Richard Reed. 1989. *Analysis socioeconomico y cultural de las poblaciones asentadas in el area de influencia del la reserva Mbaracayu.* Unpublished manuscript prepared for Fundación Moises Bertoni: Asunción.

Thigpen, Jaunita. 1996. Help wanted: Traditional wisdom required. *The Nature Conservancy.* Nov./Dec.

Treacy, Jonathon. 1982. Bora Indian agroforestry: An alternate to deforestation. *Cultural Survival Quarterly* 6(2): 16–17.

34

Moral Fibers of Farmer Cooperatives

Creating Poverty and Wealth with Cotton in Southern Mali

Scott M. Lacy

When the imminent threat of Civil War in the United States threatened to disrupt cotton exports to textile mills in France, French entrepreneurs and government officials sought alternative cotton sources in their African territories and colonies. Counter to the ambitions of the French, cotton production in African territories like the French Soudan was geared toward local consumption not export. To feed the demand of domestic textile mills, the French coerced West African farmers to increase cotton production through taxation and technological inputs. The intensification of cotton production established a cash crop, which to this day serves as a foundation to the economy of West African nations like Mali and Burkina Faso.

Development officials promote cotton production as a means to combat endemic poverty in rural Malian communities, but cotton farming can create poverty as well. When world cotton prices are high, cotton-producing countries like Mali may reap financial benefits, but when prices fall, small-scale cotton farmers pay the price. Mali ranks as one of the poorest countries in the world, and historically low cotton prices make this country's strength its weakness. In this selection, Scott Lacy examines some of the ways Malian officials have tried to assist family farmers. For decades, communities in Mali organized cotton production through farmer collectives, one per village, but starting in 2003

the government gave farmers a new option allowing the formation of smaller sub-village collectives. The freedom to choose the membership and size of one's local cotton grower association may lift some producers out of poverty, but this freedom may further complicate the economic and social viability of other producers and communities in crisis.

As you read this selection, ask yourself the following questions:

- What is the difference between cotton produced in the United States and cotton produced in Mali?
- How did colonization transform cotton production in rural Malian communities?
- How do decentralized farmer collectives (CPCs) help some farmers but harm others?
- What is the difference between the memberships of Dissan's two cotton collectives (CPCs)?
- How do fluctuations in global cotton prices impact the lives of small-scale family farmers in rural Mali?

The following terms discussed in this selection are included in the Glossary at the back of the book:

brain drain	*cooperative*
cash crop	*subsidy*

F or several centuries, cotton has been a critical component of the agricultural economy of Mali, West Africa. In fact, presidents, economists, and contemporary development officials have long promoted this

cash crop as "white gold" with the potential to lift Mali from its status as one of the poorest countries in the world. After all, Malian farmers grow some of the world's highest quality cotton, and at a fraction of the cost of international competitors; U.S. cotton growers, for example, produce lower-grade cotton and they spend nearly three times as much to produce each harvested kilo. To capitalize on this rare market advantage, in 2002 Malian officials modified national policies

Lacy, Scott M. "Moral Fibers of Farmer Cooperatives: Creating Poverty and Wealth in Southern Mali." This article was written especially for *Applying Cultural Anthropology: An Introductory Reader*, 8/e.

governing rural cotton production based on the idea that decentralizing local farm collectives would encourage farmers to bolster domestic harvests. Initially production statistics confirmed this theory, but the positive effects were short-lived. In the following pages, I describe how farmers from a village in southern Mali adapted to the decentralization of community cotton collectives, and I explore the roles of cotton and cash cropping in rural subsistence economies.

METHODS

This chapter is based on a long-term study in southern Mali starting with fifteen months of fieldwork in 2001/2 and annual follow-up studies from 2004–2008. While living and working with family farmers in the village of Dissan (11°36N, 7°31W, 344 masl,), I conducted two extensive surveys in 2001/2 to learn about household agricultural production, including farmer practices and knowledge of local crops and growing environments, household economies, and community-based farm collectives. In 2001 I surveyed all sixty-six Dissan households and conducted a comprehensive census of the community to acquire baseline data on household farm production and resources. Before the planting season, in March and April 2002, I interviewed a stratified sample of Dissan households ($n = 20$) to further investigate farmer knowledge and production practices. After completing these first two surveys, I spent a full growing season apprenticing with four households to actively learn about the resources and annual production cycle of Dissan farmers. Since 2004 I have returned to Dissan to conduct annual follow-up studies focused on crop choices, seed systems, and household farm production. Qualitative data used in this chapter come from ethnographic field notes, individual interviews, and a series of informal group interviews recorded between 2001 and 2008.

STUDY COMMUNITY

I was introduced to Dissan when I arrived there in 1994 as a Peace Corps volunteer. Dissan is a rural farming community that traces its origins back to the seventeenth century (Lacy 2004:83–85). In December 2001 there were 881 people living in sixty-six households in Dissan. The household (*du*, in Bamanakan) is an extended family that lives, eats, and works together using common resources. Depending on its size, a household either shares a single compound or a conglomeration of adjacent compounds composed of shaded

sitting areas, sleeping quarters, cooking huts, and various storage constructions. According to my 2001 census, the mean number of people per household was thirteen (SD = 8.9). Bamanakan is the primary language spoken in Dissan, however, some community members speak other languages including Arabic, French, Fulani, and Wolof.

Though Dissan is in a relatively wet region of Mali sometimes referred to as the cotton zone, even in good years when many households harvest enough grain to last the year, other households suffer food shortages. Annual rainfall throughout Mali is low and extremely variable, making rain-fed agricultural production a complex and risky enterprise. Nonetheless, every family in Dissan depends on rain-fed agriculture for subsistence, including the teachers of the village primary school who farm to supplement their salaries.

In 2007/8, Dissan households used hand-held hoes, collective labor, and animal-traction plows to cultivate a combined total of 282 hectares of field crops (not including secondary plots of peanuts and rice), including 21.5 hectares of cotton and 161 hectares of sorghum (Table 1). Farmers typically produce sorghum for household consumption and grow cotton as a cash crop or as a means for procuring agricultural inputs and short-term credit (or both). Data from the 2001 survey show that households who acquire credit and inputs through cotton production are the households that plant the most sorghum; they also are more likely to have expensive farm equipment like cultivators, seeders, plows, donkey carts, and sprayers for applying chemical pesticides and herbicides (Table 2). Despite the fact that cotton opens farmer access to

TABLE 1 Dissan Agricultural Production, 2002 vs. 2007

		2002–3	2007–8
Total hectares planted:			
	sorghum	155	161
	millet	20.5	57
	maize	89.4	42.5
	cotton	31	21.5
Number of HHs growing:			
	sorghum	58	57
	millet	14	30
	maize	54	34
	cotton	37	15

TABLE 2   Sorghum Cultivation and Ownership of Farm Equipment by Household, Dissan, 2001

	Mean sorghum hectares/HH	Percentages of households owning:				
		Plow	Cultivator	Seeder	Donkey cart	Spray pump
Cotton credit HHs, *n* = 41	2.8	88	71	46	61	49
Other HHs, *n* = 25	1.7	36	12	4	8	0

small loans and agricultural inputs, cotton production has declined sharply since 2001. In the 2007–8 growing season, only 15 Dissan households grew cotton, in contrast to the 37 households who grew this cash crop in 2002–3.

HISTORICAL OVERVIEW OF COTTON PRODUCTION IN RURAL MALI

Before the French-led intensification of cotton production in colonial West Africa, family farmers in southern Mali grew regional varieties of cotton for a strong domestic market and for self-sufficient household consumption (clothing, blankets, fishing nets, string, etc.). Starting in the 1890s, commercial and colonial interests worked for decades shaping Malian cotton production in an attempt to capture cotton harvests for French textile mills. By 1950 the colonial state was spending approximately 70 percent of its resources on the intensification of cotton production, targeting southern Mali through the introduction of new varieties, agricultural extension, price subventions, and support for rural investment in machinery and fertilizer (Roberts 1996, 280). Prior to the introduction of incentives like agricultural extension and credit for purchasing plows and agrochemicals, family farmers in Mali resisted expanding household production beyond local needs.

Dissan elders explained that cotton cash cropping came with plows; widespread extrahousehold cotton production and farmer credits followed the installation of a regional cotton processing facility in the 1960s. Local farmers first acquired plows in the 1960s from the Compagnie Malienne pour le Développement des Fibres Textiles (CMDT), a state agency created by the government of Mali's first president, Modibo Keïta. In the 1970s the CMDT worked with villages to organize cotton producer collectives and began transferring to these village associations production responsibilities such as ordering and distributing inputs, and managing credits and payments (Bingen, Serrano, and Howard 2003, 410–11). The

efficacy of the village association strategy developed by the CMDT in the 1970s eventually transformed this once regional program into a national one. Today the CMDT remains the primary agency for agricultural extension services and credit in many southern Malian communities.

CMDT and Collective Cotton Production in Dissan, 1974–2002

In 1974 the CMDT started the process of transferring to villages responsibility for cotton grading, weighing, orders for equipment and inputs, and credit management (Bingen 2000, 357). At first, the CMDT appointed existing village social organizations as the body responsible for such tasks, but by the late 1970s it had established an AV ("Village Association") system for southern Mali managed by community officers, including president, treasurer, and secretary. With World Bank financing, the CMDT organized literacy and numeracy programs in Bamanakan to teach farmers skills for effectively managing village cotton production. The AV program proved to be so efficient by CMDT standards that it eventually became national policy.

As the AV system took hold in southern Mali, many Dissan farmers began acquiring more household money through cotton production. The AV merged all Dissan farmers into a single cooperative for organizing local production, spreading individual responsibility and risk among all village cotton farmers. From the CMDT perspective, this system consolidated fiscal accounting and responsibility into manageable units; every year, after receiving one lump sum for the entire village's cotton harvest, the AV distributed crop payments to individual members. When poor harvests or household crop failures led any number of producers to default on their individual loans, the AV absorbed those debts. In 2001, for example, two Dissan households defaulted on their loans and although both households repaid over half their debts, an outstanding balance of roughly US $300 remained. Although $300 accounts for only 2.5 percent of all Dissan loans in

2001, it is substantial debt for a rural farming family in a country like Mali where annual per capita income was a mere $239 for that same year (World Bank 2003). Furthermore, these economic indicators fail to capture the social discord or peripheral economic hardships endured by individuals and communities as a result of loan defaults.

Once established, the AV system provided farmers access to credit, it established de facto community security nets for cotton farmers and gave rural populations a formidable voice in regional and national agricultural policy. Siaka Sangare, long-standing secretary of Dissan's AV, explained that in 1989, when the CMDT attempted to restructure the AV credit system, producers across the country, including Dissan, used their AVs to organize a cotton strike. Through AV leaders, the CMDT brokered a deal that was acceptable to farmers, and the strike was averted (USAID-Mali 2003). However, in 2000 many Dissan farmers joined a national cotton strike in protest of unpaid harvests and low purchase prices. The CMDT typically set purchase prices after the planting season for cotton, forcing farmers to purchase inputs on credit and organize production without any certainty of returns on their investments. Largely due to a saturated global market, not to mention enormous U.S. subsidies for industrial U.S. cotton producers, international prices for cotton fell significantly in 1998 and 1999. Falling prices translated into significant operating deficits for the CMDT, which meant farmers in Dissan and elsewhere had to bear the brunt of these economic losses. In 1998 the CMDT purchase price for cotton was 185 CFA francs (FCFA) per kilogram, and the price dropped to FCFA 150 in 1999 (USAID-Mali 2003). Secretary Sangare noted that unexpectedly lower prices in 1999 put some Dissan farmers in debt, leading many to abandon the crop the following year. However, in 2001, when the CMDT guaranteed a good purchase price before planting (FCFA 200/kg), many farmers returned to cotton production. The national cotton strike certainly influenced the favorable price of cotton in 2001, but rippling effects of the strike extended further; in late 2002 the CMDT announced the AV system would undergo major organizational changes.

The Meeting

In November 2002, shortly after most households had harvested their cotton, the CMDT extension agent who works in Dissan, visited the AV to call an important meeting. The extension agent is an agricultural engineer trained in Katiabougou, Mali, and at the University of Dijon in France. The meeting was one of thousands throughout Mali, organized to familiarize farmers with fundamental changes to the organizational structure of cotton collectives in Mali (Diallo 2004). Though renamed, the AV could still serve as a villagewide cooperative, but under the new system, the AV could be composed of any number of independently organized, subvillage collectives. Using diagrams on the chalkboard of a dilapidated one-room schoolhouse, the extension agent explained in Bamanakan how the new system would empower farmers.

With children peeking in windows and with the sounds of chickens and donkeys in the background, the extension agent sat at a table in front of thirty-five farmers seated on weathered desktops. The CMDT representative began with an announcement: after the 2002 harvest, the CMDT would encourage Malian cotton farmers to establish new collectives that permit members to associate themselves at the subvillage level. According to the agent, villagewide associations reduce incentives for skilled, large-scale producers, because these producers bear financial liability for the catastrophic crop losses and irresponsible credit management of other farmers. The agent occasionally looked down at his notes as he discussed the regulations for forming the new cotton collectives. Farmers listened patiently, a few with modest disinterest, as the agent described eight new rules.

- Each group will be called a CPC (*coopératif pour les producteurs cotonnière*).

- Each CPC must have at least five producers and/or a minimum of ten separate cotton fields.

- Each CPC must produce an annual minimum of 30 metric tons of cotton (slightly less than half of Dissan's combined total of 70.7 metric tons produced in 2002).

- CPC members must be from the same village (associations with people from multiple villages are prohibited).

- Every CPC member must have a certificate of residency (obtainable for a small fee from a regional administrator).

- Each member must sign an official document containing CPC by-laws, organizational structure, and a description of responsibilities for each CPC officer. The document, written in Bamanakan, is made official with the approval and signature of all CPC members and a CMDT officer.

- Each CPC operates for three years, after which it must be renewed as is, modified and renewed, or disbanded.

- All Dissan CPCs collectively constitute the Union des Coopératifs de Dissan.

The extension agent reinforced several CPC policies before taking questions from farmers. First, he explained some of the benefits of the new CPC system. For example, if someone in a CPC turns out to be a poor associate or a bad worker, at the end of the three-year term of the CPC, members can vote to expel the underperforming associate. Meanwhile, CPC members must pay the debts of fellow members in default, but as CPC members they would have recourse. If necessary a CPC can take legal action against members in default using a CMDT legal service available to all CPC members. Some farmers raised their eyebrows when the agent described how the CPC system deals with chronic debtors and rule breakers: in the worst cases, a judge will dispatch gendarmes to claim payment or in-kind restitution. The agent also said that the CPC system will equate to money for community improvements and projects. Under the former system the AV received from the CMDT a sum equal to 2 percent of the gross price of all Dissan cotton delivered to the CMDT scales. These funds were used according to AV by-laws for: operational costs (20 percent), officer stipends (30 percent), and community development projects (50 percent). The extension agent explained that under the CPC system, defaulted loans would no longer drain funds earmarked for community service.

Throughout the meeting, the CMDT representative focused on a central theme, the power of a strong collective voice. Farmers in attendance nodded their heads as the agent recalled how AVs unified farmers during the cotton strike of 2000. Using an intricate diagram of circles within circles, the extension agent demonstrated that the work and efforts of each CPC will have a single, strong voice, while the village collective—the Union des Cooperatives de Dissan—will have an even stronger voice to represent all Dissan CPCs. Although this well-worn selling point may sound trite, there is no doubt that AVs helped farmers organize and amplify their voices en masse in 1989 and 2000 when they successfully convinced CMDT authorities to address farmer concerns regarding AV policy and cotton prices (Lacy 2004, 107–8).

From my perspective as an observer, perhaps the most salient yet understated point raised by the extension agent during the meeting was that farmers could use the management skills they develop as members of CPCs to form cooperatives for other crops or animal husbandry. As the meeting drew to a close, some of the biggest cotton producers in Dissan voiced skeptical interest and tacit approval for the new system, but a few producers—one of whom with considerable, old cotton debts—expressed concern about the potential difficulties they may face if they hope to join a CPC to obtain credit.

Farmer Perspectives of the CPC System

The freedom to choose the membership and size of one's local cotton grower association may help some producers prevent monetary losses stemming from the crop failures of other village producers, but this freedom may further complicate the economic and social viability of producers and communities in crisis. Following the meeting I asked several farmers to describe their reactions to the new CPC program. Although most farmers voiced cautious or little interest in the new CPCs, two of them held starkly opposite opinions. The first farmer, an elder named Sidike Sangare, said he was suspicious of the new system. During the meeting Sangare remarked that farmers who default on loans eventually pay their debts, and should not be expelled from a group, chased by gendarmes, nor excluded from cotton production, particularly when their households may be in crisis. Under the CPC system the de facto safety net provided by the AV would be transformed into several smaller nets, spreading larger risks among smaller groups of producers. After the meeting Sangare predicted he would not grow cotton the following year. True to his word, elder Sangare abandoned cotton production and focused on grain for future harvests; he eventually repaid his cotton debts, but he passed away a few years later.

On the other side of the spectrum, AV officer Burama Tarawele expressed great optimism about the CPC system. Tarawele was visiting Dissan from Bougoumbala, a neighboring village, and was present at the Dissan meeting. Immediately following the meeting Tarawele said he was pleased the CMDT was finally addressing the problem he termed, "the politics of CMDT." Echoing the extension agent's words, from Tarawele's point of view, the former AV system was counterproductive for large-scale cotton producers like him. Before the formal initiation of the CPC program in the region, Tarawele had already brokered a special arrangement to create a proto-CPC in his village; he and two other farmers decided to create a subvillage collective to independently procure credit and inputs through the CMDT. Though leaving their villagewide cotton association created some quarreling in the village, Tarawele believes people now understand why he and his two partners left the Bougoumbala AV (*decentralization* was the term Tarawele used). He said that the CMDT cooperated with this decentralization because he and his cohorts—all large-scale producers—threatened to abandon cotton. Tarawele said the CPC program will be good for Mali cotton farmers, but admitted that many farmers do not have the skills to apply for, acquire, and effectively manage independent loans. He acquired his banking and management skills in CMDT workshops and as the former secretary of his village AV. Tarawele's ultimate goal is to intensify his cotton production in order to invest in cattle and animal husbandry.

Dissan Creates Two CPCs

Even though Dissan farmers were free to create their first CPCs in 2003, they chose to preserve their villagewide collective. For 2004, however, after several quarrels related to a confidential financial dispute, farmers made a decision that would not have been possible two years earlier. Because the new CPC system encouraged subvillage collectives, farmers resolved their dispute with the dissolution of the villagewide AV. Then the former AV leader formed a CPC with seven other households, while all other cotton-producing households banded together to form a second, much larger CPC. The larger of the two groups built a separate storage shed, and by the start of the 2004 growing season both CPCs were operational. Though factors like rainfall and pest control have plenty to do with successful cotton farming, they alone do not explain

why aggregate Dissan cotton harvests almost doubled in one year under the stewardship of two independent subvillage collectives (Table 3). Following wildly successful harvests, Dissan farmers reported positive initial experiences with both CPCs, but the enthusiasm of the first two years of the new system has waned.

The financial dispute that split Dissan's villagewide collective may have inspired a short-lived competition between the two CPCs which emerged from the conflict. This competition may have bolstered local harvests temporarily, but Dissan cotton production has since declined as most small-scale producers have adopted alternative cash crops such as cereals, peanut, and sesame. Per CPC rules, Dissan cotton growers re-established their CPCs in 2007–8, but many producers chose to abandon cotton. In short, all eight of the former AV leader's CPC members renewed their cooperative and grew cotton, but the second CPC membership decreased from 37 households in 2004 to seven households in 2007. The divergent fates of the two Dissan CPCs are rooted in the unique memberships of both collectives. The former AV leader's CPC attracted large-scale producers with production goals similar to Burama Tarawele, but membership was not directly based on production levels; family alliances and social relationships also played a major role. A cursory look at some of the characteristics of the CPC households indicates that the bifurcation of Dissan's AV consolidated some of the village's more wealthy households, leaving the others to fend for themselves (Table 4). Likewise, in other villages across southern Mali, cotton cultivation has been shown to exacerbate economic disparity among households (Moseley 2005, 46–49).

Do Subvillage Collectives and Cotton Increase Poverty, Wealth . . . or Both?

Every year after the CMDT has collected cotton harvests from villages all across the region, farmers listen intently as radio stations announce final production totals for local villages. Cotton is undeniably a major focus of household agricultural production in southern Mali, and transforming the AV system with subvillage cooperatives (CPCs) affects different farmers in different ways. Depending on the resources, skills, and experience of individual producers, the CPC system equates to new opportunities for some farmers, and exclusion from cotton production and farmer credit for others.

In the short term, successful cotton farmers capable of acquiring and managing credit stand to gain

TABLE 3   Aggregate Dissan Cotton Harvests Recorded at CMDT Facility, Bougouni, 2003–7

	Cotton collective system in use	Number of cotton households	Aggregate harvest (kg)	Households making $0 or debt from cotton harvest
2001/2	1 AV	41	N/A	4 (10%)
2002/3	1 AV	50	70,740	N/A
2003/4	1 AV	23	39,750	2 (9%)
2004/5	2 CPCs	47	98,521	3 (6%)
2005/6	2 CPCs	38	86,989	2 (5%)
2006/7	2 CPCs	26	58,987	6 (23%)
2007/8	2 CPCs	15	14,285	9 (60%)

TABLE 4   Smaller CPC Households Versus All Other Households, Dissan, 2001

	Small CPC HHs	Other HHs
Number of:		
Households	8	58
People per HH	23	12
Field hectares cultivated, 2001	10.3	5
Percentage of households owning:		
Plow	100	65
Cattle	100	58
Cultivator	100	46
Donkey cart	100	42
Seeder	83	25

more autonomy over production choices. Furthermore, provided they associate with other stable producers, these farmers may reduce the risk of losses from cotton profits due to crop failures or mismanagement by others. Farmers known to have defaulted on previous loans, whose households may be in crisis (labor shortage, debt, chronic crop loss), face potential difficulties if they seek CPC membership. Just as elder Sidike Sangare abandoned cotton farming because his old cotton debts made him an undesirable associate, Burama Tarawele formed his own CPC to avoid associating with unreliable or crisis-prone farmers. Cotton may not be an equally appealing nor accessible crop choice for farmers of different means.

Elder Sangare was not the only farmer to question whether cotton farming was a worthwhile endeavor. Even before the CMDT announced the changes for cotton collectives, Dissan farmers debated whether or not cotton was "worth it." The Dissan *ton* (a villagewide collective labor organization) decided in 2002 to grow peanuts instead of cotton to raise group funds. This decision was based on the idea that peanuts were a less risky crop and would not require nearly as much labor, in contrast with cotton. Equally important, peanut crops do not require major investment costs for fertilizer, herbicide, and insecticide.

As it evolves, the CPC system will generate new debates and questions about the social, ecological, and financial ramifications of household cotton production in southern Mali, but exactly how these subvillage collectives may or may not transform local production and socioeconomic dynamics has yet to be fully determined. In the long term, three critical issues will determine the success or failure of the CPC system: the exclusion principle, the efficacy of CPCs in expanding the idea and benefits of cooperatives beyond cotton fields, and the strengthening of individual and collective voices of cotton farmers. In southern Mali, responsibility for household cotton production typically excludes women and poorer households, who, as a result, have limited access to extension services and inputs (Moseley 2001, 187).

On the one hand, CPCs may lead farmers to exclude crisis-prone producers like elder Sidike Sangare, but CPCs could have the potential to open new opportunities for formerly excluded farmers. Investing in human capacity in terms of ensuring farmers who want to create a cooperative and have the financial and literacy skills necessary to protect their own interests could also, with no small effort, bring women and poorer farmers into their own credit-worthy collectives, particularly if the CPC cotton model is successful in encouraging the formation of new cooperatives for other crops and animal husbandry. After all, if literate farmers with proven track records and strong financial management skills (acquiring and managing credit) break off into subvillage collectives, as they have done in Dissan, they might be less able or less willing to assist those farmers with different skill sets and resources. This new, localized manifestation of brain drain and wealth consolidation has the potential to exacerbate social and financial inequality, rendering cotton as a crop for relatively wealthier households. In the recent past, producer organizations like cotton collectives have been shown to amplify the voices of farmers in southern Mali (Bingen, Serrano, and Howard 2003, 407). In the end, what may determine the success or failure of the CPC program is whether or not it bolsters or diminishes the voices and opportunities of all farmers.

REFERENCES

Bingen, James R. 2000. Prospects for Development and Democracy in West Africa: Agrarian Politics in Mali. In *Democracy and Development in Mali*, ed. James R. Bingen, David Robinson, and John M. Staatz, 349–368. East Lansing: Michigan State University Press.

Bingen, Jim, Alex Serrano, and Julie Howard. 2003. Linking Farmers to Markets: Different Approaches to Human Capital Development. *Food Policy* 28: 405–419.

Diallo, Madou. 2004. Situation scolaire: L'heure de vérité à Koulouba. *Le républicain*, December 8. http://www.planeteafrique.com/Web/LeDiplomate/Index.asp?affiche=newsdatabase_show.asp&cmd=articledetail&articleid=252.

Lacy, Scott M. 2004. One Finger Cannot Lift a Stone: Family Farmers and Sorghum Production in Southern Mali. PhD dissertation, University of California, Santa Barbara.

Moseley, William G. 2001. Sahelian 'White Gold' and Rural Poverty-Environment Interactions: The Political Ecology of Cotton Production, Environmental Change, and Household Food Economy in Mali. PhD dissertation, University of Georgia.

———. 2005. Global Cotton and Local Environment Management: The Political Ecology of Rich and Poor Small-Hold Farmers in Southern Mali. *Geographic Journal* 171 (1): 36–55.

Roberts, Richard. 1996. *Two Worlds of Cotton: Colonialism and the Regional Economy in the French Soudan*, 1800–1946. Stanford, CA: Stanford University Press.

USAID-Mali. 2003. Production and Export Opportunities and Constraints for Coarse Grains. www.usaid.org.ml/mes_photos/production_and_e.

World Bank. 2003. World Development Indicators 2003. Washington, DC: World Bank. CD-ROM.

35

Family Planning Outreach and Credit Programs in Rural Bangladesh

Sidney Ruth Schuler and Syed M. Hashemi

In many parts of the world, high fertility rates threaten women's health and lead to a variety of negative consequences associated with exploding populations. Many applied anthropologists argue that stabilizing population growth is critical for increased quality of life in developing nations. Yet the paradoxical coexistence of high birthrates in tandem with starvation and poverty is all too common. Governments and nongovernmental agencies spend millions and millions of dollars each year trying to reduce birthrates. Certainly there has been much success, but there is a long way to go.

As we have seen repeatedly, anthropology teaches us of the interrelationships between the various segments of our social order. If we wish to reduce the birthrate, for example, there may be ways that are less intrusive than family planning and that have additional benefits for women and their communities.

Women's participation in the economic sphere is linked to their status in society. Low status, isolation, dependence, and lack of mobility to even visit with other women limit women's opportunities and ability to act in their own interests. Empowering women by enhancing their economic role in society can have many consequences, one of which is an increased use of contraceptives.

This intriguing selection examines the case of a Grameen Bank program that provides loans for poor women in rural Bangladesh.

As you read this selection, ask yourself the following questions:

- Who should make judgments about whether the fertility rate in Bangladesh is too high? And who has the right to implement programs that change the social order?
- How does purdah limit women's access to family planning services?
- What is Grameen Bank's strategy for reducing women's isolation?
- How are economic conditions linked to the use of contraceptives?
- Should family planning workers assist women in using contraceptive methods secretly?
- What do women mean when they say that through Grameen Bank they have "learned to talk"?

The following terms discussed in this selection are included in the Glossary at the back of the book:

dependent variable *qualitative methods*
hypothesis *random sample*
purdah *TFR (total fertility rate)*

Schuler, Sidney Ruth, & Syed Hashemi. "Family Planning Outreach and Credit Programs in Rural Bangladesh." Reproduced with permission of the Society for Applied Anthropology (SfAA) from *Human Organization* 54, no. 4 (1995):455–461.

In rural Bangladesh, women's ability to seek out family planning services is limited by their isolation and their economic and social dependence on men. Large numbers of female outreach workers—about 28,000—are being employed by the government and nongovernmental programs to bring family planning services to women in their homes. Program evaluations and research studies have documented the effectiveness of this strategy, particularly in increasing use of the oral pill and other temporary contraceptive methods. Recent studies show substantial increases in contraceptive use and a decline in estimated fertility rates—from TFR[1] of about 7 in the late 1960s and early 1970s to about 5 in 1989—and attribute this change in large part to the expansion in access to family planning services in recent years, mainly through female community-based workers (Cleland et al. 1994; Larson and Mitra 1992; World Bank 1992).

While the intensive door-to-door delivery strategy has been effective in raising levels of contraceptive use from low to moderate levels (e.g., from 19% in 1983 to 40% in 1991), it is obvious that intensification of service delivery can only go so far, and that other strategies will be needed if levels of contraceptive use are to be increased to a level that would stabilize population growth. Improvements in the quality of services are needed, both for achievement of higher levels of contraceptive use, and from the perspective of women's rights to better health and reproductive autonomy. Another strategy would be interventions that increase women's ability to take an active role in getting access to services—for example, programs that strengthen women's economic roles and increase their mobility. This article examines the effects of the Grameen Bank program that provides small loans for women's self-employment activities in rural Bangladesh. Survey and ethnographic research findings are used to analyze the effects of the Grameen Bank, community-based family planning outreach, and women's relative levels of physical mobility on their practice of contraception. The effects of exposure to the Grameen Bank and home visits by family planning workers are compared for members and nonmembers living in Grameen Bank villages.

BACKGROUND

Among the poor in rural Bangladesh, women's lives are severely restricted by their social and economic dependence on men. Because of *purdah* (a system based on an ideology concerned with secluding and protecting women to uphold social standards of modesty and morality) women's contacts with the world outside of the family are extremely limited. Many cannot avail themselves of family planning, health and other services that may be available unless these services are brought to their homes. Bringing services to women in or near their homes is the principal strategy of the Bangladesh Government's family planning program and of many of the nongovernmental organizations providing family planning services in rural areas. As noted above, this strategy has been very effective in increasing contraceptive use.

Grameen Bank is a quasi-governmental organization involved in lending to the poor in nearly half of all villages in rural Bangladesh. Its two million female members (and about two hundred thousand male members) come from landless, rural, poor families, most of whom have very few assets of any kind. The program attempts to draw women out of isolation by providing them with credit, to enable them to earn a cash income through various types of self-employment activities. In addition to supporting economic activities that require interactions in the public sphere, it increases women's mobility and access to information by requiring that they attend regular meetings. The rituals of membership help women to create a sense of identity outside of the family. Grameen Bank does not provide family planning services. We have argued, based on a previous analysis, that the program influences contraceptive use by strengthening women's economic roles and contributing to their empowerment, increasing their ability to overcome obstacles to use of contraception. The same analysis suggested that BRAC (Bangladesh Rural Advancement Committee), whose program focus is similar but somewhat broader, does not have the same effect on contraceptive use because it is less effective in strengthening women's economic roles and in helping them to establish identities outside of the family (Schuler and Hashemi 1994).

A number of studies (e.g., Koenig et al. 1992) have assessed the effects of family planning outreach on use of contraception in Bangladesh. Two recent studies (Simmons et al. 1988, 1992) argue that the role of the female family planning worker in Bangladesh goes beyond the conventional concept of "supply" of family planning methods and services, so that they function as change agents in the communities where they work. In this article we focus on the effects of credit rather than family planning programs in transforming reproductive norms, and we attempt to highlight the interactive effects of the two types of interventions.

METHODOLOGY

Data Sources

The analysis is based on a survey conducted in late 1992 to measure the impact of participation in credit programs on contraceptive use. It included four separately selected samples. The first two were random samples of Grameen Bank and BRAC members.[2] . . . With a few exceptions, the women in these two samples have been members of the programs for a minimum of 18 months. The third was a comparison group consisting of nonmembers from Grameen Bank villages who would be eligible to join BRAC or Grameen Bank (i.e., poor and functionally landless). The fourth was a second comparison group consisting of women living in villages not served by either program, who would be eligible to join the programs. One adult woman was selected from each household. The interviewers were Bangladeshi women who had previous experience in conducting demographic surveys. They received more training during the process of pretesting the questionnaires. In addition to questions related to contraceptive use, the survey included questions related to women's status within the family and community, their physical mobility and their economic roles. A total of 1305 married women younger than 50 were interviewed.[3]

The data from concurrent ethnographic research in six villages describes the credit programs in operation, from the perspectives of the field research team as well as participants in the programs. The team consisted of six women and six men, all Bangladeshi, most of whom had master's degrees. The team received intensive training in qualitative research methods at the beginning of the project, and the principal investigators provided continuing informal training throughout the study. The male-female team in each village conducted in-depth interviews to document change processes, both in women's roles and status and in norms related to reproduction and use of contraception. This article is based primarily on the survey data, but data from the ethnographic study is taken into account in interpreting the survey results.

Hypotheses

The following analysis is intended to test several specific hypotheses. Underlying all of them is the more general hypothesis that women's isolation, dependence, and lack of mobility inhibit use of contraception, and that a variety of programmatic strategies can be used to lessen these effects. The specific hypotheses are:

1. Home visits by family planning fieldworkers are positively related to contraceptive use.

2. Membership in credit programs and residence in villages where such programs are present increases the likelihood that a woman will use contraception.

3. Women's relative physical mobility is positively related to use of contraception.

4. The higher level of physical mobility of credit program participants does not fully explain their greater propensity to use contraception.

Variables

Dependent Variable   The dependent variable indicates whether or not the respondent is currently using any method of contraception.

Exposure to Credit Programs   These variables indicate whether the respondent was a Grameen Bank member, a nonparticipant living in a Grameen Bank village, or a resident of a comparison village, where no credit program existed.

Control Variables   In order to distinguish between effects of credit program participation per se and effects of other variables that are believed to affect contraceptive use in Bangladesh, several control variables are included. These are respondent's age, whether she ever attended school, number of surviving children, existence of at least one surviving son, existence of at least one surviving daughter, and an indicator of the relative economic level of the respondent's household. The latter is a composite measure based on the number of items owned from the following list: bed, blanket/quilt, shawl/sweater/coat, radio/TV, cow/buffalo.

Indicators of Access to Family Planning Services
We include two indicators of access to family planning services. The first of these is whether the respondent was ever visited by a family planning worker and the second is whether she was visited in the three months prior to the survey. Because of the strong emphasis on community-based services in the Bangladesh family planning program, these are generally thought to be the best indicators of access to family planning services in rural Bangladesh.

Indicators of Women's Physical Mobility   For this analysis we consolidated the variables related to women's mobility to create a single score. In the survey interview the respondent was presented with a list of places (the market, a medical facility, the movies, outside the village) and asked if she had ever gone there. She was given one point for each place she had visited and an additional point if she had ever gone there alone. A dichotomous variable was then created, in which a respondent with a score of 3 or better was classified as "more mobile."

Frequency distributions and means, as applicable, for the dependent and independent variables are presented in Table 1.

STATISTICAL RESULTS

The first section of the analysis compares women living in villages where Grameen Bank is present with women living in villages without a credit program. As Table 1 indicates, there is a dramatic difference in levels of contraceptive use between Grameen Bank members and women living in comparison villages—a difference of 16 percentage points. . . . The presence of the Grameen Bank program in a village has a significant effect on use of contraception, both among members and nonmembers, which is not explained by the effects of outreach. Visits by family planning workers (both recent and "ever") also appear to have strong independent effects, as do age, relative wealth, and presence of a surviving son.

TABLE 1   Characteristics of Study Samples

	GB	GB Non-members	Comparison
% using contraception	59.0	48.0	43.0
Mean age (in years)	31.0	26.0	29.0
Mean no. surviving children	3.5	2.6	3.3
Mean no. surviving sons	1.8	1.3	1.7
Mean no. surviving daughters	1.7	1.3	1.6
% attended school	29.0	18.0	18.0
Mean wealth score	2.5	1.7	1.6
% ever visited by FP worker	83.0	67.0	78.0
% visited in past 3 months	36.0	38.0	35.0
Mean mobility score	2.3	2.1	1.9
Mean duration of membership (in months)	50.0	—	—
N of cases	312	315	424

. . . [Further,] women who are "more mobile" are considerably more likely to use contraception. Sixty percent of the "more mobile" group were using a contraceptive method, compared with 46% of the "less mobile" group. The relatively higher level of mobility of women in Grameen Bank villages explains, at least in part, the higher level of contraceptive use.

COMBINED EFFECTS OF GRAMEEN BANK AND FAMILY PLANNING OUTREACH

Previous studies in Bangladesh have found contact with female family planning workers to be one of the most important determinants of contraceptive use. . . . In general the findings indicate that family planning outreach has a highly significant effect on contraceptive use and that the presence of Grameen Bank in a village has an added effect. However, another dimension is added when contraceptive use rates among women who have/have not been visited by family planning workers are examined separately for each of the three groups (Figure 1).

For the comparison group and for nonmembers in Grameen Bank villages, rates of contraceptive use among women who have been visited by a family planning worker are 21 and 30 points higher, respectively, than for women who have never been visited. However, for members of Grameen Bank, the rate of contraceptive use is consistently high (59%), regardless of whether the women have ever been visited by a family planning worker. This suggests that the potential of Grameen Bank to influence contraceptive use is particularly important for women whose access to

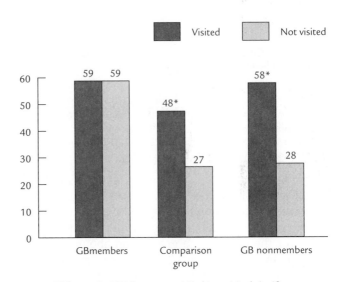

*Difference in CPR for women visited/not visited significant at $p < .001$ in chi square test.

FIGURE 1   Current contraceptive use—all methods, whether ever visited by FP worker

Schuler, Sidney Ruth & Syed Hashemi. "Family Planning Outreach and Credit Programs in Rural Bangladesh." Reproduced with permission of the Society for Applied Anthropology (SfAA) from *Human Organization* 54, no. 4 (1995):455–61.

family planning services is relatively limited. For nonparticipating women in Grameen Bank villages who have been visited by a family planning fieldworker, the rate of contraceptive use is almost as high as among Grameen Bank members in the same communities—58%, compared with 48% for women in the comparison group. For the nonparticipants, the combined effect of the presence of Grameen Bank in a village and

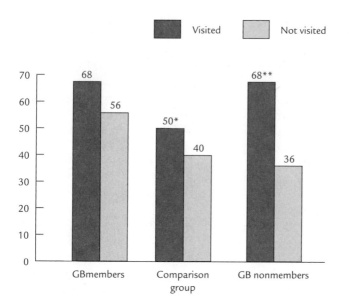

*Difference in CPR for women visited/not visited significant at $p < .05$ in chi square test.

**Difference in CPR for women visited/not visited significant at $p < .001$ in chi square test. (For GB members difference not significant at $p < .05$ level.)

FIGURE 2 Current contraceptive use—all methods, whether ever visited by FP worker past three months

Schuler, Sidney Ruth & Syed Hashemi. "Family Planning Outreach and Credit Programs in Rural Bangladesh." Reproduced with permission of the Society for Applied Anthropology (SfAA) from *Human Organization* 54, no. 4 (1995):455–61.

family planning outreach is even more evident when one looks at visits by family planning workers within the past three months (Figure 2). Among women who were not visited within the three months preceding the survey, the rates of contraceptive use are about the same for the comparison group, and about 20 points lower than among Grameen Bank members. The rates of contraceptive use among women who were visited by a family planning worker within the past three months are 9 points higher for Grameen Bank members, 11 points higher for the comparison group, and 32 points higher for Grameen Bank nonmembers (68%, 50%, and 68%, respectively).

. . . Family planning outreach is an important factor explaining the relatively high level of contraceptive use among nonparticipants in Grameen Bank villages, but . . . the even higher level of contraceptive use among participants is due to other factors.

DISCUSSION AND CONCLUSION

The strong effect of visits by community-based family planning fieldworkers on use of contraception supports the findings of previous research in Bangladesh. Because

of their social and economic dependence on men, and their limited physical mobility, most women in rural Bangladesh cannot get access to family planning methods and services without assistance. As one of the respondents put it,

> I am not allowed to go out and work even though we are so poor that we are sometimes desperate. Neither my husband nor his parents will let me go out to work . . . I had wanted to use family planning before my two daughters were born. I asked my husband several times to bring me a family planning method but he wouldn't listen . . . I am a woman—I could not get it for myself.

The ethnographic study data indicate that men often fail to provide this assistance because they are generally apathetic about fertility control, or because they fear that side effects will lead to economic losses—either by interfering with work or by incurring monetary costs for treatment. Since most women are prevented from working outside of the home, and perceived as economically nonproductive, their husbands and in-laws often feel that it is wrong for them to incur expenses (Schuler et al. 1995).

In this context the presence of a community-based fieldworker, whether employed by the government or a nongovernmental organization, can make a great difference. By providing information and services in the home, they preempt the need for most women to go to clinics or other sources for family planning methods. They provide free pills and suggest things that women can say to persuade their husbands to allow them to use contraception. In cases where persuasion seems unlikely to be effective, they often assist women in using contraceptive methods secretly.

The survey findings suggest that, in addition to "supply-side" strategies, it is possible to influence fertility through programs that decrease women's isolation and their economic dependence on men. Such programs can help women to overcome obstacles to contraceptive use such as lack of mobility, lack of cash, lack of information about contraceptive methods and services, and opposition or lack of cooperation from their husbands and other family members. Grameen Bank strengthens women's economic roles through credit, enabling them to contribute more substantially to their families' support. Even in cases where the woman hands her loan money over to her husband, there is usually some acknowledgment from the family that she is a source of income. Involvement in the program also gives women a socially legitimate purpose to participate in a group outside of the family. The opportunity for involvement in a nonfamily group can be important as a source of identity, new experiences, and ideas.

TABLE 2 Comparison of Method Mix in Grameen Bank Villages Versus Comparison Villages (N = 1051)

	Grameen Bank Villages	Comparison Villages
Modern Methods		
Pills	22%	15%
Condom	1%	—
Injectables	5%	1%
IUDs	1%	1%
Female Sterilization	18%	18%
Male Sterilization	2%	3%
Traditional Methods		
Rhythm Method	4%	4%
Withdrawal	1%	—
Abstinence	1%	—
Other	1%	1%
No Method	46%*	56%*

Totals not equal to 100% because of rounding.

The ethnographic and the survey findings from this study generally support Grameen Bank's own contention that strengthening women's economic roles gives them more autonomy and more control over important decisions affecting themselves and their families, as well as contributing to their self-confidence and propensity to plan for the future. It promotes women's relative freedom to move about in public and to travel outside of the village. Where more women are employed outside of the home, and are required to walk along roads or use buses or other forms of transport, it is less difficult for them to travel within and outside of their villages to get services.

Participation in the Grameen Bank program also makes members more experienced in interacting with men outside of the family and with authority figures. Although the interactions that take place in weekly meetings with bank staff clearly cast the women in a subservient role, this nevertheless seems to give them a certain self-confidence. In all interactions with government officials and even representatives of nongovernmental organizations, the poor are in a subservient role, and at least in this case it is the woman rather than her husband who is doing the interacting. Several of the women in our study told our field investigators that through Grameen Bank they had "learned to talk," and now they were not afraid to talk to outsiders. This probably increases their ability to avail themselves of family planning and health services.

Through a combination of intimidation and confidence-building, Grameen helps women to stand up to their husbands. Normally, any savings or asset that a women might have could be legitimately (at least from her husband's point of view) appropriated by him. Having recognized that this would be a central problem in a loan program for women, Grameen Bank tells women what to say when their husbands try to take their loan money. Case studies suggest that women who have developed the self-confidence to try to protect their assets and earnings from their husbands are more likely to take initiative in other areas, such as practicing family planning.

The Grameen Bank program can produce high rates of contraceptive use among members, even if they are not exposed to family planning outreach. The very high rates of contraceptive use among nonmembers in Grameen Bank villages who are visited by a family planning fieldworker suggest that the presence of Grameen Bank's program in a village in combination with family planning outreach can increase use of contraception dramatically, even among women who do not join Grameen Bank. The probable explanation is that reproductive norms are changing in Grameen Bank villages, but that diffusion of innovations takes time. Nonmembers, whose level of dependence on men has not been reduced because they have not participated in the program, typically require the support of family planning workers to follow the reproductive norms that are emerging (Table 2).

In considering the implications of these findings, it is important to avoid overestimating the magnitude of the changes occurring in gender relations. The vast majority of women—including those who participate in the Grameen Bank program—are able to make only small cash or kind contributions to the family's support, and many have little or no control over the income. Only a quarter of the Grameen Bank members in our survey said that their contribution represented half or more of the family's income, and only 7% of the nonmembers in Grameen Bank villages and 4% in comparison villages said this. Socially, and psychologically as well, the typical Grameen Bank member, like other women, is extremely dependent on her husband, and simply has to accept inequities, extreme limitations on her autonomy, and in some cases physical abuse. Watching the realities of poverty and gender-based subordination being played out in social life in the six ethnographic study villages, most of the members of our research team did not expect to find that the small changes occurring in women's lives as a result of Grameen Bank were having a measurable impact on contraceptive use.

Our ethnographic study provided some insight into the processes through which women are asserting themselves in making reproductive decisions, but it also revealed continuing obstacles to increased and more effective fertility control. The most significant of these seems to be fear—related to method side effects, health problems that may be perceived as side effects, and the widespread belief that contraceptive methods cause physical weakness and other problems. In some cases lingering ideas that contraceptive use may be sinful are reinforced when contraceptive users suffer from side effects or experience other types of misfortunes. In addition to physical suffering and even death, contraceptive users and their families fear inability to work, and the possibility that the problems resulting from contraceptive use will require costly medical treatments. Because most women do not have an independent income or control over money, they know that if something happens to them they will be dependent on others—in most cases their husbands—to arrange and pay for medical treatment. Generally the fieldworkers who come to their doors have limited training and are only minimally equipped to treat health problems. Women's restricted physical mobility and their economic dependence on men, as well as their general condition of poverty, limit their ability to seek treatment. In our view, a continuous and increased focus on providing economic opportunities for women and, simultaneously, on improving poor women's access to health services and improving the quality of contraceptive services is needed.

NOTES

1. TFR, or Total Fertility Rate, is the average number of children born to a woman during her lifetime.

2. Since the previous analysis suggested that BRAC does not affect the level of contraceptive use among its members it was excluded from the present analysis.

3. See Schuler and Hashemi 1994 for a more detailed description of the survey methodology.

REFERENCES

Cleland, John, James E. Phillips, Sajeda Amin, and G. M. Kasmal. 1994. The Determinants of Reproductive Change in Bangladesh: Success in a Challenging Environment. World Bank Regional and Sectoral Studies. Washington, DC: The World Bank.

Koenig, Michael A., Ubaidur Rob, Mehrab Jali Khan, J. Chakraborty, and Vincent Fauveau. 1992. Contraceptive Use in Matlab, Bangladesh in 1990: Levels, Trends, and Explanations. Studies in Family Planning 23(6): 352–364.

Larson, Ann and S. N. Mitra. 1992. Family Planning in Bangladesh: An Unlikely Success Story. International Family Planning Perspectives 18(4): 123–129.

Mauldin, W. Parker and John A. Ross. 1991. Family Planning Programs: Efforts and Results, 1982–89. Studies in Family Planning 22(6): 350–367.

Mitra, S. N., Ann Larson, Gilliam Foo, and Shahidul Islam. 1992. Bangladesh Contraceptive Prevalence Survey. July 1991: Key Findings. Dhaka: Mitra and Associates.

Schuler, Sidney Ruth and Syed M. Hashemi. 1994. Credit Programs, Women's Empowerment and Contraceptive Use in Rural Bangladesh. Studies in Family Planning 25(2): 65–76.

Schuler, Sidney Ruth, Syed M. Hashemi, and Ann Hendrix. 1995. Bangladesh's Family Planning Success Story: A Gender Perspective. International Family Planning Perspectives 27: 6.

Simmons, Ruth, Laila Baqee, Michael A. Koenig, and James E. Phillips. 1988. Beyond Supply: The Importance of Female Family Planning Workers in Rural Bangladesh. Studies in Family Planning 19(1): 29–38.

Simmons, Ruth, Rezina Mita, and Michael A. Koenig. 1992. Employment in Family Planning and Women's Status in Bangladesh. Studies in Family Planning 23(2): 97–109.

The World Bank. 1992. Population and the World Bank: Implications from Eight Case Studies. Operations Evaluations Department. Washington, DC: The World Bank.

36

The Search for Sustainable Markets

The Promise and Failures of Fair Trade

Julia Smith

Consumers who are willing to pay $3 or more for a cup of coffee might be shocked to learn that farmers who produce coffee beans sell their product for less than a dollar a pound. Despite a recent rise in world coffee prices as well as a boom in the high-price specialty coffee market, many coffee farmers in Latin America, Africa, Asia, and elsewhere struggle to make ends meet.

Fair Trade coffee certification and marketing is a strategy created by socially-minded entrepreneurs who wanted to get more of the consumer's money into the hands of the people who actually produce coffee beans. In the late 1980s when world coffee prices began to decline to the point that beans were selling for less than it cost to produce them, Fair Trade coffee certification was born in the Netherlands. The Fair Trade certification process was designed to establish a commodity chain that is fair to farmers regardless of fluctuations in global coffee prices. In particular, Fair Trade coffee differs from conventional coffee because farmers are guaranteed a fair minimum price for their beans. Since its creation, the idea of Fair Trade coffee has matured to include programs promoting community development, education, environmentalism, and healthy living.

The philosophy behind Fair Trade coffee is that the market better serves small-scale producers when farmers are guaranteed fair prices and direct access to markets. The benefits of Fair Trade coffee include improved livelihoods for coffee farmers, and closer relationships between producers and consumer. Unfortunately, not all coffee farmers have the resources and marketing skills to reap the potential benefits of Fair Trade production. In this selection, Julia Smith applies anthropological methods and understanding to see how Fair Trade impacts different farmers in different ways. While Fair Trade coffee production improves the lives of some coffee farmers, it may not serve all small-scale farmers equally.

As you read this selection, ask yourself the following questions:

- What is the process of Fair Trade certification for coffee beans?
- Why was Fair Trade coffee certification established?
- What does Fair Trade certification promise farmers? What does it promise to the consumer?
- Why is Fair Trade coffee production not an option for all small-scale coffee farmers?
- How and why did COOPABUENA farmers diversify their farm production after the failure of their cooperative?
- Has Fair Trade certification lived up to its goal of improving relationships between small-scale coffee farmers and coffee consumers? Why?

The following terms discussed in this selection are included in the Glossary at the back of the book:

commodity	*organic*
fair trade	*social justice*

The fair-trade market has been praised as having the potential to transform small-scale coffee farming by ensuring a fair price to producers, improving market access for small producers, and creating closer ties between producers and consumers. Although the roots of the fair-trade movement date back to the 1940s, the first clearly branded fair-trade coffee appeared in the 1970s and 1980s. Coffee has for many years been one of the most widely traded food commodities in the world, with a well-developed international market. Because 50 to 70 percent of the world's coffee is produced by small producers (Lines 2003; Transfair USA 2005a), the coffee market was an obvious early target for fair-trade organizers. Today the fair-trade coffee market is large and well developed, with clearly delineated standards and prices. Since that time, the fair-trade coffee market has grown from a tiny social movement to a significant segment of the world market.

However, the success of fair trade has made it difficult for organizations selling fair-trade coffee to meet the movement's goals of "build[ing] a more equitable and sustainable model of international trade that benefits producers, consumers, industry and the earth" (Transfair USA 2005b). As the volume of coffee sold has grown from a few thousand pounds to over 60 million pounds and as vendors of fair-trade coffee have shifted from small cooperative groceries to large chain grocery stores and Starbucks, the closeness of relationships between producers and consumers and the degree of collaboration between producers and purchasers of coffee have deteriorated considerably. The experience of a medium-sized cooperative in southern Costa Rica over the last decade illustrates the challenges that face the movement as both production and consumption of fair-trade products continues to grow.

Studies of the impact of fair trade have largely focused on a handful of the most successful coffee cooperatives, including studies by Laura Raynolds and her group at Colorado State University (Murray et al. 2003; Raynolds 2000, 2002) as well as others (Boot et al. 2003; Hudson and Hudson 2003; Lyon 2005; Nigh 1997). Mixed experiences with fair trade have been investigated considerably less frequently (although see Martinez 2002; Moberg 2005). The cooperative of COOPABUENA in southern Costa Rica was not selected for its fair-trade experience but rather for a different study; as such, it serves as an example of the difficulties that many cooperatives experience as they enter the fair-trade market. In addition, this case study demonstrates that the fair-trade movement has, at times, functioned essentially as any niche market, rather than transforming relationships between producers and those who buy their coffee.

GROWTH OF THE FAIR-TRADE COFFEE MARKET

The fair-trade system for coffee is fairly straightforward. "Smallholders organised in cooperatives or other organisations with a democratic, participative structure" (Fairtrade Labelling Organizations International [FLO] 2006) can apply to the FLO for certification as fair-trade producing cooperatives. To be certified and to retain certification, cooperative members must avoid using certain agrochemicals, refrain from farming practices that could damage the environment, and work toward sustainable agricultural systems. Once certified, cooperatives may sell coffee through the fair-trade market. The FLO also certifies buyers of coffee, who are given contact information for a variety of certified cooperatives. To retain certification, buyers must pay at least $1.21 per pound of conventional coffee plus a $0.05 per pound fair-trade adjustment and an extra $0.15 per pound for organic coffee. When the price of coffee rises above $1.21 per pound, the buyer must pay the market price plus the adjustments (Transfair USA 2005a).

The FLO, as well as country-based fair-trade organizations, serve as matchmakers between sellers and buyers, rather than directly buying and selling products like coffee. The intent of these fair-trade organizations was not to focus on the economics of the deal. Instead, the fair-trade movement aimed to create strong links between producers and consumers, by encouraging both sides to perceive the relationship as a collaborative one. However, as the fair-trade market has grown from a small social-justice driven movement to a broad niche market, these relationships have often diminished, and only the economic deal remains.

The growth of the fair-trade market has been truly astounding. According to Transfair USA (2006), the volume of fair-trade coffee sold in the United States has grown at 45 percent or more each year since its introduction. World trade has grown more slowly, as fair-trade coffee has a longer history in the European market, but market volume from 2003–04 grew nearly 26 percent (FLO 2005). In 2004, the fair-trade coffee market grew to 84 million pounds (Transfair USA 2006:3). In the United States, two percent of all coffee sold is fair-trade coffee; in some European countries, fair-trade coffee has exceeded four percent of coffee sold (Transfair USA 2006:4). Although the U.S. fair-trade market will likely continue to grow rapidly for a considerable time to come, this remains a tiny fraction of world coffee production.

The number of producers in certified cooperatives has increased rapidly, from 374,077 in 1999 to 684,077 in 2004 (Transfair USA 2005a:5). This growth has kept pace with the growth in consumption, so although the amount of fair-trade coffee sold per producer has increased, it remains under 90 pounds. To put these numbers into perspective, one hectare of coffee can produce thousands of pounds of coffee. Ninety pounds of fair-trade coffee generates less than $110 of income per producer in a fair-trade certified cooperative. If this income was distributed evenly, fair trade might slightly improve the lives of hundreds of thousands of producers. Of course, sales are not evenly distributed. Instead, some cooperatives have been highly successful, selling the vast majority of their coffee through the fair-trade market (Murray et al. 2003:16), whereas others have struggled to find any access to fair-trade markets.

The unevenness of impact is not intentional but results from the way the fair-trade market works. Fair-trade organizations only certify producing cooperatives and purchasing companies, and leave producers and purchasers to contact one another. Not surprisingly, this allows more experienced fair-trade producers to continue to dominate the market. They are more aware of, and hence responsive to, the concerns of U.S. and European vendors and have already developed effective communication strategies with them. In turn, the vendors are more likely to be familiar with the experienced fair-trade producers and their track record, whether through other vendors, through fair-trade Web sites, or through direct communications.

Massive growth has not been the only change in the fair-trade market; the ways in which coffee is sold have changed as well. In the early days of the fair-trade movement, coffee was largely sold through alternative food markets, such as cooperatives and small stores specializing in organic food. Today, Starbucks is the largest seller of fair-trade coffee in North America (Starbucks 2006) and much of the remaining fair-trade coffee is now sold through chain grocery stores. In addition, the distinctiveness of fair-trade coffee has been reduced by the variety of alternative coffee products. Fair-trade coffee is now found next to organic coffee, bird-friendly coffee, and shade-grown coffee, all implying support for the environment and small producers.

This change in markets also altered the relationship between buyers and sellers. Instead of small-scale purchasers traveling personally to arrange the sale of small amounts of coffee, the most important purchasers of fair-trade coffee today are buyers for large chains like Starbucks. Given the large quantities of coffee they are purchasing from many parts of the world, these buyers generally prefer relatively large cooperatives with an established track record of delivering a consistent and high quality product over a smaller cooperative new to fair-trade production. In turn, consumers are led to identify with a generic "fair-trade producer" rather than the actual producers of the coffee that people are buying. All of these factors reduce the interaction between producer, buyer, and consumer.

The market for fair-trade coffee has also grown more demanding. Increasingly, fair-trade coffee is expected to meet the standards of specialty coffee, where specific varieties of coffee are carefully managed to produce a high-quality product. Although consumers are willing to pay high prices for coffee, to compete with specialty coffee in locations like Starbucks and grocery stores, fair-trade coffee must be of the same high quality (Giovannucci 2001; Roseberry 1996). In addition, even though pests such as *broca*, an insect that lays its eggs in the developing coffee bean, are growing in virulence in Costa Rica (Borbón Martínez n.d.), fair-trade coffee must increasingly be organically produced, instead of simply in transition to sustainable production, to be marketable at all. In the past three years, between 87 and 100 percent of fair-trade coffee sold in the United States was produced organically (Transfair USA 2006).

The combination of demands puts strain both on producers who have continued to grow coffee using traditional methods and those using more modern production. Traditional methods produce a relatively organic coffee, but mix varieties of coffee and often lack some quality control, whereas modern production methods integrate pesticides and fertilizer along with higher yields and more consistent quality. The demand for organically produced, high-quality coffee comes at a time when fair-trade organizations and purchasers are providing less technical assistance and support to fair-trade producers. The FLO (2006) has chosen to support its increased costs by asking farmers to pay part of the costs of their certification as fair-trade coffee producers. The fair-trade market is growing both more demanding and more expensive for producers, acting more like other specialty coffee markets.

At the same time, vendors such as Starbucks argue that they find it difficult to find adequate supplies of high-quality fair-trade coffee (Howley 2006). These vendors want more producers certified as fair-trade producers, so that they can more easily find a broad selection of high quality coffee to offer to consumers. Programs to increase the quality of existing fair-trade producers are moving too slowly to please them. The sense that many fair-trade certified cooperatives do not produce world-class premium coffee continues to be an issue, which makes it more difficult for newly certified cooperatives of unknown quality to convince U.S. and European sellers to take a chance on them. This challenge is made worse by the fact that some cooperatives, poorly organized and inexperienced in dealing with international markets, have found themselves unable to complete contracts (Martinez 2002).

THE FAIR-TRADE EXPERIENCE OF COOPABUENA

Some of the problems with the developing fair-trade market can be seen in the experience of COOPABUENA, a cooperative of mostly small-scale coffee farmers in southern Costa Rica, founded 42 years ago in a newly colonized zone near the Panamanian border (Cole

Christensen 1997; Smith 2001). This area, located in the Pacific highlands of southern Costa Rica, was developed after WWII through two means: small-scale settlers claiming homesteads by occupying government-owned land and large-scale farmers who had been granted large farms by the government out of those same lands. Although these two groups generally interacted peacefully, their interests and land claims often came into conflict. This discussion is based on two periods of fieldwork in the communities of Agua Buena district, the first conducted for 14 months in 1997–98, the second conducted for six weeks in the summer of 2005. Research included participant-observation, interviews, and archival research.

The center of what would become COOPABUENA was one of these large coffee farms, owned by André Challe, a wealthy developer from the capital. After clearing land for the production of coffee and cattle, bringing in large numbers of workers, and building a coffee processing plant (beneficio), he found that the considerable undeveloped parts of his farm quickly became overrun by squatters seeking unoccupied land to develop as homesteads. After multiple unsuccessful attempts to remove the squatters, Challe gave up, defaulted on the mortgages on the farm, and allowed the bank to take the farm.

The debt was held by the national bank, whose representatives approached the local producers on and around Challe's farm, encouraging them to take on the property as a new cooperative—the first in the zone. In 1963, COOPABUENA was formed with a mix of medium-sized and small producers. Taking on the property and the debt left behind by Challe left the new cooperative with both substantial assets and a substantial debt. The beneficio, a state of the art wet processing facility, could easily process over a million pounds of coffee a year. Prime land, some of which was eventually sold to reduce the debt, remained in the possession of the cooperative. However, the bulk of the land that the cooperative had just acquired was occupied by squatters, many of whom were now new members of the cooperative.

The bank and cooperative formed a plan to reduce the debt: the land reform agency would take over the occupied parts of the farm, give title to the squatters living on it, and reimburse the cooperative for the land. This solution had been standard policy for squatter-occupied properties in the Costa Rican highlands. However, here it failed. Some squatters refused to pay for land they said had never legally belonged to Challe, but had been legitimately claimed as homesteads from government land. Others depended on the fact that Instituto de Tierras y Colonización (ITCO, now IDA—Instituto de Desarrollo Agrario), the land reform agency, would not actually force them from

the homes they had occupied for many years. In the end, they were right. The land reform agency and the cooperative admitted defeat; many land titling issues in the area remain unresolved to this day. This left the new cooperative responsible for the value of this land as well as the equipment they were using.

Although the founders of COOPABUENA intended to function as the main coffee cooperative for the new canton of Coto Brus, the government had other plans. COOPABUENA was quickly followed by two other cooperatives, COOPROSANVITO and COOPE-SABALITO, which formed in the central and northwestern parts of the new canton. As many members of COOPABUENA lived in these areas, the two younger cooperatives left COOPABUENA with fewer producers and less coffee than anticipated. Moreover, COO-PROSANVITO and COOPESABALITO essentially limited the area in which COOPABUENA could recruit new members, as the Costa Rican government encouraged the cooperatives not to compete directly.

Despite this setback, COOPABUENA managed to largely pay off their debt by the early 1980s, although they were forced to take on new debt in the early 1990s to improve their infrastructure and to meet changing environmental regulations. By the early 1990s, the cooperative had over 400 members delivering nearly two million pounds of coffee to the cooperative annually, significantly smaller than the other two local cooperatives that processed five million pounds or more (Smith 2001). Ten years later, it would grow to 800 members and process over three million pounds of coffee (ICAFE 2005).

These small farmers developed diversified production systems that included beans and vegetables sold in the internal Costa Rican market, meat for local consumption, and occasional forays into export crops such as tiquisque and caña india (the same strategy is described in other parts of Costa Rica by Sick 1997, 1999; and Barlett 1982). However, none of these crops replaced coffee. Export markets were small and undependable; each crop went through a brief boom before prices collapsed or the market dried up entirely (Conroy et al. 1996). Internal markets were more dependable, but the prices of these crops too rose and fell unpredictably. It was sometimes hard to find buyers for them as well. Therefore, coffee remained the dominant crop in the area, although its price too sometimes dropped.

Much of the literature on fair trade emphasizes the increase in small-farmer income made possible by cutting out middlemen and brokers within the exporting company, who often leave little income for the producers. However, the Costa Rica coffee production and marketing system had essentially accomplished this from the 1940s to the 1960s. The government encouraged small-scale coffee farmers to form cooperatives at that time, offering financial and logistical incentives (Hall 1976:163–165; Seligson 1980:74–78). COOPABUENA was formed as part of this program, as were its competitors. The quantity of coffee they produced allowed them to sell directly to exporters, ensuring that the bulk of the world market price of the coffee would go to COOPABUENA. In addition, the government of Costa Rica enacted laws that regulated the level of expenses and profits that coffee processors and sellers can deduct from the price paid to coffee producers. Even before fair trade entered the lives of the producers of COOPABUENA, they faced a relatively just situation in terms of how the world market price of coffee was distributed between producers and sellers. This serves as a reminder that, although democratically organized cooperatives are an important part of the fair-trade model for coffee, there is nothing about this sort of cooperative that depends on fair trade.

Although cooperatives like COOPABUENA had many advantages for their members, their democratic organization did not protect them when the price of coffee dropped. In response to the low coffee prices of the early 1990s, the now professional management of COOPABUENA began to seek out opportunities to sell coffee through alternative markets. They moved into the fair-trade market by joining COOCAFE, which at that time was the only fair-trade certified consortium of cooperatives in Costa Rica (COOCAFE 2006). Joining an established organization of fair-trade producers seemed likely to offer quick access to markets, as COOCAFE had an established product. COOCAFE took coffee from its member cooperatives, roasted and packaged it, and sold it as Café Forestal in European markets. Over time, in response to the demand for more differentiated coffee for the specialty market, COOCAFE began to sell less of the generically Costa Rican Café Forestal and to specialize more in coffee from single areas. This left COOPABUENA largely out in the cold. They were the "odd man out" in COOCAFE, as the other cooperatives were located in the northern part of the country, where the coffee and growing conditions were radically different from COOPABUENA's. Even worse, COOPABUENA coffee was graded lower, a medium-hard bean, than the more desirable hard bean or strictly hard bean found in the north. COOPABUENA's somewhat lower quality coffee was largely because of the high rainfall, 100 inches or more annually, although the medium altitude of 900–1,200 meters also contributed to the lower-quality product. This meant that, although their coffee was of quite good quality, it was not compatible with the product (single location coffee grown at high altitudes) that was becoming most profitable for COOCAFE as a whole. So, as some coopera-

tives increased their sales of fair-trade coffee through the late 1990s, COOPABUENA lagged behind. They would never catch up. The same factors that had led the producers of COOPABUENA to be reasonably successful in the world market doomed them in the new fair-trade market, with its increasing demands for organic coffee and higher-quality coffee. Farmers were too dependent on agrochemicals to easily switch to organic coffee. In addition, the large-scale processing equipment owned by the cooperative made it difficult to process single varieties of coffee separately, a basic requirement for specialty coffee (for further discussion of this issue, see Smith 2006).

Despite their lack of success, the management remained enthusiastic about the long-term prospects of fair trade, encouraging cooperative members to experiment with organic coffee and sustainable-production methods. At the small-scale experimental level, producers responded enthusiastically and creatively. With the assistance of government agencies and volunteers from the United States, farmers began to experiment. Early successes focused on the creation of erosion control systems and the use of nitrogen-fixing trees in coffee fields. Others experimented with the use of organic fertilizers such as compost, *bocashi* (a Japanese fermented organic fertilizer utilizing chicken manure, rice hulls, and molasses that could be made in 10–15 days), and products made from the organic waste left after coffee processing (for discussions of bocashi see Maine Organic Farmers and Gardeners Association 2007; Sustainable Harvest International 2007). Scientists from the United States carried out experiments regarding a variety of cover crops, both in coffee and in traditional slash and mulch production systems, in the area (Rosemeyer 1994; Rosemeyer and Gliessman 1992; Schlather 1998). Experiments with an entirely organic coffee were largely unsuccessful, probably because of problems with fungal disease and relatively exhausted and eroded soils. Little support for this sort of experimentation came from COOCAFE or other fair-trade sources; although COOPABUENA collaborated with the government on some projects, most of this experimentation was supported by private individuals and community-based organizations.

Through the late 1990s, as the price of conventional coffee remained high, the failure to make significant progress either alone or through COOCAFE in the fair-trade market seemed unimportant to the producers of COOPABUENA. In 1998, the manager presold nearly the entire harvest through the conventional futures market when the price reached $3 a pound. The fair-trade contract, however, was based on a lower price, so that the cooperative members earned less from the small amount of coffee sold through the fair-trade market than from coffee sold through the conventional market. However, as the price of coffee began to slide below a dollar a pound in 1999, the continued inability of COOPABUENA to develop a substantial fair-trade market became a liability. As the price of coffee slipped under the costs of production, farmers felt betrayed by the failure to find a position in the fair-trade market.

Many farmers felt that they had worked hard to develop sustainable methods of growing coffee, with the understanding that the effort would be rewarded with access to a market with better, or at least more stable, prices than those of the conventional coffee market. As prices slumped lower and lower, some began to say that they regretted the undertaking, although others argued that the effort had been worthwhile for its environmental results, even if there were no financial rewards. But even the most enthusiastic began to let their efforts to develop more sustainable-production systems slide. In extreme cases, coffee was ripped out of fields, leaving bare earth vulnerable to erosion. Some farmers were able to sustain some enthusiasm for sustainable production methods, shifting their efforts to other crops, such as vegetables and tubers. However, the cooperative, with millions of dollars in assets intended for coffee processing, storage, and sale, was in no position to shift to these markets. In any case, none of these markets were large enough to produce income for all the members of the cooperative. Moreover, earlier failures with crops such as macadamia nuts left the cooperative management convinced that sticking to what they knew was prudent. Although individual farmers diversified production, the cooperative remained committed to coffee.

A bright spot emerged in 2001, when a group of agricultural researchers at University of California, Santa Cruz (UCSC), who had previously done research into sustainable agricultural systems in the area approached COOPABUENA about setting up a direct marketing system, exporting first to the university community, then by mail order throughout the United States. Although this involved only a few hundred pounds at first, it offered a price nearly three times greater than fair-trade markets offered. It also offered things that fair-trade systems had failed to deliver to COOPABUENA: direct contacts with U.S. business owners and consumers, technical support for the development of sustainable agricultural systems, and a sense of partnership in setting prices and goals. The Santa Cruz group was formalized as the Community Agroecology Network (although I am in touch with this group, I was not part of the organization, which was led by agronomists who had worked in the area in the 1970s and 1980s).

Although these kinds of connections encouraged individual producers and revitalized movements toward sustainable coffee, the extra income was not enough to save COOPABUENA. From 2000 to 2004, the cooperative fell deeper in debt. Managers came and went; the last made an aggressive effort to increase both the volume and the quality of COOPABUENA coffee, hoping to build on their direct marketing success by making their coffee more attractive in the larger fair-trade market. However, it was not to be. In 2004, the banks that held COOPABUENA's debt refused to finance the next year's harvest, forcing COOPABUENA into bankruptcy. The banks took over the assets of COOPABUENA, leaving many members shortchanged, as they had not been paid for all of their coffee. Despite eight years of concerted effort to build a fair-trade market, COOPABUENA had been unable to sell enough coffee through that market to make a real difference to its producers, or to its survival.

Direct marketing with the assistance of their U.S. partners had been more useful. Although the financial impact remained small as well, the other forms of assistance clearly made a difference both to farmers and to the cooperative. Shortly after it became clear that the cooperative would be forced into bankruptcy, faculty and students involved with CAN—as the UCSC group was known—started encouraging local producers with whom they had collaborated to consider forming a new cooperative, for the explicit purpose of continuing to sell coffee in the United States. In the end, 50 producers out of the 800 members of COOPABUENA, agreed to form a new cooperative, COOPUEBLOS, for the sale of sustainable coffee. Income from the direct marketing system with CAN continued through the organizing period. In late 2005, the producers were still formalizing the legal organization but expected to be once again selling fair-trade coffee through COOCAFE soon. Students affiliated with CAN provided assistance with financial matters and encouraged the development of a more open organization and leadership style. COOCAFE, however, has offered little assistance, whether financial, technical, or organizational, as this group has worked to get off the ground.

The problem of volume still remains. In 2004–05, COOPEPUEBLOS has sold less than 10,000 pounds through direct marketing; in 2005–06, they expect that they might sell as much as 15,000 pounds through direct marketing and another 15,000 pounds through the COOCAFE fair-trade market. Even the 30,000 pounds they hope to sell represents only a small fraction of the production of the 50 current cooperative members, as each producer might produce 3,000 pounds of coffee or more. In comparison, COOPABUENA processed almost two million pounds of coffee through the 1990s and topped out at over three million pounds in its last year of existence. After a decade of seeking out fair-trade markets, the cooperatives have never sold more than one percent of local production through alternative markets. Realistically, alternative markets will remain a tiny percentage of sales from this area for years to come. The question is whether it will be sufficient to encourage farmers to continue investing in coffee.

In the summer of 2005, the failure of COOPABUENA weighed heavily on the community, leading many people to a deep pessimism. People muttered darkly about how cooperatives could not be trusted when the money owed them seemed unlikely to emerge. They described themselves as disillusioned and not likely to try cooperativism again. One producer standing in his now-empty coffee field swore he would never grow coffee again.

This disillusionment was largely driven by the fact that the members of the cooperative were financially hurt by the bankruptcy. Costa Rican coffee processors, both privately owned and cooperatives, pay producers through a complicated system, developed to comply with Costa Rican laws about coffee sales and the distribution of the proceeds from coffee sales. In it, producers are paid a fraction of the final sale price of the coffee the week that the coffee is harvested and delivered for processing. Then a series of "adjustments" are paid through the year, with the final payment only being paid about the time of the next harvest. In its last year, COOPABUENA allowed the value of the initial payment to vary: as the harvest progressed and more coffee was sold, more was paid out to producers. Thus, producers who waited until late in the harvest to collect their payments were paid more than farmers who collected their payments weekly. In addition, some farmers were rumored to have made "special deals" to receive more of the final payment on delivery. If all had gone well for the remainder of the year, these differences would not have mattered. But the cooperative was forced to begin liquidation before the producers were paid their adjustments, leaving many farmers feeling that the payments were handled unjustly. Although all may still be paid eventually, the payments were delayed sufficiently that people doubted that the cooperative would make good on its obligations.

The sense of disappointment ran deeper as well. Although the cooperative's financial difficulties were nothing new, it had been a local institution for over 40 years and had seemed indestructible. The coffee processing plant occupied the center of town. The cooperative's failure seemed to some the end of coffee production in the area: if the catastrophically low prices of the previous five years had been too much for the cooperative, perhaps it was too much for local farmers as well. Rumors of corruption of both the

manager and the local directors circulated through the community. In this crisis, the fair-trade movement had no help to give.

However, a small group of farmers, many of whom had come to leadership roles through COOPABUENA, continued to work with CAN. In response to the low prices of coffee after 1999, they had made agricultural diversification as a local priority. New projects focused on growing vegetables under roofs during the rainy season to sell in the neighboring lowlands, raising pigs for the market, and the revival of traditional household production, which had declined sharply across the 1980s and 1990s. They also experimented with new ways to reuse farm waste, most impressively the use of pig manure to produce cooking gas. Some early successes from these experiments are helping to build a new sense of optimism about the future. CAN further helped to build a sense of optimism by making it clear that they wanted to continue working with local farmers despite the failure of COOPABUENA.

The case of three producers helps to illustrate the range of responses to the situation in the community (all names are pseudonyms). All are small farmers with farms of less than five hectares. Carlos had been a leader in COOPABUENA, working as an inspector of members' fields. He had also been involved in some of the mid-1990s experimentation in organic agriculture, producing bocashi, the Japanese organic fertilizer, for his fields as part of an experimental group. His father and brothers went further and were involved in an unsuccessful attempt to grow organic coffee. The failure of these experiments and of the cooperative did not discourage him, in part because he was closely mentored by government agronomists and the leaders of CAN. His agricultural practice had always been reasonably diversified. In 1997–98, in addition to coffee, Carlos grew maize and beans as well as a variety of fruits and vegetables for family use. A return visit in 2005 found the diversification vastly increased. A roof made of plastic sheeting over a wooden frame protected a sizeable plot of vegetables, up from the handful of plants in 1997–98. A pen contained pigs being fattened for the market, while sugarcane to feed them grew nearby. Carlos had taken on a leadership position in COOPEPUEBLOS as well, and was eagerly pursuing new marketing opportunities for COOPEPUEBLOS coffee. Although he was aware of the many challenges ahead, he saw the formation of the new cooperative as an opportunity for a fresh start, developing smaller-scale processing methods that would be more sustainable and more flexible, making it easier to process organic coffee and other specialty coffees separately. From his perspective, the future was bright. Although his production was considerably diversified, coffee was still his mainstay. He expected that the new cooperative would soon be selling fair-trade coffee through COOCAFE.

Luis, however, had not been deeply affected by attempts to create a more sustainable coffee production system. He saw the new cooperative only as a pale shadow of COOPABUENA. He blamed corruption for the death of COOPABUENA and pointed to the continuities in leadership as evidence that the new cooperative was no better than the old. He had little hope that cooperativism on the large scale would be reborn here, although he was interested in the possibility of affiliating with one of the other large cooperatives in the canton. His farm was only moderately diversified in both 1997–98 and 2005, with vegetables and a small amount of maize for household use. However, nonfarm income from a series of business ventures was more important to his family than their declining coffee income. He was concerned about the way that CAN and COOPAPUEBLOS were favoring certain farmers, and had no intention of joining the new cooperative. From his perspective, the future of coffee production was bleak. He did not blame fair trade. From his point of view, it simply had never been important to local coffee production and marketing. Although he personally was well situated because of his investment in nonagricultural businesses, he saw the failure of coffee production as very detrimental to the zone and feared that nothing would develop to take the place of coffee.

Ernesto falls somewhere between the two. He has been interested in farm diversification for some time: in 1997–98, he was producing coffee but was also a leader in growing vegetables and marketing them in neighboring lowlands. In 2005, he had shifted his farm entirely away from coffee, and said in disgust that he would not grow coffee again. However, his farm was otherwise diversified in many of the same ways as Carlos's farm. He was growing vegetables under a roof of plastic sheeting to protect them from rain and sun; he was raising pigs and even breeding them; and he talked about managing the waste from the pigs to both fertilize his fields and provide cooking gas for his house. He spoke eloquently about the issue of sustainability, but thought that the future of the area lay somewhere other than coffee. The promise of fair trade to provide a sustainable price for coffee seemed to him simply impossible. Ernesto is a clear example of the failures of other market crops to displace coffee; although he still produces vegetables, he grows fewer than he did five years previously. His coffee fields now stand empty.

As the new cooperative rises from the old, optimism—about the future of coffee in southern Costa Rica, about the value of working toward sustainable agricultural systems, and of the long-term promise of alternative markets—is rising again. The manager of the new cooperative, a local producer, talked enthusiastically with all visitors about efforts to bring local coffee to wider attention and how visitors could help. This optimism was contagious. Three weeks after swearing he would never grow coffee again, Ernesto said that he thought he would plant coffee next year—just a quarter of a hectare, but he might try organic coffee this time.

IMPLICATIONS OF THE CHANGES IN FAIR TRADE

Fair-trade literature has focused on improving the lives of small-scale farmers, emphasizing the creation of democratically organized cooperatives that allow farmers to deal in the marketplace on favorable terms. This includes payment above market value but especially the establishment of a floor price, below which payment will not drop, as well as empowerment of Third World producers through collaboration, education, and exchange. However, fair trade did not succeed in fulfilling these promises for COOPABUENA. The first was a reality long before fair trade in coffee began. The second failed in two ways: (1) when coffee prices were high, fair trade failed to offer a better price than conventional markets, and (2) when coffee prices were low, fair trade was not a large enough percentage of sales to substantially improve small-scale farmers' incomes. Finally, fair-trade networks did not contribute significantly by assisting the producers of COOPABUENA with technical problems, by enabling direct contacts between COOPABUENA and sellers, or by providing support when COOPABUENA entered its final crisis or as the new cooperative emerged. Although fair trade was not responsible for the demise of COOPABUENA, it did little to ease the blow or to forestall COOPABUENA's demise.

Instead, for COOPABUENA, the direct marketing system with CAN played the roles that fair trade was originally intended to, building relationships between producers and consumers while supporting efforts to create more sustainable production systems. It even supported local producers as they created a new cooperative to take the place of the old one. The fair-trade market, however, functioned essentially as just a place to sell coffee at a higher price. Moreover, it was a market that was hard to enter, whose demands (for higher quality and single variety coffee) changed over time with no warning or assistance to producers to help them meet these demands. From their perspective, the promise of fair trade as something more than a market for coffee has not been fulfilled. The producers of COOPABUENA found other resources to help them develop sustainable-production systems, improve the quality of the coffee they produce, and even seek out new resources when the cooperative failed. However, this was in large part owing to luck, for example, a U.S. farmer living in the area and former Peace Corps volunteers turned academics recruited researchers and students into the zone.

It might be easy to dismiss this case as an exception or aberration. Some cooperatives have certainly had very positive and lucrative experiences with fair trade. However, the scale and structure of the fair-trade market, with its low demand per certified producer and its move toward more conventional retail outlets, guarantees that these experiences are not unusual. For many farmers around the world, fair trade remains a promise rather than a reality, revealing itself not as a supportive community, but as a demanding market.

Some producing cooperatives are big winners, selling the lion's share of their coffee in the fair-trade market, whereas others remain on the outside looking in, trying to break into this lucrative and promising market. Those big winners do receive the benefits that the fair-trade literature claims and that fair-trade buyers expect, although the outsiders find themselves excluded not only from the market but from all those other benefits that the fair-trade movement publicizes. If this were just any alternative market, this outcome would not matter—all markets have winners and losers. But in a market whose conceptual base and justification is support for small producers and cooperation between people in wealthy and poor countries, this outcome is troubling. It is even more troubling as the costs of certification are increasingly borne by producers (the basic cost for certification is now $2,000) without guarantees that the producers will have real access to buyers in the developed world.

To some extent, a shift away from building relationships between producers and consumers was inevitable as the fair-trade market grew to over two-thirds of a million producers and over 80 million pounds of coffee (not even considering other fair-trade crops). However, the implications of these shifts and how the movement might respond to these issues seem to have not been seriously considered. As fair trade continues to grow, grappling with what these changes mean for producers, consumers, and fair-trade organizations will occupy more time and attention. Whether it will become simply another specialty market, if one in which the producers and their workers are guaranteed a fair price, or whether it will continue to strive to be something more, is something that only time can tell.

REFERENCES

Barlett, Peggy F. 1982. *Agricultural Choice and Change: Decision Making in a Costa Rica Community*. New Brunswick, NJ: Rutgers University Press.

Boot, Willem, Christopher Wunderlich, and Armando Bartra. 2003. *Beneficial Impacts of Ecolabeled Mexican Coffee: Organic, Fair Trade, Rainforest Alliance, Bird Friendly*. Electronic document, http://privatizationofrisk.ssrc.org/Warren/, accessed March 29, 2006.

Borbón Martinez, Olger N.d. *Prevención y Control de la Broca del Fruto del Cafeto (Hypothenemus hampei, Ferrari, 1867) en Costa Rica*. Unpublished MS, ICAFE (Instituto del Café) Costa Rica.

Cole Christensen, Darryl. 1997. *A Place in the Rain Forest: Settling the Costa Rican Frontier*. Austin: University of Texas Press.

Conroy, Michael, Douglas Murray, and Peter Rosset. 1996. *A Cautionary Tale: Failed U.S. Development Policy in Central America*. Boulder, CO: Lynne Rienner.

COOCAFE. 2006. *Nuestra Misión*. Electronic document, http://www.coocafe.com/inicio.htm, accessed March 29, 2006.

Fairtrade Labelling Organizations International (FLO). 2005. *Delivering Opportunities: Annual Report 2004–2005*. Electronic document, http://www.fairtrade.net/sites/news/FLO_AR_2004_05.pdf, accessed March 29, 2006.

——. 2006. Standards. Electronic document, http://www.fairtrade.net/sites/standards/general.html, accessed March 29, 2006.

Giovannucci, Daniele. 2001. *Sustainable Coffee Survey of the North American Specialty Coffee Industry*. Electronic document, http://www.scaa.org/pdfs/Sustainable_Coffee_Report_NA.pdf, accessed March 29, 2006.

Hall, Carolyn. 1976. *El Café y el Desarrollo Histórico-Geográfico de Costa Rica*. San José: Editorial Costa Rica.

Howley, Kerry. 2006. *Absolution in Your Cup. The Real Meaning of Fair Trade Coffee*. Electronic document, http://www.reason.com/0603/fe.kh.absolution.shtml, accessed March 29, 2006.

Hudson, Ian, and Mark Hudson. 2003. Removing the Veil? Commodity Fetishism, Fair Trade, and the Environment. *Organization and Environment* 16(4): 413–430.

Instituto del Café de Costa Rica (ICAFE). 2005. *Café Recibido Acumulado Cosecha 0405*. Electronic document, http://www.icafe.go.cr/newsite.nsf/Reprint001b? OpenForm, accessed November 25.

Lines, Thomas. 2003. *Europe and the Coffee Crisis: A Plan for Action*. Electronic document, http://www.oxfam.org/en/files/bp030226_EUcoffee10.pdf/download, accessed March 29, 2006.

Lyon, Sarah. 2005. *Maya Coffee Farmers and the Fair Trade Commodity Chain*. Ph.D. dissertation, Department of Anthropology, Emory University.

Maine Organic Farmers and Gardeners Association. 2007. *Tips: Bocashi Boosts Growth.* Electronic document, http://www.mofga.org/mofga/other/mofgj05x.html, accessed March 15.

Martinez, Maria Elena. 2002. *Poverty Alleviation through Participation in Fair Trade Coffee Networks: The Case of the Tzotzilotic Tzobolotic Coffee Coop Chiapas, Mexico.* Electronic document, http://www.colostate.edu/Depts/Sociology/FairTradeResearchGroup/doc/tzotzilotic.pdf, accessed March 29, 2006.

Moberg, Mark. 2005. Fair Trade and Eastern Caribbean Banana Farmers: Rhetoric and Reality in the Anti-Globalization Movement. *Human Organization* 64(1): 4–15.

Murray, Douglas, Laura T. Raynolds, and Peter Leigh Taylor. 2003. *One Cup at a Time: Poverty Alleviation and Fair Trade Coffee in Latin America.* Electronic document, http://www.colostate.edu/Depts/Sociology/FairTradeResearchGroup/doc/fairtrade.pdf, accessed March 29, 2006.

Nigh, Ronald. 1997. Organic Agriculture and Globalization: A Maya Associative Corporation in Chiapas, Mexico. *Human Organization* 56(4): 427–436.

Raynolds, Laura. 2000. Re-Embedding Global Agriculture: The International Organic and Fair Trade Movements. *Agriculture and Human Values* 17: 297–309.

———. 2002. Consumer/Producer Links in Fair Trade Coffee Networks. *Sociologia Ruralis* 42(4): 404–424.

Roseberry, William. 1996. The Rise of Yuppie Coffees and the Reimagination of Class in the United States. *American Anthropologist* 98(4): 762–775.

Rosemeyer, Martha. 1994. Yield, Nodulation and Mycorrhizal Establishment in Slash/Mulch vs. Row-Cropped Beans. In *Tapado, Slash/Mulch: How Farmers Use It and What Researchers Know About It*, eds. H. David Thurston, M. Smith, G. Abawi, and S. Kearl, 169–178. Ithaca, NY: CIIFAD and CATIE.

Rosemeyer, Martha, and Steven Gliessman. 1992. Modifying Traditional and High-Input Agroeco-systems for Optimization of Microbial Symbiosis: A Case Study of Dry Beans in Costa Rica. *Agriculture, Ecosystems, and Environment* 40: 322–331.

Schlather, Ken. 1998. *The Dynamics and Cycling of Phosphorus in Mulched and Unmulched Bean Production Systems Indigenous to the Humid Tropics of Central America.* Ph.D. dissertation, Department of Soil, Crop and Atmospheric Sciences, Cornell University.

Seligson, Mitchell. 1980. *El Campesino y el Capitalismo Agrario de Costa Rica.* San José, Costa Rica: Editorial Costa Rica.

Sick, Deborah. 1997. Coping with Crisis: Costa Rican Households and the International Coffee Market. *Ethnology* 36(3): 255–276.

———. 1999. *Farmers of the Golden Bean: Costa Rican Households and the Global Coffee Economy.* DeKalb: Northern Illinois University Press.

Smith, Julia. 2001. *Towards Sustainability: Small Scale Coffee Production Beyond the Green Revolution.* Ph.D. dissertation, Department of Anthropology, University of Pittsburgh.

———. 2006. Small Producers in the Specialty Coffee Market. Paper presented at the 105th Annual Meeting of the American Anthropological Association, San Jose, CA, November 16.

Specialty Coffee Association of America (SCAA). 2006. *U.S. Coffee Retail Sales, Electronic document,* http://www.scaa.org/pdfs/news/specialtycoffeeretail.pdf, accessed March 29, 2006.

Starbucks. 2006. *Starbucks, Fair Trade, and Coffee Social Responsibility.* Electronic document, http://www.starbucks.com/aboutus/StarbucksAndFairTrade.pdf, accessed May 21.

Sustainable Harvest International. 2007. *Bocashi: Mixing Magic.* Electronic document, http://www.sustainable-harvest.org/bocashi.cfm, accessed March 15.

Transfair USA. 2005a. *FAST FACTS: Fair Trade Certified™ Coffee.* Electronic document, http://www.transfairusa.org/pdfs/fastfacts_coffee.pdf, accessed November 25.

———. 2005b. *TransFair USA's Mission.* Electronic document, http://www.transfairusa.org/content/about/overview.php, accessed November 25.

———. 2006. *Fair Trade Almanac.* Electronic document, http://www.transfairusa.org/pdfs/2005FTAlmanac3.17.06.pdf, accessed March 29.

37

Globalization from the Ground Up

David Crawford

Doing anthropology can be a romantically nostalgic practice. Long-term participant observation and cultural immersion require unexpected physical, emotional, as well as intellectual challenges. For anthropologists who follow Malinowski and Boas into the quotidian lives of their research communities, fieldwork is more than a data collection exercise. Immersing oneself in the daily life of a community, and gaining the trust and participation of your hosts, is far more challenging than our carefully constructed research designs might suggest. Cultural immersion requires experiencing research subjects as hosts, friends, experts, and teachers. Some people mischaracterize this model of cultural anthropology as "hanging out in the village." More accurately, cultural immersion produces emotional bonds created through months, and then years, of shared laughs, meals, tragedies, holidays, funerals, weddings, births, and more. Not so different from a first love, the community that hosts an anthropologist's dissertation research forever remains in that anthropologist's heart.

As anthropologists and communities age, they will say goodbye to a generation of elders and kids they've known from birth who begin having families of their own. It's not difficult to empathize with an anthropologist's nostalgia as passing years, births, and deaths transform the village. For example, the arrival of electricity and outdoor lighting might cast a new florescent glow over what was once a picturesque moonlit village. Similarly, elders (anthropologists and others) may sometimes bemoan youth musical tastes as local traditional musicians become less popular than Rihanna, Lil Wayne, and Akon.

Nostalgic memories aside, our study communities are not living museums frozen in time. Anthropologists and others who may be inclined to romanticize an "authentic" past free from Coca-Cola, cell phones, and reality television must embrace the larger historical truth: globalization is nothing new, and our host communities have been changing for generations. The places we think of as only recently entering the modern world have always been modern, and they've always been connected to the world through regional and long-distance trade networks. In this selection, anthropologist David Crawford presents a fresh perspective on globalization and culture change that comes from the Atlas Mountains in Morocco. In addition, Crawford's chapter presents a unique behind-the-scenes account of how cultural anthropologists work tirelessly to make sense of their study communities, from figuring out where to "use the bathroom" to organizing surveys and interviews.

As you read this selection, ask yourself the following questions:

- How did the author arrange for meals during his field research?

- Based on the author's account, what are some of the difficulties of doing anthropology field research?

- After returning to his study community years after his original study, what changes did the author notice in Tagharghist?

- What did the people of Tagharghist think about the changes in their community? How would someone from this community define globalization?

- List and describe the three types of globalization as discussed by the author.

The following terms discussed in this section are included in the Glossary in the back of the book:

agency	hybridity
Berber	globalization
cultural diffusion	souk

Crawford, David. "Globalization from the Ground Up." This article was written especially for *Applying Cultural Anthropology: An Introductory Reader*, 9th ed.

FIELDWORK: GETTING STARTED

I first came to Morocco's Agoundis Valley in the mountains south of Marrakech in 1995. It was only a short visit. In those days there was no road, only a narrow mule path etched into the rugged cliffs. People lived in houses of compressed mud, and they stayed alive by farming barley in hundreds of tiny, steeply terraced plots. They had an elaborate system of canals and ditches that brought snowmelt from the plunging Agoundis River to the fields. There was no electricity, no plumbing, and no potable water except for one frog-filled spring. It seemed like an ideal place to examine rural Moroccan life, a place that was literally and figuratively "off the grid." My belief was that if you wanted to understand the global, you needed to begin from some specific locale. While I didn't explicitly plan to test theories of globalization when I arrived, it was clear that rural Morocco was changing rapidly and would provide a useful vantage point on social change.

I returned to Morocco in 1998 to do research and settled in the village of Tagharghist, a small place of a couple hundred people living high in the mountains, about 5,000 feet above sea level. During my first visit a man named Abdurrahman had invited me to stay. I spoke no Berber, the language of the indigenous people of Morocco, but I did speak some Arabic, and Abdurrahman spoke some, so I rented a room and began asking for lessons in Berber. Within a few weeks we dropped the Arabic and continued our exchanges exclusively in Berber.

The most difficult thing at first was figuring out how to feed myself, and how to compensate people for their help and hospitality. I had my room, and a small stove, but there was no place to buy food, and anyway it was lonely—and pretty weird from a local perspective—to eat alone. Several families began a kind of competition to take me in as their guest, and I didn't want to offend anyone so I sometimes ended up eating several dinners in one night and then nothing the next. Slowly I worked out a system where I ate at only three of my neighbors' houses: one who was pretty well off, one kind of middle class for the village, and one very poor. I was officially a guest so it would be an insult to offer money for their hospitality, but villagers had very little food and I didn't want to take advantage of their generosity. So, each Thursday, market day, I would walk 20 kilometers to *souk* and bring back a kilogram or two of meat for each of my hosts. Families rarely had meat, so they really liked this. It was the same quantity for everybody no matter how much or how little I ate at a particular house. This allowed them to be generous hosts and me to eat without depriving them of calories. It also avoided the kind of cash for food exchange that would move us from a guest/host relationship to one of a paying client and service provider.

Another dilemma was that most people went to the bathroom in the stable below their house or out in their fields when they were working. I was only renting a room, so I had no stable and no fields to use as a bathroom. Where was I supposed to go? I figured out where there were some private areas behind boulders or trees that were not too far a walk from my house, and old ladies taught me to throw rocks at rude children who would try and follow me. Once I was able to speak some of the language, eat, and go to the bathroom I could move on with the research.

I began collecting genealogies and making kinship charts, diagrams that showed all of the family relations. This is pretty classic, old school anthropology and it made sense in my context. Kinship charts were useful for keeping track of the social landscape. I asked "who is the father of x" and "who is the mother of x" over and over again hundreds of times until I knew everyone in the village at that time, and hundreds of dead ancestors. This turned out to be very helpful because it allowed me to understand how people were related to one another—and in a village, everyone is related. Old men would quiz me by asking about obscure relatives, things like, "who married Mohammed the son of Hussein Ait l'Haj?" and when I looked at my charts and knew the answer, they thought I was really clever. It made me proud that the old men called me "smart." Along the way my Berber started to get better. These charts also helped me to understand the patrilineages, the lines of male ancestors that villagers used to organize work groups when they needed to build a new canal or repair the mosque.

The next step was to find out about the political and economic structure of the village. Who was powerful and who was not? Who had economic resources? To understand how villagers were connected to global processes, I needed to understand their local social and political structures first. You can't tell how something is changing until you know some basics about it. By eating and working with people it became clear that the village was very gendered, by which I mean that men and women usually worked, sometimes ate, and almost always socialized separately. Men who controlled households (usually grandfathers) considered themselves equal to one another, but within households there were strict hierarchies by age. Older men controlled younger men and boys, and younger men were very deferential to their elders. Older women dominated younger women in the same way.

To understand the differences between households I tried counting and measuring all the fields (there were over 1,411 tiny plots that fed the village), and I spent a lot of time analyzing the irrigation system to see who got how much water. By adding up the irrigation time that each household controlled, I discovered that the men who insisted that they were all equal to one another had very different amounts of land. This matters a lot in a farming society. Everyone was desperately poor by world standards—well below the World Bank's official poverty line. But still there was economic hierarchy, even if people denied it. This reminded me of the United States, where everyone believes they are part of the "middle class" despite dramatic economic inequalities.

I also did household surveys, where I asked who contributed to a household's income, who ate there, and what sorts of resources they had (cows, goats and so forth). I also figured out dependency ratios within a household, which means how many children versus how many workers are around to feed them. This is complicated, however, because children start working at a very young age, especially girls. Through household surveys I found out that many households had "absent members" who went to the city to work. These were often children, especially girls who were sent to live as nannies in the homes of the Moroccan middle class. All their wages were returned to the households in the village. This was a major sign that this seemingly isolated village was more deeply connected to the larger economy than I imagined. When I would read about theories of globalization, I would think about these girls and wonder how they fit in.

The more I talked with villagers, the more I understood their perspective on the world. Unsurprisingly, their concerns often focused on important things they lacked, which included everything from warm clothes and shoes to medicine and dental care. Villagers told me again and again how hard life was farming barley, how little they had, how determinedly they had to work to stay alive. A constant refrain was "life in the mountains is hard."

I lived in Tagharghist for 14 months and worked diligently to find out everything I could about it. Then for the next decade I came back for periodic visits. During these visits it became apparent that the village was changing dramatically. A road was built, and a school. Trucks came in and out of the valley. Some people began planting fruit trees and selling the fruit at market. The traditional village saint was ignored as new, urban understandings of religion took hold. And most importantly, ever more people went to work in the city. It became common for households to send their children to work in Marrakech or Casablanca and send money back to the village, and the villagers came to rely on the money earned through wage labor.

I asked villagers what they thought of the changes. I had them tell me "life histories," where in an open-ended way they would relate how things had changed over their lifetimes, and I tape recorded their answers. I also asked them to compare village life to city life, and comment on whether they preferred life in the village (i.e. the "traditional" world) or the city. I also asked about village history, how and why the village formed, where their ancestors came from, and so forth. I do not have space here to detail all their answers, but they bear on the massively widespread process we call "globalization." To fully appreciate the lessons on globalization that the people of Tagharghist shared with me, I considered how their ideas fit within three major theories of globalization.

THREE THEORIES OF GLOBALIZATION

Everyone agrees that the world is changing. The questions are how and why? There is a large, complicated scholarly literature on globalization so I will focus on the three theories most common today. Other explanations might be more convincing, and it may be that different parts of each theory are necessary to explain the data. An important role of anthropological research is to apply what we learn "in the field" to theories that emerge from universities. Anthropological data is often interesting in its own right—it's fascinating to see how different people think and behave—but this kind of information is also vital for evaluating scholarly assertions about how the contemporary world works.

Probably the most common theory of globalization is *McDonaldization*, from the title of a book by sociologist George Ritzer (1993). The argument is that huge corporations are selling similar products in similar ways, organizing people to produce these products in similar ways, and thereby swamping local cultural distinctiveness with an overwhelming uniformity. In short, cultures come to be organized like fast-food restaurants: same product, same way of making it no matter where you are. New values on efficiency and uniformity take over so that people, too, become part of this homogenizing cultural system. It is not just food, either. The McDonald's mentality produces everything—from Windows computer software and Avon beauty products to Kalishnakov rifles and Marlboro cigarettes. Politicians who favor this theory tend to present it as inevitable, the "only game in town." Some even argue that it is essentially good that formerly distinct people now shop for the same products as everyone else, but most anthropologists find this disturbing.

This tendency towards homogeneity is blamed on big business, or more expansively, capitalism. Massive corporations—from oil companies to film studios—control the political process in most of the nations of the world, and they also work through global institutions like the International Monetary Fund (IMF) and the World Trade Organization (WTO). Their goal is to free businesses to make more commodities more cheaply, and to sell these commodities anywhere they want. The result is that local cultures cannot resist or escape. Corporate logic inflicts a general global culture on formerly diverse local communities.

A second theory of globalization is the "clash of civilizations" hypothesis, and its main proponent is Samuel Huntington (1996). Here communities are not being fused into a single global culture, but instead they consolidate into large cultural blocs, or "civilizations." Huntington believes that one bloc—"the West," he calls it—is culturally incompatible with others, most notably "Islamic civilization." For him it does not matter if there are McDonald's restaurants in Riyadh and Jarkarta, or if Muslims text on cell phones while eating at Pizza Hut. Huntington sees Muslims as essentially different from people in the West, and the two civilizations as inherently antagonistic towards one another. This theory is often cited by politicians who favor aggressive action against nations in other civilizational blocs.

The "clash of civilizations" theory explains these divisions by asserting the power of culture over people. Adherents of this theory believe that vast groups—literally billions in the case of Muslims—share very specific values among themselves. Since these values are special to them, and since they cannot be combined or compromised, such people cannot be expected to get along with those in other civilizations. It is not clear in this theory why culture should all of a sudden become so powerful, why civilizations would be consolidating at this particular historical moment, or why the contours of the civilizations are drawn as they are. Most anthropologists find this theory unconvincing, even racist, but it is very popular in some sectors of the media.

The theory of globalization most accepted by anthropologists focuses on "hybridity," the mixing of cultural elements. This idea has many current proponents, but the core of it goes all the way back to the early 20th century and Franz Boas, one of the first professional anthropologists (1938). While Boas did not use the term "hybrid," his ideas of "diffusion" and "historical particularism" are very close to it (Hatch 1973). For Boas and most of his students cultural elements "diffuse," or travel, more or less independently. So, for example, it is possible for a culture to adopt the fashion of wearing baseball caps while ignoring the sport of baseball itself. From this perspective cultures are always borrowing from one another and assembling the borrowed pieces in their own "historically particular" ways. That's why so many people around the world use Arabic numerals without considering themselves culturally Arab. (Try doing algebra using Roman numerals!) Once a cultural trait is borrowed, people tend to believe it was always their own.

Two things drive hybridity today. The first is agency (the ability of people to choose what they want) and the second is technology (especially communications technology). Technology is thought to "compress space and time" (Harvey 1989). For example, planes allow us to travel anywhere in the world in less than a day, and the Internet makes it simple to send information everywhere virtually instantly. This allows people more choices than ever before, and thus allows culture to change at dizzying speeds. For example, rap music became popular around the world very quickly because people like it (they have agency and they choose it) and because both artists and songs can be quickly sent from one end of the globe to the other. Proponents of hybridity emphasize that the meaning of rap—the lyrics, rhymes, and political projects—are unique to each culture. From this perspective cultures are not becoming a single homogeneous thing, nor are they consolidating into huge civilizations. Instead they are doing what they always have done: borrowing elements from one another and forming their own unique combinations. The process is moving faster than it ever has, however, and this leads to some novel cultural forms.

WHAT AN OUT OF THE WAY VILLAGE TELLS US ABOUT GLOBALIZATION

By 2011 I had been working in Tagharghist for well over a decade and there was clearly change going on. Clearly "globalization" was happening in some sense and I wanted to find out how and why. I continued to do household surveys. I interviewed villagers about life in the city, and I interviewed some migrants. I tried to fit the ethnographic data together with what I understood from the scholarly literature, but the fit is far from perfect. I asked myself what theories of globalization tell us about this one small part of the globe, and what this small place tells us about theories of globalization? Below are some of my conclusions. You may ask yourself how they accord with what you understand from your own life, and from other ethnographic contexts you might have read about. You might also look around for other theories of globalization. For now, though, here is what I learned:

1. For the world's poor, life has few good options. The people in Tagharghist are not "choosing" in a consumerist way because they are on the edge of survival. They have two tough options: move

to the city to take low-paid, often dangerous, and demanding work or remain in the village to labor long and hard before they are old enough to relax and let the young work for them. The city offers rewards sooner (a paycheck every week, an escape from the dominating fathers of the village) but no long term security. The village offers long term security in exchange for a lifetime of serving elders. I have argued elsewhere that each option has a different "temporality of inequality," by which I mean they are both unfair in different ways, over different time periods (Crawford 2008). Globalization theories that emphasize choosing *commodities* miss crucial elements of the experience of the world's poor. Theirs is not a life of shifting tastes in consumption, but shifting strategies for survival.

2. Tagharghist has long been a part of "the global." Abdurrahman told me about his family history beginning in the 12th century, when his ancestors came to the mountains from the plains. I had not expected this. Abdurrahman's ancestors were Arabs who *became* Berbers, which suggests that we shouldn't think of any culture as being what it is or remaining the same from time immemorial, even indigenous peoples. Everyone has history; everything changes. Some people, like these illiterate villagers, know far more of their history than most people I meet at universities.

3. Also, during the 12th century these mountains were "the center of Islam." I learned from the villagers that a leader named Ibn Tumart had made his home at the base of the valley and launched what became the vast Almohad Empire. The Almohads eventually controlled most of Spain and almost all of North Africa and founded one of the world's great civilizations. Ibn Tumart was a Berber, like my friends in the village. He converted this region to Islam over eight hundred years ago and made it the center of what was then an Islamic world system. What is marginal today was not so in the past. Our world system is not the only one to ever exist.

4. The motivations for the current changes in Tagharghist are both economic and cultural in a complicated way. On the economic side, fathers send their children down to the city to work because families need the wages. This is fully culturally sensible since children are supposed to support parents rather than the other way around. Some of these children break away from their families and start new lives in the city. However, they tell me that this is not because of a sudden change in culture, a desire to own flashy new products or otherwise "become modern." Rather, it is because young people want to choose husbands and wives to start their own families. In the village they have to wait because the fathers own all the land. If a father wants his son to marry, he might get him a wife and she can move into the father's household, but many young men and women want to choose their own spouse and be independent. It is important to emphasize that this is a normal cultural thing to want; it's just not always possible. When young people break away, they are doing so in pursuit of a traditional village goal (marriage and children) by putting new resources to work (wage labor). This is how the capitalist economy sucks the life out of villages and globalization expands. Wage labor removes the young who serve the old, and the rural social order starts to collapse. The primary motivation for wage labor is not that young people want to live in the "modern world," but that they want to live out their traditional goals more quickly.

How does all this fit with theories of globalization? They all have something to say, but none of them captures everything. The McDonaldization theorists are right that wage labor may have a homogenizing effect, that capitalism sometimes destroys other social worlds. But young people seem to be choosing wage labor in many cases, trading a lifetime of hard work with a secure reward (owning your own land) for the immediate reward of a weekly paycheck and the ability to get married and start families.

Culture is important, as the "clash of civilizations" people suggest, but not in the way they think. People in Tagharghist do not primarily think of themselves as Muslims any more than Westerners wake up and ponder how to "be Western" each day. Islam forms the backdrop of daily life, much like Christianity in the United States, but that's about all there is to it. Villagers live in relation to larger civilizations, but their lives are much richer and more complex than simply being a member of a culture or civilization or religion.

The hybridity model provides a unique perspective that underscores the significance of the day-to-day choices of people. However, this model can obscure one critical fact: wealthier people have many more choices than poor people. So, examples about hybrid music or the transformative role of the Internet are simply not applicable to the lives of billions of people who live on the equivalent of a couple dollars a day. What is hybrid for the poor are strategies for survival.

Finally, an important lesson about globalization that we can take from Tagharghist is that the Western, capitalist era is not the only "global system" in history, and not the only game in town. Islamic civilization was also "global," and is global now. It offers a common language and civilization that stretches across continents, and influences many hundreds of millions of people. Local cultures always exist in relation to the outside and to larger forces, to widespread phenomena like "capitalism" or Islam—or capitalism and Islam at the same time.

It would seem from the evidence in Tagharghist that globalization theories tend to overemphasize the isolation of traditional cultures, unduly stress the uniqueness of our era and the monolithic nature of our economy, and vastly overstate the cultural importance of "the West."

REFERENCES

Boas, Franz, ed. 1938. *General Anthropology*. New York: D.C. Heath and Company.

Crawford, David. 2008. *Moroccan Households in the World Economy*. Baton Rouge: LSU Press.

Harvey, David. 1990. *The Condition of Postmodernity*. Oxford: Blackwell Press.

Hatch, Elvin. 1973. *Theories of Man and Culture*. New York: Columbia University Press.

Huntington, Samuel P. *The Clash of Civilizations and the Remaking of World Order*. New York, NY: Simon and Schuster, 1996.

Ritzer, George. 2011. *The McDonaldization of Society*, sixth edition. Newbery Park, CA: Pine Forge Press.

38

The Price of Progress

John H. Bodley

Anthropologists are not against progress: We do not want everyone to return to the "good old days" of our Paleolithic ancestors. On the other hand, the discoveries of cultural anthropologists have made us painfully aware of the human costs of unplanned social and economic change. Anthropologists do not want our society to plunge blindly into the future, unaware and unconcerned about how our present decisions will affect other people or future generations. Cultures are always changing, and the direction of that change is toward a single world system. Cultures change because a society's economy is pulled into the world economy. "Progress" is a label placed on cultural and economic change, but whether something represents "progress" or not depends on one's perspective.

In this selection, John Bodley reviews some of the unexpected consequences of economic development in terms of health, ecological change, quality of life, and relative deprivation. We have seen this same theme in several previous selections—the invention of agriculture, for example. The benefits of economic development are not equally distributed within a developing society. In this selection, we see the relative costs and benefits of economic progress for some of the most marginalized people of the world—the tribal peoples who have been the traditional focus of cultural anthropology research. We believe that the problems detailed here should make our society think about the way cultural change can make people's lives worse; these are issues of social justice.

Anthropologists have been active in seeking solutions to many serious problems. At the same time, most anthropologists believe that tribal peoples have a right to lead their traditional lifestyles and not to be forced into change. In this regard, an organization called Cultural Survival has been active in the international political arena in protecting the land and rights of native peoples.

As you read this selection, ask yourself the following questions:

- What is meant by quality of life? Why might it increase or decrease for a population?

- What are the three ways in which economic development can change the distribution of disease?

- Why do people's diets change? Do people choose diets and behaviors that are harmful to them?

- What is meant by relative deprivation? Can you think of other examples of this process?

- Are tribal peoples more vulnerable to the negative impact of social and economic change than larger industrial societies?

The following terms discussed in this selection are included in the Glossary at the back of the book:

dental anthropology	relative deprivation
ecosystem	self-sufficient
ethnocentrism	swidden cultivation
nomadic band	tribe
population pressure	urbanization

In aiming at progress . . . you must let no one suffer by too drastic a measure, nor pay too high a price in upheaval and devastation, for your innovation.

—Maunier, 1949:725

Bodley, John H. "The Price of Progress." From *Victims of Progress*, 4th ed., 1999. Reprinted by permission of Rowman & Littlefield Publishers, Inc.

Until recently, government planners have always considered economic development and progress beneficial goals that all societies should want to strive toward. The social advantages of progress—as defined in terms of increased incomes, higher standards of living, greater security, and better health—are thought to be positive, *universal* goods, to be obtained at any price. Although one may argue that tribal peoples must sacrifice their traditional cultures to obtain these benefits, government planners generally feel that this is a small price to pay for such obvious advantages.

In earlier chapters, evidence was presented to demonstrate that autonomous tribal peoples have not *chosen* progress to enjoy its advantages, but that governments have *pushed* progress upon them to obtain tribal resources, not primarily to share with the tribal peoples the benefits of progress. It has also been shown that the price of forcing progress on unwilling recipients has involved the deaths of millions of tribal people, as well as their loss of land, political sovereignty, and the right to follow their own life style. This chapter does not attempt to further summarize that aspect of the cost of progress, but instead analyzes the specific effects of the participation of tribal peoples in the world-market economy. In direct opposition to the usual interpretation, it is argued here that the benefits of progress are often both illusory and detrimental to tribal peoples when they have not been allowed to control their own resources and define their relationship to the market economy.

PROGRESS AND THE QUALITY OF LIFE

One of the primary difficulties in assessing the benefits of progress and economic development for any culture is that of establishing a meaningful measure of both benefit and detriment. It is widely recognized that *standard of living*, which is the most frequently used measure of progress, is an intrinsically ethnocentric concept relying heavily upon indicators that lack universal cultural relevance. Such factors as GNP, per capita income, capital formation, employment rates, literacy, formal education, consumption of manufactured goods, number of doctors and hospital beds per thousand persons, and the amount of money spent on government welfare and health programs may be irrelevant measures of actual *quality* of life for autonomous or even semiautonomous tribal cultures. In its 1954 report, the Trust Territory government indicated that since the Micronesian population was still largely satisfying its own needs within a cashless subsistence economy, "Money income is not a significant measure of living standards, production, or well-being in this area" (TTR 1953:44). Unfortunately, within a short time the government began to rely on an enumeration of certain imported goods as indicators of a higher standard of living in the islands, even though many tradition-oriented islanders felt that these new goods symbolized a lowering of the quality of life.

A more useful measure of the benefits of progress might be based on a formula for evaluating cultures devised by Goldschmidt (1952:135). According to these less ethnocentric criteria, the important question to ask is: Does progress or economic development increase or decrease a given culture's ability to satisfy the physical and psychological needs of its population, or its stability? This question is a far more direct measure of quality of life than are the standard economic correlates of development, and it is universally relevant. Specific indication of this *standard* of living could be found for any society in the nutritional status and general physical and mental health of its population, the incidence of crime and delinquency, the demographic structure, family stability, and the society's relationship to its natural resource base. A society with high rates of malnutrition and crime, and one degrading its natural environment to the extent of threatening its continued existence, might be described as at a lower standard of living than is another society where these problems did not exist.

Careful examination of the data, which compare, on these specific points, the former condition of self-sufficient tribal peoples with their condition following their incorporation into the world-market economy, leads to the conclusion that their standard of living is *lowered*, not raised, by economic progress—and often to a dramatic degree. This is perhaps the most outstanding and inescapable fact to emerge from the years of research that anthropologists have devoted to the study of culture change and modernization. Despite the best intentions of those who have promoted change and improvement, all too often the results have been poverty, longer working hours and much greater physical exertion, poor health, social disorder, discontent, discrimination, overpopulation, and environmental deterioration—combined with the destruction of the traditional culture.

DISEASES OF DEVELOPMENT

> Perhaps it would be useful for public health specialists to start talking about a new category of diseases. . . . Such diseases could be called the "diseases of development" and would consist of those pathological conditions which are based on the usually unanticipated consequences of the implementation of development schemes (Hughes & Hunter, 1972:93).

Economic development increases the disease rate of affected peoples in at least three ways. First, to the extent that development is successful, it makes developed populations suddenly become vulnerable to all of the diseases suffered almost exclusively by "advanced" peoples. Among these are diabetes, obesity, hypertension, and a variety of circulatory problems. Second, development disturbs traditional environmental balances and may dramatically increase certain bacterial and parasite diseases. Finally, when development goals prove unattainable, an assortment of poverty diseases may appear in association with the crowded conditions of urban slums and the general breakdown in traditional socioeconomic systems.

Outstanding examples of the first situation can be seen in the Pacific, where some of the most successfully developed native peoples are found. In Micronesia, where development has progressed more rapidly than perhaps anywhere else, between 1958 and 1972 the population doubled, but the number of patients treated for heart disease in the local hospitals nearly tripled, mental disorder increased eightfold, and by 1972 hypertension and nutritional deficiencies began to make significant appearances for the first time (TTR 1959, 1973, statistical tables).

Although some critics argue that the Micronesian figures simply represent better health monitoring due to economic progress, rigorously controlled data from Polynesia show a similar trend. The progressive acquisition of modern degenerative diseases was documented by an eight-member team of New Zealand medical specialists, anthropologists, and nutritionists, whose research was funded by the Medical Research Council of New Zealand and the World Health Organization. These researchers investigated the health status of a genetically related population at various points along a continuum of increasing cash income, modernizing diet, and urbanization. The extremes on this acculturation continuum were represented by the relatively traditional Pukapukans of the Cook Islands and the essentially Europeanized New Zealand Maori, while the busily developing Rarotongans, also of the Cook Islands, occupied the intermediate position. In 1971, after eight years of work, the team's preliminary findings were summarized by Dr. Ian Prior, cardiologist and leader of the research, as follows:

> We are beginning to observe that the more an islander takes on the ways of the West, the more prone he is to succumb to our degenerative diseases. In fact, it does not seem too much to say our evidence now shows that the farther the Pacific natives move from the quiet, carefree life of their ancestors, the closer they come to gout, diabetes, atherosclerosis, obesity, and hypertension (Prior 1971:2).

In Pukapuka, where progress was limited by the island's small size and its isolated location some 480 kilometers from the nearest port, the annual per capita income was only about thirty-six dollars and the economy remained essentially at a subsistence level. Resources were limited and the area was visited by trading ships only three or four times a year; thus, there was little opportunity for intensive economic development. Predictably, the population of Pukapuka was characterized by relatively low levels of imported sugar and salt intake, and a presumably related low level of heart disease, high blood pressure, and diabetes. In Rarotonga, where economic success was introducing town life, imported food, and motorcycles, sugar and salt intakes nearly tripled, high blood pressure increased approximately ninefold, diabetes two- to threefold, and heart disease doubled for men and more than quadrupled for women, while the number of grossly obese women increased more than tenfold. Among the New Zealand Maori, sugar intake was nearly eight times that of the Pukapukans, gout in men was nearly double its rate on Pukapuka, and diabetes in men was more than fivefold higher, while heart disease in women had increased more than sixfold. The Maori were, in fact, dying of "European" diseases at a greater rate than was the average New Zealand European.

Government development policies designed to bring about changes in local hydrology, vegetation, and settlement patterns and to increase population mobility, and even programs aimed at reducing certain diseases, have frequently led to dramatic increases in disease rates because of the unforeseen effects of disturbing the preexisting order. Hughes and Hunter (1972) published an excellent survey of cases in which development led directly to increased disease rates in Africa. They concluded that hasty development intervention in relatively balanced local cultures and environments resulted in "a drastic deterioration in the social and economic conditions of life."

Traditional populations in general have presumably learned to live with the endemic pathogens of their environments, and in some cases they have evolved genetic adaptations to specific diseases, such as the sickle-cell trait, which provided an immunity to malaria. Unfortunately, however, outside intervention has entirely changed this picture. In the late 1960s, sleeping sickness suddenly increased in many areas of Africa and even spread to areas where it did not formerly occur, due to the building of new roads and migratory labor, both of which caused increased population movement. Large-scale relocation schemes, such as the Zande Scheme, had disastrous results when natives were moved from their traditional disease-free refuges into infected areas. Dams and irrigation developments inadvertently created ideal conditions for the rapid proliferation of snails carrying schistosomiasis (a liver fluke disease), and major epidemics suddenly occurred in areas where this disease had never before been a problem. DDT spraying programs have been temporarily successful in controlling malaria, but there is often a rebound effect that increases the problem when spraying is discontinued, and the malarial mosquitoes are continually evolving resistant strains.

Urbanization is one of the prime measures of development, but it is a mixed blessing for most former tribal peoples. Urban health standards are abysmally poor and generally worse than in rural areas for the detribalized individuals who have crowded into the towns and cities throughout Africa, Asia, and Latin America seeking wage employment out of new economic necessity. Infectious diseases related to crowding and poor sanitation are rampant in urban centers, while greatly increased stress and poor nutrition aggravate a variety of other health problems. Malnutrition and other diet-related conditions are, in fact, one of the characteristic hazards of progress faced by tribal peoples and are discussed in the following sections.

The Hazards of Dietary Change

The traditional diets of tribal peoples are admirably adapted to their nutritional needs and available food resources. Even though these diets may seem bizarre, absurd, and unpalatable to outsiders, they are unlikely to be improved by drastic modifications. Given the delicate balances and complexities involved in any subsistence system, change always involves risks, but for tribal people the effects of dietary change have been catastrophic.

Under normal conditions, food habits are remarkably resistant to change, and indeed people are unlikely to abandon their traditional diets voluntarily in favor of dependence on difficult-to-obtain exotic imports. In some cases it is true that imported foods may be identified with powerful outsiders and are therefore sought as symbols of greater prestige. This may lead to such absurdities as Amazonian Indians choosing to consume imported canned tunafish when abundant high-quality fish is available in their own rivers. Another example of this situation occurs in tribes where mothers prefer to feed their infants expensive and nutritionally inadequate canned milk from unsanitary, but *high status,* baby bottles. The high status of these items is often promoted by clever traders and clever advertising campaigns.

Aside from these apparently voluntary changes, it appears that more often dietary changes are forced upon unwilling tribal peoples by circumstances beyond their control. In some areas, new food crops have been introduced by government decree, or as a consequence of forced relocation or other policies designed to end hunting, pastoralism, or shifting cultivation. Food habits have also been modified by massive disruption of the natural environment by outsiders—as when sheepherders transformed the Australian Aborigine's foraging territory or when European invaders destroyed the bison herds that were the primary element in the Plains Indians' subsistence patterns. Perhaps the most frequent cause of diet change occurs when formerly self-sufficient peoples find that wage labor, cash cropping, and other economic development activities that feed tribal resources into the world-market economy must inevitably divert time and energy away from the production of subsistence foods. Many developing peoples suddenly discover that, like it or not, they are unable to secure traditional foods and must spend their newly acquired cash on costly, and often nutritionally inferior, manufactured foods.

Overall, the available data seem to indicate that the dietary changes that are linked to involvement in the world-market economy have tended to *lower* rather than raise the nutritional levels of the affected tribal peoples. Specifically, the vitamin, mineral, and protein components of their diets are often drastically reduced and replaced by enormous increases in starch and carbohydrates, often in the form of white flour and refined sugar.

Any deterioration in the quality of a given population's diet is almost certain to be reflected in an increase in deficiency diseases and a general decline in health status. Indeed, as tribal peoples have shifted to a diet based on imported manufactured or processed foods, there has been a dramatic rise in malnutrition, a massive increase in dental problems, and a variety of other nutrition-related disorders. Nutritional physiology is so complex that even well-meaning dietary changes have had tragic consequences. In many areas of Southeast Asia, government-sponsored protein supplementation programs supplying milk to protein-deficient populations caused unexpected health problems and increased mortality. Officials failed to anticipate that in cultures where adults do not normally drink milk, the enzymes needed to digest it are no longer produced and milk *intolerance* results (Davis & Bolin 1972). In Brazil, a similar milk distribution program caused an epidemic of permanent blindness by aggravating a preexisting vitamin A deficiency (Bunce 1972).

Teeth and Progress

> There is nothing new in the observation that savages, or peoples living under primitive conditions, have, in general excellent teeth. . . . Nor is it news that most civilized populations possess wretched teeth which begin to decay almost before they have erupted completely, and that dental caries is likely to be accompanied by periodontal disease with further reaching complications (Hooton 1945:xviii).

Anthropologists have long recognized that undisturbed tribal peoples are often in excellent physical condition. And it has often been noted specifically that

because where tribals can retain or regain their status as local majorities they may be in a more favorable position to defend their resources against intruders.

Swidden systems and pastoralism, both highly successful economic systems under traditional conditions, have proven particularly vulnerable to increased population pressures and outside efforts to raise productivity beyond its natural limits. Research in Amazonia demonstrates that population pressures and related resource depletion can be created indirectly by official policies that restrict swidden peoples to smaller territories. Resource depletion itself can then become a powerful means of forcing tribal people into participating in the world-market economy—thus leading to further resource depletion. For example, Bodley and Benson (1979) showed how the Shipibo Indians in Peru were forced to further deplete their forest resources by cash cropping in the forest area to replace the resources that had been destroyed earlier by the intensive cash cropping necessitated by the narrow confines of their reserve. In this case, a certain species of palm trees that had provided critical housing materials were destroyed by forest clearing and had to be replaced by costly purchased materials. Research by Gross and others (1979) showed similar processes at work among four tribal groups in central Brazil and demonstrated that the degree of market involvement increases directly with increases in resource depletion.

The settling of nomadic herders and the removal of prior controls on herd size have often led to serious overgrazing and erosion problems where these had not previously occurred. There are indications that the desertification problem in the Sahel region of Africa was aggravated by programs designed to settle nomads. The first sign of imbalance in a swidden system appears when the planting cycles are shortened to the point that garden plots are reused before sufficient forest regrowth can occur. If reclearing and planting continue in the same area, the natural pattern of forest succession may be disturbed irreversibly and the soil can be impaired permanently. An extensive tract of tropical rainforest in the lower Amazon of Brazil was reduced to a semiarid desert in just fifty years through such a process (Ackermann 1964). The soils in the Azande area are also now seriously threatened with laterization and other problems as a result of the government-promoted cotton development scheme (McNeil 1972).

The dangers of overdevelopment and the vulnerability of local resource systems have long been recognized by both anthropologists and tribal peoples themselves, but the pressures for change have been overwhelming. In 1948 the Maya villagers of Chan Kom complained to Redfield (1962) about the shortening of their swidden cycles, which they correctly attributed to increasing population pressures. Redfield told them, however, that they had no choice but to go "forward with technology" (Redfield 1962:178). In Assam, swidden cycles were shortened from an average of twelve years to only two or three within just twenty years, and anthropologists warned that the limits of swiddening would soon be reached (Burling 1963:311–312). In the Pacific, anthropologists warned of population pressures on limited resources as early as the 1930s (Keesing 1941:64–65). These warnings seemed fully justified, considering the fact that the crowded Tikopians were prompted by population pressures on their tiny island to suggest that infanticide be legalized. The warnings have been dramatically reinforced since then by the doubling of Micronesia's population in just the fourteen years between 1958 and 1972, from 70,600 to 114,645, while consumption levels have soared. By 1985 Micronesia's population had reached 162,321.

The environmental hazards of economic development and rapid population growth have become generally recognized only since worldwide concerns over environmental issues began in the early 1970s. Unfortunately, there is as yet little indication that the leaders of the now developing nations are sufficiently concerned with environmental limitations. On the contrary governments are forcing tribal peoples into a self-reinforcing spiral of population growth and intensified resource exploitation, which may be stopped only by environmental disaster or the total impoverishment of the tribals.

The reality of ecocide certainly focuses attention on the fundamental contrasts between tribal and industrial systems in their use of natural resources. In many respects the entire "victims of progress" issue hinges on natural resources, who controls them, and how they are managed. Tribal peoples are victimized because they control resources that outsiders demand. The resources exist because tribals managed them conservatively. However, as with the issue of the health consequences of detribalization, some anthropologists minimize the adaptive achievements of tribal groups and seem unwilling to concede that ecocide might be a consequence of cultural change. Critics attack an exaggerated "noble savage" image of tribals living in perfect harmony with nature and having no visible impact on their surroundings. They then show that tribals do in fact modify the environment, and they conclude that there is no significant difference between how tribals and industrial societies treat their environments. For example, Charles Wagley declared that Brazilian Indians such as the Tapirape

> are not "natural men." They have human vices just as we do. . . . They do not live "in tune" with nature any more than I do; in fact, they can often be as destructive

of their environment, within their limitations, as some civilized men. The Tapirape are not innocent or child-like in any way (Wagley 1977:302).

Anthropologist Terry Rambo demonstrated that the Semang of the Malaysian rain forests have measurable impact on their environment. In his monograph *Primitive Polluters*, Rambo (1985) reported that the Semang live in smoke-filled houses. They sneeze and spread germs, breathe, and thus emit carbon dioxide. They clear small gardens, contributing "particulate matter" to the air and disturbing the local climate because cleared areas proved measurably warmer and drier than the shady forest. Rambo concluded that his research "demonstrated the essential functional similarity of the environmental interactions of primitive and civilized societies" (1985:78) in contrast to a "noble savage" view (Bodley 1983) which, according to Rambo (1985:2), mistakenly "claims that traditional peoples almost always live in essential harmony with their environment."

This is surely a false issue. To stress, as I do, that tribals tend to manage their resources for sustained yield within relatively self-sufficient subsistence economies is not to make them either innocent children or natural men. Nor is it to deny that tribals "disrupt" their environment and may never be in absolute "balance" with nature.

The ecocide issue is perhaps most dramatically illustrated by two sets of satellite photos taken over the Brazilian rain forests of Rôndonia (Allard & McIntyre 1988:780–781). Photos taken in 1973, when Rôndonia was still a tribal domain, show virtually unbroken rain forest. The 1987 satellite photos, taken after just fifteen years of highway construction and "development" by outsiders, show more than 20 percent of the forest destroyed. The surviving Indians were being concentrated by FUNAI (Brazil's national Indian foundation) into what would soon become mere islands of forest in a ravaged landscape. It is irrelevant to quibble about whether tribals are noble, childlike, or innocent, or about the precise meaning of balance with nature, carrying capacity, or adaptation, to recognize that for the past 200 years rapid environmental deterioration on an unprecedented global scale has followed the wresting of control of vast areas of the world from tribal groups by resource-hungry industrial societies.

DEPRIVATION AND DISCRIMINATION

Contact with European culture has given them a knowledge of great wealth, opportunity and privilege, but only very limited avenues by which to acquire these things (Crocombe 1968).

Unwittingly, tribal peoples have had the burden of perpetual relative deprivation thrust upon them by acceptance—either by themselves or by the governments administering them—of the standards of socioeconomic progress set for them by industrial civilizations. By comparison with the material wealth of industrial societies, tribal societies become, by definition, impoverished. They are then forced to transform their cultures and work to achieve what many economists now acknowledge to be unattainable goals. Even though in many cases the modest GNP goals set by development planners for the developing nations during the "development decade" of the 1960s were often met, the results were hardly noticeable for most of the tribal people involved. Population growth, environmental limitations, inequitable distribution of wealth, and the continued rapid growth of the industrialized nations have all meant that both the absolute and the relative gap between the rich and poor in the world is steadily widening. The prospect that tribal peoples will actually be able to attain the levels of resource consumption to which they are being encouraged to aspire is remote indeed except for those few groups who have retained effective control over strategic mineral resources.

Tribal peoples feel deprivation not only when the economic goals they have been encouraged to seek fail to materialize, but also when they discover that they are powerless, second-class citizens who are discriminated against and exploited by the dominant society. At the same time, they are denied the satisfactions of their traditional cultures, because these have been sacrificed in the process of modernization. Under the impact of major economic change family life is disrupted, traditional social controls are often lost, and many indicators of social anomie such as alcoholism, crime, delinquency, suicide, emotional disorders, and despair may increase. The inevitable frustration resulting from this continual deprivation finds expression in the cargo cults, revitalization movements, and a variety of other political and religious movements that have been widespread among tribal peoples following their disruption by industrial civilization.

REFERENCES

Ackermann, F. L. 1964. *Geologia e Fisiografia da Região Bragantina, Estado do Pará*. Manaus, Brazil: Conselho Nacional de Pesquisas, Instituto Nacional de Pesquisas da Amazônia.

Allard, William Albert, and Loren McIntyre. 1988. Rôndonia's settlers invade Brazil's imperiled rain forest. *National Geographic* 174(6): 772–799.

Bodley, John H. 1983. The World Bank tribal policy: Criticisms and recommendations. *Congressional Record*, serial no. 98-37, 515–521. (Reprinted in Bodley, 1988.)

Bodley, John H., and Foley C. Benson. 1979. Cultural ecology of Amazonian palms. *Reports of Investigations, no. 56.* Pullman: Laboratory of Anthropology, Washington State University.

Bunce, George E. 1972. Aggravation of vitamin A deficiency following distribution of non-fortified skim milk: An example of nutrient interaction. In *The Careless Technology: Ecology and International Development*, ed. M. T. Farvar and John P. Milton, 53–60. Garden City, N.Y.: Natural History Press.

Burling, Robbins. 1963. *Rengsanggri: Family and Kinship in a Garo Village.* Philadelphia: University of Pennsylvania Press.

Crocombe, Ron. 1968. Bougainville!: Copper, R. R. A. and secessionism. *New Guinea* 3(3): 39–49.

Davis, A. E., and T. D. Bolin. 1972. Lactose intolerance in Southeast Asia. In *The Careless Technology: Ecology and International Development*, ed. M. T. Farvar and John P. Milton, 61–68. Garden City, N.Y.: Natural History Press.

Dennett, Glenn, and John Connell. 1988. Acculturation and health in the highlands of Papua New Guinea. *Current Anthropology* 29(2): 273–299.

Goldschmidt, Walter R. 1952. The interrelations between cultural factors and acquisition of new technical skills. In *The Progress of Underdeveloped Areas*, ed. Bert F. Hoselitz, 135–151. Chicago: University of Chicago Press.

Gross, Daniel R., and Barbara A. Underwood. 1971. Technological change and caloric costs: Sisal agriculture. *American Anthropologist* 73(3): 725–740.

Gross, Daniel R., et al. 1979. Ecology and acculturation among native peoples of Central Brazil. *Science* 206(4422): 1043–1050.

Hooton, Earnest A. 1945. Introduction. In *Nutrition and Physical Degeneration: A Comparison of Primitive and Modern Diets and Their Effects* by Weston A. Price. Redlands, Calif.: The author.

Hughes, Charles C., and John M. Hunter. 1972. The role of technological development in promoting disease in Africa. In *The Careless Technology: Ecology and International Development*, ed. M. T. Farvar and John P. Milton, 69–101. Garden City, N.Y.: Natural History Press.

Jones, J. D. Rheinallt. 1934. Economic condition of the urban native. In *Western Civilization and the Natives of South Africa*, ed. I. Schapera, 159–192. London: George Routledge and Sons.

Keesing, Felix M. 1941. *The South Seas in the Modern World.* Institute of Pacific Relations International Research Series. New York: John Day.

Kroeger, Axel, and Françoise Barbira-Freedman. 1982. *Culture Change and Health: The Case of South American Rainforest Indians.* Frankfurt am Main: Verlag Peter Lang. (Reprinted in Bodley, 1988: 221–236.)

Maunier, René. 1949. *The Sociology of Colonies.* Vol. 2. London: Routledge and Kegan Paul.

McNeil, Mary. 1972. Lateritic soils in distinct tropical environments: Southern Sudan and Brazil. In *The Careless Technology: Ecology and International Development*, ed. M. T. Farvar and John P. Milton, 591–608. Garden City, N.Y.: Natural History Press.

Mönckeberg, F. 1968. Mental retardation from malnutrition. *Journal of the American Medical Association* 206: 30–31.

Montagu, Ashley. 1972. Sociogenic brain damage. *American Anthropologist* 74(5): 1045–1061.

Price, Weston Andrew. 1945. *Nutrition and Physical Degeneration: A Comparison of Primitive and Modern Diets and Their Effects.* Redlands, Calif.: The author.

Prior, Ian A. M. 1971. The price of civilization. *Nutrition Today* 6(4): 2–11.

Rambo, A. Terry. 1985. *Primitive Polluters: Semang Impact on the Malaysian Tropical Rain Forest Ecosystem.* Anthropological Papers no. 76, Museum of Anthropology, University of Michigan.

Redfield, Robert. 1962. *A Village That Chose Progress: Chan Kom Revisited.* Chicago: University of Chicago Press, Phoenix Books.

Reinhard, K. R. 1976. Resource exploitation and the health of western arctic man. In *Circumpolar Health: Proceedings of the Third International Symposium, Yellowknife, Northwest Territories*, ed. Roy J. Shephard and S. Itoh, 617–627. Toronto: University of Toronto Press. (Reprinted in Bodley, 1988.)

Smith, Wilberforce. 1894. The teeth of ten Sioux Indians. *Journal of the Royal Anthropological Institute* 24: 109–116.

TTR: TTR, United States, Department of the Interior, Office of the Territories. 1953. Report on the Administration of the trust territories of the Pacific Islands for the period of July 1, 1951 to June 30, 1952.

United States, Department of State. 1955. *Seventh Annual Report to the United Nations on the Administration of the Trust Territory of the Pacific Islands* (July 1, 1953, to June 30, 1954).

———. 1959. *Eleventh Annual Report to the United Nations on the Administration of the Trust Territory of the Pacific Islands* (July 1, 1957, to June 30, 1958).

———. 1973. *Twenty-Fifth Annual Report to the United Nations on the Administration of the Trust Territory of the Pacific Islands* (July 1, 1971, to June 30, 1972).

Wagley, C. 1977. *Welcome of Tears: The Tapirape Indians of Central Brazil.* New York: Oxford University Press.

Wirsing, R. 1985. The health of traditional societies and the effects of acculturation. *Current Anthropology* 26: 303–322.

Glossary

acculturation   The process of extensive borrowing of aspects of another culture, usually as a result of external pressure, and often resulting in the decline of traditional culture.

adaptation   The process by which an organism or a culture is modified, usually through selection, enhancing the ability of individuals to survive and reproduce in a particular environment.

adipose tissue   Fat. A physiological mechanism of energy storage; some adipose tissue, especially when deposited on the central body, is associated with chronic diseases.

adjudication   A process of handling disputes in which the ultimate decision is made by a third party appointed by the legal system.

affinal   Related by marriage (as opposed to biology).

affinal kin   A kin relationship created by marriage.

affines   Individuals related to one another because of marriage between their families; related through marriage rather than birth.

Afrocentric   An explanation based on African origins.

age grade   A social category of people who fall within a particular culturally distinguished age range; age grades often undergo life cycle rituals as a group.

agency   The means, capacity, condition, or state of exerting power.

aggression   A forceful action, sometimes involving physical violence, intended for social domination.

agnates   Individuals sharing a patrilineal kinship tie; people related through the male line.

agnatic   Related through the male kinship line.

agrarian   Relating to agriculture.

agricultural development   Changes in agricultural production intended to improve the system by producing more harvest per unit of land.

AIDS   Acquired immune deficiency syndrome, a fatal disease caused by the human immunodeficiency virus (HIV) and usually transmitted through semen or blood.

Amerindian   Native American populations.

anorexia nervosa   An eating disorder characterized by extreme dieting and a feeling of being fat even though one is underweight.

anthropology   The systematic study of humans, including their biology and culture, both past and present.

anthropometry   Science of the measurement of the human body, including measurement of bones, muscle, fat, and other body tissues.

applied research   Study directed at gaining valid knowledge to help in the solution of human problems.

arable land   Land suitable for cultivation.

arbitration   The hearing and determination of a dispute by a person chosen by the parties or appointed by the legal system with the consent of the parties.

archaeology   The field of anthropology concerned with cultural history; includes the systematic retrieval, identification, and study of the physical and cultural remains deposited in the earth.

argot   A specialized, sometimes secret, vocabulary peculiar to a particular group.

artifact   An object manufactured and used by human beings for a culturally defined goal.

asexual   Without sexual desire, or in terms of sexual identity, someone with no apparent sexual drive.

asylum   The process by which immigrants are allowed to remain legally in their host country because of "persecution or a well-founded fear of persecution" in their country of origin.

atoll   A string of small coral islands that seals off or partially encloses a lagoon.

australopithecine   A member of the genus *Australopithecus,* the hominid ancestors of humans.

autonomy   Independence; being self-governing, self-directing.

Ayurvedic medicine   Traditional medical system of India.

AZT   An antiviral drug used to slow down the replication of HIV, the human immunodeficiency virus that causes AIDS; AZT is very expensive.

basic research   Study directed toward gaining scientific knowledge primarily for its own sake.

beer-drink   A communal beer drinking occasion among the Xhosa of southern Africa.

behavioral ecology   An ecological and evolutionary approach to understanding animal behavior in terms of how animal behavior contributes to an animal's or a species' survival/evolutionary fitness.

Berber   A descriptive term for the language, people, or identity of a group of people who have lived in Morocco and throughout Northern Africa for millennia.

berdache   An anthropological term which refers to "two spirit" Native Americans (Native Americans who fulfill mixed gender roles).

big men   Political leaders in tribal-level societies whose status has been achieved and whose authority is limited.

biogenetic   Genetic.

biological anthropology   Subfield of anthropology that studies the biological nature of humans and includes primatology, paleoanthropology, population genetics, anthropometry, and human biology.

biomedicine   Modern medicine as practiced in the United States and Europe; emphasizes the biological causation and remedy for illness.

biophysical diversity   Outward biological appearance resulting from interaction of genes and environment; phenotype.

biotic community   Plants and animals sharing a niche within an ecosystem.

blended family   A non-traditional family that may includes step children, adopted children, foster children, step parents, step grandparents, and fictive kin.

blood relatives   A folk term referring to consanguineal kin, that is, kin related through birth.

brain drain   The out-migration of highly skilled and educated people from economically marginalized communities and countries to economically advanced areas and countries.

brideprice   See *bridewealth.*

bridewealth   The presentation of goods or money by the groom's family to the bride's family at the time of marriage; an economic exchange that legitimates the marriage and offspring as members of the father's patrilineage.

burqa   A head-to-toe veil common in Afghanistan, often made of cotton and covering most of the body, including the face.

bush-fallow   A technique used by horticulturalists that allows a garden plot to return to the wild state after a period of cultivation.

cadastral   A government survey and record-keeping system for recording land ownership and property boundaries.

canton   A small territorial division of a country.

capitalism   An economic system characteristic of modern state societies where land, labor, and capital all become commodities exchanged on the market and in which socioeconomic inequality is a constant feature.

carrying capacity   The maximum population size that can be maintained in a given area without causing environmental degradation of the ecology.

cash crop   An agricultural product grown for money instead of food or subsistence.

caste   A ranked group, sometimes linked to a particular occupation, with membership determined at birth and with marriage restricted to others within the group.

ceremony   Public events involving special symbols that signify important cultural values or beliefs.

chief   The political leader of a society that is more complex than a tribal society and is characterized by social ranking, a redistributive economy, and a centralized political authority.

chiefdom   A society more complex than a tribal society, characterized by social ranking, a redistributive economy, and a centralized political authority.

CITES   Convention on International Trade and Endangered Species. An international agreement to limit the capture of endangered animals, including whales, and regulate the market for endangered species; related to the International Commission for the Conservation of Atlantic Tunas (ICCAT) that assigns quotas for tuna fishermen.

civilization   The culture of state-level societies characterized by the following elements: (1) agriculture; (2) urban living; (3) a high degree of occupational specialization and differentiation; (4) social stratification; and (5) literacy.

clan   A kinship group whose members assume, but need not demonstrate, descent from a common ancestor.

class   An economically, socially, and politically similar group of people, e.g., middle class.

clines   A gradient of morphological or physiological change in a group of related organisms, usually along a line of environmental or geographic transition.

clitorectomy (clitoridectomy)   Removal of the clitoris.

Clovis   A term used to describe a Paleo-American culture that distinguished itself by its unique projectile points (fluted points) made of obsidian and chalcedony. The term refers to a city in eastern New Mexico.

Clovis point   A large lancelike projectile fluted at the base and flanked at both sides.

clustering   In epidemiology, the concentration of cases by place of residence and time of diagnosis.

cognates   Words that belong to different languages but have similar sounds and meanings.

cognatic kin   Kinship traced simultaneously through the male and female lines in a nonunilineal pattern of descent.

collective behavior   Patterns of social action.

colonialism   The establishment of government of sovereign rule in a territory through political, social, economic, and cultural domination by a foreign power.

commodification   The transformation of a good or service into something that can be bought and sold with money.

commodity   Products such as food or fuel which can be traded for money or for other products.

communal   Shared with a group.

commune   A general term describing a cooperative community whose members collectively share property, labor, and income.

comparative framework   An analytical approach in anthropology using the comparison of cultures across time and place.

complementary schismogenesis   Forms of social interaction between people or groups that complement or "feed into" one another. Complementary schismogenesis occurs when language and/or cultural differences become exaggerated when two cultures, languages, or personalities come into contact.

constructions of femininity   The warp in which a given culture defines appropriate ways of thinking and acting for women. See *gender roles*.

consumable commodity   Something that can be bought or sold, and then used up.

consumer society   A characteristic of modern capitalist societies in which the purchase of non-essential material goods and services is an important marker of social status and identity.

consumption   The act of consuming goods or resources.

contingent truths   Truth based upon the best scientific evidence available at the time and subject to revision as knowledge expands.

conversational analysis   A technique in sociolinguistics that focuses on the social and symbolic attributes of verbal interactions.

cooperative   An organization or enterprise assembled for the production and marketing of goods, and for mutual support, benefits, and the distribution of risk.

corporate culture   The cultural characteristics of a workplace.

corporate kin groups   Social groups, like lineages, that share political responsibilities and access to land; characteristic of tribal societies.

correlate   A variable that stands in a consistent observed relationship with another variable.

correlation   A statistical relationship between two variables.

corvée   A system of required labor; characteristic of ancient states.

creole   A type of language that results from the widespread adoption of a pidgin language as the primary language of a group.

Cro-Magnon   A term broadly referring to the first anatomically modern humans, from roughly 40,000 to 10,000 B.C.; named after a site in southwestern France.

cross-cultural   A standard form of anthropological analysis using the comparison of traditions and practices from different societies.

cross-cultural research   The exploration of cultural variation by using ethnographic data from many societies.

cross-cutting ties   Affinal or trading relationships that serve to counteract the political isolation of social groups in tribal societies.

cross-sectional   Research done across different geographic locales.

cultural anthropology   A field of anthropology emphasizing the study of the cultural diversity of contemporary societies, including their economies, sociopolitical systems, and belief systems.

cultural diffusion   A process by which a custom, idea, folklore, or behavior pattern is spread from one society to another.

cultural dissonance   A situation arising from the incompatibility of two or more interacting cultural systems.

cultural evolution   The process of invention, diffusion, and elaboration of the behavior that is learned and taught in groups and is transmitted from generation to generation; often used to refer to the development of social complexity.

cultural ideals   A valued characteristic or belief of a society.

cultural materialism   The idea, often associated with Marvin Harris, that cultural behaviors are best explained in relation to material constraints (including food-producing technology) to which humans are subjected.

cultural mediation   The social processes through which someone learns or acquires the normative, shared behaviors and knowledge of a particular group or population.

cultural pluralism   The simultaneous existence of two or more cultural systems within a single society; multiculturalism.

cultural relativism/cultural relativity   The principle that all cultural systems are inherently equal in value and, therefore, that each cultural item must be understood on its own terms.

cultural reproduction   The process by which cultural behaviors and beliefs are regenerated across generations or spread among people of the same generation; cultural construction creates reality.

cultural validators   Actions or performances that enhance a sense of identity and belonging within a community or organization.

cultural values   Ideas, beliefs, values, and attitudes learned as a member of a social group.

culture   Learned patterns of thought and behavior characteristic of a particular social group.

culture area   A largely outmoded idea that the world can be divided into a limited number of geographical regions, each defined by a certain set of cultural features that result from common ecological adaptation or history and are shared by all groups in the region.

culture broker   An individual who attempts to negotiate and translate between two cultural groups, particularly in contexts of miscommunication or potential miscommunication.

culture shock   The experience of stress and confusion resulting from moving one culture to another; the removal or distortion of familiar cues and the substitution of strange cues.

decotion   The extraction of flavor by boiling.

demography   The statistical study of human populations, including size, growth, migration, density, distribution, and vital statistics.

dental anthropology   A specialization within biological anthropology; the study of the morphology of teeth across time and populations.

dependency   A theory of international economic relations in which an economically powerful nation creates ties with other nations in ways that reduce the possibility of economic independence of the poorer nations.

Defense of Marriage Act   A federal U.S. law that states that: (a) the federal government may not recognize same-sex or polygamous marriages for any purpose, and (b) no state is obliged to recognize a same-sex marriage conducted or recognized in another state. This law was passed by the U.S. Congress and signed by President Bill Clinton on 21 September 1996.

dependent variable   The resultant phenomenon that is explained by its relationship with an independent variable.

devoted actor   Actors willing to make extreme sacrifices independent of their prospects for success.

dialect   A regional or class-based version of a spoken language, although the difference between dialect and language can be influenced by historical and political considerations.

diffusion   A process of cultural change by which traits of one society are borrowed by another; the spread of cultural traits.

discourse   A verbal exchange of ideas, or it can refer to any speech unit longer than a sentence (such as a story or a joke).

diseases of civilization   Chronic diseases, such as cardiovascular disease and obesity, that characterize the epidemiological profile of modern capitalist societies and are the result of infrequent exercise and high fat diets.

dividual   As opposed to "individual," someone whose identity or selfhood is tied to his or her relationships with other people.

divination   A practice that foresees future events or discovers special knowledge through rituals, spirit possession, and supernatural perception or knowledge.

diviner   A practitioner of divination (see definition). One who uses traditional rituals or practices to foresee the future or to communicate with the supernatural for some other purpose(s).

domestic labor   Work performed in the home, such as cooking, cleaning, and taking care of children.

domestication of plants and animals   The invention of farming.

dowry   Presentation of goods or money by the bride's family to the bride, the groom, or the groom's family.

Ebonics   The rule-based and pattern dialect of English spoken by many working-class urban African Americans; black English vernacular.

economy   The production, distribution, and consumption of resources, labor, and wealth within a society.

ecology   Technically, ecology is a branch of science that examines the interconnectedness of organisms and their environment. In anthropology, ecology typically refers to the interrelationship between humans and the environment, natural and built.

ecosystem   A community of plants and animals, including humans, within a physical environment and the relationship of organisms to one another.

edutainment   A marketing technique in consumer-oriented societies in which consumerism and education are simultaneously valued.

egalitarian   A society organized around the principle of social equality; characteristic social formation of food foraging groups.

egalitarian society   A society that emphasizes the social equality of members and makes achieved statuses accessible to all adults.

embodied   Human experience inside an individual body and the expression of culture through the body.

embodied knowledge   Knowledge that seems to reside "in the body" and does not require conscious thought (for example, riding a bike).

emic   Describing or understanding a specific culture from the subjective point of view of someone living within that culture.

epidemic   Higher than normal occurrence of a disease in a particular area.

epidemiological transition   The historical change in the primary cause of mortality in a population from infectious disease to chronic disease.

epidemiology   A science that studies the incidence, distribution, and control of disease in a population.

epistemology   The study of the nature of knowledge and its limits.

ergonomics   Human engineering; an applied science concerned with the anthropometric characteristics of people in the design of technology for improved human-machine interaction and safety.

essentialist   A view of reality based on a single inherent fact rather than a socially constructed reality.

essentialize   The assumption that all individuals of the same social category (e.g., class, caste, race, gender) have the same beliefs, values, experiences, and other characteristics.

Ethiopian birr   The unit of currency in Ethiopia, which is one of the most frequently used African currencies.

ethnic groups   A group of people within a larger society with a distinct cultural or historical identity; ethnicity is a common mechanism of social separation in complex, heterogeneous societies.

ethnocentrism   The assumption that one's own group's lifestyle, values, and patterns of adaptation are superior to all others.

ethnocide   The attempt to exterminate an entire ethnic group (similar to genocide).

ethnographic   See ethnographic methods.

ethnographic methods   The research techniques of cultural anthropology based on long-term participant observations, yielding a description of another culture.

ethnography   An anthropological method that generally involves living in a place for an extended period of time, participating in and observing daily life, and then writing about the culture or the place.

ethnology   The study and explanation of cultural similarities and differences.

ethnomedicine   The medical theories, diagnosis systems, and therapeutic practices of a culture or ethnic group.

ethnopediatrics   The study of how differing parenting styles affect infant health and growth.

ethos   The worldview of a particular society, including its distinctive character, sentiments, and values.

etic   Describing or understanding a specific culture from an outsider/external (sometimes neutral) point of view.

etiology   The theory of causation of a disease or illness.

eugenics   The genetic improvement of the human race through control of breeding.

Eurocentric   Interpreting the world in terms of Western and especially European values and experiences.

evaluation researcher   A researcher who assesses (evaluates) the impact or outcome of a treatment or program.

evolutionary medicine   An anthropological approach to disease, symptoms, and medical care based upon our evolutionary heritage.

exchange   A social system for the distribution of goods; reciprocity is a widespread system of exchange between social equals while markets act as a mode of exchange between strangers.

excision   One of three forms of female circumcision; includes clitorectomy and removal of some or all of the labia minora and labia majora.

exogamous   Relating to a custom that forbids members of a specific group from selecting a spouse from within that group.

explanatory model   A patient's cognitive scheme for understanding his or her illness.

extended family   A domestic unit created by the linking together of two or more nuclear families.

fair trade   An economic partnership which serves marginalized and/or impoverished producers by providing market incentives including: access to markets, guaranteed minimum purchase prices, social and health programs, environmental stewardship, and improved relationships between consumers and producers.

fallow   The period during which a unit of agricultural land is not cultivated so that nutrients can be restored to the soil.

family of origin   Nuclear family into which an individual is born and in which he or she is reared.

fecundity   A demographic characteristic of a society referring to its overall capacity for reproduction.

feral   Living in, or pertaining to, the wild; without the benefit of society or culture.

feud   A pattern of reciprocal hostility between families or kin groups, usually involving retribution for past wrongs or deaths; such as blood feud.

FGM   Female genital mutilation or female genital modification; *see* sunna circumcision, excision, infibulation.

fieldwork   The hallmark of research in cultural anthropology, it usually involves long-term residence with the people being studied.

fission   The splitting of a descent group—a residential unit based on shared kinship—into two or more new descent groups or domestic units.

focus groups   A research strategy in which an investigator leads a small group in discussion on a particular topic; frequently used in market research.

folk taxonomy   A culture's system of classification or grouping of objects, which can reveal the cognitive categories of that group.

food foragers   People living in a society with an economic pattern harvesting of wild food resources, usually by gathering plants or hunting animals; hunting and gathering.

food insecurity   The lack of sufficient food and/or resources to meet the energy requirements of a population. Based on the definition of food security created at the 1996 World Food Summit, food insecurity is the inability of people or nations to have access to "safe, nutritious food to maintain a healthy and active life."

food scarcity   The lack of sufficient food to meet the energy requirements of a population; may be the result of failed food production or a socially unequal distribution system.

foraging   Hunting and gathering; the original human economic system relying on the collection of natural plant and animal food sources.

fraternal polyandry   An uncommon form of plural marriage in which a woman is married to two or more brothers at one time.

gender   The social classification of masculine or feminine.

gender dimorphism   Physical and physiological differences between males and females; sexual dimorphism.

gender roles   Accepted models of behavior, thoughts, and emotions associated with masculinity and femininity that are culturally defined and learned over the course of one's upbringing and socialization.

genealogy   The systematic study of the consanguineal and affinal kin of a particular person, including his or her ancestors; a common method used in anthropological field studies.

gestation   The carrying of young in the uterus from conception to delivery.

ghetto   A subsection of a city in which members of a minority group live because of social, legal, or economic pressure.

globalization   A dynamic and enduring trend toward cultural and linguistic homogeneity produced through ever-increasing international links between people and communities across the globe.

Gordian knot   A highly intractable problem or impasse; in Greek legend, a knot tied by King Gordius of Phrygia and cut by Alexander the Great, after an oracle had said it could be untied only by the next ruler of Asia.

gris-gris   An amulet or talisman, typically of African origins, worn or otherwise carried as protection against disease and evil.

hallucinogen   A substance that induces visions or auditory hallucinations in normal individuals.

hearth   The floor of a fireplace.

hierarchy   The categorization of a group of people according to status, whether it be ascribed at birth or achieved. A hierarchy refers to groups organized in this way.

HIV   The human immunodeficiency virus that causes AIDS.

holistic   Refers to viewing the whole society as an integrated and interdependent system; an important characteristic of the anthropological approach to understanding humans.

hominid   An erect-walking bipedal primate that is either human, an extinct ancestor to humans, or a collateral relative to humans.

Homo sapiens   Hominid species including modern humans and immediate archaic ancestors (Neandertals).

horticulture   A plant cultivation system based upon relatively low energy input, like gardening by using only the hoe or digging stick; often involves use of the slash-and-burn technique.

hot-cold humoral system   Traditional ethnomedical system of the Indo-European world.

human rights   Related to a post–WWII international movement begun by the United Nations and associated with the 1948 International Declaration of Universal Human Rights. The rights enumerated include: equality before the law; protection against arbitrary arrest; the right to a fair trial; freedom from *ex-post-facto* criminal laws; the right to own property; freedom of thought, conscience, and religion; freedom of opinion and expression; freedom of peaceful assembly and association; also included in the document economic, social, and cultural rights as the right to work and to choose one's work freely, the right to equal pay for equal work, the right to form and join trade unions, the right to rest and leisure, the right to an adequate standard of living, and the right to education. During the 1990s, human rights efforts often emphasized women's rights.

human universal   A trait or behavior found in all human cultures.

Human Terrain Team   An experimental and controversial U.S. military program that assigns anthropologists to work with American combat units in Afghanistan and Iraq.

hunter-gatherers   Peoples who subsist on the collection of naturally occurring plants and animals; food foragers.

hybridity   A fusion of ideas, technology, genetics, languages, or any multitude of cultural expressions.

hypothesis   A tentative assumption or proposition about the relationship(s) between specific events or phenomena, tentatively set forth as a "target" to be tested.

ideal body images   Culturally defined standards for attractive body shapes.

indicators   Measurements that anthropologists and other social scientists use to assess the achievement of specific goals and objectives. Life expectancy rates, for example, "indicate" the length of an average lifespan in a given community or country.

indigenistas   Individuals and organizations that work on behalf of indigenous people.

indigenous   The original or native population of a particular region or environment.

indigenized   The reconceptualization of a foreign cultural construct or idea to make it fit within a local/indigenous worldview.

infanticide   Killing a baby soon after birth.

infibulation   One of three forms of female circumcision; includes circumcisions and excision, followed by the sewing up of the sides of the vulva so that scar tissue covers the vaginal opening, except for a small gap for urination and menstruation; requiring some surgical opening for first intercourse and birth; also called pharaonic circumcision.

infidel   A nonbeliever with respect to a particular religion.

informant   A member of a society who has established a working relationship with an anthropological field-worker and who provides information about the culture; the subject of intensive interviewing.

institutions   Formal organizations within a society.

intensive interviewing   The ethnographic method of repeated interviews with a single informant.

intercultural communication   The exchange of meanings and messages between people from different societies characterized by different underlying ideas, beliefs, and worldviews; may or may not be complicated by the speaking of different languages.

intonation   Deploying changes in vocal pitch or melody to convey grammatical information (a question versus a statement) or expressive meaning (happiness versus anxiety).

intragroup solidarity   A measure of in-group social cohesion.

Islam   The religious faith of Muslims who profess belief in Allah as the sole deity and in Mohammad as the prophet of Allah.

jirga   Meeting of tribal leaders (typically male elders).

key respondent   A subject that a researcher finds particularly knowledgeable and amenable to multiple interviews.

kibbutz   A collective settlement owned and operated by members who eschew private property in service to the well-being and sustainability of the community itself. While they may not earn money for their work, members typically receive housing, clothing, educational opportunities, food, and medical services.

kinship/kinship systems   A network of culturally recognized relationships among individuals, either through affinial or consanguineal ties.

Koran   The sacred text of Islam.

kula   Traditional long-distance trading network for valuable objects among Trobriand islanders first described by B. Malinowski.

lactose intolerance   The inability of adults to digest milk because they no longer produce the enzyme lactase; a biological characteristic of a large proportion of the world's population.

land concentration   The degree to which land ownership is concentrated among a small number of people in a society.

land tenure   A system of land ownership and inheritance.

language   A rule-based and patterned system of communication.

late capitalism   A form of capitalism emerging in the second half of the twentieth century, characterized by finance capital, globalization, and technological innovation.

latifundistas   Large landowners who use low-cost native labor to make enormous profits.

levirate   The practice by which a man is expected to marry the wife or wives of a deceased brother; commonly found in patrilineal descent systems.

lexicon   The vocabulary set characteristic of a group; argot.

life history   A methodological technique of cultural anthropologists in which a key informant's biography is compiled using multiple interviews.

liminal period   An intermediate phase or condition.

lineage   Refers to a kin group tracing common descent through one sex from a known ancestor.

lingua franca   A language used by populations beyond the region and scope of its native speakers. A single and dominant language used by members of multiple linguistic backgrounds becomes the lingua franca of that multi-ethnic population.

linguistic anthropology   A subfield of anthropology entailing the study of language forms across space and time and their relation to culture and social behavior.

linguistic relativity   A principle of anthropological linguistics referring to the fact that all languages are equally adequate as systems of communication.

linguistics   The study of language, consisting of: (1) historical linguistics, which is concerned with the evolution of lan- guages and language groups through time; (2) descriptive linguistics, which focuses on recording and analysis of the structures of language; (3) sociolinguistics, the way in which speech patterns reflect social phenomena; and (4) ethnosemantics, the study of the connection between reality, thought, and language.

literacy   The ability to read; not possible for people who speak unwritten languages.

lithic   Referring to stone, especially with regard to artifacts.

longitudinal   A research strategy that examines changes in a particular group over time.

luxury   A consumer good primarily purchased as a marker of social status.

mana   A supernatural force inhabiting objects or people.

manioc   A root crop or tuber that is often called cassava. In many countries throughout the world, people east manioc root as a staple crop; in the United States, we commonly find manioc in the form of tapioca.

marriage   A culturally constructed institution through which interpersonal and usually intimate relationships are sanc- tioned and recognized by social, religious, and/or government authority.

maternalism   Having or demonstrating characteristics associated with mothers and mothering.

matrilineal   Relating to, based on, or tracing descent through the maternal line.

mediator   The role of a disinterested third party in dispute settlement.

medical anthropology   The study of health and medical systems in a cross-cultural perspective; includes the study of biocultural adaptations to disease, ethnomedical systems, and cultural factors in health-seeking behavior.

mercenary   A person, typically a soldier hired to fight for a foreign army, who works exclusively for financial gain.

meritocracy   A system in which advancement is purport-edly based upon ability or achievement of the individual.

metalinguistics   Elements of communication beyond verbal speech; includes the use of gesture, personal space, silence, and nonlinguistic sounds.

metamessages   An underlying message communicated through body language, intonation, or any combination of nonverbal communication. For example, a person who says he is not tired may communicate the exact opposite message if he simultaneously has difficulty keeping his eyes open.

microeconomics   Small-scale or individual economic decisions and patterns, such as the ways that individuals budget their cell phone expenditures.

micropolitics of social inequality   Small-scale patterns of power between individuals or small groups, the ways that inequalities between people are played out on a personal level.

miscegenation   Marriage or sexual intercourse between a woman and a man of different races, particularly between a white and an African American in the United States.

moiety system   A social system in which the entire group is divided into two kinship units, which are usually based on unilineal descent and exogamous.

monogamy   Marriage between one man and one woman at a given time.

moot   A public hearing or community assembly to decide local problems and administer justice.

morphology   The study of form as structure as opposed to function.

mosque   An Islamic place of public religious worship.

Muslim   An adherent of or believer in Islam.

multiculturalism   A movement to broaden the range of cultures we study, in reaction to the prevailing opinion that the great accomplishments have been made almost exclusively by males of European descent.

multiple paternity   The concept, occurring in several South American cultures, that every man who has intercourse with a woman during her pregnancy contributes to the formation of the child; therefore, a child may have multiple fathers.

multiplex relationships   Complex social relations characterized by multiple patterns of interaction, for example by kinship, business, political party, ethnicity, and religion.

national character studies   Descriptions of the cultural belief and "typical" personality of people from another culture, an approach used by the culture and personality school of anthropology.

natural selection   The primary force of evolution, first described by Darwin and Wallace, that causes changes in gene frequencies for environmentally adaptive traits due to relative decreases in mortality for certain individuals.

negotiation   The use of direct argument and compromise by the parties to a dispute to voluntarily arrive at a mutually satisfactory agreement.

neocolonial   After the age of colonialism, this refers to continued economic and political policies by which a great power indirectly maintains or extends its influence over other areas or people.

Neolithic   A stage in cultural evolution marked by the appearance of ground stone tools and, more importantly, the domestication of plants and animals, starting some 10,000 years ago.

nomadic band   A food-foraging group that moves among a variety of campsites; a society without sedentary villages.

nonreactive measure of behavior   Various methods for collecting social science data that are unobtrusive and unsubjected to bias introduced by the population under study.

norms   Standards of behavior characteristic of a society or social group to which members are expected to conform.

nuclear family   A basic social grouping consisting of a husband and wife and their children, typical of societies with monogamous marriage with the family living at a distance from the parents of the husband and wife.

obesity   A medically defined condition of excessive fat storage.

observational research   Research conducted by documenting what is observed (as opposed to other research techniques such as interviews, questionnaires, or laboratory tests).

Operation Khyber   a 15-day U.S. military campaign in Afghanistan in which anthropologists joined 1,000 U.S. and Afghan soldiers to clear out more than 200 Taliban insurgents and secure a major road in southeast Afghanistan.

organic   a mode of agricultural production which promotes biodiversity, minimal use of chemical inputs such as fertilizer and pesticides, and environmental stewardship.

origin myth   A story found in most cultures that explains the creation and population of the world.

orthography   The way in which words in a particular language are written phonetically to include sounds (phonemes) not represented in our alphabet; anthropological linguists usually use the International Phonetic Alphabet (IPA).

othering   A stigmatizing process of defining one's self-identity in opposition to one's perceived characteristics of someone else.

ovulation   The part of the menstrual cycle in which the egg (ovum) is released and fertilization can occur.

pacification   In tribal areas like New Guinea, the establishment by outside authorities of peace from blood-feud warfare.

palaver   A discussion for purposes of dispute settlement, typically informal and following customary law.

paleoanthropology   The study of human fossil remains.

Paleolithic   Old stone age; the archaeological period that includes the beginning of culture to the end of the Pleistocene glaciation.

paleontology   The study of the fossils of ancient, usually extinct, animals and plants.

paleopathology   The study of disease patterns in extinct populations, primarily through the examination of skeletal remains.

paramount chief   In a ranked society of ascribed statuses, the position at the top of the hierarchy.

participant observation   The primary research method of cultural anthropology, involving long-term observations conducted in natural settings.

parturient   Bringing forth or about to bring forth young.

pathogen   An agent that causes disease.

patriarchy   A form of social organization in which power and authority are vested in the males and in which descent is usually in the male line.

patrilineal   Descent traced exclusively through the male line for purposes of group membership or inheritance.

patrilocal   A postmarital residence rule by which a newly wed couple takes up permanent residence with or near the groom's father's family.

peasants   Rural, agricultural populations of state-level societies who maintain parts of their traditional culture while they are tied into the wider economic system of the whole society through economic links of rent, taxes, and markets.

pedagogy   The methods and techniques of teaching.

physical anthropology   Another term for biological anthropology; includes the study of paleoanthropology, population genetics, human adaptation, and primatology.

Pleistocene   The geological period approximately from 600,000 years ago to 12,000 years ago, characterized by recurrent glaciations.

pollution   The act of defilement, uncleanness.

polyandry   A relatively rare form of plural marriage in which one woman is married to two or more men.

polygamy   A general term for plural marriage, either polygyny or polyandry.

polygyny   A common form of plural marriage in which one man is married to two or more women; in societies that permit polygyny, the majority of marital unions are monogamous. Extended families may be formed through polygyny.

polytheism   The belief or worship of multiple deities.

population   In genetics and biological anthropology, a discrete demographic unit often characterized by in-marriage.

population density   The ratio of the number of people per area of land; closely related to carrying capacity.

population pressure   The situation of population growth in a limited geographical area causing a decline in food production and resources and sometimes triggering technological change.

potlatch   A feast given by a Northwest Coast Native American chief often involving competitive gift-giving, first described by Franz Boas.

prehistoric   The time before written records.

primatology   The study of nonhuman primates.

primogeniture   A rule of inheritance in which the homestead is passed down to the firstborn (male) child.

primordial   Belonging to or characteristic of the earliest stage of development; first in sequence of time.

principal investigator   The lead researcher in a large research project.

privilege   A special advantage, immunity, permission, right, or benefit granted to or enjoyed by an individual, class, caste, or race. Such advantage may be held consciously or unconsciously and exercised to the exclusion or detriment of others.

probability sampling   A data collection sampling technique based on the known proportions of various social groups.

proletariat   The working class in a state-level society, usually residing in urban areas.

psychoactive drugs   Chemicals that affect the mind or behavior and that may cause, among other things, hallucinations.

purdah   The Hindu or Muslim system of sex segregation, which is practiced by keeping women in seclusion.

qualitative methods   Research strategies that emphasize description, in-depth interviewing, and participant observation.

quantitative methods   Research methods that translate behaviors or attitudes into reliable and valid numeric measures suitable for statistical analysis for hypothesis testing.

race   A folk category of the English language that refers to discrete groups of human beings who are uniformly separated from one another on the basis of arbitrarily selected phenotypic traits.

radiocarbon dating   A method of absolute dating in archaeology using organic material and based on the decay rate of the radioactive isotope Carbon-14; useful for objects less than 50,000 years old.

random sample   A data sample selected by a method in which all individuals in a population have equal chance of being selected.

rational actor model   A conflict resolution model in which the state is understood as a sole actor which makes decisions based on the state's goals, preferences, and a desire to maximize potential benefits.

reciprocal gift   A mechanism of establishing or reinforcing social ties between equals involving a "present," which is repaid at a later date.

reciprocity   A system of mutual interaction involving the regular exchange of goods or services (for example, inviting someone over for dinner because they previously had you over for dinner).

reforestation   To renew forest cover by seeding or planting.

refugee   According to international law, someone residing outside of his/her country of nationality, or who has no nationality, because of "persecution or a well-founded fear of persecution."

regional economy   As opposed to globalization, this refers to the production, distribution, and consumption of goods and services in a distinct and limited geographical context.

relative deprivation   A concept wherein individuals perceive that they are less well off only in relation to another group or to their own expectations.

religion   Attitudes, beliefs, and practices related to supernatural powers.

rapid eye movement (REM)   The part of the sleep cycle when dreaming is done.

reproductive success   A variable used in Darwinian analyses referring to an individual's overall achievement in reproduction of their own genes (through direct offspring or kin).

rites of passage   Religious rituals that mark important changes in individual status or social position at different points in the life cycle, such as birth, marriage, or death.

ritual   A set of acts, usually involving religion or magic, following a sequence established by tradition.

sacred   A descriptive term for something worthy of religious respect or veneration.

sacred values   Beliefs that motivate action in ways disassociated with prospects for success.

sample   A subpopulation that is studied in order to make generalizations.

sanctions   Generally negative responses by a social group as a consequence of an individual's behavior; used to maintain social control.

séance   A ritual, usually held at night, designed to promote direct contact between people and spirits.

secret society   A social organization or association whose members hide their activities from nonmembers.

secular   A descriptive term for something that is explicitly not related to religion or religious beliefs.

segmentary system   A hierarchy of more and more inclusive lineages; functions primarily in contexts of conflict between groups.

self-sufficient   Refers to a characteristic of most pre-state societies; the ability to maintain a viable economy and social system with minimal outside contact.

serial monogamy   The marriage of one woman and one man at a time but in a sequence, usually made possible through divorce.

seropositive   Testing positive for a given disease (such as HIV infection) based on a blood test.

seroprevalence   The prevalence (proportion of people infected in a population) of a given disease based on blood tests.

sex   Determined by biological characteristics, such as external genitalia and having XX or XY chromosomes (contrast with *gender*).

sex roles   Learned social activities and expectations made on the basis of gender.

sexual dimorphism   A condition of having the two sexes dissimilar in appearance.

shaman   A part-time religious practitioner typical of tribal societies who goes into trance to directly communicate with the spirit world for the benefit of the community.

shifting agriculture   A form of cultivation (horticulture) with recurrent, alternate clearing and burning of vegetation and planting of crops in the burnt fields.

sickle-cell anemia   An often fatal genetic disease caused by a chemical mutation that changes one of the amino acids in normal hemoglobin; the mutant sickle-cell gene occurs with unusually high frequency in parts of Africa where malaria is present.

SIDA   The Spanish, French, Italian, and Haitian Creole acronym for AIDS.

SIDS   Sudden infant death syndrome—the sudden and unexpected death of an infant, also known as crib death.

signaling theory of ritual   A theory which predicts that groups that impose the greatest demands on their members will elicit the highest levels of devotion and commitment.

single-interest relationship   A relationship based solely on one connection, such as landlord-tenant.

situated   Formed by a given person's experiences, based on context.

slang   A small set of new and usually short-lived words in the vocabulary of a dialect of a language.

slash-and-burn techniques   Shifting form of cultivation (horticulture) with recurrent, alternate clearing and burning of vegetation and planting in the burnt fields; swidden.

social capital   A shared network of resources, norms, knowledge, and institutions that enable mutually beneficial cooperation for those who possess it. Rather than monetary wealth, someone rich in social capital has a network of family and friends who will always be there to lend a hand.

social class   In state-level societies, a stratum in a social hierarchy based on differential group access to means of production and control over distribution; often endogamous.

social cohesion   The process by which a social group binds itself together, producing greater cooperation and conformity.

social construction   A reality that is created and agreed on by interpersonal interaction and discourse; opposite of essentialist.

social control   Practices that induce members of a society to conform to the expected behavior patterns of their culture; includes informal mechanisms, like gossip, legal systems, and punishment.

social justice   A philosophy or application of laws and values which promote an egalitarian, fair, and harmonious society.

socialization   The development, through the influence of parents and others, of patterns of thought and behavior in children that conform to beliefs and values of a particular culture.

socially validated   Approved or recognized by the culture of a particular social group.

social mobility   The upward or downward movement of individuals or groups in a society characterized by social stratification.

social networks   An informal pattern of organization based on the complex web of social relations linking individuals; includes factors like kinship, friendship, economics, and political ties.

social organization   A culturally inherited system that orders social relations within social groups.

social status   A person's level of prestige in society. Social status is associated with factors like education and employment as well as higher and lower levels of wealth or power. In the United States, for instance, doctors tend to have higher social status than cooks at McDonald's.

social stratification   An arrangement of statuses or groups within a society into a pattern of socially superior and inferior ranks; based on differential access to strategic resources.

society   A socially bounded, spacially contiguous group of people who interact in basic economic and political institutions and share a particular culture; societies retain relative stability across generations.

sociobiology   The study of animal and human social behavior based on the theory that behavior is linked to genetics.

sociocultural   Refers to the complex combination of social and cultural factors.

sociolinguistics   A subfield of anthropological linguistics emphasizing the study of the social correlates to variations in speech patterns.

solidarity   Unity based on community interest, objectives, and culture.

somatic   Having to do with the body.

somatization   The physical expression of psycho-social problems.

sorcery   The use of supernatural knowledge or power for purposes of evil, for example causing sickness; used to further the sorcerer's individual social goals.

souk   Arabic term for an open-air market.

species   The largest naturally occurring population that is capable of interbreeding and producing fully fertile offspring.

spurious   Not an actual or causal relationship, as in the correlation between the number of storks and birthrate.

staple foods/staples   A type of food that is a dominant part of a regional or national diet. Maize (corn) is a staple food in the United States, while drought-resistant crops like sorghum and millet are staple foods for farming families living in extremely dry climates.

stasis   A state of equilibrium or balance between opposing forces.

states   A complex society characterized by urban centers, agricultural production, labor specialization, standing armies, permanent boundaries, taxation, centralized authority, public works, and laws designed to maintain the status quo.

status   Position in a social system that is characterized by certain rights, obligations, expected behaviors (roles), and certain social symbols.

stigma   Socially constructed shame or discredit.

stratified societies   A society in which groups experience structured inequality of access not only to power and prestige but also to economically important resources.

stroll   A street where prostitution activity is concentrated.

structure   In anthropology, generally referring to social institutions and patterns of organization.

subculture   The culture of a subgroup of a society that has its own distinctive ideas, beliefs, values, and worldview.

subsidy   Financial aid given by a government to a person or group to support an enterprise deemed essential to the public interest. The U.S. government, for example, provides subsidies to farmers and transportation businesses like Amtrak because they provide essential public services which otherwise may not be profitable.

sunna circumcision   One of three forms of female circumcision; this procedure includes clitorectomy (removal of clitoris and hood) and sometimes refers only to the cutting of the hood (prepuce); the name *sunna* relates the practice to Islamic traditions, although most Muslim scholars and theologians deny any Koranic justification for female circumcision.

superstructure   In the theory of cultural materialism, refers to a society's ideology.

sushi   A traditional Japanese food of rice and thinly sliced raw fish and other ingredients rolled in seaweed and artfully presented to the diner, eaten with a horseradish sauce.

swidden cultivation   A tropical gardening system, also known as slash-and-burn horticulture in which forest is cleared, burned, cultivated, and then left for bush-fallow.

symbol   A sign that consistently but arbitrarily represents an object or meaning; the basis of communication within a culture.

symbolic concession   A non-material incentive, such as a formal apology, offered to promote a peaceful and enduring resolution to an unresolved conflict.

syntax   The word order or pattern of word order in a phrase or sentence.

taboo   A supernaturally forbidden act as defined by a culture, violation of which can have severe negative consequences.

TFR (total fertility rate)   The average number of children born to a woman during her lifetime.

third/fourth gender   Third gender typically refers to male and sometimes female berdaches, while fourth gender only refers to female berdaches.

time-allocation study   A quantitative method that identifies what people do and how much time they spend doing various activities; useful for cross-cultural comparison.

toddy   A generic name for alcoholic drinks traditionally made from fermented palm or coconut shoot sap.

totem   A symbolic plant or animal associated with a social group (clan) used for identification and religious expression.

transmission   Passing of an infectious agent to an uninfected person from an infected group or individual.

transnational culture   A pattern of cultural beliefs and behaviors characteristic of elites throughout the world and often spread through mass media.

tribe   A relatively small, usually horticultural, society organized on principles of kinship, characterized by little social stratification and no centralized political authority, and whose members share a culture and language.

trophic exchanges   Relationships between organisms having to do with food; eating or being eaten.

UNAIDS   A United Nations program with global partners who advocate and work to achieve universal access to HIV prevention, treatment, and care.

universalism   The understanding that certain beliefs, values, rights, or conditions are or should be universal.

urbanization   The worldwide process of the growth of cities at the expense of rural populations.

urban villages   Small (usually segregated) communities of minorities or rural migrants located in cities.

usufruct rights   The legal right of using land (or resources on land) that is not one's private property.

utopia   An ideal society, whether imagined or implemented. The term is derived from the Greek word for "no-place."

validity   The quality of a measurement tool or variable actually measuring what is intended.

values   The ideas of a culture that are concerned with appropriate goals and behavior.

virilocal residence   Patrilocal postmarital residence.

waganga   Diviners or healers who, according to Giriama (Kenya) spiritual beliefs, can harness supernatural powers and win favors from ancestors. They are specialists who mediate between the visible and invisible worlds.

walkabout   A custom of Australian Aborigines involving a long circular journey to sacred places and a return to home.

war   Violence between political entities, such as nations, using soldiers; to be distinguished from the smaller scale feud.

weaning   Acclimating someone (as a child) to take food other than by nursing.

Western culture   A generic term referring to the common beliefs, values, and traditions of Europeans and their descendants.

World Health Organization (WHO)   An institutional branch of the United Nations; its primary objective is to provide leadership and support on global health issues.

worldview   The particular way in which a society constructs ideas of space, time, social relationship, and the meaning of life.

Xhosa   A South African cultural group belonging to the Bantu language family. The Xhosa were traditionally farmers in the regional division of labor.

yerba mate   *Ilex Paraguayensis*. A tea made from the small branches and leaves of this species of tree is consumed hot or cold. Widespread use of this refreshment throughout colonial Latin America made it Paraguay's main export for four hundred years.

yerbateros   People who collect yerba mate, usually in uncultivated stands in the tropical forest.

zeitgeist   The general intellectual, moral, and cultural climate of an era.

Index